RICHARD BURTON

A Life

Melvyn Bragg

WARNER BOOKS

A Warner Communications Company

WARNER BOOKS EDITION

This Warner Books Edition is published by arrangement with Little, Brown and Company, 200 West Street, Waltham, MA 02154.

Cover design by Anne Twomey
Cover photo by Ken Regan/Camera 5

Warner Books, Inc.
666 Fifth Avenue
New York, N.Y. 10103

 A Warner Communications Company

Printed in the United States of America

First Warner Books Printing: July, 1990

10 9 8 7 6 5 4 3 2 1

To Ion Trewin
The Highgate man of letters
and a remorseless editor

Contents

Foreword

In writing this book I have discovered a much grander, much bigger, an altogether more compelling man than I had anticipated.

I had the benefit of many interviews with those close to him who have never before spoken in public: of new letters and reminiscences, and quantities of detailed business contracts which draw their own peculiar graph of his life. There was access to new and crucial medical evidence. There was the invaluable help of his family. I had the good fortune to be given Philip Burton's hitherto unpublished memoirs. These provided a lengthy and dramatic insight into critical periods in his life. Sally Burton speaking for the first time in depth about her husband proved a vivid source: unconsciously, perhaps, she had, during their time together, become his chronicler.

It was she who gave me total and unrestrained access to the Notebooks, hundreds of thousands of words which, over great stretches of his life, tell Burton's own story in his own words. In part, these record the life of a man obsessed with one woman—Elizabeth Taylor. The switchback course of this obsession, its often unbearable frankness and its extraordinary passion testify to the uniqueness of a marriage which, for many years, mesmerized the public. There are sensational revelations but, equally, the Notebooks show a man hidden to the world of photographers and publicists, a man as private and quietly complex as can be imagined.

Like very few—men or women—Richard Burton led many lives. In his one span he soared and fell, triumphed, failed and fought on in a way which I found moving, painful and exhilarating to behold.

MELVYN BRAGG

PART
ONE

1
Welsh Jenkins

"Pwy sy'n fel ni?" his father would ask as he squatted outside the Miner's Arms on a summer's evening, nicely, melancholy, drunk.

"Neb," replied his friends, miners all, like him.

"Pwy sy'n fel fi?"

"Neb."

"Who is like us?"

"Nobody."

"Who is like me?"

"Nobody."

There was nobody like Richard Walter Jenkins. Not to his eleven children. Not to his neighbours. Not to his mates. Dic, he was called, or Dic Bach y Saer—"Little Dick the Carpenter"—after his grandfather who made pit-props: "Daddy Ni"—"our Daddy" —to his sons and daughters. Five feet three, immensely strong— "could pick up a thirteen-stone man by the seat of his pants"—a craftsman collier—"he would look at the seam of coal . . . take a Number Two mandrel [a half-headed pick] and if he hit it just right, something like twenty tons of coal would fall out of the coal face"—and a man with a "love of words, the longer the better."

"He looked very much like me," claimed his most famous son, also named Richard Walter Jenkins, later to be known as Richard Burton. "That is, he was pockmarked, devious and smiled a great deal when he was in trouble." Most others insist that the young Richard got his looks from his mother, Edith, a fair-haired

3

girl, taller by far than Dic, a sweet beauty, "a very strong woman," to whom her husband was absolutely faithful and utterly irresponsible: as he was to all his family.

For there was nobody like Daddy Ni as a drinker, heroic, a "twelve pints a day man," often away for nights on end—"met a friend"—incapable of passing a pub, and a gambler too—"the dogs"—leaving wife and children short and maybe desperate when times were hard enough already. Yet his charm always took the curse off it. "No nastiness in him." However much the family sat and planned and prepared to scold him after a frightening bender, he would soon have them all melted with his gypsy stories. Snared rabbits: slept in a chicken coop: down in the underworld of docks. They protected him. Dic Bach y Saer was put to bed by the older children he so serenely neglected, whispering, "I've got children in a thousand, good as gold."

"And the whole family, all of them," says a neighbour, "were lovely, so pleasant, quite outstanding."

The Jenkins family was one of the clans of Wales. "Nobody like us"—he meant the Welsh. In their grander moments the Welsh would claim most ancient associations—the luminous legendary King Arthur—and boast they had supplied England with its greatest monarchs—out of Owen Tudor—Henry VII, Henry VIII, Elizabeth I. "They are an alien race," wrote Burton, "and nobody knows where they came from or what they are." The lost tribe of Israel? Carthaginians blown north by the Gulf Stream? Celts, certainly, who had shrugged off the occupation of the Romans. Or did they come straight down from antique gods? They needed myths. For the twentieth-century facts were that they were a small, oppressed, poor and exploited people, in thrall to the then all-mighty English, and their sole singularity was the Welsh language and only a quarter of them spoke that.

Dic's family was of that portion. In the language they aggrandised their past, they made their history legend, they cherished themselves—as minorities always have done: the Jews, the American blacks, the Basques, the Sikhs—and looked out for Redeemers, Messiahs or, in the case of the Welsh, Heroes. Richard Burton, Actor, was and is now a Welsh Hero. "There are so few of us," he wrote, "and God knows we can't afford to give many of us away." He was never to give Wales away.

Outside the family, being Welsh was the greatest blessing he had and he held to it. It was to him first and last a land full of Heroes. Grim glory, matchless strength, and the wit to confuse, the charms to transform any invader. Heroes all. Down the pit, on the rugby football field, in the pub, telling stories, singing anthems as if they were war songs, and finding poetry—Dylan Thomas, Gwyn Thomas, R. S. Thomas—in the country of the Red Dragon. Every Sunday of his childhood he was at chapel hearing the Bible in Welsh and singing in that intricate melodious tongue. From the age of awareness he looked out over his Welsh battlements at a foreign culture, for English and the monied English siege were all about him. He was born a blood member of what then seemed a condemned and irrelevant tribe: he never forgot that. Revenge and restoration were part of his duty.

As if, in part, to fight back at their crushing fate, the Welsh families in those industrial valleys bred and grew and savoured their own with biblical fruitfulness and devotion. Dic Jenkins and Edith married on Christmas Eve in 1900, had thirteen children in twenty-six years. Thomas Henry in 1901, Cecilia in 1905, Ifor in 1906, two girls—both Margaret Hannah, both died in infancy—William in 1911, David in 1914, Verdun in 1916, Hilda in 1918, Catherine in 1921, Edith in 1922, Richard Walter in 1925, Graham in 1927. It was a small army as much as a large family. Edith Thomas was married at seventeen: she had been working as a barmaid at the Miner's Arms and she was married from there. Her parents disapproved of the match to the twenty-four-year-old miner. The Jenkinses were supposed to be beneath the Thomases. Yet both were the first in either family to sign the marriage register with more than a cross. Both families had been transformed from what might be called a lumpen peasantry into what Marx did call the lumpen proletariat. The individuality and richness of their lives—given a glance of a chance—mocked such lumpen labels.

Just as the young Richard—the name means Rule-Hard—saw the Man as Hero in struggle and song, so the child's eye view saw the Woman as Noble, Wonderful and infinitely Capable. Edith fitted that. She provided full meals and basic decency for her many children. She made the clothes, baked, cooked, brewed beer and sold it, made butter and sold it, decorated others' houses, took in others' washing and brought up her remarkable family with little help from her husband, often penniless a few hours after getting his wage packet, a greater child, perhaps, than any of her own. Richard, as a baby, would never let her out of his sight, cried if she left him.

The men were granite figures, fearless in the primitive and dangerous under-earth world of coal: the women were half way to heaven—and in command. And all of this world woven into the Welshness because only Welsh men were *so* hard; only Welsh women *so* beautiful. And only the Welsh had *such* stories. Nobody like them.

The Jenkins family had their own stories. Stories which Richard Burton brought out again and again because he was proud to celebrate his past and would not let any bounty or glamour of the present put it in the shade. And the greater the gap between his colossal global success and the terraced cottages of South Wales, the more determined he was to employ the grappling irons of loyalty and haul his past alongside. This was where he came from—not in any self-pity—(although there could have been an excuse for that, in the bitter harvest of the coalfields)—nor with any attempt to show off (although the battles he had fought and won to achieve what he did deserved a boast)—those stories were told and retold to keep the faith.

In 1970, being interviewed, with Elizabeth Taylor, by David Frost:

> Occasionally my father would take off on what is known as a bat. I have sufficient intellectual control so that my bats only last about three days—his would last sometimes as long as three weeks. He took off one Friday, disappeared. We waited for him all Saturday. We were very poor. It was during the Depression, round about 1930, I should think. And one of the great things Welsh miners have and had is greyhound racing. The old man didn't turn up for a week, and then two weeks and then three weeks and everybody was fairly in despair. After all there were, in those days, eleven children. And suddenly the kitchen door—we all lived in the kitchen—burst open, and standing there was my father with the most effulgent smile on his face. He stared with his stupendously stoned eyes at the assembled and stricken family. He had a piece of orange rope: this was the lead for a dog which was a

greyhound, which was at least twenty-four years old. It had no teeth. And, as one of my brothers said, if you took it for a walk it panted. He looked at his stricken family and he patted this mangy dog very fondly on the back and said: "Boys, our troubles are over!"

Other stories about Dic, Little Dick the Carpenter—how he never got to a rugby match because there were too many pubs on the way, how he was burnt all over in a pit explosion, wrapped in bandages so that only his eyes and nostrils showed through—and bathed slowly back to health by his daughters who poured olive oil over him all the time, how he took his daughter Cecilia (Cis) to eisteddfods because he loved to hear her sing but how she pleaded with him "not to stop anywhere and not to leave her in the hall." And how he could work up to his thighs in water in a two-foot seam of coal.

The Miner's Arms was the campfire for story-telling: and often the setting. Richard's grandfather, Tom, who had been crippled in the mines and had a wheelchair, had a great win on a horse called Black Sambo. Into the Miner's Arms—drinks all round—and again—and again. Out, drunk, hoisted into the wheelchair, downhill all the way home, whipping the air and calling out "Come on Black Sambo!," out of control, crashed into a wall: killed instantly. Always told as a comic story.

The tragic stories—the quiet or violent deaths of the unrecorded poor—were rarely told. But the place was a battlefield. Crippled men; worn-out women; tuberculosis in the walls; pneumoconiosis in the lungs; malnutrition, despair, unnecessary death. One sure and certain way to combat all that was money.

The man who at one stage was thought to be among the top half dozen money earners in the world was born on November 10th, 1925 at 2 Dan-y-Bont, Pontrhydyfen. His father was forty-nine, his mother forty-two and he weighed twelve pounds—remarkable for that time and place. Two years later, after the birth of another child, the mother died "of puerperal fever" her son was to say, grimly, "which is hygiene neglect." Money and the knowledge money can buy would have saved her.

Pontrhydyfen—"pont," a bridge; "rhyd," a ford; "fen," a cart—is high in the valley of the River Afan. Its gentle green bosomy hills were obliterated in the mid-nineteenth century by pit-heads, ironworks and regiments of cheap terraced housing. The countryside lapped the grimy shore of the town and Richard's father and some of his family had that Lawrencian link of black industry and green pasture. Not so Richard. Wales to him—physical Wales—was the catacombs of coal, the engines and architecture of massive wealth creation, rain-soaked narrow streets, hillsides leaking black, and occasionally a soaring aqueduct such as that in Pontrhydyfen under which still stands the house in which he was born. They've tried to put a plaque there but it gets stolen.

The *place*, then, a most unlikely nursery for one who was to play Hamlet at the Old Vic, Arthur in *Camelot*, both of them a record number of times on Broadway, a man who was to understand claret and enjoy meetings of several kinds with several princesses. The *time* even less welcoming. He was born heir to the betrayed promise of the Great War, after which another Welshman had assured the returning British soldier of a "home fit for heroes to live in." Instead, South Wales, like the other furnaces and engine rooms of Britain, was being hammered by a gathering Depression. In 1926 would be the General Strike when Welsh miners marched the two hundred miles to London, their trail easy to follow by the black-blood spat along the road, while back at home the troops moved in for fear of revolution. How far such seismic social pressures come through to a child may be impossible to judge. But the Jenkins family, part of the great mass, were trapped in the middle of it. Burton's occasional flarings of radicalism, which persisted undiminished throughout his increasingly affluent career, were as tap-rooted in Pontrhydyfen as his love of the subversive language spoken there.

The death of the mother was the test of the family. Dic, Our Daddy, walked away from it and ended up moving between his daughters—"You never noticed him if he didn't speak"—putting a shilling on the horses, reading anything that came to hand, off on his benders, neglecting all his children and loved and welcomed by all his daughters, a kind of successful King Lear of the Welsh coalfields.

Fifty years later, a friend of all the children and a neighbour throughout the years still recalls with awe the way they behaved. "They were just marvellous," she says. "Marvellous how well they did it. The boys went their own way. The girls brought themselves up. The little ones were farmed out. Nothing was lacking. They were very strong, you see, the Jenkins in Pontrhydyfen. They kept the chapel going and they cleaned it as well. They were all very funny, they could all perform, you know, do a turn. Quite unself-conscious. Quite outstanding,'' she said, as she had said before. All Dic's "golden children" stayed true through their great loss.

If parents are your primary role models, then Richard Jenkins was formed by an alcoholic father and a beloved mother who died and left him when he was two. They say that in such a case you search for your mother for the rest of your life. Oddly, though he could never bear to be out of her sight and cried whenever she left him, as soon as his eldest sister, the faithful Cis, got him to her own home he ceased to cry. To his great sorrow he could never recall his mother.

You can measure the greatness of a life by the length and quality of the journey taken. The journey Jenkins-Burton took was epic. The odds against him were all but unimaginable. How many millions similar to him have given up the ghost of ambition or had it driven out of them?

If you are moulded by a place then for him that place was a bleak black valley in Welsh-speaking South Wales, the trenches of the industrial battleground. He never lost the pride and pleasure in the tales of his deep, working, glittering-tongued Welsh past. It was wonderful to him. It is still wonderful—both how far he moved from it and how he never abandoned it at all.

Richard Walter Jenkins Junior was to dine with the Duke and Duchess of Windsor, yet keep the common touch, be courted by Presidents and praised by the greatest Prime Minister of the century. He was to be hugely admired on the classical stage by Sir Laurence Olivier, John Neville, Sir John Gielgud and Sir Peter Hall, loved on film by Humphrey Bogart, Clint Eastwood, John Huston, Mike Nichols. He would outbid Aristotle Onassis for a jewel and marry the highest-paid film star in the world, twice. He was a famous lover and notorious drinker on several continents. He was driven by a devil that he never knew but he never stopped fighting, a maker of his own myths, Celtic, Faustian, an Icarus and a Don Juan, coming out from his beloved Wales like a mystical warrior to rove the world for conquests, forever unsettled, forever daring.

But his first recorded journey, crying all the way, aged two, was with his sister Cecilia, on a bus, poor as mice, travelling the four miles from the Welsh heartland of Pontrhydyfen, with its magical stories, its heroes, its dragons, to Port Talbot, tough steel town, English-speaking, grind and grime. He stopped crying when they arrived at the house. Cis's touch. Nobody like her either. *Neb*.

2
"A Bell In Every Tooth"

Richard, or "Rich" as he was called, went to live with Cis in 1927. He stayed for fifteen years. He would be grateful and loving to her throughout his life. In 1965 he published *A Christmas Story* and wrote:

> My sister was no ordinary woman—no woman ever is, but to me, my sister less than any. When my mother had died she, my sister, had become my mother, and more mother to me than any mother could ever have been. I was immensely proud of her. I shone in the reflection of her green-eyed, black-haired, gypsy beauty. She sang at her work in a voice so pure that the local men said she had a bell in every tooth, and was gifted by God . . . She was innocent and guileless and infinitely protectable . . . She felt all tragedies except her own.

Later in that passage he wrote: "It wasn't until thirty years later when I saw her in another woman [Elizabeth Taylor] that I realised I had been searching for her all my life."

When you meet Cis now, you can still see her clearly in that eulogy. "The thing about Rich," she said, the face still lovely, the voice still pure, "is I couldn't help myself. I loved my husband. And he was a fine man, a good man. But if it came to an argument

—well, I looked at Rich and I couldn't help myself. There it is. Nobody knows how much I cried over him.''

"Cis was so busy,'' said a neighbour, "she didn't have time to cough. There were so many of them.''

She and her husband Elfed James, a miner, after renting a couple of rooms, soon ended up at 73 Caradoc Street, the top end, the scullery butting against a mountain leaking coal juice known as "the Side.'' The Side, an unlovely, but beloved spot was where the miners met to squat and smoke and gossip: Burton recollected it warmly as a fraternal masculine club, much cherished. You had to cherish what was in front of you in Port Talbot, with one of the biggest steel works in Europe belching out smoke and the wind crossing Swansea Bay to bring the remorseless rain. Taibach, where Cis and Elfed lived, was largely a cluster of small cheap terraced cottages since demolished and unmourned. The great task, for someone such as Cis, was to make of her own house—a three-bedroom semi-detached in which they were the first occupiers—a place of comfort and gleaming triumph against the odds.

They were high. She had a "very plump'' and soon exceedingly dependent and vigorous two-year-old boy. Back in Pontrhydyfen she had brothers and sisters she saw it her duty to cook and wash for. There was Daddy Ni. The chapel. Little money. And Elfed, her new husband, married only a few months and heir to a clan of claimants.

Cis lives now with her two daughters Marian (three years younger than Richard) and Rhianon (six years younger). Their draughts of memory were clear and generous but the daughters—in truth Richard's nieces but brought up as his sisters—thought there were points with which they did not wish to embarrass their mother and after our talks Rhianon wrote:

> It is a pity but my father, Elfed, has been given very little credit in articles and books. He was a good father, strict at times but also a bit of a softie. He did have a very hard time which we, as children, could not understand . . . they took care of Richard as you know but my mother also had to look after the children left in 2 Dân-y-bont, Pontrhydyfen, travelling there at least twice a week on two separate buses with Richard, a two-year-old, in tow. Many times after cooking and cleaning there, she would

have to bring suitcases of washing back to our house in Taibach to get it ready for the next visit.

With all the work she had to do my mother could not do a sloppy job. Everything in our house was spotlessly clean. Her brothers' shirts and collars were always starched and ironed to perfection. I am told that she always looked attractive and very well turned out even at this particular time . . .

My father had a very hard tough job underground, earning a small wage. He was probably very frustrated too as his bride, who had little time to be with him, was struggling to keep two homes running. She was exhausted with work and grief over her mother's early death, a mother she loved very much. There were financial problems too.

My father could read sol-fa and old notation as could most people in our chapel. He was conductor in Noddfa Chapel, Taibach, which we all attended. He had a good tenor voice and he belonged to a male voice glee party. He was also on the committee of the Taibach Co-operative Society and the local hospital. He had a sense of humour. He encouraged the three of us to recite, and sing and play the harmonium. He was firm with the three of us, but Richard seemed to get into trouble being a strong minded boy and rugby mad. "Trouble" being dirtying or tearing his best clothes, or kicking the soles off his shoes in the field on the way home. Whenever my father reprimanded Richard, my mother would defend him there and then, right or wrong. This must have infuriated my father and undermined his authority. He never used physical violence on us . . . My mother has said many times in our adult life that although she loved our father and should have stood by him, as far as Richard was concerned, "she could not help herself."

That last phrase occurred time and again. Burton himself often used it of her, proudly. He had a tendency, even a compulsion to repeat short phrases which seemed particularly apt: to hammer at them as if something was being shaped on an anvil, or as if each phrase was a key which unlocked whole galleries of memory. Cis's helpless adoration of her child-brother was fully returned.

There were several who thought that Rich was too much of a burden to expect Elfed to bear.

And the older Richard got, the greater the adolescent turbulence, the fiercer the rebellion, the more he clashed with Elfed and the more he provoked Cis's displays of loyalty. The cross-complications were dangerous and Elfed's part has suffered. Rhianon's account, I think, is wholly convincing. Decent and teetotal, Elfed has been underestimated unjustly and sometimes, in comparisons, by Richard himself. Partly because he had to take the daily grind and brunt of this hugely assured and powerful boy's pains of growth. Partly, more simply, more painfully, because he was not a Jenkins. Not a faded but once, surely, glorious hero like Daddy Ni to whom Elfed would give his best chair in the house: nor Ifor, the new male fixed point in young Rich's universe.

Ifor was the third child, born in 1906, and nineteen years Richard's senior. When he was a child Ifor became Rich's North Star. Ifor was a great coal hewer. A rugby football hero. The Rock of Jenkins. Ifor stayed in the family stronghold in Pontrhydyfen. Ifor was loved and revered by the small brother whom he in turn saw as the family's great hope of true escape, a conqueror, the one who would show them. Their deep friendship would be lifelong.

So many talked with warmth and unchallengeable admiration about Ifor: Lauren Bacall in Los Angeles, Brook Williams in Switzerland, Emlyn Williams in London, John Neville in Stratford, Ontario, Kate Burton in New York, Robert Hardy in London— "Ifor," they said, "Ifor was marvellous." It is worth mentioning the spread of opinion—and it would be easy to enlarge it—because his was that rare character which stamped itself effortlessly and in the same way on every sort of company. And worth spreading it out geographically too: Ifor was to travel the world with Richard. To Rich, from earliest childhood, as Cis was "more mother to me than any mother could ever have been" so Ifor was the chieftain brother, indomitable protector in the rough and wreckage of those valleys.

A friend of many years' standing has said that, "Ifor would have loved to have stayed on at school. He was good at school. But he had to leave when he was thirteen. He had to go down the mines and he stuck it out. He was in the strikes of 1921 and 1926 when they were all unemployed. He left the mines eventually and got a job with a builder—he could turn his hand to anything—one of those men, you know, plumbing, anything. He learnt how to take a car to pieces. Always punctual. Never wasted time. He was a very very strict person, Ifor. Very fit. They were all a bit afraid of what Ifor would say if they did wrong. When he came back in a temper sometimes, or been drinking, Cis told me they would put Rich on the kitchen table and tell him to dance. That always made Ifor laugh. He was very fond of poetry—he could read it as good as Rich and maybe better. They would have whole nights just reading poetry. He had a lovely voice. And he was in the rugby football team—Rich was proud as proud. Rich was crazy about football. He idolised Ifor. He had a bad back as well, you know, just like Rich. He injured it in the Normandy landings. Those Jenkins boys all had trouble with their bones.''

These three were the major domestic figures in the dominating childhood of Rich Jenkins. Cis, who ''could not help herself'' and was then and forever his perfect woman. Elfed, a sober and upright man who was to become unfairly the sounding board for Richard's first rebellions. Ifor, straight from the Welsh mists of mythology, a hero in poetry and war, and everything his father failed to be. Cis was also his first conquest. Elfed his rival in love. Ifor the idol he would one day have to dislodge. Work was all about those three, the exhaustion and boredom of work, the fear of losing it, the meagreness of its rewards. But so was joy—in song, sport, and the infinite fictions of the family and neighbours. Money was the key not to happiness—they were too fine for that—but unashamedly the answer to material necessity. Chapel filled the spirit but not the belly. To a romantic affectionate boy such as Rich, watching the wear of work, sensing the tensions of poverty, longing for everything to be given to those who cared for him so much, money could seem the sole solution, the salvation. He began to make himself a few pence early on—running messages, collecting newspapers for the chip shops and horse dung for fertiliser, finding the pay-penny cracks in life on the narrow streets. Picked up expensive habits, too. Started to smoke at eight.

Outside that powerful triangle was a constant swish of family, extended family, neighbours, friends, gangs, clubs. As a man he became a compulsive house buyer. As a child, he shuttled between two houses—Port Talbot and, most weekends, back to Pontrhyd-yfen. Shared beds. ''Here's our real little Welshman,'' Daddy Ni would say. The boy would reply in the language of the country, ''I am glad to be in your house, Daddy Ni." There were all the other brothers and sisters, Edith who was good at arithmetic and sorted things out for all and sundry, David who was to become a police inspector, Hilda and Cassie who delighted in their roguish little brother—threepence here, sixpence there. They were a remarkable family. Verdun was to lose half a foot in the pits and use the £300 compensation to buy an upright piano (although he could not play it). "This caused great excitement," said Cis. He made Rich a boneshaker which thundered down Caradoc Street. Noddfa Chapel in Taibach. Three times on Sundays.

Children not much younger than Rich arriving to be his nephews, nieces, playmates. There was a cousin Dilwyn from whom he became inseparable (they even shared a pair of roller skates) and to whom he gave the greatest tribute of affection by constantly getting him into trouble. Various aunts of terrible aspect who would threaten and alarm—tales of scorching with a flat iron for minor mischiefs —and kind uncles who would be a sure bet for a sweet or a copper or two. Di Doodle Alley Tap whom the war had made wrong in the head, Tom Francis who kept pigs, lived rough, smoked a cabbage pipe with them. The boy lived on a roundabout of encircling affections, complex loyalties, quick on the emotional draw, switching from role to role as bolder boys scramble from horse to horse on a carousel: and always, it seemed, outside the house of Elfed, Richard was the bringer of good fortune. "Rich was the only one who could get round *her*," Rhianon said of a particularly fierce aunt. "He would stand there, with his Just William cap on and sing—no movements, just natural, and it made you forget the world."

As he was, in part, to become a "man's man" so he was a boy's boy. Nobody I have talked to thought he had any "side," or curried any favours. And although he himself often said he was "spoilt," "a little lord," nobody else accused him of that. He was hell bent in fact on what there was to be done in the village and in the town: didn't stop to cough. Totally absorbed in the wild delights of the streets, the railway lines, the alleys, the adult, seductive adventure playgrounds of an industrial landscape. He soaked up the action and tone of what was, looking on it now, and especially given the circumstances, a remarkably fertile culture. Provided you were not ground down by illness or poverty.

The Jenkinses were not poor. You would have been a brave man to accuse them of it. They were respectable, in their own arena of life, as respectable as any and more than most. Never to be pitied. But the pressure of surrounding poverty and the fear of it were as inescapable as a shadow. And there had been very hard times indeed when Daddy Ni was drunk and away for days on end and no one else in the family was earning: except the mother slaving in beatified drudgery. Richard's brothers and sisters would certainly have passed on tales of quiet desperation: but by the time he was seven or eight, things were easier. His five older brothers were in work; so, inter- mittently, was his father; so was Elfed.

The boy found himself in a peculiar position. The immediate past and the constant threat was poverty. Not quite the poverty of no shoes, of basic and meagre food, no possessions other than the most rudimentary necessities—but too near that for comfort and he knew plenty who were in that condition. Poverty was always out there ready to get you. And yet, as a partial recovery took place in the 1930s and the Jenkins clan bit the bone that was thrown at them, the small boy's world became a wonderland of gifts, large and small, of treats, tips, goodies.

This can be seen quite clearly by looking at a passage in the autobiographical *A Christmas Story*, and comparing it with an un- published hand-scrawled manuscript I found in his papers. In *A Christmas Story* he writes, wondering about the present he might get:

> Pray God it wasn't Tommy Elliot's farm, which I'd played with for two years and which I feared—from glances and whispers that I'd caught between my sister and Mrs. Elliot—was going to be cleaned up and bought for me for Christmas. It would be shameful to have a secondhand present. Everyone would know.

That had indeed happened to him once: when very young.

In the unpublished manuscript—a cluster of unorganised mem- ories about Christmas (and, incidentally, like most of his private jottings, more vivid than anything he published)—he describes what became more and more the norm.

> Then, in bed, fighting to sleep and to forget the miracle of the morning to come. Saying, if I get a farm with cows and sheep and a five-bar gate and chickens and a coop

and a metal stream and a few trees about the place and a
green field made of billiard cloth and a dog or two and a
cat—never mind the cat—and perhaps a fox on a hill . . .
if I get this, with a pair of ball-bearing roller skates so
that I can gleam and flash and go backwards through the
heavy Friday traffic and be as glamorous as Boy Davids
from the Park . . . If I get those things and a book or
two—I will go to Wednesday night chapel for a whole
year. And I got them and I did!

It got even better.

One year I topped everybody. My brother Ifor gave me a
beautiful bicycle—hub-braked and dynamoed, a thing of
beauty and a joy for a couple or three years. I have never
ceased to be proud of that winged machine. I allowed
everybody to ride it. I went to Swansea on it and Newport.
I cycled on it to Aberdare and Mountain Ash.

It was typical of him that he "allowed everybody to ride it." From
the beginning, all the recollections and anecdotes speak of his open-
handedness. Just as he had no "side" so he seemed to have no
possessiveness. Possessions—yes—he had those and he loved them.
But it was always easy come, easy go: easy-going in many ways,
it seems—a characteristic which developed into that "repose" and
"utter confidence in himself" that so many actors and writers remarked on.

"There was never anything nasty about him," said Cis's daughter
Marian, who was his niece but, she said, "felt like his sister." With
Rhianon she made up his first fan-club: but even so—as with all
the others I talked to who came from Richard's past—there was no
"soft soap": sadness because he was gone—much of that—but no
false sentiment. "I used to have a terribly runny nose," said Marian,
"and I was that much younger than him and he would be landed
with me by Mam. 'Take Marian to the park, Rich,' she would say
and he would grumble but off he'd go. And then he'd meet the boys
and want to play football—he was mad about rugby football, he
would play with a tin can if there was nothing else. And I would
be standing there with my runny nose. So he'd make an effort and
play a game. And then he'd suggest hide-and-seek. I was to do the

counting—up to a hundred (I couldn't count up to a hundred, I had to do it in tens) and when I opened my eyes he'd have disappeared. Gone to play football in another part of the park. But I could always find him. Even in the streets I could always find him. And he was never nasty. He'd just say—'oh, here she is!' and take me in.''

"He used to help us with our homework," said Rhianon. "He was very quick. He would say to us—'I've told you *once*!' ''

There are plenty of stories of his singing. Very few about his acting until his adolescence. "The first time I remember was at home," said Marian. "Mam had asked him to look after us and there were just the three children in the house. He told us to sit by the fire. Then he went out and came back with his eyes all black and slitted, his face streaked with soot, a blanket around him and he shouted, 'I am Charlie Chan!' and pulled out the carving knife. We were nearly hysterical. He got very worried, had to calm us down before Cis came back."

The acting he saw as a boy was at the local cinema, popularly known as the "Cach"—the "Shithouse." Cis did her best to call it correctly the Picturedrome, but alas . . . From seven or eight onwards he would go with his cousin Dilwyn, spend some of his hard-earned money on a packet of five Woodbines, and hope for action. Cowboy films were the favourite: love stories despised. "Bloody love," he would say in disgust when asked why he had not enjoyed the film. "Bloody love." Burton never—to my knowledge—spoke of the early mass of films he had seen with any of that significant affection other actors give to their earliest influences. I suspect his own life was more than a match for the movies, although he did like to imitate Hopalong Cassidy. The camera does not seem to have made the take-over bid for his active imagination that other people record. But the celluloid dreams filtered through. Like the politics of the miners which seamed through the talk of his brothers, never as vivid as the "stories" but always there, those early films provided him with examples of acting which he must have absorbed willy-nilly. When he needed a political opinion he never had to reach far for it—there it was in that treasure trove of a Welsh childhood. So perhaps when he needed to fly by instinct in deciding the course of his career, there was the Cach, the action, the absorbed attention of everybody he knew and the glamour of illicit cigarette smoke uncoiling in the beam of the projector.

Sport was his passion. Girls were all right and, Marian says, he "always had a fan-club. True, you know. From about twelve, I would say, there would be girls around the house and crying and Cis would say, 'I've had Phyllis here and you promised to meet her.' 'Sorry, Cis—been playing football.' " Cricket was greatly loved—and he became captain of cricket; Ifor taught him tennis; at table tennis he had been well coached—locally, of course—and could be fanatical. But football—Welsh rugby football—the amateur game that put fifteen men in red jerseys to take on England most especially at Cardiff Arms Park and *beat the hell out of them!*—football was his passion. "I would rather have played for Wales at Cardiff Arms Park than Hamlet at the Old Vic," he said later.

He just might have done. As a schoolboy it was thought he would have been in line for an International cap had the war not prevented all that. In the RAF he played for a representative Welsh side with a famous senior International, Bleddyn Williams.

On page 37 of his volume of reminiscences [Burton was to write in an article on rugby], Mr. Williams is kind enough to suggest that I had distinct possibilities as a player were it not for the lure of tinsel and paint and money and fame and so on. Incidentally, one of the curious phenomena of my library is that when you take out Bleddyn's autobiography from the shelves it automatically opens at the very page mentioned above. Friends have often remarked on this and wondered afresh at the wizardry of the Welsh. It is in fact the only notice I cherish.

As a boy he knew the names of the players in all the Welsh teams, the local teams, the world-beating teams.

I come from a fanatically rugby-conscious Welsh miner's family; five of my six brothers played it with some distinction. I even knew a Welsh woman from Taibach who before a home match at Aberavon would drop goals from around forty yards with either foot to entertain the crowd and her name, I remember, was Annie More . . . What's more, I knew people like a one-armed inside half—he'd lost an arm in the First World War—who played with murderous brilliance for Caernarvon for years when I was a boy. He was particularly adept, this one, at stopping a forward bursting through from the line-out with a startling iron-hard thrust from his stump as he pulled him on to it with the other . . . Jimmy-One-Arm . . . a great many people who played unwarily against him died unexpectedly in their early forties.

He was dismissive about his own ability.

In my teens I had lived precariously on the lip of first class rugby by virtue of knowing every trick in the canon, evil and otherwise, by being a bad bad loser, but chiefly and perhaps *only* because I was very nippy off the mark. I was 5'10½" in height in bare feet and weighed soaking wet no more than 12½ stone and since I played in the park, usually at open side wing forward, and since I played against genuinely big men, it therefore followed I had to be galvanically quick. When faced with bigger and faster forwards I was doomed. R. T. Evans of Newport, Wales and the Universe, for instance—a racy 14½ stone and 6'1½", was a nightmare to play against and shaming to play with, both of which agonies I suffered a lot, mostly, thank God, the latter, lesser cauchemar. Genuine class, of course, doesn't need size, though sometimes I forget this.

On the day of his first marriage, his wife went off to perform in a matinée and Burton listened to the International match. Wales lost. He was reliably reported to be badly out of sorts for the rest of the evening. Wherever he was in the world he managed to get hold of all the important rugby results. Just as whatever production he worked on, his contract specified that he would never work on St. David's Day—the Welsh National Day. Cliff Morgan, a marvellously tricky Welsh stand-off half, became a pal late in Richard's life and told me "there was no doubting his passion for the game. Or his knowledge. He loved the complexities of it all. I asked around about him as a player and they said he was 'rough and fearless.' "

The consequences of this passion were widespread, comical and partly tragic. Once when he had to play a matinée at the Old Vic, for instance, in *Hamlet*, scarcely offstage for a moment, there was a Welsh International match. Burton had a portable radio in the wings and for some reason Lord Hamlet kept straying across stage to those wings all afternoon. But that was not enough. Other actors were instructed to bring on the score. It was said that Gertrude gave him the final result.

He used to go down to Cardiff from London for big games, rarely missing an International unless someone like Hamlet intervened. After one such day, on the journey back, he and his brother Ifor ended up in a nasty fight with several English supporters and it was to this that he traced the beginning of his lifelong, terribly painful and ultimately crushing spinal problems.

Neck and back injuries are, in any case, very common among rugby players. Particularly vulnerable are those—like Richard—who play, as it were, "out of their weight." He was light for what he did and played in a place and at a time when very heavy tackling was the chief feature of the game. After all, many of those he was up against would have been miners, like his five brothers, like Ifor who could carry a bag of cement under each arm. Burton was deep-chested, as strongly built as a Welsh pit-pony, but his very virtues—"fearless"—and his total commitment probably threw him into impact tackles which, together with the grinding wear and tear of the game, did his bones no favours. I was interested in the anonymous neighbour's comment on Ifor that "all the Jenkins boys had trouble with their bones." We are talking of a period and of a class in which nutritional deficiencies were commonplace.

Most important of all, though, rugby football gave Burton a real and early taste of fame. You couldn't fake it out there on a cold bleak field with twenty-nine others and despite his modesty, Burton was among the best. Several others have testified to his trouble-shooting capacities. When one friend was being picked on and hacked by a bullying and much bigger opponent, Burton laid the bully out; when the referee was not looking, of course. To be a hero on the field and to aspire to the red jersey of Wales was far and away the most dashing thing you could do. Burton put himself alongside that select company.

Rugby sank a deep shaft to masculine and sporting company and he drew on that for pleasure and refreshment throughout his life. By his mid-teens, just after war broke out, he was a star. The school magazine put it in writing: "R. Jenkins has been a tower of strength in Rugby and under normal circumstances would probably have gained an International cap. He is without doubt worthy of the honour.''

It was also the cause of much of the trouble with Elfed. ''Coming home from school he had to cross the park,'' said Cis, ''and he would always play football without coming home to change his clothes. Ruin his shoes. Very expensive to replace. He always promised to come home first but then, he would say, 'Sorry, Cis. I just got carried away.' Elfed got mad.'' But Cis took his side. And there was Ifor, part of the greatness of the town team. And all of the family starting to watch the boy more closely as he sailed or forced himself through one limit after the other—a talent, it was beginning to seem, in every pocket. Watched over by Cis ''who couldn't help herself.''

3
A Working-Class Hero

He had won first prize at the eisteddfod as a boy soprano. He was of International standard as a rugby player and captain of cricket. He had girl friends from the age of twelve and was rumoured to drink beer not long afterwards. At school he dared answer back to the Headmaster—politely—when he felt he was in the right. And one way and another he got together, in most weeks, as much spending money as a young working miner. None of this, though, for Ifor or for Cis or, I presume, for the rest of the family, was to be compared with the fact that Richard Walter Jenkins Junior, aged eleven, passed a scholarship to the Secondary School and went there: the first Jenkins of that line ever to do so. *That* was glory.

Throughout his life he was deeply impressed by writers and scholars. He tried to be the former and his Notebooks show his struggle: the latter he knew he could never be but always revered. Ifor worked in the mines, played his rugby and read poetry: dangerous work, hard sport and learning; a masculine ideal come down unalloyed from Ancient Greece to Pontrhydyfen. Burton always had a calm, lofty perspective on his work as an actor. This came partly from that confidence built up in the wide affection of the large family, partly perhaps from the arrogance of the supreme athlete, mostly, though, from his view that writing and learning were the real thing: acting was fine and dandy but not in the same league.

Burton was always a great reader. Pride of his house in Swit-

zerland was a library. It is the lair of a glutton for reading, full of
hardbacks and paperbacks bought, read, discussed in his Notebooks
and in the case of poetry, often and remarkably remembered in large
and eloquent part—from John Donne, Edward Thomas, John Betjeman, Gerard Manley Hopkins, William Dunbar and others including
of course Shakespeare and Dylan Thomas. Dylan, his first independent discovery, later became, wonderfully, a friend. He was a
man brought up a bus ride away from Taibach, a word-clotted surreal
dark comedy Welshman whom Burton adored. It is terrible news
for publicists and headline hunters everywhere but the secret has to
be revealed. Even at the perilous height of his Drunk Welsh Star
with Mega Diamond Wife Shocks Sin City headline-hugging period,
he liked to be in front of a fire with a pile of new paperbacks and
maybe, but by no means compulsively, a glass of wine: often undrunk. Everywhere he went he took a book-bag. Everyone I have
spoken to about him—without exception—brought up his reading,
the breadth of it, the compulsion, and the evangelical enjoyment he
took in passing on what he had read the night before. He was a
light sleeper, for long periods an insomniac. Print absorbed many
of the hours of solitary darkness.

He went to Eastern Infants School where the playing field was a
concrete yard and you trained for football by being slammed against
a brick wall. Classes were about fifty strong but discipline, we are
told, was excellent. If the teacher criticised or even hit you then the
last thing to do was complain at home because the certainty was
you would be criticised or hit again. The industrial mass was then
a drilled mass and what it also knew was that to survive you had
to take no chances: the best thing to say was nothing. Burton's local
fame grew in contradicting this up to a point—but only up to a
point. By later blackboard-jungle classroom-rebel standards he
would have appeared as disciplined as a fearful nun.

He read hard from the beginning—everything from the most
popular to the most awesome works. That was his own drive. His
luck—and he would have a lot of luck (which he acknowledged
generously and constantly)—was to meet here the first of many
teachers who set him on his way.

Some thought Meredith Jones a rough, bullying master, picking
out the brightest boys to train them up for the scholarship class
and by their results inflate his own ego. Burton would have none

of that. Jones was, he wrote, "a recognisable spiritual descendant of Geraldus Cambrensis and Shakespeare's Fluellen—passionate, fluent, something of a scholar . . . of remarkable vitality and afraid of nobody." Nor was Burton afraid of him: Jones appreciated that.

To pass the scholarship was to enter a fine world. You need not then be a miner, a butcher's boy, a shop assistant, go into the steel works, do dirty work. You were set on a different road: you could even become—who knows?—a schoolteacher. Jones drummed old-time learning into his chosen corps and, in March 1937, Richard sat the scholarship and passed it. That autumn, he entered Port Talbot Secondary School. "Without Meredith Jones I would never have gone to University," he said. Joy, at 73 Caradoc Street, was unconfined.

Over the next four and a half years Burton, like a young shark eating all before it, devoured the sport, the small-town adventure life, the clubs and choirs and outings available. He was good enough at the schoolwork but not at all outstanding. He acted a little, played an American Mr. Vanhattan in Shaw's *The Apple Cart*—but his true worlds were the sports field and the streets. Out of this time came the first stories of his boldness—answering back to a teacher, taking out girls, and of course the all-dazzling displays at rugby and cricket. Then in his fifth year at the school, when he ought to have been aiming for his school certificate which was the next and essential passport for that golden educated future, he left abruptly to work as a haberdasher's assistant in the local Co-operative store. It was a terrible fall: humiliating and very painful. It was, in one sense, his first serious test of character. Everything until then had come easy. Now he was down and he hated it.

Tennessee Williams has written about several football heroes who suddenly drop through the floor at the height of their prowess. And there's Biff in Arthur Miller's *Death of a Salesman*. What those and others have in common—and their authors understood—was the greatness of that adolescent fall, the sheerness of the descent from the podium of acclaim to a life sentence committed to the stock room of a Co-operative store in a provincial town. In class and cultural terms, it was one of those occupational zones with no way out. How had his star fallen? And where were Cis and Ifor?

It is not easy to be precise here as a gentle curtain is drawn. All that Burton himself would say (much later) was that "something of a small family crisis demanded that I should leave school and go to work." Elfed, it appears, was ill and off work. He had borne the brunt of Rich's upbringing for almost fourteen years and the boy was past "normal" school-leaving age. He was a difficult boy. No master pleaded for his future: it seemed that he had traded in his scholarship for that foreign and rather dangerous element—self-expression. Elfed could and did pull strings on the local Co-operative committee. At twenty-eight shillings a week, "it was considered a good position," says Marian, his daughter. "It was a collar-and-tie job. It was a job for life. It was *practically* pensionable!"

There is no record of anyone in the family resisting this move. Perhaps they felt that it had been a dream all along, always doomed, this fantastical idea that their young brother would go on and get himself a serious education, even go to college. Out of reach, and all of them too busy with their own lives . . . But they must have seen how he hated it. "I broke my heart over him when he went to the shop," said Cis. "He *hated* it. Oh—he *hated* it."

Perhaps the consensus was that as Elfed had borne the burden, he had the right to make the decision. Older brothers had offered to help out along the way and—as the Christmas bounty proved—presents had come along and sixpences and treats. But Elfed had persevered. However, the boy was hard to handle, smoking, and drinking most likely, out with girls, too grown up for school.

Daddy Ni, as ever, drifted about the edges of the conflict, concentrating on the dogs, the pubs . . .

There are two versions of Rich's tearaway youth. One that it is rather a myth. That won't wash. At fifteen he was an independent, tough and troublesome man-boy. Teachers, relatives and friends enough testify to that. But it has to be in proportion. Being a rebel in Taibach's mining and chapel community was coming in at 10.50 when you had promised to be in by 10.15. It was taking out a girl with a trail of boasts littering the streets behind you, although you both returned as virginal as you had set off but usually much colder. "He had class," the girls said. "He was never a groper." Being a rebel was answering back—often countering idiotic commands with common sense but "answering back" all the same when parade-ground obedience was demanded from all budding industrial soldiers. It was the threat of disturbing the order—an order hard worked for and not to be upset because surely worse would replace it. Hold what you had. Keep ambition low. Look after your own. Keep yourself to yourself . . . Dour survivalist precepts. In the chapels the favoured Book of Revelations was interpreted by the Welsh bardic preachers to portend the overthrow of the bosses, the rout of present power, the rise to glory and authority of the congregations of the oppressed. But that was not allowed to leak out of the chapel. Rich was a threat. Most of all to himself. Put him out to work: that would school him. And Elfed was right: it did. In his own way.

He could have stuck in. It was a decent wage, an easy job, plenty of energy left over for rugby, for girls, for the play-acting in which he was becoming interested. The haberdashery counter could have been a useful enough base for his operations. Or he could at least have appeared to accept it and put on a show: he was already capable enough of that. But he did neither. And his reaction was, I think, the first self-defining move of his life—and undoubtedly the most crucial.

First of all he let nothing stand in the way of his true feelings. He felt humiliated—apart from everything else, the soppiness of being a shop assistant in a family of miners brought out a terrible blush for his masculinity: absurd, you might think, but not so absurd if that was your world. His brothers came back with stories of heaving and hacking coal: even Daddy Ni still worked at the face: even Elfed, seen as the over-restraining killjoy, worked down there. And Rich? Rich delivered boxes of socks and learnt how to fold a suit. He would linger on those delivery trips and stay for dinner or tea or come back via the Talbot, the pub across the road, although he was under age. He engineered a reputation for being "hopeless." He showed his world his contempt for the job by doing it very badly. He cannot have been unaware of the risk. "He hated it," repeated Cis, still afflicted by the memory.

He took a much greater and more serious risk, one which his relatives to this day gloss over or fudge. But the fact is he acted illegally. Had he been caught or had he panicked he could well have been in very serious trouble: the charming young tearaway could have become a court case.

It was wartime and there were government coupons for almost

everything. Certainly for clothes. You paid your money but you also paid your coupons—ensuring some stab at equality and some effort at control. No coupons, no goods. But not at the Co-op when Rich was alone. A nod was as good as a wink. Friends of the family discovered their coupons returned or were relieved of the duty of delivering them. His fame grew. Difficult to prove at this stage when so many clam up but I have a distinct feeling that it was not only coupons that were being given away.

What was he up to? Well, there was the devilment of it, and the showing off and the natural generosity—all mingled together in the mischief and excitement of an act of illegality. Crime, like boxing, is one of the ways working-class boys get their feet under tables otherwise forbidden to them. It is also seductive—the achingly boring days in the Co-operative were suddenly spiced by the conspiring behind the haberdashery counter. Working-class heroes have often flirted with delinquency in adolescence: it is hard to find the right channel for extraordinary energy. Some would say it was a cry for help. He was certainly clever enough and wise enough to know the risk he was taking and yet he took it. Cis, who knew about it, was scared stiff.

I think that he was pulling himself down to touch the pit of his character. "He hated that shop, hated it." They all tell you that. Like someone pulling a blanket over his head and defying nature to do its worst, he sank and pushed himself down as far as he could go. If he was going to be a failure, then let the full extent of his failure be experienced. It was a way of imposing some sort of initiation ceremony on himself. Oh—it was high spirits and daft and cocky, of course: but it was also self-abasement. The sort of abasement novices have to go through before they are admitted to an order. It was as if he were scouring all the weakness out of himself by an equivalent to giving himself the disease. Like Thomas Hardy, I think, he held "that if way to the Better there be, it exacts a full look at the worst." And they did notice him.

He was not much of a prospect. Suffering badly—as usual— from boils (he gave them all nicknames)—"it's the badness coming out," they would say—disenfranchised in the great educational paperchase, neither a macho miner nor a successful exception, he was a nobody in the middle of nowhere with no prospects. But having let himself sink as far as he could go, he began to rise and with such gathering force and fury that he not only routed all who had disbelieved in him, he left even the believers agape. He would miss no more opportunities. Acting was the escape tunnel.

Meredith Jones had begun a youth centre for boys and girls. It met in the evenings in the leaking old Eastern Infants School. This was the site on which Burton regrouped. He was a fierce table-tennis player, he boxed, he sang, he larked around and lent a hand and, boils and all, emerged as one of the natural leaders in that competitive group. That lavish endowment of talent, which had been blotted up in sport and intense boyish preoccupations, was now called up in all its force and it did not let him down. The club's pivot was the drama: its master was Leo Lloyd—the second of those men who were to promote the career of so many boys and girls from the Afan valley.

Lloyd did not patronise them. The youth of Port Talbot were broken in on great drama and fired, from the beginning, to reach for the sky. Perhaps, like Meredith Jones, Lloyd's natural interest and generosity were spurred on both by the obvious scarcity of opportunity for the children in that industrial beehive and by the war which had just broken out. The peers of these teachers and the relatives of the boys were dying for their country—all the more need to help its future generation. Burton wrote, with typical flaring generosity (like his fellow Welshman, Henry VII, he never forgot those who had been with him around the campfire when the crown was hardly even a dream in unreal England):

> Leo Lloyd was monastically devoted to his job—it is difficult for me to realise it was all done in his spare time—. . . he persuaded me that acting was infinitely fascinating. He taught me the fundamentals of the job . . . unsparingly . . . he channelled my discontent and made me want to be an actor.

Rich was brilliant as a count in a one-act play based on *Les Misérables*. And he appeared in a radio documentary about the Air Training Corps of which he was a member.* But he was still a haberdasher's assistant.

*The Air Training Corps (ATC) was set up throughout the country to pre-train the older schoolboys for their war service.

Cis was coming out of the Co-op one day (hoping that Rich had not, yet again, taken some cigarettes and put them on her account), when she met a bristle-moustached Meredith Jones who demanded, "How can you let him do it?" Even today as she tells the story, she is harassed. "I told him—my husband had a hard job, he wasn't working for a time. I told him . . ."

"He could be a good actor," said Meredith Jones, confounding Cis utterly. "I'll see what I can do."

It is more than likely that Cis had never seen her young brother/ son act in any formal sense at this time. Hence her bafflement. But she held her peace and waited for the miracle.

Meredith Jones's decision and subsequent determination are a remarkable tribute to him. What it says about the young tearaway is even more remarkable. Not only had he made a unique and convulsing impact on this generous but hardheaded man, he had made it as an *actor*. Something he had done rarely and with no great sense that "this was it." Yet it was as an actor that he was now seen. Not a footballer—for which there was much more evidence—nor a scholar unfortunately lapsed—for which, judging from his reading alone, there was also much evidence of promise at least. But as an actor. Already he was capable, it seemed, of making that impact on the stage which was, in record time, to put him at the top of his treacherous profession and bring on the applause of his finest contemporaries. In his time of exile, he had found a focus. The boy of all talents, the hero without a quest, the "natural" who failed had found a purpose. He would not let go of it. And meanwhile, Mr. Jones told Cis he would see what he could do.

What Meredith Jones did took some months and what he did was unprecedented. He persuaded the Chairman of the Glamorgan Education Committee, Llewellyn Heycock, to have the boy readmitted to the grammar school. "He came home," said Cis. "I was upstairs. Cis! Cis! Nobody's done this before. Cis! Something wonderful has happened! There's a chance. They're going to take me back!"

Eighteen months after he had left, he went back to complete unfinished business. He was a man among children but he swallowed that. He was there on sufferance and most likely on trial and he knew that. His reputation went before him and it was not auspicious. A teacher, Philip Burton, a friend of Meredith Jones and Richard's commanding officer in the ATC, was asked to keep a special eye on this extremely rough—diamond? They were taking a chance. Rich marked his first day back at school by opening the door and wanging a gym shoe violently across the classroom: it broke a window. He had come out of a nightmare with something of the steel town's steel inside him. He was back: but, the gym shoe signalled, on his own terms.

4
The Man Who
Gave Him His Name

The Jenkins family network had failed. True, Elfed had swung him a collar-and-tie job that was "practically pensionable": true, Cis was always there and the other brothers and sisters would look out for him. But sixteen was a man and when he had begun to drown as a man there was nothing they could or did do to step in and help. Richard would never blame them for that. But he never forgot that for almost a year he sank like a stone and would have disappeared without trace but for outside intervention. From now on he would take care of himself and, as time went on, to ensure family solidarity, he would take care of the family. Indeed much of his life was spent creating and caring for families of one kind or another. The system would not let him down again. He would listen to outsiders. He would go further: he would seek out those who could help. Philip Burton was to be the most powerful of these.

This is the time when Rich's life was reshaped. He went back to school a misfit, troublesome, confused, way behind in his studies, far too independent for his own good and on trial. Less than a year later he was embarked on a career which would take him from the industrial grime of Taibach into films and on to the West End with hardly a pause for breath. Philip Burton engineered all that.

He could not have done it, of course, without the raw material and that is what he found in Rich and that, at first, is how he treated him. Until love and then awe came in.

Richard was engaged on what must often have appeared to him to be a bewildering balancing act. First there was the character he had become. Everyone who knew him in those schooldays—men and women alike—speak with affection of him: stories tumble out like clothes spilling out of a split suitcase—Richard peeing out of the train window as the engine roared by the station platform, Richard taking a girl up on to a mountain and scaring her to flight at his howl as a passionate hand landed on one of his more angry boils, Rich, reeking of beer, rolling into school and being sent home. Rich the larrikin, the local hero, star of the rugby field and the club— who did it all out of infinitely pardonable devilment. And the moody Rich who would take a girl out to sit by a river, leave her as untouched as a Madonna in a Lady Chapel and read poetry aloud. One of the impressive things about all this is that everyone agrees about his modesty, his lack of show. Later, at Oxford, Robert ("Tim") Hardy, who came from an extremely well-connected family, talked, emphatically, about Richard as a "natural aristocrat: born to command." Grand though this sounds, it seems to be borne out by those who knew him about that time. One of many seeming contradictions.

This core of his character was formed. He had "found himself" young and firmly held on to that; as he was to do with remarkable consistency. Yet he had to bend that independent character of a man to the urgent and cropping world of the educational imperative. It was up in the morning and back to school. Grateful though he was—and there are few examples of anyone more grateful and generous than he was to those who had in any way helped him or even just been around in the bad times—he was not going to be craven or knuckle down like a goody-two-shoes. Anyway he could not. His character would not let him. Meredith Jones—who relished his protégé's roughness—was aware of that and told his friend Philip Burton to keep an eye on him, make sure he did not let slip this second and last chance.

He was strung between a character which threatened to spoil his opportunity and an opportunity which threatened to shear away his character. He had the added confusion of not knowing what he wanted to be and when an ambition did dawn, not knowing how he could possibly achieve it. On returning to the Secondary School he had told the staff that his ambition was to become a teacher, which was politic. But after some success at Meredith Jones's youth club and after getting on terms with Philip Burton, the great tide of energy which just wanted *release*, to get *on*, to get *out*, funnelled into the notion that he might be an actor. For the twelfth child of Daddy Ni, in wartime Wales, with conscription the order of almost everyone's day, it was an audacious ambition.

But not entirely fantastical. After all, there was Owen Jones. Jones had won a scholarship to the Royal Academy of Dramatic Art in London. Jones had played Laertes to Olivier's Hamlet at the Old Vic. Other boys from Port Talbot Secondary had been escorted through the mysterious gates into the fabled world of professional acting—the man who had done all that was Philip Burton. Burton was Richard's opportunity; Richard was Burton's great chance.

It is not too difficult an exercise to set out Philip and Rich as violent opposites—a mismatch made in mischief. But their need for each other was the basis of Rich's affection for Philip and the source of the older man's power over the boy who would gratefully take his teacher's name and put it up in lights half way around the world. They were to call each other "father" and "son" and be friends with one sole interruption until Richard's death. All they had in common, to begin with, was this terrible need: Rich for a mentor who would make him grow, Philip for a pupil who would take on the weight of unspent devotion. But that was some way off: at the start and on the surface . . . chalk and cheese, day and night, sun and moon.

Philip Burton's early life had been calculated to bring him up as "a spotless youth." His parents were Anglo-Welsh, his father a beer-drinking, musical miner killed in a pit accident when the boy was fourteen; his mother dogged, the one who bound a steel hoop of gentility around her Philip, the one who somehow saw him to the University of Wales from which he emerged aged twenty with a double honours degree in History and Mathematics. There was talk of some grandeur in the English past and some evidence of middle-class money which did not come to the aid of Philip. He had his living to make and he came to Port Talbot to make it as a teacher. By that time he had been twice smitten. Firstly by the theatre; secondly by what he called his Pygmalion, even his Svengali, complex. He wrote plays and sent them off to West End managements and kept writing when they were rejected: he did some work as a freelance writer, producer and actor on BBC Radio which had studios in Cardiff. And there were the school plays. As for

Svengali, Owen Jones was one of several who had been mesmerised out of Port Talbot by Burton's powers. He could be very fierce in pursuit of his ideals.

He lived the life "of a spotless bachelor." Ma Smith took in gentlemen paying guests and for his outlay he had a bedroom, a personal sitting room and the dedicated service of the widowed Mrs. Smith and her daughters. His hours were long and strict. In addition to his school life and his theatrical life and his special coaching of the boys, he would play the organ in church (*not* chapel: he was an Anglican) and several times a week work with his boys in the Air Training Corps which he turned into one of the finest in the principality, often called on for show parades. He read deeply and liked his own company. He used to tell Mrs. Smith that "a cultured person is never lonely." When Richard returned to school, Philip was thirty-eight, formidable and, locally, not a little feared.

Philip was sternly drilled in his ways. Richard was like a gusher of newly tapped oil spraying about in all directions. Philip's emotional background was tight, controlled, everything in its proper place, unhappy and deeply unaffectionate. Rich roared out of a conflagration of overlapping, overspilling, competing and confusing flailing emotions in which little was as it seemed. Philip was austere, Rich profligate, Philip clean and tidy, Rich, at that time, smelly-socked and rough. Rich was restless, active, an athlete, Philip a man of the desk and the study, interested only in things of the mind. Philip always very cautious, Richard always extremely careless.

Yet within a few months of Richard's returning to school he had moved in with Philip, leaving his own family to do so. However much he struggled—which he did—he was lashed into line by Philip and finally took his name. This man from Mountain Ash pointed him not only towards the theatre but to his own Olympus of ambition—the University of Oxford of which, in those days, a miner's son could not even afford to dream.

The steel in Philip Burton—and it had to be steel for the young Jenkins to take instruction—was his scholarship. Meredith Jones was a great talker and on the way back home from the youth club he

> would talk for instance [Richard later wrote] of the "Love Song of J. Alfred Prufrock" and hold us all, a group of

young boys, spellbound as he unfolded with conscious looks of wonder the marvellous courage of the man Eliot to write the poem "Prufrock" at the time he did. "No 'If I should die think only this of me' or Sassoon and Owen and Thomas with their beautiful bitterness but 'I have measured out my life in coffee spoons.' What a gesture, gentlemen."

Meredith in the high flow of his talk would describe anybody of whatever age or sex as "gentlemen" as if at a council meeting. "What quiet bravery and who's to say, who will argue with me, who will deny that Prufrock's slow death was not the more terrible." But Philip Burton was a proven scholar and a writer and an opener of doors thought slammed shut forever in the face of a hungry and rough Welsh Jenkins. Meredith Jones could shove you out of the Co-op and back to school: Philip Burton might take you to Xanadu.

Philip now lives in Key West. He became an American citizen many years ago, ran an acting school in New York, wrote books, produced plays, leaving the confined valleys of Wales where superabundant energy and effort were needed to achieve quite ordinary goals, for the land of opportunity and plenty. He has done well.

Now in his eighties but crackling alert, he is happy alike to talk about his view of Hamlet and his literary friends in the town, the work he was doing in the church, the essays he was writing: there is an irresistible donnish delight in his manner and calmness, the repose of the greatly confident—a quality which was later attributed to Richard. You could see that the "rough and fearless" young rugby player, the suspicious street boy now, despite his pock-fretten skin, coming into a youthful handsomeness which men and women alike would call "beauty," would break like a wave on the serenity of Philip's rock of scholarship. Scholarship and sport and money and poetry: four of the things that mattered to the young Welshman, and something else he needed more: opportunity. He had been given and had himself taken an immense amount out of that mining culture. But his was still a subject class. He and Philip Burton conducted what could be looked on as some kind of elaborate courtship ritual which would result in his hurtling on to a world stage.

After we had talked, Philip read to me from an unpublished memoir which he had entitled "The Two Burtons." His voice is well-trained, clear, very "English" it would be thought. Unlike Richard he was not brought up in Welsh but learnt it as a foreign language. Richard had the opposite experience: to him English was the foreign language, the tongue of the occupying race, and he conquered it completely. Philip told what is, in fact, an extraordinary tale beginning as the not uncommon (for those times) attempt to rescue a poor but talented boy from his circumstances and ending as some sort of love story. A few months later he decided not to publish the book but with tremendous generosity said that I could use whatever I wanted from it.

One day in 1964, while Richard was playing in *Hamlet* on Broadway, he and I were interviewed jointly in a private corner of an Eighth Avenue bar and restaurant much frequented by theatre people. We had a live audience of one, Richard's wife, Elizabeth Taylor. One of the questions aimed at me was, "How did you come to adopt him?" For reasons that will become apparent I hesitated in order to make a true and careful answer, and Richard jumped in with "He didn't adopt me; I adopted him." There was much truth in that. He needed me, and, as I realised later, he set out to get me.

Years later he found a diary he had kept as a schoolboy in 1940, two years before I became really aware of him, and he gave it to me. There are thirteen references to me in it, all of them complimentary; sometimes I appear as "Burton" and at other times as "Mr. Burton."

Nearly every Sunday starts with the entry "Chapel all day." Welsh was the language of the chapel Richard attended, and he and many others found a weekly joy in the singing. Even after he came to live with me, he still joined the family at chapel every Sunday.

There are frequent references in his diary to air-raids, sometimes two or three in the same day. Port Talbot had a large and vital steelworks, and moonlit nights almost always brought the Luftwaffe, but they also came in daylight. The diary records no fear of the bombings. I remember that, a few years later, when I took Richard to London for the first time, we experienced a very heavy raid. I thought he was following me and other hotel-guests to the shelter, but he wasn't; he had gone up to the roof "to watch it all." The diary records that even when the family went to a nearby shelter he would stay in bed.

To Elfed, Richard was a potential wage-earner, and there he was in school, costing money not earning it. There are several references in the diary to rows with Elfed. Sometimes the causes were trifling, as when Richard returned some books to the library including one that Elfed had wanted to read.

There's a very revealing entry for Tuesday, May 21st. Elfed must have got hold of the diary. I don't know how much of it he read, but the entry for May 20th must have galled him because it told him that the potential wage-earner had spent much of the day in playing cricket. In pencil he wrote, "At four o'clock Richard Walter shits his pants." Since this was written in pencil, why didn't Richard erase it? It seems he wanted to preserve the evidence of Elfed's attitude to him. He even added a comment: "This was written by Elfed in an attempt to spoil the Book, but it will remain if I live to be 100."

That diary is filled in on every single day throughout that year— 1940. He was fourteen. Not a line is wasted. On May 22nd (the day following his terrible vow against Elfed) he writes up a typical entry: "Went to see *As You Like It* as performed by Form 4. It was very good. Trevor George [a close pal] was the star of the evening as Touchstone the clown. The war has taken a serious turn against us. The Huns are only fifteen miles from the Channel. But am confident we'll pull through." Shakespeare, stardom, pals and the war—much of his adolescence is there. Every single Sunday of that year records "Chapel all day." Fights are chronicled. Modesty asserted—he is selected to run in several events for his school against Mountain Ash and he writes: "I hope there are no crack runners because I am no crack." The mischief is there. "Bought a pipe for a bit of fun—smoked it for a bet." Philip, understandably, selects those passages revealing his uneasy situation in the house of Cis and Elfed.

A poignant reflection on the situation occurs in the entries for Thursday and Friday, October 10th and 11th. Thursday: "Had a terrible row today; Elfed told me to go back to Pontrhydyfen. I walked as far as Cwmavon. I hate the sight of Elfed. I am going to ask Daddy to take me back home where I can go to work. I could never stay home now." Friday: "I intended to go to Ponty but I have cooled off a bit now. Cis wants me to go if I want to. But I am sure that wherever I go I will not be wanted, the same as here."

Richard returned to school a month before his seventeenth birthday. As a result of his lost schooling he couldn't return to his previous class, and so was at least a year older than the other boys and girls in the class to which he was now assigned. With his experience of the world he was now a young man among kids.

He took two steps which brought him into contact with me: he joined the ATC Squadron, and he saw to it that he did Fire-Watch duty on my nights. Every night some of the older boys, under the charge of a master, had to maintain watch at the school because of the air-raids. In particular they had to deal with a fire-bomb that might get lodged on the roof. Richard's fire-watching finally resulted in his coming to live with me.

During our fire-watching, Richard seized every opportunity for private talks with me, which were often interrupted by air-raid warnings. I soon became very interested by his undoubted potential—but for what? He was developing an acute social and political conscience, and I could see him devoting his life to the Labour Party. When he told me that he wanted to be an actor like Owen Jones, I was very surprised but instinctively excited and challenged.

I told Richard that, if he wanted to become a professional actor, he first had to change both the quality of his voice and his speech, and that would involve hard and tiresome work. His response was, "All right; change 'em."

He began to tell me the difficulties of his life at home, and finally he told me that he had tried more than once to find a home with another brother or sister, but they had persuaded him to return to Cis and Elfed. I am sure that they had a twofold motivation: reluctance to be burdened with a teenager who wasn't earning a wage, and the consideration of how much he meant to Cis. One night I was so touched by yet another account of his plight that I said, without realising the full implications of what I was saying, that there was a spare bedroom in Mrs. Smith's house. (The bank clerk who had occupied it had been called up to the army.) He seized on it and asked when he could move in. I immediately backtracked, and he said with a sorrow that made me feel guilty, "When push comes to shove, nobody wants me." I began to defend my withdrawal. I said that soon he would be in the Air Force and no longer a financial burden on Elfed, and, even more than that, when the war was over he would be a wage-earner at something or other, and would be able to help Elfed and Cis; what was more, Elfed would be already well aware that the liability he resented would become an asset he welcomed. I felt sure that Elfed, and still more Cis, would now be unwilling for him to leave. His reply was, "Ask Elfed; that's all; ask 'im." I had to agree to do so, and it was arranged that I would go to the Taibach house the following Sunday afternoon.

I have vivid memories of that Sunday afternoon meeting with Elfed and Cis in the front room of 73 Caradoc Street. I had gone there determined to use every argument I could muster to retain the situation of Richard's living with the James family. I had not met Cis or Elfed before.

Richard was not in the room. My first impression was of the Madonna-like beauty of Cis. She sat silent while the vigorous Elfed did all the talking with me. His answer to everything I said was, "You take 'im, Mr. Burton, you take 'im." I promised that his further education would be no burden to them, and that after the war, I would see to it that he received a free college education, which should not be denied him, but all I got was "You take 'im, Mr. Burton, you take 'im." Finally, in order to have a word with the silent Cis, I asked Elfed to fetch Richard, who had been awaiting in the kitchen the result of the meeting.

Reluctantly Elfed left the room and I said to Cis, "Ritchie is your son much more than your brother, and I know how much you love each other. What do you want me to do?" Her answer, which changed not only Richard's life but mine too, was, "If you take him it would be the answer to my prayers." When Elfed returned with Richard, I told them I would do as they all wished, and the room seemed to be filled with the happiness of relief.

He moved into 6 Connaught Street, Port Talbot, on March 1st, 1943, St. David's Day. His landlady was Mrs. Smith.

In Philip Burton's version, from then on, all was sweetness; Richard occasionally went back to the house of Cis and Elfed (on Sunday mornings) and the two of them got on with the transformation of the street boy into the stage man. But it is not the only version.

Even today, Cis's face grows dark at the memory. "We could have coped," she said. "We could've managed." It would have been surprising had there *not* been a ripple of unease running through the Jenkins family. There was a sort of shame in it: however much you could point to this being done before by dedicated teachers for brilliantly promising pupils—there was still a sort of shame in the boy being farmed out. And he had been taken from them. "Nobody knows how much I cried," said Cis, whose mothering of him was now over.

She had given him an ideal; she had given him what appears to have been unfailing and uncritical support: he was never as an adult to be easy without one woman on whom he could totally rely. Cis had also now given him perfect freedom.

He would come home (to her home) after school for his tea "but I would send him off to Mrs. Smith's. I said, 'Rich, it isn't fair. If you're going to stay there, you have to stay there properly.' He wasn't a happy boy. Why weren't you happy, Rich? He would tap his head. Too much of this, Cis: have to use this a lot now." Philip grew fiercely ambitious for the boy. The moulding was hard and marked him for life.

Contemporaries remember him coming scowling to school after what had clearly been rows with his patron. Richard has described this period as "pure hell" and "the hardest work I ever did in my life." Philip was relentless and the boy had no alternative: he obeyed or he would fail. However much he bucked against it, in the end, if he wanted to survive in this world, let alone succeed, he had to do everything the schoolteacher instructed him to do. The intellectual domination and the emotional charge which carried it rapidly whipped him out of his old ways.

It is essential to stress that although Philip's dedication to Richard became intense, it was part of a larger compulsion which preceded and succeeded Richard—to help young people get out and get on through education. Mr. G. Dear, who was at school with Richard, told me: "We learnt more in class from his talking above and beyond the subject matter than from others who stuck to the syllabuses . . . it was an honour to be selected for the annual school play . . ."

Later on as a teacher Mr. Dear was once called on to teach English and, "Naturally used Phil's methods. It so happened that the results were incredibly good—29 out of 30 pupils passed in the English Language paper, 27 in English Literature . . . I feel sure Phil was indirectly responsible! I want to acknowledge a personal debt to him. I am only one of the many who owe so much to the man."

Philip coached Richard in his schoolwork so efficiently that he was to pass the required certificate with ease despite having missed school for eighteen months. In Philip's two honours subjects, Maths and History, he did particularly well but he also passed in five other subjects including Welsh and his loathed Chemistry. To achieve that from a standing start in nine months meant application as well as ability. But in this period, his several talents, which had shone so clearly when he was much younger and somehow been lost in the scrum of his long adolescence, began to regroup.

For beside the schoolwork, Philip was as good as his word about turning Richard into an actor. "His voice," he wrote, "was rough to begin with but with constant practice it became memorably beautiful." It was the source of his acting genius. They practised in the living room on psalms and Shakespeare, sometimes the pitch rising so high that the Widow Smith feared her much-favoured gentleman paying guest and that charming but coarse Jenkins boy might be arguing. (Richard lacked refinement, Mrs. Smith thought: his table manners were not as nice as they should have been, he turned the lavatory in the garden into a smoker's den and he was so spoiled! Practically his first request to her had been to ask her to clean his shoes!) But Philip also took Richard out on to the hills and up to the top of Welsh mountains like master and disciple in some biblical parable. The boy would speak "say the Chorus from *Henry V* and I would go further and further away from him, forcing him not to shout but to make certain I could hear him. He soon learned that it was distinctness, not volume, that mattered." The voice changed: darkened, soared over the valley.

Philip has spoken of Richard's "wonderful, curious mind. I soon discovered he had a natural feeling for poetry. One Sunday morning after he had gone to his chapel and I to my church, he came back excitedly waving a newspaper and said 'Listen to this,' and he read the Dylan Thomas poem 'The force that through the green fuse drives the flower.' When he had finished I asked him what it meant. He replied, 'I don't know, but isn't it beautiful?' The poem was published several years before the incident. He used to collect old newspapers for fish-and-chip shops. I don't know where he had got it. All I do know is that it truly happened."

It began to matter to Philip that Richard was a "natural": just as it mattered to the boy himself. To have a gift somehow eased the soft and suspect business of being an aspiring actor in a dark and sweaty coal-steel town. To have a gift was superior, naturally aristocratic, it was to be a chosen one. When you were born as a scarcely distinguishable blob in the smoked ranks of the industrial army of the poor, when privilege was not only out of sight but in the hands of a foreign country, when you saw the daily cost of a necessary daily grind, then to have a "gift" was perhaps the only sure way to see an escape. Only through such an accidental, miraculous chance could anyone expect to shake off the yoke of grimly limited prospects. To Philip the boy's "gift" justified the increasing extravagance of his devotion and the growing bond of his love. For surely someone as gifted as that deserved all that could be done for him: and "the gift" put it above any gossip about an overkeen schoolmaster bringing on a bright pupil and overrode any chatter about the besotted nature of his devotion. Philip would sprinkle sugar on Richard's morning cereal; lend him clothes; buy him an expensive raincoat—although he was a thrifty man. (Richard lost the expensive raincoat the same night in a snooker hall.) If the boy had a "gift" then it was everyone's duty to see that it was not wasted. Because the gifted were rare and no sacrifice was too much.

It cannot have been easy for either of them. Philip confirms the continuation of Richard's subterranean drag of melancholy: the Welsh word is "hiraeth." Once, for example, having forgotten his key, he spent the night, he said, at his grandmother's grave, on the bank of a stream, the Frwdwyllt, the Wild Stream. And there was already the fear and the regret at the distance he seemed to be travelling from Ifor; the utter ignorance of what was going to happen when or if he *did* finally and two years late pass the examination. There would be active service in the war—without question. But then what?

And would there be anything at all? The bombs fell on South Wales and reports came in of young men killed in the air, on land, at sea. The war inside himself was a small conflagration compared with the bombardments he saw for himself and read about daily. Turbulence and violent death haunted his adolescence just as repression and hard tack had besieged his childhood.

Rich was now half way through his eighteenth year. His body was broad, strong, at ease with itself. The skin was bad and boils would still stalk the neck and shoulders. His eyes, blue-green, were set widely apart on a face which was defining itself rapidly now as unforgettable. Although his encounters with girls were way above average for the time and place and company he moved in, they were still sexually unsuccessful. Yet the charisma was already fuelled in large part by that sexual eagerness and masculine vulnerability which beat across the footlights and through the lens for years to come. Philip was in his prime. A chaste bachelor—impropriety unthinkable. And yet between these two, from what has been said and written and recollected by both, an intense and governing bond grew up unlikely though it had at first seemed. It was yet another layer in what was to become the bountiful and complex nature of Burton's attitude to sex, to authority, to love and to loyalty.

If there is one word—with hindsight—which describes the young boy throughout this most critical year, it would have to be "conqueror." There was always that about him—the Welsh chieftain down from the hills on a raid to seize the bounty of the fat rich oppressor and then ride home back into the trackless labyrinths of his past. As a stage actor his greatness was for Heroes: as a screen actor too—Alexander, Antony, Becket, Trotsky: or Anti-heroes—

George in *Who's Afraid Of Virginia Woolf?*, Jimmy Porter, Leamas in *The Spy Who Came In From The Cold*; Comic Heroes—Petruchio; Cartoon Heroes—*The Wild Geese*; Fallen Heroes—Edwin Booth. The role began early in life. Here, he honed it.

He conquered the man who had got Owen Jones to London and to RADA and to the Old Vic. He conquered him so completely that the man now housed him, clothed, fed and supported him and used every spare minute to coach and prepare him for some as yet unrevealed greatness. The man rewrote a radio play for him and got him early professional experience. Rich had conquered his own temper enough to take and not to spoil this rare second shot at school. He conquered his tongue and—with excellent irony—was directed by Mr. Pygmalion Philip Burton to play the long and taxing role of Professor Higgins—expert on English speech—in *Pygmalion*. He was accent perfect. Even a minor incident reveals his desperate determination to overcome, the desperation of the poor. Philip tells the story:

> While he was in school I gave him every chance I could to play before an audience, both in the school and in the local YMCA. He loved performing. When he first came to live with me he showed some envy of his young brother Graham's success as a soprano in the local eisteddfodau, the Welsh competitive festivals. I pointed out that his voice had certainly ceased to be soprano, but he pestered me to teach him the solo for the next eisteddfod. It was Sullivan's "Orpheus with his lute." One evening I reluctantly agreed to go back to school and attempt to teach him the solo. (I was the pianist for the school assembly which began the morning.) The piano was on the platform of the assembly hall and parallel to the side walls. Richard faced the non-existent audience and so couldn't see my reaction as he gave vent to excruciating sounds. At last I could contain my laughter no longer. He turned to me in dumbfounded fury. Then he stalked out angrily, exclaiming, "I'll show you. Someday I'll show you." And he did. On the first night of *Camelot* on Broadway, on December 3rd, 1960, I went into his crowded dressing room after the performance and he greeted me with: "Well, I showed you, didn't I?" I didn't know what he was talking about.

But Richard had not forgotten and seventeen years later he wanted it remembered—however lightheartedly—that he had conquered there, too.

With all this he retained his poise, his special modest confident quality, concealing the melancholy and resisting any temptation to swank. His eyes were peeled for the main chance—but where was it? And what was it? And would it ever come?

Philip Burton's manuscript takes his disciple through the golden gates:

> My Squadron 499 of the Air Training Corps became very successful, so much so that I was awarded a national honour, a Member of the British Empire, MBE (Military). I mention this because it brought me into favoured touch with the Commanding Officer for Wales, and through him I was able to gain admittance for Richard to Exeter College, Oxford, for six months prior to his joining the Royal Air Force, a privilege granted to very few cadets. If they made a good impression during that brief stay at the University, they would be given priority of consideration for becoming undergraduates when they were demobilised. But my Commanding Officer brought up an important issue: the question-raising ambiguity of my relationship to Richard: he had another home and his father was still alive; it would be better and easier all round if I adopted him. When I raised the question with Richard he readily agreed to become my adopted son. I put the matter in the hands of a local lawyer, and he took it up with the magistrates. I was well-known locally and they found no objection to the adoption. But when it was found that I was twenty days short of being twenty-one years older than Richard, legal adoption was ruled out. The alternative was that Richard become my legal ward, and for that his father's signed agreement was necessary. David Jenkins, a brother of Richard and a police officer, undertook to secure this and did so with no difficulty. Then Richard's name was legally changed by deed-poll to Burton.

The document states that Richard Walter Jenkins shall ''absolutely renounce and abandon the use of the surname of the parent and shall bear the surname of the adopter and shall be held out to the world and in all respects treated as if he were in fact the child of the adopter.''

''In later years,'' Philip wrote, ''he always referred to me as his father. He told me that, when he heard in 1957 that his father was dead, his immediate reaction was 'Which?' ''

5
Settling for Acting

If Richard Burton was lucky in his background it was because he made his luck. Hundreds of thousands the industrialised world over barely rose above the daily survival—hard enough in many cases. To get out was a considerable achievement: to go on to etch his own personality on the world was so rare as to be wonderful: but to do it on his own terms, in his own way and to do exactly as he wanted was astounding. No surprise that every single person who met him wanted to turn that meeting into an incident, an anecdote, an event. His genius was above all in what he was. Burton soared: he made it look effortless, and he put no one down in the process. And few cared to try to put him down.

Out of his family's travails he helped to make a fastness of domestic security—Cis, Ifor and the barricades of brothers, sisters, cousins, aunts, ever-open houses . . . out of the outwardly unpromising landscape of a war-battered, low-waged steel, coal and chapel culture he took a fine voice, musical knowledge, a skill in many sports, a love for learning: and he never forgot that a few shillings would and did make the difference between dignity and pity, poverty and decent comfort. He impressed Meredith Jones as he impressed Philip Burton—both to an extent that they had never been impressed before, driving them to help him help himself. He was a memorable mixture of inner repose and outer restlessness, of calculation, even shrewdness, and a princely carelessness, of something certain, never to be shaken, only perhaps tested and eroded as the years went by, and something uncertain, game for everything and willing to push himself to the point of self-destruction. Life was for the living and Rich seized it.

If we live out much of our developing years in imitation—especially of those most close to us—then Burton very soon outstripped guiding example. The tenacity of his loyalty brought him back again and again to the perfect womanliness of Cis and the unmatchable maleness of Ifor, but in his wider field of operation they were no more than a couple of reference points: the rest of the map had to be filled in—by Philip, by Meredith, by rugby heroes, by the poets, but most of all, and as he went along, by himself.

One thing is clear. He went at it very hard: punishingly, perhaps even at that stage, dangerously hard. Though physically a lightly built rugby player, he never hesitated to go for the top league and would be bounced and shaken regularly. He drank when young and while still young drank a lot, challenging himself to knock off all comers, but most of all to align himself with the legendary drinking miners who could and did sweat it off down the pit while Richard had to force it off in games. And perhaps through the drinking he sought to meet his father of whom he spoke so little and to whom it seemed, the older he grew, he meant so little. He smoked a lot which hit the hard-worked lungs while the boils surged up out of a weakness in nutrition which, together with the ill-starred Jenkins bones, augured ill for long life and clean living. Neither seemed to interest him much.

That outer evidence of strain and clash was balanced by the hugely admired stillness, the self-possession. That came most from his wide-apart blue-green eyes, the sculptured bones covered with wasted skin, the rare smile. The finest expression of himself lay in his love for language.

In one respect, it was a particular and technical interest. He was a crossword fiend, an acrostic fanatic, an inveterate amateur etymologist and a Berlitz blitzer on new tongues. The constant bookbag was a working kit. Even for a short weekend trip, Sally, his widow, wrote there would be "a dictionary, the complete works of Shakespeare, the *Oxford Book of English Verse*, the Koran, a Larousse, an atlas, together with paperback copies of the *Oxford Book of Quotations*, a reader's encyclopaedia . . ." and then there were the new novels and biographies and history bought in paperback raids.

In his heyday he had a memory like a clamp. Put to it, he could recite some of Shakespeare's sonnets backwards: that was one of his party tricks. Tumultuous chunks of the Bible in English and then in Welsh, the great monologues of Shakespeare, Manley Hopkins, Baudelaire, Rimbaud, Donne, Dylan Thomas—those could all be turned to account and were. But the passion was no party show. If he had one talent above all—Alec Guinness has singled it out as his greatest gift—it was for reading verse with intelligence and passion. He did it because he was intoxicated by it: and he had found it for himself. It was the force that through the green fuse . . . drove him. "The only thing in life is language," he said— with Elizabeth Taylor in tears beside him. "Not love. Not anything else."

The acting was almost a by-product of that and had it not been for a fortuitous advertisement in Cardiff's *Western Mail*, it might have remained just that. Oxford, the scholarship, would then have been the defining influence, become the place in which he could have planted his flag and redrawn himself. As it was, another Welsh wizard was to pipe him away. The announcement proclaimed that Welsh actors and actresses were needed by the eminent playwright, director and actor Emlyn Williams, to fill "small parts in his new play which will open in London in the autumn." In particular, he wanted a "Welsh boy actor."

Philip Burton sent off Richard's name immediately.

His boy was in good shape. Anxious—waiting for the results of his examination—with varied experience in school plays. Mime (in *Les Misérables*), a big leading role (Professor Higgins), a virtuoso turn (as an American businessman in *Youth At The Helm*, he had impressed everyone by talking into five telephones at once—everybody in Taibach talked about it: Cis heard accounts "up and down the street"), work on the radio and, above all, those scrupulous sessions in Ma Smith's front room and on the high hills, schoolteacher and pupil, two sons of miners in Wales, striving to speak the language of Shakespeare faultlessly.

He walked it.

Also, all of seventeen, he made a pass at the attractive, sophisticated casting director, Daphne Rye—the most influential casting director in Great Britain. Three years later it was she who gave him his passport, from the limbo of a long RAF demobilisation process, to the West End.

But it was Emlyn Williams he conquered at that stage and Emlyn Williams mattered. He was to give him a part which would take him into the West End a few months after leaving school, write a special role for him in what would be his first film, introduce him to his future wife and, through one of his sons, Brook, provide him with a lifelong younger "brother." More than all that, though, he showed Richard the way. By some terrific fluke Richard came face to face with his future at the precise time he most needed to see it. For Emlyn Williams had walked where Richard began to realise he now wanted to tread. Williams pointed in a direction and Richard followed it.

Williams himself—a miner's son—had found his way out of Wales and out of the pits via a schoolteacher, a woman, on whom he had based his hit play *The Corn Is Green*. In the play a boy from the pits is discovered by the schoolteacher and after furious efforts, gets into Oxford University. And in Oxford, the Welsh boy had launched himself as a nationally acclaimed actor and playwright. Emlyn Williams was precisely the right man to be the next guru. But once again Burton had to win and hold his luck.

Williams recalled that first audition vividly.

"He was a most spectacular-looking boy. Marvellous green-blue eyes and he had Repose. Nothing precocious. Nothing smart-alec. Almost shy but *sure* of himself, you know." It was Williams's perceptive and remarkable schoolteacher, Sarah Grace Cooke, who met him and said to Emlyn, "He's like you: but he has the devil in him. You haven't."

It was a devil longing to get out and Emlyn's gentle comedy, *The Druid's Rest*, gave the devil its chance. The boy saw what fun and mischief was to be had. The devil grabbed it and was on the loose for ever after. Burton's devil was a terrible and limitless sense of driving pleasure: it was fuelled by awesome capacity and the hunger of those who cannot believe that such fortune will not vanish before their appetite is appeased. He was barely eighteen, he was to go on a tour of the fabled cities of England; he was to be thrown in with chorus girls, drink with vagabonds of the stage, have the money for floosies and low bars, time to read and time to talk and be praised for doing this stage work which was not work at all. Acting was Open Sesame.

And he had a friend in this Celtic lust for life: Stanley Baker, his understudy, another son of a miner, much poorer than Richard's family, and again someone plucked from that army of industrialised subjects by a schoolteacher. A couple of years younger, Baker looked older, and had already appeared in a film. The two boys from the puritan villages of Wales set themselves up as hell-raisers to the world.

Windows were smashed clean out in fourth-floor dressing rooms as actor and understudy flared up into a fight. Dreadful punishments were promised by Emlyn. Next night the same. Dock pubs in Liverpool in wartime full of enthralling and wicked characters. Train journeys to cold suburbs and the first recorded attempt at love-making—ending in fear of eternal damnation as he dozed off in front of the fire afterwards and his socks began to smoulder. So sex sent you straight to hell! Torn between a huge urge to do everything and a huge ignorance about how to go about it. Leaning through their window to sting the breasts of the sunning chorus girls with ammo from their pea-shooters in the morning: in the evening beer all round and trying to coax them up an alley. Quite dizzy with the glamour of it all. Philip came up to keep an eye on him for a week or so. So did Ifor. But he was out on his own now. "He was the most beautiful boy I'd ever seen," said Gladys Henson, who played his stage mother. "He was always lolling about, always so calm. He took everything in his stride . . . the theatre was quite secondary to his interest in rugby; he never stopped talking about the game! . . . I said to him: don't go to sleep in the middle of rehearsals! And he said: 'Oh you know me, Glad. I go my own way.' "

Burton was living off the land and he loved it. An almighty cloudburst of possibilities had cascaded over his head and he loved that too. Emlyn Williams might have pointed his finger to Art, to the Theatre, to Magic and Burton had time for all three: but later. What hit him most was what hit him first. What a *life*, what *fun*, what pickings were there here! Perhaps it did not in truth add up to very much. A few smashed windows, drink, a fight or two, umpteen girls almost "conquered," long tall stories almost believed—but compared with what he had been used to it was the lure of the Orient, freedom, the cry of the Sirens. And all he had to do was be this other person and convince everybody. Which he did.

"In a wretched part [he played Glan, the elder son of publicans] Richard Burton showed exceptional ability," wrote the *New Statesman*. He would claim that it was the sentence which changed his life, convinced him that acting was worth doing. All *that* and an accolade from *the* intellectual socialist weekly! If only he could keep in touch with that centre of himself, which somehow, mysteriously, enabled him to do this acting business—then all the rest would be his.

Far from arriving at Exeter College, Oxford, in April 1944 as a grateful Jude the Obscure, he roared into the University apparently ready for anybody. The RAF training was no sweat, thanks to Philip's crack preparation in the ATC. The University work was not difficult—English and Italian. It was out of season for rugby and so he had plenty of roving time and the nights were growing longer. And yet he has confessed to feeling "terror."

This cannot be doubted—even though he soon overcame it. Oxford University, home of scholars since the days of Alfred the Great, was an all but religious ideal for generation on generation of humble schoolmasters and their pupils: Thomas Hardy's tragedy of Jude is based on that assumption—to enter Oxford was to enter the Golden Kingdom. But here he was, son of Dic Bach y Saer and a barmaid, nervous of a fish knife and coal Welsh from Taibach—in a city of colleges, quadrangles, domes, spires, towers, Big Tom, All Souls, the Radcliffe Camera, the Bodleian Library, the Parks, punts, the Union, the seeding ground of Prime Ministers and Viceroys, the growing place for Bishops, the earthly centre of scholarship. And though the place was leavened by servicemen on short courses and all the liveliness of that well-reported wartime gaiety, it was still dominated by public-school men with backgrounds of privilege and wealth quite foreign to Burton and smacking too sharply of the oppressor, with accents of command and futures of rule. The people against whom his brothers and their friends had struck in the Twenties, the people who had stood by the Army in the Valleys, the people who had let his people go to hell in war and in peace. These thoughts could always be called up, as they were many years later in his attack on Churchill.

But Burton's radicalism was soon overtaken by the inevitable favours bought him by his talents. Yet for a short time his arrival at Oxford threw him back on the hunkers of his class and family. It was his strength that he was never to lose that capacity to measure everything against his past—however much others might sneer at it. He always needed that: without it he could not feel easy in himself. And if *that* went—as, later, it threatened to do—then his access to that gift, that way with speaking, with "being" another person and totally convincing an audience—that would be in danger. Pontrhyd-yfen was tap root and talisman. In the end, Oxford was just another obstacle in the path: he took it, as always, by a full frontal attack.

Through beer, talk and that danger referred to by Robert Hardy, ("he breathed the very air of danger"), he became a man to reckon with. Having to absorb this phenomenon—for such the eighteen-and-a-half-year-old became within a month or two, despite all the swirl of competition (from local airfields and ancient academies)—the Oxford undergraduates graciously *invented* a school and back-ground which made it easier for them to justify taking him on board. "Burton of Blundles" they called him rather sportingly.

His time for revenge and the peculiarly genuine appearance of it would come eventually. Meanwhile he got on with what he found inside the citadel.

He found of course that not all undergraduates were of a kind. There was one, Robert Hardy, for instance, rumoured to be twelfth or was it twentieth in line to the throne? Anyway, indisputably well-connected and a "toff" and after an initial spat (very common with Burton, the initial spat with those who later became good pals), they became and remained fast friends. To this day, Hardy, himself having achieved the double of classical and popular success as an actor, speaks of him at that time with unaffected adulation. "I had never met anyone like him before nor have I since. He was, gen-uinely, a great man, a leader, he had so much *size*. Put half a dozen hell-raisers in a room with him and he would be their chief in ten minutes. Have your best conversationalists around to tea or dinner and Richard would wipe the floor with them. And there was so much danger about him—on stage and off stage—it was intoxi-cating. We all went after girls: Richard always got them. We all drank: Richard out-drank us. You may think I am exaggerating but I am telling you the truth as clearly as I remember it and I remember it very clearly. He had more 'size,' more originality than anyone I had ever encountered."

Hardy is generous to the memory of his friend but he is no sentimentalist. There are areas and times of Burton's life which he doesn't think much of and he says so. If there was a certain element of the Prince and the Pauper in all this, it worked both ways. You cannot be aware of class without being aware of snobbery and the young Burton could be temporarily affected by that. On the other hand he made his position clear and crude—as he always did later in similar situations—by making it plain that he was the control, he was the paymaster. It was he who lent Hardy the money to go to Paris: he who decided to take Hardy's hopeful acting career under his wing and get him an audition with "my father" down at the Cardiff studios, where Philip's radio play gave him an entrée. Interestingly, Hardy thinks this may have been a set-up by a protective Burton to put his new posh friend off acting altogether: for Philip discouraged Hardy. By chance another producer was there who encouraged him. "When he discovered I wanted to be an actor he felt deeply responsible and thought I must be stopped." Hardy is amused that Richard did not see the steel beneath the silk. I think the odds are that Rich was showing off his new toff as a pal to Philip and throwing in the favour of an audition along the way.

What held the two men together—apart from that click of friendship—was an unaffected and deeply worked love for *Henry IV*, Parts I and II, and *Henry V*. They had arrived independently at a similar view on the character of Prince Hal and the way in which that should be developed through the three plays. Both were to exercise their joint theory in memorable performances. Meanwhile excited discussion—which was to go on, intermittently, over three or four years—cemented the high-minded low fun of their close friendship. Indeed, they could have been Hal and his rascally crew.

There is no shortage of anecdote or incident at Oxford. Burton's reputation as a drinker is deceitfully challenged by some idiot who spikes his beer with wood alcohol: he crashes down a flight of stairs and hurts his back. "His back problem was already very much in evidence then," recalls Hardy. He holds pubs in thrall to his Welsh past—the stories which would be told afresh for a lifetime now emerge in their first edition—and his childhood, far from seeming a ball and chain in this airy court of privilege, glowed into a magic kingdom to match any of them. Grandfathers and coal-hewing cousins, brothers and the front row of Neath, Homeric schoolteachers and sopranos whose voices had a bell in every tooth made their entrance on to the Oxford stage, mixed in with chorus girls from Cardiff, waterfront villains from Liverpool and the twenty-two-carat glitz of the West End, where he had opened in *The Druid's Rest* in January 1944 with fires in the sky at night, bombs falling from the Luftwaffe and pubs and clubs burning excitement under the blackout. Ygarth the wild cat which savaged sheep and escaped drowning made its entrance as did the Burton trick of sinking a sconce (two pints) of college beer in ten seconds ("never been beaten"). Deprived—fortunately as it turned out, for otherwise he would have had no spare time at all—of the pleasures of the rugby field, he played a little squash and tennis (developing his "cannonball serve: that's all you need, see: they never get it back") and "chatting up." It was at Oxford, he said later, that he met an older woman who "sorted him out about all that. No trouble ever since."

We only have Burton's spoken word for this and the obliging older woman is untraceable. It is not uncommon in life: it is not uncommon in fiction. What is interesting is that Burton was prepared to talk about it publicly in a way which implied that he had sexual problems before this date. It is that which inclines us to believe him.

And he loved simple and dramatic solutions to everything: especially if they could be retailed in conversation. Just as he had had the nerve to try to pick up the casting director at his first audition, so he had the taste and—in sociological terms—the cheek to seek out the stylish and lovely Nina Bawden, later the novelist. He hinted at a weekend in London at Emlyn Williams's. She gave him the gentle brush-off: how could this boil-necked boyo know Emlyn Williams?

But what did you believe? It was not that he boasted—or not very much. But what he *did* do was to embroider, to fantasise. "He loved to change direction," said Hardy, "he loved to test people, to see where their pretensions were—it was all terrific fun to him, serious and not-serious both at the same time, the way very very good comics are. He should have played more comedy." (Emlyn Williams confirmed that: "He had the timing, the perfect timing that comedy needs: and dead-pan, classic dead-pan.") His comedy went into those Welsh and newly minted theatrical stories at Oxford where he had the time of his life. "Drinking produced a vein of brilliance in him," Hardy said. Burton was in his Valhalla: a company largely of men, a chosen few, who could endure ancient and god-like debauches, sing old songs, recite the enduring poetry of the race, spin yarns which threaded together truth and fiction in a seamless flow of talk—while outside there was world war and the danger of war to which they were all headed and of which they were all unafraid. Oxford remained a beacon throughout his life.

"This boy is a genius and will be a great actor. He is outstandingly handsome and robust, very masculine and with deep inward fire, and extremely reserved."

That was the judgment of the scholar Nevill Coghill, Fellow in English Literature and director of the Friends of the Oxford University Dramatic Society, which, in effect, put on the most lavish undergraduate productions—a tradition which had sent out many actors on to the London stage. Coghill was to do *Measure For Measure*. Burton asked for an audition and did one despite being told that all the parts were taken. He recited "To be or not to be." "Out came the most perfect rendering I had ever heard," said Coghill, "except that given a short while before by John Gielgud in his Haymarket *Hamlet*. But it was not just an imitation of Gielgud."

Coghill allowed him to understudy the leading part, "the complicated sex-driven Puritan," Angelo. The young man who was to have done it fell ill and Burton stepped forward. He had sent for Philip who had raced up from Wales to coach and instruct this miraculous son in a great Shakespearian role to be performed in an Oxford college before an audience of West End luminaries (Gielgud, Terence Rattigan): "We worked on it line by line, hour after hour, into the early morning . . . I never ceased to be astounded by how quickly and thoroughly he absorbed the notes I gave him."

Many thought his Angelo a triumph. "There were moments when he totally commanded the audience," Hardy recalls, "by this stillness. And the voice which would sing like a violin and with a bass which could shake the floor." At the party afterwards Binkie Beaumont, far and away London's biggest impresario (he had put on *The Druid's Rest*), asked the boy if he wanted to be a professional actor. Burton was unsure and non-committal. "If you've made up your mind by the end of the war," said Binkie, "look me up."

Philip went back to Richard's rooms in college to wait for him on this night of undreamt-of triumph, to enjoy it with him, to talk it through. Richard did not turn up until dawn, the first birds chirping over the lush, dewy college lawns. His trousers were ripped, his leg bleeding, he had spiked himself sliding over the college railings. He had gone on to a party at a rich woman's house, he explained, and seen a display of drinks such as he had never seen on earth before. Compelled to try them all, he had then passed out. "Sorry, Phil," he said. Philip forgave him. He had been repaid in plenty.

What a year! The West End, the school certificate, Oxford, Angelo, Gielgud applauding, Coghill calling him a "genius" and Binkie Beaumont making an offer. All this for an eighteen-year-old who, just over a year before, had been feared—in the context of the time—unmanageable and a little while before that had been sunk down without trace behind the haberdashery counter in Port Talbot's Co-operative shop. Philip had a great deal to be pleased about.

But Richard had still not settled for being an actor.

The foreground of Burton's life is so vivid that it is easy to forget the dramatic and hugely influential background against which it is being played out. As a boy he lived through a Depression inside an industrial monster clanking and heaving its passage through an increasingly ungrateful century. As a young man the context was war. His time in the ATC meant that he was targeted for the Air Force. His inclination meant that he would aim to be a pilot. The area around Oxford was buzzing with trainee pilots and tales of bombing raids and the relentless statistics of casualties, young men in their late teens, budding twenties. The thought of risk and high danger was exciting but it must also have been distorting. Burton's Welsh and hungry and visceral sense that everything had to be grabbed or it would be lost forever would be reinforced at this critical stage in his life by the fatalistically hedonistic mood which infected so many.

He left Oxford in autumn 1944 to do his training at Torquay. His eyesight was below par which disqualified him from being a pilot —and annoyed him a lot—but he passed out as a navigator. (He had left Oxford, incidentally, as one of the twelve prize-winning cadets.) The mysterious pattern of war decreed that he sail to Canada on the *Aquitania*. Soon after he got there the atom bomb all but ended the issue and certainly ended all active prospects for the latest intake of air crew. They were not even given their wings and for the next two years, on the "last in last out" principle, they had to endure the insufferable tedium of waiting for demobilisation. These years, like the first few years at the Secondary School, see Burton relapsing quite cheerfully into that boyo-larrikin-rugby-skiving coast through life: not a care, it appeared, in the world—Tom Jones at large.

Before Richard had left for Canada, Philip had secured a pass for him to come to Cardiff to star in a radio production of *The Corn Is Green*. He could scarcely have given him a firmer hint if he had hit him over the head with a mallet. There was both their backgrounds—a boy taken from a bleak past into a glorious future by a dedicated schoolteacher—and furthermore this acting business got him off duty, paid him as much cash as a miner's weekly wage for a few hours' easy work and had a satisfying tint of glamour . . .

Burton filed it away. He was still not committing himself. There was a war to be fought; and after that possibility evaporated, there was fun to be pirated wherever it showed its flag. From Winnipeg —where he had to work a bootlegging ruse to get a drink—he hitched to New York to stay with some friends of Philip: they were in Vermont and so he busked a few days in Manhattan, perhaps even sang for his supper in Greenwich Village. It would not be the first or the last time. He had no nerves and no shame about singing or performing when "the necessary" was in short supply. His voice was now re-forming into a pleasant tenor and his clamp of a memory could breeze him through Welsh songs and hymns, music-hall ditties and comic specialities half the night. He also did imitations—Churchill a *pièce de résistance*.

One of the best authorities for the next couple of years of Burton's life—back in the UK, waiting for the demob in various rural localities—is the actor Warren Mitchell. He too had been at Oxford, studying Science, and he was another of the twelve prize recruits who marched away from the City of Dreaming Spires. He was then known as Mick Misell, came from the East End, and bristled when an officer, asking Burton if he was going to be an actor, was rebuffed by the reply, "Probably not, sir. The trouble is the whole theatre's controlled by the Jews."

Mitchell remembers this affectionately and wisely. "It was probably something he'd heard an old actor say," he said. "There wasn't a ha'porth of prejudice in him—except that the Welsh were marvellous and especially the Welsh-speaking Welsh and most particularly those from Pontrhydyfen and most of all the Jenkins family. That apart, he ended up with a black dresser, Irish drinking pals, Jewish bosom friends (he once introduced Elizabeth Taylor to my father—'Have you met my little Jewish girl friend, Mr. Misell?') and so it went on. He couldn't give a damn about anybody—that was one of the things that was so attractive about him. Not about *anybody*. It could be frightening. But anyway I flared up and said that sort of remark was what we were supposed to be fighting the war about and I went for him. And he backed down. In public, there and then—shook hands, apologised, excused his stupidity and we were friends."

Like Robert Hardy—and like Hardy, Mitchell is an intelligent, thoughtful and trustworthy man—he has few qualifications about Burton at this stage: Burton would be nineteen, twenty, twenty-one. "There was a sense of wonderment about the man," he says. "Whether he knew it or not, he was one of those people you can't help looking at. One Air Force Day we were putting up stands for a show and he leapt up and did about half a dozen speeches from *Henry IV* and *Henry V*. I couldn't believe it. And I looked at all the rest of them—a tough lot, I can tell you—*they couldn't believe it either. They were intoxicated.*" The basic passions were still unrestrained. "It was rugby, rugby and rugby with all those fellas. He played in a team with ten Internationals. Then they'd go drinking. Then they'd come back and talk about rugby half the night and all you heard was 'came around the bloody blind side and bang!' " Now that there would be no war, he seems to have lost interest in navigation (if he ever had much). "I heard him over the intercom once—we were on an exercise—up in the clouds—saying, 'sorry, Oggy, forgot my ruler!' Forgets his bloody ruler and he's the navigator! And there was this aircraft recognition test. Maximum score 100—lose six points if you shot a friend, lose eight if you failed to shoot an enemy. 'Burton!' 'Yes, sir.' 'Your score, Burton.' 'Minus two hundred and fifty-four, sir!' "

There was also the curious incident where Burton defended an Italian POW. The man had been accused of raping a local girl and was in very serious trouble. Burton, who had studied Italian at Oxford, undertook to defend him. Either because of the man's dialect or Burton's patchy command of the language, detailed communication was not possible. However, Burton discovered he knew the lady in question. So did most of the camp. He persuaded the court that *she* must have raped *him*. The case was dismissed.

Burton then asked the defendant, whom he had nicknamed the SOB (Son of the Barber), to sing an aria. Which he did. Burton replied with a song in Welsh.

Burton started a Welsh male voice choir—"although at one time there were only two Welshmen in the camp"—and at one stage, up at Docking in Norfolk, he seems to have done everything but declare the place an independent colony.

Robert Hardy—who had arranged a nifty transfer to London—confirms this. "I went down to see him. It was like visiting a Tartar camp! And this terrible boy at the centre of it all! They went to the pub with Air Marshal's ranking chalked on their uniforms, windows were smashed to prove that broken glass need not draw blood, there were tremendous fights, he lived at the local hall, there was game, there were bounties we never saw in London—he sailed very very close to the law during that period." "He *was* in residence at the local hall," confirms Mitchell, "because he was in bed with the cook." "I tried to get him to come to London," said Hardy, "but he wouldn't. He had all the rugby he wanted, he said. And he was translating a novel into Welsh, producing one of Phil's plays with that shambolic crew up there—reading first editions borrowed from the Hall." "He passed on one of his girl friends to me," Mitchell said. "He'd got too many as usual. I had to pretend I was him! Put on the Welsh, spout a bit of Shakespeare—'You're a bit small to be a skipper,' she said. 'It's not size, it's the way you hit them,' I said. A hairdresser she was, very classy, lots of money. 'Hullo, Mick,' the lads would say. 'Mick? Mick?' 'They mean Dick. It's a way they have. We all get nicknames.' Kept it up for three weeks. I was Richard Burton. I thought, if you could be Welsh *and* a Jew, you'd have everything going for you!"

The bottom line was that there was nothing for them to do and those thoroughbred young men were too bright and too vigorous to put up with endless bull. They were given an inch or two. Burton by all accounts took several miles. "He had this feeling of danger," said Hardy more than once, "on and off the stage. And most people were willing to accept his leadership because the *rewards* were so great: it was exciting: it was the size of the thing, the scale he brought to it." Aircraftman First Class Burton got away with it even—it was said—when caught undisguised *in flagrante* with a leading officer's wife.

There was, in this period, a time of steady courtship. The girl—a few years older than him—was the actress Eleanor Summerfield. He would take frustrating and puzzling journeys on the serpentine British railways to see her for a snatched fraction of a weekend in a provincial rep. She took him to her home in a middle-class London suburb and her mother disapproved. Nevertheless they regarded themselves as unofficially engaged. It did not last but the parting seems to have been no terrible pain, the memory very fond.

Meanwhile back in Wales, Philip Burton had taken the plunge, moved to Cardiff and gone to work full-time at the BBC as a producer. But he let nothing get in the way of his chief purpose. Richard was taken to Stratford-upon-Avon for a week where they saw Marlowe's *Dr. Faustus* and the ex-schoolteacher had his ward up in the morning in the hotel gardens to study and learn by heart the great speeches. *The Corn Is Green* was to be done on the new medium of television in 1946 and somehow Philip wangled leave of absence from the RAF for Richard who yet again played Morgan Evans and yet again was pulled back from the gypsy snares of freewheeling pleasure to the source and the purpose of it all. In 1947 he was staying with his "father" when, by chance, a new play by P. H. Burton called *The Rescuers* was being produced. The story was obliquely based on the death of Philip's father and told of miners digging their way to their trapped workmates. Still, though, the young man hovered. Should he get back into Oxford and try for a First and a Rugby Blue? (The trouble with that was that so many All Blacks and Springboks and older British Internationals were at the University he would be better advised to wait a year or two.) Or should he write? He already had the entry ticket of a couple of rejection slips—one from the BBC. He kept Philip's intense pressure at bay.

What he was to do next was always to be a serious problem for Burton. His nose was pressed to the pane of his present blinding experience. His mind and spirit wandered far from the crowd of contemporary detail. This split made him simultaneously very alert and extremely absent-minded, now on the ball, now off in a world of his own. The future was always a foreign country, always took him by surprise and was always challenged and met with a charge. Perhaps one of the reasons for his impact—as a man—on so many varied people was this great and lordly carelessness about where he was "going": as if a mapped-out course was just a waste of precious time. The time to *be* and the time to brood: that is what he wanted. What he was to become—that was a chore.

Yet it was around this time that he settled for being an actor. "He had a lack of esteem for actors and an actor's life," said Robert Hardy, "but he liked the *parts*." What might well have fixed it was a radio play, *In Parenthesis*, by David Jones, produced for the BBC Third Programme by Douglas Cleverdon in 1948.

It is so good. The play is based on David Jones's book—an epic poem centred on the First World War but bringing in Welsh military history and mythological references from Roman times. It is a complex and profound tour de force which carried much of its weight over to radio in Cleverdon's adaptation and production. Burton always thought it the finest thing he ever did. And to hear him now, that biting, intelligent, comprehending and passionate voice—he was right. It had everything he loved—the Welshness, wonderful poetry, drama on the heroic scale and a sure unflinching sense of literature.

Philip Burton was also in it (no doubt he got his ward the part) and so was Dylan Thomas. And this, I think, was the final clincher. The great poet became his friend.

Though from a much more comfortable background than Burton, Dylan Thomas had been brought up just the other side of Swansea Bay, a few years older than the man who would become his greatest reader. Burton discovered Dylan Thomas for himself. He startled Philip with him, so impressed Emlyn Williams with a recitation on a London street in a blackout that Williams could recall it precisely forty years later, and introduced anybody he thought would appreciate it to the dark-vowelled, consonant-cracking language of the man whose most famous work would be *Under Milk Wood*, whose first performance—on radio and stage—would star Richard Burton.

Dylan Thomas was a real poet—in direct line from John Donne; he was Welsh; he drank; and he became a friend. Burton was deeply proud of that.

Dylan Thomas would act now and then to pay the bills. He was in this production of *In Parenthesis* and Burton has described a highlight from Thomas's performance.

"Dylan as an actor and as an explosive performing force was a dangerous rival for other actors, as I know, for I worked with him a few times or several, and once for instance a director [Douglas Cleverdon] said to him—we were rehearsing a radio play at the time—Dylan, will you take the words 'Mam! Mam!' and scream them for me. You understand that you are dying in no man's land, and when you hear the Royal Welch sing, I will give you a cue light and then scream for me, woodjew, there's a good chap. And the Royal Welch did sing in the rehearsal, it was a record of course, and they sang of what you could see from the hills above Jerusalem, and it was in the minor key and sad as the devil or death, and the green light flickered, and Dylan, short, bandy, prime, obese, and famous among the bars, screamed as I have never heard, but sometimes imagined a scream, and we were all appalled, our pencils silent above the crossword puzzles, and invisible centuries-gone atavistic hair rose on our backs. And there was a funny silence and

Dylan said that he'd bet I couldn't do that scream like that with a cigarette in my mouth and I shook off the centuries, stopped staring, smiled a little, noted that he had indeed monumentally screamed with a cigarette in his mouth and went stunned back to my crossword.''

So. If acting was good enough for Dylan Thomas, who was probably his lifetime's hero, if it was the world of words of David Jones and the wish of dear old Phil—then all in all he might as well give it a try.

And another thing. Binkie Beaumont, good as his word, saw that he had a contract a few weeks after he was finally demobbed in 1947. Burton met Warren Mitchell in the street very soon after. "£500 a year," he exulted—it was more than any of his family had ever made in their lives. "Can't believe it. £500 a year—whether I work or *not*!"

That settled it.

6
Sybil Among the Women

"And where were you last night?" Emlyn Williams asked.

"Out drinking." Richard was never afraid to tell Emlyn the truth. "And with some floosies."

"Why don't you find a nice girl?"

"Dunno."

"There are plenty all around you. Over there. Sybil Williams she's called—go and introduce yourself to her."

He did so. They were married a few months later. Sybil was nineteen. Burton was twenty-three.

This happened on the film set of *The Last Days of Dolwyn*—Burton's celluloid debut in a part written especially for him. He had been taken up by and was much impressed and influenced by Emlyn Williams—working-class Welshman become writer/actor/director/ Oxford University graduate—but Williams's guidance was not always so effective.

"People have been coming to me and saying 'He's drinking, you know.' "

"Have they, Emlyn?"

"Yes. Oh, I say, what is he drinking? 'Beer,' they say. 'But a lot of beer.' "

"That's true, Emlyn."

"Well. I like a drink myself but we have to watch it. People will be jealous of you. People will not miss anything that gives you an Achilles' heel. Do you understand?"

"Yes."

"Watch it then, won't you?"

"Yes. I will, Emlyn."

"And he just stood there," Emlyn concluded, "looking so desperate that I gave us both an enormous gin and tonic!"

The one problem appeared to be solved. The other did not seem to be a real problem at all. Alcoholism was then barely acknowledged and certainly not a widespread and alarming medical issue. It was not the harm he might do himself but the slips he might make along the way which alerted Emlyn.

Sybil Williams, though, seemed indeed a solution. And for many years of their marriage it seemed that she was. Burton had once again followed the directive of an older man.

For much of his life Burton had an unslakeable appetite for sex, a great talent for affection, and a genius to arouse. Since coming back to London on his £10 a week contract he had teamed up again with Stanley Baker and they had gone on the rampage. Star studs at the Streatham Palais de Danse, hawks in the dovecots of Irish nurses, pickers-up of usherettes, shopgirls, actresses, chorus girls . . . how far they "went," how much they "did" lies mercifully buried under the silt of time—but boyos they were.

It was expected. That they were having more than their fair share—that at the very least, seems beyond all possible doubt. But the imperative was common at that time, for some years beyond and in some quarters still today. Crudely put, it directed the young male of the species to "get as much as he could" before marriage cut off every tap but one. And if you came from a chapel and puritanical background of dark and moral mills where the only promised warmth was hell-fire, then—given the opportunity—you skidded all over the field like a jackpot rabbit. And if you found that you had entered the company of players, of actors, of those descended from strolling vagabonds and historically always noted and envied for the looseness of their morals, then all your Christmases came at once.

It should need no stressing that even today, when more and more actors (those in work) are aiming at the regular working-day/mortgage belt, affairs, amours and just plain sex inside a company is not unknown. The brief encounter often comes with the brief stopover in the oasis of a job. More so at that time when companies were culled from post-war part-blackout part-music hall Britain to cling together for a while on what usually became the wreckage of a production. Perhaps an analyst might say that the casual sexual connection in this context was the only thing that kept the group going. Another view would be that it was a hail and farewell community, and while it was together it was open all hours. And because it *is* the tradition, it all seems at once brisker and more tender, easier and less crucial than in the outside world: though this may be an error; the easiness might be an art too. But the central and critical point is that the sexual gavotte tended to go with the theatre like pinstripes and a bowler (then) went with the City.

Burton's sexuality, which many have pointed to as the source of his power on stage and, at his best, on screen, became notorious in its more scandalous manifestation in his love for women. This was apparent from quite early on. Even now his contemporaries raise their eyes and murmur "Ssshh" because there are still alive those whose feelings might be hurt and the extent of it all is better buried under the marriages and the more undeniable liaisons.

Don Juan today has lost whatever sympathetic press the years of male domination gave him. Feminism and a greater acknowledged (though not necessarily practised) awareness of the equality and independence of sexual rights have becalmed the Don as a fool of time. Psychology has dissected him to death. AIDS has ousted him out of history. But there is little point, for instance, in turning on an artistic, enlightened medieval king because he also enjoyed slaughtering hundreds of deer in a day's hunt and daubing the fresh blood on his own face and those of his friends. Examples can be multiplied. To yank someone entirely out of their time and smack them around for not being of *our* time is perhaps a salutary but only a limited exercise. Yet the times have indeed changed: and Burton's early sexual insatiability, his later infidelities, his many women and his concurrent devotion to monogamy all need some explaining.

Not, though, apologising for. To begin with the obvious, there is no record that he forced a woman to bed against her will—none; there is no rumble of the stain of real deceit—it seems he always made the rules of the arrangement clear. Self-delusion was something else. As his reputation went before him like a brass band in front of a carnival, from the age of twenty no woman he met could possibly have been unaware of it.

There is a more speculative, perhaps deeper point. Burton had grown up surrounded by multiple tensions, multiple obligations, multiple loyalties. Cis, as he sadly said, "was wonderful, but she was not my mother." His father had first been replaced by an elder brother, then by one teacher, then another dominating man . . . his younger sisters were his nieces, his older sisters more like aunts, the brothers like uncles, the cousins like brothers, the real aunts like mothers . . . he had many alternative worlds. This was not insecurity, it was a world of pleasing affectionate options. Singularity, like, later, monogamy, was a difficult thing, a strain, almost an oddity: perhaps that was its appeal for him, but why did it have to be so? Complexity, elaboration, alternatives, parallel lives, that was the way it had always been; that was his "norm." Did Sybil realise this? I think so. And she saw there was good in it—if it could be kept away from conflagration.

Perhaps she saw something else. That in all this—in the maelstrom which he had managed to turn into a benevolent vortex—his real preoccupation at that time was to be a man. Men, essentially, were miners. They could be steel workers. They were always sportsmen. As children they were spoiled—how can a five-, seven-, eleven-year-old be blamed for the lifelong influence of having his shoes cleaned, his tea-cup passed across a table, his hair combed, his every want anticipated by the mother he ached for because she was already so worn out and was not, in the end, his mother? Men were the providers. They were not to be questioned: what they did was supply the pillars for the system. And if they dillied, or dallied, and if they tarried a little—then blame, surely, and shame, if caught out, but it was all trivial and irrelevant compared with the necessity to be a man. Sybil knew where all that came from.

There has been the usual talk of "insecurity" and maybe so, although this fashionable "insecurity" is a very glib key which seems to fit every known lock. More interestingly, those who knew him well speak of his outstanding security. "He was not insecure *at* all," said Emlyn Williams. "He was very very strong." He knew who he was and what he wanted to do way before most people. What he wanted to *be*, what the answer was to his particular puzzlement and pain—that was different. But his steely sense of his outward self was his most envied quality.

It is also true that he was lost without a woman around him. He could neither cook nor sew. In the tribal fashion of her place and times, giving the best cuts to the master, serving the young lord, Cis had spoiled him.

Burton was very secure—over-confident perhaps—in his body and its appetites. He believed that his body was a good guide to his character and he punished it and indulged it by turns. Sport, little sleep (never a good sleeper), drink (though he thought of this as a treat for the machine), cigarettes (heavy) and general hooliganism was punishment. Sex was one of the pleasures. Like money, it was the "real thing."

He seems to have been a great romancer. "He laughed them into bed," Warren Mitchell said. "There was the poetry, the stories, the *fun* of him," said Robert Hardy. And he was a hunter. But he was never a man intent on building up a score. He was, it appears, neither rapacious nor peremptory, no "for kicks," no "wham bam, thank you, mam!"—he tried to make sure both of them enjoyed the time; and he was fun. Most of all, perhaps, as the woman behind these anonymous observations concludes, "When you were with him, you were all he was ever interested in, even though you knew that a week or two later it would be somebody else. His *concentration* on you was a charge in itself." He could also, like anyone else, behave very badly.

Curiously enough, though—and most curious of all, given the world of intense cohabitation in which he grew up—Burton hated to be touched. He was no hugger, no fondler, no arms around the lads or groping the girls. His physical aloofness made him "nerve-racked" and "full of the horrors" on stage when he had to kiss someone. He hated changing in front of others—and this from a man who played rugby with fourteen other men week in week out for years and must have huddled with them in the cramped and corrugated spaces of dressing rooms up and down the country. That aversion to touch was coupled with the distance he could put between himself and others, the withdrawal. Perhaps the centre of it was indeed some intimation of doom: his mother dead so soon after his birth, his father indifferent, best joked about, his context a wasteland of the Western world. Was that branding so early and deep that nothing would heal over it? In which case, what better, what other remedy than to push yourself as hard as you could towards all extremes to feel alive, but keep the centre inviolate?

Daphne Rye, the top casting director, looked after him following his demob and in 1948 ushered him into the West End in a literary play—from a book by Elizabeth Bowen—*Castle Anna*, which Daphne herself directed. Burton had a small part, did it competently, met Richard Leech, a young Irish doctor, who had taken to the boards. Leech, who had expected a generous-minded rival, was amazed at Burton's blunt declaration that if he could not make the acting game pay well and soon, he would be off. And he was missing his rugby. Warren Mitchell went around to see him after a performance and was amused—following Burton's initial reaction to the money—when he grumbled, "You won't believe all they give me for this? A miserable £500 a year!"

Stories told about Burton at this time are necessarily retrospective and tend to suffer from retrospective grandeur and glamour. The other side of the roaring boy, the young Hal and poetry-loving bruiser, the devil in bed and pub, was a young man who felt alone in London, knowing that he had to look out for himself and look out sharply. London was full of young men from the war with connections new and old, quicker at the game, civilian spivs, career barrow-boys; to get what you wanted you had to be hard and fast: no lingering. He had no time to stand about in the theatre if it did not deliver. He had to make his own terms.

Ten years later Burton would have been as happy as Larry. In the late Fifties, early Sixties, following *Look Back In Anger, Roots, A Taste of Honey, Saturday Night And Sunday Morning, Lucky Jim, Room At The Top*, a young Burton would have been a dream ticket. Provincial accents were then acceptable, even for a brief moment preferred; writers were making memorable works out of a background much nearer that of Burton. Most importantly, there was a cluster of writers, directors, actors and critics who gathered around an idea of a realistic, passionate, intellectual theatre which would have been a most fertile ground for Burton. There is a study to be made of men and women born "out of their time." It is a recurring phenomenon and perhaps when you miss that particular notch you have to adopt original even eccentric strategies to bring the times and yourself together in the big bang of true fame and real success.

Bryan Forbes, the writer and director, came into the London theatre at the same time as Burton and knew him then. He describes the West End theatre which he and Burton were heir to as "Binkie's. Binkie Beaumont was H. M. Tennent and directly and indirectly he controlled about a dozen theatres. He had good taste. He paid about fourpence if he could get away with it. And you had to be with them. The prevailing tone was homosexual—there was no doubt about that. You did not have to *be* one—but it helped. Richard, of course, never deferential, never awed, totally fearless, just played the other way flat out! Went his own way. There was nothing they could do about him. And they were not fools: they could spot talent. But it was a very distinctive and pervasive tone: the Hollywood casting couch was for starlets in the States and stud boys in London. Thank God for Daphne Rye: she saved us."

As Burton loved to live in opposition—it made him feel most alive and it could be argued that he lived in serious opposition to his own body for long stretches of his life—it is interesting to speculate whether the homosexual network gave yet another spin to his heterosexuality. More importantly, it *was* a network. Burton knew about networks. Networks, he was beginning to see, were what made the world go round. Meredith Jones had worked the educational network; Philip had engineered the ATC cadet to Oxford on another network; Emlyn Williams was the centre of a growing Welsh network, the "Tafia"; Binkie Beaumont (who had started work in a theatre in Cardiff—the Welsh connection may have helped Burton once again) was the unlikely Godfather of the London network: Burton himself was to become a Godfather and enjoy it enormously. This was the way the world as he saw it worked. He accepted that and worked it. Daphne Rye was his way through.

Burton used to make up affectionate calypsos about Daphne Rye. He was one of what were known as "Daphne's hoofers." Richard Leech and Bryan Forbes were also part of the club. "Daphne protected us," says Forbes, "those of us who needed it." She prised Burton out of digs in Streatham to install him on the top floor of her house in Pelham Crescent—just a few doors down from Emlyn Williams. Daphne was his sort: she was interested in quality production and worked with the artistic "Company of Four" which did *Castle Anna* by Elizabeth Bowen and John Perry which opened in February 1948 and *Dark Summer* by Wynyard Brown. Burton got good parts. She was interested in promoting the careers of young stars. And she was Rabelaisian, rather surprising, liberated fun.

Almost immediately, it seemed, Burton got his first film break —still only a few months out of the RAF. "Came out on a Monday, in a play on a Tuesday, star on a Wednesday: never looked back," he would say, later, when he enjoyed teasing around with his reputation and idly sowing mischief.

He had some way to go but Emlyn Williams was determined to help him. The part of the young boy in the film *The Last Days of Dolwyn* was written especially for him. Emlyn had some difficulty in persuading Rank and the producers, Alexander Korda and Anatole de Grunwald, to take on this new boy. He arranged for Burton to have a screen test. "I prepared it very carefully. Korda and de Grunwald were startled. I sent Richard a telegram, 'You have won the scholarship'—it's a line from *The Corn Is Green*. You know, he didn't even bother to reply!"

Those who were with him on the tour of *Dark Summer* at the time were equally astounded. Not even to *reply*! He drop-kicked the telegram away, went out for a drink and turned up months later on the first day of filming amiable as an old soldier. "I'd almost given you up," said Emlyn, half nettled, half intrigued. Careless, confident, his own man even then.

"He was a natural," says Williams, continuing in the long line of those men and women of experience and the most foxy intelligence, who could not analyse Burton's gift any more clearly than that. "The only thing he couldn't do was to look longingly innocent. He didn't have it in him. He couldn't be vulnerable. He had to look through a window and see the girl dancing—but he could only look 'fierce.' " Maybe he had never been innocent. Sly cigarettes from the age of eight.

"And that was another thing," said Williams. "His smoking. We were shooting the film in North Wales in a terrible wet month in a tiny village and he smoked and read and did his crosswords and smoked. I said, 'Richard—you have a good voice—you really should stop smoking. If you stop for three months, I'll give you £100'—a lot of money in those days, 1948—£1,000 now? £2,500? – anyway. His face lit up. After two months he gave in. Came and told me—no cheating. Self-indulgence overcame greed!"

Sybil Williams had been born in Wales. Her father, an official in a coal mine, had died when she was young and she was brought up and well educated by "academic" sisters. Her background was a few rungs up from the Jenkinses and that elementary social fact helped to give her a poise in the face of his ever-increasing sureness. Many found her consistent equilibrium the most surprising of her many qualities. She came to England to stay with a sister, went to acting school in London and through a teacher who knew how to persuade Emlyn Williams, was all but smuggled into *The Last Days of Dolwyn* as the sixth girl extra "when only five had been budgeted for. But then I thought—Alexander Korda can afford six," said Emlyn, doing a favour for the female line of the Tafia.

She was petite, going silver-haired, vivacious, bright, and willing to take Richard on trust. After the first date he said he would phone her: she waited by the telephone until after midnight. No call. Next day. Where were you? Phoned all day, he said, you'd better get the engineers to look at that telephone of yours. She accepted that. They began to go out together.

It is not only that no one on the planet has a bad word to say about Sybil: people trip over their superlatives. Her life and career after she and Burton split up confirms the opinion of her energy and flair—and her directness. She took on Richard Burton and it is impossible that she did not know—quite soon—that there were flaws: she knew about theatrical affairs and knew that most of them were no more than vessels bumping in the night or for the run of the play. And he would mostly take very good care not to be found out. "Mustn't hurt Sybil." There were rules when she *did* find out. "The first week I say don't hurt her: the second, don't hurt me," she is reported to have said. But all that is way below the surface when people talk about her.

The family liked her—Cis and Hilda, Ifor and David, Pontrhydyfen and Port Talbot: she was Welsh and so pleasant and easy, lovely personality, beautiful voice, could make you laugh, just what Rich needed, just right for him. A great woman, says Lauren Bacall, she had balls, she still has. She was too good for him. My mother is a very nurturing woman, says Kate Burton, their elder daughter, I know that they just suited each other perfectly at that time. "Marvellous," says Robert Hardy, and the word rings like an echo around every friend you meet. On and on it goes and goes on still. He had met a jewel and he snapped her up. She was soon to give up her own acting career—which she never took seriously—to—spoil him? Support him? Manage him? More mundanely, most likely, prepare to have the family for which they had to wait many wearing years.

I don't know how she coped, they say—Rich telling her he'd be back for lunch and not turning up till dinner and *then* with Stanley or some other pals. He took such chances, they say, but Syb never seemed to bother. They would sing Welsh songs together, she would take up the descant, he would make up verses with just a little edge to them. Photographs show them beaming at the camera, oddly alike, almost a brother and sister likeness. Nobody ever got through Sybil's guard.

Syb was "wonderful," he told his friends. "I've met this marvellous girl." Activity on all other fronts was called off immediately. He wooed her and wed her within a few months. And yet the night before the wedding his detachment or his melancholy reasserted itself when he told Stanley Baker that he was marrying her only "because she expected it." She was a nice girl and she expected the ring.

But he wanted a nice girl who expected the ring. When told to settle down—and Emlyn Williams, who had to a large extent taken over the parental role from Philip Burton at this stage, *did* instruct him to do that—it clicked with something and he thought—well, why not? And the girl turned out to be "wonderful."

Interesting that he had married precisely the sort of girl he would have married had he stayed at home. For surely back in Port Talbot a smart young man would have looked a notch or two up the ring-ridden ladder of class and hauled himself up—in his pride—one or two places. That was the way of it. And that was the beauty of it. She was home but, like him, an exile: together they made up a little principality but it was inside the great metropolis. He knew her every move and she had seen and heard of his like since childhood.

They were married in February 1949 and Daphne Rye, who had given them the reception, encouraged Sybil to move into Pelham Crescent. Early in the following year, with Daphne's help, they bought a house, 24 Lyndhurst Road in Hampstead, North London, an area which attracted writers, painters, actors, a taste of bohemia and, most importantly, immigrants, especially from Eastern Europe, but still with its own Cockney Pearly King and Queen. Just the melting pot for the young Welsh couple. The Burtons let off part of the house and lived in the rest. It was all very sensible and creditable.

Hampstead was a dashing address. Sybil was "like Cis." In Sybil he had rejoined his past but he transplanted it to an artistic suburb of London which had been the haunt of legendary highwaymen, was now the roost of exiles and writers and only fifteen minutes from the West End theatre. Sybil was home.

7
Making It

In less than three years after his demob from the self-indulgent pastures of the peacetime RAF, Richard Burton turned himself into a great young classical actor—*the* heir and very apparent to Gielgud and Olivier; *and* Hollywood was on the line, fishing for a new star. It was another violent shift in a life and a career which never had an even, an easy or predictable pattern. And it was done with an extraordinary vault of achievement. He had appeared in only five stage plays as a professional adult when he was called to Stratford-upon-Avon to play a full season of major Shakespearian roles. Most important of all, he did them so well that those who saw him then still today, thirty-seven years on, speak of him with awe. "He was just astounding, miraculous," says Peter Hall. "He *was* Prince Hal." Son of drunken Dic, son again of stern Philip the teacher, he transformed himself into an heroic king of England, and the theatrical court bowed the knee.

He played *Henry V* in February 1949 on his beloved BBC radio, the home of the Word and poetry and all that mattered. Alec Guinness, who first met him at this time, considers that reading poetry on radio was the best thing he did. The play was directed by a fellow Welshman, Frank Hauser, a young intellectual and committed man of the theatre. "It was interesting because he arrived for the audition clearly drunk," said Hauser. "He was pockmarked, gleaming with nerves and drunk. He did a poor audition. Robert Hardy had recommended him. We gave him the part in the end and I think it was a great boost for him. There'd been the Scofield incident you see. I think Rich had lost his nerve—probably for the first time in his life."

"The Scofield incident" referred to—and never yet totally explained—was a play, *Adventure Story*, by Terence Rattigan, as bankable then as Tom Stoppard is today. The subject was Alexander the Great, and Paul Scofield was to have the leading part. Burton was given the considerable role of Alexander's friend, Hephaestion. Daphne Rye once again had pointed him in the right direction. It was everything that Burton could have hoped for in the West End at that time. But Peter Glenville—a noted, respected director—fired him. His explanation was very simple: Burton was too short, he said, when Scofield spoke of him as " 'my rock, on which I lean' . . . he went to lean and went down about two feet." Burton himself had several versions: "I was supposed to play Paul Scofield's older friend," he said, "but how can anyone . . . he looks a hundred and eight to begin with." At other times he said that Glenville needed a more mature and a wiser actor. At the time he was badly thrown. But he could always get work in good old BBC radio: that was his stamping ground. Hauser's offer was balm.

"He had the essential selfishness of a star actor," says Hauser. "But then he had a very attractive self. He had to have space around him—and he could create his own space—and then he could work. At that time he didn't have the guns to storm the big parts. Henry V was about right for him."

What shook Burton was not that he would appear to "the World," i.e. the metropolitan thespians, as someone who had failed in a straight contest with another rising young actor, Scofield—although that made him angry and inflamed his competitive instincts—what shook him was that he had no real idea why it had happened. He had early and with total certainty come to the conclusion that whatever he had as an actor was beyond his comprehension. Superstitiously, perhaps, protectively more like, he did not care to explain it or examine it much and he would not interfere with it at all. Nor would he allow anyone else to do so. It was a gift. As mysterious and as simple as that. And if the pieces were in place—the right words, above all, and then the right part—he could make it work. But to be told that he could not make it was to be told that this gift could disappear as unpredictably as it had arrived. That shook him.

Daphne Rye bailed him out again. *The Lady's Not For Burning* by Christopher Fry was to be directed by John Gielgud at the Globe in May 1949 and Richard auditioned for the "orphaned clerk." Written in verse, the play was set in the Middle Ages and told of a soldier back from seven years in the wars who wanted to die and a beautiful witch who wanted to live. The audition was held at the end of an afternoon and Burton discovered that he was not alone: a very young actress, Claire Bloom, was auditioning for another of the minor roles. She recalled Burton trying to tell a few "feeble jokes," but his hands were shaking. *Adventure Story* was still taking its toll. And he may have taken a drink or two to steady his nerves. He would mysteriously shake so badly sometimes that old-timers recommended a large brandy. The audition went badly. Pamela Brown, who was to co-star with Gielgud, remembered saying "the girl but not the boy." Gielgud gave him another chance, asked him to come back the next day and do it again. Fry himself intervened, struck by the boy's intelligence and independence. Gielgud took him on.

Whether Gielgud was persuaded by Fry or Daphne Rye or Binkie Beaumont—whose production it was—or whether he saw talent obscured by nerves, he does not remember. It was a small part, he was in a hurry, the boy was very striking to look at, quite "a dream Prince," says Gielgud. That may have been enough. It was certainly enough to change utterly Burton's fortunes on the stage.

For despite empty houses on its provincial tour, this wordy, intelligent, seemingly uncommercial verse drama was a success in London, ran for a year and then went over to Broadway. Burton was in a hit—and a classy hit—and in the tonnage of reviews he rarely failed to be mentioned, often praised. Moreover for a year he shared a stage with one of the greatest and the best-loved English stage actors of the century. This was his acting university. Gielgud was his tutor and forever after, his idol.

It was after this that Vere Barker, his rather grand agent, helped him to get the house in Hampstead and began to up his fees even for radio—for which he continued to work—poems, plays, schools radio, £10, £12, £20 sometimes: it all totted up. In the increasingly middle-class and English world in which he was moving, the notion of earned money, cash for work, was thought vulgar. To want to be a millionaire was coarse, even ridiculous; money somehow floated down from Daddy or was waiting in a will at the end of an estate —that, though rarely the reality, was a prevailing view, and rather attractive in its unworldly dimension. Another, more understandable, view was that there was not a lot of it about and the trick was to get your hands on it. This was still the post-war England of austerity and ration books—full of those coupons that young Jenkins of the Port Talbot Co-op had treated in such a cavalier manner. Burton had no middle-class expectations, and certainly no desire to ape aristocratic ways he was not heir to. But he had a keen interest in a deal. This, too, set him apart.

When he landed the part with Gielgud, for instance, Binkie Beaumont offered him £10 a week. Burton asked for £20. It was a prestige production aimed at the West End. And, after all, *The Last Days of Dolwyn* had made him something of a film star. £17. 10s. was finally agreed. Burton was so elated at his tough bargaining that he took a rare taxi back to Pelham Crescent, where he met his neighbour, Emlyn Williams, who winkled the details out of him and sent him back for £30. Burton describes being "between the two men I most feared" but nevertheless, and with all that was hanging on the part, he went back for more. Eventually he got £30 and as he left the room, Binkie said, "*I* know: that old Welsh pit-pony has just been at you."

In one short lesson, then, Burton found that he could turn a decent offer of £10 into a "fortune" of £30 a week. So he was right to drive a hard bargain. Even the genial Binkie Beaumont was prepared to pay him a third of what the experienced Emlyn Williams knew he was worth and could get. The theatre and film world was mined with rip-off merchants, however nice they seemed. Burton accepted that and learnt from it. And in those early days he was careful with money. Except in pubs.

The purchase of his house was a purchase on security. He could never believe his luck, just as he could never explain his talent. He was to be at the mercy of both and early on he knew it. At that stage he seems to have cut his natural philosophy from the worsted clichés of a poor childhood: "never rely on anybody else," "make yourself independent as soon as you can," "put a bit by for a rainy day," "don't let the good times run away with you." There was fantastical talk (in 1949!) of being a millionaire. He would say that his driving demon was "the poverty of Wales"—grandiose but no less true for that. Money mattered. "Making it" also meant making money. There was that black future to fend off: there was the endless black past to staunch and help.

Now as then, Gielgud is acute, highly intelligent and concerned to help draw a full portrait. He was a friend of Burton's throughout his life, directed his record-breaking *Hamlet* on Broadway, appeared with him in *Wagner*, met and studied him. As a snapshot of the young Burton, aged twenty-four, Gielgud's account is valuable. "He was marvellous at rehearsals. There was the true theatrical instinct. You only had to indicate—scarcely even that. He would get it and he never changed it. There was this rather famous instance where he had to scrub the floor while Pamela and I were having a long and involved discussion, but I was told that people couldn't take their eyes off *him*. Alec Guinness told me that. Many other actors did. It comes along very rarely, that particular unmistakable talent. And of course it can be very dangerous because it's so difficult to control." Of his character: "He was very sunny, no vanity, so confident. He boasted now and then, but in a pub way, you know, a Welsh way, for fun. He was a real pub boy. Loved to talk: never boring. Highly intelligent—read a great deal. Had a great stable of ladies. Always very respectful to me." One further observation: "He was always careless. At the first morning of rehearsal he began yawning and looking at his watch, wanting to be off for a drink. It was a marvellous opportunity for him but he was careless." And bored.

"He was already a star," says Claire Bloom. "A fact he didn't question."

He was to go to Brighton for a fortnight in another play, in 1950, *A Phoenix Too Frequent* by Christopher Fry, whose well-wrought and "difficult" verse dramas had so unexpectedly caught the taste of the public. He did films—at this time, 1949 to '51—*Now Barabbas Was A Robber*, *Waterfront*, *Green Grow The Rushes* and *The Woman With No Name*. Like Olivier before him, he took more or less whatever came his way. He had to. Korda signed him to a seven-year contract, after the very encouraging reviews of *Dolwyn*, and he was put to work.

What comes out of those films is his willingness to do films. The British film industry was in a melting-pot—thrashing about, often vigorously. But curious growths appeared: *Green Grow The Rushes* (1951) was the film technicians' union's attempt to make a go of it. Burton joined in what was a disaster. *Waterfront* (1950) had a certain social realist clout and his reviews were not bad.

The fact was that there was no place in British films for an actor of Burton's particular quality and no director to take him up. The quality of passionate and intelligent realism he could bring to a part was not in demand until many years later. Kind hearts and coronets ruled and that was fine, but to Burton it was a closed shop.

One film, however, *Now Barabbas Was A Robber*, directed by Gordon Parry from the play by William Douglas Home, brought him his best review yet from the finest film critic of her day, C. A. Lejeune, in *The Observer*. "To my mind," she wrote, "he has all the qualities of a leading man that the British film industry badly needs at this juncture: youth, good looks, a photogenic face, obviously alert intelligence and a trick of getting the maximum effect with the minimum of fuss." On its American release, the *New York Times* also picked out Burton.

Films, in London at the time, for theatrical types, were considered as little more than perks. You were paid the money and you ran with the game. You joked about it. You affected to look down on it. You were secretly terrified of it but you kept that *very* secret. Films did not count. The Theatre mattered. Burton may well have been stained by those prejudices—it would have been hard not to be: and once again it is important to understand the circumstances in which he found himself.

As a boy in Taibach he had gone to the Cach to see his screen heroes. Movies were magic. To be *in* them—unbelievable! And yet there was no school of thought which cultivated and refined that enthusiasm, no influential and witty group of young film makers who could draw him in and use him as C. A. Lejeune perceptively realised he could be used. And whereas on the stage he had the words of Christopher Fry or the presence of John Gielgud—both of which drew out his respect and so his best shots—in films generally he would have a leaky script and brief takes—neither giving him the chance to wind up and deliver. He did not complain. It was a start. He was well noticed, he had the beginnings of a fan-club, and back home the Welsh papers gave him full-page spreads. Ifor came up now and then to keep an eye on him.

The films were shot during the day. The theatre played in the evenings, the nights were for drinking. Life was scythed down relentlessly. Sybil, up in Hampstead or with one of her many friends, kept the home fire burning and joined the gang when they had a special bash. She was deciding to devote herself to supporting him as he leapt from one peak to another. One after the other the towers of prestige and glamour were falling to him.

Yet it was a most unlikely vehicle which took him to his first truly national conquest: a cart. A wheelbarrow, to be exact, which carried an old woman backwards and forwards across a bare stage —pushed by Richard Burton, her son, in search of a sign from God. The one-acter—*The Boy With A Cart* in January 1950 by Christopher Fry—was chosen by Gielgud to feed the Fry boom. Burton was the Boy. "He was simply splendid at it," says Gielgud. "Absolutely no question. It was a wonderful *succès d'estime* for him and his miming—he had to mime building a cathedral—was spell-binding." Burton has declared that it was when he was performing that scene on the stage that he felt the hairs on his neck stand on end and knew for the first time the power he could have over an audience.

Anthony Quayle—on the hunt for a young lead to star in his Festival of Britain Shakespeare season—came to see it and was conquered. "There he was. Bang off. Prince Hal." Quayle was already well established as an actor of considerable stature, a director of intelligence and an unusually good administrator. The Festival of Britain, 1951, was designed to tell the world that we were back in business, full of vim and zip, bursting with new ideas, new teeth in the new bulldog, through another war with honour and into the second half of the twentieth century with eagerness and confidence. Shakespeare was called in to play his part: Quayle was commissioned to serve up Shakespeare in Stratford: Burton was discovered to complement Quayle.

Quayle was Falstaff—the most loved, the richest comic part in Shakespeare. In *Henry IV*, Parts I and II, he has the time of his life. Alongside rich, corrupt and irresistible Sir Jack Falstaff is the young Prince Hal, wandering far from his true royal path, mixing with thieves and wastrels when he ought to have been studying to be a king. In most productions, young Hal is the disciple and accomplice of Falstaff, a broth of a boy, a young man who has turned his back on respectability and on his destiny.

Again Philip Burton came up from Cardiff to spend time with Richard on the part. Robert Hardy was there to re-rehearse the discussions they had held on desolate airfields during the war. Burton dug into himself and, as he always did with work he reverenced, laid all he had at the service of the part. His Hal would be no

rollicking dropout. His Hal would be a truant Prince, perhaps, a
man disobedient to his father and contemptuous of the popular expectation, but no less a Prince for that, always watching, always
using the lines to cut out a space for himself. Burton arrived at the
first rehearsal word-perfect and with the part already sewn on him
like a skin.

There were reports—denied by Quayle but confirmed by Richard
Burton and, in his book, by Philip Burton—that Quayle and Burton
quarrelled over the interpretation. It is only fair, I think, to hand
over to Philip Burton's unpublished memoir here. This was the part
he had dreamt of night after night in that living room and now—
astoundingly—it was to come true in the birthplace of Shakespeare
with a great company all around his son. This was Philip's reward.
He wrote:

> My conception of the part, especially since we were seeing
> its full development in the three plays, was that even in
> his wild days the Prince must sometimes be aware of the
> burden of kingship which lay ahead. There was one mo-
> ment of which I was particularly proud, and Richard made
> it a magic one. It occurs in *Henry IV*, Part 1. Falstaff and
> the Prince are having a high old time by pretending in
> turn to be the King chastising Hal for his association with
> Falstaff. At the end Falstaff pleads with Hal as the King
> never to banish Falstaff: "Banish plump Jack, and banish
> all the world!" I wanted Richard to take a moment to let
> the words have their full impact on the Prince, and then
> to say to himself, "I do, I will." And inevitably he does
> when he becomes King.

> Richard told me that his interpretation of Prince Hal
> caused some trouble with the director who was himself
> playing Falstaff and consequently wanted no serious note
> to disturb the comedy of the tavern scenes.

> Some entries in my small diary express my joy at Rich-
> ard's success in that 1951 Stratford season:

> *Sunday, April 8th.* (In London.) A quiet day at home,
> luxuriating in Rich's Stratford notices; they are miracu-
> lous.

> *Friday, May 11th.* Saw *Henry IV*, Part 1. Rich was
> magnificent and Sybil delightful. (Sybil had the small part

of Lady Mortimer who speaks only in Welsh. Shakespeare doesn't even give her speeches in an English translation.) This is bliss indeed.

Monday, May 14th. A doleful day. I had very reluctantly to leave Stratford after an idyllic weekend. I don't want a bit to go to America now. But I did go to America and so I didn't see the climax of the series, *Henry V*, until . . .

Saturday, September 22nd. Up early to go to Stratford. Rich and Syb met me at the station. Saw Part 2 at the matinée; it is much better; "Oh, polished perturbation" soliloquy particularly impressive. Very moved in the evening by *Henry V*: there's no doubt about R.'s greatness. I feel proud, humble, and awed by God's mysterious ways.

It would have been puzzling had Anthony Quayle *not* been disturbed. Falstaff's laughs, his command, were undercut by Burton's proud Prince. The established actor whose plays they ought to have been was out-manoeuvred. Quayle recognised Burton's immovability. Once the younger man had decided on the part he would not—because he could not—change it. And once he was on stage, no one could make him do what he did not want to do. Again and again Burton spoke of "being on your own out there," "fighting for your life," "it's you against them." Although a pleasant and a modest man, he was also a compulsive competitor—in pints, in sex, in stories, in sport, on the stage. Quayle, who was director, star and patron, had every reason to feel dismayed: Burton got in his light. Yet he recognised the depths that Burton was drawing on—"the Welshness"—and he was one of the first to spot and to note the uncanny, superstitious, even mystical relationship he had with his talent. "I don't know where it comes from. I don't know what it is. Just a knack," Burton told him. And it might go away if he didn't listen keenly, feed it perhaps with the energy of his life, stoke it up with risks to his health and even to his sanity.

The Welshness was another key to what Sybil called "that wonderful summer." "There were nightingales," says Robert Hardy, who was also so infected by the prevailing Welshness that his own Archbishop Scrope had a coal valley lilt, "there was laughter." It was here that Richard bought his first car—a Flying Standard. Robert Hardy taught him to drive and *that* produced enough stories for half a night's drinking in Stratford's actors' pub, the Dirty Duck. Richard at that time was openly delighted at the prospect of posh motors. A year later he bought a Lea-Francis—the Flying Standard had collapsed—then a Mark 10 Jaguar, then a Cadillac, then the red MG which he never sold and took to Switzerland. That summer in Stratford was a Welsh heaven.

Hugh Griffith, an outsize and very grand Welsh actor with eyebrows like handlebar grips, was there in full bucolic magnificence: there was a Welsh harpist who pretended to be a ghost, Rachel Roberts teamed up with Sybil as "Lady Something or other" and they gossiped, knitted the acting village together, went on stage wearing wristwatches and nail varnish. It was here that Sybil decided to give up acting altogether and dedicate herself to Richard's career and the eagerly expected family. There was naked bathing on a hot summer's night after a stirring performance, there were wondering Welsh friends and neighbours up to see this phenomenon and afraid that his Welshness might be too loud: "The English are afraid of us," said Burton and brawled, now and then, to prove it. The merry scoundrel pleasure-court of Sir John Falstaff was mirrored in the company of Hugh Griffith and the Welsh contingent, with Burton playing the key figure in both.

Wonder accelerated to amazement when Humphrey Bogart and Lauren Bacall turned up, saw the plays, and fell for Burton. "He was just marvellous," Lauren Bacall says. "Marvellous. But even then he was trouble, you know. He'd only met Bogie and I—over in the pub, the Dirty Duck, for about half an hour when he insisted on taking me round to Shakespeare's birthplace. Recited great lines on the spot of course. It wasn't exactly a pass, but what the hell was Bogie to make of it? But Bogie loved him. We all did. You had no alternative."

Some of the critics were a little cool. Some disparaging. He was too wooden, too overt. But there was one critic, Kenneth Tynan, to be the defining critic of British theatre in the Fifties and Sixties, who took his wife Elaine Dundy up to Stratford and went backstage to congratulate, to talk, later to drink. Then came a review which made a bonfire of all the others and lit up Burton's name in flames in the English theatre of the day.

His playing of Prince Hal . . . turned interested speculation to awe as soon as he started to speak: in the first intermission the local critics stood agape in the lobbies.

Burton is a still brimming pool, running disturbingly deep; at twenty-five he commands a repose and can make silence garrulous. His Prince Hal is never a roaring boy: he sits hunched or sprawled, with dark unwinking eyes: he hopes to be amused by his bully companions, but the eyes constantly muse beyond them into the time when he must steady himself for the crown. "He brings his cathedral with him," said one dazed member of the company. For all his bold chivalry this watchful Celt seems surely to have strayed from a wayside pulpit. Fluent and sparing of gesture, compact and spruce of build, Burton smiles where other Hals have guffawed, relaxes where they have strained, and Falstaff (played with affectionate obesity by Anthony Quayle) must work hard to divert him. In battle, Burton's voice cuts urgent and keen—always likeable, always amiable.

His gifts were now in place. His public role and character were now fully marked out.

The presence: the "magnificent head and shoulders" noticed by the alchemist of shrewdness, Alec Guinness: "the cathedral" he brought with him, as a fellow cast member observed. The Voice. The stillness, the sexual aura, that high-definition presence which is found in men and women heterosexual and homosexual and recognised equally by all: at its rawest and most baffling—"star quality."

So there he stood in the Dirty Duck, opposite Shakespeare's Memorial Theatre in Stratford-upon-Avon, 1951, Prince of the heap. "He came from nowhere," says Gielgud. "Very rare." Dreams of Hollywood stardom—which would come: of more great roles on the stage—which would come: of more glorious drunken evenings in great company—which would come, and women and money and fame—all would be given to this pockmarked child of a miner from Welsh-speaking Wales, born with "the devil in him" as Emlyn Williams's tutelary genius Sarah Grace Cooke observed. Now the devil was out; and at large.

8
Hot for Hollywood

"I didn't want him to be an actor," said Cis. "I thought it was too hard. I was frightened for him." She had every reason to be frightened. She could see into him. Burton was hurling himself on the course most likely to tempt and test him to the limit. He was going to play tricks and take risks with his life and personality and do so in an increasingly wilful and dangerous way. To some extent we all do: to a greater extent, perhaps, all actors do this. The difference with Burton came from the scale on which he did it, the talents he gambled, the colossal winnings, the rupturing losses, the public glare in which increasingly it took place and the undeniable fact that in the middle of this maelstrom was always a quiet, reading man whom Cis would have recognised with relief as the boy sitting beside the fire, buried in a book.

"I can be loud or soft," he said of his voice at this time. "I have no middle range." That had been rather pointedly obvious when he played Ferdinand in *The Tempest* at Stratford in the glorious summer of 1951: a lightweight romantic figure with no menace or drama about him—Burton was not good. Even his devoted admirer and friend Robert Hardy was reduced to praising the ruff he wore! Nor had the more mature, quiet paragon of Henry V escaped from censure. As Prince Hal—wonderful, but as the tempered King—"he lacked inches," said one reviewer. The wound was salved a little when Olivier sent word that he too had been accused of "lacking inches" in the same role and by the same critic! Gielgud, too, through the agency of his mother, produced reviews to prove that the golden oldies of the classic past with whom Burton was being compared to his disadvantage had been just as slammed in their time.

The middle range, perhaps, was where a comfortable, accomplished actor could exist and grow. Burton was neither. He made it *seem* easy—that was different: that was the pride of the macho Valley rugby player. He had class: but that too was neither comfortable nor craftsmanly accomplished. The actor William Squire, who worked with him often in films and on the stage, speaks of his "*lack* of craft, his *lack* of tricks and knowledge of the trade. He was what he was and that was it. When it worked of course—and it did, many times—he was marvellous. But although he talked of acting as a craft, he took no trouble over it."

It is essential at this point to try to understand what is happening to Burton since so much of his public life flows from the tensions between Hollywood and the English stage, between money and art, as it was thought, between philandering and fidelity, between a public and a private life. Very soon he will be known as one of the greatest seducers of our times and in a town—Los Angeles—not known for the lack of competition. Very soon he will be outfacing the all-powerful Darryl Zanuck and spurning a millionaire's bribe while privately scheming to join that six-zero club. Very soon he will be up for Oscars and head over heels in the switchback strip of movies. On the London stage, the great roles will be plucked like plums, in the Welsh valleys his fame will swell like the fortissimo of a chapel organ and his acts of generosity, recklessness, coarseness and excellent manners tossed on to the fiery legend like dry logs. It is quite remarkable that from so early an age with so short a track record he should have inspired such an industry of interest.

What he relied on, I think, and what he always came back to was that "natural" self which he did not understand nor at this stage want to understand, but which gave him his power. It was like an Aladdin's lamp. A gift. Somehow he had acquired it and when the need arose he would use it. The genie would appear: and all would be solved. In this sense, Burton was drawing on something profound and perhaps dangerous in himself. He was, perhaps unwisely, fearless about using—and abusing—this gift.

Somewhere in that unknown territory where acts of will, instinct and habit mingle with inheritance, chemistry, biology, is the struggle—if it is a struggle: many can't or won't or don't—to "make something" of yourself. The battle is like the tragic acts in a Greek drama—always vital, always offstage. It is there that the most ordinary-seeming ingredients can be re-ordered and re-energised into extraordinary explosions of personality. Burton pulled the struggle out into the open and made this "thing" that was himself stand up to as many trials as he could imagine. It was like the course of trials which underline so many of the great myths and fairy stories and narratives.

He saw his life as a succession of tests, mostly invented by himself. One way to get out of your past is to invent a future you aim for. Burton's was based on the Celtic hero. The hero must be challenged and tormented, he must be bamboozled and tried up to breaking point before he is permitted to claim the prize, before, in fact, he is able properly to call himself a hero. Burton put himself on trial, later on public trial, either because he was driven to it by a daemon he could not command or because he willed the daemon to come out and fight. Now one, now the other, I suspect.

And so he always laid himself on the line. Film directors were even to complain—as stage directors complained—that Burton had no "tricks," that he played no games. He sank into the part with total conviction or—just the opposite—he put it on with open contempt and boredom. It worked or it did not work. Somehow it was not his business and certainly it was not his business to pander to it. He dared life to deliver its best and to do its worst. It was this rawness, though, which was at the root of his appeal and of his greatness as an actor, his power as a man.

He was aware of the courage he needed. Although he had the pride and the carriage to make it look easy, he was often terrified. He described himself being "scared witless" when he went to Oxford, for example. Yet he conquered it. He was shaking with nerves when he did the most critical audition of his career—for John Gielgud and *The Lady's Not For Burning*—and yet he forced himself through it. None of this is all that unusual. What distinguishes Burton was the formidable nature of the obstacles he set himself and the growing weaknesses of body which he ignored. He was forever daring himself to succeed in "the big league" and, almost equally, prepared to throw it all away. He was a conqueror who loved conquest but soon became bored with the spoils.

From the first he used himself as an open laboratory. The experiments became increasingly harmful. He was Jekyll and Hyde to himself, swallowing the compounds and mixtures of his own fantasies and terrors and watching what happened. He was quite prepared to go wild. In drink he could be aggressive and thoroughly nasty. Satan could capture his tongue. Some of the interviews he began to give to journalists are the equivalent of psychoanalysis—in which, of course, he expressed no confidence. But to a passing journalist he would free-associate in a way which would have held Freud entranced. His childhood, for instance, became an infinitely fictitious country, now like Gorki's *Lower Depths*, now like the Chicago stockyard slums, now like an occupied country burgeoning with guerilla units, now a place of giants, spotless princesses, poetry and song. His drinking became vengeful. And there was always the shadow of illness, the occasional disturbing blankness, the spasms of physical distress.

One course above all he set himself: or perhaps he could not help it. There was to be no hypocrisy, no pussyfooting around, no pretence at all—not with himself. If he were to discover the nature and the limits of this person he was—and, as time went by, stave off the *timor mortis*—fear of death—then he would go for the nerve and the bone, draw blood. Small wonder that Cis was "frightened for him." He was taking himself to the limit and then pushing on from there.

He had been across to New York with *The Lady's Not For Burning*, just before the Stratford season. The play had done quite well and he was noticed in the small part. To a post-war austerity-rationed Welshman, America was lush Eden and the fleshpots of Egypt combined. He loved it and although he was obedient to his great theatrical challenge and returned to Stratford, he was happy to go back after Stratford to star in *Legend Of Lovers*, a play by Jean Anouilh which had begun life as *Eurydice*. It was the sort of part which would often come his way. Wordy and intellectual, with only a small chance of success: the sort of play a cynic would say that producers put on so that they can feel good. The public gave it early notice: the critics were again kind to Burton. At that stage in his career no one was looking for a hit-machine: the longer heads realised that it was a difficult job to scale the face of Broadway—as it was in the

West End—with so few footholds and even fewer helping ropes dangling down to give you a lift.

Back in London he starred in another prestige production—*Montserrat*, adapted by Lillian Hellman. Daphne Rye got him the part, Binkie Beaumont was the producer, the play opened at the Lyric, Hammersmith, on April 8th, 1952. Burton played the anguished but heroic young captain who would not betray the revolutionary leader despite the systematic slaughter of six hostages. It had a limited run of six weeks. Once again the reviews for Burton were excellent. Those who saw the performance thought it memorable—Burton alone against the Establishment, the powerful of the oppressor: his most convincing role. But not many people did see it and he was left with a clutch of good notices, a prospect of the West End which would say no, most times, to the sort of plays he was right for and a generous offer from Anthony Quayle to come back to Shakespeare in Stratford and tackle the next range of roles.

Burton declined for two reasons. The first was that he said he wanted an interval before he "took on" Shakespeare again. This was surely sensible. The 1951 Stratford season had been such a success, it would have been foolish to have followed it with any lesser thing. He needed to regroup. But there was a simpler reason than that: his hunch told him he was not in the mood for it. The instinct said no. So there was no argument.

Korda told him he was ready for a first crack at Hollywood. The money, at that time, was tremendous. Korda let him out on a three-picture deal with Fox, continued to pay him $15,000 a year but would take a large slice of what Fox paid him: from the three pictures Richard would earn about £80,000. In 1952 you might have bought Buckingham Palace for £80,000. "He just couldn't believe there was that much money in the world and it was coming to him," said Sybil at the time. He totted up the figures night after night, and "he would take that piece of paper out of his pocket and look at it again and again." This was not only copper-bottomed security, it was a chance to play with the big numbers and see what happened.

Korda gave him a leaving party which left everyone paralytic. Poured on to the plane, alone, Burton was humped for thirteen hours across the Atlantic, assuaged by alcohol; stopped over for a few drinks in New York and then taken on an eleven-hour trip to Los Angeles which was made tolerable by more alcohol. He sank into the waiting limo unshaven, crumpled, white-faced, nervous, shattered and by the time he got to the posh Beverly Hills Hotel, in need of the complimentary bottle of Scotch a thoughtful management had left in his room. A few hours later he was at a mega Hollywood party, the Welsh wonder from Stratford-upon-Avon, declaiming Shakespeare, drinking soundly, reciting Dylan Thomas, singing, story-telling, perhaps a little over the top, one or two thought, but to the majority a marvellous new whirlwind of talent and animal energy. Those forty-eight hours were a small opening shot in the game of chance and challenge he played with his stamina over the next thirty years. "My liver is to be buried separately from the rest of me, with full honours," he was to say in a later film.

Lauren Bacall and Humphrey Bogart were his welcoming party and he was immediately at the centre of the fastest set in town. "He was great fun," says Lauren Bacall, "the stories, the energy, the poetry. He was different. Bogie just adored him." So who would say him nay? Certainly not a considerable number of ladies, according to hot gossip and well informed rumour. On the other hand, Burton stoutly denied that he had broken up nine marriages: why, he did not even know three of the couples aforementioned. Sybil papered the loo with that article and others.

The little hard evidence we have of Sybil at this time points to a tough and cheerful woman who had made her deal and stood by it. Despite his lone pursuits of happiness, the greater impression is that they worked the Hollywood field together, for Burton's material rewards, seeing it as a treasure trove best plundered before it disappeared. She remained the faithful wife but Richard certainly appears to have had the licence to rove.

The laws of libel and courtesy to the living provide that a decorous Fifties-style Hollywood curtain be drawn over some of these matters. It was a time when a bare ankle could not be shot stepping out of a robe for the implication would be "nakedness," the consequence "sex" and the inevitable result—the destruction of the nation. Burton's amours were widely touted "with this guy you bring your own mattress," a well-used crack but at Burton, well aimed. There was a relationship between Jean Simmons (then married to Stewart Granger) and Burton which was so close that he continued embracing her, publicly, after the stroke of midnight one New Year's Eve, only to look up to a slap in the face from Sybil, who instantly left the party—for New York. A few days later he joined her. When they returned, the Burtons, who had been sharing the Simmons–

Granger household, moved out to a minute bungalow which they rented from the James Masons.

There were those who thought that Burton was a shit. Lauren Bacall, looking back, speaks of a "big pro-Sybil lobby." "People didn't like his going around town with one after the other." Lauren Bacall cannot be doubted. On the other hand her present emphasis may be retrospectively the harder because she was so emphatic in the Sixties when Burton "crucified Sybil" by leaving her for Elizabeth Taylor. She is unequivocally pro-Sybil. Nevertheless it is not difficult to imagine that there was a Burton-is-an-expletive-deleted faction among the Hollywood wives, mistresses, starlets and full supporting cast.

Burton expected—and usually got—"cover" from his friends and complicity in the cover-up from the women. He said persistently, "I'll never hurt Syb. I'll never leave Syb." This was repeated endlessly, a vow, a charm, a prayer? But as time went on he seemed not to mind who saw him, who heard about his infidelities. That was life as he lived it and that was that.

Setting out his own terms was a constant provocation. At this time, he said, "All I wanted to do was to live, pick up a new Jag, and act at the Old Vic." The British theatrical Establishment who thought he aspired to be their new idol would be puzzled over "All I wanted to do was to live"—but they would have let it pass as a Welsh eccentricity; "to act at the Old Vic" would have drawn beams of approval. But "pick up a new Jag"—that would not do. No matter they had, or aspired to, Bentleys and Rolls and MGs and Rovers—no matter they somehow winkled out the wherewithal to obtain the vehicles—Burton's *saying* it was somehow too vulgar. It is likely that he knew that and said it with all the more relish. Like the Hollywood Establishment—though for different reasons—they too had their doubts about this bold new boy.

Burton loved women. "You must first love, or *think* you love the woman," he said. "When you are with the *only* woman—the only one you *think* there is for that moment—you must love her and know her body as you would think a great musician would orchestrate a divine theme. You must use everything you possess —your hands, your fingers, your speech: seductively, poetically, sometimes brutally, but always with a demoniacal passion." This is the testament of an erotic fundamentalist.

Love was one of the realities in life and he went for it. "All I wanted to do was to live . . ."

Sybil's reaction has to be assumed: she has said very little. She seems to have dealt with it in a remarkably successful manner. They were invited to Hollywood parties together and they left together: when one broke into song, the other took up the harmonising line. Their calypsos were enjoyed and their company was sought. Emlyn Williams, who stayed with them in this period while he was on a tour with his Charles Dickens readings, describes scenes of domestic industry and felicity. Richard swore by Sybil: "She'll never leave me." Sybil's very few utterances seem fatalistic. Her actions—as with Jean Simmons—could be dramatic: her forgivingness, though, seemed to be infinite. The further assumption must be that they gave each other a great deal that was worth having and keeping. They called each other "Boot," short for the comic Welsh pronunciation of Beautiful—Bootiful! But he was already pushing it and Lauren Bacall saw that and did not like it. "I'll never divorce Sybil," he said, "and she'll never divorce me . . . she thinks I'm a genius."

His nerve was in excellent shape. He went to one party where Cole Porter played the piano, Judy Garland sang and, invited to follow *that*, the young Welsh unknown blenched not, stood forward and slammed the room silent with "To be or not to be" spoken in Welsh. He exchanged jokes with Greta Garbo, whom he did not recognise, and put his hand on the goddess's knee. He wore the battered corduroy trousers and old tweed jacket of the skint London actor, not for effect but because buying clothes was a waste of money. He was prepared to be known as a "tight-wad." He and Sybil lived carefully, borrowed cars to save renting them, accepted hospitality, incurred and endured some cutting remarks of the wealthy but kept steadfast to their aim to make some money and run back to London to act and feed the security bank. You never knew when your luck would turn—another mean Taibach slogan to see him through these dazzling fields of honey and clover. Money mattered: those who had never had any know the value. The bleak wisdom of bare and poor streets were still his commandments. You had to go for it. Poverty was still a dread.

One of his compulsive gambits was to challenge everyone at the first meeting. He made a few gamey remarks to his first Hollywood leading lady, Olivia de Havilland, and she announced to the world that he was "a coarse-grained man with a coarse-grained charm and a talent not completely developed."

He would have agreed with that. Indeed at one stage he banged his head against the studio wall in frustration. The camera then as always gave him a major problem.

He could photograph marvellously and at times the camera "loved" him. Arthur Ibbetson, the English cameraman who worked with him on several occasions, first notes how alarmed he was to discover what a bad skin Richard had and then enthuses without pause about the shape of his face, his professionalism, his patience. Yet others—Burton included—thought that he never "came over" on the camera as he did on stage. That is as may be. He certainly "came over" with considerable force on several occasions—*Virginia Woolf, The Night Of The Iguana, The Spy Who Came In From The Cold, Look Back In Anger*. He found it very easy to be "professional" in the sense of doing the job competently while being totally uninvolved, and often the lack of involvement showed. In his way—at times—he was directing us to his distance from the script, the movie, the work—"Look! I hate this rubbish," he was saying, but that was not much help to the performance. He performed best when he had well-written lines and was acting with someone he respected. And even then he could appear awkward. Those ingratiating nudges to the audience, all those lovable, identifiable tricks and traits, the camera-wise knowingness—he never learned. Either he could not—which, given his wit and his intelligence and, above all, perhaps, his shrewdness—is unlikely; or he would not—which, given the obstinacy and tenacity with which he stuck to his own version of himself, is much more likely. Once again, he was his own man, went his own way which meant he often lacked utterly the pleasing, the plasticine complicity a great screen actor needs. The camera wanted everything: Burton wasn't having that.

If the camera is a lie detector—and it can be—then it told the truth about Burton's essential reserve. That secret self which he drew on, and which he would draw out and test as time went on, was not for public display *unless Burton willed it*. Then, fine. It is useful, I think, to point out again how much he disliked being touched. His first girl friend said he was "not a groper: too much class." Kissing women on stage or on screen—with very very few exceptions—Claire Bloom one, Elizabeth Taylor another—"gives me the horrors." It seems odd that a man with so much of a reputation for sexual encounters should cringe from public contact, but it was all part of his reserve. Just as his repeated and heartfelt defences of monogamy are all part of the complex and muddled or profound idea he had of the division of responsibility and territory between different degrees of love, different qualities of sexual encounter.

Similarly, directors have noted how rare it was for him to bring his natural rage into play on screen. Anger could sweep across him like a storm cloud in fast motion and burst all about him in a fury of violently well-picked epithets. And he was a fist-fighting man in his twenties and thirties. But he was most sparing with the anger on celluloid: would rather fake it than summon it up. Partly out of shyness, partly because he kept to himself what he felt he most needed, he would not let it out and some performances suffered. It was yet another indication of where his deepest interest lay: in his life, not in his career. In being who he was: that was his vocation, and discovering how far he could go and even, fatally, what he could get away with.

Burton was goose meat for the publicity machine. The stories of poverty and struggle got wilder and ever wilder in the publicity office until his family came crawling out of the Middle Ages on all fours! He had an irrepressible tendency to send up his interviewers: if they were daft enough to believe it—so much the worse for them. He kept forgetting they would write it down: he seems to have thought—most of the time—that they had just turned up for a friendly drink. He ignored the great truth—jokes don't cross frontiers. He often came out as a bit of a bighead and, accused of this at the time, took a tape-measure and agreed that his head had indeed expanded by one-eighth of an inch since leaving Wales. At one stage his entire family of fourteen were reported as having lived on a dollar a week! Hollywood was the biggest carnival he had ever seen and he was like a box of fireworks set off all at once.

And the films? Three. *My Cousin Rachel* (1952), *Desert Rats* (1953) and *The Robe* (1953).

My Cousin Rachel, from a Daphne du Maurier novel, was a vehicle for Olivia de Havilland. Burton climbed on board and, even in a rather clumsy performance, made enough of a mark to be nominated for an Oscar. They dressed and lit him against his character—softening where they ought to have emphasised the toughness—and they gave him a part with no verbal bite and no guts but even so it was not a bad first break for the boy from the snooker halls of Port Talbot.

In *The Desert Rats* as the young English captain who put paid to that upstart Rommel by turning him back at a crucial moment in the whole North African Campaign (set in Palm Springs), he was fine. He was always fine as a soldier or a man of action. There were no frills and producers regretted that: they yearned for the signature of a Wayne and, later, an Eastwood, a Marvin. Burton did the job on screen as efficiently, one felt, as he would have done it in real life. There was an admirable lack of bullshit in Burton's performances. In action he was excellent. He played that aspect of himself which could well have been in a war—after all he had trained long enough for it—and the result was the sort of performance he was to deliver several times in his film career and none the worse for that: professional, convincing. He loved being in the same film as James Mason. Robert Wise, the director of *The Desert Rats*, found Burton as agreeable and hard-working and as reliable, as had Henry Koster in *Rachel*. He was a good soldier.

The third film in this three-picture deal which was to bring him "more money than he thought there was in the world" was *The Robe*. This was the Big One.

Hollywood's many attempts to grapple with God would make a well-judged study of the interaction between America's dream world and its view of authority and the Promised Land. *The Robe* was intended to be the boldest and grandest yet—as epic as de Mille but with a serious and intelligent slant on the story of Christ. Of course it was also intended to make a fortune, and win awards for integrity and holiness. It is always easy to be sceptical about Hollywood and God and it is right to be so. There is no doubt, though, that inside the declaration to make a blockbuster was the whisper of an ideal.

The pre-filming budget had gone up to the then astronomical sixteen million dollars with Tyrone Power cast in the lead. Koster came in to direct, cut the budget to six million dollars, and either passed over Olivier for Burton (whom he admired) or went for Burton after Olivier turned it down. Burton certainly saw the part as a "catch" in the competitive stakes. He wanted it. A great deal was riding on it: some said the Fox studio was at stake. Burton appreciated that. It was to be a spiritual *Ben Hur*, Christianity on the new Cinemascope and for adults.

He played the part of Marcellus, a noble Roman who is converted to Christianity and chooses to die for his new religion. Jean Simmons plays the woman who first misunderstands and finally adores him. Victor Mature it was, no less, who led him to the Lord.

It is important to hold on to our hats and remember that it was quite well reviewed at the time. The religious community sent its messengers on to the set and Burton obliged with such whoppers ("playing Marcellus is like playing Hamlet") that his reputation as an honest interviewee ought to have ended there and then. He was told not to smoke on set because it spoiled the image: he smoked. There was little he could do about the image. Much of the time on the screen he wanders around helplessly in a freshly starched little Dior number looking for a line worth saying. Of Jesus Christ, someone says: "We gotta find out where he holes up at night." Marcellus starts off the film as a drunk, a womaniser, a detached outsider amid the (very decorous) antics of Ancient corrupt Rome—but alas he is converted. Victor Mature, who has given so much pleasure in his day that nothing must be said against him, is, however, not wholly convincing sitting in a cell wearing a leather mini-skirt, reading Pythagoras. At other times he looks at the sky, his jaw clenching and unclenching as if working a particularly stubborn wad of chewing gum while the Kansas City Glee Club harmonises solemn music: perhaps he wants to turn it off—but they are unstoppable. Burton at one stage goes quite powerfully mad and no wonder.

He became friends with Mature: they played craps on the set. There is an awed and yet a sickly innocence, a pasteboard period falseness about the whole enterprise, and lines like lead which today make *The Robe* seem older, more quaint than silent movies. Insofar as the film was held together, Burton held it together: was it worth holding?

Well, that was what they made, then. Back in England, although his friends might snicker, they were still impressed: he was up there, a Hollywood star in a big Hollywood epic. Many of his fellow British actors—throughout the years—only affected to despise the movies: they themselves were not asked to do them or, if asked, played minor roles or did not get the hang of it at all. Envy and sour grapes had their customary party.

It was unfortunate, in a way, that Burton *did* hold it together. Just as *Rachel* gave Hollywood an inkling of his class, and *Desert Rats* reassured them as to his reliability, *The Robe* showed that he could almost carry what were really the worn-out carcases of a clapped-out era. *The Robe* had been shot in Cinemascope in order to tempt the new television viewers back into the cinemas. The studios were rocking from an earthquake none of them believed was happening. The old studio system which had produced good writers, good directors, good stars, good movies, was breaking up and bits of it were sliding all over the ancient and sacred lots. At first television did for celluloid what the San Francisco earthquake had done for property. It was obviously time for a change. Television was beginning a thirty-year triumphant march. The artistic initiative in cinema was about to shift to Europe. The later young saving brats of the American film industry had not arrived. One of Hollywood's major strategies in the face of all this was to re-create the hits of the past in larger-than-life packs and Burton was useful for that.

His moment came at a time when shoring up the old seemed all that mattered or all that anyone could think of. His potential for convincing, intense, even poetic realism was not to be conveyed for some time. Pageants were to be the salvation of the studios. So they hoped.

It is a touch unfair to use hindsight to criticise what faced an eager hungry young Welsh unknown in the piranha-filled goldfish bowl of Hollywood in the early Fifties. The remarkable thing is that with such thin material and from such a long way back, he came through so quickly. But there is a sense in which he complied with what was being asked of him. After all, the local cinema, the Cach, had been his dream world and here he was in the biggest Cach in the world doing more or less what he had seen "the greats" doing in the Thirties. His background, too, reached out for the security of tradition. New moves tend to come from middle-class artists who have had the opportunity to absorb a great deal early and feel sufficiently confident in an educational and financially secure context to move it along. Working-class artists are brought up with traditional—at best, and if they can get it. And they always know it can disappear overnight.

On the whole, in that first year in Hollywood, Burton made a fair shot at it. His feet were on the ladder; he had gatecrashed at the top. They would ask him back.

He did one thing in Hollywood for which he has not been given anything like sufficient credit. He turned down flat the king's ransom, the pot of gold, the answer to his poverty-prayers he had always dreamt of. And in the process he showed his steel of independence.

Fox, through Darryl Zanuck—one of Hollywood's few surviving super barons, head of Fox, a star-maker—offered him a seven-picture deal (at the time of *The Desert Rats*). This was to cover a seven-year period. He would have some time to slip over to London to act. The fee was a million dollars: there could also be percentages. True, he still had the Korda minimum deal to fall back on, but this new offer was in a wildly different category.

This was 1953. In order to put that offer in perspective we have to imagine a young unknown with rumours of a short classical stage success to his credit, no films worth mentioning and no bankability whatsoever, being offered, in 1988, about twelve to fifteen million dollars. Yet the offer seems to have given Burton no pause. Fifteen million dollars. Burton said that he had promised to go back to the Old Vic for £45 a week to do *Hamlet*, and he was sticking to it. It was a big decision.

Burton never disguised his respect for what money would bring. Let all the well-heeled English pooh-pooh it as they may, *he* knew that pounds, shillings and pence bought warmth, desirable goods and security and he wanted that for himself, for his family and, as time went on, for an ever-increasing host of dependents. This offer was a real and unarguable fortune. In one bound he would be free of all financial worries. And all he had to do was to stay in the sun and turn up on the lot when a suitable—or unsuitable (he was used to taking the rough with the smooth)—script came up. It was a tremendous act of strength to refuse that and a real financial sacrifice and gamble. None of those who sniped at his film career were ever to be so lasciviously tempted.

The great imperial Zanuck was not amused at Boyo Burton's refusal and tried to force his hand. On occasions like these, friends of Burton reported, he would counter-attack by releasing his temper, tearing up the room and making it quite clear and genuinely credible that *whatever* they did, said or tried on *he* would do just whatever he wanted. "He never backed down," Emlyn's son, Brook Williams, said, "not in front of anybody." Burton's own version is milder:

> On one side of the courtroom was Darryl Zanuck and half the corporation boys in America. On the other side was

me, alone; I didn't have a lawyer. I played it very English, very Ronald Colman.

At one point one of the lawyers jumped up and shook his fist at me and said, "You shook hands with Mr. Zanuck on this agreement. You shook hands with Mr. Zanuck in his own office."

And I said, "I don't believe Mr. Zanuck said that because he's an honourable man. But if he did say it, then he's a fucking liar."

The place broke up in complete confusion. Strong men fainted and were carried off by weak men . . .

The story rocketed around Hollywood and outgunned all the gossip of crawling up drainpipes, being visited in his dressing room by naked ladies, drinking day and night, smashing his head against a wall. He had integrity! Back to the Old Vic.

A felicitous footnote to that incident is that he got his cake after all. He did go back to London; he did defy the might of Zanuck, but the canny Alex Korda in London stitched up the contract later which, yes, was to give him a million dollars, but also tie him to some terrible films. This was the rule of the day. If you worked in movies in America you worked in the studios and you were their property. Attempts to buck that system would end in the courtrooms or, as likely, unemployment. It was star-slave labour. But at the crucial moment, Burton *had* bucked the system. There were powerful men in Hollywood who never forgave him and exercised their revenge for years.

Filming of *The Robe* was arduous and he was exhausted towards the end of it. He and Sybil took off for a few weeks' holiday before going back to London. When all the shouting died down, it was always—back to Syb.

It had been a hell of a year. Three big movies; drinking with Bogie; flirting with Garbo; taken up by Hedda Hopper, "the most exciting success story since Gregory Peck's contracts of ten years back"; liked by directors; known as his own man and a tough one; married to a charmer and, now at peace with Olivia de Havilland, sitting on the floor at a last party telling her that he was "terrified" of going back to play Hamlet, would wake up in the middle of the night sweating and shaking at the thought, unable to go back to sleep. The terror of the live theatre, and all those powerful professionals waiting for him: it was all that concerned, even consumed him. There is no reason to believe he was other than sincere. He had fixed his star on the great Shakespearian roles—that, in his professional life, was what he lived by, that was how he tested himself to the limit. One of the biggest of all was about to challenge him and he knew what it would take.

About twelve years after this first Hollywood year, he wrote about it. He described a party.

The house in California—it was in the Bel Air district of Los Angeles, I think—looked as if it had been flung by a giant hand against the side of a hill and had stuck.

From the main living room, master bedroom, guest bedrooms, dining room, kitchen level, the house jutted and dropped one floor to a "playroom."

The "playroom" was not for children.

It was complete with bar and barman, hot-dog simmerer, king-sized double-doored two-tone refrigerator, drugstore hotplates, big-game trophies on the walls (the host was a big-game hunter who acted in his spare time), and huge, deep, low divans and easy chairs—villainously uncomfortable for men, but marvellously made for cute little women who could tuck their cute little legs away and blazingly efface their cute little pretty little pouting little personalities in niches of the vast furniture and make like cute little pussycats.

Below the "playroom" the house again jutted and dropped to the swimming pool, the showers and the changing rooms.

It was my first time in California and my first visit to a swank house. There were quite a lot of people in and around the pool, all suntanned and all drinking the Sunday morning liveners—Bloody Marys, boilermakers, highballs, iced beer. I knew some of the people and was introduced to the others. Wet brown arms reached out of the pool and shook my hand. The people were all friendly, and they called me Dick immediately. I asked if they would please call me Richard—Dick, I said, made me feel like a symbol of some kind. They laughed, some of them. It was, of course, Sunday morning and I was nervous.

I was enjoying this small social triumph, but then a girl sitting on the other side of the pool lowered her book, took off her sunglasses and looked at me. She was so extraordinarily beautiful that I nearly laughed out loud . . .

She sipped some beer and went back to her book. I affected to become social with the others but out of the corner of my mind—while I played for the others the part of a poor miner's son who was puzzled, but delighted by the attention these lovely people paid to him—I had her under close observation . . .

She was unquestionably gorgeous . . . She was lavish. She was a dark unyielding largesse. She was, in short, too bloody much, and not only that, she was totally ignoring me. I became frustrated almost to screaming when I had finished a well-received and humorous story about the death of my grandfather and found that she was turned away in deep conversation with another woman.

Elizabeth Taylor remembers that brief encounter too.

"My first impression was that he was rather full of himself," she says. "I seem to remember that he never stopped talking and I had given him the cold fish eye."

He left alone as he had arrived. Sybil had gone on ahead to London a week or so before. The Hampstead house needed to be opened up. Burton was heading back for base.

9
When the Going Was Good

Burton returned in 1953 as the conquering hero and went down to Wales to see and be seen. Cis was still there, of course, and Hilda, Tom still worked in the pits, David was in the police, Verdun a machinist, Graham a clerk, Ifor a bricklayer. All of them turned out for him; 73 Caradoc Street was given a June spring clean and Sybil and Richard moved in for a few days. Taibach and Pontrhyd-yfen were proud of him and he was unaffectedly pleased to be home. The beer and the stories flowed. Photographers snapped the strapping young giant crossing a bridge with his bemused and diminutive father, looking wary in the pub as his father waved a finger over a pint, glancing obligingly into the middle distance as the wind from Swansea Bay blew his hair. There were presents all round.

There always would be—for those he loved. And, later, for charities, for stricken individuals whose paths crossed his, prodigal amounts, and for down and out old acquaintances from way back. He was a tight-wad in Hollywood, surrounded by those swimming pools of golden sun and projected dollars. Back home he was King Wenceslas, all the year round. Cis had a song when Rich was small, a song which ended up saying that if ever she had the money, she would buy a Russian squirrel coat. There it was, wrapped up in a box "too good to open: all the way from the USA." It was probably on this trip that he conceived the plan—which he would execute – to set up, in their own houses or businesses, *all* his brothers and sisters.

In truth he was a little depressed by this visit to Wales, largely on account of Dic, his father. Burton was never heard to say a word against him and would boast about his "capacity" and his gypsy adventures, but the old man's indifference—"How are you, Rich?" "I could have been away in Swansea for the weekend"—was disturbingly offhand, even oppressive. Much as he loved Wales and never betrayed it, he could be happier in foreign countries now. The time of contradictions was on him. There was rarely a time when multiple tensions were not vying for supremacy.

Aged twenty-eight, dragging old defeats with him, full of new victories, he was in a state of turbulent fury.

It was time for *Hamlet*.

Just before Burton's return, Kenneth Tynan had reappraised the young actor whose Prince Hal at Stratford he had so eloquently praised:

> Burton is first and last an animal actor, with an animal's accidental grace and unsentimental passions . . . His Hal, like himself, was a princeling of tenacious ambition, lightened and relieved by stubborn good sense: and the good sense, even now that Hollywood and the Waterloo Road [site of the Old Vic Theatre] are en fête for him, is still unimpaired. He has lashed himself to his own main-mast, steering directly by his own star, the star of absolute self-trust which is within all the best actors and whose courses are unalterable, even by failure.

Strange how Tynan, like Robert Hardy and so many others, insisted on calling the son of the miner a "princeling," an "aristocrat" as if his true origin simply could not account for his gifts. So enter now—Lord Hamlet, London, 1953.

Once more into reach came Philip Burton with text, notes and theory. "On June 28th I received the script of the cut version which was to be used, and on June 30th we began to work. According to my diary, we had seven sessions, some of those long ones . . ." Once again Richard arrived at the first rehearsal word perfect and the director glided over the monologues, saying, "They're yours." It is a remarkable testament to the bond between these two that after blowing up Darryl Zanuck, boxing with Bogie and more or less picking his roles in the most powerful classical company in the land, he would still sit and listen to Philip's scholarly interpretation and, it seems, abide by it.

Philip saw *Hamlet* as essentially a "revenge play which has a formula as fixed as that of a modern mystery play in which, at its best, the culprit proves to be the least suspected and the most convincing." Devoted to revenge, Hamlet's obstacle is to be *certain* of the murderer: the ghost has given him the name but

> . . . The spirit I have seen
> May be a devil, and the Devil hath power
> T'assume a pleasing shape . . .

So was the ghost reliable? Furthermore, if the murderer, the culprit, is the new *King*, then his revenge must involve regicide—the ultimate crime in Shakespeare's day:

> There's such divinity doth hedge a king
> That treason can but peep to what it would,
> Acts little of his will . . .

This Hamlet, then, is not the hyper-sensitive and poetical young prince of Gielgud (much admired though it was by Philip): *this* Hamlet is out for vengeance but baulked by false trails and the fear of committing an even greater crime than that he was revenging. The sense, the ferocity of the lines were to be stressed, not languor, not indecision but the careful working out of the plot. Even in his reflections, he seeks action.

Burton was to be criticised for "taking the poetry out of the lines" in almost exactly the same way in which, in the Thirties, Olivier was criticised as Romeo. Both of them went for a greater realism. While Olivier's came from what he saw the role needed as he melted and disappeared into it, Burton's came from what he could give as the role was moulded to his personality. Olivier always strove to be different: Burton was always himself. Olivier lived through the many parts he played: Burton made the parts live through him. Olivier, perhaps, wanted to lose himself: Burton to find himself.

Claire Bloom was his Ophelia. "It was the happiest I ever saw him," says William Squire, who was in the company with him. "And it was the first time Sybil was in danger."

Since being with Burton in *The Lady's Not For Burning*, Claire

Bloom had gone on to begin to build up what was to become a distinguished and skilfully organised career as a serious actress. Charlie Chaplin had turned her into an international name in *Limelight* and yet here she was back at the Old Vic down behind Waterloo Station taking her chance with the best and toughest actors and actresses in town.

As always with Burton, you hack through to any particular emotional moment through tropical undergrowth of anecdotes apocryphal and plausible. Claire Bloom is supposed to have called him "that uncouth man" and he is supposed to have sworn to make her pay for it, and the sex came off them like a floodlight. Yet he could be odd about that. There is a reliable anecdote—from Brook Williams—that after a day's filming some time later, "the lads" with a nod and a wink and a "how's yer father" indicated to Rich that it would be worth his while to stay behind. Brook stayed with him and they sat crowded uncomfortably in a small airless cutting room through an hour or two of hard blue movies—the first, it transpired, that Burton had seen. Much guffawing went on and Burton, appealed to at every turn, as it were, nodded like an umpire. Afterwards, in the car on the way back, he was depressed. "But I had to go, Brookie," he said, "had to join in. They'd have taken it the wrong way if I didn't." He hated pornography but—or allied to that—his interest in sex was undisguised. His appetite, according to seasoned statisticians, was Juanian. His sense of competition—once challenged—was limitless.

There was something electric about Claire Bloom when she arrived at the Old Vic. William Squire was chosen to be her guardian. "You will keep him away from me, won't you, Billy?" she asked. Squire stuck close to her. In the Olive Branch, the pub across the way from the Old Vic, Burton, sensing mischief perhaps, asked, most gruffly, "Gettin' on well with Claire, then?"

Words to the effect of "just good friends" rather frostily met this nosey matiness. Eventually, "Look, it's no good, Rich. She won't do it with anybody. Especially not you," said Squire.

Squire would not explain more but enough had been said. Burton's dander was up.

"I bet I'll get there."

"You won't."

"What you bet?"

"A pint," said Squire.

"You're on."

Later in the week, Squire reports, he was sitting at the back of the stalls watching Burton rehearse when Claire, beside him, remarked: "You have to admit. He *is* rather marvellous."

"Yes," said Squire, seeing his ship go down the slipway, "he is rather marvellous."

"There was a system," he said. "The stage manager alerted him when Sybil was on the way in and Claire would leap off his knee and back into her own dressing room."

Soon it became painfully, embarrassingly or worryingly clear to their circle that they were extraordinarily happy together. Sybil kept her distance: did not pursue Richard to where she knew he would be with Claire. It is not known what she said in private but the view of Sybil, the uniquely tolerant—which seems undeniable—began to be yoked with Sybil the martyr, which was potentially dangerous. Martyrs often provoke explosive guilt in those they seem to save. Claire Bloom likewise and quite reasonably has put up the shutters against any discussion of a relationship which seems over the years to have gone from genuinely innocent adolescent friendship through sexual obsession to humiliations, bitter broken promises, exhausted recriminations and finally a violent rupture followed by total silence on both sides. In photographs at that time, though, of his Hamlet and her Ophelia, they look enraptured with each other.

There is one view which says that the wonder is that Burton held on to Sybil so tenaciously. It is commonplace, especially in the ego-brimming insecurity of the theatrical, showbiz world, for the wife who helps the husband to rise, the ladder to his climb, to be cast aside when he gains some height. The classiness of Claire Bloom, her undoubted talent, quality, beauty, promise, made her, in that world of sexual roulette, a winner to break the home. There were no children in the way; and Burton was not a religious man. Times were far far stricter then but actors were not expected to behave themselves. Yet Sybil held him and he held unto her. The bond between them was proof against tremendous pressure.

Hamlet opened in Edinburgh. Squire remembers walking down the street with Robert Hardy, seeing Richard and Claire embracing wildly under a lamp-post and spinning Hardy around so that he wouldn't catch sight of it. These were early days and Hardy was a friend equally of Richard and Sybil. And it *was* the Fifties. But soon, it was out. Tales, in Edinburgh, of Burton's frightening stamina: up all night drinking—*all* night—into rehearsal, a matinée, an evening performance, out at a party with Claire, into a studio the next morning, still with Claire, still with no sleep, set to do the title role in a radio play, a couple of stiffeners and up at the microphone steady, willing and able.

He had turned down a fabulous mountain of money to devote himself to the great roles of Shakespeare but the future great role of Burton was also under cultivation. There is no question, however, at that time in the early Fifties, but that he was out to seize the crown, pitting his performance against the best ever seen on the English stage. Olivier especially was in his sights. The production moved down into the cockpit of English theatre—the Old Vic.

His Hamlet on the whole was well received. He was "moody, virile and baleful," he had "dash, attack and verve." John Gielgud did not like it much. After he had seen it he came around to Richard's dressing room to take him to dinner, and observing he was beset by visitors, said, "Shall I go ahead or wait until you're better—I mean, ready?" Burton loved to re-tell that story. Winston Churchill came and is said to have sat in the front stalls and muttered the lines along with the Prince and when he came backstage, request, "My Lord Hamlet, may I use your facilities?" That too was retailed. As was the story of two of the supporting cast who were supposed to lower a flag over Hamlet during his final dying monologue. Stage discipline had been getting slack—Burton, for instance, had imitated Gielgud throughout one performance—and Michael Benthall, the director, had issued severe warnings. As the flag was being lowered, the house hushed and the dark and tragic Prince of Denmark uttering his last words, Burton the Prince looked to one of those two rather camp gentlemen who murmured out of the side of his mouth: "So who's the boy in black?" He loved the stories as much as the acting.

Michael Hordern acted with him then and many times afterwards. He was Polonius to Burton's Hamlet. I mentioned to Hordern that although the critics had been good, there was a certain coolness about the reaction. Hordern would have none of it. "I immensely admired his Hamlet. Really, at that time, he only had to walk on to the stage and open his mouth and the rest of us could have gone home. It's one of those things you can't explain at all: people call it charisma or—star quality. And I never found him a hogger. Very generous on stage. Unless you tried to put him down."

Robert Hardy, who was Laertes, was one of those who thought

his Hamlet was *not* his best performance—good but "too strong, I thought." The Prince of Vengeance was perhaps too much of a shock. But Hardy is eager to record one thing. "In the fencing at the end. I was something of a swordsman—taken lessons, practised, that kind of thing. When we duelled, there were over a hundred passes—some quite complicated—and we did it more than a hundred times—and sometimes Richard had a drop taken along the way—and he knew *nothing* about fencing. But he never lost his way or forgot a single pass, not once! And by God I had to fight for my life!" "He was so young, so vital, I was in tears," said Emlyn Williams. "I hadn't dared to hope he would be *so* good."

Hardy reserved his bouquet for Burton's Coriolanus in that marvellous 1953–4 season directed by Michael Benthall. Coriolanus—the proud, unbending Roman hero who will not gain office by seeking favours from the mob, who despises them and is contemptuous of all such sucking-up to "the people."

"His Coriolanus is quite *easily* the best I've ever seen. Without parallel," says Hardy. "But, you couldn't rely on it happening the next night." Already he was quickly, openly bored. Once the puzzle was cracked, the conquest made, the enemy taken—interest fell away.

He took a lot of persuading to do Coriolanus. At first he refused. Michael Benthall rang Philip Burton to ask for help. The play and its cast had been announced but Burton had decided that he would not do it. Could Philip get him to change his mind.

> I said I'd try. Richard had not discussed it with me but I guessed what was wrong. He could find no jot of sympathy for the character whose unmitigated contempt for ordinary folk, to him the amorphous mob, was so completely at variance with Richard's abiding identification with the working class . . . there followed a never-to-be-forgotten long night of discussion. I pointed out that it was the very lack of ambivalence in the character that was admirable . . . He had no ulterior motive: he refused to benefit from his victories. He was a man of action, happy only in action . . . He was the quintessential soldier's hero.

Richard went out and did it and according to Philip, Olivier himself agreed that it was the greatest Coriolanus he had ever seen.

Now he was a torrent in full spate. The queues grew around the Old Vic. Burton attracted an intelligent appreciative young audience. They were also rabidly enthusiastic. Philip noted: "The last night of the Old Vic season: Richard's fans nearly tore the place apart. He had to be smuggled away in a taxi."

In that thirty-nine-week season he had played three other taxing roles. In *Twelfth Night* he was a disappointing Toby Belch. "*I* couldn't wear a crown," said Michael Hordern. "Richard couldn't wear a wig." He added, significantly, "Disguise diminished him." And he knew it. "He didn't know about make-up at the time," said William Squire. "He'd had no training in that. Nor in voice projection: and I think he *never* did get the hang of make-up."

In *The Tempest* he played the animal man Caliban and once again the good reviews rolled. But as Ariel, an almost naked sprite, Robert Hardy was violently slammed by shocked critics. A scandal threatened. Burton steadied him, told him to ignore the critics—"Don't read them: they don't understand"—do what he wanted, don't back down. Hardy remains grateful thirty-four years later. In *King John* he played the Bastard. George Devine, the director, had the idea of leaving Burton on stage throughout as a "Chorus." This had to be abandoned, as Philip Burton happily recorded, because "Nobody could take their eyes off Richard." Silent and stuck at the side of the stage with the best of British classical actors about him, he would still demand the audience's full attention.

The company took *Hamlet* to Elsinore. There were high jinks and mad nights. Burton had been warned off work by a doctor—exhaustion was the diagnosis—and had pulled out of a few performances but typically he ignored the advice and went back on to lead the troops and take the Danes by storm.

As a first season in London it had been breathtaking. With less stage experience than the average dedicated amateur actor of his age, and following a year's lay-off in the cine-city of California, Burton had taken on some of the most demanding roles ever written and in at least one realised heights which no one who saw him ever forgot. Two others—Caliban and the Bastard—were greatly applauded: Hamlet convinced many but not all. Only Belch flopped. He was now, beyond any doubt, the heir to Olivier and Gielgud both. He had catapulted himself from Meredith Jones's roof-leaking youth club through Ma Smith's quiet respectable living room by way of Daphne Rye's few Lyric offerings and a short bout at Stratford, right to the front of a jealous, talented, overcrowded and intensely competitive profession.

During that glorious run, his hero died—Dylan Thomas, poet, of "an insult to the brain": alcoholic poisoning.

Later in New York, "where he went, I went," Burton wrote in an essay on Thomas:

> He was the master and I was the follower . . . he always made straight for the White Horse Tavern . . . and we all gathered around like vultures, including those who really didn't care for him at all . . . He was an extraordinary talker . . . the best talker I think I ever knew. One spent endless hours with Dylan just to hear him talk and get a new audience and tell an outrageous story that he concocted right out of the air. The whole bar listened while his great voice rumbled on and on with fresh-minted images pulled right out of the back of his hat.

There were, Burton emphasised, two Dylans: the one who did not talk nor did he drink but laboured at his poetry. The other of the White Horse Tavern.

Thomas's early death shook Burton badly. He was in some way involved. Dylan Thomas had rung him up drunk asking for £200 "for the education of my children": Burton did not have the money. Thomas said that there was a new play he had written which Burton could have (*Under Milk Wood*)—but Burton simply did not have the money. Thomas then went to America and was soon dead.

It is inconceivable that Burton would have refused the loan had he had the cash. He adored Dylan Thomas. He longed to be the writer, the talker, the *figure* that Thomas was and he saw the poet as the best of talented, anarchic, outlaw—Wales. The small amount of money left him by the ninety-two per cent taxman after his first year in Hollywood had gone on the house, the presents, on a car, on booze . . . It seems to me significant that after this, Burton always has money about him: that he was forever pressing it on friends: that up until the end of his life he would ask those he knew well or had known well and loved in some way, "You OK for cash?" It became a compulsion. Even on the *Wagner* film, when John Gielgud was in his late seventies and wealthy from stage, television, films, books, he still asked him, "OK for cash, John?"—and in all seriousness.

It could seem that Dylan Thomas had died on November 9th, 1953, for want of £200: aged thirty-nine.

Douglas Cleverdon, the BBC producer who had coaxed and nursed Dylan Thomas through years of writing and rewriting of "the play" which he had offered Burton—*Under Milk Wood*—put together the first performance. Everyone did it free. All the royalties and fees were to go to Dylan's widow Caitlin and the children. Richard played the part that Dylan himself would have played: Sybil was in it, as was Philip.

> To begin at the beginning:
> It is spring, moonless night in the small town,
> starless and bible-black, the cobblestones silent

The voice is an elegy for his own past, for his dream of Wales and for his true hero, a poet, dead of drink, lacking £200 "for the education of my children."

And it was about this time that the family came back to him or he to claim them. He went down to Wales, for rugby—of course —and to see the brothers, the sisters, nieces, nephews, his father Dic—took him out in the Jag: "What you think of the car, our Daddy?" "It isn't a car, mon, it's a bloody bo-at." Cis came to see him at the Old Vic and cried proudly throughout the performance.

Ifor was nineteen years older than Richard, the same build (he could wear Richard's suits), bald, physically tough, devoted and entirely loyal to Gwen, his wife, a man who could turn his hand to any skilled job—carpentry, plumbing, building, electricity, a great reader of poetry, once a powerful rugby player and coalminer, a big drinker—the embodiment of the best of Richard's childhood but also a relentless reminder of it. Soon it was more or less official: he was going to look after Richard for the duration.

There is no doubt that Richard loved his brother Ifor and admired, even adored him. As with Sybil, it is impossible to find anyone with any slightest criticism of Ifor, not a blemish, not a spot. Richard saw him as a rock. So did others. Perhaps though it was Ifor who leaned on Richard, he who, up from the bleak small town of Port Talbot, saw Richard as the power whose charge would light up *his* life. Richard was glad to pay and provide for him and no doubt Ifor earned what he got one hundred times over. Nevertheless the past had clutched him to itself. From then on—happily, freely, but unremittingly—Richard Burton was to repay debts real and imaginary beyond any reasonable, any generous expectation. As if driven to it: driven to obliterate the past he had known and make it what he had longed for it to be: unable, unwilling to part from it, driven to rewrite it and reward it.

Any chance of breaking the dominating emotional circuit of his childhood was gone. He had escaped the prison but taken the walls with him. He had left Wales, but Wales had tracked him down and found him out: and he embraced it. Ifor was family. Ifor was also guilt. His marital steadiness highlighted and reproached Richard's infinite capacity to fall in love. More importantly, Rich was to become utterly responsible for Ifor. Richard was to fear that he had taken Ifor from Wales, from a safe and stable place and put him at risk. The consequences of this were to be tragic.

Sybil and he were now thinking of adopting children. Ifor and Gwen too were childless. Syb is shadowy in these years. Her total post-marital silence has not been compensated for by the chatter or the revelations of her friends. She saw a lot of Stanley Baker's wife; she was friendly with Rachel Roberts; she had her own circle and was always made welcome by Richard's current cast. "I don't know how she coped with him," one or two said, but none of them thought her misguided to want to. "Mustn't hurt Syb," he'd say again and again. "He'll never leave Syb," they'd say. "It was lovely to see them together," said Emlyn Williams. "Made you smile."

After the Old Vic season, Burton still had three movies to make in his seven-movie contract with Korda and the first of these was *The Prince Of Players* about the actor Edwin Booth, brother of John Wilkes Booth who shot President Lincoln. Once again Korda sent him back to Hollywood.

This part at last seemed made for Burton. Philip Dunne, the director and producer, had seen him in *The Lady's Not For Burning* and loved him then. *The Robe* was a hit and even though there were murmurings of worry about Burton's impact on the screen, he was still regarded—and by some star-calloused movie men—as one of the few really great actors. They saw it in the studio. They saw it on the set. The cameramen told them how good he looked and when they squinted down the lens—there was that fine head, the blue-green eyes wide apart, the strong nose and the arrogant mouth, the poor skin well disguised by make-up. The flow of ladies to and from the Burton dressing room—so gossip had it—was like river traffic around New Orleans at Mardi Gras and that mattered too: he had It. The problem was to put It up on the screen and surely all those old hands in Hollywood so praised by Orson Welles and so well used by the Hustons and Wilders and Hitchcocks—surely they could do the magic.

Philip Burton read the script of *Prince Of Players* "until three a.m. It is . . . a disgrace." His opinion of the film was the same. It has been described as "the first flop in Cinemascope."

It could have been so good and so right for Burton. Even now the extracts from Shakespeare hold the attention. And there are moments all along when Burton is exactly right. Yet it never surmounted a terrible script and indifferent direction. Again and again Burton was to be landed in this dilemma. There will always be those who say that it was always his own fault, that he should have been a better picker, that you make your own luck. Up to a point. But here he was playing an historically fascinating actor; he was acting Shakespeare; he was being directed by someone thought to be good—but the script, the story development, simply did not hold and because Burton was in the middle of it, he took the splat.

As he went off for his next role, though, he had hopes that he was leaving behind a fine film.

Now Fox loaned him to United Artists to work with the Oscar-winning director—(for *All The King's Men*)—Robert Rossen. Rossen wanted to take on that recurring Hollywood heavyweight, the Epic. This time not the Bible but the Greeks. A story "So Mighty it Staggers the Imagination"—Alexander the Great.

The Hollywood of *Prince Of Players* had been movie town revisited. Sybil had come out and they had taken a modest house; the Bogarts had been welcoming and new tales of the Old Vic provided a good Chapter Two to the previous Tales from Stratford-upon-Avon. International success has its own tom-toms and real fame is unmistakable. Acclaim is the true Esperanto. Burton came into town as a big catch. Edwin Booth was the perfect combination of America, Acting, Shakespeare and History. Perhaps the pro-Sybil lobby grew, although once the Don Juan was seen to be someone who could hold down a marriage as well, then somehow, given the time, the place, the opportunities . . . that was acceptable. And it *did* provide fruity gossip. Never dull, the man Burton. Just as he was a drinker who could hold down his drink . . . a talker who could hold his audience . . . a sportsman—tennis, table tennis, cricket—who could deliver . . . and anyway all those young men who had lost years in the war were spending a little longer back on the prairies of bachelor hunting grounds . . .

But *Alexander The Great* was to be shot in Spain between February and July 1955. It was Mega and it was going to trail-blaze. Burton, of course, was to be the heroic Alexander. Rossen—who was to go on to direct one of Burton's all-time favourite films, *The Hustler* (from which he quoted huge chunks as he played billiards)—was deeply impressed by Burton's intelligence and especially by the range of his reading. It is difficult to keep in mind that throughout the helter-skelter life and the deep plunges into concentration for months on end for the big Shakespearian roles, and despite the drink, the affairs, the raids into radio to pick up the odd £20—Burton was reading three or four books a week. He researched Alexander thoroughly and loved to discuss the man and the period with Rossen. Together they would finally crack the Epic.

Burton here for the first of many many times shares his good fortune with his pals. Everybody was to come out to play in the Spanish sun. Sybil joined him immediately. Ifor, Gwen and Valerie Douglas, his new personal assistant, followed. There were to be later films in which, when you bought Burton, you bought his entire court. Now, though, it was "the lads." A word in Rossen's ear about some of the actors back home and—lo!—we discover Michael Hordern, William Squire and Stanley Baker turning up. A high old time was clearly in the offing. There has been speculation that Burton put fun before everything else and there is no question that it is a legitimate charge. Fredric March was Philip, Alexander's father, and Claire Bloom arrived in Spain to play Barsinoe, one of his three wives—"really his mistress," she said helpfully in a press interview. Sybil went back to London soon afterwards.

Burton was fitted out with a blond cowpat wig which was a mistake. Despite Rossen's much-claimed years of research, the entire cast looked as if they had been dressed by someone whose enquiries into period had been to fast-run a Cecil B. de Mille film. Everything—the set, the costumes, the action—seemed laundered out of life. There was lots of riding across maps with ancient names thereon, lots of golden oldies: "Greetings, Aristotle!" and mind-stoppering questions: "What thoughts drive through your storm-tossed brain?'' Burton, blandly blond and in a lady's tennis tunic fashionable at Wimbledon in the Thirties, looked on helplessly as an unstoppable rush of clichés fled from his lips.

The attempt to tell the *whole* of Alexander's story was mistaken; the dramatic tension was imperceptible; the big set pieces looked set in plastic; and Burton—made to make more speeches than a presidential candidate—was to get the blame.

But Spain was left on a high. As in *Prince Of Players*, he thought he was leaving good work behind him. Back to Hollywood for another Fox movie, *The Rains Of Ranchipur*. Burton was to play a Hindu doctor. He was very bad. The film was very bad. ''It never rains but it Ranchipurs,'' quipped a desperately upbeat Burton as he fled back to London and the Old Vic where he could earn in about fifteen years what *Alexander* and *Ranchipur* each had made for him in as many weeks.

An interesting point about *Ranchipur* is that, as with Sir Toby Belch, Burton could not be bothered to attempt to do a character part. Or he had not the talent. His method was to imagine that the character was himself and that he, Burton, could do those things: could conquer an empire, recite Shakespeare in a brothel, be the Prince of Denmark or Caliban the savage animal man on the magic isle of Prospero: yes to all of those—no to a part which, like a wig, diminished him.

He was scathing about most of his films, saw very few of them and felt, with some justification, that he was persistently hammered for taking chances which did not come off. It could be argued that his instincts were bold: he was not skulking behind a proven marketable talent. He was aiming high—the big Epic, the Difficult Film (*Prince Of Players*—''special material,'' Zanuck called it, insuring himself cannily), and he often went into these cinematic battles with directors and producers of reputation and ambition. Words, though, kept failing him and without the words Burton was just about done: he could deliver action—but it had to be hard, fast, man-bang action, not slow drums and trumpets to set it all up. ''None of my films has done me any good,'' he said at one stage and he rubbished his movies with a kind of doleful exuberance, like a boy from the back row of Taibach Cach complaining all the way home: ''Bloody love!''

While he had been away, his friend Robert Hardy had enjoyed great success as Prince Hal. Burton was down to play Henry V at the Old Vic. In what was a typical gesture of generosity, probably unique to him, he wrote to his pal saying that *he*, Hardy, should take on Henry V—the plum role—instead of himself. "He thought he'd had his crack at it in Stratford a few years before and I should have mine now. Extraordinary, wasn't it? I can't think of anyone else who would dream of doing that. Then, now or ever," says Hardy. "I refused, of course."

"Family" was back in the centre of frame and pals were family. Nothing was too good for them: no sacrifice too much: the back-to-back solidarity of the depressed Valleys became the ark of the covenant he was forging with his new life.

In December 1955, Burton played Henry V at the Old Vic and theatrical London went mad. *The Times* began its review by pointing out the defects in Burton's Henry V at Stratford and went on:

> Mr. Burton's progress as an actor is such that already he is able to make good all the lacks of a few short years ago . . . what was gratingly metallic has been transformed into a steely strength which becomes the martial ring and hard brilliance of the patriotic verse. There now appears a romantic sense of a high kingly mission and the clear cognisance of the capacity to fulfil it . . . the whole performance—a most satisfyingly romantic one—is firmly under the control of the imagination.

Tynan, fast becoming the arbiter of theatrical reputation, said that Burton was "now the natural successor to Olivier." He went further. In time, he said, he would be regarded as the greatest living classical actor. "He is pure anti-romantic, ingrowing rather than outgoing. Within this actor there is always something reserved, a rooted solitude which his Welsh blood tinges with mystery. Inside those limits he is master." And he added, importantly, "Beyond them he has much to learn." In January 1956 he was given the *Evening Standard* Drama Award for his Henry V—the best performance of the year.

He needed those reviews. *Ranchipur* and *Alexander* belly-flopped: Burton was not movie box-office. Back in Hollywood the bad word was out.

His next venture at the Old Vic in February 1956 was to alternate the parts of Iago and Othello with John Neville. This had been attempted before—by Irving and Booth, for example—but not on successive nights. It was an unnecessary and even a ridiculous challenge. But, by then, Neville and Burton were fast friends, known as the Welsh Wizard and the Willesden Wonder—Neville was brought up in an unfashionable northern suburb of London, Willesden, best or rather only known for the number of its railway lines and the fame of its Junction. As Othello, Burton was soundly reviewed but also criticised again—as with Hamlet—for being less than poetical with the verse. As Iago, he was fully praised.

It was while he was doing Othello that Frank Hauser went to see him on a curious mission. Hauser—who had produced Burton's radio version of *Henry V*—was attempting to revive the Oxford Playhouse Theatre and needed money. Burton had promised £2,000: he had a respect for and devotion to Oxford—and also, to help was somehow to put it in his debt rather than the other way around. It was to pay it back—in both senses. It was gratitude and sweet revenge—both. £2,000 in 1955 is approximately £25,000 to £30,000 today, probably more: in any circumstances it was a princely and grand gift, given the hammering that Burton was taking from the taxman—£6,000 left out of £82,000 earned—a third of all he had earned from a year's filming. It was a lordly gesture. But Professor Nevill Coghill, another old friend, was involved and Hauser *did* come from Wales.

Hauser went to the Old Vic to collect the money. Burton persuaded Hauser to stay and see his Othello and meet him afterwards. Hauser is and always has been a man of cutting judgment, slow to convince, an untainted intellectual whose interest lies in drama. He will have nothing to do, for instance, with the sloppy notion that "Burton was a failed genius. There is no such thing as a failed genius. Either you are or you aren't."

As a director, he had always been rather worried about Richard. "Directors don't really want to buy the performance when they sign the contract." Not a believer in luck, he noted that Burton had worked with several weak directors (there were strong ones too: he omitted those) "because he did not want to be pushed around."

Hauser began to watch *Othello* rather grumpily. He was supposed to be at a party following a friend's wedding and he had heard that while Burton was remarkable as Iago, his Othello was merely commendable. "But he was marvellous in that performance. Very free: passionate. You look for *moments* with the very greatest actors. What they actually *do* at a specific moment. Here, when Othello murders Desdemona and realises that he has made a terrible mistake—he suddenly leapt on to the bed and held her—like an animal—'nobody's going to take her away from me'—very moving, memorable.''

In the dressing room Burton handed over the £2,000 (and never mentioned it again: the information on this all comes from Hauser) and then asked Hauser to have dinner with Valerie Douglas—his personal assistant, whom he had brought from Hollywood. There was an offer on the table. The offer to Hauser was to come in and direct Richard's next production. It was just and whisperingly hinted that if he *did* become Richard's director and did *not* pursue the Oxford Playhouse idea then the money might be returned. ''Perfect manners,'' says Hauser admiringly. ''He made the promise and kept it. Quite possibly—in those days money was much much tighter— he found that he simply could not afford it. But he insisted on keeping his word. Too good-mannered even to be party to that very delicate salvage operation.'' Hauser refused the directing offer, took the money and for a time made a huge success of the Playhouse, where he was Director until 1973. ''You know,'' said Burton, years later, ''in Hollywood at the time I was being told to put $500 here and $2,000 there: all those smart brokers and accountants were telling me how to invest and make millions. Everything I touched went bust—except the Oxford Playhouse.''

After that season together at the Old Vic, John Neville's career took an entirely different course from that of Burton. A director of several theatres—in the English Midlands, in Nova Scotia, he now lives in Canada. Often, to his fury, compared favourably with Burton. He looks the same thoughtful, handsome, classical, matinée idol he had been in the mid-Fifties when he and Burton at the Old Vic and Johnnie Ray at the London Palladium had, between them, wrapped up the ''bobby-soxers.''

These are Neville's impressions of Burton at that time, 1955–6: ''He was always a little reserved unless you knew him very well. But there was that glow of success about him. He first heard me when I was Fortinbras in his *Hamlet*. I'll always remember the look he gave me on stage when he turned around and saw me. When I asked him about it, later, he said he'd thought, 'Here's someone to reckon with.' We were both from working-class homes and that was unquestionably a bond. Whatever happened to Richard for the rest of his life was strongly rooted in that background. He said, 'I'll work till I get every one of them'—his family—'out of it.' It was an extraordinary thing *at that time*, you know, to be Welsh or a Cockney and unashamed of it. We took to each other—and with Richard that was that. He was serious about friendship.

"I met all the family. When my three children were very young, Cis looked after them—at Richard's suggestion!—so that my wife could come with us all on a trip to New York. They came back speaking in a strong Welsh accent with Cis crying on the doorstep because she didn't want to let them go! What people!

"He had a wonderful mind—in another league from that of any other actor around. He would do the performance—Othello, Iago —we would go out around the pubs and then the drinking clubs— always beer then—and punctually in next morning for rehearsal, me hungover, Richard telling me about *A History of Mathematics* which he'd dug into when he finally reached home. His stamina and his energy . . .

"He was a *wonderful* actor. Sometimes it was amazing. He would just walk on to the stage and there would be a 'presence,' an aura. It was a great deal to do with sexual attraction: I put that very high on the list of attributes for greatness in acting.

"He was lazy, though: didn't have to work at it, bored, talked a little—very shyly—about being a writer.

"He was such *fun*. A lot of young people were introduced to the classical theatre by him. You couldn't resist him. We went out and did the pubs. Sybil would phone Caroline, my wife: 'Is Richard with you?' Caroline: 'I thought John was with *you*.' We played a double game.

"And there was this generosity. We were up in Hampstead at his home one night and he was fretting and nagging me about my car. He had a Jaguar. I had an old oblong Austin 16 the wife's cousin had given me.

'You ought to have a proper car,' Richard said.

'I'm very happy with the car I've got.'

'That's not a car—what car would you like if you lost this one?'

'A convertible Morris Minor.'

'How much is that?'

'£680,' said Neville. A *fortune*. You could still buy a good small terraced house in a decent district of London for that.

'Come on then,' said Burton.

"We went into his bedroom and from under the bed he hauled a suitcase stuffed with notes. It was like being in a gangster movie. He counted out £680.

'Had a good day today,' he said.

'I'll pay you back.'

'Don't worry. Don't worry.' ''

Neville did pay him back. Scores did not and now never will. He never brought it up. ''Richard said: 'You're the only man in the world who's ever paid me back!' '' Later there was to be another —again, oddly, a working-class pal—Stanley Baker, with his background tougher even than that of Burton or Neville. He paid Burton back *with interest*!

''Richard did what he wanted to do,'' says Neville. ''All that talk about 'letting his talent down' is neither here nor there. He chose the path he wanted and he stuck to it, however much they sniped and tried to put him down: he had the blinkers on and he went his own way. Acting wasn't the most important thing to him. Living was: and he hoped one day to be a writer or a scholar. But he was a *STAR*. And the Old Vic proved it beyond all question. It was unmistakable. He just had to walk on to the stage. Nobody can take that away.''

10
The Retreat

After the Old Vic season he began to plan to move out of London and set up in Switzerland. The main reason for that was money: the better to accumulate it.

In his Hollywood year he had earned about £82,000, out of which the British taxman let him keep £6,000. This was a Conservative Government. The Labour Government had similarly taxed wealthy individuals. There seemed no prospect of change.

Given that one of the objects of making films was making money this was not altogether satisfactory. He now had Ifor and Gwen on his payroll; Sybil did not work; there was the determination to help the many brothers and sisters back in Wales; children were hoped for and impulsive acts of generosity—largesse indeed—were not conducive to steady saving. Some of his older contemporaries kept more of what they earned by living abroad—in Hollywood, a large English community there—or in Europe. Others had very smart accountants or found ways to institutionalise the wealth—British taxmen were much softer on institutions and companies than on individuals. Burton's problem was that he had the prospect of what, for him, was riches. The reality was a handsome but comparatively small sum left at the end of that particular rainbow.

Film-making was precarious. And he did not need to be told that he was a long way from being "God's gift" to the screen. He ridiculed the films in which he appeared but he did not want the source to dry up. Anyway it is a mistake to take his interview-word about films—or indeed about anything much. He spoke the truth to his very closest friends, to one or two in his family and later to his Notebooks. These can be relied on. The rest was as the mood took him—flannel, fibs, mischief, jokes, outrageous statements, anything to have fun. Of course he wanted to be a great film actor. The jokes about film-making were an insurance against failure: a common enough tactic. Denigrating the film industry served the same purpose: again, common enough in whatever sphere. He hated to fail and in films he was failing.

Being enough of an actor to know the essential value of an unfractured ego, he had no option: the industry had to be to blame. Not him. Laurence Olivier had gone over exactly the same course —but for longer—in the Twenties and Thirties. What had changed Olivier had been his great good fortune in running into the brickwall talent of William Wyler who broke him, as a screen actor, in *Wuthering Heights* for which at first Olivier never forgave him and then never ceased to be grateful. Wyler forced Olivier to respect the camera and the medium. No Wyler had yet surfaced for Burton and he was being thrown to the critics in those static stupefied epics, raw meat for jackals. Burton's problem was different from Olivier's because for some reason, on the set (unlike Olivier pre-Wyler) he *seemed* fine: and he *looked* fine—a natural: it was the *inward*, personal Burton, the thing he was, that Welsh reserve which held out distrustfully against the camera like a man of iron will-power against a hypnotist. He would not go under. He would always be himself. He had to find a script which would allow him—as Shakespeare allowed him, as Christopher Fry and Lillian Hellman had allowed him—to be himself and be the part at one and the same time. Then he would make it work.

Meanwhile he would be aware that the bloom might be going off the new rose. Hollywood was in some ways a careful, even a fair place and it knew that here was an extraordinary actor. No one from studio head to extra said any different. There was a problem, though: how did you get that talent on to the screen . . .

Stage acting was precarious enough: film acting must now have begun to seem even more of a gamble. If he was to get together the "necessary" to deliver the security he wanted for Sybil and himself and the release he wanted for others, he might only have a short time. Reputations struck and then the hour passed and they were gone. It was not a steady or pensionable job—something which many of those who criticised him for being "unpatriotic" in leaving England undoubtedly enjoyed. Nor was he in the public school network—so comically well documented by Evelyn Waugh in *Decline and Fall*—which would guarantee him against all manner of misfortune. He came "from nowhere"; he was always an outsider; he had thrown in his lot with players, vagabonds, charmers; he had to look out for himself. And he was emerging as a clan chief, a Welsh mafia Godfather: he had to look after others.

The decision made itself.

True he had a house (still half let off and bought pre-Hollywood) in Hampstead, a Jag at the door and the occasional suitcases of fivers under the bed. True he would impetuously act like the Aga Khan and never express a regret. But the wealth was not there: a touch humiliating, in a funny way. After *The Robe* and *Alexander*, "So Mighty it Staggers the Imagination," and tales of Garbo and Bogie: all that life-spending belt of energy. All that burn of himself. What had he made from it all? Half a house. He had some of the trappings of budding international success without the wealth which ought to have underpinned it.

One consequence was the beginnings of a financial entourage of the kind that could be very costly. He had an expensive New York lawyer, Aaron Frosch; the assistant-cum-business manager, Valerie Douglas, who would arrange the Swiss move. His English agent, Vere Barker. A soon-to-be-hired Swiss agent, Maurice Solowitz . . .

He could of course have cast them all aside, settled for what he had, smoked his pipe and read his paperbacks. Which is to say he could have been someone else but Richard Burton.

His strategy was to bust through; to make another conquest; to tackle the problem head on and overcome it. To get to Switzerland for a few years, get his hands on money (in Switzerland at that time, the £82,000 would have yielded him about £80,000, or thirteen times more than he got in England), set up the family and return to London "independent," "secure," "invulnerable"—the dreams of all men and women who have been brought up with no expectation of any of these. Money was the key. He had seen that in Taibach. He had seen that in the relaxed ease of his better-off London acquaintances. Hollywood, USA, unashamedly told him that. The death of Dylan Thomas put the seal on it. He was on his way.

There was another reason. Since leaving the RAF in 1948, he

had hurtled through a space created by himself like a comet. Everything had been sensation. He had decided to put himself to the task
of acting and poured all his awe-inspiring energy into being an actor:
this included being a rake, a hell-raiser, a princely friend, a stroppy
enemy, a world-championship boozer, a man who explored and
tested his manliness to the limit. There had been little time for
reflection. Reading appears to have been as gobbled raw as everything else. There was no time for dreaming. Another day, another
contract. There was no time for being alone: his world moved in
self-protective clusters. He needed silence and calm.

He planned and hoped that Switzerland would give him that also.
Ifor would come along of course, and Gwen . . . there would be
walking and talk, logs on the fire, late-night lazy reading, new books
coming with the weekend post, nobody to nab you for a quick radio
or a useless meeting. And indeed he *did* have those times; continued
to have them for the rest of his life. They were some of his most
relished moments. The move to Switzerland indicated the two broad
divisions of his character and stamped them in geography. When
he was in the world he was a hunter in the jungle and little was
spared although he rarely seems to have broken his code of honour.
When he was out of "the world" he was available to the spells of
poets and scholars and dreamed of joining them if only through
reading them with the care they demanded.

It was a move made for the future. There was not a great deal of
money salted away in that suitcase under the bed. He had to make
more movies to justify the move. It would be humiliating if he went
through all the "Farewell England" and "We hate unpatriotic tax-
dodgers" hypocrisy and discomfort with nothing to show for it! He
left (in 1957) to bad publicity.

Roberto Rossellini requested him for a film, *Sea Wife*, to be shot
in Jamaica. Rossellini was a very good name, good director, good
money, good location, goodbye London or rather au revoir.

Rossellini was "off the film" before a shot was taken.

Joan Collins was the nun and his co-star in what turned out to be
a dreadful shipwreck story. Philip Burton saw it and recorded that
he was "ashamed" of it. It is a stinker. But in the hands of Rossellini . . . ?

Joan Collins later wrote that Burton had made a pass at her which
she had rejected. She reported that Burton (a) talked to her at length
about the fact that women "always succumbed" and (b) was in-

stantly coupling with every woman on the island. "I believe you would screw a snake," quoth Joan. "Only if it was wearing a skirt," riposted Richard, gallantly keeping up the standard of the repartee. This is supposed to rebound *against* Burton: I think he managed to turn a lousy line into a passable quip.

I am sure that Burton was as puzzled as everyone else at times by his remorseless sexual appetite and just as puzzled at the fact that so often it could be satisfied. As a man from the puritanical wastes of chapel-bound Wales, he must have been shocked at his own behaviour. But that did not slow him down.

He can too easily seem merely macho, boorish, boozy and short on sensitivity. Yet there is confusing evidence. All the more reason to trust the friends who then and now smile as they remember the sexual escapades and others—trying to take a horse upstairs in a restaurant, drenching his armour with the contents of his bladder after a particularly beer-driven performance of *Henry V*, taking on bets (for a pint!) about what would turn out to be a pivotal and punishing affair—because they automatically link them with the man who gave them and others so much joy. And of his talent, as he moved to Céligny, on the wrong side of Geneva, there was no question.

He called the new house Le Pays de Galles (Wales).

> In January 1957 [Philip Burton wrote], I received the first letter from Richard written in his new Swiss home, and I was deeply disturbed by it. My instinctive reaction had been against the move because it would take Richard away from the world in which he was at his best and happiest, the London theatre. For Valerie Douglas Richard's world was Hollywood which existed to make big money which should be protected by all possible means. I described the letter in my diary as "world weary." I think it sprung from perhaps a subconscious realisation of the significance of the move he had made.

Richard cut himself off from a great deal. The theatre, the pubs, the rugby, the handy company, the radio work, the latest stories. He also cut himself off from a renaissance in English theatre and cinema which could have been of considerable material benefit. The drive of the Royal Court writers and the new British film industry was precisely for the sort of committed realism with a romantic flair, the anti-hero Outsider hero who Burton *was*. He became the Prince across the water.

He also cut himself off from easy metropolitan liaisons. Perhaps that was part of the intention, to devote all or at any rate much more of his time to Sybil. Céligny was a small unfashionable quiet village. Their unpretentious and rather cramped house was about a hundred yards from a railway line and half a mile from Lake Geneva. The house was to be modestly enlarged. Ifor was to build a guest chalet in the garden. The upper part of a barn was to be turned into a library. It was not a Beverly Hills "swank house," nor ever would be, nor was meant to be. The only place to score was across at the Café de la Gare and both he and Sybil were soon close friends with the owners. It was far too close to home. He had little alternative but to be a domestic animal.

And then early in 1957, Sybil became pregnant: they had waited a long time. Both of them were "tremendously happy."

Brook Williams began to visit them quite early on. If Emlyn saw his young self in Richard, Brook saw something of a father, elder brother, hero and later close friend whom he could serve in Richard who used to go to the Williamses' cottage at the end of the Forties. Brook has lived at Céligny with Sybil, with Suzy Hunt (Elizabeth Taylor came but never lived there—stayed in her own place up in the mountains in Gstaad—now *that* was a swank Swiss village, fashionable, unquiet, and full of château-chalets) and now with Sally. He became a central part of that larger Burton "family" which used to move into a film rather like a platoon of roving mercenaries—hairdresser, dresser, actor pals, stuntmen . . . When Brook was a boy, Richard seemed in some way to look out for him: Brook repaid this by looking out for Richard over many years.

When Brook was about ten, Richard took him in hand. "He taught me to shave. I used to watch him shaving and so he would foam up my face, give me a razor without a blade in it, and then we would stand side by side in front of the mirror, him showing me how to do a clean sweep, stretch up the chin, play face golf, chat 'man to man,' and me imitating him."

There were tips galore. "He would say, 'Do you know how to immobilise a man, Brookie? Pull his jacket over his arms and then—bop! Good tip that.' " Or at tennis. "He taught me how to do the 'cannonball serve'—'That's all you need to learn about tennis, Brookie. They never get it back.' " He would go to Brook's school to see him in school plays. "He took an ordinary flask—the sort you use for tea—but his would have a stiff pint of martini in it. He'd pour it out into a plastic cup and blow on it!''

Emlyn was away a great deal: Burton knew what it was to have an absent father and knew also through Ifor the value of a much older brother. Brook was the beneficiary and never lost that status.

We re-created some of Richard's routines. Out in the red MG—still working well—on a fine Sunday morning; drive the twenty minutes into Geneva Airport, having phoned the newspaper booth beforehand to make sure the Sundays were there. Perhaps a *petit blanc* in the bar, scanning the sports pages, the book pages, the reviews, marking down the longer pieces for later. A first stab at the crossword puzzle. Past the bookshop and a quick purchase or two—"You read this one, Brookie? Bloody good. I'll get it for you. And I'll have those two here"—back into the car and perhaps loop back through a favourite village for another *petit blanc* or maybe a vodka in the bar with the locals and return for lunch as likely as not over at the Café de la Gare and the local fish dish with the local wine. Boules in the afternoon, a game of tennis or table tennis in which no quarter was given, and then reading into the night, a glass or maybe two . . .

As Burton's time in Céligny grew longer—at first it had been thought of as a snatch-and-grab raid—he welcomed increasingly and most of all ''stories'' about the actors he knew and enjoyed. Best of all if they were funny. "He loved them and loved to tell them over and over again. All Gielgud's gaffes—best of all those that put Richard down: 'When you get better . . . I mean, ready.' '' Brook Williams has become the Keeper of the Stories.

"Anything to do with Hugh Griffith.'' Griffith was a mighty Welsh actor of the period in the same sulphurous and thundersome style as Donald Wolfit, face like an Easter Island statue whose mother had mated with a gargoyle, body big as a mattress, Welsh to the tips of his black locks. "He was the Archbishop at Stratford in *Henry V*. That long boring speech at the beginning. Richard did this wonderful vault for 'Once more unto the breach'—the lights blinked, he hit a hidden springboard and—bang!—he was on the horse. Magic! All very precise; quite tricky. This time Hugh shuffled back on disguised as a soldier and moved the horse! Richard—brilliantly—still managed to hook one leg over it, but he was upside down, in agony, marriage prospects severely bruised: and winded. 'Once more unto the—ouch!—breach.' Griffith's cackle in the wings could be heard all over Stratford. Of course Richard got him back—I don't remember how." Or Griffith, fed up with what he thought of as "amateur" work in an American production, stalking off, announcing he would go home to "Welsh Wales." "Richard told everybody not to worry, Hugh would be back: he had no idea what Hugh *would* do. At the end of the afternoon a drunken bearded figure could be spotted jinking down the centre aisle. Then it stopped. 'I have come back because I am not Jesus Christ and I cannot walk across the Atlantic Ocean'—each syllable banged out on the Welsh anvil. When Griffith was nominated for a Tony Award for *Look Homeward Angel* he was asked if he was a Method actor. 'No, no. But I *am* a Methodist.' "

Burton's speciality, it seems, was as much in the telling as in the tale itself. Like many actors, he was a wicked mimic and collected mannerisms and tricks of speech like train numbers. His stories were embellished by baroque adjectival flights, apparently unnecessary but plot-binding digressions and the tremendous vision of someone who loved whatever was anarchic, outsize, careless, destructive, mad.

He adored Robert Newton, the star of *Oliver Twist*—as Bill Sikes—and the ultimate villain, Long John Silver, in *Treasure Island*. Newton took to drink furiously. It was a time when drink proved not only machismo but independence and a contempt for the opinion of the world—two of the qualities most longed for by actors in their perpetual bondage to the four thongs of the telephone, the contract, the reviews, the applause. Drink was a sovereign unto its own. At that court Newton for a time was King.

"He and Richard used to go to the studios together at one time," Brook recalled. "He would give Richard a lift in this ancient Bentley. This morning Richard turned up at 5.30 a.m. and Newton appeared, flask in hand, unslept, unshaven, ready to drive them out of London to Pinewood. The Bentley wouldn't start. Covered in frost. Winter. Newton hands Richard the large flask—brandy—goes back into the house, comes out with a horse-whip and lays about the bonnet! Gets back in the car: it starts. Richard starts to laugh —Newton glares at him and they drink and drive to Pinewood where Newton suddenly insists he will *not* go through the studio gate. He would go through the window of the security box. Finally they all heave him through—by this time he is late. His dresser, in a flurry and fussing about and very camp, hurries him along, puts on the frock coat, puts on the cravat and then Newton hears the bell and starts for the stage—makes for the set. The dresser rushing along beside him desperately trying to tell him that he is not wearing any trousers nor any underpants. Finally the poor man says 'Mr. Newton, sir'—they are on the set by now—technicians, directors, actors everywhere—'Oh Mr. Newton, you can't go on like that, sir' 'And why not?' The Long John eye opens its widest. 'Because, sir'—the dresser terrified—'there's something missing, sir.' 'Missing? *Missing*?' Newton bellows, looks down at his front shirt tail and then turns to his dresser and nods. 'Thank you,' he says, 'for pointing it out. Very grateful.' And he lifts up his shirt and yells, 'Make-up!' ''

"Newton hated it all by then, you see," Brook said. "Anything to break the boredom."

Anybody rare or strange or who didn't give a damn. Victor Mature became a pal while they were in *The Robe*. Mature taught Burton to play craps, Burton out-manoeuvred Mature when he was going for a poignant close-up and they scrapped cheerfully. He loved Mature's stories against himself: as when Mature attempted to join an exclusive golf club and was turned down on the grounds that actors were not acceptable. "I am not an actor," Mature wrote by return, "and I have sixty films to prove it." Or Ernest Thesiger in Moscow on an Old Vic tour, with Scofield as Hamlet and Mary Ure as Ophelia, hanging back on an excursion to the Kremlin to chalk on the walls "BURGESS LOVES MACLEAN." Or the writer with the unlikely name, Count Robert Farquharson, of the Holy Roman Empire; or Jack Dillon the producer and the poet Louis MacNeice in the George around the corner from BBC Broadcasting House or Esmond Knight, whose glass eye kept falling out in *The Lady's Not For Burning*—"Well, pick it up, dear boy, pick it up!" Or the Hamlet who jumped in the grave alas dug too deep and heaved himself up to say "It is I"—and fell down: back up—"Hamlet"—fell again—"the Dane." Utterly disappeared for several minutes.

Stories about favourite friends were non-stop and to be redelivered and refined at any opportunity. Gielgud, of course, was the fa-vourite's favourite. On the disastrous first night of *Othello* with Ian Bannen (scenery fell down: an actor cut his hand) the play, already running over four and a half hours, had still some scenes to go.

Bannen attempted to cut. "Rodrigo's dead, my lord," he announced. (Rodrigo had two scenes to play.) Gielgud withered him. "*Dead*, sayst thou?" Bannen/Iago: "Well, not dead. Just not very well, my lord."

Gielgud's steely and intelligent stage presence intimidated many. Towards the end of one play, on came a messenger with vital news and dried completely. Gielgud glared. The poor man forgot the century, his mother, his name, everything. Gielgud: "Hast thou naught to say?" Long pause. Messenger: "Naught, my lord."

Another favourite was Michael Redgrave, whose occasional absent-mindedness was a source of joy. At the end of one play he is left with a retainer on stage; he is about to commit suicide. Redgrave had worked up the audience and himself to a high tension. He moved hypnotically towards the final line which he spoke haltingly but clearly: the line was supposed to be "Bring me a pint of port and a pistol." The retainer would go off: the curtain would fall slowly. In his climactic euphoria, Redgrave declared, "Bring me a pint of piss and a portal." The retainer, a young actor, desperately tried a salvage job. "A pint of *piss*, my lord?" "Aye," rounded Redgrave, furiously, "*and* a portal."

He loved to hear and to tell stories, especially with a drink to hand. He was still able to stun himself with alcohol, sleep for a few hours, get up at a coalminer's five a.m., with a hangover, and do a day's work. The back and neck problem which was to torment his last years and dominate him for more time than he would ever admit, was no more than a sudden pain, a tightening of the shoulder muscles, a lack of looseness in his swing when he served one of his "cannonballs." Drink was an anaesthetic.

You could look on Céligny in two lights and he did. One was to see it as an unwise move—cutting himself off from the work, the gossip, the mates, the chatter, the fun he so much enjoyed, taking on the part of the melodramatic villain of post-war austerity—the tax exile. (Quips to journalists about actors being entitled to be exempt from tax did not help much.) Out of it. Or you could see it as a very necessary and wise pause. In less than ten years he had turned himself from an uncommercial layabout in the RAF into the undisputed great young classical actor of his generation, a very useful West End property, a film name if not yet a Hollywood star, a brilliant radio actor and reader of poetry, a man well off by the Fifties' standards of his friends and full to bursting with experiences sexual, alcoholic, social, sporting and intellectual: a time to digest. Time to take his own Wales abroad and plant it deep. Time to read and have Ifor and Gwen about him, think of the rest of the family, start up a new offshore family of agents and lawyers, aides and actor pals of his own. At Céligny he would have time to decide, as he always had to decide and redefine, what it was he really wanted to do. This acting was all very well—sometimes it was sublime— but was that all there was to life?

Baffled by his talent and superstitious of it, he always needed time to adjust to himself, to discover whether it was really still *there*. It was time to start again. He was forever starting again.

Swiftly and deeply he dug in. When his father died ("Which one?") aged eighty-one, a few months after the move to Céligny, neither he nor Ifor went to the funeral. For such a family-story-telling man, this was a tremendous decision and his joking excuses will not do. The decision indicates clearly that the two brothers were finally antagonised by the rejection of their father. Dic the Carpenter, Little Dic. Dic the Drunk carried home by Ifor through the disapproving gaslit streets. A silent faraway figure to Richard, who protected him in stories but saw in him the wreckage of a woman's life, his mother's. It was a rare slap in the face of his past. It indicates a decline which grew into despair with the vanity of life.

But in September 1957, Kate was born. The longed-for first child. Burton had made a film with Nicholas Ray, hoping—alas mistakenly—that the director of *Rebel Without A Cause* would do something distinguished. But *Bitter Victory*—a war story—was not good. Some would see the title as a rueful comment on his over-hasty move. Burton himself would have disagreed. He had packed up his tents and left to settle as and where he wanted: Pays de Galles—Wales—abroad, like a crusader bound for the golden city.

11

On the Road
to Camelot

The birth of Kate reanimated the life of Richard and Sybil. Sybil now seemed absolutely secure. She knew what she had, what she wanted and what she would put up with. Many of her friends with more respectability, more reliability, more fidelity had less fun, less poetry, less sex, less life. She knew her man. He wanted both monogamy and an infinite access to affairs: not uncommon. What was uncommon was the range of Burton's lust and the intensity of his devotion to Sybil. Kate both represented and confirmed that.

Several "theories" have been advanced for his behaviour and top of the list of course is that old reliable "he wanted to be loved" and "the bigger the star the more they need to be loved." Perhaps. As a boy he found himself adored by older sisters and was a good catch for the girls. As a man Burton saw women as part of a great and delightful hunt. A born hunter and conqueror, the world he inherited left him no better battleground than that between the sexes. There is plenty of evidence that he would chat away about his lesser escapades, like an old campaigner. Offensive, no doubt, outside a conniving masculine society, deeply unappealing in a post-feminist world and unattractive to those men and women whose creed is to keep private matters private. But to Burton it was not always private. He was by birth, by temperament and by choice a member of that club which strives to be "manly" and sees the testing of that quality as the salt of life. Willing women, game for play, were part of that battle.

Moreover, sex was guaranteed pleasure and that was never to be resisted. He smoked, he drank, he seized the day. He also read, wrote, sifted through life.

He was a warrior; and his wars were those ancient engagements first with the other sex and finally, increasingly ferociously, with himself. But war of some kind there had to be or the life of a man had no meaning.

Yet for a short while—during the pregnancy—he seemed to have found a peace. Kate, his daughter, speaks of her father with a penetrating warmth and variety of appreciation. If a "good father" can be judged by his children then he was a good father: Kate certainly believes so. His close friends, recognising how much "family" meant to him, saw the birth of Kate in Switzerland as the finest fortune possible. Everything was now in place. Ifor was building a guest chalet in the garden; Gwen was there, company for Sybil; Kate was a bright baby; the Café de la Gare provided good wine, good fish, a short stroll: Switzerland was empty of temptations.

But *Bitter Victory* was a flop and the word was out that Burton was not box-office, not bankable. All set up to exploit his tax nest, to enrich his domestic nest with judicious raids abroad into the pirate fields of fat-loot films, he found himself becalmed. The telephone did not ring. The scripts did not hit the mat in the hall. He was all dressed up with nowhere to go.

The easiest part of an actor's life to understand is the uncertainty. It is something that most of us spend most of our lives attempting to insure against. All but a very few actors have to build uncertainty into their career thinking. It can be humiliating—if you allow it to be: there you are, a marvellous actor or actress and nobody wants you, nobody recognises your talent, nobody gives a damn. Burton was unused to idleness. At a point of maximum charge in his adult life, and optimum possibility for some sort of refreshed domestic contentment, he found himself out in the cold.

When the offer came late in 1957 to do a play in America he took it immediately. It would make good money and set him up again. It was by a playwright then widely thought of as an intellectual of the theatre, Jean Anouilh: the play was a comedy, *Time Remembered*. His co-star was Helen Hayes. The young actress in it was Susan Strasberg. He got off the ship and went straight into an affair with her which she recorded in detail in her memoirs, *Bitter Sweet*. For the first time we have a woman's side of a Burton romance.

It is an extraordinary account: generous, honest, illuminating. Susan Strasberg was the daughter of powerful parents—Lee and Paula—who lived for and through great art, particularly great performance, and who believed in great creative experiences above all else. In the case of Lee Strasberg, it produced the Actors' Studio and some very fine American actors indebted to his teaching— Brando outstandingly. In the case of Paula Strasberg it produced, most notably, the later Marilyn Monroe, who came to the font that had blessed Brando and Co. and entered into a long, demanding and complex relationship with Paula. Art was the ideal and the excuse for all excesses. It was a household which was to accept— in Paula's case welcome and in Lee's case take intense interest in —what was on the most obvious level a rampaging affair between Burton, a married and family man in his thirties, a noted lover, and their nineteen-year-old daughter, coupling wildly at a time when Nice Girls Didn't.

It was also a household capable of delivering their daughter, aged fifteen, into a starring role on Broadway where, as Anne Frank, she gave a star performance. The same household could commit the crass act of piling into their daughter's dressing room after a difficult opening night of *Time Remembered* and tell her she had been "terrible," refuse to let her even *touch* them, her mother saying "How could you do this to me?" In her moment of need, Susan saw that Paula would leave her and fly West to be on the set with Marilyn, her star pupil.

In *Time Remembered* Burton played the Prince, she the young and naive girl swept off her feet. It is tempting to say that the same thing happened offstage but there are at least two qualifications: Susan was not a virgin nor was she a stranger to "older" (i.e. over-thirty and married) men. And Burton was prepared, at all times but most especially at the beginning, to put up with obstacles which would surely have been either a deterrent or a goad to a mere copybook Casanova. For though Ms. Strasberg fell in love with him and went into beds with him when they were on the road, she left her diaphragm in New York and these beddings were unconsummated.

Burton—from her account, and this is corroborated—fell for her in an apparently guiltless and public way. There was a private apartment—but there were no hiding places. Nightclubs, well-known theatre hangouts, a Sunday lunch en famille with the Strasbergs, parties with Olivier, Ustinov, Philip Burton, Fonda. Under Helen Hayes's disapproving eye—she feared that Richard was squandering his talent and Susan was jeopardising her marriage-ability—Richard in his dressing room conducted what became the longest running bar on Broadway, Susan behaved like a bride-to-be and the play rumbled on to some good reviews (Burton was surprised; he told Philip he was depressed about the part) but no profit. The producer complained that the stars were being paid too much.

He introduced Susan to Sybil's brother David and, as instructed, she said, in Welsh, that she loved him more than anyone in the world. He gave a surprise party for her in a theatre and the cast included most of the best of Broadway. He bought her a diamond pin, which she loved and wore always; a satin lounge suit which she hated because it made her feel like a mistress; and a white mink muff and scarf which was marvellous until she found out that Sybil had been bought a white mink coat. Were they a set?

Above all he gave her words—his own, Shakespeare's, Shelley's, Dylan Thomas's—and promises. To love her forever; to be with her until she grew old; never to let her go. He appears to have been as possessive as she was jealous. Perhaps he meant it.

He certainly sounded as if he meant it, but then he was often—no, as Ms. Strasberg herself gracefully concedes—*always* full of spirits when the most lavish of these bouquets was landed at her feet. *In vino veritas?* Why not? It was the Assyrians, I think, who insisted on discussing all serious matters twice: once drunk, once sober. And split the difference? The sober Burton brought Sybil and the baby Kate over to New York, installed them in an apartment and gave a spectacular Hawaiian family party. He very rarely if at all slept the full night away from home and, when the run of the play ended, he sailed back to Switzerland en famille after a late-night drive in a horse and carriage through Central Park with Susan under a flea-infested blanket. Yet Burton had promised the girl the moon.

He can be called a shit in the manner in which one is prepared to write off someone's character for that particular transgression of the socio-moral code. He can be called greedy. He can be called a little mad, a little lunatic, a Dr. Jekyll sober, a Mr. Hyde drunk and indeed he feared that he was boring sober and, by implication, less boring drunk.

Perhaps drink was an escape. More likely it was the entry to a more agreeable and magical personality. In drink—while you are strong enough to take it—there can be the oriental experience of a continuous present. "I love you forever" means that the moment is forever and the love will always exist in that seemingly profound sense. Never mind more linear chronology. "You are the woman I have to live for" means just that, at precisely that moment: desperately. Of course it was "unfair" on Susan Strasberg but she knew about Sybil and Kate. She met Sybil. She knew Burton's vow: "I'll never leave Syb." She was heartbroken when he left, but a frank friend remarked, "Susan has often been heartbroken."

What is interesting is the intensity and sincerity which Burton put into this. He took far far more public risks than he need have done. Said far more than expected. Acted, appeared, *was* in love. It was not so much a "need to be loved" with Burton (though who has not got that to some degree?), it was a huge appetite for love, for the loving: he was in love with love itself. Later in his life, drunk? sober? he talked about how he loved all sorts of women—old, young, fat, smooth, hairy, lovely, ugly, all creeds, colours, ages and types—and he loved to make love to all of them. Perhaps the act of loving lay in some key balance with his hatred of being touched. It certainly points to the separation of his self into many selves, which could co-exist, at this stage, happily. It also underlines that his interest was more in taking risks with his life, in exploring the limits of his personality in the street, in bars, in bed than on the stage.

Inside the Strasberg account there is a telling reference to Burton's drinking. It is clear that, aged thirty-two, he is already well aware that it has a grip on him. He is also writing to Sybil that he begins to see it as a problem. When he does not drink then the glass of champagne he holds on stage shakes in a hand that could be palsied. He writes to Susan that he is afraid that he will die of drink. But he must not die—he must live to love her. But the will to drive himself, to take what he could as it passed—the temptation and usually the ruin of most of those rocketed to success from materially barren backgrounds—and the enjoyment in testing himself in this one man's way open to him, was irresistible.

In *Time Remembered* in New York, Burton the frighteningly heavy drinker, the wooer of women, the story-teller and the generous benefactor (he ran free classes on Shakespeare for the cast and their friends) finally became Burton the legend. Survivors of those days still shake their heads over the legend in sorrow and astonishment, but they always remember the huge fun. Burton was a source of energy which lit up the minds and lives of many who passed his way.

This revelation about drinking is important since it shows that he was concerned about it earlier than he admitted. If he did not drink, he might collapse in some way—that was also a dread. Fear of the blackout. Drink was a force in his life. At this stage, it does not seem to have stopped him doing anything he wanted to do—work or play. But like the increasing pain from his back and neck, the growing worry about drink foreshadowed the serious struggles which would become the monsters of his middle age. It was a medicine that could kill.

In New York the picture we get is of Burton as a driven man determined it seemed to define himself by the forces of excess and opposition. Just as a great athlete pushes himself until he reaches the absolute climax of his possibilities, so Burton drove himself at this time. His drinking was way beyond the social or the swaggering. He would arrive well primed at a bar at midnight and be re-encountered there the next morning still holding forth, still downing the double vodkas and beer chasers. His infatuation for Susan Strasberg was not a mean little affair, nor a harmless one or two nights' stand but a testing, public "honest" passion. At the same time he had a sound marriage—everybody said so—and Sybil oiled the wheels of an agreeable family social life—visits, picnics, parties. He would talk at length to Lee Strasberg about acting—Strasberg was a great admirer of his—and then think it through carefully in his own way and stick to what he had intuited for himself. But everything was being explored, pushed.

For a multitude of reasons, most of them darkly buried, he was hammering himself and hammering his way through life like some Celtic demon. Daring himself to do his best and his most and life to do its damnedest. His life was way beyond what was accepted and what was acceptable as any "norm." His own man, he went his own way. At this time it suited him to live several different lives—simultaneously flat out.

While he was in *Time Remembered* he did an American television version of *Wuthering Heights*. The reviews and reports of this were excellent. Philip Burton—not unbiased but not entirely uncritical —thought he was "magnificent." There were those who thought it better than the Olivier performance. Olivier was a friend, an admirer and someone to whom, at that time, Burton felt junior but by no means unequal. Gielgud he relished and loved both for the man he was and for the early help he had given him. To Olivier he was potentially a rival—especially in films where the part would be offered to one and then the other. Neither had consistently struck star form; yet both were still considered great actors. Like Olivier he was still a little defensively snobbish about movies. Later, Burton was to find film-makers he could respect. At this time he settled for what they wanted—beefcake with a high IQ—and what he could get.

Hollywood was the film industry and Burton knew that survival was as much to do with deals as with delivery. He became a hard dealer. And even in the late Fifties, his career seemed nowhere, the black kept coming up and the wheels kept turning round. It was about that time he began augmenting his embryonic group of advisers, lawyers, agents—to Aaron Frosch and Valerie Douglas he added Norman Gyre of Goring, Gyre, Tyre, Rudin and Brown in the USA, Pierre Folliet in Switzerland, Hugh French in London.

To survive in business he became a businessman and the yellow files swell with jargon, deals, figures, percentages and claims for services. This too, true to form, he did flat out at first and at the end of the Fifties, after what for him was a poor run, he could say he had put one million dollars in that fabled Swiss bank account whose mysteries he would unravel to spellbound English reporters still imprisoned in the land of ninety-eight per cent tax, a £50 limit on personal spending when you went abroad, where the dream of great wealth was the £75,000 jackpot on the football pools.

Burton's insistence on going his own way and making no secret of his desire to amass a fortune while the going was good got him into trouble. Colleagues whose talents would never lead them to the temptations of success blamed him for what they saw as yielding to them. A minority of snide critics were always barking at his heels and used the stick of his money-making to beat what they really detested about him—his Welsh working-class origins, his successes, not least with women, and his non-"English" talent and manner. As always the best—Olivier, Gielgud, Neville, Tynan, Hall, Brook—had most time and understanding for him. They had some idea of how difficult and how interesting it was for a man like Burton to battle his way to what he wanted while never giving up what he really cherished. Which included what he saw as his debts and responsibilities to his family and his loyalty to his own instincts.

Burton is still today criticised in those vast and draughty halls of English hypocrisy for merely "going for the money." Three times already—and for substantial periods—he had walked away from what his critics would have ogled and perhaps even accepted as a king's ransom to come back to the Old Vic Company on £45 a week. Now he did much the same again. This time, in its way, was even more impressive.

Olivier had given a party in New York—hired a boat, cockles and mussels, English as Cockney, starry as Sunset Boulevard—and Burton had met John Osborne. Osborne was the most influential British playwright since the war. *Look Back In Anger* had defined a generation, provided a watershed in Britain's view of itself and brought him into the public prints as a controversial, dangerous figure. He was and is a beguiling mixture of strict intellectual and highly strung cavalry officer, at once fastidious and wonderfully rude: an original. Burton was intoxicated by him as he, at first, was drawn to Burton. Would he play the lead part, Jimmy Porter, in *Look Back In Anger*? This would secure the backing and make the film possible and, who knows? profitable. Burton said yes immediately.

His advisers were dismayed. A three-picture deal with Warners was being carefully constructed and Burton walked away from it. The deal would have netted him about $450,000. For *Look Back In Anger* he received less than $100,000. Therefore he turned his back on approximately $350,000: to get a contemporary (1988) equivalent it would be necessary to multiply by at least twelve. The sum rejected then becomes over $4 million. This was at a time when Burton was intent on building up his wealth and when, in Hollywood terms, the Warner deal would have been good news. For a man supposedly nailed to the cross of commercialism it was rather an impressive decision.

For quality of language he would drop anything. Another of his activities while in *Time Remembered* in New York (little wonder that he wrote to Susan Strasberg that he had lost touch with sleep) was an attempt to set up a film based on *Coriolanus*. This was dreamed up with Philip who brought Richard the story of Simon Bolivar, the central character in the South American independence movement of the early nineteenth century. Philip worked on a screenplay of Coriolanus—Bolivar—while Richard tried to raise money for the project. He failed but the energy he put into what could have been an original and audacious venture underlines the consistency of his concern with the finest material. *Look Back In Anger* was certainly that.

It was directed by Oxford-educated (that mattered to the intellectually snobbish side of Burton) Tony Richardson. Richardson was then in very fine form: he was to get an Oscar soon afterwards for *Tom Jones*. It co-starred Claire Bloom and Mary Ure. Burton plays the part of Jimmy Porter audaciously—not quelling his own sexual power, but dilating and perverting it. The fury of his class resentment against what he sees as the unearned privileges society gives the woman he has married compared with the mean deal issued to the beloved figure of his old landlady is coruscating. It is, in ways, a revenge marriage, Burton/Porter taking his revenge on the whole unjust hierarchic complacent closed shop of the English upper classes in the citadel of its prime institution—the family. Burton takes enormous risks—making no attempt to curry favour with the camera or the public. He comes over as a man consuming the world and himself in an anger which feeds on every swallow of oxygen he takes. And he manages to portray, with ferocity, the hopelessness of idealistic love. The performance restored and reinforced his reputation in England.

He was unusually pleased with the whole experience. To Philip Burton he wrote:

> the filming seems to have gone well tho' I know to my cost there's many a slip twixt cutter and flick. Still, everybody is delighted with themselves, and I have had two letters from Tony Richardson and John Osborne which are worthy of Edmund Kean and might indeed have been

written about him. I go full out and have I hope extracted every ounce of comedy. It contains, one forgets, a great deal of mad savage humour . . . And I promise you that there isn't a shred of self-pity in my performance. I am for the first time *ever* looking forward to seeing a film in which I play.

Most of the American critics hated it and disliked Burton—long past being the flavour of the month. Commercially it flopped. Harry Saltzman, the producer, blamed Burton, saying he was "monumentally miscast." Mr. Saltzman is monumentally mistaken. Tony Richardson's direction brought out the bleak, Victorian, squalid, depressed, London-local-dank-street life aspect of the film, playing up its social conscience at every opportunity: Burton delivered lines such as "I hope the baby dies," "I don't care if the baby has two heads" with venom. It was virtually impossible to *like*. You admired and you were shaken or you ran away. To blame Burton is ridiculously unjust and yet some of the mud stuck. Opinion hardened further that he was a no-go on the screen, even in "art house" movies.

Claire Bloom appears to have come back into his life as well as into the movie. When Susan Strasberg arrived at the studio to meet her lover after long weeks of waiting and scheming to get across the Atlantic to him she was bundled out of his dressing room and into the adjacent WC just before Claire Bloom came in. Immediately Burton made it clear that the game was up. Susan went on to Waterloo Bridge, anguished by the humiliation in the lavatory. She contemplated hurling herself in the Thames and then took hold of her nineteen years and caught the next plane out. Whether Burton's discretion was due to an *embarras de maîtresses*, whether he thought of London as a home ground on which you played differently or whether, as seems most likely, he had fallen out of love, is not clear. Nor is the attitude of Sybil, whose view of all this was and remains mysterious. Friends differ. Some say she knew and cared but didn't act; others that she knew and did not much care; others that she knew only a fraction and bore with that; others that the two of them always had a brother-sister, two Welsh kids taking on the world relationship which could see off anything as long as the main purpose was being served and ground gained.

It is worth noting that in *Look Back In Anger* Burton on screen was a much different proposition to the Burton of, say, five years earlier in *The Robe*. Now the hairy chest is unshaven, the chubbiness is gone, the boyish glamour looks are forsaken. He is a mature, virile, wonderfully and intelligently handsome man who is generous but also dangerous. The cold look in the eyes, the holding back, the lash of the tongue—he could see himself in Jimmy Porter and it is a self which reveals more than all his drinking and friendly Welsh boasting. It is a tormented and furious self somehow forked on pain and able to vault over it only by that "savage humour." It is also someone who thinks he has the devil by the tail and can twist and twist and still evade the jaws of hell.

When Burton was in England for the filming he slipped contentedly back into old ways. He did a Welsh radio play *Brad* (Treason) by the Welsh writer Saunders Lewis, a friend and contemporary of one of Burton's idols, the poet and painter David Jones. He was very proud of the fact that his Welsh was still up to it. Once again it is worth pausing to look at the uniqueness of a man who would turn down the equivalent of four million dollars from Hollywood one day and be pleased to take the equivalent of four or five hundred pounds from BBC Radio the next. And of course he went back to Wales.

When Burton went back to Wales there was no coy modesty. He was expected to be the Big Star and certainly in Wales he was regarded as top of the tree. ("Brando? What you think of this Brando boy?" a friend of his brother's asked in the pub. "Very good," said Burton, who liked Brando a lot. "Very good indeed." "I know," said the Welshman, "but Rich, can you *beat* him?") He would not be so churlish as to let them down.

He arrived in a Rolls-Royce of course, which went straight up to the pub and an old friend of his father's who dreamt of being Pierrepoint the hangman sat in it for hours contentedly patting the upholstery. Didn't want to drive anywhere. Just wanted to sit there alone. Drinks all round of course and stories of the glittering and famous tumbling all over the bar. For those back home, Burton was prepared to give as much and more than he would give to a major movie. Ancient rugby matches were replayed; old characters did their turn: Burton's love of his home base was unaffected and contagious. He kept faith by going back as the person he had become: he made no pretence that he was still "one of them"; he did not need to pretend. But he had changed and would change and he paid them the compliment not only of revealing that but of celebrating it with them.

The family were now receiving what were to be the opening shots in a campaign of care which was to embrace them, their children, other relatives and Welsh friends up until, and after, his death. Cis and Elfed were bought a house. There was money for all. Ifor and Gwen were settled in Squire's Mount in Hampstead; Tom got a bungalow, Hilda her terraced house, cars for Will, Verdun, David and Graham, cheques all round and especially at Christmas, outings for the old folk of Caradoc Street . . .

He himself continued to live modestly. The house in Switzerland was no more sumptuous than many a detached small villa along a decent stretch of English coast. There were no antiques, no expensive paintings, no Persian rugs, Ming jars, rare volumes, extraordinary cellar, executive excess in health equipment or horses or fashion-house clothing. The books were impressive in number but largely paperback; booze was at most a dozen or two bottles of claret, some vodka, general drinks for guests but best of all—over the road to the Café de la Gare. The furniture was good but unpretentious, just as his clothes were off the peg, absent-minded, typical of a man. Cars *were* a luxury. He kept the fire-engine-red MG and always had a big one besides—Cadillac, or Rolls. Apart from that, Burton hoarded for financial security—which he very soon acquired—and then for spending on family and friends. Directed at first to houses, pensions, cash and then to daft extravagances—an airlift of the family to New York, to Budapest, the hiring of a floor of the Dorchester for all of them . . .

The year following *Look Back In Anger*, 1959, Burton made two films, *The Bramble Bush* and *Ice Palace*, directed by Vincent Sherman. For each of them he received a basic $125,000 with overtime, which in the case of *Ice Palace* all but doubled his fee. Daniel Petrie, who had directed him in *Wuthering Heights*, and now in *The Bramble Bush*, again concluded that though Burton was "pound for pound one of the greatest actors in the world" it did not come over on the screen. It could have been something to do with the director or the fact that the US Censor chopped off the ending, making nonsense of it. On paper it had seemed a fair stab at a "problem" film—this time about euthanasia. Like most other directors, Petrie admired Burton's professionalism—no messing, no tantrums, his punctuality, his concern for other actors, his giving the director exactly what he wanted. Like most other directors, he did not test or challenge Burton.

By now Burton had a man to "look after him." This was Bob Wilson, a slim black six-footer from New Jersey, one of whose chores was to make sure that on the stroke of five p.m. a large vodka and tonic, the first of the day, hit Burton's outstretched hand. At this time he never drank before five when filming: on the other hand, nothing would stop him taking that first drink on the dot.

Vincent Sherman, who directed *Ice Palace*, adapted from an Edna Ferber novel, compared Burton with Clark Gable: the same professional ease, he noted, the lack of fuss, the men liking him, his toughness, dirt under the nails, his boldness and fun, the women throwing themselves at him, the pleasantness of the man. The location shooting in Alaska was not easy. Up at five a.m. (Burton often evaded this hurdle by drinking his way through the night), action in sub-zero temperatures, take and re-take, freezing waiting around. From Burton—no complaints at all. "Here we are," said Burton to Jim Backus (the voice of Mr. Magoo), who had become a drinking pal, "drinking at three o'clock in the morning, sitting on top of the world and making this piece of shit." Which it was. Once again the interest is to see how far Burton can keep his contempt for the material from his professional delivery of a performance. Even here, though, he has fine moments—especially as the defender of the workers. Late one night when the real workers in an Alaskan bar were cutting up rough, Burton turned on them and addressed to them a powerful strip of Shakespeare, which brought silence and respect. No one like him.

While he was filming, his second daughter, Jessica, was born. Philip describes how Sybil had to get on the phone to reconcile Burton into accepting the fact that he had not been there.

Céligny in Switzerland was now settling down as a home. He treated it like a Welsh hill chieftain might treat his castle. It was the anchor and the centre of a life unquestioningly devoted to expedition and conquest. Down from the hillside, out of the redoubt, all men were foreigners, all were potential enemies. The thing was to strike for a prize, secure it and live off the land while doing so, coming home with booty, seeking refreshment and ease and the love of the pure woman and children in whose name terrible deeds could be done. Outside Le Pays de Galles was a state of permanent warfare in which gain went to the strongest and all was for the taking. Only the rules of war—courtesy, chivalry, fair warning—applied. Inside the domestic walls was the world of peace, the real world, the world you conquered to secure.

Burton in Le Pays de Galles was a man who would have genuinely disappointed the reporters and columnists already delighted with him as a source of quotes and gossip—new starlets, old cracks, new rumours, plenty of action. In Céligny he read greedily, he practised writing, never ceasing to hope that this deep but diffident ambition could one day be teased out. Jessica was a beautiful baby. The Scofields came to stay—Paul Scofield, with whom, like John Neville, he was to be increasingly unfavourably compared although both men admired and continue to admire him and neither had anything like the opportunities and offers in films which came Burton's way. They found Rich and Syb very good together, cheerful, devoted to the two girls, still calling each other "Boot," still singing Welsh songs, Ifor and Gwen snug in the guest chalet, and Richard talking seriously about finding a modern and convincing way to portray Lear, Macbeth, Richard II, in touch with Peter Hall and Peter Brook about possibilities—no one doubting he would soon return to the classical stage as he had done before.

He was a fortunate man and he had the intelligence to know it, the sense to enjoy it and the energy to keep all the pieces in play. Although there were rumblings about his box-office capacity, he was still ahead of Olivier on most lists and, as he cheerfully said, he was one of those they turned to when Brando passed up a part. Brando was an actor who greatly respected Burton's nerve. Brando, like other young Turks, had started on the stage and kept threatening to return seriously to it but never did. Burton did. All of them knew what balls that took especially after the soft lights and fat nights of Hollywood. So although he was both disappointed and disappointing, Burton could say that the films served his purpose. By now he was well over his snobbery—although for devilment he would re-adopt it now and then just as he would claim he was descended from Jews or say his family lived on five shillings a week or anything else that sent up a gullible journalist and took the boredom out of an interview—and he wanted to do good work. *Look Back In Anger* had been a treat.

Another treat from the same duo—writer Osborne and director Tony Richardson—was a BBC Television play: *A Subject Of Scandal And Concern*, in 1960. For this the BBC paid him the unprecedented sum of £1,000. This sad, almost elegiac drama was based on a true story, that of George Jacob Holyoake, a nineteenth-century schoolteacher, who ruined his own life and that of his family for his principles. Burton here was directed to play a character role and responded so well that you could imagine he had been doing it all his life. Once again, given the words and the director, he seized the chances. Alas, after one or two showings, the film was shoved in the archives, unable to spin on his reputation.

But as long as he could do *A Subject Of Scandal And Concern* and, to a lesser extent, another television play, *Fifth Column* with Maximilian Schell in the USA, nothing much was amiss. The stage, of course, needed to be revisited soon—but for which part . . . ?

Plump at his feet like wind-dropped fruit came the offer from Moss Hart to play King Arthur in what was finally to be known as *Camelot*. Julie Andrews would be Guinevere. Moss Hart, who had adapted *Prince Of Players* and much admired him, convinced Lerner and Loewe, lyricist and composer of *Camelot*, that Burton's singing voice (heard at a Hollywood party in duet with Sybil) was well up to the mark. Burton consulted Olivier, who nodded it through: to appear in a Broadway musical was the fantasy of most British actors, however classical. Burton was to get $4,000 a week plus a percentage.

As he began to ease his way into *Camelot*, he recorded the voice-over for a twenty-six-part series entitled *The Valiant Years*. Based on Churchill's account of the war, Jack le Vien, the producer, wanted a Churchill "type" of voice. Burton's version was hugely acclaimed as a brilliant solution and an enormous factor in ensuring the success of the series. He decided against impersonation—although he prided himself on his "Churchill"—and instead found a voice from the most unlikely source. "I based my voice slightly on a Peter Sellers imitation I once heard of an upper-class Englishman dropping aitches and changing 'Rs' into 'Ws.' " Later, Burton was to be troubled by Churchill and his own apparent identification with him. Even on this occasion he lost no opportunity in telling reporters that he was far removed from Churchill socially and politically: in the terms of the British caste system, they were natural enemies and Burton was uneasy lest anyone forget it. He knew that the success of anything he did depended on the degree to which he could find himself in the part and part of him was an imperious, dictatorial, even tyrannical leader. Therefore praise of "his" Churchill was praise of what he least liked in himself: and condemnation was condemnation of his own character. He fed his potential lives, but non-lived lives, through the parts he played. Churchill must not be seen to be too close: he had to keep open the road back to Pontrhydyfen. He was paid $100,000.

The Valiant Years was a smash hit in America, which was what he needed and where it most mattered at that time. The voice, some thought the best part of him, could always conjure up his greatness. It was indeed a wonderful instrument—stagey, you think for a few moments as you put on the records today or drift unexpectedly into a film: but then the petty cloak of fashion falls away and you re-cognise a great gift—sound *and* sense in what seems to be perfect balance, force *and* intelligence, pause and calculation all riding on that throb of instinctive rhythm, all textured by what you could happily fantasise as an irresistible mix of mining valleys, poetry, cigarettes, vodka, passion and the rough end of a long night.

The advances for *Camelot*—the follow-up to Lerner and Loewe's *My Fair Lady*—were record-breaking. The show itself seemed set to break those involved. It was based on T. H. White's romantic, even magical view of the trials and court of the legendary King Arthur. Burton played the King, the lead. It soon became known as "Costalot" the Musical or "Medical." Moss Hart had a heart attack; Loewe had a severe haemorrhage which hospitalised him for a crucial fortnight; Lerner was in the middle of another miscarriage of a marriage; the sets and costumes cost more than King Arthur's royal court; at one stage the show ran for almost five hours. Burton emerged as the saviour and the leader, seen, acknowledged and praised as such on all sides. The situation was made for him.

"He could have been a great commander," Robert Hardy said; and again and again people called up leadership titles to describe him. Olivier more than once talked to him about taking over the National Theatre. At this time Burton was considering moving into production. Yet always his most absorbing battles were the fight he was having with the world OUT THERE and the trials he was forcing on himself.

In *Camelot*, as in every stage production, he had prepared his ground well beforehand. Burton never underestimated the nakedness of the stage—especially for a star. To be there, to have to deliver, night after night, aware that you are being scrutinised—both criti-cally and sympathetically—and to convince all the people to suspend disbelief: that took nerve and energy. Skill could see you through but except for his infinite vocal power, Burton was not a craft actor. His basic training had been in Ma Smith's sitting room. What he did was that almost magical thing which the few great high-definition performers can do, usually at great cost to themselves: that is to draw on their own fundamental and secret reserves, to will themselves into the part so profoundly that a kind of mesmerism takes over the audience. A spell is cast. When it is broken the performer—singer, actor, musician, entertainer—is either uncontrollably high, utterly drained or, dislocatingly, both. Burton knew the dangers of calling up those forces but his pride in *doing* just that made him go for it despite them. It was what made him great and he had to keep proving it—to himself as well as to everyone else. The basic precaution he always took was to absorb the part before any director got to him. And more often than not, he worked, still, amazingly, after all this time, with Philip.

Philip was now fully resident in New York. He arranged Sybil and Richard's apartment for the duration of *Camelot*. His own cleaning lady, Madge, would ''do'' for them. He wrote:

> Richard arrived six days before Sybil and the children and spent most of the time with me.
>
> As soon as Richard got hold of the script and score of *Camelot* we set to work on his three big solos and duet. There was a piano in the apartment. In my youth I had taught myself to play the piano and was a fairly good sight-reader . . . my mind flashed back to the time when, at Richard's insistent request, I had taught him finger-by-finger to play the First Movement of Beethoven's Moonlight Sonata and he had become sufficiently adept at it to surprise people when the show-off mood was on him . . . I had some pleasant sessions with Richard in going over his lines. I liked the potential of the show.

When he arrived on the first day of rehearsal for *Camelot*, he was, as he liked to be, way ahead of the field. Ready for the gladiatorial stage.

The stage confirmed his unassailable belief that you were on your own and had total responsibility for yourself. It was man against man or woman, one individual against another, horns locked for supremacy, and that was the world he lived in. It somehow reclaimed him, for although the stage was wildly distant from the mines and could not be mentioned in the same breath, similar and related qualities were demanded. He could do his fighting on the stage; he could take his public risks there. He could feel danger and know fear. He liked that.

And yet. Fellow actors emphasise and insist that he was not a stealer of scenes, an upstager, did not throw his star weight about. Particularly not to those he liked. They were "family" and although he would rough and tumble he was just as willing to hold out a hand. The closer you come to Burton the man it is apparent that the tightrope he trod was strung between oppositions, often extreme, often violent.

Quite simply, it appears, Burton held *Camelot* together on what proved a disturbing and chaotic tour. It was his leadership alone which got it to Broadway. When Moss Hart collapsed and Loewe went down, Burton drafted in Philip as a director. Several weeks' work between them saw the production through one of its roughest periods. Philip took 1½ hours off the running time. Three new songs were added. There was a new set. Typically, when Philip was asked if Moss Hart could retain full credit, he said yes. Burton seems to have thrived on the difficulties. He took the understudy rehearsals; he never let a drink cross his lips. Without Burton, Lerner said again and again, the show would never have made it. When his own part was slashed right back, he made not the slightest objection, relearnt it in his dressing room in an afternoon and did it that same evening. When bankers were wailing and ambulances toing and froing, Burton's response was always, "Don't worry, luv, we'll get through." All this, it seems, without antagonising anyone. "I can't remember any actor," Lerner wrote—and he had a tremendous range of experience—"as loved by a company as he was." The battle, the critical thumbs-down on the road, all the daily strain that such mega-musicals are heir to, seems to have suited Burton down to the ground. Lerner thought he was magnificent. "God knows what would have happened if it were not for Richard Burton," Lerner wrote. "If ever a star behaved like a star, it was he . . . *Camelot* might never have reached New York had it not been for him."

Lerner also watched him closely on stage. "I've never known *anyone* with that kind of presence on stage," he wrote. "There was a moment when he was merely standing by the fire, supposedly in deep thought, while others in the scene were speaking. But I saw no one was interested in what was being said. His peculiar power of concentration was so great that he just sucked all the energy of the stage into him." Lerner changed that scene to involve Burton actively in it.

He studied Burton in every way. Having tried to keep up with him for one night only in drinking and failed utterly, Lerner said, "I would have matched him drink for drink against anybody in the world."

One matinée day Burton took on a bet that he could drink a bottle of vodka during the matinée and another during the evening performance—while acting—with no effect. Julie Andrews—unaware of this—was to be the judge. "What did you think I was like today then, luv?" he asked at the end of the day. "A little better than usual," she replied.

The show came in to mixed reviews. Burton was well liked by some of the critics, but the audience did not smell success and the drift to the exits often began before the interval. The huge advances kept it going but it did not look as if it would be a hit until a twenty-minute extract appeared on the *Ed Sullivan Show*. Immediate sell-out. Round-the-block queues. Burton invited everywhere—toast of the town, King of Broadway, Tony Award for best actor in a musical. He let rip.

"Burton's Bar" opened up in his dressing room (which he and Sybil refurbished with $700 of his own money). *Le tout* New York came for drinks and chat, followed by *le tout* Hollywood and London when in town, and the party went on to bars, to clubs. Women hung around. There was Pat Tunder, for instance, a long-legged beauty of a dancer from the Copacabana Club, whose relationship was well publicised at the time and has been much commented on since. He would sometimes arrive croaking and clearly sleepless, but out came the pass-phrase "don't worry, luv" and as Lerner watched incredulously, he would control the shakes, get on stage, whisper for a moment or two and then *will* the voice, the alcohol-pushed, sex 'n' bed-sotted body into action and the performance would be word perfect, often good. Lerner made his notes. So did the chorus. The song "I wonder what the King is doing tonight" often sounded surprisingly like "I wonder who the King is screwing tonight."

"He was a driven man," said the perceptive Lerner, "a remarkable fellow and a remarkable actor."

Settled in for a long successful run, Burton built up his paperback mountain and began to think more seriously of producing. For $8,000 he bought the rights to Dylan Thomas's *The Beach Of Felesin* and paid Philip to do a first-draft screenplay. Alas, nothing came of this. He sorted out his business affairs, putting aside trusts for the children, pumping more back to Wales, and discovered that in the five years since leaving London he had become that then totally fabulous being, a millionaire. The contract films, the solid saving and now *Camelot* had totted up the zeros.

The record of the show soared in the charts and yet another pinnacle had been reached. He had acted at the Old Vic, sung on Broadway, recited on BBC Radio and, given the trauma of Hollywood in the first television decade, at least kept his face on the screen.

His Prince Hal at Stratford had represented *the* new way to realise Shakespeare for our time. He was Jimmy Porter in the film of the play of the decade and although *Look Back In Anger* continues to be remounted and redesigned to the mood of the time, Burton's savage performance helps make it one of the best British films of the Fifties and gives a view of Porter which seen now is surprisingly relevant.

And in *Camelot*—liked by the Kennedys; Burton was invited to the White House—he was where America wanted to be. In a Kingdom of Grace and Righteousness, surrounded by monsters and dark enemies but triumphing over them all, the Democracy of Good over the Empire of Evil, with a big sword and a song.

You might take it further. His private behaviour was not altogether unusual. What was unique was his boldness—something which would become a great virtue in the puzzling-to-be-honest and permissive society of the Sixties. Perhaps the sympathy with which his antics were met, by and large, was due in no small degree to the fact that people scented that he was the herald of a new time coming on. Certainly his openness prefigured what were thought of as the healthy and necessary upheavals soon to come in the Sixties. The ancient world dominated by Doris Day-values was breaking up. Divorce rates rocketed, the ideal of sanitised suburban stability began to seem limited, respect for authority plummeted. The idea of the men or women who went their own way rumbled in the near distance and hedonism ceased to be a total sin. In that sense, Burton's lust, his apparent mission to screw the world and all that moved thereon, and to do it for what to him were good and sufficient reasons, chimed in perfectly with the era. He came out of the closets of the Fifties fully primed for the new decade.

His drinking kept faith with the heroes of his youth and his stories and boasting kept everybody on their toes. The only area which he had not hit in the centre was in the movies. He had been miscast: he had had bad luck—good directors on bad form, good scripts in poor hands, ambitious projects which ran out of energy. But excuses apart, he had not scored—save in *Look Back In Anger*, in *Desert Rats* and, in isolated sequences, some talk of *Alexander*. Not enough to convince the inside track that he could make it. If he could get away with *not* giving all he had—then he did so. Moreover, like an Indian or an Arab he seemed to fear the camera's demands on his soul.

But here he was in 1960, thirty-five and, taken all in all, he had achieved everything he could have dreamed of. The best actors in England accepted him as a leading member of a very small crack corps. In Hollywood though not box-office he was by no means out of the running. His ambition to write was growing. He had discovered how to make mounds of cash and keep much of it. He had a faithful, loving wife and two beautiful children. And there was the world of the other life, the night world of excess, of poets, of sex, song, wild talk, a fantastical whirligig in which he whipped himself on harder and faster.

Most of all was the relief and the triumph. He had come back on stage, and he had made it. *Camelot* was a great big hit . . .

Now word came that the monstrous film *Cleopatra*, started in London, was in trouble and Burton was requested to play Antony. It meant cutting short his contract in *Camelot* but Lerner and Loewe could not have been more helpful—they knew what they owed him. With Richard's connivance they even secured $50,000 compensation out of the film company. Everybody was taking the film company. Elizabeth Taylor had asked for an unprecedented $1,000,000 plus imperial expenses. Again, multiply by twelve and the size of it hits the solar plexus.

Burton was happy to go to Rome. There would be a home on the

Appian Way for Sybil and the family. The money was very good
—$250,000 plus lots of overage should it run on. As it undoubtedly
would. He was on top of the world. After this he thought he would
go back on to the English stage. The *Cleopatra* money would finally
secure his future. It would be a Roman Holiday.

12
Cleopatra

Cleopatra changed Burton's life. Not only in the obvious ways: the divorce, the notoriety, the box-office, the Burton–Taylor circus . . . but also in ways more profound. For long, perhaps for ever, afterwards he was poisoned by guilt: equally, he was obsessed by one woman who brought out the finest and the most destructive forces in him. Most importantly of all, he seems to have made the decision to burn: to go for the heat wherever it was; to confuse his life in the present and let the devil take the consequences. After *Cleopatra* he found himself on a world stage and discovered that the man he was gave the public the part they wanted. He became the driven flawed hero of passion, riot and adventure, locked in a death-battle with himself even as he seemed to be taking on the world. Only in his notebooks and in the books of others did he seem to find peace. The rest was war. The first battle took place in Rome.

The forces that were called up were impressive. There was *Cleopatra* the film—the most expensive ever made—on which the future of a great studio, Fox, increasingly appeared to depend. Boardroom manoeuvres in the USA were hurled against location strategies in the Cinecittà Studios. Spyros Skouras, now head of Fox (Darryl Zanuck had left, but was waiting in the wings), Walter Wanger and Joe Mankiewicz on the set—four powerful players circling the body of Cleopatra, each with his supporters, now fearing it to be a corpse, now seeing it as the magical solution to years of problems. The money flowed faster than the fountains of Rome and soon the public was to be hooked on what the writer Brenda Maddox has called "the most public adultery in the world." What made it tantalising and finally compulsive to a thousand magazine and newspaper editors who knew what their public wanted was the cast list: Antony and Cleopatra who became and were "equalled" by Burton and Taylor. And there were exciting complications on that basic theme: Taylor and Fisher, Burton and Sybil, Taylor and her favourite professor Max Lerner, Burton and his favourite dancer Pat Tunder . . . Wales came in to battle for Sybil—Philip, Emlyn, Ifor: Taylor called up her Hollywood-boned megastardom and fired on all guns. There were children, four on one side, two on the other, the Vatican hoisted its flag, the American Congress was advised to banish Burton–Taylor from the innocent shores of the USA, publicity men shaped it, sat on it, attempted to control it and finally watched, like everyone else, helplessly, as the titanic Event—"Le Scandale," as Burton called it—proceeded in all its slow and rending inevitability . . . there were suicide attempts, false trails, denials, decent gestures, drink, brave promises, utter deceit, flaunting, skulking and undeniable painful passion.

The paparazzi of Rome were on the loose like avenging Bacchae and when the film was over, Burton had been transported to a different world. Or had he transported himself? The film, finally, had three and a half hours chopped out of it—most of it containing Burton's best scenes which are somewhere in a Twentieth Century-Fox vault. According to Joe Mankiewicz, the writer-director, they show Burton giving a remarkable performance. So what he came originally and finally to prove—that the great intellectual epic was possible—landed on a cutting room floor on the West Coast. He was left with a part which required neither screen nor theatre—just himself, herself and the public. Fiction became fact, which would outbid any fiction for years to come.

There had been several film stabs at Cleopatra before. Claudette Colbert had been in Cecil B. de Mille's version, Vivien Leigh in that of George Bernard Shaw. The story of the Queen of the Nile who conquered her conquerors, first Caesar and then Antony, whom she led to his defeat followed by her suicide, was irresistible, especially at the end of the Fifties when Hollywood was in a flutter and floundering. This one began in England in 1958 as a cheapo— one million dollars the lot, to be directed by Rouben Mamoulian at

Pinewood Studios. It ended costing forty million dollars (some say sixty-five million dollars). If we apply the most modest of multiples between 1963 and 1988—say four?—that makes it a hundred and sixty million dollars at current prices. It makes *Heaven's Gate*—which crashed in at about fifty million dollars and almost brought down United Artists—seem like a short.

Twentieth Century-Fox, who were making the picture, were badly broke: dreadful movies, the panic of an industry suddenly bypassed by television, mounting losses, maddened shareholders. As *Cleopatra* went on from one extravagance to another it was increasingly unclear which drowning body was clinging to which. All that seemed obvious to outsiders was that both appeared to be sinking. The budget increased forty-fold. Elizabeth Taylor, having negotiated one million unprecedented dollars, ended up with very nearly three. Joseph Mankiewicz, brought in to replace Rouben Mamoulian, cost three million dollars to pay him and have him extricated from current contracts. The sets on the rain-sodden backlot at Pinewood were mercifully abandoned and Rome became the prime location. Millions—some estimated seven—had been spent without a usable foot of film to show for it. As the production dragged on and boardroom battles grew fiercer than anything at the mouth of the Nile, it became clear that unless the film was a hit then Fox would perish. Between England and Italy the casting changed: Peter Finch as Caesar was replaced by Rex Harrison, Stephen Boyd by Burton. With some deep corporate cunning and even deeper desperation, Fox did hold on and the film eventually made money. The desperate gamble was to work. Superstition triumphed over sense; folly overcame foresight: in the end, utter and loathsome self-indulgence sorted the whole thing out. Hollywood at its worst triumphed.

Joe Mankiewicz had a real picture in mind. He had won his Oscars, he had written his winners, he had the trust of Taylor (rare), the admiration of Burton (rare), the respect of Rex Harrison (rare) and a budget which could have recreated all the Pharaohs with change still left over for the beauty of the Nile. The big white Hollywood hunter was out to bag the Thinking Epic. There was something gigantic and touching about these worldwide cinema epics, something tremendous about the reach of this new imperial medium which felt that it needed to gather in the greatest stories ever told and recircuit them around the planet in all the glory of technicolour.

Mankiewicz was widely read and commendably ambitious. But he had too much to take on. To direct a film on that scale—thousands of miles from his home base, doing everything in two languages, coping one day with the cast of thousands, elephants and all, and the next with the legitimate illnesses of the star—multiply by a hundred and has he still time to put the necessary pressure into the direction? He was also writing it! Writing at night, directing by day—for months. You could call it megalomania or another variety of madness: yet you could not blame him for trying to seize this occasion to make something massive and memorable. Soon he saw it as two films: each of three hours: Part One with Caesar, Part Two with Antony. This, which could have been a viable option given the publicity the film attracted, was vetoed. The final cut owed much less to Mankiewicz than to Zanuck who had by then succeeded Skouras at Twentieth Century Fox. Mankiewicz had been captivated by Burton's performance and never ceased to regret that it was never seen by the public. He still says today that Burton influenced the way in which he wrote the part, "the world's greatest loser."

Had Mankiewicz had a little more time to write—then perhaps the truly modern major epic might have been made: had he been allowed to go his bold six hours' way—then Burton's own essays in that region might have been crowned with the evidence of real achievement. As it was, between the push and the rush, between the panic and the alarm button, out went all the pacing, the flighting, balancing subtleties that Mankiewicz had aimed for. The film succeeded at the box-office largely because of the publicity and that was generated because of Burton–Taylor as themselves, as Antony and Cleo, and as richly hyped media megastars. He hadn't realised, said Burton, that "she was so fucking famous." She even knocked Khrushchev off the front page.

Elizabeth Taylor had been one of MGM's most successful child stars. Born in middle-class London, in Wildwood Road, Hampstead, brought over to America in 1939 when she was six, propelled into showbusiness by an alarmingly ambitious mum, adored by a handsome father who dealt in paintings, she was the little rich girl type. Rich called out to rich. And that perfect, privileged English heiress had always been plunder for a rough Celtic marauder from over the border.

Not only was she extraordinarily beautiful, she photographed marvellously well and took her film acting seriously. She held her own with Lassie. She came through the worst part in *Little Women*—as the spoilt brat—with the audience still on her side. On the horse in *National Velvet* she swept past the winning post into the hearts of the cinema nation which was then the world. It was a "classic" popular Hollywood movie and the legend began. She had made herself grow three inches in a few months in order to secure the role, it was said. She *became* the character. The horse was given her as a present after the film. She pleaded for it: she loved it so. Later she bitched loudly at what it cost her to feed and maintain.

Education at the MGM school was not rigorous. There are stories of spectacular under-achievement. But Taylor was always shrewd. She would denigrate her lack of brains—but never undervalue her store of cunning. What the MGM kiddies' school may have failed to do, MGM Studios more than compensated for. Her education there was a total and successful course in riding and exploiting the world of celluloid fantasies, Monopoly money and mafioso deals. The pretty little rich girl who liked presents and would demand them when they were not forthcoming, the movie-mad, pet-mad, astoundingly polite child seems to have been rather like a ventriloquist's doll and fulfilment dream to her mother until well into her teens. Kitty Kelley, in a biography, reports that when Elizabeth was asked a question, even "How are you?," Mrs. T. would reply, "Elizabeth is a little feverish today." Mrs. T. was on the payroll—not unusual with child stars.

Mother was inspired in all she did by a single-minded wish for a wonderful future for Elizabeth. She introduced her to the two notorious gossip columnists of Hollywood. She chaperoned her towards rich young men. She encouraged the concentration on appearance, appearance and appearance. Between the unreal movie world which was *her* real world and the hothouse ambition of her devoted mother which was the centre of her family life, Elizabeth grew up in a fantasy land. She was like a princess in a fabulous story, pampered and petted, schemed over and manipulated, made to please as exactingly as the foot of a Chinese child would be strap-bandaged to perfect tininess. The miracle is that she retained any real contact at all. But money, as often, was a contact. That was real. Sex, too, when it arrived on the first night of the marriage. Money and marriage were her twin guidelines.

When she engineered her first screen kiss in *Cynthia*, America's young men cheered aloud. They knew the Hollywood code. Liz was going to be laid. That extraordinary bond between the public and the few great stars they follow throughout their lives with the attention—conscious and unconscious—of a "special relative" was already dug in. Elizabeth Taylor herself began the double public life of screen actress and public personality: the private life had to fight for any space between. In a sense, like a few others, it is no exaggeration to say that she belonged to the nation. They treated her as the fairy sister, daughter of the family—to be idolised and idealised but also to be whipped cruelly when the mood came or the magic failed to please. She had to learn to live with all that and, unlike many others, although she bent she did not break.

She crossed the chasm between child star and adult star without breaking her stride. She banished her mother for some penal time. She gatecrashed adolescence and came out of her cocoon greedy for life. We read that at that time she discovered foul and obscene language and threw it around like mud pies. She practised slovenliness. Her unhousetrained dogs shat everywhere. Perhaps it was her revenge on Lassie. She exercised her power in such wearing capers as being constantly late. She gave the world what it said it wanted—the wicked sweetness, the stolen sugar, the privilege of undeniable beauty: for herself she hoarded the squalor with glee. For another self she developed the business nerve of a world-class poker player. Inside that pretty little head, a great deal that was tough, violent and remarkably impressive stirred and spat at the world which had bondage-plastered her to the image of painted perfection. Somehow—as with Burton—these often conflicting and warring selves were kept together. She was quite remarkable but hardly anyone noticed anything below the surface. She was thought of as simply a star.

By the time she and Burton met on the set in Rome she had been through four marriages, more than a score of illnesses, some very serious indeed (in one she described how, clinically, she had "died" four times), three extremely painful births, affairs, a queen's ransom and some excellent films in which her adult career took off. *A Place In The Sun, Suddenly Last Summer, Cat On A Hot Tin Roof* (for which she deserved an Oscar) and *Butterfield 8* (for which she got one, but only, as she herself said, because she had almost "died" those four times and, conveniently, in the run-up to the awards)— these more than compensated for the mediocre quota all but the very luckiest contract stars had to do.

Her husbands were (i) the extremely rich Hilton heir, Nicky, a gambler who seems to have been a good lover but someone who beat her and altogether seems as spoilt in his way as she was in hers; (ii) the extremely charming Michael Wilding, almost twenty years older than her, an English matinée idol with all the drawing power that signifies, very like her handsome deep background father, it appears, idle and easy, two children a necessary interlude, a bridge to motherhood; (iii) Mike Todd, biggest of the big shots, earned and lost one million dollars by the time he was nineteen, he said, ostentation writ in colours of Cecil B. de Mille style—a hugely generous donor of orientally expensive baubles to his wife; to please him she became Jewish, after having been a Catholic after having been raised a Christian Scientist; they had one child. Then the tragic death of Todd in a plane crash after making *Around The World In Eighty Days* which paid off a fortune in debts and set out to make a new fortune in royalties; (iv) Eddie Fisher, crooner extraordinaire, husband of Debbie Reynolds, best friends of the late Mike and Elizabeth Todd: one child, adopted.

All the marriages were publicly declared to be eternal: all husbands the love of her life—again in public. Public fidelity and eternal love were part of the MGM contract. You spent the life, but they owned it.

From these marriages she had gained even more wealth, much sexual experience—hugely appreciated—motherhood, tragedy and scandal. Her breaking up of the Fisher marriage brought upon her the wrath of American Righteousness—a powerful and much feared force. She was not yet thirty.

The complex, perhaps impenetrable, web of mystery, lies, publicity, truth and talent which spun her into a star was already in place. She had become an American icon. Andy Warhol would celebrate her; Michael Jackson would be besotted by her; illnesses would trigger off pantechnicons of fan mail; marriages would release another flush of front-page pics, headlines, interviews; she was as much part of the world of publicity as the world of films and her life based so largely on fantasy was not only legitimised by, but even encouraged by the public. She became one of their dreams.

Professor Max Lerner later wrote about her status in America. Lerner was one of her lovers, an intellectual who had a steady affair with her while she was married to Fisher. This rather punctures the ideas that (a) she was a serial monogamist and (b) she had to marry every man she slept with. Lerner, incidentally, was married at the time, another rebuttal of that notion that she only went to bed with her husbands, a notion designed to give a certain respectability to the sexual and marital tornado of her life. But it was an effective publicity stroke at the time. In his piece Max Lerner described Taylor as a legend, Monroe as a myth. Taylor gave him hell: why was she "only a lousy legend"?

For she was passionately self-absorbed and acutely aware of herself. This was essential to her celluloid power. One of her major preoccupations as a young woman was to sit in front of a mirror trying out new looks. As a performer she would trudge dutifully through the rehearsal hitting her marks, noting the steps to the left or the right, deeply puzzling for anyone who had come to see an actress. Only when the camera purred did she act and as Paul Newman, one of many, said at the transformation, "Now, hold on a minute. I wasn't ready for that." She was and is razor sharp on her own image. With Burton, for a number of years, she was confident enough to run totally counter to it.

Not only was there no "normality" in her life—there never had been and there never could be. She was as pinned to her public stardom as a traditionally trapped suburban housewife to her kitchen. On the movie living was almost always on expenses, away from home. And directed to project an indefinable charisma. The sex appeal, the ability to transmit through the camera a musk of sensuality, seems to be one undeniable key. Another is to do with the trade-off, the willingness to give yourself away, to do a Faustian deal with the camera, to float yourself off. It is a strange, even a chilling, phenomenon and the more successfully you dare to do it, the more heavily you pay, it seems.

And equally, the more heavily you can *be* paid, if you get the right gang of lawyers and agents. She did.

When Elizabeth Taylor had demanded one million dollars (more than the total budget of the original film) she cried when she could not get it. Her tears paid off—they usually did and, as we have seen, she ended up—after overage—with about three million dollars for the film plus all the usual perks and "her presents." Should a producer fail to produce a "spontaneous" gift, he would be keelhauled and bawled out by one of the most frightening sounds in Hollywood—Taylor at full tilt, epithets like Exocets bearing in on the enemy. All was fair in the jungle of Hollywood—she knew that. And she was the jungle's own cat.

It is as easy to dismiss her as appearing spoilt, greedy, selfish and mean as it is to dismiss Burton as seeming boastful, faithless, a poseur and a drunk. Far too easy. For we must recognise that these two people were subject to seductive and ravishing opportunities, to strains beyond the comprehension of most, to temptations of the flesh, the press, the purse. They go where few could or dare to go and it is their dicing with survival as much as their surfing with their own success which draws us in. The primitive and the sophisticated are constantly colliding.

Here as everywhere else, Elizabeth Taylor gave full measure. In the movie of her life she threatened to disappear at the end of many a chapter. There is a sense in which you can include these illnesses in the script she wrote for herself. *She* did. Her near fatal illness at the Dorchester while in London with Fisher to do *Cleopatra* Mark I—which turned to pneumonia and needed and luckily got an urgent tracheotomy—was explained as part of her wish to live in a "dream world" with the deceased Mike Todd rather than the "real world" with "Poor Eddie." The notion that those who represent the people so luxuriously ought to seem fatally dependent on the public was drummed into her at the MGM school. The allied notion that they wanted you to glitter and shine but also loved it when you threatened to gutter out was her own. Her licence to play was bonded with her licence as a plaything. Understandably, many of her close friends were homosexual: there could be an equality here, i.e. no sexual contests.

She arrived in Rome with the Million Dollars held aloft like the Roman Eagle itself before many another conqueror entering the Pagan and then the Holy City. Dogs, cats, children, bodyguards, secretaries, nannies, hairdressers and all settled down in luxury which soon turned to what many thought to be glitzy squalor. All the animals sprawled with each other and the pups would lick her children awake with her full approval: she saw this as healthy. Joe Mankiewicz had been waiting and writing. Rex Harrison was there with his new wife Rachel Roberts and his own not inconsiderable demands. Meanwhile the elephants and extras were all lined up. Burton had not yet arrived.

Anyone approaching the Burton–Taylor story is met by the contradictions of many memories, the confusions of hundreds of newspaper reports, first-hand accounts which can differ radically and finally the elusive and rapidly changing moods, panics and decisions of the two principals. *The Cleopatra Papers* by Jack Brodsky and Nathan Weiss provides medium close-ups from the film's two chief publicists. There is Mankiewicz's version, and of course, Burton's own version; the recollections of Emlyn Williams or Brook, his son, or Philip Burton give alternative angles. Long shots are plentiful. The true close-up is difficult, not least because the affair went through so many different phases. That was one of its fascinations.

"I must don my armour once more to play against Miss Tits," Burton is reported to have said, uncharacteristically ungallant—nerves? Or another misquote? Then he sat around idly in Rome in the autumn of 1961 while Rex Caesar Harrison went to Cleopatra before him.

By the time Burton came to do any real work—in January 1962—he was on overage, which was very agreeable. It would double his fee. Stanley Baker was in Rome; so was Rachel Roberts, a long-time friend of Sybil's from the glorious Stratford days; Caitlin Thomas, widow of the poet, was there; Roddy McDowall, whom Richard had suggested and had been winkled out of *Camelot* to play Octavius, shared a house with the Burtons. Ifor and Gwen came too. Lots of drinking and gossiping. Serious talk of a new play in London by Christopher Fry, promises of work with Peter Brook, two children now—Kate and Jessica—Ifor to drink and talk with, all rather boring but expense-account boredom and good company. Burton's gambles—get the money to Switzerland, keep the tap root to classy theatre in London, feed the family and peg away at the movies—was paying off. On a good day it could even look like a strategy.

And then he donned his armour. There's a sense in which he never again took it off.

Had they "known" each other before? Rumours persist about bumps in the night when he was in New York as King Arthur: even before in Hollywood. I doubt them. The evidence points to a "first time" here. Brook Williams states firmly that "at first Richard couldn't stand her." Remarks to Joe Mankiewicz, including "Miss Tits" and "I expect she shaves"—a rude rugby bar reference to the stubbornness and spread of her hair (she had been born "covered in black hair," reported Kitty Kelley, and her mother had despaired:

much patience and skill had gone into keeping it at bay) tend to support that. Besides, his whole public stance was that she was just another star. He had met them all: which he had. He was impressed only by eloquent talent: which he had not yet discovered in her.

Elizabeth Taylor's version is that at first he made a standard pass—"Has anybody told you what a pretty girl you are?"—and she could not wait to rush back to make-up and tell "the girls" what a duffer this poetic Welshman, this great Shakespearian classical actor, really was. Linked with that is the statement that her heart went out to him in the last week of January 1962 when they played their very first scene together. The studio describes it as an "electrifying encounter." He was shaking from a titanic night on the town, he was grey, he forgot his lines, he was "vulnerable." At first she laughed—and then became sympathetic. It was then, she said, that she fell for him.

Friends of *his* report that it was seeing her naked in the bathing scene which had him rubbing his hands. She pursued *him* and intensely, because at first he was clearly unimpressed, one camp claims; he pounded after her not so much for the flesh as for the glamour, says another. He was blitzed by her wealth and power in the movie world, they said—Mankiewicz is still of that school—and in their contemporary *Cleopatra Papers* Jack Brodsky and Nathan Weiss put forward this opinion several times. Her contract, said the journalist David Lewin, intoxicated him as much as her body and he talked about it for hours. The portrait they draw is of the canny Celt seeing a way to double his fee and pursue his lust simultaneously.

When filming started, both were occupied elsewhere. Whatever her later, accepted version that "poor Eddie" was a rebound from the spectacular Mike Todd, a mere hyphen between Todd and Burton, there is plenty of evidence that Eddie and Liz enjoyed each other. The sex—from anecdote and memoir—seems to have been good. Fisher's main trouble may have been that his own career took him away from her. At that time and for many years afterwards, Elizabeth Taylor could not endure being alone. There was always Max Lerner, in his mid-fifties, a syndicated columnist—but he was in the States: there was some gossip of "sex with her ex"—Nicky Hilton.

But the Brodsky–Weiss book declares the Fishers to be "very much in love" when the filming began in Rome. Other observers agree. And after all it had been seeing Eddie beside her bed every time she had surfaced in that last illness (which had commanded ten doctors including the Queen's surgeon), which she said had saved her. Moreover although public favour had been restored and an Oscar bestowed, her habit of busting marriages had wounded her reputation badly after the ousting of Debbie Reynolds. For many reasons, it is safer to conclude that she was well enough married for these first few months. And there was the part to play—a colossal role on which the picture, the studio, the reputation of the director and her own fortune—paid a million dollars and then flopped?—depended. She was altogether otherwise engaged.

Burton was still seeing Pat Tunder, the Copacabana blonde beauty, whom he had met while he was in *Camelot*. He may well have expressed his interest in others. He was in the full tide of his Don Juan phase—the fantasies of a Welsh chapel boy had turned into reality and his rich love for women, his longing to turn desire into conquest and his delight that so many complied were all at their height. Clearly he had a huge taste for all manner and depth of lust and affection towards the opposite sex—not a common gift. A shame, he seemed to think, not to exercise it. Perhaps his success was as much a reflection of a widespread feminine need for a man such as him as an indication of cheerfully admitted pleasing promiscuity. Few men were as deeply intrigued by women, or as capable of pleasing them.

And there was Sybil. Now with two daughters, the younger, Jessica, increasingly worrying. An awareness of her terrible illness began to dawn on them. Photographs of them together in Rome seem happy enough but these photographs, like interviews and anecdotes and memoirs, are only partially reliable. From the fierceness with which Sybil summoned him when the Taylor rumours began and the alacrity with which he came, from the terrible rows he had later with Ifor and Philip, with Stanley Baker and Emlyn, all of whom were on her side, one can deduce at least that the expectation of their private continuity was powerful. And possible. Burton's ease in the roundness of his success coupled with his concern for both of his daughters made for a strengthening of bonds with Sybil. However it was, he kept away from his leading lady for some months.

When you meet Elizabeth Taylor there is no question of the beauty of the woman—those violet eyes, the jet hair, the beguiling cross of macho shoulders and earth-mother bosom: fun, sex and danger beam off her as directly as the shaft from a lighthouse. In her manner too she is like no one else. It is half as if she is encased still in the studio world, a jewelled chip off the old screen Royalty, one who has seen and known them all, while the other half makes it up as she goes along and is capable of nothing and everything. If ever there was a call for a "cynosure for neighbouring eyes" to be cast, Taylor would be the number-one contender.

Those who met Burton say that a similar singularity of presence, a unique mixture of solidity and total unexpectedness was characteristic of him too, especially in this, the first great stretch of his adulthood.

When the two of them did turn and see and go and bed with each other, the clash of eyes, the locking of horniness, the bays of triumph and pleasure would be heard all over the jungle.

Publicists, producer, the studio, lawyers and friends attempted to drown and deny the story. At first, with some success.

For at first Burton seems to have treated it as just another affair: and that may have been what deeply stung her into action. He laid her; she guilty: must get him as a husband—Mankiewicz's version. A few weeks after their first "electrifying" moment on the set, when he could hardly stand up straight, came St. David's Day—March 1st—a day which Burton always insisted he had off. To celebrate the glory and honour of Wales he went on a record-breaking bar tour. He turned up with Pat Tunder on the set the next morning and when Taylor told him off for being late he warned her not to set his temper going and besides it would do her good to wait for others for a change. "When you are in a cage with two tigers," said the director, Mankiewicz, who had a great deal of time for both of them, "you don't let them know that you are terrified."

Mankiewicz was not only terrified that his star would go ill again—although one of her more protracted illnesses could sink the financially floundering movie and its ailing parent in the USA. He feared the reaction of the Great American Public. When Ingrid Bergman had run off with Rossellini ten years earlier, it had wrecked her Hollywood career. The prudes and the Bible-belt censors were still in command and maybe even fiercer now with some sixth sense that the rules might soon be changing. Brodsky and Weiss write about serious and justified commercial hysteria. Described as "this cancer," the affair could wreck the movie: the churches and their congregations could boycott it. Elizabeth Taylor had only just survived the consequences of her marriage to Eddie Fisher (the husband of her best friend and America's sweetheart!) by "dying" four times. Now here she was again after a married man with children . . . and there were her own children . . . and the newly adopted Maria, the crippled child whom she and Fisher had taken up.

The truth seems to be that the two of them fell for each other violently. At different speeds: stop-go: now a retreat, now a headlong charge: gradually—and then suddenly.

Elizabeth loved Burton's fun in drinking—Burton's Bar was of course in full spate in Rome as in New York and when Burton tricked Eddie Fisher (who was trying to control Elizabeth's own drinking) by switching full glasses for empty ones, she said, "I love this man." Burton began to be fascinated by her power—Pat Tunder left a couple of days after St. David's Day. He was genuinely and increasingly impressed by Elizabeth's screen talent. And they giggled a lot together.

It began to gather pace. Sybil left Rome temporarily for London with the children and when Richard learned of this he "went pale" and took a frightened-looking Elizabeth to her dressing room to tell her that the game was up. But a week later they were together again. Burton was now in deep.

His friends began to issue very heavy warnings about hurting Sybil, leaving her with one child, Kate, whom he adored and was adored by and the other, Jessica, who was now discovered to be schizophrenic and autistic. She would never speak and Burton was devastated. She would need special care all her life and he would provide it, but she would never know a minute's "normality." He blamed himself. One of Sybil's few quoted remarks for this period was that the paparazzi were so devouring, groping at the windows, prowling about the house day and night, that Jessica screamed in terror at them. So had his affair toppled the child into an eternal fastness of horror? Guilt stalked him forever after.

Fisher fought his corner clumsily but hard. He rushed to Elizabeth's bedside for what the Brodsky and Weiss department called a sudden attack of "food poisoning" (to the alarm and fury of the woman who ran the restaurant in which Elizabeth had eaten) and there was a reconciliation. It had been a suicide attempt. She had been determined to prove to Burton how much she loved him. The restaurant received a public apology. But when, a little later in New

York, Fisher asked his wife on the telephone to assure him of her love, she refused. Elizabeth prided herself on her truth-telling. He wanted publicly to prove he was a man. He had called in reporters to record this phone call. They did.

Later Sybil also made an attempt on her life. Like Elizabeth, it was with pills. It was in Céligny. Richard was in Gstaad. Ifor coped with everything. At this moment she fled to Philip for help. He came down firmly on her side, but Richard—now isolated and deeply disturbed—blew him out of the water. Even Philip. He would not speak to him again for more than two years. It was that serious.

And everywhere the paparazzi. Gossip spreading like fallout from an atmospheric test. When Richard and Elizabeth tried to sneak away for the day they were discovered, harassed, snapped and driven back to base. The effect of the pressure on their behaviour was, understandably, bad. Burton, the forever "good guy" on the set, the man who was as cool as Gable, became irritable and nervy. Elizabeth tormented the publicists by giving them no help, no cover at all. She was after Burton.

But was he after her? In love with her, yes, and wildly intoxicated. Yet he was still telling friends he could handle it, still convincing himself and fewer and fewer others that once the film was over the affair with the leading lady would end as it had done so many times before. He would never have told Sybil in bed what Kitty Kelley says that Taylor told Fisher. When Eddie asked her if she really loved Burton she said (softly) yes. Not so softly she brought Burton back to their Roman villa and answered yes again and again in front of Fisher while Burton drank the man's brandy. Burton never took Elizabeth anywhere near his own villa although, earlier in the movie, in the quiet days of Rex Harrison and Caesar, the Burtons, the Fishers and others had enjoyed the occasional dinner, met at a party. At one of the early ones Sybil saw Richard looking intently at Elizabeth and thought: "Hello." But he would never leave her. Not Syb. All his friends always said that; he himself said that: "Couldn't leave Syb." Everybody knew that. It was part of the Agreement. He was on lease. The freehold was hers.

Now Sybil knew she was badly threatened. She called up her family. Emlyn Williams flew out from London—"at my own expense" he said—to put the case for a "nice little affair" between Antony and Cleopatra. Elizabeth was not amused. Thinking she was out of hearing he remarked that she walked "like a chorus girl."

(Later he remembered that he himself had married a chorus girl.) Williams's observation echoes several other stories—of Elizabeth putting on a blonde wig and, wrapped only in a towel, rushing into Richard's dressing room while he was in the shower: "How much do you charge?" was his question when he saw her. Sexual fun and games were well under way and sexual obsession was not too far off. He told Williams in Welsh, *"Dwi am broidi'r eneth ma"*—"I am going to marry this girl." It is the first evidence we have of his new and totally unexpected seriousness.

His acting pals in theatrical London thought he was off his head, setting up with a monster, making a terrible error. He ignored them. Indeed, at a certain time, opposition seems to have steadied him and cleared his mind. Stanley Baker—the old fellow miner's son from the Valleys of Wales and the bare theatrical boards and broads of England they had romped through together—also tried. He too was ignored.

So, most importantly, was Ifor. Ifor was four square for Sybil and the children. Ifor spoke for the family and the family "rued the day," said Cis, "when he met Elizabeth." Ifor had always been seen to be in charge. Now the reality broke through. Richard was his own man and always had been. The family, even Ifor, were a sincerely cherished, even over-cherished, part of his past; but he stood apart from them. It was reported that he and Ifor came to blows. Ifor and Gwen left Rome with Sybil and the children.

Yet still Burton would not fully commit. The agreement seemed to be that Sybil would keep out of the way until the picture was over and then they would get together again. Friends thought that too. Harder-nosed gamblers on the film set put their money on Liz. Richard and Sybil gave bland interviews swearing eternal devotion and laughing it all off. Elizabeth went wild.

The lines were feeding the parts. When Elizabeth had to go mad—as Cleopatra—at the news that Antony had married the sister of Octavius, it was reported that she cried "Sybil!" as she slashed the set to ribbons. Mankiewicz, seeing that he could not control it, wisely tried to ride it and was accused of putting in lines which were deliberately ambiguous. Said Cleopatra: "To have waited so long, to know so suddenly, it hurts." Said Antony: "Everything that I want to hold or love or have or be is here with me now." And: "Without you, Antony," she says, "this is not a world I want to live in." The studio quailed. Mankiewicz called "Cut!" several times but their embrace went on. "You make me feel like an intruder," he said.

Burton was fighting for his life: his old life. One of his characteristics as a stage actor was his need to create a space around himself. He tried to create a space at this time. In the middle of the maelstrom, he isolated himself. Another characteristic was the capacity—which must have drawn on every power he had—suddenly to *make* himself leap into another world: *make* himself into a great classical actor with a ridiculously meagre amount of training; *make* himself change that rough coal valley common voice into a sound which can still lift the hairs on the back of your neck and please constantly with its intelligence; *make* himself a star rugby player although, in that league, too light and weak-boned; *make* himself into a quite awesomely big drinker despite the heavy tax it made: on it went. In every area of his life, save when he was sitting down with a book, privately pottering at the typewriter, or possibly, at ease with Sybil, Burton was someone who had to *make, invent* himself. "He came out of nowhere," said Gielgud. Now those early, defining models were left way behind, and their substitutes, Ifor and Emlyn, Sybil and Gwen, were ordered away. He was making a new man of himself.

What he was doing was pitting everything he had gained against the gamble of a life with Elizabeth Taylor. The sounds of confused interviews, painful confrontation, raw upset over the next two years were the sounds of roots being ripped out screaming. He had made his life and himself, his family and his career into all that he wanted and more than he had dreamed of; indeed he lived inside old adolescent dreams of desire and wonderful sexual independence. Elizabeth Taylor would destroy that.

Like Antony, he would have to give up everything.

He knew that very well and yet *"Dwi am briodi'r eneth ma"*— "I am going to marry that girl." Said—for the first time—in Welsh.

In several accounts of this time it had been suggested that Burton was cynical. That he was knocked out by Taylor's stardom and saw the association with her as a very useful leg-up. There was a partial truth in that at the outset. One of the few accounts we have of Sybil at the time is to the effect that it would all blow over and they'd end up a million dollars richer. Burton, like every survivor in that completely bizarre, now sentimental, now cruel industry, had to fight his corner at all times. He knew that playing between Rex

Harrison and Elizabeth Taylor in a mega-movie directed by Joe Mankiewicz would up his fee. That was one of the reasons he wanted to do it. It was the celluloid equivalent of playing Young Hal at Stratford, or Coriolanus at the Old Vic. It was perfect. An epic subject, great stars, fine director. Lots of publicity and, bonus on bonus, an excellently realised part.

But to say that he went for Taylor because of her stardom is to underestimate him. Burton, remember, in his complete appearance of self-confidence, "You know me, I go my own way," and with that innate sense of equality and the experience, usually, of superiority, had known the greatest stars in London, Gielgud and Olivier, and from the first moment he got off the plane in Los Angeles, the Hollywood top set accepted that he was one of them.

He was fascinated by her contract. Every actor in the world was fascinated by this first $1,000,000 deal. With its imperious demands for penthouses and commissaries and nannies and all the court of a tsarina—it revealed to him a tough, sod-them, diamond-hard element in Taylor he had never suspected. Welsh Jenkins had come to Hollywood and eventually found out that it was mafia, it was street crime and it was slush: he had coped well. But Taylor had been fed and bred there and he now realised what a major operator that had made her. She was the queen of those mean streets. He knew how tough it was to get your way, the gamble with your career and even yourself. The contract was the equivalent of her diary. Was she tough!

And her power on the set intrigued him—not because he had not seen it before in others: but because it was expressed through this painted sugar doll. He began to discover a unique woman and he scented that she had never been discovered before: she was his true America and, he sensed, unexplored. As an interesting, beguiling woman, she was virgin territory. He scented also that to go for her it would be necessary to slough off the selves which had taken so much will and fury to get. He would indeed have to keep on the armour of Antony, the man who lost everything for love of the woman he knew could destroy him.

Still in Rome, the filming going on despite threats from the boardroom that it ought to be closed down and rumours gathering like cavalry about to charge on a titillated world, Burton was in torment. A man who had such a compelling debt to his family that he had regenerated it was called on to abandon his family: not only Syb but Kate, the bright child he adored and Jessica, the afflicted child who set off morbid fears about "bad blood" and opened wide the sluice gates of guilt. The struggle was between Kate and Liz, he was to write: the daughter of reality and the woman of fantasy.

None of this is unusual: hundreds of thousands of men who have quit families will recognise the portrait. Perhaps in Burton's case it was intensified because of the central and essential place he had always claimed for the family—but that too is not uncommon.

What is rarer is the way it had to be played out in public and the absolute nature of the choice which he sensed before him: and what is rarest of all is the Elizabeth Taylor factor. What did she represent?

Sexual lust: there can be no question of that. And all the degrees of sensual appreciation, a tactile paradise. Fun—a fellow boozer, joker, sport, anarchist; a several-layered personality who found no trouble in switching from one to the other and whose "gift" like his own was unaccountable. Above all, a mystery and an adventure. He had everything he wanted in life: now he could have everything he imagined. Yet he could not imagine what life would be like with Taylor. She was all the Sirens and also the princess who laid down the challenge. He was hypnotised by her.

And she, openly, by him. It was impossible for hardened observers to distinguish between them. Alan Jay Lerner spoke of seeing them and their relating a dream they had shared: of a boat capsizing, each, in panic, looking for the other; waking up out of the shared nightmare. They were, he concluded, deeply bound together. Hollis Alpert of the *Saturday Review* gained an interview with them and saw them as a married couple, relaxed, even bored, overwhelmingly normal—and this when the hysteria of the press and the pressure of their lives was pounding them like cannon night and day. They had become a unit, a republic of two, increasingly a law and a state on their own.

She pointed out a diamond in Bulgari's in Rome. He bought it for her. (Eddie Fisher had assured the world that she could be kept happy for up to four days if you bought her a diamond. Mike Todd bought her diamonds as doting fathers buy chocolate for children.) It cost $150,000. Burton forked out. In its own crude way it was the fee of recognition that he was prepared to cross over into another world. For Sybil, at Elizabeth's urging, he also bought a piece of jewellery, at a quarter the price. "I introduced her to beer," he said. "She introduced me to Bulgari's."

Having banished from Rome all who could help him, Burton tried to keep the cap on the volcano. With all his might he wanted it to be just another affair. There is evidence from Burton's later interviews that Elizabeth, too, was—or said she was—willing to give it up so as not to hurt Sybil, Kate, Jessica, not to mention her own families. They kept up the pretence. But one night, hunted, penned in, rent by frustrations, "I just got fed up with everyone telling us to be discreet," said Burton. "I said to Liz, 'Fuck it, let's go out to fucking Alfredo's and have some fucking fettuccine.' " The prey was on the street.

Alfredo's on the Via Veneto was the paparazzi's playground. The photographs flashed around the globe faster than the satellites. "Le Scandale" went public. It was now on the market, a stock to be quoted on all exchanges. "It's an insane asylum here," wrote Brodsky.

Taylor made majestic promises of abdication should he want her to, of anonymity, poverty, serfdom. She would stop acting; stay at home; sit in the stalls at the Old Vic for ever and just watch him. Burton, plagued to death by his own doubts and the flattering fury of her determination, did not buckle. The film would end and so would the affair. Fox talked of "the crisis." Mankiewicz was convinced that Burton was giving one of the great screen performances of the decade. The paparazzi went ape. The Vatican fired a warning shot, as did the spokespersons for American morality. Fox drew up plans to sue.

Again, according to Burton later, they agreed that they would part. Too many people had been hurt, too many would be hurt. On the surface Elizabeth Taylor stood to lose far less than Burton but that was not how she saw it. He had become the centre of her life and she had never been as balked, never been as held off, never had to bend the knee in this way. Yet, she agreed, Sybil must not be harmed.

They went to Ischia for the sea-battle scenes, arriving in a helicopter and taking adjacent suites in the prime hotel. A successful producer took them out for lunch on his yacht and placed hidden cameras to capture the moment. Taylor, of course, cinema's child, nosed them out. Burton, quite rightly, went for their host. But everybody wanted a piece of the great romance. To be away from the photographers and reporters, they had to take measures—helicopters, ostentatious disguises—or go to places—bugged yachts, high-security parties—which brought them yet more publicity.

Sybil waited: and not in vain it seemed.

When Taylor's filming ended she spent the last night on Ischia with an ambulance on standby outside. It was neurotic; it was absurd; it was rotten with self-indulgence; but it was serious. Both these totems of self had been deeply bitten by the poison of their mutual attraction: Taylor then swore she would go away for ever.

They were together again in a few weeks and spent time with Rex Harrison and Rachel Roberts at Portofino. Then Burton's filming ended too and they parted. She wrote him a letter saying that they had to stop; they had hurt too many people.

Both of them to Switzerland. He to Céligny where Sybil and the children, Ifor and Gwen, the family, were waiting at Le Pays de Galles. He had come home. But it was a grim exhausted hearth.

Elizabeth to Gstaad in order, she said, to be near her children at school in Switzerland. She phoned a wrecked and unmanned Eddie Fisher, kept him, just, in play.

She was waiting. She would live in the cheapest flat to be with him. She would surrender anything for him: pride, career. She would be there when he wanted her. Waiting eternally. The Sleeping Princess.

Céligny to Gstaad is about eighty-five twisting Alpine miles.

After a few weeks they began seeing each other.

Céligny was now the grim vault of guilt. Gstaad with Elizabeth and the lovely Liza—Mike Todd's daughter—a pleasure dome in the clouds.

Both were being drawn in. Was she the spider patiently constructing the sexual web in the fairy mountains of Gstaad, spinning out lines to Céligny beside Lake Geneva below? Had he hypnotised her, charmed her to such a degree that she did what she had never done before: "I was there when he wanted me," she said. They seem to have made serious efforts to behave "well," to be "decent" to those who would be hurt. They saw that what concerned and delighted them would wound and even destroy others. But as Cis had said of Rich—that "I couldn't help myself"—so here, from all the evidence, by now, it seemed, they couldn't help themselves. The sincerity and strength of the passion, despite their serious attempts to control it, brake it, divert it, convinced those closest, even those most disapproving, that it had gone way beyond sexual games, career tactics, or fun on the set. They needed each other badly now and nothing less would do. Who telephoned? Some say her. Who arranged lunch? Some say him.

Cars racing through the autumn night Alps—one more meeting, one more betrayal.

By now they were possessed by each other. "Like Romeo and Juliet," a greeting card would soon say in America, "like Antony and Cleopatra, like Liz and Dick—Love is forever." Burton was on his way to another, a dangerous intoxicating world.

13
"No More Marriages"

When Burton began his move towards Taylor, he was leaving the well-built fortress of his adult ambitions to go back into the no man's land of adolescent dreams. He had arrived at Céligny with meagre resources but in five years built up the total security he craved: *Camelot* cemented it, *Cleopatra* gave him an extra wall. He had his first child, Kate, a total, proud delight. With Sybil he had survived many of his crazy years. Ifor and Gwen were just down the garden in the chalet. There was money for the brothers and sisters in Wales. Broadway had been breached and Hollywood was still interested. Moreover, although he was regarded in London by his contemporaries as a rascal and man to shake your head over, he was still wanted by the best of the day. He was not yet a renegade. The classical stage was open to him: the best parts were on offer, the best directors courted him. He had everything he had ever wanted.

Elizabeth Taylor redrew the maps of his ambition and of his fantasies. Most importantly, she teased him out of the fortress, down on to the plains where he would have to reinvent himself again and fight for his life in new battles, new wars. Reluctantly, angrily, he came to see that he wanted the risk as much as he wanted the woman. He would leave everything for her; or did he leave "everything" for himself? Boredom was always a curse and security could be seen as a prison cell.

Was it a Faustian deal? Did he sell his undoubted talent for fame, wealth and the love of "the world's most beautiful woman"? And was it that which made so much of his later life so agonising, some of his later work so depressingly bad, and his death so premature? There is a sense in which all this is true. There was also the extra dimension of his knowing the end as he set out at the beginning. Certainly his London pals told him to "beware," she would "eat him up," she was a "monster." This was not just cocktail party chatter. People *can* be destroyed; talent *can* be corrupted; there *are* monsters who swallow up the personalities of others. Perhaps those in showbusiness and the theatre are more vivid in expressing their understanding of it, but it happens all the time and everywhere. People can take on too much or the wrong struggle and, at first unaware of this, soon be wounded, even annihilated. Burton was aware that she might do this to him.

But those who most firmly warned him of this and those he most surely trusted—Ifor, Emlyn, Philip, Stanley Baker and, one assumes, Sybil—he now avoided. He wanted to be alone. Perhaps he never was to be so alone.

Was he doing it for wealth? In the event he gave up *all* he had earned over ten careful and chancy years and came to Taylor as beggared as a bankrupt. He could have had no idea then of their future joint earning capacity; nor was he the sort of man to live off her wealth (which anyway, at that time, despite the paper millions in *Cleopatra*, was draining away in debts and extravagances). He *gave up* wealth for her. And fame? Yes, she had a most powerful press and movie fame. But for Burton, fame was Dylan Thomas; fame was Evelyn Waugh; fame was writing finely and movingly and brilliantly. Movie fame was dandy but not in the same league. Not even Elizabeth's.

It was the woman herself who finally drew him out, the mystery and, as he saw it, the wonderful undiscovered country of Elizabeth Taylor which drew him on. But it was his own curiosity and sense of adventure which kept him there. If it was a Faustian deal—and it is that which has given his life such a mythic shape—it was his own adaptation of it. Less crude, perhaps, less obvious. And yet, as the consequences took shape, as the Burton–Taylor show got under way and developed, then paradoxically it did grow more and more like the old story of the man who sold his soul for the secret of great wealth and fame. The part was waiting for him. "I am Faustus," he said—later.

All this was in the future, though, as the two of them began the long and wounding road to divorce and marriage.

Curiously, although there are several contemporaries who will point out the attraction which Burton held for Taylor, fewer see what she held for him outside the glitz. Yet in everything he wrote and in all we can observe, they seem to dovetail and join in remarkable equality. The main distinction 'was that while she was prone to obsessive love, he was not: he was capable of ''falling'' for someone privately—Claire Bloom—even foolishly—Susan Strasberg—and certainly flauntingly—Pat Tunder—and for fun, for the hell of it—a cast of hundreds. But the obsessive character, the all but suffocating character of Elizabeth Taylor's addiction (at first) to all her husbands was beyond him. He had never totally ''lost himself'' in anyone else. Nor had he experienced the battery of assault that Taylor brought to bear. On both these counts, therefore, it seems to me that the long and slow path he took to divorce was a double testing. Of her—was this no more than another infatuation à la Hilton or even the stronger bond that held her for some years to Michael Wilding; was it as much if not more than Mike Todd? And of himself—did he *really* feel like this—once he had peeled away the Roman carnival, the diamonds and the paparazzi, the excitement of deception and the aphrodisiac of publicity? Burton, knowing well that the stakes were the highest he had ever played for, knowing that he would be giving up everything he had so fiercely built up, took his time and waited to see if the obsession would wear away.

Meanwhile they seemed made for each other, as perfect opposites can be. Elizabeth Taylor was the ultimate Feminine—pampered almost from birth, told that the sweetness of a smile, the touch of an eyebrow, the lie of the hair, the curve of a waist, the body, the face, the Thing she was would bring the world to her feet. In terms of attention, success, admiration, money and all she saw around her, it had done so. Only Royalty or one or two others who got their fame at second hand could out-match Taylor and the select few who had become the young tsarinas of Hollywood and its empire of celluloid. She knew that her body was a tabernacle, her reputation a shrine.

Burton loved all that, was ravished by it and loved to ravish in return. All the whispers are that they could not take their hands and everything else off each other in the early years. But for him the body was a sham. His own was pocked, banged about, a receptacle for abuse through alcohol and nicotine and "a joke: strong men collapse in tears of laughter when they see me stripped for action." He hated stripping for action. His marvellous looks were a fluke, no more to be cosseted than the equally mysterious fluke of his talent. Yet each was intrigued by the other's difference. It was a superficial example of the ways in which they found new territory in each other.

At its simplest, he was a macho rugby-playing Welsh working-class hero of whom it was demanded that he be *hard*. She was an utterly feminine classless Hollywood starlet, star, megastar of whom it was demanded that she be utterly *yielding*. He seemed independent, although he could be as dependent as a leaf on a tree. She, entirely dependent, although she could be as tough as granite.

The "attraction of opposites"—the fascination with what was different—spiralled on. He was soundly educated and although he had a tendency to stick loyally to the same score of familiar poets, he was constantly diving into bookshops, scanning the waterfront of print. She had been weaned on gravy gossip which in comparison seemed thin and insubstantial before his starchy intellectualism, his relish of eloquence and love for the polysyllable. She longed for an education and Burton's first part on the school stage had been Professor Higgins. He loved to teach as much as to learn. Yet her streetwise experience and cunning far outboxed him. For every plus there seemed to be a satisfying minus, an equilibrium.

She was bred in movies, he clove to the stage. She knew that a look, a silence, a gesture could carry all the impact she wanted. He saw words as the only certain communication. He seemed rooted in a race, a place, a family, a culture, a language, a time, a deep and rich seam. She, like some fairy thing fabricated out of candyfloss fantasy, floating on a tide of publicity, attached and rooted to nothing more than the fickle desires of the audience.

He was punctual, puritanically tidy. She appeared to be incapable of punctuality and slovenly, the clothes stopped where they dropped. He was domestic. She was a gypsy. He was careless about his choice of parts. To her such decisions were given the thought that presidents give to a NATO treaty. He was a cheerful bar-room boaster; she punctilious for the truth.

They were in awe of each other's virtues: delighted with each other's shortcomings.

And there were as many points at which they coincided. Both drank and loved the intoxication which came from it. She was foul-mouthed and he, from calling a spade a spade began, it was noticed, to call a f...ing spade a f...ing spade. Meanwhile her English accent grew stronger.

Both loved sex and made no secret of it and, when they met, were in good shape. Neither was fussy about money. In what can be called "the realities" there was much common ground.

Both were thought to be astoundingly beautiful and both had the cross-sexual potency. Elizabeth Taylor was adored by women as well as men, Burton by men as well as women. After years of observing the effect of the phenomenon of their mere looks, both were sharply aware of the impact they made and knew the pain and the strain of wearing that mask.

More importantly, Burton and Taylor knew what it was to be not only exceptional but even rather freakish. As he himself had said to Anthony Quayle, "I have this knack." His looks, his "knack," the eternally regenerative force of his will—all that came from a mysterious source best left unexplored but it had launched him from Pontrhydyfen to Rome, from the boil-stricken virgin of a haberdasher's assistant to the millionaire lover of "the most beautiful woman in the world." She had led a life at least equal in its singularity, schooled and cosseted as only great figures of Royalty or sacrificial victims had been in the past, plucked out for her uniqueness and manufactured to be a common icon, disciplined and spoiled way beyond normality. Strange, in some ways unreal creatures, Burton and Taylor recognised twin souls.

In even deeper ways too, they knew the lust and envy of those around them, the beat of the public and the unreliable call of fame. They knew about being isolated and wanting never to be alone, constantly to be reassured, through sex, through a sympathetic entourage. They knew that such a degree of exposure and envied fame is hard to tolerate especially when it is not institutionalised like Royalty or pegged to outstanding wealth and breeding, but dependent entirely on performance. They had always to be giving parallel performances: and that which they gave off-screen for the public was the most dangerous and the most demanding.

But both were at a stage to want what was most dangerous and demanding. Taylor did not want just another husband. She wanted Burton for ever and was prepared to abase herself to get him. The suicide attempt was serious. On the last night of filming an ambulance had indeed stood by. She would publicly be his *mistress*— with all the humiliation that word meant for her at that time—and, more, she would simply "*be there*." At his pleasure.

He was quietly, slowly, very slowly, to cast off the life he had made at such expense of spirit and fury. To exile friends, to abandon all real hope of the London stage, to ignore, even turn his back on, the pleas of Ifor and finally Cis.

That hard crystal calculating centre, a compound of "genius," according to Professor Nevill Coghill, "carelessness" according to an equally admiring Gielgud, and the unaccountable selfness, "I go my own way, luv," had been melted by Elizabeth Taylor. She had got to the devil in him and now she worked on it.

And her vehement passion had equally been bent to order by him. He had taken possession of her. She was fascinated by his fascination with her. She was literally prepared to lay down her life for him or, harder for her, simply wait until and on whatever terms he wanted her. She would be the Sleeping Princess to be awakened only by *his* kiss.

And inside the tumult of the next two years, which Burton has referred to as "a war," which stunned both of them with the force of public attention so that at times they were like prisoners in the spotlights, inside all that was a mutual feeling of adventure and a perilous attraction to the high risk of it all. Every obstacle was a goad. Every sensible conversation which ended in a sensible parting took them one step nearer the fire that both of them longed to play with. Every prospect of destruction and chaos was alluring. Both were Faustus—they had made a compact. Out there, together, was a life to be seized. What would it be?

For the next two years until the divorces came through it was life on the run, life in a jitter, two lives for Burton some of the time, a life roasted in searchlights, lives which seemed the laboratory of contemporary morality. It would have killed most people. Burton had his drinking. Elizabeth had that inexplicable vacuum of essential power. Accumulations of stress—severe illness, divorce, death of friends, domestic uproar, more illness, which would debilitate most people and cripple some—she sawed through them like a diamond cutter through stone. When Mike Todd was killed, for instance, her howling grief was heard over Beverly Hills, her cry that she wished to go with him, her frenzy of mourning: and yet a few days later she went back to the set and completed *Cat On A Hot Tin Roof*. Then took Eddie Fisher from her best girl friend. Then "almost died" four times. Then took on Cleopatra and Rome. No wonder the thousands of Roman extras cried "LEEZ! LEEZ!" instead of "Cleopatra!" when she did her triumphant entry. She waved, of course, and cried and the mob roared again. "Home wrecker!" they shouted in the streets, but she was still Queen of the Streets. The furore they created in the press—sometimes whimpering with rage at its own thraldom to their notoriety—resembled and, in quantity, outreached the Duke and Duchess of Windsor's saga. Taylor and Burton, Burton and Taylor became the licentious Royalty of the sexy Sixties.

After their meetings in Switzerland it was next stop Paris where Burton did a recording for BBC Radio (for a record-breaking £150) and Elizabeth Taylor did some work on *Cleopatra*. They stayed at the Lancaster Hotel. They were playing hide and seek with the press and at this stage "hiding" quite successfully. Burton's public statements either denied he was leaving Sybil or denied he would marry Elizabeth. She gave fewer, sharper statements. Sybil sent out breezy signals from Céligny: Richard was a terrible boyo but he always came home.

The fallout from *Cleopatra* was still there in that autumn of 1964. Whom could they trust? Servants had hidden cameras; a leading producer had invited them to lunch and run a camera on them from behind a closed door; there was talk of pirate private tapes, of intimate conversations going the rounds and the price for a naughty or nasty pic of Burton and Taylor drew in the hungriest and luckiest photo-pornographers. Then there were the lawsuits. Fox were suing the stars, the stars counter-sued, the lawyers blessed the movies.

Zanuck had a massive go at Taylor and Burton. He had re-inherited Fox after the collapse of Skouras—who had lost the board-room battle—and was taking personal control of everything. With *The Longest Day* on its way (in which Burton played another military role with his usual exemplary efficiency) Zanuck turned his guns on *Cleopatra*: and Antony. He came in heavily and legalistically. They heard Zanuck's lawyers out. Heard how their conduct had prejudiced the potential sales of the film. And indeed there were worries. In the US Congress, Representative Iris Blitch introduced a bill to have Burton and Taylor banned from entering the USA. *Il Tempo* called Taylor "this vamp who destroys families and sucks on husbands like a praying mantis." The Vatican Radio (naming no names) said that publicity given to recent marital scandals and divorces "endangers the moral health of society." This was very serious stuff. The American market was composed of many many Catholics: global markets too could be threatened. And Hollywood itself—founded on the idealisation of a Jewish American wholesome family life—could join in a fit of moral fervour and disown its sick child. Fox seemed a loser anyway. Elizabeth Taylor felt that she was not loved. "I will never go back to America," she said helpfully. "I hate America and America hates me."

And then *L'Osservatore della Domenica*, the Vatican City's weekly, weighed in with a planted letter naming Elizabeth Taylor directly: "If your marriage is dead, we must say, according to Roman usage, it was killed dead. The trouble is, my lady, you are killing too many . . . Where will you finish? In erotic vagrancy? And your poor children . . ." Headlines all over the USA; editorials; on TV; radio: "erotic vagrancy." Was this a titillation or a lure? In 1962 no one could be sure and the money was on the moral majority. As Louella Parsons wrote: "It ought to have killed them."

So Zanuck's lawyers had real worries and possibly a case. Again, as in Hollywood, Burton was there for his own defence and when the Zanuck–Fox case had been outlined he pointed out that his side would now investigate and reveal the private doings of Mr. Zanuck and every other top executive. The case went away. Soon afterwards Zanuck said, "I think the Taylor–Burton association is quite constructive for our organisation." Quite, in America, meaning very. Zanuck, the shrewdest Fox, had seen what the smart gutter press had picked up and the public loved. Burton and Taylor had moved out of movies and into a self-contained media event which was unpurchasable publicity. They had moved off the showbiz pages and into the hard news. They were up there with Kennedy and Khrushchev and the Cuban missiles.

A great deal of this must be to do with that complex but possibly unfathomable bonding which occurs between a contemporary public and a contemporary icon. Hype? Glitter? Need? The flattering democratic notion that anybody could soar that high? That they were the people's choice? The power-fulfilling notion that there are man-made gods and goddesses who can be pulled down by the same hands that raised them up? The deep need for kings and queens to walk among us and the preference for those who make it for themselves rather than having it thrust upon them? And what about the persisting notion that societies always need sacrifices and choose their victims with care? All this, undoubtedly, with the sexy and thrilling twentieth-century medium of celluloid to belt them around the globe. And the power of Burton and Taylor as individuals—two fairy stories, not one; two comets, not one; two freaks of fortune, not one. And the expectation of an explosion. And there was one other most potent factor: "Le Scandale" hit the nerve of the morality of the time like a needle. Its timing was potent and perfect.

The Sixties was to pride itself on being a decade of honesty, of openness, an end to hypocrisy, an overturning of the public and domestic shams and lies (as its spokesmen/women saw it) which had corrupted marriage, sex and the family for so long. Pretence was out. The sexual cover-up was exposed in article after book after research document. Burton and Taylor, in their public adultery, seemed to be saying, "We love each other, we know we are destroying marriages and disrupting families, but love is all you need and all that counts and we are not going to hide it. Furthermore, folks, we don't give a damn." That was the message and it was as a voice from the heaven of the future to those who felt that the years and the times had suppressed them too long. "Sexual intercourse began," wrote Philip Larkin, "in 1963. Which was just too late for me." Not for others. The brave flaunted it and the Burtons were the first of the brave. Older generations may have envied them in secret; younger generations openly applauded.

The message of open love was only half-true. They tried like anything to hide it. They—both, but Burton especially—gave an almighty damn every day of the week at the time. But it was what they *seemed* that mattered. And they never let their new public down.

Looks, fairy stories, fame, illness, drink: whatever they did was accepted as part of the pattern because they were breaking a mould. Had they tried it ten, even five, years before it would certainly have harmed them, and perhaps destroyed their careers. As most people's morality is at least ten years behind the times, they appeared to be taking the most astonishing risks. And they flaunted it.

She was the vengeful dark survivor—her only rival was the blonde angel Marilyn, the innocent victim. Taylor was the sinful executioner. On most of her publicity photographs at this time she stares almost balefully at the camera. Nothing given away. She punched Burton a lot, shouted at him, swore and called him "Taffy," "a burnt-out Welshman." "Fatty," he responded, or "my little Jewish tart." But mostly he called her "Ocean," because to him she was boundless. Yet the fights were what the legend needed and the proof came in her black eyes, cut lips, screaming matches and apparent willingness to dice with death in many ways. She was the dark lady of the press. She was fantasy's favourite rich girl. His was the dream of all poor boys in the back streets of Rio, of Naples, of Pittsburgh, of Birmingham, of any tenement in the world. It was better than any soap opera could hope to be. Who would win? Who would survive?

And how they flaunted it, even at the beginning as they stepped out not so gingerly up the Via Veneto and began their act on the public stage. Jewellery for her; a $257,000 Van Gogh from her to him (again use a multiple for current figures: thirty would be useful in the case of the Van Gogh). She took three hundred dresses with her to Rome and then sent to Paris for more. She was to give him the only present he said he wanted—a complete edition of the classic Everyman Library, five hundred volumes, all rebound in varying shades of leather. He dressed like a scruff, which men liked. She could take all day to do her hair. But most of all they got out front and did it. The audience—through the press—could not get enough. Society was changing before their very eyes and Burton and Taylor were proving it.

Burton had always been an interviewer's gift. If you use only the clippings (as distinct from a few thoughtful interviews he gave where he was clearly on his best behaviour) you can make him look seven sorts of a clot. It was a miracle he wasn't a homosexual, he would say; or, he would give five thousand pounds to the woman who would have his baby; or, Olivier had sent him a telegram: "Do you want to be a famous actor or a household name?" Both, he had replied—or had he? The bar-room boasts were the way he talked: on a stool with a few drinking pals such quips were neither here nor there and his Welsh or acting cronies would have been very disappointed had he not over-egged the pudding. That was the fun of the bars. "He was not always truthful," confessed Philip Burton. Nor did he intend to be. Except in his notebooks.

But the Welsh way was to talk it up: Celtic stories were tall stories and if your audience was daft enough to swallow it whole—so much the worse for them. He truly didn't give a damn. Which was a little tricky when you were faced with, drinking with, or on at least one vividly recorded occasion, in bed for a few days with a willing female reporter jotting down everything you said. "Every time I talk to anybody," he complained, cheerfully, "I've got to tell them my biography." If he was challenged on what he was reported to have said he would say that he had been drunk at the time and that, for him, as, he assumed, for anybody who knew what was really what, put an end to the matter. And so he stoked the fires with gunpowder: "I will marry Elizabeth," "I will never leave Sybil," "Elizabeth is like a mistress," "Richard can never leave me," (Sybil), "I will marry Richard" (Elizabeth). And then he would pop out for a drink. The boozing was prodigious but for reasons which escaped the doctors who checked him out at the time, he seemed to be walking through the furnace of alcohol unscathed. The system took everything he threw at it. Bloody Marys at ten thirty. On to the second bottle of vodka in the afternoon. If he was working, it was a different routine but, it seems, only a little less drink. Another layer was added to the story: that of the hero taunting the fires of destruction and proving himself to be indestructible.

At this time—throughout his thirties and early forties—he pushed his body through new limits of strain and abuse and yet his deep powers of full recovery seemed unimpaired. This must have been another gift, another knack. As such, it was out of his control. Therefore he would drive it, the pocked and troublesome body, until it fought back or collapsed. It was as if he saw it as a thing outside himself. Its remarkable strength meant that it withstood the punishment and demands for too long. What drove him on was the most ancient cry of all, the cry to live, to take the one life and give it all he had. This must be related to his vivid awareness of death, his obsession with its imminence. The skull beneath the flesh. It was as if he sent along his body into the lists and dared death to do its worst.

Because of "Le Scandale," Burton declared, nobody would give him a job for months. Perhaps the film world was waiting for a signal after the monster stories of the past year. Zanuck gave it. "Quite constructive" was a very hot inside tip. Anatole de Grunwald was on the phone.

De Grunwald had been persuaded by Emlyn Williams to give the young Richard Burton his first film role in *The Last Days of Dolwyn*. He now offered Richard a part in *The VIPs* from a script by Terence Rattigan, a slight comedy full of guest appearances. Sophia Loren was supposed to play opposite Richard. "Let Sophia stay in Rome," suggested Elizabeth, helpfully. She herself was in Paris with Richard: "I'll do it." For a million dollars. And Richard wanted his new price—half a million. De Grunwald anticipated the publicity furore which would surround the release of *Cleopatra*, made a great number of transatlantic calls (twenty-seven, he claimed, in one afternoon) and worked out that a fast shoot (ten weeks), a quick edit and a smart campaign could see Richard and Elizabeth out as "VIPs" about the same time as *Cleopatra* and for an eighth or tenth the cost.

They came to London. They arrived together by train and set off in separate limousines for adjoining penthouse suites in the same hotel—the Dorchester, where Elizabeth had always stayed since her days as a child star. One of its staff made all her arrangements: always. A fortnight later, Sybil and the girls slipped into town, to Hampstead. It was December. Sybil prepared for Christmas with Ifor and Gwen. "It was neither one thing nor the other," complained Elizabeth. "He wouldn't leave his family. We were all there."

The adjoining suites ("twice as expensive to hire," Burton grumbled) were a genuflection to the prevailing morality. The presence of Sybil in the Welsh camp up on the hill beside Hampstead Heath was like a task force of conscience. Burton grappled with the several lives he was now conducting.

To Elizabeth he showed the London he loved. Actor pals were hauled in—Robert Hardy, of course ("Don't hate me, Tim," she said, when they left his Chelsea house)—and writers—Rattigan, Robert Bolt—who were as delighted to meet her as she was impressed to meet and talk to them. Or, sometimes, be talked to. Yet she could always redeem herself. Not only because she was *their* screen goddess too but, most importantly, she had the wit to know and seize a chance. After one discussion about the theatre in which she had remained silent for hours, as if excommunicated, she confessed, "I know nothing about the theatre," and then threw an arm across over her forehead in a dramatic gesture, to add, "But I don't need to. I'm a Star." She was. They loved her for it.

John Morgan, left-wing journalist and intellectual, Welsh pal of Burton and shrewd observer, wrote of her at that time, "Sober, she can be a boring woman. The tedium of her conversation is noticeable. She talks about her children mainly. But when she's got a few drinks in her she becomes very lively and flirtatious. Sexually attractive? I'll say." And the "boring" woman would disappear as she worked on it. Burton was her university. "Poor Elizabeth," Burton would say, only half-mockingly, "she was educated at MGM." She was a hungry pupil. She loved his London circle, surprisingly ranged from the Marquess of Bute, whose ancestors had owned half Cardiff, to socialist scribes, from the Chelsea home of Tim Hardy to pubs where only rugby was talked and only pints were supped and women were supposed to knit together women's talk in the corner.

But there was Sybil and the forces she could range against him. Burton still loved his family although he thought that they were giving him a hard time and probably thought they were right to do so. He strongly disapproved of himself at this time. He was "maddened by guilt": he went up to Hampstead to try to repair the breach with Ifor but was reduced to standing out in Squire's Mount, bending down and shouting through the letterbox. The door remained locked. "My name is writ in water," he lamented as the vodkas went down and Elizabeth forced a boiled egg into his hand. He was being torn apart. For it was not only Sybil to whom he owed so much: it was Kate, bright Kate whom he doted on; and Jessica, sad autistic Jessica about whom he would always feel bewildered and guilty. Had his life . . . Had the press intrusions . . . had his infidelity . . . had "Le Scandale" . . . had it all wounded the child? She was very pale-skinned; black hair. The only word of hers which is recorded was uttered when Sybil took her across the Atlantic. In tears and sobbing wildly—which was not usual—the little girl kept crying out "Rich!" "Rich!" Later, when she was about six, she was to go into the hospital of the Devereux Foundation. She is still there. In 1976 Burton did the commentary for a film which explained the Foundation's work.

The Stanley Bakers took action and asked the Burtons to dinner. Richard picked up Sybil. They went to the Bakers and though Sybil looked strained, Richard seemed cheerful. Elizabeth phoned four times during the evening. Richard dropped Sybil off in Hampstead and sped down the six miles back to the Dorchester to meet "the woman I had been looking for all my life." He was experiencing emotional pain in a way which had never happened to him before save possibly in early childhood. Where was his centre now? Or then? He was having to make the hardest private decisions a husband and father can make. And he had to do it in public.

As 1963 arrived with no promises or, worse, promises all round, he was spending some days with Sybil up beside the Heath and some with Elizabeth down beside the Park. When the two paths crossed there was a crisis. He went into the Park with Sybil and the children and all Elizabeth's entourage jumped into panic for fear she would look out of the window and see them. Sybil went to dinner with Robert Hardy, who drove back to the Heath via the Park. As they passed the Dorchester, Sybil cried, "Oh, get him out! Get him out!" Right, said Tim, slewed the car around and stormed the foyer (together with his pet dog) in the not so very early hours of the morning. The management refused to put his call through and the dog peed on the foyer carpet. Hardy swept out.

Elizabeth brought *her* family into the battle—Dad, Mum, brother, the whole clan which veered so wildly between iron ambition (Mum) and deep easy-goingness (Dad). She had obeyed them, imitated them, rejected them and abandoned them but they were there whenever she needed them and over they came to join her court—or was it an army now?—of secretaries, bodyguards, hairdressers, pets, children, nanny, nurse, tutor . . .

Burton did not find it so welcoming back on his old pitch. There was a growing circle of sneerers. His tax exile, his tremendous success, and now Taylor—all this from a Welsh working-class arriviste! It was too much. "This is a man who has sold out," said one Harvey Orkin, a London-based American agent, loftily. It was a judgment nodded through by many then as now long-serving members of the court of envy. Burton lashed back but the knives were out.

Down to Wales then to see an International, stand in the crowd, yell and sing "Sospan Fach" and talk with men who knew what they were talking about. A great day—in January—but getting off the train at Paddington Station he was involved in a vicious fight with several youths and his back was damaged again. He himself dated the later serious back troubles from that brawl. Elizabeth dabbed his cuts and iced his bruises expertly. If you were in trouble she was a wonderful nurse. And her mixture of Christian Science (Mother) and Jewish Momma (by adoption) was guaranteed to make you want to get well soonest.

And *The VIPs*? Directed by Anthony Asquith from the script of a very able and applauded playwright, Rattigan, it ought to have been better. Orson Welles, Maggie Smith and Margaret Rutherford were among the cameo parts. Burton and Taylor were fine but not firing. Her mind seemed largely elsewhere and somehow she seemed awkwardly on her best behaviour. The market research team had discovered that *International Affair* had much more box-office appeal than *The VIPs*. But reluctantly bowing to the old morality, de Grunwald kept the old title. It was not a disgrace. If you make so many films some will come in as average: this was above average and nostalgia may give it more qualities. De Grunwald's financial gamble came off. The film opened a week after *Cleopatra* and cleaned up. The Burton–Taylors made about $3 million out of it. And even in a film such as *The VIPs* there are those who saw Burton's quality. David Lean said of Burton's performance in that film, "He was such a star! Saw it again the other night on television and he just leapt out at you. Marvellous! Real star quality."

Elizabeth had done the film uninsured. Lloyd's of London had been driven into despair over the insurance on *Cleopatra* and insuring her would have been a major addition to the budget. Elizabeth behaved impeccably—to show she could.

And this was England. Her birthplace. Her accent became more English. She presented a programme in London for American television ($500,000—record fee) and was criticised back home both for her intrusiveness and for the new plumminess in her voice. But she knew how to behave. Richard took over the foul language for the moment. Nor would she intrude. Richard's career came first. "I'm just a broad," she said. "I didn't know I was destroying a famous actor." London was not going to accuse her of vulgarity. She advised him to go back to Shakespeare and turned her attention to his film-making.

All the while she was nursing her hopes about *Cleopatra*—as was Burton. Both of them had been much impressed by Mankiewicz. Elizabeth thought that she would get at least an Academy Award nomination for the part—maybe another Oscar, better than the one she had from *Butterfield 8*. Burton too thought that at last he had cracked the Epic—so spoofed up and messed up by Hollywood despite all the money and research and talent thrown at it. Messages from the cutting room that Mankiewicz had been pushed aside by Zanuck, whose conception of *Cleopatra* did not include her being dominating ("I'd cut off the genitals of any woman who talked to me like that"), were not reassuring. But their hopes continued high.

Meanwhile Richard steeled himself to split with Sybil and went into *Becket*. He took a few days off drinking to write about it for an American magazine. After referring to Tennyson, T. S. Eliot and Christopher Fry—credentials firmly established!—he goes on:

> Jean Anouilh, in his version, makes no attempt to use a made-up language . . . to suggest a bygone era. He is as colloquial as last week and as coarse, when he wants to be, as the age of which he writes . . . it is obvious that Anouilh intends this play-film to take place here and now and that the theme is now and eternal, local and universal, the old old theme of the battle between Good and Evil.

He elaborates on the part he was to play:

> This battle and transformation from the temporal to the spiritual in the man Thomas Becket is as fascinating to the actor as it is to the writer and as difficult to realise. It is comparatively easy to be a red, roaring man. But it is not so easy to change into a little pale man, alone, burned by the fury of his own awful and terrible belief, moving uncertainly towards unattainable and impossible saintliness . . . He must be taciturn, spare, meagre and miserly in his dispensation of beautiful words. This is the writer's and the actor's problem with a part like Becket—to keep him as silent as possible and still interesting.

In this piece we find one of the rare times when he seems to be talking soberly about acting. More often than not he would discuss it as no fit job for a grown man; something disgusting about putting on make-up and pulling on tights or learning "tedious lines written by some boring man." Now he is a touch more considered.

> I think it is essential in any performance . . . that rapport between players should be absolute. I find it impossible

to give my best if I am forced to act with someone I cannot
admire and respect. Therefore . . . it was essential that
the man playing Becket and the man playing King Henry
should at least get on well with each other. In this case
they got on well—I give you my word—they got on very
well. They may have failed but they got on very well.

Peter O'Toole played King Henry—fresh from his triumph in David
Lean's *Lawrence Of Arabia*. Burton had seen him at the Bristol Old
Vic as Edmund in *King Lear*.

He looked like a beautiful, emaciated secretary bird . . .
his voice had a crack like a whip . . . most important of
all you couldn't take your eyes off him . . . Acting is
usually regarded as a craft and I claim it to be nothing
more except in the hands of the odd few men and women
who, once or twice in a lifetime, elevate it into something
odd and mystical and deeply disturbing. I believe Peter
O'Toole to have this strange quality.

Few actors would have been as generous of near rivals. Burton then
gives some insider gossip.

We had the reputation—ill-deserved, I must say—for terrible wildness. So our colleagues were quite surprised to
see us hold nothing but teacups for ten days. When it
became clear that the two of us did have a common rapport
I put on my best Irish accent and said, "Peter, me boy,
I think we deserve a little snifter." Then we drank for
two nights and one day. We appeared quite blasted for
the scene wherein the King puts the ring on Becket's finger
making him Chancellor of England. There was no dialogue
so that was no problem. But O'Toole had a dreadful time
putting that ring on me. It was rather like trying to thread
a needle wearing boxing gloves.

Peter Glenville was the director. Years before he had fired Burton
from *Adventure Story* in which he appeared with Paul Scofield.
Burton accepted the part of Becket "provided I don't get fired
again." His idol, Sir John Gielgud, was to play the King of France.

He is the only actor I've ever met who makes me feel
slightly uncomfortable with awe . . . In truth from my
earliest years I modelled my acting on Gielgud's though,
because of our vast differences in temperament, voice and
body, nobody has ever remarked on it.

Sir Donald Wolfit was in the film, Pamela Brown, Martita Hunt—
"big league company," noted Burton, happily.

Olivier had played Becket and later King Henry with great success
on Broadway with Anthony Quinn and he had been tipped for the
film role. It was yet another example of the several instances when
the two of them were in direct competition as equals. That in itself
is a measure of the pace Burton had set himself and the impression
he had made in such a short time.

O'Toole was the joy of it. The two of them—as can be seen in
the film—rollicked like boys let loose for the first time. Elizabeth
was enchanted by it all—the pub lunches, the champagne and
brandy, the pub crawl back to the hotel, the wonderful monologues
from Shakespeare they would throw at each other and the Celtic
bravura of stories true, false and fantastical. This was a world she
had not dreamed of. She came to the set every day and never let
Richard out of her sight, drank when he drank and still had the sense
and energy to guide him back across the broken glass of his guilt-
strewn London to the adjoining suites of the Dorchester Hotel.

In writing about *Becket* he paid the earliest of what were to be
many tributes to her.

I believe and hope Elizabeth Taylor taught me subtleties
in film-making I never knew existed and which, maddeningly, I could have discovered for myself in my previous dozen films or so, had I not the timid arrogance
and the reluctant awed belligerent refusal to learn from
great film stars. That is one of the brand marks of the
secretly envious stage actor. Among other things she
taught me the value of absolute stillness and that my very
penetrating voice need not be pitched louder than a telephone conversation. But chiefly she taught me to regard
the making of a film as exacting and as serious as playing
Shakespeare on stage.

What a change was here! It is that last sentence, I think, which counts for most. And the results were to be seen immediately. In *Becket*, despite some scenes in which the strain of separation from Sybil, the shame and the "maddening guilt" are perceptible and doused under a waterfall of alcohol, his portrayal has sequences of screen greatness. He was on his way again.

He must have felt he needed a new life or he would not at such expense have cast off the proven comforts and rewards of the old. In March 1963 he met Sybil in the foyer of the Savoy Hotel and finally told her that he wanted a separation. He had chosen Elizabeth.

Sybil called a couple of friends to help her pack and went to New York.

She had already shown her ability to be publicly independent. She had taken a flat in Brompton Square and hit the town. She became the star of the Ad Lib nightclub, she was great friends with Burt Shevelove, whose *A Funny Thing Happened On The Way To The Forum* was hitting the West End. Her circle included Snowdon, Princess Margaret, Dirk Bogarde, Rex Harrison—and she scooped the pool of old pals, the Bakers, the Williamses, Robert Hardy and his wife . . . In New York she exploded into action. Having said of Richard, "He's tied hand and foot, like so much lend-lease. I'm not going to cut the lease and when I get him back he will be two million dollars richer," she now announced a separation. But there would be no divorce, she said. Elizabeth would be denied. Richard confirmed that there would be no divorce and said that he had no plans to marry Elizabeth Taylor. "Liz and I aren't made for marriage. She's not had much luck in her love life. Apart from Mike Todd and myself, of course, she hasn't known any real men."

With that out of the way, Sybil backed a small off-Broadway theatre, opened and ran Arthur's, which became the most successful nightclub in New York, and a few years later married the leader of a band she employed there. They had a daughter, Amy, and are still married. Apart from a few off-the-cuff and brief remarks to reporters in the early days she has never talked publicly about her life with Richard Burton. When it was clear that it was all over, she said, "I'll survive it better than Rich. My family's always had more class than his."

Sybil in America gathered a great army of support, among the public—she was an instant celebrity in her own right. Her success fanned the success-greedy flame, and the film world rallied round her. Elizabeth Taylor was envied and disliked: considered much too much the pampered princess and an unforgivable marriage buster. Trail-blazing she may have been for those reaching out for the love beads which would take them through the Sixties, but the film world was still twin-bed and hypocrisy. Burton too was not entirely popular out on the West Coast. He had made it clear from his early days that he rather disdained their beloved medium and even though he had now changed, it was too late and they were not listening. He had offended producers by his independence and the list of ladies enjoyed or rejected made up a fifth column of wives and mistresses of the Hollywood mafia who had a thing or two to say about or a score to settle with Mr. Burton. He was never their man.

I find it still today among the older Hollywood community. I am sure that it was this personal antipathy which worked against his ever getting an Oscar despite being nominated seven times and seeing inferior actors get it for standing up straight. In 1969 John Wayne at least had the grace to bash down Burton's door and thrust the statuette for *True Grit* into his hands and say, "You should have this, not me." Burton was touched. He had given Hollywood a going over: they got him back. It confirmed his view of the world out there. Sybil was the heroine. "Hello, Mrs. Burton," said Joan Crawford, in an expensive store. "I admire you. You have integrity." "Thank you, Miss Crawford." "You know what integrity means?" "Yes, Miss Crawford."

It was the end of what had been a marvellous boy-girl provincial romance, beginning in cheerful, broke hopes and then gathering to a totally unanticipated climax of fame and wealth. They had travelled a long road together. Until the end, those who knew Richard well were betting that he would come back to Sybil and for some time more he was still to cling to the possibility by delaying the divorce. He should have had two wives and two families, some said—and indeed had that solution been culturally acceptable it could have worked quite well . . . with anyone but Elizabeth Taylor. She wanted Burton entirely for herself. Whatever Liz wanted, Liz got. That had been the story since *National Velvet* and it was the only story she knew. She wanted him: not today, not tomorrow; but the time would come.

There would have been no problem but for Elizabeth Taylor. She was the only woman in the world for whom he would have left Sybil

and then only after long thought and only *then* after it finally dawned
on him that for the first time in his adult life he was truly, deeply
and hopelessly in love, exhilaratingly out of control: all that the
poets had described.

Meanwhile, Burton worked on *Becket* and tried to kill the pain
in the only way he knew how—drink. Mike Maidlin was the publicist on the film. All publicists who work with the big stars are as
case-hardened as a judge in the criminal courts. But Maidlin was
awed at the drinking. He had never seen anything like it. "It was
something to behold," he said solemnly. In great detail he describes
an occasion on which Burton was finally persuaded to go on the
great *Ed Sullivan Show*: Sullivan, the man who decided on stars for
the American public and pumped life into a thousand reputations.
It was his show which made Elvis Presley famous and acceptable
and turned *Camelot* from a borderline success into a smash hit.
During this persuasion exercise, Burton and Taylor drank themselves
stupid in the foyer of the Dorchester. While reciting poetry Burton
was suddenly, violently, sick. "Oh my dear," said Taylor loudly,
jumping instantly to her feet, "I think you have a fever. You haven't
thrown the flu yet." Otto Preminger, arriving like the US Cavalry
to save the situation, was told to "Fuck off! Just fuck off!" by a
humiliated Burton. He fled and never forgot or forgave. Waiters
cleared up the mess: they were used to it in Elizabeth's room—but
this was supposed to be a safe area. There were no safe areas any
more as Burton staggered through the process of tearing his past
out of his mind. Hours late for the interview, caught flat drunk,
trying to struggle into a pair of tights (over his trousers) while an
equally drunk Taylor giggled uncontrollably, he went on the set,
insulted O'Toole, forgot where, who, what, when and they returned
to America with what they described politely as "unusable footage."
A major publicity occasion blown and he didn't even notice.

There was undoubtedly something all but insane about him at that
time. The devil was out and it was driving him mad. He gave a
lengthy interview to Kenneth Tynan which reads in part like the
ravings of D. H. Lawrence's less clear-headed heroes. Tynan interviewed him in the suite overlooking Hyde Park. At lunch, Laurence Olivier had come to their table and Burton had told Olivier
that he was going to make *Macbeth*. Olivier had wished him good
luck. *Macbeth* was the film for which Olivier could not raise funds
and it signalled the end of his ambition to make films of Shake-

speare's plays. Burton knew this. He never could resist a spat. He was a "mischief maker," as Lauren Bacall observed.

The interview ranged over "being interviewed." "Actors should keep their mouths shut and hope for the best. Mostly they're afraid to talk and for very good reasons." Drink. "I love drinking in pubs and bars and restaurants with friends about me. I can't stand the empty kind of drinking." Politics. "Essentially, of course, I'm a socialist and I always will be because I don't have the moral courage not to be." Elizabeth Taylor ("who floated in and out wearing pink lounging pyjamas and no make-up"). "She gives you a sense of danger . . . she's one of the selected few who aren't actors by our standards but if you put them on a screen they emanate something —something I frankly don't understand . . . she's a pretty girl, of course. She has wonderful eyes and a double chin and an overdeveloped chest and she's rather short in the leg." So far so sane.

It was when he talked of marriage that the lunacy became rife, the strain showing like an X-ray.

"Monogamy is absolutely imperative," he said, as, presumably, Elizabeth "floated in and out" in her pyjamas. "It's the one thing we must always abide by. The minute you go against the idea of monogamy, nothing satisfies any more . . . sexually the relationship may cease but you must never move outside it . . . you may find other solutions but you mustn't violate the idea of monogamy. If you do it destroys you . . . there's no such thing as a more fascinating girl, they're all the same and our appetites are all the same. Sex is no excuse. There is no excuse for infidelity. One of the things that annoyed me most about the cover story in *Time* magazine was that the man said I was unfaithful to my wife. I never have been, not for a moment." And, presumably, Elizabeth continued to come and go, pink pyjamas, no make-up and all . . . then he came to the kernel of his argument, which puzzled his friends and brought a mischievous Peter O'Toole, article in hand, to his dressing room. What did it mean? "All of us have been brought up on the idea that one should be absolutely faithful to one other person because of the sexual act. Right? Now the moment you go against that idea . . . you must get a little feeling of guilt. It's fascinating to do what I do which is to move outside the idea of monogamy without physically investing the other person with anything that makes me feel guilty. So I remain inviolate, untouched."

Sex, then, is utterly unimportant. Monogamy is a mystical and unbreakable bond. Those with whom he has "invested himself physically" are of no account. He is untouched by that. Monogamy remains.

It has its own logic although to class sleeping with other women as not being "unfaithful" could be said to be little more than redefining the word. However, it does reveal the depth of his attachment still to Sybil and the seriousness of the counter-forces he was throwing against Elizabeth.

How would she take it? "I'm not mad at Richard," she said, boring in as O'Toole interrogated his hungover friend on the meaning of "inviolate." "I'm in love with Richard," she said. "I'm going to marry Richard," she said. Did he have a chance?

Cleopatra was released in June while Burton was filming and Elizabeth was obliged to host a special viewing for the visiting Bolshoi Ballet. She said that after the showing she just made the Dorchester in time to vomit. It seemed to both of them that everything they had done which had been any good had landed on the cutting-room floor. Taylor was as upset for Richard who "looked like a drunken sot on a campus"—as she was for herself. The rumour that she refused to leave her suite for several days appears to be true. The reviews were not nice: possibly the worst she had ever, would ever or could ever receive. "Overweight, overbosomed, overpaid and undertalented, she set the acting profession back a decade." "Miss Taylor is monotony in a slit skirt." "She is an essentially physical creature, no depth of emotion apparent in her kohl-laden eyes, no modulation in her voice that too often rises to fishwife levels." Then they got worse. Burton, too, was slammed (although one or two of the critics spoke up for him) but he retreated into his stronghold of contempt, probably, at that stage, mocking himself for ever expecting that anything half decent would come out of the movies. Elizabeth's phone calls to the set of *Becket* were now so frantic that they interfered with the production. She needed help. She was badly shaken. Burton took action. "I will marry her," he said, at large, "no ifs, no buts." Gallantry decided the matter.

With *Becket* over and the last binge with O'Toole faithfully undertaken and a last conversation with Gielgud about the *Hamlet* they intended to do in America the following year, Burton took a few days off to show Elizabeth some life. Wales was the first stop. It was a brief and difficult encounter, but her genuine delight in the place, her willingness to please, her real interest in what went on and the fact that Richard was clearly in love with her meant that it served. By now all the brothers and sisters were moving up in the world and Richard's regular cheques, twice a year with presents an extra, were most useful. Next, Oxford to see Nevill Coghill, lunch in a pub of course, and a look rather wistfully at the place he loved so much but in which he had spent a mere six months. His terribly old-fashioned respect for "Oxford men," which he never lost, is the touching reminder, or the scar, of that grafting scholarship.

In return Elizabeth took Richard down into posh Kent to meet the Cazalets. Sheran was her old friend—she was to marry Simon Hornby in 1968: father Peter was the Queen Mother's racehorse trainer. Burton, never the snappy dresser (Taylor would have a sustained go to change that), bought a suit, professed nerves and conquered all the company in minutes. There was a lot "out there" on the social scene which they could give each other as well.

Somewhere a guest appearance in the film *What's New Pussycat?* was slotted in. "Haven't you seen me somewhere before?" asks Burton. "Give my regards to Whatsername," says O'Toole. And that's all there is of him. But it is a small pointer to what was going to grow and grow and come to fascinate him as scholarship and women and wealth fascinated him: the forces of worldwide popularity, the public power and face of success; the playing to an audience without the necessity of a theatre, a camera, a microphone; playing at being the self the public wanted and then wrong-footing them. Flirting with the image: like making faces in the mirror until you don't recognise yourself. A form of self-hypnosis, and yet also an experiment to see what you could bear and a dare to test what the "world" could actually do.

He had signed to do a film with John Huston—*The Night Of The Iguana*, based on Tennessee Williams's play—and in September they set out for Mexico City. The two Wilding boys were packed off to school in California; Liza Todd went with them; Maria, the crippled girl adopted by Elizabeth, was to remain in London with a nurse for more hip operations. Maria was, in one way, Elizabeth's proof that she could deal with a badly afflicted child. Although she had begun adoption proceedings while with Eddie Fisher, it was while "with" Burton that she concluded them and insisted on them. Perhaps in some way it was to equalise Jessica—to show that she could cope? To give Richard a child to save? To find an immediate joint body to bind them together? The power and utter obsessiveness of her love for him can never be underestimated.

At the airport in Mexico City they did not dare get off the plane because of the size of the mob waiting for them. Eventually, with confusions coming perilously close to hysteria, they made a run for it. Elizabeth was manhandled badly; Burton fought back, bare knuckles, lashing out. They refused to attend a press conference but Richard issued a statement: "This is my first visit to Mexico. I trust it shall be my last." Outside Rome it was their first real taste of the mobbings they were to receive from now on, for years, wherever they went. This expresses the notion that the stars belong to the people, that their monarchy is validated by mob adulation which expresses itself, when unrestrained, in assault. These fans are the modern Furies and those on the receiving end have every reason to be afraid: the mob wants a real piece.

Later, in Puerto Vallarta, a fishing village three hundred miles north of Acapulco, they changed their minds about Mexico and, as a consequence, forever changed Puerto Vallarta. That too was to be one of their penalties. They came to an unspoilt fishing village, loved it despite the flies and the lack of modern conveniences, loved it because of its isolation and unsanitised life and yet as soon as they bought a house and were seen to be regular visitors, it mushroomed into a Mexican St. Tropez. Those whom the gods want to destroy they first make megasuccessful.

But that was later. The early days were like all early days in a beloved place—retrospectively idyllic. The house they rented, the Casa Kimberley, had six bedrooms and, miracles, six bathrooms. And one mosquito net. Later they bought the house: buying houses became a hobby. Work was done before they arrived—all the (two) best stores in town were raided, the place was made ready for as many eventualities as could be coped with. The entourage was already well experienced in looking after Elizabeth as if she were a Maharani: now they had a Maharajah who was remarkably undemanding but on whom they insisted on lavishing so much energy and attention that he would quite often flee the house for a bit of peace and quiet. And find a bar.

Throughout this time he had the whip hand with Elizabeth. She wanted to marry. He was in no hurry. She wanted to get her man. He considered himself got and that was good enough for him. She would not relent. He was lazier than she was but he was beginning to fall ever more desperately in love with her. But he still called that one shot—the wedding ring. She devoted herself to him like an Egyptian handmaiden. Hot lunches were brought to him on the set every day and if she were late he would grumble loudly, ignoring the fact that her journey by boat and up a mountainside to the jungle location was no easy trip. She fussed over his hair. He poured a bottle of beer over it. She was never away from the filming for a day.

One reason could have been the cast. Deborah Kerr, Ava Gardner and Sue ("Lolita") Lyon were the three principal women. Burton played the fallen priest. One hundred and thirty journalists turned up at one time or another despite the limitations of one aeroplane a day and one telephone only in the local cantina. Fewer would have come for a large earthquake. Celebrity on the scale of Burton–Taylor had become a staple ingredient of the press and needed feeding. These were the new courtiers: the "stars" the new Sun King and Queen—or rather, mistress.

Burton's acting improved markedly with *Becket* and *The Night Of The Iguana*, and with one or two rubbishy exceptions was to continue on a high for the next few years. Generously he attributed it all to Elizabeth's teaching him a few tricks and convincing him of the seriousness of the medium. He would always deflect praise by expressing gratitude to others. But here it was, I think, especially unjustified.

Film, it seems, demands a confessional, opened-up response from the actor. Perhaps it was simply the sex which gave Burton his new power. Both of them loved sex. Or perhaps it was the fact that Elizabeth moved and excited him, exposed and disturbed him so strongly that the hard centre, which had always held aloof—"the canny Welshman," "I go my own way"—melted somewhat into the camera. And a great screen actor was born. His characterisation of the priest in *The Night Of The Iguana* was brilliant: moving, concise, tense, desperate, saying the Tennessee Williams lines greedily, like a man unused to such verbal nourishment, playing delicately off Deborah Kerr, twistedly off Sue Lyon and with great affectionate world weariness off Ava Gardner.

He drank a lot—even for him—towards the end of this appalling yet wonderful year: a recipe for a Burton cocktail began "First take your twenty-one Tequilas . . ." He refused to go to New York to rehearse *Hamlet*, knowing that the knives would be out and he would rather go with the play in good shape. With Gielgud, the director, in Australia, Burton near Acapulco and the producer, Alexander Cohen, in New York, it was thought sensible to open in Toronto.

Elizabeth was monitored daily by a secretary of John Huston who detailed her exotic costumes—she seems to have dressed now like Minnehaha, now like a bosomy pin-up, now like a French lady of the streets. "She's seducing me again," Burton said contentedly. The cunning secretary noticed most perceptively that Elizabeth had rolls of fat spilling over her forty bikinis. She did not note that Taylor did not give a damn. She was a star! Fat could be burned off in a week. The tactic with Richard was to keep him in her sights at every possible moment. He asked her permission to take photographs of the women in the cast "because I am afraid of you" — she would drink with him, sleep with him, feed him, pet him, listen to the repeats of Dylan Thomas. And work on the divorces.

Richard was determined that his would cost him all he had. There was a need to purge himself and also, he wanted his family to have as much of the protective element of money as he could muster. It is well substantiated that he gave Sybil everything he had so carefully and astutely clawed together since his professional career began. Apart from properties, this came to about $1,500,000. There was also the undertaking to deliver a substantial annual sum. Sybil did not want the house at Céligny in Switzerland—New York was to be her base and Switzerland included Elizabeth at Gstaad.

When he discovered that even with these round figures there was money left over he gave it away to his Welsh family and, more, to charities. What had once represented the most he could aim for became the least he could do. He presented himself for marriage to Elizabeth Taylor as a man of no wealth, no inheritance, worth what his wits and his talent would fetch him. At that precise time, after the critical debacle of Cleopatra and the critical disappointment of The VIPs, these did not seem to be worth very much. Becket and Iguana, which were to bring him the right sort of film fame, were not yet released. And he was off to play Hamlet in Canada—not a traditional money-spinner. Yet at the same time, as he said, he expected to "look after Liz," to be the Port Talbot breadwinner. "I felt it was my job to support them even though I had nothing." A new family loomed.

Elizabeth, never to be outdone, claimed that she too was broke. It is difficult to see how she could be. But the Todd estate had, apparently, been left in considerable disarray with his extravagances not yet paid for by his profits. On the other hand she had the jewels, a collection which was already beginning to vie with those of oriental potentates; she had her Impressionist paintings, helped here by her father whose guidance put together a collection worth a great deal then and a dizzying amount today; there were royalties and there were properties. Yet other people's finances, especially at the "get rich quick" end, are often chimerical though from a distance they look like safe little tropical tax havens. She chose to let it be known that she too was no heiress. It gave her parity. Perhaps it was done to spare his feelings. It also gave them both a dynamo: get out there and earn.

And yet the first thing they did was spend. Bought Casa Kimberley at Puerto Vallarta, thus earning the eternal gratitude of the Mexican Tourist Board, brought over Elizabeth's brother and his five children, her own four children, retainers, bodyguards . . .

The filming came to an end ahead of schedule and with no disruptions on the set. John Huston gave each of his principals a gold-plated gun with silver-plated bullets each of which carried one of their names—none were used—and meanwhile Elizabeth was setting about wresting a divorce from Eddie Fisher. She did it in a way that makes the blood run cold.

Fisher did not want to make it easy. He remembered the day he had telephoned to Rome from New York in front of reporters and asked her to deny the Burton rumours. Taylor prides herself on being truthful. She would not deny them. The next day the headlines jeered at him across the United States. He remembered Burton taunting him. And his wife, in bed, confessing that she loved this Welshman, and the pills she swallowed for Burton and her woundingly abrupt dismissal of himself. Fisher could think he had been used, time and again. Kept hanging about, for example, just long enough for her to secure the adoption of the crippled little Maria; pulled back to Rome whenever she needed cover; dialled in Las Vegas when the fist of Burton seemed too evidently against her. "I'm going to show her I'm a man," he kept saying; but she would not be convinced. Now he nursed his badly hurt pride—the affair had dented his popularity too: the backlash of celebrity is as intriguing a study as its full frontal effect—and he wished to show strength.

There was also a little number he was doing around the nightclubs called "Cleo the Nympho of the Nile" with Juliet Prowse—one of his new girl friends; Ann-Margret was another—kicking up a skit on "Liz." At that time the columns and clubs and bars throughout America were full of Dick 'n' Eddie 'n' Liz jokes—most at her expense—and she got to hear about it. Hence, partly, the "I hate America" declaration. But "Cleo the Nympho" struck hard. And besides, Richard, at long last, was getting a divorce. At last he was tearing himself free from the greatest rival she would ever have, a grey-haired Welshwoman who liked best of all to stay at home and chat with girl friends. It had been an epoch in the brief but action-packed history of the loves of Miss Taylor and now Eddie Fisher was taunting her and above all defying her. Whatever Elizabeth wanted—as producers who had been forced to fork out unscheduled presents knew; as other actors knew; as hairdressers and the press and multi-million-dollar executives knew—Elizabeth got.

She flayed Fisher now. She let it be known that she had never loved him, that he was merely a handy staunch while she mourned Mike Todd, that he had not really existed for her, that he was no man, that he was mean and silly and . . . furthermore she wanted *everything* from the settlement. Kitty Kelley reports that she wanted the green Rolls-Royce that *she* had given *him*! She wanted the very expensive chalet they had bought together in Gstaad. She wanted sole custody of Maria and somehow it transpired that Eddie had never been a legal partner to the adoption at all. She wanted him out of the trusts and financial pacts they had made.

Burton joined in. All he saw was a man being churlish. It was precisely the impression of dark, unbridled Jacobean vengeance, this genius of hers which entertained and intrigued him. But he also saw it more simply. It was a straight case for Welsh rugby-club morality. The man did the decent thing in those circumstances—he paid up, pushed off and shut up. "Burton deserves an Oscar for sheer gall," said a shaken Eddie Fisher. But he stood no chance.

Taylor and Burton meanwhile were sorting out their own future financial arrangements with Aaron Frosch and the files of contracts were to fill Burton's Céligny cellars. They were, at this stage, only dimly aware of their earning potential—they were to become the biggest box-office stars of the Sixties with Burton ahead of Taylor for quite a while. They were also, according to some calculations, to become among the highest income earners in the world for a few years. At this stage it was a case of securing the future in a careful

way and taking a full look at the worst case. All this was done in
Puerto Vallarta, where they built a second house connected to the
first by a bridge modelled on the Bridge of Sighs.

In December 1963, Burton finally got his divorce from Sybil and
Elizabeth instantly asked the woman who had designed her dresses
for *Cleopatra* to work on her wedding dress.

In January 1964, Fisher capitulated. By then Burton was into
rehearsals for *Hamlet*.

John Gielgud was the director—the man so many think of as the
definitive Hamlet of the century. Still today his recollection of the
experience is pinpoint sharp and most affectionate. "That sort of
celebrity is so very hard to cope with. They had to exercise the dogs
on the roof. There was a man with a machine gun in the corridor
outside their room. All very unusual and it made them very hard
to get hold of. And impossible to entertain. They always entertained you. One night I did take them out to a nice bistro—lots
of champagne. The manager wouldn't give me a bill! He said that
there had been four or five hundred people outside—in sub zero
temperatures—just waiting for a glimpse of them. So you see! But
he was wonderfully respectful to me and frightfully nice to the
company and they adored him. And her. They never pushed themselves forward. Nor did he in the part. Never vain. And it went on
to be the most enormous success, you know: broke my own record
in New York—rather upset me." He smiled and then talked about
the production.

The central idea was to do it as if it were the last run-through
before the first dress rehearsal. Not a "modern setting": a rehearsal
room with, Gielgud hoped, all the clutter and individuality which
came through in that context. It was a bold idea and Burton's hatred
of tights and dressing up dovetailed into it with great relief.

The rehearsal process was written up in *Letters From An Actor*
by William Redfield who played Guildenstern. He accentuates
Gielgud's obsession with detail and apparent reluctance to give the
cast the overview, the metaphysical pep talk, the key to the drama
that they expected. It was all "Straighten your back, do," or
"Don't play with your sword" or "Gabbled a bit there." He could
be very firm on pronouns: "Yes, John loves pronouns," said Richard, but Gielgud was bewilderingly simple on the whys and hows.
Redfield adored and admired Gielgud, as did the company, and
by every account it seems to have been a very happy one. "The

cast loved Richard," said Gielgud. "And he was very good with them."

Just how good we can see in Redfield's book. "He is a deeply educated and remarkably unselfconscious man," Redfield wrote of Burton. "He combines education with intuition to a remarkable degree. He is a brilliant actor (in fact, is he *all* actor) but he is also an enemy to vulgarity and a man at war with boredom." Redfield's perception of Burton's character is precise and convincing.

Over the weeks of rehearsal there were many stories. Gielgud's direction was hard to latch on to. There was the absurd but very real threat that the play would never be able to transfer because Burton would not be allowed in New York. As the *Washington Post* wrote: "Congressman Michael A. Feighan of Ohio strongly feels that the State Department ought to show its regard for propriety by revoking the visa issued to Mr. Richard Burton the British actor." A precursor of the move against John Lennon—and in both cases it gave the men an outlaw glamour which, ironically, was most valued in the United States itself. Nevertheless at the time it was a nasty one. And there were the mob pressures; the divorce pressures; the colossal strain which came from break-up. Through all this Burton's nerve rarely seems to have frayed. Nor did that of Elizabeth Taylor.

It was she who shuffled the actors around at the end of the day and invited them up for drinks (to the "Royal Suite"). Often had them stay on for dinner—champagne—theatre talk. Richard loved all this—Ralph Richardson anecdotes were traded in for Barrymore, Olivier was countered by Brando. Elizabeth seems to have been "possessed of a modesty and self-effacement which surprised me a great deal," wrote Redfield, ". . . I believed her softness to be genuine." Taylor, in truth, was having the time of her life. Gielgud admired and respected her. She was surrounded by real actors; she was gobbling up Shakespeare. She was Den Mother to a young American cast. She was not the star; her man was: soon to become, in her phrase, "the Frank Sinatra of Shakespeare." And she was going to be married in the morning.

Redfield checks up with Burton on some of his theatrical stories of the night before and often as not they fall apart. Burton is completely unfazed by this and it is a useful reminder. In his cups he was a story-teller and embellished wherever necessary, and expected the brighter listeners to understand the art.

Redfield's book reveals that Burton had difficulty learning the whole part well. The great monologues seem to have come easily. The spare prose—much more difficult. He became excessively nervous. Unsurprising. That sort and that level of classical acting is like top-class mountaineering or ballet. You get out of condition. The stamina to hold the centre of the stage for three and a half to four hours; the memory to hold not only your words but everyone else's; and the moves, and the sword fight and the lighting plot and the . . . Burton was out of practice. There was also the drink. This tremendous difficulty of re-entry, suddenly out there on the boards, alone in front of an audience and for *hours*—has kept many great screen actors from returning to the stage. Brando, the great young hope of the American theatre, is the most prominent example. But Burton did it. Again and again. He wanted to be up there with Olivier and Gielgud. More importantly, it interested him, drove away boredom, startled and tormented and tested him. And Shakespeare was his great love.

But he was failing. Elizabeth took action. She phoned Philip Burton whom Richard had not seen nor spoken to for two years. Philip was in New York, trying to set up an acting school and at fifty-nine about to apply for US citizenship. His unpublished manuscript records what happened.

Philip had devoted himself to Sybil and Kate and Jessica. He gave the quality of support that counts. He took Kate into the park every Sunday; he helped Sybil deal with Jessica and settle into her apartment—in the same block were Aaron Frosch (still her lawyer too) and Roddy McDowall, an old friend. He stuck by his estrangement from Richard to prove his loyalty to Sybil and although he suffered from it he did not complain.

"I foresaw trouble when I was told that Sir John Gielgud was to be the director," is his first entry in the matter of *Hamlet*. "Their conceptions of the character are contradictory." He saw *Becket* which caused him to "weep with pride." Then on Saturday, February 2nd, while having dinner with friends, he received a phone call which had been transferred from his house.

> It was Elizabeth Taylor. As I had anticipated, Richard was having trouble with Hamlet. He said I was the only one who could help him. Would I come up? . . . I was torn in my loyalties. Then Richard came on the line and that

soon settled it . . . Later I spoke to Sybil about it: she
said "Of course you must go: he needs you." I think that
incident bears testimony to the fine quality of both Elizabeth and Sybil . . .

He went to Toronto immediately. "I knew it would be an impossible
situation," Philip says today. "Gielgud would be trying to get *his*
Hamlet out of Richard." A chauffeur met and took him, by mistake,
not to the threatre, but to the hotel.

. . . at the hotel suite, after a nervous delay, Elizabeth
came out to meet me. Although it was a tentative meeting
on both sides it was a good one and it was to lead to a
warm and enduring friendship. I was to discover that her
character, values, intelligence and talent matched her famous beauty.

He went to the theatre alone. Richard thought Elizabeth would
distract him. At the interval there was a very long delay. Polonius
in a dressing gown came and led Philip backstage. "He said that
Richard was in such a state he couldn't go on without a word from
me. I gave him one, and a very strong one. Boy, did I tell him!"
   Philip disapproved of the production, made his notes and went
back to drill his son.

As usual in such circumstances, we talked for hours. I
gave him detailed comments and suggestions but my main
purpose was to restore his confidence . . . It was a great
relief to get a phone call from one of his colleagues on
Tuesday morning [Philip had been forced to return to New
York to take out his citizenship]. "He gave a wonderful
performance last night. We're all talking about it. It's put
new life in the show."

It is by any standards quite remarkable that Richard, so far along in
his career, should need so badly to call up Philip for a repeat of the
Ma Smith's sitting-room discussion. But characteristic. Burton was
always vividly aware of his roots and when in doubt or danger he
would strike back for them. Or was it that he truly trusted only very
few? The distinguishing aspect of his life with Elizabeth was that

as it went on he drifted away from those roots—too many people around him, too much money, travel, baggage, booze . . . but more importantly, I think, he came to *want* to cut off, to try "the Ocean." For Hamlet in Toronto, though, he still called up Philip, his guiding voice.

And then they were married. Bob Wilson, his super-powered black dresser, was the best man. Elizabeth arrived at Richard's side unescorted, ravishing. And very late. "She'll be late for the last bloody judgment," said Richard. She was wearing "a low-cut bright yellow chiffon gown," reports Kitty Kelley, "with the $150,000 emerald brooch Richard had given her in their *Cleopatra* days. For her birthday he had given her an emerald and diamond necklace and now for a wedding present he gave her matching emerald and diamond earrings."

He loved to deck her with jewellery. He would boast of its cost as if he were still the goggle-eyed boy from Pontrhydyfen pressing his nose to the window of some goodie shop and hoping he had enough to buy a present for Cis. Elizabeth, he was to say, was the woman he had been looking for since the time of Cis.

She had got her man. She the man-eater. He still the man who was marrying her to humour her. She was in thrall to him yet.

He was ridiculously handsome. The blue-green eyes, the sculpted face, the young but ravaged looks that swept women under his spell. His sense of tremendous force and adventure matching her softness and aura of danger. Like two prize beasts reared for prime breeding. Though that, alas, perhaps fatally for them, was not to be.

He had even bought a new suit.

He had also got drunk on the plane up to Montreal where they had at last found a Unitarian minister prepared to risk the wrath of God and his congregation by splicing through the multiple divorces. "Why's he so nervous?" asked Elizabeth of Richard. "We've been sleeping together for two years." Afterwards, she did not disappoint her fans. Here it came once again—"this marriage will last for ever."

Indeed it seemed it might. They had no idea of the quite relentless disproportionate public pressures that would be put on them. Richard's boredom seemed at bay and Elizabeth beckoned as a fathomless love, a study, a pupil, a pal. Against the odds the two of them seemed hell bent on monogamy.

He came back after a brief weekend honeymoon—on the Tuesday. "And they said it wouldn't last," he observed to Redfield.

Elizabeth now had everything she wanted: before her, she knew, was a million dollars a movie, and a new life—actors, plays, talk, interesting rows, and Richard whom she would never let out of her sight.

He was deliriously happy. Robert Misil, who played Horatio, reports that "they couldn't take their hands off each other . . . she was captivated by his poetic brilliance and he was—to the extreme—inordinately proud that he, Richard Burton, the twelfth of thirteen children born to a barmaid and a Welsh coalminer, had married the most beautiful and most famous woman in the world."

The Welsh lad had come out of the Valleys with a vengeance: the prize had been taken, the "boy from nowhere" had swept her away. He was part of a fairy tale, part of a dream.

That first night back after taking his applause from a packed and appreciative audience he turned to the wings and beckoned for Elizabeth. She had been banned from sitting in the audience because it delayed the curtain up: posses of women would come up and stare and say "but her eyes are blue."

Now she came on to centre stage. He took her hand and reached out for a line from the play. Looked around. His new reality was to be like this—a confluence of fact and fiction. None of the dramas they played in would ever hold the public as spellbound as the drama they were. It was here that he joined together the actor and the husband of Elizabeth Taylor and acknowledged that from now on the world was indeed their stage.

His voice rang out, the voice trained on the Welsh hilltops above the steel town, the voice which many thought his greatest gift: now he set himself, themselves, square to the world, Liz and Dick, Cleopatra and Antony, Taffy and Ocean: "I say, we will have no more marriages," he said. The applause rocked the theatre. It was their coronation.

PART
TWO

14
"The New Elizabethans"

At Boston's Logan Airport they were once again seriously mobbed. There were three thousand "fans." They tore at Elizabeth's hair, wrenched at her earrings, slammed her against a wall. Burton punched his way through to her. In the hotel lobby it was worse. He had thought that "once the somewhat illicit quality of our relationship" had been resolved in marriage then the public interest would dissipate. It intensified. When *Hamlet* opened in New York the police had to block off the street after the performance so that Burton, with Taylor, could walk in safety the few yards to his stretch limousine. "Why?" Burton asked of Truman Capote. "Because they're sex maniacs," said Taylor, brought up on the tough-tittie, one-liner view of the masses, "and we're sinners and freaks." Frank Sinatra swore that his bobby-soxer crowds had not been as big or as demanding.

Bodyguards were hired. Security men became part of their life. For the next five years the Burtons moved around with the protective cover of a minor head of state. It hemmed them in. But with kidnapping scares—the four children were often with them—and the mania they provoked, it was necessary. It cut them off. Soon their friends would find it all but impossible to get through to them. When they succeeded, Burton was as affable as ever but the entourage—the secretaries, hairdressers, dressers, bodyguards, nanny, tutor—was as protective as any Ottoman court. Alec Guinness describes several occasions on which messages and even presents appear not to have got through. "It was most peculiar," he says. Even the perennially loyal Philip, even the deeply admired Nevill Coghill, even Tim Hardy had the greatest difficulty penetrating what became a laager. And of course eventually the best people would cease to bother. It was all aggravated by Burton's distaste for the telephone. He hated using it. And by his drinking. But the principal cause was understandable. Out there—they were at risk.

The isolation was buttressed by the immense claims they made on each other's time and presence. Elizabeth said that she would never leave his side and appears to have made a hundred per cent success of that. She was not only on the set of *The Night Of The Iguana* every day, she was by his side in the bar every night. She was in the wings for every performance on the road with *Hamlet* and went to the Lunt-Fontanne to see the play forty times (Richard appeared a hundred and thirty-four times), each time in a different dress. The other ninety-four nights she turned up afterwards and escorted him from the stage door to the limousine. He professed his love for her from the rooftops of any newspaper column in tow. After confessing his anxiety: "What I was concerned about was whether I could stay faithful, because I had been a great womaniser—knocking off everyone there had been in sight," he moved into overdrive: "She brings me repose," he told David Lewin. "Since being with her I have never wanted another woman and I've never *had* another woman."

They bid each other up. "Richard is a very sexy man," said Elizabeth. "He's got that jungle essence that one can sense." "If you don't know what a woman such as this woman is like," said Burton, "you have missed a great deal in life." "I rely on him totally," said Elizabeth, "ask him about everything, even to say which dress do you like best. I love not being me, not being Elizabeth Taylor, but being Richard's wife." Burton lavished his hoarded vocabulary on her as freely as he was to buy her jewels. After the marriages and disasters she had been through and after the ripping away from Sybil and Kate and Jessica and Wales which had left a wound all but impossible to staunch, it *had* to be the marriage of the century. Nothing less could justify it. Both of them set to work at it with all their energy. This was to be the triumph of monogamous, sexy fame.

Their mutual absorption at first cut out everyone including the children. Paul Neshankin was a young tutor taken on at the time of

Iguana and in the entourage which went to Canada, New York, Paris, London, Bavaria, Dublin . . . What he described to Kitty Kelley was a sad world for the children. These were Michael and Christopher Wilding, on the verge of teenage, who had hopped around so many schools that they were behind and undisciplined; Liza Todd who at seven could not read; Maria, four, who could not yet speak English and whose life centred on complex hip operations. Burton wanted to send one of the boys to an English boarding school but Elizabeth wanted her family around her. Unfortunately there seems to have been very little time for them. When they take a couple of floors at the Lancaster Hotel in Paris, for instance, the tutor reports that time would go by without Burton and Taylor seeing their children and when they *did* see them it was like a Royal visit. Meanwhile an elderly governess had freedom to discipline them, he reports.

Burton was right. It was no place for children. But Taylor had her point. She wanted her family about her. Burton had just discovered the guilt but also the liberation of having no family. Taylor had found a man whose track record as a domestic Godfather was impressive. There were clashes and screaming matches from early on but Taylor described them as "exhilarating," saying they made her feel "like his intellectual equal which of course I'm not." The gypsy life—they bought several houses but rarely stayed in them for more than a few weeks—made it very awkward. Their determination to love each other to death, drink each other under the table and investigate the wonder of what the other had brought into their lives simply burned up time. The children suffered. Later Burton and Taylor took much more interest, more care. But the life they lived was never going to be ordered.

In the first year or two of marriage, they explored more fully what they had found attractive about each other during the "illicit" period. Part of the public's interest in them—mirrored in the literally thousands of articles and photographs, scores of interviews and front-page covers, dazzling successes at the box-office—was that despite the guards and the entourage, they conducted this exploration, partly, in public. And for the public? Just as they had anticipated the public mood change by their open adultery, so they anticipated that next change when the fashion was to come "upfront" and talk about your feelings. Soon they were to epitomise yet another major change of mood and fashion—the notion that hedonism was good for you, that flaunting it was fun, that material gains should be enjoyed and good luck to them. The Burtons, in the first half of the Sixties at least, *were* the action.

One of his friends, John Morgan, has said that Taylor "added five years to Richard's life." She gave him a project, diverted his boredom; fascinated him. Her belting honesty dazed him. No nuance, no treachery, no lies, no welshing: straight. Her toughness was adorable. She had no doubt that films were a business, that money was the basis of the racket, that she was a money-maker and liable to be exploited unless she fought her hardest. Whatever they offered was less than they would make out of her and so she demanded more. A present was an essential bonus as well as an investment (tax-free) as well as a childish reassurance. Usually she chose the presents herself. She had no qualms about all this. Whereas Richard was grateful and always impressed by the size of the fee, she was neither.

As for her, she loved the fact that he "paid the bills," that he did *The Times* crossword every morning and corresponded with writers, Isherwood, Spender; directors, Brook, Hall; actors, Olivier, Gielgud, all on equal terms. He was to deck her with jewels: he also bedecked her with public and private compliments. She became his willing pupil. She became his daughter—would call him Dad. She mothered him as no one but Cis had done and in *A Christmas Story*, written in 1964, he wrote (of Cis) "I knew that I had a bounden duty to protect her above all other creatures. It wasn't until thirty years later, when I saw her in another woman, that I realized I had been searching for her all my life." She was his "tart"—a word he would use with its Welsh childhood connotations, when a "tart" was the girl you took out, a slangy but not necessarily derogatory expression.

They would exchange names. He would call her Sam or Fred; she would call him Agatha. This began soon in their affair and seems to have drawn strength two years later from *Virginia Woolf* as did a great deal of the darker side of their lives. But the darker side too was attractive. He swam in this utterly present, fresh, uncluttered, sensual woman, avaricious for life, able to bite the head off a producer and cosset a sickly kitten, so armour-plated that stresses which kill people appeared to leave her undented, so easy to move and bruise that any knock made an instant mark. She bewildered and intoxicated him.

They laid claim to each other. "She wants to play Hamlet and I want to earn two million dollars a picture," said Burton. And to the tutor one night he said, "I want to be rich, rich, rich!" The notion of wealth intrigued him although when he got it he gave most of it away, often to a passing acquaintance down on his luck. It is in these years that the big trusts were set up for all the children. Regular annual cheques were organised for even more members of the family back in Wales—plus Christmas cheques—and unexpected bonuses. Elizabeth. Money. Drink. Pals were lacking at first but as his power grew—in the mid-Sixties he was called "The New Mr. Box-Office" and went into the Top Ten pullers, with a higher ranking than Elizabeth!—he brought the pals into the films with him.

At the centre of it, though, was this acute passion. Whether for reasons of potential danger or for a terrible kind of mutual interdependency, they could not be away from each other. The passion had to take the burden of their energy and all the expectation of their dreams. The miracle is that for a few years it did that.

Those years included *The Sandpiper*, *The Spy Who Came In From The Cold*, *Who's Afraid Of Virginia Woolf?*, *Doctor Faustus*, and *The Taming Of The Shrew*. They included the realisation that they would never have a child of their own: Elizabeth's previous experiences had made that too dangerous. They set up two companies which over the next eight years brought them more than fifty million dollars with royalties continuing to roar in. (And again we have to multiply that figure by five or six times to get its present-day weight—$300—400 million?) Elizabeth became a British national after a great deal of worry about reneging on her oath of allegiance to the USA. She said it was because she "liked the British the best." Others pointed out that the tax advantages at the time to a Briton living abroad were very considerable indeed.

Their entourage settled around them as a permanent feature: Elizabeth's secretary Dick Hanley and his secretary John Lee; Burton's own two secretaries, Bob Wilson, his dresser and assistant; Gianni Bozzachi, her personal photographer; his wife Claudie, one of the hairdressers; Ron Berkeley, make-up; Gaston, the French chauffeur; the tutor, the governess, the nurse for Maria and the regular bodyguard, Bobby la Salle, an ex-boxer who wore slip-on bow ties, so that he could not be throttled by his own necktie, and high-heeled pointed shoes for crowd combat. Gaston was also a help here: he had the Croix de Guerre and a black belt. The larger security force changed from location to location.

And behind the domestic entourage, of course, were the lawyers, agents, publicity men—Aaron Frosch, Valerie Douglas, John Heyman, John Springer . . . it can and does look excessive on paper. But when you tot up the size of the family and the variety of its needs; the number of moves and movies they made and the hundreds of different contracts—not to mention the demands made on skills by "the most beautiful woman in the world," then it approaches some relation to comprehensibility. For Burton, quite soon, it all became another family to which he would become almost as devoted and feel almost as responsible as he did to the brothers and sisters back in Port Talbot and Pontrhydyfen.

These then were "rich, rich, rich" years: possibly the richest of his adult life: and at the end, when everything came together, Shakespeare, Elizabeth and a film, he began his Notebooks. If there is a single theme over these early years, it is of Richard giving to Elizabeth. His love and his fascination were expressed in gifts: and the biggest of these was to her confidence as a woman and as an actress. In Hollywood she had been the beautiful broad. Now she was with the intelligent and smart set. Her confidence in herself grew. He never ceased to prime it and he did it in such a way as to make others too realise her value. He pushed her towards two of the highspots of her acting life: doing Martha in *Virginia Woolf*, and, for her own self-esteem, reading poetry with him on the New York stage.

Philip Burton was in trouble. His American Musical and Dramatic Academy was chronically short of funds. His American gamble looked doomed. Richard prepared to bail him out and suggested Elizabeth should join him. She had never appeared on stage before. Never been "live." As for reading poetry—even skilled actors come out in a rash at the thought. Shrewdly she enrolled Philip as her tutor and he coached her over several weeks. He was on stage with them—introducing the poems.

Everyone was there. Montgomery Clift, Mayor Lindsay, Carol Channing, Eunice Kennedy Shriver, Anita Loos. Seats, one hundred dollars. Elizabeth Taylor appeared in an off-the-shoulder Grecian gown, diamonds and sapphires flashing and flaunting. She never was one to sneak in. Burton began with "To His Coy Mistress"—

Marvell; then D. H. Lawrence, "The Snake." It was a well-worked-out programme. His first section ended with the St. Crispin's Day speech. Elizabeth—without a microphone on the Lunt-Fontanne stage where Richard as Hamlet had been deluged with reviews any actor would dream of—took on Thomas Hardy, "The Ruined Maid," Robert Frost, Elizabeth Barrett Browning . . . "I didn't know she was going to be this good," said Richard. Bea Lillie, sitting in front of Emlyn Williams, whispered to her companion, "If she doesn't get bad pretty soon people are going to start leaving." She didn't. They stayed.

For Act II she appeared rerobed, hair full of jewelled ornaments. They closed with the Twenty-third Psalm: she fluffed the opening. "Sorry," she said, "let me begin again. I sure screwed that one up." To her verse in English he responded with a verse in Welsh. The ovation was tremendous. Elizabeth, Liz, that dumb broad empty-head from Hollywood, superior clothespeg, jewel-hunter and husband-shopper, envied and joked about, was there bowing graciously to Le Tout Manhattan after having given them a bouquet of English literature. On her arm the man who not only got astounding reviews for his Hamlet—"Electrifying," "Brilliant," "The best-equipped actor in the English speaking world"—but from the film of *Hamlet* would take fifteen per cent of an estimated six million dollars. Fame *and* money. She had returned to her "hated" America and she had showed them. And how. While he, the rich little poor boy who never forgot how near the depressed Welsh Valleys were, had on his arm a bejewelled woman whom the world had elected as its Queen of Sex, a legend. At the party they both got splendidly drunk.

There was a lot of drink around. And massive curiosity. Part of the apocrypha reports that an enterprising couple rented the apartment below the Burtons and climbed on chairs to press glasses to the ceiling and tune in. They were rewarded with several drunken explosions and shouting matches. Taylor declared that she loved them. They could be comic. Burton was once enraged that a single anonymous person had booed his performance as Hamlet; Elizabeth, uninterruptedly watching television, was less perturbed than she ought to have been. The stresses and often quite lunatic over-sensitivity of live performance was not her experience. He put his foot through the television and cut a toe to the bone. As he suffered slightly from haemophilia, it was worrying for a while but the eavesdroppers were rewarded with curses from him and huge laughter from her.

When Burton came out of *Hamlet* after a hundred and thirty-four performances the box-office indicated he could have done a hundred and thirty-four more. They turned down two million dollars for ninety days' work in Israel and instead, at Elizabeth's insistence, agreed to do *The Sandpiper*. She had not made a movie since *The VIPs*. The reception of *Cleopatra* had scared her. Now her nerve was back—though not yet her judgment—but, as she rather unwisely said, "It's always a giggle to pick up a million dollars." Richard got half a million. Both received substantial percentages. She had her usual heavy expenses bartered down to the last hairdresser—her own costume designer and make-up artist and hairdresser. Taxes indicated it be shot in Big Sur, California, for a few weeks and then in Paris. The Lancaster Hotel braced itself.

Two events notable in Burton's life, though not headline news, occurred in New York during *Hamlet*. Firstly, Elizabeth, determined to build bridges, went out of her way to bring Emlyn Williams back into his friendship with Richard. Williams was delighted: "In Rome you met Mr. Hyde," he said, "now meet Dr. Jekyll." "I preferred Mr. Hyde," said Elizabeth the truth-teller, but the bond was reforged. She went further and flew over to New York as many of Richard's brothers and sisters (plus wives and husbands) as were available, put them up in style, took them to *Hamlet* and fussed over them. She was particularly attentive to Cis and made her a confidante. Cis praised a new pearl necklace which Elizabeth had just bought in that morning's shopping. Elizabeth agreed that it *was* pretty and, pal to pal, confessed: "It only cost seventy-five thousand dollars." Richard was now fully restored to the Welsh.

The other news can be found as a throwaway remark he made in a late interview. "Playing Hamlet last year," he recalled, "I was tearing along waving my arms and ripping out the lines when the arthritis struck me. I stopped absolutely rigid in mid-flight, one arm raised above my head. You can't imagine the pain. I reached up gingerly with one arm and pulled the other down and then I shuffled off stage sideways like an old man. Fortunately Liz knows all the doctors in the world and she got me a man who fixed me up so I missed only a couple of performances." The "weak Jenkins bones," the back which had been over-jarred in rugby football, injured again in the fight on Paddington Station, was giving a clear warning. Burton ignored it, just as he ignored every admonition about his drinking. He could cut down on it—and did —though it was hard: and as for the back it was a matter of a few walks, some table tennis: no worries. He was travelling too fast to stop for repairs.

He was bored with *Hamlet* by the time he left it. To amuse himself he had tried out several different interpretations during the run, including a homosexual Hamlet. He would also insert lines from Marlowe or in German to see if anybody noticed. It was always hard for him to sustain an interest once he had cracked a problem. He went out to conquer, did so, and was then often indifferent. Elizabeth and money and writing—they were the infinitely interesting matters.

The Sandpiper—about a married priest attracted to a bohemian woman artist whose son he takes into his school—could have been above average. Dalton Trumbo had a hand in the script. Vincente Minnelli was directing. The movie exploited his Sybil–Elizabeth conflict but need not have been the worse for that. It was, said the critics. Subsequent writers have been no kinder.

Elizabeth thought that Richard looked "beautiful and strong" in it and that when they were together on screen in a group he made "us all look better than we are." "I'm not even ashamed of what I did," she mentioned.

It is true that Burton looks wonderful—it was at this time that whole roomfuls of young matrons were reported to be "hot" for him. It is also true that he manages to get through enemy lines of dialogue with that wire-cutting voice which defies the mockery they deserve. There are worse stories and worse films. What is really interesting is that the Burtons were prepared to let so much of the dialogue adopt and peddle innuendo which referred directly to their private lives. This taunting or dangerous or exhibitionist streak was to continue right through until *Private Lives* itself, Richard's last and unnecessary and utterly debilitating stage experience.

In *The Sandpiper* Burton plays a man in love with two women: his dutiful and good wife and this rare creature Elizabeth Taylor or E.T., as she became known by one of her nicknames, from the other space of freedom, spontaneity, art. He is pedantic, relishing words. "The miracle of man . . . ," he says, "facing the mystery of time and the implausibility of death, can still rage, create, love." "Good for him," E.T. says. "Men have been staring at me and rubbing up against me since I was twelve," says the heroine of *National Velvet*, all too aware that middle-aged American males who took their children to that incredibly popular movie were not looking at the horse. She was Lolita in jodhpurs. "I've always been too eager for praise," she says. "I've lost my sense of sin," says Richard, "and become one of the world's most accomplished liars." Married wives are "unfulfilled" says Elizabeth . . . The film's considerable box-office success was wholly due to the off-screen Burton–Taylor duo; its mediocrity to their on-screen presence.

But the public and the two stars were making a deal. They would come to see Burton and Taylor together (or singly. Burton did *not* need Taylor to be a star, as *Iguana* and *Spy* proved beyond doubt). And they could appear in inferior material provided that on film the couple signalled what was going on in their private lives. Just as in newspaper interviews Elizabeth would dish out headline grabbers such as "This Vile Man . . . ruined me" (the article would then double back and show it was a "joke") so in some of their films they were using the public occasion to enjoy, play with and shape the soap opera that their private-lives-in-public had become. Elizabeth had flaunted her jewels and now she would be as open about her man. Richard, in interviews, treated the newspapers as a long-running confessional and was prepared to tell the world and its mother what he thought of Elizabeth. During one row with Minnelli (it was not a happy film: Burton saw through the script and was bored with it; he was also boorish), he said, "For the money we will dance." Interestingly, though, for the film, to flesh it out, to divert himself, he acted his own life through the lines and gave a peculiarly resonant sub-text to a rather mechanical pro-hippy movie. Like playing Hamlet every which way, he looked for risks to take: anything to beat back the boredom.

Sometimes this would grip him in a melancholy that was impenetrable. One or two of his acquaintances have suggested that there was some sort of clinical imbalance. The much later and reluctant admission of early attacks of mild epilepsy could account for this. He could do nothing about such black moods. "The Black Dog" of childhood echoes around the Celtic gloom of many a grounded drunken poet. It was nonetheless distressing for that. There were times when he felt an unaccountable misery that was almost insupportable.

That Christmas gave him the best news he had had for years. *A Christmas Story* was published. He boasted that a publisher offered him $100,000 for a novel. The idea of being a writer, something which his canniness and modesty had kept him from, now began to grow a little. A diary was purchased, bound in leather and kept, intermittently, for 1965. Laconic stuff.

They are up in Gstaad.

Health is the preoccupation—as it was to be so often. Elizabeth's father has a heart condition. Elizabeth herself walks into an open cupboard door and receives two lovely black eyes.

The film in the offing is *The Spy Who Came In From The Cold* and Burton goes to London to meet Martin Ritt, the director, and begins discussions: he is to play Alec Leamas. He has lunch with Ritt and Claire Bloom who will co-star. "She was nervous, but was all right," he writes, with considerable relief, on January 7th.

The next entry is not until the 3rd May. In between he was giving one of his finest performances. *The Spy Who Came In From The Cold* was not a happy picture and the central reason for that is alluded to in the diary: Claire Bloom.

According to William Squire and several others, Claire Bloom had been the first and until Elizabeth the only real "threat to Sybil." Elizabeth's jealousy and possessiveness at this critical stage in their as yet honeymoonless marriage were at their fullest pitch. Burton was in the ring with both of them and it was raw-knuckled stuff. Claire Bloom knew him from that time when he seemed to have made a serendipitous pact between monogamy and compulsive rutting. Now, with Elizabeth, he was bent on finding both and all of these in the one woman.

Elizabeth had to play wife, mother, daughter, sister, slut, whore, paragon, debating partner, pupil, mistress, quick fling, nurse, avenger and equal; and she was able and prepared to do it. Burton, though, was not prepared for Claire Bloom and he found it very difficult to handle. Elizabeth would call "Richard!" across the set in a shrill squawk which Claire Bloom could imitate well. Claire would be subject to intense concern from Elizabeth over her need to wear false eyelashes. The make-up was mixed in blood. Later Claire made a well-reported and very cutting summary of it all: "He hadn't changed at all, except physically," she told Sheilah Graham, who had dogged the Burton–Taylor affair through Rome and never got to Elizabeth, who hated her. "He was still drinking, still boasting, he was still late, still reciting the same poems and telling the same stories as when he was twenty-three . . . It was obvious that he was going to be a huge star which is not the same as being a great actor. He has confused them." Shown the article and asked his opinion, Burton simply said, "Hell hath no fury . . ."

Burton himself had tried for the rights in *Spy*. Martin Ritt and Paul Newman acquired them. Ritt says, "I fought for Burton. His agents were asking three quarters of a million for him. Finally Paramount agreed to pay it." You would have expected Ritt and Burton to get on. Both men from working-class backgrounds: Ritt, a man of integrity who had stood and then suffered for his principles in the McCarthy hearings. But he did not approve of Burton's heavy drinking and Burton resented that. Nor was Burton absolutely convinced that Ritt's decision to flatten him out completely as a character, "make him anonymous," would work. It is very hard for an actor—especially an intelligent and powerful actor like Burton—to take on trust a demand which eradicates many of the characteristics on which he has built his reputation. No strong sex for Burton this time; no oratory; no action; no charm. Ritt regretted they did not hit it off, but it was the Claire Bloom–Elizabeth business which poisoned the making of the film. Ritt took Claire Bloom's side and blamed Burton for being offhand and cool with her. But what else could he do? Elizabeth Taylor was like a one-woman emotional KGB: he was under twenty-four-hour surveillance. She monitored every wink.

I have a couple of witnesses to Burton during the first long shoot in Dublin. Frank Delaney, the writer, spent "some small time with him" and found in him a "terrible melancholy . . . a permanent anxiety . . . and then he was a great flirt, the waitresses, a friend of mine, any woman. You could see that Elizabeth Taylor was besotted by him . . . I felt sorry for him because when he was in the company he was so dominant that he had to do all the talking . . . a great stress . . . no wonder he repeated his stories . . ." No one could match him, many say that. "He truly loved words," said Delaney. "He would chew over them—'mellifluous,' 'servile' . . . and he was not always drunk, not at all, although once he did try to take a horse into an upstairs restaurant . . . he would be the best company . . . but it was the memory that most impressed me—not just Shakespeare and the Welsh poets, you'd expect that—but 'Tintern Abbey,' I remember, reams of it, and Joyce, the opening of *Ulysses*, paragraph after paragraph, word perfect."

The other witness is the book's author, John le Carré. "Marty Ritt rang me up—I was in Vienna—would I come to Ardmore? [The studio near Dublin.] Richard thought the lines lacked punch. I'd never written a line of screenplay before. But I went and met him for a pub lunch. Magnus Linklater [then a *Sunday Times* journalist] was there as well. Burton treated us both to a 'poor little me' monologue: 'I can't go to a pub any more. Elizabeth is more famous than the Queen. I wish none of it had ever happened.' We drank a lot." Was he right to complain about the dialogue, I asked. "Oh yes. It was all too prolix. It was a matter of tightening it and giving it balls." And Elizabeth? "They were living out their marriage in public at the time. Yul Brynner came out, I think, and Harvey Orkin: there were shouting matches in restaurants . . . and there was the Night Shoot."

In this sequence Burton had to come out of a corner shop and walk down a street. The street had been damped down to give it a gloss for the black and white shoot. Ritt told le Carré that Burton had been rowing with Elizabeth all day and was drunk: would he, le Carré, look after him? So le Carré went to the shop. "He had a bottle of Scotch in his raincoat pocket, possibly another in the other pocket. He did the take several times—it was about ten, eleven at night. It was the biggest free show in Dublin—the fire brigade, the police, crowds. But it was under control. When all of a sudden—the white Rolls-Royce appeared with Gaston the French chauffeur and Elizabeth looking like a million dollars. She drove on to the set! The crowd was out of control and surged up to her. Richard put on his British officer voice: 'My God! There's my little girl!' and he rushed across to the Rolls, screaming at the crowd and then screaming, in French, not very good French, at Gaston—to get the hell out. And then at Elizabeth! So they went. And he came back for more takes. We drank a lot more.

"Back to the Gresham Hotel in the small hours. I was in my room when there's this phone call. Come up for a drink. Elizabeth wants to meet you. Very embarrassing. All that British bit . . . So I took off my pyjamas, up I went and there he was, alone, in this vast sitting room. There was a rather ethereal conversation. 'Richard?' 'Yes, darling?' 'Who's all here?' 'The writer.' I realised they had the place wired up! They were talking on the intercom! So he went into the bedroom to get her and they had a mother and father of a row. Sounds of slapping. All of that. And all coming through on this intercom! Anyway eventually she arrived in the sort of fluffy wraparound dressing gown you send away for, bare footed, rather broadarsed, but extremely cuddly, extraordinarily attractive—those beautiful eyes, far more beautiful off screen than on. And she gave me one of those little-girl handshakes, 'How'd you do?' and left! Burton was wonderfully embarrassed: 'Do you mind? Elizabeth is, I think, not feeling . . .' "

Le Carré's summary is that "knowing him was impossible. There was something about him that was unapproachable. He had much more reality than one gave him credit for. I had the impression that it wasn't much fun any more—it had been fun—fighting and fucking his way up but now it just wasn't any more . . . I saw him a few months later on the beach at Scheveningen in Holland. It was shocking to see how he had deteriorated in that time. He talked a little bit about writing: he'd just had one or two stories published." Le Carré had wanted Trevor Howard or James Mason for the part of Leamas. "Somebody more embattled. I thought Burton looked like somebody who had lived too well rather than somebody who had lived a lot. But I was wrong."

Burton's performance is brilliant: and who knows? The booze, the "shocking deterioration" le Carré speaks of, the "no fun any more"—all of that might have been in the service of finding the character. Burton's way was always to make the part *be* him. He *was* Hamlet, he said; he *was* Leamas for that time; he was to *be* George in *Virginia Woolf*.

The journal starts up again on the penultimate day of the shooting of *Spy*—Elizabeth is in hospital, Richard is "nervous all day worrying about her." Elizabeth says that she knows how much he hates "ill people" but he has been "wonderful with me." She is also rejoicing that *maybe* another operation will enable her to have a child with Richard. "I want that more than anything in the whole world." Sincere and expansive declarations of mutual love are abundant. They headed to the Riviera for a break. The children joined them and Burton—relieved for a while from the high wire act of acting and the circus of film-making—got down to family.

Went tramping with Michael, Christopher, Liza, after having watched them at the riding school. Liza and Mike
splendid but Christopher started to show panic and with
my usual hatred of watching others humiliated I left with
Maria for a stroll to the river. E. feeling the same, came
out shortly afterwards. Chris obviously upset at the end
of the ride. Asked me if I would ride for pleasure. I said,
no, I'd rather read a good book. I think he agrees heartily
but he mustn't be stopped, the shame of it. Dined at home.
Fried chicken.

They went back to Gstaad. He learns a dice game called Yahtsee
in the bar at The Olden, teaches the children and they play "ferociously" for hours. They amble around, Burton still trying to sta-
bilise himself after the great "scandale."

But after the embattled *Spy* which, by all accounts, frayed his
temper and tested him hard, he was about to play the part which
his friends said would tear him apart, George to Elizabeth's Martha
in Albee's *Who's Afraid Of Virginia Woolf*? Yet over these two
holiday months they potter on happily enough. He is worried about
his "continual late sleeping" but that's the sum of the complaints.
Elizabeth is referred to as Burt. "Went for walk with Burt to local
which is a bar on the sands a mile and a bit from the house. Burt
walked there and back. What next?"

He begins to record his reading. He makes a tentative foray into
what will become a central preoccupation of the Notebooks—his
intimate relationship with Elizabeth. But the big news, in June, is
that Sybil is to marry "a member of a 'pop' group called 'The Wild
Ones.'" Burton worries that the man, Jordan, is eleven years
younger than Sybil. Elizabeth assures him that this need be no bar.
Burton's main hope is that this new arrangement will allow him to
see more of Kate.

Sybil gave up her vast alimony payment—Elizabeth was a little
bewildered by this. But it all swept past as the new project reared
up before them. *Virginia Woolf* was waiting. They set up house
in L.A.

It was Richard who encouraged Elizabeth to go for *Virginia
Woolf*—"This could be your *Hamlet*." It was Elizabeth who winkled him into the co-starring role against considerable opposition.

And it was Elizabeth who picked out Mike Nichols—who had never before made a film—to be the director. Haskell Wexler was hired as cameraman despite being vetoed at first by Richard who feared that Wexler's famous naturalistic and merciless style would highlight all the pockmarks on his face. (Gore Vidal told me that whenever he met Richard Burton, he [R.B.] would go into "an extravagant aria about why he was not homosexual. I'd listen as long as I could and then say, 'Who cares, Richard? Let's talk about dermatology. Now there's a subject!' ") Ernest Lehman, the writer and producer, had made an excellent job of turning Albee's claustrophobic play into a film script. It would be a closed set. It would also be the most expensive black and white film ever made and one of the key films of the decade.

Anxieties clamped on to the production throughout. Could Nichols direct? Would the play "transfer"? Would the play's "language" survive the censor? Could the heroic Burton transform himself into a broken, provincial, castrated American lecturer? And could Elizabeth Perfection-and-Ice-Topping Taylor convince as the fat, foulmouthed and sluttish Martha? Would the public like what they saw? And would the Burtons' private life survive? Yes to the first six. The seventh deserves a more complicated response.

Taylor got $1.1 million with all the usual perks, including security police. She would have done it for nothing she said (truthfully) but she'd had a shot at a bigger-than-*Cleopatra* fee "for fun." "We took you!" she said exultantly to the producer once the contract was signed. "We really took you!" Burton got three-quarters of a million. Great money, plus perks and, like Elizabeth, a healthy percentage. Filming over-ran by thirty-five days and the Burtons could have claimed more than a million dollars in overage. They waived it. Elizabeth let Jack Warner know she would appreciate an eighty-thousand-dollar brooch as her present. "For what I'm paying her she can buy her own brooch," said Warner, one of her few equals in the Hollywood version of poker.

Elizabeth got a second Oscar for the part of which Richard had said, "You have to do it to stop anyone else doing it." Richard was nominated—as he was six times—but an excellent performance by his friend Paul Scofield in *A Man For All Seasons* pipped him. He could be forgiven a certain ruefulness.

His performance as George was superlative. "I *am* George," he said to Mike Nichols, and once again with a script he respected and a director he respected he bent his will to it and the result is riveting. There is one sequence when, alone, under a tree, he tells the story of the boy. It was done in a single take. Nichols was overwhelmed. He deserved an Oscar for that sequence alone. But he had fought too many battles in Hollywood, made no attempt to be the favoured son, gone his own way. Mike Nichols says, "He was the loneliest man I had met."

The broken, tender yet brutally tongued man here spoke words which echoed his own life and which ricocheted off the set and into the dressing rooms, into the house. Elizabeth went up to a hundred and fifty-five pounds and transformed herself into what Richard often called her—in fun?—a termagant. Their rows were nasty. "Monkey nipples," he called her. "For Chrissakes shut your fucking mouth!" They treated the world as a private kitchen. Gossip about their rows was on the daily exchange. Nichols thought that although Taylor might have been a necessary stage for him, she was already wearing him down.

What struck me most forcibly seeing it again is how much Burton supports Taylor's performance. It is extraordinary and touching how he often holds her up. The crack of the dialogue—no doubt well rehearsed by Nichols—is entirely paced by Burton. He hammocks almost every sentence she speaks and lifts what could have been mere shrillness into that damaging desperation. This is not to disparage her performance which, for the public and for most of Hollywood, emerged as totally unexpected, bold and powerful. It is just worth noting that as well as giving one of the finest performances of his film-making career, he kept a strict and helpful eye on "my girl," "Burt," "Ocean." When he saw the film he was dissatisfied with his own performance.

Yet not only did it provide him with precisely the sort of good part he needed, it added to the Burton–Taylor ever-rolling press snowball. *Were* they George and Martha? Enough nudges and winks took you in that direction. Whether they were or not they were Burton and Taylor up there on screen, heaving up the guts of a marriage at a time when the whole of the Western world seemed to be shaking itself loose of its matrimonial bonds. Once again they hit the mood of the day and helped perhaps to define it.

Virginia Woolf was notable for "language" which by the standards of the time was thought utterly unacceptable. Paul Ferris in his book on Burton writes:

A meeting with Jack Warner produced a list of words that
would have to go, among them thirteen Goddams, twelve
variations on Christ and Jesus, including a Jesus H. Christ,
three bastards, seven buggers, four screws and screwings,
four sons-of-bitches and SOBs, two scrotums and a right
ball, together with such phrases as "must have made it in
the sack" and "on the living room rug."

The film was shot with the "language" more or less intact and to
Warner's astonishment it was passed. No one under eighteen could
be admitted without an adult, but that was as much an inducement
as a bar. The movies would never be the same and yet again Burton
seemed in the van when it mattered.

But *Virginia Woolf* took a toll. When they separated for the first
time (years ahead), Elizabeth said that she was "tired of playing
Martha." Richard in his journals admits to a nature which, and
not only in drink, could be "picky," "twisty," "nasty," "quar-
relsome" and the film licensed that. In one scene she had to spit
in his face. Nichols demanded take after take and Elizabeth eventually cracked up, wept, couldn't do it any more. Again on one
occasion, Burton simply could not leave his dressing room—not
drunk—couldn't find the nerve to suffer the exposure that the part
brought.

By any acting standards, George following Leamas with only a
few weeks between was a strain: add to that the remarriage of Sybil
and worries over Kate, the multiplying difficulties of educating the
children, the nomadic life . . . he was in need of a rest—and after
all he had become forty during *Woolf*.

Instead, in February 1966, the Burtons came to Oxford and put
up at the Randolph Hotel just a few doors along from the Oxford
Playhouse. They were there to fulfil a promise Burton had made to
Nevill Coghill, the don who had called him, with Auden, a "genius"
and who had directed him in *Measure For Measure* during his brief
Oxford days. At times it seems as if Burton is working his way
through a shopping list of those who have in any way done him a
favour: to them shall bounty be given one hundredfold. Burton was
to star in an otherwise student production of Marlowe's *Doctor
Faustus*. One way and another due to *Doctor Faustus*, the Oxford
Playhouse, Coghill's hobby horse, was to receive a hundred thousand dollars.

There had been talk of *Coriolanus* and *Lear*—Burton was keeping to the pattern of coming back to the stage, keeping in touch, in trim. But the film business was spinning along so *well* . . . and he was more proud of his film work now. Marlowe's massive role—with ten days' rehearsal and a week's performance—would have to do. *The Taming Of The Shrew* was in the offing and writing was now beginning to preoccupy him. There was a piece he had written for the *New York Herald Tribune* on Constantine Fitzgibbon's biography of Dylan Thomas, other articles in the pipeline, the idea of an autobiography or a journal was taking shape.

Oxford was yet another gift to Elizabeth. Nevill Coghill adored her and she him. The undergraduates found the Burtons modest, accessible, generous and amusing. To this day the journalist Peter Hillmore can repeat stories he heard from Burton at that time and he still gets a laugh. The actress Maria Aitken who was in the production thought they were marvellous fun and loved the eccentricity of Bob Wilson, the tall slim black dresser, standing in the wings with a Scotch to refresh Doctor Faustus as he rushed offstage in a welter of verse.

"This is Professor Coghill's last year at Oxford," said Richard at the press conference which attracted fifty photographers, television cameras and scores of reporters. "Since he started me off I think I should finish him off." And Faustus? "I think the last speech is the greatest speech in the history of literature," said Burton dutifully. And the man? "All men are tempted in some way or other at some time. Everybody is offered a choice—one way being easy the other difficult." The bonus for the PR men was that Elizabeth was to play Helen of Troy, a non-speaking part. "I have never acted on stage before, so I'm starting the easy way. It's a marvellous opportunity." It could be seen as another gift from Burton to Taylor.

Burton never managed to learn the whole part—it is rumoured he gave himself only ten days and treated the event as a spree. The carelessness that Gielgud noted at the outset was still with him: as was the detachment, the calculation. But now he was in a swirl of Elizabeth.

The play was panned by Irving Wardle in *The Times*: "University drama at its worst," highly praised by Harold Hobson in the *Sunday Times*. Burton was accused by another critic, Alan Brien, of scaling himself down to the level of the amateur actors. He was acclaimed

by a young Oxford don in the *Western Mail* for "the best performance of his career"—Coghill thought him brilliant. Burton had
tremendous nerve to take it all on—the role, the undergraduates,
the short rehearsal time . . . John Crosby in the *Observer* handed
out a witty accolade of the speech in which Faustus asks God to be
merciful. Couldn't he—he asks God—cut his sentence to a mere
hundred thousand years? "It takes a great actor to deliver that speech
without wringing a strangled sob of laughter out of one. But Burton
did it." Elizabeth was also used by critics as a knife-sharpening
exercise, but there again there were those who thought the little she
had to do she did superbly . . . It was a selfless and generous gesture
on both their parts.

Generosity in various ways was to be one of their characteristics.
The announcement of large gifts of money by Elizabeth was not
always followed through but if you were any sort of friend in any
sort of trouble she was there. While they were in Dublin the son of
Gaston the chauffeur was shot accidentally in France. Elizabeth went
to France with Gaston, stayed with him for a week, pulled him
through. Her friend Montgomery Clift, terribly ill and totally un-
bankable, was coaxed back into an interest in life by Elizabeth. She
put up her own money as a guarantee for him in a picture, *Reflections
In A Golden Eye*, in which she insisted that he be her co-star. He
died before the film was made.

At the time of *Doctor Faustus* David Lewin interviewed both of
them on television and asked Richard if he saw a parallel between
himself and Faustus. "You bastard, David! I knew you'd ask
that," quoth Helen of Troy. Richard was more politic and spoke
of temptation and choice and pointed out that he still returned to
the stage. Would I be selling out, Elizabeth asked, if I deserted
films for the stage? But the plot was laid. Burton having played
Prince Hal for his generation and then "the working-class hero"
and then Don Juan and attempted Renaissance Man, was now
Doctor Faustus, the man who sold his art for money. It coincided
with a truer analysis—that of a man being drawn slowly but, it
appeared, helplessly into a deeply seductive and romantic circle of
self-destruction.

But that was some time ahead. *The Spy* and *Virginia Woolf* were
to show producers that what they had hoped for and then despaired
of in the Fifties was now on the big screen. And his quality could
also be big box-office. They would continue to make films together

for some time—"Must we *always* make films together?" Burton grumbled. "We'll end up like Laurel and Hardy." "What's wrong with Laurel and Hardy?" Elizabeth the Ocean replied and off they went to Italy for Shakespeare. The most famous couple in the world: all human life seemed there: all the world their stage.

15
A Roman Holiday

They returned to Rome in 1966 with eight extra security guards and a private police escort all paid for by Burton. Having sworn never to return to the Holy City they were back in force: "I guess we just got sloshed and forgot," he said.

While in Rome they filmed *The Taming Of The Shrew*, which Franco Zeffirelli directed; and *Doctor Faustus* which Burton co-directed with Nevill Coghill. They also made the deal to do Graham Green's *The Comedians* and Richard did the narration for a film on the Florence flood disaster which raised many millions.

The Shrew was financed by the Burtons' waiving their fees and taking a percentage. Burton himself found some of the money for *Doctor Faustus*, fees were waived entirely—all profits to go to the Oxford Playhouse. And the Florence film was done for nothing.

It is here that the Notebooks proper begin. He had kept a journal now and then in the previous year. The Notebooks too take the form of a journal at the outset but eventually loosen up into a commonplace book, and, most importantly I think, simply a place where he could write. The notion of being a writer had always lurked, modestly. Now that he had come through the worst of the batter over Elizabeth–Sybil; now that their finances seemed to be rolling on (although at this particular time the royalties from the films which were to be successful were still some way off); now that he had some sort of *base*—ironically in Rome—he took up his pen.

Over the next years—most fully in his time with Elizabeth—

238

these Notebooks became more and more the first sketches for the autobiography he eventually wished to write. It is significant that he took to them when his life with Elizabeth was sealed. He wanted to chart these unknown waters and keep a logbook. Sometimes the detail and the intimate revelations can appear too intrusive, but it is essential to use them. For here is a man trying to put down the truth of himself, in sickness and in health. The whole truth. He may have wanted to do this as a counterpoint to the ceaseless bombast and contradictory mischief he ladled out to so many reporters. At least there would be a true record somewhere, an authorised version. And there was the vacuum to fill. Now that he and Elizabeth were embarked on a life which made it clear to all others that the two of them together were the centre of everything they became cocooned and—there were many dull moments, even weeks. For the way they led their lives meant that there were no real equals around them, and only very occasional pals he could intellectually work out with. The Notebooks became a way of holding an intelligent conversation—with himself.

It is because of their substance and, as time went on, intensifying attempt to see himself plainly that this part of the book increasingly veers towards autobiography. Sometimes Burton reflects on his past and these passages both illuminate what has already been written and, more importantly, show how he was shaping up to see and present himself. The Notebooks provide a remarkable opportunity to give a man the opportunity to speak of his own life inside a life being written about him. The double perspective—for the next stretch of the book—parallels the increasingly marked double life Burton was living. More and more the property of the public as success and fame piled up around Elizabeth and himself. More and more private as he tried to take soundings of himself in these dangerous waters.

At first he did indeed write with a pen. Back to basics. A neat grammar-school hand. Dates underlined in red ink. From March 18th to November 19th, a hundred and sixteen pages; school exercise book, sometimes three hundred words a page, writing on both sides of the paper—thrift, or habit? Perhaps it is significant that he was no longer the castrated George in *Virginia Woolf* nor the embittered Alec in *The Spy*, the conscience-shredded priest in *Sandpiper* nor the whisky-stoned priest in *Iguana*, but Petruchio, macho man's macho for any woman born, the man who tamed the shrew. Burton had to find the roles in himself; they had to "click" in some way. When that seemed far away from him the strain of wrenching himself into position—rather like a receiving dish had to be skewed around and steeply angled to take a distant signal—it could have a "shocking" effect, as John le Carré noted in *The Spy*. Burton was fond of saying, "I am George, George is me" or "I am Faust, Faust is me." He was given to bombast but these statements fit in with what he had always said about acting—to Anthony Quayle at Stratford as Young Hal, to John Neville at the Old Vic, to Gielgud in New York. Philip knew that. When Philip was sent for it was to earth him. Now he "was Petruchio" and it was a role that took him straight back to the rugby club, Shakespeare-loving, broad-living past.

It is perhaps no coincidence that the Notebooks begin when he is working on Shakespeare. His strength in the plays was always in the great soliloquies. The Notebooks become like soliloquies and, like them, they tell the audience the truth. Whatever else is said elsewhere in mischief, as a white lie, in confusion, as a false boast, here he speaks as truthfully as he can.

It was Zeffirelli's first major film and on the surface a risky choice. Though noted as an opera director, and designer, he would not only be moving into a new medium but the language itself could be a problem. But not, as it turned out, as important as the question of who designed the clothes. As so often happened with those he came to like very much, Burton was aggressive at the outset.

The first sentence of the first entry, March 18th, sets it up.

> Lunched at home with Franco Zeffirelli, Allessandre de Paris, Irene Sharaff and Dick McWhorter [production manager]. Irene [the costume designer for Elizabeth] is a funny contradiction. And enormously concerned with her own dignity.

A fortnight later the rumblings begin.

> (March 30) Some agonising on the part of Franco Z. about my initial costume. I hope he's not going to be a bore when we start to work. They are changing or rather adapting the present costume. I wish I had Larry's and

John's—indeed most actors' love of dressing up and all
that goes with it—the fittings, the finicky fussing, etc.

And builds up the day after.

(March 31) Today I received a letter from Franco saying
that he felt better able to write his thoughts than speak
them as his English is not too reliable. A very good excuse
for not facing somebody with something unpleasant.
Wasn't it Winston Churchill who always fired his under-
lings by letter? Who would have thought the Old Man to
have had so much milk in him. Anyway the letter said
that he had designed and had had made a new first costume
for me and would I come in at 4.00 to try it. I went and
of course waited twenty minutes. At first I was dismayed
by its weight and size but having tried it on felt better at
once. I tested it immediately and will see the result tomorrow at about 11.00 o'clock. It had better be good.
Irene Sharaff is obviously upset. Old Snapshot adores her
and I must use tact and so on to keep her.

"Old Snapshot" is one of his new nicknames for Elizabeth: "Quicktake" is another. Sharaff was there at her insistence. In his autobiography, Zeffirelli criticises Taylor for keeping them waiting but
praises her for always getting it in one take. Then Burton sorted it
out.

(April 1) Z. described her costume as 1930 touring version
of *Shrew* in America. I said, as far as I was concerned,
he could do all the bloody costumes but E. was adamant
re Irene's clothes and I told Zeffirelli that if she turned
cold on him that that would be the end of her performance.
If there were any more hold-ups I said due to costume
problems somebody, I said straight in his eyes, would
have to go. We had invested $2,000,000 in this venture
and I didn't want another Cleopatra.

As so often happened when Burton encountered a dominating
man—especially one from another culture or a strongly differing
physical type—he was initially aggressive. Though he was to end

up liking Zeffirelli and enjoying the operatic flutings of the man, in the beginning it was locked horns and the matter of the costumes became a battleground. That seemed to resolve it. There also appears that rather unlovely characteristic—"the stirrer"—noted earlier by Lauren Bacall. At a certain stage Burton clearly revelled in the explosions going on. The bloodcurdling and slanderous exchanges were undoubtedly relished. He continued to have serious doubts about the film for a while.

> (May 11) I'm starting to feel afeard about it. We chose, possibly, a bad one. Snapshot is fine, and I think I'm alright, but I worry about the other performers almost all of whom are brilliant but ill-served by the director.

He carried a grudge against Zeffirelli for a while.

> (April 21) I'm not sure I like Zeffirelli. As a mind and personality he's not a patch on M. Nichols. But he has flair, shall we say. He has a sense of the spectacular. He will succeed. Yesterday he was worried again about his billing. I told him for the umpty ninth time to fix it with Columbia and that whatever was mutually agreeable to them was also so to us. But his grumbling was put into letter form. He couldn't tell me direct.

But by the end of the shoot all was well. The Burtons moved on to film *Doctor Faustus*. Zeffirelli went to the Met in New York to direct a new opera by Samuel Barber: *Antony and Cleopatra*.

> (Sept. 22) F. Zeff. arrives back from his triumphant disaster at the Met.—the new one in N.Y. We should see him shortly. Looking forward to it too. How one changes. He has written many outrageously campy letters from N.Y.

Altogether typical of Burton who would begin many new friendships with an attempt to unsettle this man or woman and then—point made—live and let live.

Zeffirelli became a considerable admirer of both the Burtons. Shakespeare's original play was cut in half, romped up and acted *con brio*. It is an irresistible knockabout version with Burton like a jolly but stern father watching "his girl" take the jumps. She had some trouble with lines but Burton's cracking got her through. His grip on Shakespeare's verses was still astounding. Zeffirelli remembers one evening. Robert Kennedy was with them—*Camelot* had taken Burton's court into the Kennedy circle and they discovered a mutual interest in poetry. Well oiled, Burton and—of all unlikely people—Kennedy began to compete over recitals of the sonnets. Burton eventually won by employing his old party trick—reciting the fifteenth sonnet word for word, backwards.

Meetings are recorded briefly but tellingly.

> (March 19) We dawdled about all day until dinner in Rome with Zeffirelli, Albee and his friend.
>
> Albee was very flattering, especially to E. about *V. Woolf* and, for him, was very talkative. They were doing a swift tour of Europe—a day here, a day there. He says that he is ⅔ through a new play which should be going on Broadway in the autumn. It contains 4 men and 2 women. He said that it was "a very curious play, a very curious play indeed." After *Tiny Alice* and *V. Woolf* how curious can you, as they say, get. He told us that he thinks about a play for 6 months approx. and then writes it in about 3. There is no second draft. It is as it is, and so remains.

After dinner they were hunted by the press.

> We had a hair-raising drive pursued by paparazzi all the way. I think Mario the driver takes too much notice of these butterflies of the gutter. They risk their lives too. Why don't they go where there's real risk. Like a war. Like Vietnam. Like anywhere.

As he settles in, the journal becomes domestic and nesty.

> (March 22) I took Liza and Maria to school this morning and then went to the bookshop on the Via Veneto and bought some 20 or 30 paperbacks. Half a dozen detective stories. Ludovic Kennedy's *Trial of Stephen Ward*, a gen-

uine Establishment horror story. And a palpably unjust
trial—nightmarishly so. Harry S. Truman's *Memoirs*. In-
genuous to the point of admiration, and also wonder that
a man of such common (but tough) intellect could ever
have become the President. *And* done so well. Perhaps
office really can make the man.

We sat quietly at home for the evening and read. We
dined *á deux* and read and sometimes talked to each other
and read out interesting bits to each other even while we
ate.

Because of his friendship with Nureyev he goes, reluctantly, to the
ballet:

How he makes the others seem like carthorses.

Back home he is struggling with Barzini, the author of

The Italians . . . intolerably prolix and self-congratula-
tory. I'll try it again and make another desperate attempt
to like *The Italians* and the Italians.

International rugby scores are noted. He writes of being distant and
melancholy and then suddenly lashes out:

I worry enormously about the fact that we have no money.
I worry that I will not be able to look after my wife and
my children after I'm dead—nobody else will.

There are summaries of the sort of conversations which often spiral
into intimacies while actors hang around half the day for their two
or three minutes of "take"—like racehorses waiting for their brief
gallop. He had brought many of the old mates into *The Shrew*—
Michael Hordern, from the Old Vic days, aboard at Burton's request
once more—"It was as easy as falling off a log for Richard: but,
do you know, I don't think he was what they call these days, I
believe, a stud," Hordern said. "He wouldn't have been my sort
of chap if he had been." (But he was everybody's sort of chap when
he wanted to be: that was the trick and the trial, that was the fun
and that was the exhaustion.) And Cyril Cusack.

(April 4) I had a remarkable sex and religion conversation with Cyril who is vastly tempted by some Roman woman. He is, I think, and he thinks so too, immature sexually. He does not have my wide experience of rabid wild oats. I told him that *I* couldn't, but then I am impervious to that kind of temptation since I fell in love with Quicktake.

I became very drunk later and shouted a lot. At E. I don't know what about. Just plain sloshed.

Old friends and new celebrations were constantly around the film which, as always with the Burtons, became a running party, a press nest, an ever-extending family.

(April 5) Mia Farrow & Mike Nichols arrived from N.Y. That M. Nichols really gets the girls. I wish Farrow would put on 15lbs & grow her hair.

(May 8) Last night we went to see *The Bible*. I expected to be thoroughly bored but I wasn't. It is a good honest film though it failed to move me at all except at the very opening at the creation of order out of chaos. I hope it's successful. The kids should see it if only for the Noah section with all those animals. Sweetly done.

After it was over we left very quickly. Before it started we met Gore Vidal, a tall dark and handsome fellow. Too handsome, I would have thought, to be a good writer which he is.

The Aberfan disaster is brooded over—what's to be done to help? And the flooding of Florence.

(Nov. 17) At 2.30 I met Sheila Pickles and the Italian TV man re the documentary on Florence. I have agreed to do it on Friday here in Rome. I will try to do the narration in Italian for the Italians and in English for UK & USA. I fear I'll have to write it too—not in Italian of course, they'll translate that. I looked up Florence and flood in the *Oxford Dict of Quotations*—there is practically nothing that is apt except from Inge.

One touching concern which comes through is his devotion to Maria. The crippled little adopted girl, now seven, was getting slowly, very slowly, better. Burton gave her time. He would take her for outings, think about her, note down his observations—always tender and practical.

> (April 11) Maria is invested with every conceivable kind of fear or, as her very competent nurse Karen says, "She scares easy." She saw a lizard today and cried with fright. What's to do. Leave it to love, I suppose, and time. The other day, with me on a walk, she refused to walk over a line of tiny ants, out of terror. I had to get her over by totally ignoring her and walking on. She was as animated and talkative about this experience as if she'd just crossed the Atlantic single-handed in a rubber dinghy.

As often, an on-form Burton could salvage a great deal out of a potential bummer.

> (June 4) We got up early slightly nervous about Maria's school sports. What would she be like? I made Bloody Marys for Karen, Eliz. and self to steady our nerves. It was a very warm day. We arrived about 5 mins before the start. Maria, with about 20 other children, danced with two chiffon scarves in each hand. She firmly, however, kept her right hand thumb in her mouth throughout. With style and grace, and much interest in the other competitors, she came last in the 25 yd. dash. They had sack races, bean-bag throwing, obstacle races. The colours were truly international. From the pinko-grey of N. Europe to Chinese yellow via black-as-nights. I entered the fathers' race which due to the devious machinations of a black [African], an ambassador, and three Bloody Marys, I lost. We had to pick up a balloon in one corner of the ground, a flag in another, a Coca Cola bottle at the gate, a chiffon scarf on route and a paper flower elsewhere. I quickly arranged with this black bloody Iago, this coloured Judas, to pick up two balloons, two paper flowers, while he picked up two bottles and two flags which, I rapidly explained, would cut the race in half as we would exchange with each other. But race-memory, atavism, took over inside his boiling black head and I had a double journey

for the bottles. His side of the bargain ceased to exist after he'd given me *one* flag and I had given him one balloon *and* one paper flower. Such cheating is soul destroying. How can they rule themselves if they are such cheats. No wonder Africa is going to the dogs. Result: the black diplomat 19th and me 20th. From now on I only cheat with Welshmen. I'm starting to train now for next year's race.

A collector's item of non-racist boisterous good humour which does not teeter into coyness or self-consciousness. He is so certain of his non-racism he can joke about it.

As time went on Burton was to become increasingly open in these Notebooks. He would admit to W. C. Fields's feelings. He would try to grapple with the not uncommon problem: how is it that you can adore children so much and yet feel almost insane with irritation at their presence? Yet, at this stage, he is calling the clan together, setting up a new Burton family which will embrace not only Wales but America too, Mexico, the Mediterranean and everywhere the gypsy tribe of bodyguards, hairdressers, secretaries and friends travel along. His old friends are now seriously complaining that they cannot get messages through. The entourage, like the mute eunuchs who guarded emperors and harems, seem to be there solely for their master's purpose. But the fact is that Burton was never a particularly sociable creature: a few pals in a pub, some talk of books and sport, and the theatre, and he was well home. He had enough now in the travelling circus of acts which was his caravan home to satisfy, even to satiate, his social energies. Elizabeth was his boozing companion.

The dearest though were the nearest and none, ever, nearer than Kate. At times during the struggle over leaving Sybil it is clear that the real fight in his mind is not between Elizabeth and Sybil but between Elizabeth and Kate. When she talks of him now—and she can look very like him—she is thoughtful and more than willing to laugh at his terrible temper, his fussy insistence on her complete education—but basically she is radiant at his memory. The Notebooks show his feelings even in the most workaday references.

(Sept. 27) Kate came to stay with us, from London (in July ?) with Ifor and Gwen as guardians. She looked bonny

and long-legged and freckled and slightly pigeon-toed. She
is so far physically so like us (who's like us?) [Back to
his own father: Who's like us? Nobody.] that she takes
my breath away. There is no sign of Syb in her at all
except for the mannerisms of proximity. She is loving and
quite clearly loves E. and E. her. (Say that fast.) They
spent one entire gossipy day together in bed, both with
temps, both with some "flu" or other. I had to carry K
to her bed at the end of the day because cunningly she
thought, perhaps, that she could sleep the whole night
with E. if she, Kate, were already asleep. But I was firm
and took her away. Neeeeeks! Neeeeeeks is Maria's version
of the word "snakes" when she sees worms.

In this first sweep of extracts, it is noteworthy how important the
Welsh family is to him.

(Sept. 23) My sister Edith (Edie) died at the age of 43.
She was the youngest sister and the funniest. She died
from an unsuspected clot of blood that formed after she
had been operated on for a weak heart. We thought she
had recovered from the operation (it seemed she had) but
5 or 6 days later she went out like a candlelight. She is
the first child of my parents to die since 1907 approx. The
shock was considerable though I was less close to her than
to Ifor and Cis for instance. We flew to London for the
funeral—all my brothers were there, Ivor (who came with
us from Rome), Dai, Will, Tom, Graham and Verdun.
Ron, the husband, was in a pitiful state. As were all the
sisters and Edie's children. All the men, heads carefully
bowed so that they could see nothing but neutral dispassionate carpet or chapel floor in the crematorium, were
stoic. I had to harrumph and snort a few times to stop the
weeping.

In the solution to the waiting time a film actor endures lies his sanity.
Elizabeth seems to have occupied it in a self-mesmerisingly long
preparation of externals—the hairpiece, the costume, the make-up—
blotting up the tensions while her mind worked on the moment when
the camera turned: and then—Shazam!—"Snapshot." There's a

lot of card-playing, astrology, palm-reading, gossip by the bucket-ful, affairs of course and phoning the agent about the next job. Burton was like Gielgud—from whom the not so careless about everything Welsh boy took a lot: they did crossword puzzles, they enjoyed theatrical chat but, mostly, they read.

> (April 29) I was called in for make-up at 12.00 noon. E. was called for 10.30. But Alexandre didn't get her hair-piece ready till 11.30 and she managed one shot before lunch. As a result of this late start I didn't work at all. I read Auden's latest collection of verse, *About The House*. And read some of a new poem called "Christ." The latter poet, as well, oddly enough, as Auden, are pupils of Nevill's. "Christ," in dipping into, seems fairly hu-mourless.

A better example of the fury with which he read is in his contest with the American heavyweight scholar and essayist, Edmund Wil-son.

> (Oct. 29) Have been reading all kinds of books. *Europe Without Baedeker* by that pompous bastard Edmund Wil-son. He seems to be wrong about everything—his book deals a lot with immediate post-war Europe. His reflections on national character are puerile. He seems to have talked only to journalists and second rate artistic people (San-tayana, an exception) and from them has received these earth-shaking impressions. He talks about the overwhelm-ing American influence on English writing for instance and writes more like an Englishman than almost anyone I know. He is also lacking in humour. He is a bore. See his book on Internal Revenue. *Memoirs of Hecate County* is unreadable.

Part of the interest in this lies in the fact that Burton was clearly marooned, set apart from the friendships and society which could give him any sort of literary-intellectual conversation. At the very time when his deeper instinct was telling him to look for survival in writing and in reflection, his will to find new worlds to conquer took him further and further away from what would have properly nourished him. A sub-text of isolation and its consequence, lone-liness, is already setting in, even this early in the marriage of the century. Wilson's ideas had to be wrestled with, unsatisfactorily, alone.

> The above was written in something like impotent fury—he is much better than that—but his determination to prove that the Decline of the West stops its headlong flight just west of the British Isles and Ireland is startling to read. His misunderstanding of the British is colossal. *And* he doesn't have the courage to say "I hate the British" but all his stories about them with about two or three excep-tions among 100 show them as snob-ridden bores of the traditional, as he describes one Englishman himself, "Mu-sic Hall" kind. He has a mindless short story in it about an English woman and an American woman both working for UNRRA, in which the warm homespun democracy of the American and the cold dispassion and cynicism of the Englishwoman are juxtaposed. Need I say who the winner is. He is a sour man who seems to rely for ecstasy entirely on fugitive glimpses of slender women in caught attitudes. He is quite nice for once about an English girl called coyly "G." He is, I think, like Hemingway, fascinated by the passionately dispassionate prep school, finishing school, mater and pater sexiness of the middle and upper class British woman.
>
> He is, as I have already stated, a bad writer but his single-minded determination to destroy all who are not American is compulsive. Though I fling the book across the room a dozen times (metaphorically) I have to retrieve it and go on reading.

There is also his interest in meals. On many a day, the chicken or the eggs or whatever is detailed—briskly—but it is there. Nothing was too trivial to be excluded.

> (Oct. 16) Lunch today was splendid. Zuppa di Vongole (clam soup with the clams in their shells) and a delicious little pasta called Crêpes al Formaggio. Light pancakes

stuffed with molten cheese and prosciutto. Cake to follow.
All good. Rivera to drink.

But meals in restaurants could lead to further complications.

The whole thing was slightly marred by fans, a couple of
parties of rowdy ones and a very persistent middle-aged
whining female photographer.

The interest in food might be due to a growing preoccupation with
his health. He is reluctant to write about this and it surfaces rather
shyly.

(Sept. 24) E. has bur, arthr, or fibro situs and has great
discomfort with her left shoulder and arm. Don't I know
it. It is peculiarly maddening because you have nothing
to show for it. No swelling, no wound, no bruise to boast
of—just nagging infuriating pain.

This is a preoccupation he kept from everyone but Elizabeth. The
other worry was the continuing lousiness of his skin.

(Sept. 24) Ron Berkeley, every night, after I've taken my
hot shower and my pores are open, rubs my spotty back
with alcohol. It will be interesting to see if it cleans up
the skin.

The skin problems don't get better.

(Oct. 8) The lump on my cheek broke this morning and
I spent ½ hr putting boiling hot water on it and squeezing
it out. That's the first on my face for twenty odd years.
What is it? I eat the same. I drink less or hardly at all
nowadays. Is it nerves? It can't be hygiene—that's my
fetish. I exercise. Ah well. Think clean, Richard. Take
your vitamins and think pure thoughts.

He exercises regularly, calling on the old RAF PT routines even
after a night when he "became thoroughly drunk."

(Oct. 11) Woke at 6.45 feeling drugged. Splashed myself
with cold water. Ran in place for a count of hundred, did
20 push-ups, 20 knees bends, 20 touch-toes, 20 arms fling,
20 sideways bends. And felt better.

The more worrying fact re-emerges, just once more, near the very
end of the diary.

(Nov. 18) I ran or rather jogged about ½ mile, having
already done my PT in a fury when I got up. Will my
arms ever come back to what they were? I don't so much
mean their looks as their strength. Four years of atrophy
from pinched nerves? Bursitis? Arthritis is a long time to
make up at 41. Well, keep on trying anyway.

Unfortunately Burton hated doctors. Speaking of them in the context
of Elizabeth's illness, he writes:

(April 20) I'm sick of these bloody doctors. I'll have to
have a really insupportable smash before I'll ever send for
one of these ill-trained, drunken, condescending, semi-
literate sods. The only pain I'd like them to remove is the
pain in the arse they give me.

And so he would not go—yet another good old macho ultimately
self-destructive working-class tradition he held on to. The consequence was that he had already been suffering for four years from
one of the more painful, under-researched and, certainly then, unknown illnesses—a form of arthritis or fibrositis. This, I think, as
much as anything, accounts for the unexpected and savage depressions he records. It may also have been a factor in his drinking—
since alcohol would alleviate the pain. His much-quoted remark that
he was afraid to stop drinking in case people found him boring when
sober is utterly unsupported by the (long) sober stretches of the
Notebooks and by those who knew him drunk *and* sober. The drive
to drink may well have come from the need to ease pain: just as
opium was used in previous centuries.

This is confirmed, for me, by the good sense and lightness of
touch with which he refers to his drinking habit here.

(May 10) I drank steadily all day long yesterday. Today I shall not drink at all while working. I don't know why I drink so much. I'm not unhappy and I really don't like it very much—I mean the booze itself.

Interestingly, a few weeks later, May 30th, he writes:

One of my awful unaccountable days of savage ill-humour . . . Eliz. joined us at lunch. She was gay and sweet but nothing could drag me out of my tantrum.

No drink is mentioned at all. On September 26th:

Astonishingly I have lost, temporarily I hope, my taste for alcohol in any form. I shall force a campari-soda-vodka between my clenched teeth before dinner or bust. I feel better without it but I look ghastly, great bags under my eyes. E. is enjoying her booze as usual and I don't resent it—much.

And it continues.

(Oct. 1) I cannot imagine what I'm going to do with myself in ten days' time when *Faustus* and *Shrew* (extra shots) is over. I can learn *Comedians*. Later I can learn the songs, etc, of *Mr. Chips*. [He was planning to star in a musical of James Hilton's *Goodbye Mr. Chips*, a role later taken by Peter O'Toole.] Maybe I'll write something other than this. Maybe I'll just read and read and read. I have hardly had a drink for about two weeks. An occasional beer and twice I became mildly sloshed on a couple or three goops. Not only do I *not* miss it I actually feel as if I never want to booze again. Drink yes, booze no.

The benders are there but they seem jolly, under control, nothing more than the occasional indulgence of a bout drinker and always associated with a lot of gossip and fun.

(Nov. 2) I have been more or less drunk for two days. I don't know why but I enjoyed it thoroughly. I didn't do too much harm except that I was rude to Bob Wilson on Monday and he sulked all day yesterday (Tues.). I also made a feeble pass at Karen, our Maria's nurse, and apologised immediately and straightaway told E. who thought it funny but probably harmful to K. I apologised again the next morning in front of E. Now what on earth possessed me to do that? It must be my impending 41st birthday. I think no permanent damage has been done to Karen, I hope to God; she's such a very good person.

I also attacked Marlon B. for embarrassing R. [Ray] Stark [the producer] by taking off his boot to demonstrate that poor Stark wears lifts. I accused Marlon of wearing them too. I think he does tho what the devil harm there is in it I don't know. Women wear lifts all the time and I wore them throughout *Shrew* to make myself look bigger. Also I don't much like looking up at people especially those who were born to be looked down on.

It is there, part of his life, but he is aware of it, like a fox who's caught the sound and scent of the hounds and quietly slid away to pursue his foxy way elsewhere.

Illness, drink, the family, preoccupations certainly but a good portion of these first Notebooks is breezy chat.

(Sept. 28) . . . Hence the Dino de L. [Laurentiis] suit against Fellini. There is a huge set on the back lot which may now be unusable [for Fellini's 8½]. Dino will figure out a way to come out smiling. Betcha.

3.00 p.m. Just had lunch with P. Glenville [the director of *Becket*]. Baked ham, pommes au gratin, salad, creamed spinach. Lots of gossip from Peter G. About Tony Richardson, Jeanne Moreau and a Greek gigolo. Have also heard that Fellini has found another backer. He will make the film at de L. Studios but as an outsider. I betcha and I was righta!

(Oct. 24) We woke about 9.30. I bathed and packed. We are going back with a lot more than we had arriving —sweaters, slacks for E., books, etc. We were going to stop en route for lunch but finally since E., as usual, took an incredible time to bath and make-up we decided to lunch at the beach and leave after lunch. There we saw Tony and Eve Britton [the actor and his wife] who introduced us to a marvellously forthright slightly strabismatic lady of ferocious English upper classness. Her husband is VIP in Arabic and to the Arabs. "Do you love Arabs?" I said. "I loathe them," she said. "Do you speak Arabic?" "Four words only after 25 years, and those with reluctance, and I'm glad to say that I don't understand *one* word." "Does your husband love the Arab?" "Hates them with a passion, my dear." I said Een So [Burton's pekingese] was subject to false pregnancies and acquired milk in her breasts. "Smear her tits with Epsom salts or vinegar & water," she said. "I was here a few winters ago and it was pissing down." "It was what?" said a Roman girl. "Teeming, my dear, teeming," "The Town likes you," she said. "Come back." So I suppose we'll have to go. E. adored her.

They were becoming collectors of eccentrics, the more inconsequentially outrageous, the better. Any connection with normality was dwindling rapidly.

Marlon Brando hove up to play opposite Elizabeth in *Reflections In A Golden Eye*.

(Oct. 29) We've seen a lot of Brando who is very nice— much nicer than he used to be—and very engaging and silly after a couple of small drinks. After 1½ vodkas the other day he said that "unquestionably the *easliest language* to learn was Spanish and not" as I had asserted "English."

Another meeting a few days later and Brando goes even higher up the Burton scale.

(Nov. 3) Marlon's immorality, his attitude to it, is honest and clean. He is a genuinely good man I suspect and he is intelligent. He has depth. It's no accident that he is such a compelling actor. He puts on acts of course and pretends to be vaguer than he is. Very little misses him as I've noticed.

A fortnight later the pact was fixed.

> (Nov. 16) Marlon B. and Christian Marquand came to
> dinner on Sat night. Everybody became sloshed to the gills
> and a thoroughly forgettable time (literally "forgettable"
> as no two people remember what happened at the same
> time) was had by all.

About the time of the new Brando friendship, Eddie Fisher sued
Elizabeth over a property settlement and demanded custody of Liza
Todd ("over my dead body," said Burton). Burton himself has
more or less finished as Faust and he has accepted—sight unseen
—a part in *The Comedians*, simply because he admires Graham
Greene who wrote the script from his own novel. Aaron Frosch
comes down for days to talk business. "Aaron is sad because he
says that he knows he bores me." Burton with the director John
Frankenheimer tries to buy and set up Malamud's novel *The Fixer*.
Gielgud wants him to be Caliban in *The Tempest*: he agrees. Josh
Logan offers him *Camelot* on film—he's not so keen. His Notebooks
rove over Lord Thomson buying *The Times*, the British elections
—this is 1966—and writing.

> (Oct. 20) Ron [Berkeley] and E. bet me I couldn't write
> a publishable book of not less than 100 pages by Xmas
> this year. $1000 is the bet. $900 E., $100 Ron. We'll see.
> I have so many books to write I'll probably end up not
> writing one.

As he has a little more time on his hands, entries lengthen. Passages
like these are rough drafts or well-worked notes:

> (Nov. 17) I have just read *Tread Softly For You Tread On
> My Jokes*—ghastly title by Malcolm Muggeridge. It's a
> series of articles collected over the years from newspapers
> and magazines and shows it. He repeats himself quite a
> bit and is peculiarly engrossed by pornography and sex.
> I have the feeling that he is not being honest in his re-
> actions. Why does he not like pornography? Because, acc
> to the Oxford Dict it gives rise to lewd thoughts? So what?
> We'd have lewd thoughts anyway, pornography or no

pornography. If you're lonely and unwanted it can solace you, and with a companion to share it it can become unimaginably delightful. The unctuous rubbishy shit written about pornography is nonsense. Practically all good pornography is best selling, so I understand, and yet I have never found anyone who when asked if they enjoyed it will ever admit it. They will say that they've read it— *Fanny Hill, Chatterley's Lover, Tropics of Capricorn, Cancer, Candy*, etc. But they're still too inhibited to say it gave them pleasure of a sexual kind. Blah. I know bloody well it did. I've heard too many men talk in too many barracks and Nissen huts and clubs not to know what *they* think, and too many honest women have confessed to me things they've thought and heard from other women not to know what they think either. There are, doubtless, pure souls who through some act of God are physically neuter, or who have had sexual normality scourged out of them in youth, or are too old to care, who may genuinely be horrified by pornography. I'm sorry for them. Journalists of course are pornography's greatest scourge, working for newspapers who wouldn't dream of having one issue without at least one scantily clad model or actress in the middle pages. How they play in the dark we'll never know.

There is the argument that pornography can make a man a sex maniac or something perverted. Well now I am, I understand, a potently sexy man but it hasn't turned me .into a sex fiend, a sex killer, a sex sadist or a sex masochist and I've been reading the stuff for years—at least twenty. I knew a girl once married to an older man with whom she'd fallen out of physical love but still loved otherwise who relied upon reading pornography urgently and quickly in the bathroom before going in to his bed to satisfy his desires and to inflame her own. The moralists would flay her alive if she had left him for another man to marry. They would excoriate her if she had extra-marital affairs. So? And what's the difference between reading it and thinking it. I myself have had in my time to make love in the dark to women by whom I was bored, desperately trying to imagine they were somebody else. And doubtless some women have had to do the same with me. Muggeridge quotes Hugh Kingsmill as saying that the act of love is ludicrous and disgusting. Speak for yourself, Kingsmill. I love its disgustingness and comicality. Put some jaundice in your eyes and the act of walking is ludicrous and obscene, and swimming and, above all, eating. All those muscles, in most people, 50 per cent atrophied, sluggishly propelling people over land or through water or gulping oysters. Come off it.

I've written the above carelessly but will elaborate on it one day. It is an important thing to kill cant and humbug even if one is a humbug oneself.

And there is indeed some humbug in Burton. He disliked pornographic *films*: he seems to have had little if any interest in the pornography which assails the public from certain bookshops. Seeing it bored or offended him. Reading about it, though, was a different matter. And that is where the humbug stops because he is prepared to give his frank reaction to this and trade in his observations against the theories and pieties he discovers in Malcolm Muggeridge.

Throughout this time the Burtons are constantly protected by security guards and hemmed in by the paparazzi. If not the paparazzi, the public. They slip off to Positano—Burton goes for a walk.

(Oct. 16) Later, without E., I took Een So for a walk up the hill from the hotel but, since I literally stopped traffic, I went back after a couple of hundred yards. Let's hope it's just weekend crowds otherwise we'll have to move on or back. Why do they do it? I never gaped at anybody in my life and much as I admire certain famed people, Churchill, and various writers—R.S., Gwyn and Dylan Thomas, T. S. Eliot, Spender, Greene, MacNeice, etc., etc., I have never asked them for an autograph. I actually feel as embarrassed seeing a public figure as being one.

And then so many people turn up to see them.

My anti-social tendencies, even with people I know well, are going to be very strained—unless I get drunk. And I don't feel like it.

Nevertheless and despite the far-flung family, the worrying finances (none of the winners were yet coming in and *The Shrew* and *Faustus* seemed losers) and all the counterforce of the life they led, Burton got down to learning Italian, setting up house and, above all, living with Elizabeth as a proper husband to a doting wife. Both of them were utterly determined to transplant leafy suburban domestic bliss into the heartlands of licence, uncertainty, panic, greed and envy.

She is the Notebooks' thread. They share their upset about the death of one of their dogs.

> (March 25) I felt dreadful all day long—melancholy and distant—and so did E. Georgie died. He must have caught something from some alien dog in the pound he was at. Now Een So is ill. Pray God she's alright. I love that old Chinese lady.

This sincere sentimentality was one of the most binding common instincts.

Real alarm sets in at the beginning of April.

> (April 6 and 7) E. who was supposed to TV for M. Todd Junior very ill from that bloody bleeding. We have sent for a doctor from London. I went to bed in a huge depression and nightmares of her dying.

From now on there are regular reports on the course of this latest illness.

> (April 8) E. has blood pressure of 90—very low apparently—from loss of blood.

On April 12th, she has to have an operation.

> (April 12) E. to go into hosp tomorrow for curettage. Came to lunch with me and felt sick and faint. On arriving home bled. Middleton-Price flying in from London to knock her out. Poor little thing. I shouted and bawled at her for being "unfit" for lack of discipline, for taking too much booze. I think I was talking about myself—out of fear for her. God get tomorrow over rapidly.

The next day.

> (April 13) I lunched alone in my room, did some Italian, and waited for the phone to ring. And waited. And waited. I read a whole book, rather precious, by Arthur Machen called *The London Adventure*. Then the blower blew and joy of joys it was herself on the other end and the operation was over and she was in pain but alive and will live to be shouted at another day.
>
> I finished work at 4.00. Showered. Had my vodka and tonic. Sped to the hosp. Before arriving home I stopped (Mario drove) in St. Peters and stared at the whole huge thing and muttered under my breath.

Elizabeth was his chief preoccupation at this time and his fascination with her is charted in detail and lovingly.

A couple of weeks later she appears fully recovered.

> (April 28) We dined at home quietly and made lovely love. The first time for a month because of E.'s condition. What a magnificent relief and release.

On set he monitors her progress as Kate in *The Shrew* without fussing about it—and makes sure that her first day's unsatisfactory work is reshot.

> Saw E's close-ups etc at the windows. She is splendid now and is bringing up her big guns (no offence). It is one hundred per cent more effective than the previous shots. She is going to be Kate.

He describes idyllic times with her, just stopping at a quiet local restaurant, having some rough cheese and wine, listening to the voices of a choir from the nearby church of the Madonna of Divine Love, speculating about the one or two other customers:

> one . . . a distinguished oldish man, well dressed, who sat alone at a terrace table and neither ate nor drank nor moved . . . the voices of the choir drifted on the air like an invisible mist, like unseen tumbleweed, like a dream.

We stopped eating our fare (raw kidney beans) and rough cheese and we stopped drinking our vin de pays to listen. It was one of those moments which are nostalgia before they're over.

Elizabeth has described the time of *The Shrew* as "one long honeymoon."

> (May 29) Both Eliz. and I agreed solemnly that we never want to work again but simply loll our lives away in a sort of eternal Sunday. Quite right too. We are both bone-lazy. And enjoy it.

He takes her friendships seriously and when Montgomery Clift ("E.'s greatest friend") dies he is totally sympathetic.

> (Sept. 24) His companion, nurse and major domo very kindly sent E. his (Monty's) handkerchiefs which he had only recently bought in Paris and which he loved, delicate white on white. And to me—Monty's favourite soap! Should I use it or keep it? E. was very upset and still cannot believe he's dead. A little Monty Clift cult has started since his death. It would have been more useful when he was alive. He couldn't get a decent job for the last 5 yrs of his life. Poor sod. I didn't know him very well but he seemed a good man. E. has received a couple of lovely letters from his mother.

He encourages her to cook, praises her cooking, passes books on to her, and tries to avoid her when he is too "savage"—then he will hive off to another bed, often creeping back at about four in the morning. He showed her off to friends: "Elizabeth cooked this meal herself." It could be irritating.

After a day of reading commentary for the Florence documentary, Burton has some drinks and blows up at the fuss being made over the two-day visit of himself and Elizabeth to London.

> (Nov. 19) Became furious, nerves nerves nerves, because of what I considered to be over packing. For *two* nights in London we have *two* large suitcases. But that wasn't

the reason really. It was nerves from a hard day and nerves about flying and nerves about the Aberfan show [the charity concert to raise money for the victims of the disaster].

Smoked myself furiously to sleep and before doing told E. she was not to come with me to London. Leave me alone, I screamed as I slammed doors. Give me some peace! What nerves and booze will do. I couldn't go without her.

That is the final entry in this first Notebook.

The most striking thing of all is how hard Burton is trying to create the conditions for a decent and viable married life. Circumstances are so heavily against him that it can be laughable. His own past is not at all promising and nor is that of Elizabeth. The complications brought on by the consequences of everything they do and the unremitting public interest in who they are seem to bar them from what they most want. But he goes for it. Limbering up for the writing; conducting the family. Being domestic when he can. Unable to resist the bender but apparently just as happy with a good book. Suffering a lot in silence from a debilitating and painful disease. Wonderful company on his day—and those seem to have been many.

At the end of *The Taming Of The Shrew* Kate makes her speech of obedience. Petruchio has "tamed" her and she gives a sermon on the duty of a wife:

> "Thy husband is thy lord, thy life, thy keeper,
> Thy head, thy sovereign; one that cares for thee, . . .
> And when she's forward, peevish, sullen, sour,
> And not obedient to his honest will,
> What is she but a foul contending rebel
> And graceless traitor to her loving lord?"

In the film, Elizabeth Taylor does that speech without irony, in all sincerity. After the take, she looked at her husband and said, "Of course, I can't say it in words like that, but my heart is there." He glowed. And her statement had to be made in public: it gave it credibility. That was much of their—joint—life.

But there was a shadow over Burton. Not only was the "pinched nerve" "arthritis" refusing to abate, he refused to take steps to check it. More than that. He feared epilepsy. There is evidence that he had first had a mild fit early in his career and since then had been aware and afraid of it. Later he was to take pills in case of an attack. It was only a distant warning, but it could strike again. Epilepsy— the terrible biblical disease of the working class—was also rumoured to be a sign of demonic possession. To those who endured it, it was a nightmare forever imminent. Together with the magnificent head and the utterly careless, audacious physical drive, Burton had an astounding constitution. He also carried the seeds of his own self-destruction in deep childhood fears. For too many years his will-power allowed him to ignore them.

And now that power willed him to reach out completely to faraway Kate and support her fully, which he did; to provide a place where Jessica could at least live and be cared for, which he did; to bring all the Welsh family and especially Ifor and Gwen who now depended on him, Bob Wilson and his wife and so many other aides who became, increasingly, dependants; to help Maria in her illness, Liza in the loss of father, Michael and Christopher in their drifting adolescence and, above all, to love Elizabeth fully and to explore that love as faithfully as he could. To make much money and a career he could respect. He was at his fullest stretch.

16
Laurel and Hardy

Elizabeth tries to be a shrew [he wrote], wants to be an autocrat and unsuccessfully attempts tyranny in little things. She often tells me off in front of people when I upset her. She is also very jealous and doesn't fancy my taking two looks at some pretty girl. She gives me hard kicks under the table but I go on looking because it does her good to feel a little humiliation at times.

1967 seemed the vintage year. The notices and profits from *The Night Of The Iguana* and *Virginia Woolf* were coming in. They were achieving that enviable double: critical acclaim and box-office success. Immense and, even better, justified critical acclaim and scarcely imaginable box-office success. That Burton was the new Number One fulfilled all the expectations of those old Hollywood producers of the early Fifties who had rightly noted the talent but been unable then to market it. They had just done *Shrew* and as 1967 unfolded, that, too, was to prove a hit—good (though not unmixedly good) notices—lots of enjoyable attention and at least a twelve-million-dollar return on their two-million-dollar investment. Ten million dollars profit (again, to get the full effect, multiply by about eight). *Doctor Faustus* was less certain but then it had been done on a different set of ground rules (Burton said that he would never again direct: he needed too many hands) and those who saw the early cuts thought that *he* was fine and *she* looked wonderful: pity about the film. That could be lived with even when the critics assassinated it.

There seems little doubt that although he was drawn into what he saw as the mystery and fun of Elizabeth he was the dominating partner. She soothed him. She sought him in bars. He flung decisions overboard. On films and film business he took her advice most carefully, as he took that of Aaron Frosch on contracts: experts were to be listened to. Philip had branded that on his brow. "We never had any question of who was boss. She always realised I was to run the show," he said. The remark seems based on truth. The Notebooks for this year show him in the driving seat. His rhythm, his idea of the life they should lead—her willing co-operation, her equality demonstrated by insistence on the presence of her own personality and style: the dogs, the entourage, the luggage: the family. The family—his and hers—became one of his preoccupations. They could ravish him, irritate him, inflame him, move him to great tenderness and he was never the standard father, nor could he be. But those children today look back on him with affection and gratitude and here, in the 1967 Notebooks, again and again we see him trying to provide some stability, some direction, some context for what was inevitably a life of global vagabondage. Burton and Taylor became the first strolling players of the jet-set age.

He is still interested in the theatre—in an interview with Kenneth Tynan at the end of 1966 he observes that he is "frightened" at the thought of going back on the stage but shrewdly self-aware it is just that fear which makes it necessary for him to try. He also points out yet again that Elizabeth has made him a better film actor, made him take films seriously.

There were very few film actors he admired. And even fewer directors. He watched very few films and Elkan Allan, the critic, talking to him about this much later in his life, thought that it was this neglect as much as anything else which accounted for the poor choices. He did not see that film knowledge could be as useful to an actor as book knowledge. This arrogance did not do him much good but at last with Huston and Nichols and Taylor he began to accept that an enterprise worth respecting was under way.

You could scarcely blame him or any sensible person for being sceptical. Time and again he had been given what looked like good scripts by those whose track record as directors had been fine, only to discover on the screen that he looked like a lulu and the film crashed. Very few people know how a script will turn out. Even among the best, they do not know. The alchemy of script, director, technicians, and the public mood is so volatile that you need much more than the modern Delphic oracle of the poll-preview. At least on stage you could—if you were Burton—control the words and control and direct the audience's attention. On celluloid your performance can be cut, literally, to shreds. Remember Antony! It can make you lose heart or resort to all manner of tricks. Burton was too grand for tricks. And although he often had a genuine enthusiasm at the beginning of a movie, his bullshit scanner would soon probe out the weakness and lies and cover-ups. He would grow bored. Then the enterprise would be reduced to making money. "For the money," as he had said, on *Sandpiper*, "we will dance." It could be a grim tango.

One of the very few film actors he *did* admire was Brando. He would come to the set of *Reflections In A Golden Eye*, occasionally, to pick up Elizabeth and arrive early to watch Brando at work. Rumours of course flew about that he was jealous of the Brando–Elizabeth scenes; that he hated Brando. From the Notebooks and all subsequent talk, this seems to have been the opposite of the case. He was intrigued by Brando.

The shank of 1967 was to be two films by writers Burton and Taylor trusted. Burton loved thriller writers, good literature and literary men: all three are combined in Graham Greene. Burton revered him. To play in a Greene script from a Greene novel, with Alec Guinness—another actor on the very short list he had any time for—and Peter Glenville (of *Becket*) directing, seemed both a joy and a certain hit. Taylor loved Tennessee Williams, "the Bird," as he was nicknamed, the wild talent, the honesty, the camp, the lush concern with illness and talking about illness. *Suddenly Last Summer* and *Cat On A Hot Tin Roof* had done her very proud. Now there was to be a film from the less successful stage play *The Milk Train Doesn't Stop Here Any More*—eventually retitled *Boom*. Joe Losey, impeccable credentials, was to direct. Sardinia was to be the location. Another cert—and a delight. But they had to be together and this did not help either movie.

Elizabeth came into *The Comedians*—one version is that Glenville forced her in; *her* version is that she was talked into it. She gave one of her more unconvincing performances. Richard was hauled, reluctantly, into *Boom*, in which as the ambiguous handsome young stranger he was adrift and unconvincing. But these were to be later judgments. Taking the luck as it came, they seemed to be extremely fortunate in the two scripts which had come their way. And well paid. The package for the two of them on *Boom* was two million dollars plus the usual high expenses and percentages. On *The Comedians* Burton got three-quarters of a million dollars, Taylor half a million, with, again, luxurious expenses and unusually high percentages. It was the first time he was paid more than her.

But it was not only the year of the family and films; 1967 was the year when the Burtons began to go publicly mega-rich. Over the next few years they were to play a dangerous high-wire act with the public. In my opinion they decided to flaunt it. "Them as has 'em wears 'em," said Elizabeth of her monarchical collection of jewellery. A dress would cost a year's wage in all but a few Western countries and would be worn once. Extravagance and the deliberate teasing of the public with extravagance would grow. It was rather like watching a matador with a bull: as if the Burtons— *driven* in this instance by Richard, although Elizabeth was a wonderful model and pupil—were determined to see just how much the public would take. It is part of Burton's testing character. They had the money, they would spend it conspicuously. They would not scurry around in grey suits and share options and offshore deals, the Cayman Islands, Liechtenstein and amalgamated buy-outs. They would live out the old-fashioned fairy tale; live it out glutinously, disgracefully, and see whether the public would be delighted in their "truth" or sickened by what they could rightly call indulgence. It was another trial. Something of a game. Burton was a fanatical games-player, puzzle-solver, test-setter, competitor, teaser.

A yacht was bought; a jet was bought; high European society— from the Windsors through the Rothschilds to the Rainiers—was embraced. In Wales, never forgetting Wales, he put £100,000 into a bid for an independent television station (what would become Harlech TV). In Paris, a boutique was purchased. Charities and individuals benefited enormously. At a Royal Command Performance in London for *The Taming Of The Shrew*, not only did the charity benefit, one hundred and fifty individuals were brought up from Wales. Family, of course; outer relatives, friends of, pals with, known about . . . one hundred and fifty. All put up in the Dorchester Hotel—fresh flowers in the rooms, courtesy Mrs. Burton, the party lasting all night and a new party starting in the morning as Richard and Elizabeth flew out and the Welsh went back to the Valleys, polishing the stories every mile of the way.

The Burtons, in 1967, can be seen to be establishing a floating island of a home with sea and air links: relishing the pleasure of working in ''sure-fire'' and intelligently written films: enjoying and adding to all the gossip. The Notebooks are best dipped into as a continuous commentary on what was one of their happiest years.

With only the hint of a cloud. Burton's arthritis was named now—but only in his Notebooks. The epilepsy was never mentioned. Not even in the Notebooks. The drinking is under scrutiny. Burton is increasingly aware of this Jekyll and Hyde division in his behaviour. When he was the wrong sort of drunk (usually he would be amiably sloshed), he could be nasty, vicious and violent. The viciousness would be allied to a certain stinging sense. He would attack people for their ''snobbery,'' their ''pretentiousness,'' weaknesses, blind-nesses, which were not without a residue of truth. But they were not the sort of things one said: certainly not in public and especially not if you were increasingly playing the game of going into Society. There is more than a whisper of desperation: more than a hint that, as someone whose life's work and survival was to be attuned most sensitively to what he *was*, he sensed his time might be limited. He had a present and pressing sense of death. *Timor mortis*. One skin too few: and that a blemished skin. He also had a vivid and often reckless lust for life.

The 1967 Notebooks run from January to November—again the exercise book, both sides, neat handwriting, now and then a gap of a week or so but increasingly not only a record but a try-out for ''the book.''

Before going to Dahomey for *The Comedians*, he did his home-work. Read up on it. Tried to sort out African politics. Just as in Italy he read Barzini and studied Italian so here he homes in on the President. The first entry, however, picks out Elizabeth.

> (Jan. 9th) E. is looking gorgeous—she blooms in hot climates. It must be that Italian blood. I didn't drink a single drop yesterday and consequently had profound ''shakes.'' I must take it easy with the booze.
>
> In Dahomey: (Jan. 10th) Yesterday we went to the Pal-

ace to be received by the President called by all his staff "*Mon General.*" He is very black (married tho' to a white wife and has seven children) about 5'8" tall, slightly bow-legged, stockily built. His clothes were ill made though his Cabinet members were impeccably dressed. I understand that coups d'état are the thing here, as in most of the new African states, so that he may not be the boss for long. At the moment it is something of a dictatorship—when I asked him how many *députés* there were in Congress he said "*aucune.*" Whoops! I thought. He obviously likes women and was forever taking E. by the arm. She of course was charming and very feminine. We both found the experience oddly moving. Here was this huge mosaic'ed palace, only completed 3 years ago, and outside the immense Salle de Reception, capable of receiving 3000 people at one time, there was washing on the line.

He showed us with great pride the "Chinese" room which was so cluttered with furniture and bric à brac from, he said proudly, "*mon grand ami Chiang Kai-shek*" that we could barely move between the furniture. With equal pride he showed us his own and his family's living quarters which were poky and small. He showed us his wife's clothes closet and brought a lump to E.'s throat when with a flourish he opened a door to show a perfectly ordinary rack for shoes.

He asked E. to step on to a mat on the way out and chuckled with delight as two wall lights automatically came on. E. simulated astonishment and he was very pleased. By this time I was sweating like a bull and was glad to leave.

The English are a cold lot. We had lunch afterwards with Guinness and Glenville and I'm sure that had we not said immediately how impressed and moved we were they were ready to send the whole thing up.

Although he writes later of the President, who visits the set and squeezes "E.'s" arm some more, we feel he has lost interest. It is not complicated enough. He has sussed it out and the rest is indifference. Even in that entry there is another, rather rugby-horny reference to "E."

> I am madly "in love" with her at the moment, as distinct
> from always loving her, and want to make love to her
> every minute but alas it is not possible for a couple of
> days. She'll have trouble walking in a couple or three
> days.

The advantage of Dahomey was that they were unpestered. There
were other intruders, "scores of minute mosquitoes which even if
they didn't bother you made you feel itchy." The disadvantage—
shared by ninety-five per cent of films—was that there was a lot of
time in which to do nothing. This set in early on.

> (Jan. 11th) Later we sat at home with the publicity man
> who is, so far, a bore, and Gaston and Ron and Frank
> Larue [another member of the entourage] and after the
> aforesaid pub man had left started talking very seriously
> and equally very drunkenly of the obligation one has to
> one's fellow beings. Should one have a child if one has
> a history of insanity in the family? Etcetera. All this laced
> with profound lectures from me and Elizabeth. Stupen-
> dously smug.

A lot of champagne was drunk. Elizabeth would often have to set
out around the very few bars in town to find Richard jarring with
the lads. After the trials of directing and filming *Doctor Faustus*,
the perils of Zeffirelli, there was a backlash and he did little but the
film work. His usual overspilling energy—buying, plotting, reading
ahead, meeting up—was abated and he liked nothing better than a
few drinks. The Notebooks dry up. One thrice-verified anecdote
which was a Burton favourite comes from this time. Elizabeth was
ringing round various bars to get hold of him. "Richard Burton,"
she said in her high firm voice; it was late at night/early in the
morning. "Who?" "Richard Burton. Is—he—in—your—bar?"
"Is he black or white, madam?"

Guinness, like other old and true friends, found the entourage
rather unlovely. Even though it was down to a minimum it was still
a presence. It was not just that it was thought to be showy—"Why
do the Burtons have to be so filthily ostentatious?" asked Rex
Harrison—it was positively disliked. There are too many stories of
the entourage appearing to behave in a high-handed manner. It is

doubtful whether that sort of thing got back to Their Majesties. It seems to be becoming a court on the over-protective and self-inflated model of the eighteenth-century German princelings. As we have seen, Guinness had tried to get through once or twice in the past and received no acknowledgment of his approaches—"Very rum," he says. "I didn't know what to think." When Burton *did* see him he was "perfectly genuinely," says Guinness, delighted, and again genuinely puzzled that messages, even presents, had not "got through."

Guinness, in *The Comedians*, paid Burton a great compliment. He had to do a long take—about four minutes—and Burton, off camera, had to listen: nothing else. But the quality of the attention can determine the quality of the performance. "It was the greatest support I've had from an actor ever in my life," said Guinness. A remarkable number of superlative compliments came his way from superlative peers. In Burton's Notebook are regular fleeting compliments to Alec or A. Guinness: "He looks remarkable as a negress. Quite deceived me at first." But for all their mutual respect they were opposites—Guinness the fine line etching, Burton the Rubensesque oil, Guinness the dry observer, Burton the roaring instigator. It was their intelligence and literary interest which gave them mutual respect and ease.

> (Good Friday, March 1967, St. Jean Cap Ferrat.) What a huge lapse. We spent some more weeks in Dahomey getting hotter and hotter, with most people getting sicker and sicker. E. won the N.Y. Critics award for *V.W.* (I was runner-up to P. Scofield) and cabled M. Brando, who was staying in Gstaad at our house, to ask if he would pick the award up for her. He did and then, if you please, flew to Dahomey to deliver it personally! He apparently made a speech attacking the assembled critics for not acknowledging E. before and not giving me the award now. Funny fellow.

His laconic reference to his failure to win a major award is rather impressive.

> We still retain a certain amount of nostalgia for Dahomey. The house, the lizards, the palm trees, the unit intrigues,

the arrogance of the American Negroes with the West Africans, the dangerous fascinating sea only a couple of sand tumps away from the house, the mad Palace, the President and his dowdy provincial wife. The Palace receptions and the fetes.

A big, though unwritten, fear was that of kidnapping. Graham Greene's novel—set in Haiti—had stirred up a lot of threats. The Burtons received two or three kidnapping alarms a week and each of their children had a policeman earmarked to guard them on location, which meant everywhere outside Gstaad and their schools. They were now finishing off The Comedians at the studios in Nice. The Mediterranean set began to present itself—Prince Rainier and Grace Kelly.

(March 31) Last Monday night we had drinks at the Palace at Monaco and then went on to the Hotel de Paris to a banquet in aid of the British American Hospital, at which we were the guests of honour. I enjoyed but don't remember too much about it. He was tubby and smiled kindly and seemed nice. She was pretty and young looking and very short-sighted. Her eyes indeed are terribly weak and at the end of the evening were shot bright with blood.

On the same day he does a "catch-up" which, in a few lines, sketches the switchback nature of his life:

Things that stick out:
We were both nominated for Oscars for V.W.—the film itself getting 13 nominations.
We had dinner with the D. and Duchess of Windsor who came back afterwards to our apt in the Plaza. We all got on famously.
We went to London for the opening night of Shrew. A huge success almost totally spoiled by Frank Flanagan's sudden death the morning of the opening night, which incidentally was E.'s birthday. He died quickly, thank God, of a heart attack. [Frank was the husband of Agnes—Elizabeth's dresser.]

A couple of weeks later Sally Wilson [Bob's wife] died in N.Y. of leukaemia or a sinister relation.

Bob and Agnes are both with us here in the house at St. Jean Cap Ferrat recovering from the terrible shock. Bob is strong and suffers in relative silence.

With the Duke of Windsor in Paris. We went back to our apt after dinner and the Duke and I sang the Welsh National Anthem in atrocious harmony. I referred disloyally to the Queen as ''her dumpy majesty'' and neither the Duke or Duchess seemed to mind.

What is notable here is not only the effortless sense of equality with which Burton swings between writing of the Windsors and then of Elizabeth's dresser—but the tone in which he does it. The weight of interest and sympathy is with Bob Wilson and Agnes Flanagan. The Windsors are boasted of, but he cannot resist teasing them about the Queen. His little store of snobbery soon exhausted itself. Always he was his own man. And the thirteen Oscar nominations for *Virginia Woolf* get shortest shrift of all.

Then came the yacht!

(May 21) We are going to buy this M.Y. [motor yacht.] It is old—60 years—is 130 feet long, three engines, 260—80 tons. She will do 14 knots. There are 7 bedrooms two of them with large double beds and will sleep 14 passengers. There are 8 crew, tho' that includes a cook, maid, waiter. The boat itself needs only 4—at the most 5—crew to run it efficiently. I estimate it will cost 25-30,000 dollars a year to run it. Not too bad when one considers our last house (rented) cost $10,000 a month plus approx $1,000 a week for food and staff, etc! If we can use it as much as possible instead of hotels we could actually save money.

It had belonged, so the tale went, to an eccentric Englishman who had installed an organ and driven out to sea in stormy conditions in order to play Bach. That suited Richard very well. For the rest of the year, the yacht was to be the toy but also, in some only half-formed way, a proper floating home for the dogs, the children, and Elizabeth and himself. Nothing went as planned, of course. The designer—Barbosa, hired by Elizabeth—was a perfectionist and also had to meet increasingly extravagant demands as the boat turned into a five-star French hotel. And there was a lot of sea-sickness about. Still, the boat was bought and Burton was off on the High Seas of public extravagance.

> (May 24, Portofino Harbour) E. anxious that I write about her so here goes: she is a nice fat girl who loves mosquitos and hates pustular carbuncular Welshmen, loathes boats and loves planes, has tiny blackcurrant eyes and minute breasts and has no sense of humour. She is prudish, priggish and painfully self-conscious.

There's talk of Cary Grant doing a film with Elizabeth—but "only if I direct! He must be frightened of her or something. Perhaps he's a little strange in the head." Gossip begins to ferment: Hugh French "told us that James Mason has left his agency after 17 (?) years because they, the agency, were getting all the plum parts for me. Well, well."

The world came to the boat. The boat, incidentally, was called *Kalizma*, after *Ka*te, *Liz*a and *Mar*ia.

> (June 1) We were in St. Marguerita yesterday for watering and fuelling and just as well as it gave us a chance to get away from Rex and Rachel [Harrison and Roberts who lived in Portofino]. We had spent Sunday up at their house and, as usual, it was very liquid. Rachel is still maniacal. We saw them again on Monday evening at La Gritta Bar in the port. Fortunately before Rachel became totally demented they left for home and dinner at about 9.30. By this time Tennessee Williams and his friend Bill had arrived and Joe Losey and J. Heyman [*Boom*] and H. French. Tennessee, who now prefers to be called Tom, seemed sloshed and spoke in a loud voice, powerful, penetrating and incoherent and somewhat embarrassing. E. told him to lower his voice a few times. We were in the Pitosforo at the time, and we attract enough attention as it is. Have now decided to do *Boom* with E. We start Aug. 14. I hope I'm right. On Tuesday evening everybody came on board. Rachel became stupendously drunk and was or became

totally uncontrollable. The strangers, T. Williams, Losey,
Bill, French, Heyman, left in disgust. She insulted Rex
sexually, morally, physically and in every way. She lay
on the floor in the bar and barked like a dog. At one time
she started to masturbate her basset hound—a lovely
sloppy old dog called Omar. E. lectured her, I did, Rex
did. All to no avail. She bitterly harangued the memories
of Carole Landis and Kay Kendall, hurled imprecations
at Lili Palmer. Christ.

Burton's disdain is clear. He insists on being an honest recorder,
but the tone distances him decisively.

Tennessee and Bill came too. Again the former seemed
to be tipsy. He is certainly not very prepossessing phys-
ically. Heyman told us he tried to kill himself a few weeks
ago but was saved by Bill. There were no details. I asked
Tenn if diarhyl (?) pills depressed him.
"I have no way of knowing," he said.
"Because," I said, "you're depressed all the time."
"Right," he said.
They left about 4 and we read in bed (at least E. was
in bed) for the rest of the day.

On June 2nd things looked up.

The two dogs have been making love now since last Sunday at least 3 times a day. Who would have thought that
dogs in heat went on so long. They remain locked after
each coition for about 10—12—15 mins. They are very
serious about it and Oh Fie's penis is beginning to look
the worse for wear.

Three days later, June 5th, "Dogs still at it!"
The previous day, the Harrisons had called again.

(June 4) Rach became pretty drunk again on Punt e Mes
and gin and started to strip off at one point. The people
on the roadway above started to cheer, thinking it was E.,
no doubt. I stopped her.

I can't see—*we* can't see how Rex can put up with her behaviour if she is continually like this. It has reached the point tho,' as they both told me, where Rex, after her behaviour last Tuesday (?) wrote her a letter. She's basically a good girl but she should not drink. I was surprised to find she's 40 years old. I thought she was about 37. Rex is fantastically tolerant of her drunken idiocies. She wouldn't last 48 hours with me and he's had it for 7 years.

Rachel was Welsh. Rich here is speaking for the clan—as a clan chief. A brief entry on June 5th.

Reading back through this Notebook I see that I wasn't writing when we heard that E. had won the Oscar and I hadn't! Bloody cheek. But P. Scofield won so that's alright. I sent him a cable and he me. Will write of the days of the Oscar later today perhaps. I must go ashore and buy some clothes for myself.

There was a great deal of speculation and rumour around this. Burton, it was said—sources unidentified—"desperately" wanted an Oscar. Taylor equally desperately wanted them to get "the double." That year she had little competition. Burton was in the ring with several contenders, most especially Paul Scofield whose *A Man For All Seasons* by Robert Bolt, directed by Fred Zinnemann, had all the qualities the Oscar-givers wanted. Burton, it is said, got wind that he would lose, could not bear the humiliation and dissuaded Elizabeth from going. Jack Warner pleaded with her, "DON'T BURN THE BRIDGES YOU HAVE BUILT." Turning up at the Oscars was a heavy three-line whip. It would be her second Oscar—a great honour in a city which takes its honours with high seriousness. Burton, it is said, dreamt that if she went she would be killed in an aeroplane crash. For whatever reason, Elizabeth did not go and missed what for her would have been an extremely sweet moment of triumph and revenge. She was indeed devoted to him and stayed with him. "But then," said Bob Hope at the ceremony "leaving Richard Burton alone on the Riviera is like leaving Jackie Gleason alone in a delicatessen." It was a good crack but Burton was in Dahomey at the time.

(June 13) Kate arrived from N.Y. with Aaron. K. was, as usual, enchanting and very pretty and excited and she immediately re-established warm "lovins" with E.

(June 14) Kate went to the hospital with E. while the latter had her leg replastered. Kate jumping all over the place and slept with us the night. I finally went to sleep downstairs in K.'s room. Aaron and Bob came on board and took up residence. We leave for Portofino tomorrow, weather permitting.

(June 21) We have been in Portofino a week roughly and leave tomorrow for Monte Carlo. E. and K. have been shopping like lunatics. E. has bought umpty-nine watches, sweaters, "puccis." K has bought hats and watches (two, I think) and has been giggling steadily from dawn till dusk. Giggling with her has been Elizabeth. What a pair! They each think the other is the funniest comedian in the world. Washarino.

In Monte Carlo the world continues to wash up as they drift around the Mediterranean.

(June 24) Orson Welles, gargantuanly fat, joined us for a minute or two. He said that every film he'd directed in his life had cost him money, that he'd never received any money from any of his films and that *Chimes At Midnight* had cost him $75,000 personally out of his own pocket. He left the table suddenly and dramatically with a *sotto voce* "Darling" to E. and a conspiratorial squeeze of my shoulder. I wondered to E. how he could possibly make love.

Back in Gstaad there is one of the periodic attempts to sort out the children's education.

(July 20) On the 5th July we picked the boys up at the school. A horrible day—Michael has definitely been sacked and Chris is everybody's darling, winning two prizes, one for Art. I loathed the headmaster. A very big man, Swiss, with an emaciated wife and, as compensation, a lovely chubby baby daughter. Ava Gardner was there with Ricardo (Madrid) who tends to be a bit of a know-all. He had a son there of 19 who still had not (or just had maybe) graduated. Mike is lethargic, sluggish and graceless but he's very loving and intelligent enough to hold his own in Le Rosay. We shall try and get him into Millfield. Fred [Norma, Heyman's wife] has talked to the head, and we might get him in there. If we can keep him in school for another 2½ years we shall be satisfied. He's probably a slow starter like his Uncle Howard [Elizabeth's brother].

Arthritis strikes again, this time in his wrist, so badly that he goes to see a doctor: "For *me* to see a doctor! I guessed it was arthritis and it is. I hope it doesn't last as long as the other dose I had in my back."

(July 21) The effect of these pills on the arthritic arm is fantastic—for about an hour you think somebody is carefully and sadistically slitting open all the veins and that your arm is about to fall off. To counteract this I took ½ tablets of E.'s Empirin and Codine. It helped a little.

He goes to London to get the Wilding boys, Michael and Christopher, into Millfield.

(July 28) Yesterday we had lunch—the whole purpose of the visit was to see him—with [the] headmaster of Millfield. He was disappointing. I had imagined a much wiser, more authoritative man. This man was tall, thin, very English, nervous in gesture and a compulsive talker. One white liar recognises another and I found some of his stories a little too highly polished. He made E. and Michael very nervous but didn't me—perhaps because my respect was mildly tinged with contempt. Anyway it seems that the boys are acceptable. I think they'll be alright there. What bores headmasters generally are. For ½ the yr they lord it over children and it must have a distorting effect on their relationship with adults. All their little jokes are laughed at, their little bursts of anger trembled at. Still, he's obviously good at his job. I became a little tetchy once or twice.

On the way back to Sicily:

> (July 28) On the plane we found Peter and Sian O'Toole and we proceeded to get drunk. Peter asked me how many nominations I'd had. I said truthfully FIVE. He said, holding up his fingers to point it, that he'd had *four*. I know he's only had two. Does he think we're idiots?

They were headed for Taormina to pick up various awards, "surrounded by publicity and paparazzi, we live in a blaze of floodlights all day long." It was on occasions like this that his admiration for her was reverent: and it spilled over.

> (July 30) E. has become very slim and I can barely keep my hands off her. It turns out that she's not that less in weight but, as a result of massage and exercise the weight has been redistributed. She is at the moment among the most dishiest girls I've ever seen. The most. I mean dishiest.

They wound up business in Rome.

> (Aug. 2) What a dreadful and terrible day and good too. All my pettiness and resentment and idiocy all rolled up into one day. I'll blame it on Rome. All the bad things that have happened to me have almost always happened in Rome. Something to do with its elevation perhaps. It is too near sea level. Or maybe the lamentable dirty remnants of the people who beat the people, by stealth not courage, who beat the Romans. These who remain cannot be Romans. They must be servants who in one wild night slew the real Romans while they were asleep in the dark. I don't like them.

He added:

> In the middle of the early night Elizabeth and I exchanged insults in which I said that she was not "a woman but a

man" and in which she called me "little girl." A lovely
charming decadent hopeless couple.

And then, like a howl of confession:

I am stupendously disappointed in myself. Something
went wrong in my head at the wrong time. Anyway . . .
something went wrong. And will never be put right. I am,
I think, sublimely selfish.

This is Burton speaking true. What was it? This "thing" which
went "wrong in my head at the wrong time"—leaving Sybil and
Kate and Jessica? Going out blindly to screw the world? Or something more simple, medical, of which he dare not even write? The
fear of epilepsy? It is a despairing cry. The howl of horror at seeing
the terrible brief nakedness of what we are.

But life went on.

(Aug. 11) A terrible day, frantically, disorganised, thousands of bags all over the place, nine children, six adults
all on one plane, Howard [Elizabeth's brother] and Mara's
[his wife] incessant screaming, my and E.'s pre-film
nerves, nine children, plane-fear, Gaston has fallen in love
again, dwarfly serious, with Patricia's mother (Patricia is
Christopher's girl friend), nine children, the *Kalizma*
hasn't arrived, nobody at the airport to meet us, nine
children (Dick Hanley, Bob Wilson, John Lee cost us
roughly $1,000 a week) and hot and a small room and a
multi-zillion dollar picture and I screamed "*fuck*" out of
drunkenness in the hotel lobby . . . To scream "fuck" in
the lobby was the only possible way to meet the justice
of the day.

They got permission to go to Venice for a ball—otherwise they
worked steadily on *Boom*. Although Burton did not at first trust
Losey—he had a tendency to beadiness about directors unless and
until they proved themselves—Elizabeth seems to have positively
disliked him. This meant, as Burton always warned, that she found
it very hard to deliver a performance. She knew her own talent to
a hair: she had to be cosseted to deliver—no matter how self-

indulgent that was, no matter how babyish it seemed, that was the case and when things went right she could deliver with the very best screen actresses. Without the cotton wool she hardened. But they were, as Noël Coward, who joined them, would always say "good pros: none of this Method nonsense." Yet in a way Burton and Taylor—good pros though they were on the surface—both drew on themselves and their own lives in ways which would have been immediately recognised by Stanislavsky. This was one of the reasons for the Strasbergs' adoration for Richard.

(Sept. 19) Worked like dogs and did 7½ minutes—we are nearly ⅔ of the way through the script after only 3½ weeks or 4.

Nasty incident that everyone laughed at when Michael Dunne the dwarf was pulled off his feet by Robbie the Giant Schnauzer dog. He carried it off very well, calling the dog a dumb head.

E. did a remarkable scene in which she nearly coughed her lungs up. Everybody very impressed.

Noël Coward arrived looking very old and slightly sloshed and proceeded to get more sloshed. He embraced us both (separately) and lavished compliments on E. about her beauty and her brilliance as an actress. Occasionally he threw a bone to me. He is a most generous man but sadly he is beginning to lose the fine edge of his wit or perhaps like me he repeats himself when tipsy. He moves like an old man but I suddenly remembered that he's always moved like an old man. Stoop-shouldered non-necked, he has the curved body of a very tall man but in actual fact he is no taller than I. He is now almost completely bald and the bags under his eyes have made his eyes even more asiatic than hitherto. He calls himself "the oldest Chinese character actress in the world." Coming off the plane he was asked how his journey was (it has taken him two days to fly from Suisse, there is an Alitalia strike) and he said, peering his way towards customs, "My whole life has been an extravaganza." He is a delightful man. "I am completely muddled," he said, "by J. Heyman. I have talked to him on the phone and communicated with him by letter and I had firmly made up my mind that

J. Heyman was a short hairy greasy Jewish gentleman, running rapidly to fat. Instead of which I find a golden boy. It is most off-putting."

(Sept. 20) E. and N. Coward are madly in love with each other, particularly he with her. He thinks her most beautiful which she is, and a magnificent actress which she also is. We all saw rushes and some assemblage last night. It looks perverse and interesting. I think we are due for another success, particularly E. I was worried about her being too young but it doesn't seem to matter at all. Wrote a long letter to Phil which I still haven't finished. Finish it today perhaps. Went to bed late—about 2.00 I suppose.

With Coward came gossip.

(Sept. 21) We talked about D. Niven and how, though they had been fast friends, he cut E. dead for seven months when she was involved in the "scandal" with E. Fisher and how though we were still friendly it could never be the same again. Noël told a story of a woman who was the leading lady of a play he was in when he was very young and how he needed £40 desperately for his mother who was running a boarding house. The actress said yes he could have the money. He went home exultantly to his mother. Next day the actress said that somebody had forged a cheque of hers for £40 and that she had just returned from the nearest police station to report it. Noël said, "Exactly £40?" "Yes, exactly £40." Noël went to the police station and asked if the actress had been there to report the fraudulent cheque. They said no they'd never seen her. "We are still friends," said Noël, "and that was in 1923 but it was never the same again." He is a good man.

Elizabeth continued to besot Burton.

(Sept. 24) Elizabeth was looking infinitely sexy. She wore mesh white leotards and the shortest mini-skirt I've ever seen. It barely, and when she moved didn't, cover her crotch. The beach boys around, who all appeared to be stoned, were beside themselves. And as we left they shouted various invitations to her and offered to kiss her in various parts of her anatomy—the mini-dress was also very low cut—including sundry offers of fornication. They were careful that I was on the boat and moving rapidly away before these generous offers were made.

It is almost sweet that he calls up his street macho. The sexual intoxication and possessive jealousy is heavily in evidence and clearly Burton is in thrall to her at this time.

Whenever Burton came near a good writer he is respectful, and always alert to whatever the writer says. He was, by reports, talking a little, and very modestly, about writing at this time and he had certainly opened up markets for his articles and stories in quality magazines. Noël Coward—whom he had known on and off for about twenty years—was a rich seam.

(Sept. 26) Last night, out of my usual loyalty (!), stayed up all night with E. and N. Coward and Co. I wrote, typed, a long letter to Howard and Mara as to what they should do with the 100 G. we gave them as a present. Occasionally I joined E. and Noël for chat and gossip. Noël says that the longest he'd ever taken to write a play was 10 days for *Cavalcade*. The shortest 5 days for *Blithe Spirit* which he wrote in Portmeirion. He had the idea on the train journey to Wales and had it written in his head before he sat down to the typewriter. Joyce Carey (actress) was with him and was writing, he says vaguely, something about Keats or something. *Private Lives* took a week. *Hay Fever* 6 days. Astonishing.

In Paris they are the toast of the smart set and on amiable joshing terms with the Duke and Duchess of Windsor. The Burtons were there to launch the *Shrew* and had a quiet dinner with the Windsors, the Rothschilds and one or two others. The next day they woke up, drank beer to dissipate the hangover, and prepared for the film and the gala that evening.

(Sept. 30) We were told that the whole of Paris was agog
with expectation and from the point of view of the press
it certainly seemed to be true. We had as much, if not
more, attention as we used to have in Rome, Paris, etc.,
during "Le Scandale." They had put crush barriers around
the streets looking on to the Opera and there must have
been several hundreds if not thousands of spectators. A
lot of people had stayed up all the previous night to ensure
a vantage point.

However at about 12.00 noon this same day I did something beyond outrage. I bought Elizabeth the jet plane we
flew in yesterday. It costs, brand new, $960,000. She was
not displeased. I think we can operate it at a reasonably
practicable rate—perhaps with luck almost nothing. This
might sound suspiciously like famous last words but I feel
safe in it. It can, in 12 to 15 hours, and with one or two
stops depending on weather, cross the Atlantic. It can land
on any small airfield including unpaved ones. It can land
e.g. at Abingdon when we go to Oxford next month. *It
can land at Saanen* [Switzerland]. It also means that we
never have to land at that horrible London Airport ever
again. Hurray!

But about the evening of the film and gala. It was an
outstanding success and the press coverage was enormous.
The film is widely praised and apart from a carp or two
in the *Herald Tribune* and one French paper—not very
important—the critical reaction was joyous. E. wore a
diadem specially created for her by the De Beers company
of Van Cleef and Arpels, designed by Alexandre, which
cost $1,200,000. With her other jewellery she wore a total
of roughly $1,500,000. When we left the hotel, sur-
rounded by 8 guards, all the hotel guests were forming an
aisle to the street. There were many photographers. But
at the Opera it was a madhouse. Despite the presence of
5 ministers of the Govt., one of whom gave us a message
purporting to come from de Gaulle himself, and numerous
luminaries of the cinema, stage, and society and the arts
E. was unquestionably the Queen of the evening. They
hardly ever photographed anyone else. [Burton knew how
much the smart set loved publicity: to beat them on their

own turf was satisfying.] I did quite well too and the flattery we were subjected to was very rich and heady. It however, I hope, has not gone to our heads. It was nevertheless sweet revenge for the social ostracism we endured such a relatively little time ago.

A few weeks later they were in Oxford.

Flew in the 125 to Oxford last Friday, landing, by special permission, at Abingdon and went straight to "The Bear" at Woodstock.

They were there for the premiere of *Doctor Faustus*.

(Oct. 20) We were nerve-racked and nightmared at the prospect of 48 hours of solid public exposure. On Saturday we televised with D. Lewin, Alexander Walker, Jim Something-or-other, N. Coghill, Lord D. Cecil, and a Professor Rosenberg of Berkeley, California. Cecil was a joy and both E. and I quite fell in love with him. He is the best kind of well-bred eccentric, sane, a compassionate but acerbic brilliant maiden aunt—tho' married and clearly male. Nevill said, upon being asked on TV, that E. would have made a fine scholar because she was among "the most intelligent creatures he'd ever met" and was paradoxically "an instinctive intellectual." So there. He said that I was among the three greatest Welshmen he'd known, the other two being Dylan and David (*In Parenthesis*) Jones. He didn't realise—and I didn't correct him—that Jones is a Cockney.

On Sunday morning I read poetry at the Union with Wystan Auden. He read a great deal of his own poetry including his poems to Coghill and MacNeice. Both very fine conversation pieces I thought but read in that peculiar sing-song tonelessness colourless way that most poets have. I remember Yeats and Eliot and MacLeish, who read their most evocative poems with such monotony as to stun the brain. Only Dylan could read his own stuff. Auden has a remarkable face and an equally remarkable intelligence but I fancy, tho' his poetry like all true poetry

is all embracingly and astringently universal, his private
conceit is monumental. The standing ovation I got with
"The Boast of Dai" of D. Jones's *In Parenthesis* left a
look on his seamed face, riven with a ghastly smile, that
was compact of surprise, malice and envy. Afterwards he
said to me, "How can you, where did you, how did you
learn to speak with a Cockney accent?" In the whole piece
of some 300 lines only about 5 are in Cockney.

Jeremy Treglown, now editor of *The Times Literary Supplement*,
remembers it a little differently. Burton was quite enjoyable, he
says, if rather short-winded; Auden was utterly compelling.

Auden is not a nice man but then only one poet I have
ever met was—Archie MacLeish. Dylan was uncomfortable unless he was semi drunk and "on." MacNeice was
no longer a poet when I got to know him and was permanently drunk. Eliot was clerically cut with a vengeance.
The only nice poets I've ever met were bad poets and a
bad poet is not a poet at all—ergo I've never met a nice
poet. That may include MacLeish. For instance R. S.
Thomas is a true minor poet but I'd rather share my journey
to the other life with somebody more congenial. I think
the last tight smile that he allowed to grimace his features
was at the age of six when he realised with delight that
death was inevitable. He has consigned his wife to hell
for a long time. She will recognise it when she goes there.
    And so to Sunday evening and the opening of *Faustus*.
It rained like mad, as usual in that splendid climate, and
there were lots of people outside the theatre in macs and
under umbrellas who applauded, etc. A nurse, it was a
charity performance for the Nuffield Hospital, and therefore a nurse, presented E. with a bouquet of flowers and
if you please curtsied. E. and I were delighted. I met
Quintin Hogg and thinking him to be Boothby asked him,
"Where is your Sardinian wife." He replied that he was
not Boothby. I recovered fast, told him I was pulling his
leg and asked, "Why aren't you the leader of the Tory
Party." He: "They had their chance in 1963 and lost it.

Now I'm too old at 59." Me: "Winston didn't become
PM till he was 65–66." He: "Hmm."

The Duke and Duchess of Kent arrived and were all
presented. The Duchess is adorable and both E. and I
loved her. She was frantically nervous as we all were but
she showed it in close-up. Muscles twitched uncontrollably around her mouth. He was shy. The show went
alright.

The party afterwards was alright but exhausting—between us we must have met a 1000 people. Incidentally
when we entered the theatre we were greeted by a fanfare
of trumpets, then silence as we took our seats and then
another fanfare for the D. and Duch of Kent. I record that
because it shows the idiocy of fame. 5 years ago we'd
have had a fanfare of raspberries. If we were lucky.

The notices next day, he said, were "money but mixed." Some
said splendid, some said vulgar but none dismissed it.

Ken Tynan came up from London to discuss the controversial Churchill play *Soldiers*. Will write about that later.

The weather was dreadful and made me feel that I never
wish to see England again. We had to land at Gatwick to
clear customs and the wind was so strong that I had to
hold Liza up. But within an hour we were over France
and the Med and it was blue again and halcyon. Don't
think out of choice that I would live in England again
even if they paid me to.

Am in a violent temper. E., as usual, has to combat
everything I do or say in front of the children. I wish to
Christ she'd not contradict me in front of them and wish
likewise that I didn't do likewise. But it's the Status Quo.
I'd best shut up.

In all this, Elizabeth's public comments were as honest as his private
jottings. "Sometimes it's not easy to be with Richard especially
when he's angry," she said. "Then I think he's capable of almost
anything. Sometimes he drinks too much. Richard is very independent. I let him do what he wants."

Towards the end of that year he took a small part in a trendy nonsense called *Candy*, jokingly blaming Brando (who was also in it, as was Walter Matthau) for leading him astray. But the film world seemed utterly secure. He thought *Boom* would be a big hit and *The Comedians* make a good critical showing and perhaps a bit of profit. Oxford had received him as a conquering hero: Paris had put on its best show for the Burtons: Ifor (who, one day, reached "into the depth of his bowels and brought out a cosmic fart that shattered the eardrums. E. was delighted and tried to respond but her netherland was not talking") and Gwen were back in place and the Jenkins Welsh had been brought up to the Dorchester for a Night To Remember. The yacht ("The first time I've been able to carry my books with me") and the jet were lined up. There was a world out there to be astonished and he was developing the taste to astonish and alarm. The devil was now firmly in the driving seat.

Elizabeth was still the central preoccupation. "When she cooks for an hour it takes me 4 hours to clean up afterwards," he wrote. They could indeed have made a good Laurel and Hardy series about their domestic lives. But the dark tone still there: and sometimes desperation. Yet leonine Burton is still rampant and never more himself than when he is paterfamilias, even to a child not his own.

> (Oct. 21) An obeisance to little Liza who bought, out of her allowance, a quite expensive present for Maria—our new Anglo-Welsh stewardess—and the conversation went like this:
> Me: You're a good girl, Liza. How much did it cost?
> She: I'm not going to tell you.
> Me: Why not?
> She: Because you'll pay me back what I spent.
> Now you can't hardly be better than that.

It was all working. And, at the heart of it, best of all, the family was being sorted out.

17
1968

The Burtons had blazed through the Sixties. Not only were they stars, box-office, a continual success, headlines the world over, they were also fun, wild, high-wire, unexpected, the taste of the times. Ladies and gentlemen, the fabulous Burtons! First their immorality and then their monogamy entranced the growing world of gossip. And where would the story end? Would the greatest Don Juan of his day be faithful to the "little Jewish tart" who extorted fidelity as the price of marriage? Would she, four times married before the age of thirty, finally rest content in a state which had suited her so badly? Meanwhile they peppered the papers with declarations of love, despair, foreboding: hostages to fortune. "I will love him/her forever"; boomerangs: "Now we have the plane we can hop over to Nice for lunch." "Everyone should pay taxes—except actors." They made it so easy for reporters that their names should be entered in some heavenly glossy magazine, for their contribution to newsprint. "All You Need Is Love," sang the Beatles—Ringo, their metronome, became a friend of the Burtons—and as the pop nostalgia of the Sexy Sixties swungalong regardless, the Burtons rode on the crest of the vogue.

Disasters, moonshots, wars, malnutrition, oppression, man's normal round of savagery to man had not quit the ring—but the pretence of those pined-for and derided early Sixties was that they had. "Peace, man." Hold out the flower like the crucifix to Dracula and evil will disappear in a puff of smoke, Tunisian marijuana for preference. LSD became acceptable—hallucination a form of intellectual exploration and the despised money a source of harmless fun. 1968 changed that. Vietnam changed that. The student revolution across Europe and America and even into India and Japan changed that. The Seventies were to be more and more "serious" side up.

It is no more than a coincidence that the Burtons began to wane at this precise moment, but coincidence it is. In 1968, *Boom, The Comedians* and *Doctor Faustus* all came out: all were commercial flops and none was a critical success. There was a whiff of the lynch mob in the air. *Doctor Faustus*, for instance, is not a good film but as a student romp to raise money for a university playhouse it is a remarkable attempt: nor is Burton wholly terrible. He carries too much of the film and is badly constrained by the over-significance of the part but he was drummed out of court. *Boom is* eccentric, no one is on their finest form: the same goes for *The Comedians*— but once again seeing these films today, there is something to enjoy and admire. For all their quirks and lapses they carry more interest than more applauded contemporary films. In *The Comedians* Burton is fine as Brown: trying perhaps too hard, unable quite to "click" with the part as he had done in *The Night Of The Iguana*, but worth anybody's time. In *Boom* he is badly miscast but gamely pulls his weight. Neither deserved the offhand treatment they received. But the word was out that their time was up. They would take a very long time a-dying.

It was Taylor's star which began to decline most markedly after this year. Again and again—right to the end—Burton would do a performance, as in 1984, which would shake the critics, bring back the public, re-establish himself as a force. Taylor, partly because of the physical hammering she took during this year, began on a decline which in acting seems irreversible. Her unique fame, though, is still a huge—limitless—credit to be drawn on whenever and apparently forever.

The newspapers were out looking for cracks in a relationship built on chasms. The *New York Times* man in Africa had caught up with them in Dahomey and was there when the news came of the Apollo astronauts dying in the capsule while still on the ground. "Good God, that's horrible," said Burton. "And they got it, just sitting there, right on the pad . . . not even an honest death." Taylor: "Oh, their poor *children*. What a pity they had to die like that, if only

they . . ." Burton (sharply): "It's not a pity they had to *die*, Elizabeth. And it's got nothing to do with children. It's a pity the way
they died." The atmosphere, we are told, "suddenly chilled." Taylor (eyes blazing): "Christ, that's what I was *going* to say, what a
pity they . . ." Burton (shouting): "It's not that they *died*. Can't
you see that? The poor bastards couldn't even die in *space*! If I die
I want to die in space or as an old man with my feet up reading
philosophy or even with a gun in my hand fighting another man.
But you can't seem to . . ." Taylor (also shouting): "That's *just*
what I was saying, what a pity they were on the ground deprived
of . . ." Glenville (arriving to take them down to the Honorary
British Consul's house): "Ready everyone?"

Interesting that in the same piece, Gaston the chauffeur volunteers
this encomium on Burton. "He was born poor. I was born poor.
He worked his way to Oxford, and well, I had to work, I became
—how you say it?—a *manual*. I tell you, if every *manual* had a
boss like Richard there'd be no Communism today."

Rows were common. Elizabeth professed to enjoy them. From
the Notebooks we see that the overwhelming majority were provoked
by Richard and most of those when he was drunk. What no one
picked up on were the peculiar strains of their situation. On Sardinia,
for instance, during *Boom*, there were kidnap threats out on all the
four children, each of whom had a personal security guard to make
certain they did not sheer off for a moment or two. Half an hour's
absence provoked serious and understandable alarm.

The Burtons seem at this time to be turning part of their lives
over to the public. Out there was a real, a vast audience to be teased
and entertained. Another specialised audience grew up—the Rothschilds, the Windsors, European society, politicians, the top swirl
of actors and writers—to be enjoyed. They began to play the
field—partly for the fun of it, partly perhaps because they were
tired of the business of making films, partly because they knew by
1968 that they were rich enough to retire: and partly because they
must have intuited that the film world was about to pass by their
joint style. It was unconsciously well calculated.

Easy Rider, The Graduate, the comparatively inexpensive, hip,
deliberately non-starry, all young American youth culture for the
fourteen- to twenty-year-olds era was becoming the only game in
town. Burton on his own showed considerable cunning and powers

of survival despite making some appalling blunders over the next ten years.

As if to mark their acceptance of a role on the world stage, this was the year of the diamonds. One explanation was that they were an investment. "A safe bet," said Burton, "and portable." That was for the lawyers and accountants. The truth, as Burton cheerfully and ruefully admitted, was that he loved decorating Elizabeth in diamonds and she loved getting them and showing them off. Both were primitively rooted. The custom is found in most remote tribes. He took great delight in her beauty and wanted her to be "the best": especially, perhaps, given his quick sense, this year when she was scarcely perceptibly on the skids, and was, for some of the time, in awful pain.

The Krupp diamond was 33.19 carats and cost him, in 1961, $305,000. Again, to hoist it up to 1988 figures you have to multiply (current values) by anything between six and twelve. As a "named" diamond it could be worth much more. How nice, said Elizabeth, that such a Germanic diamond should end up with a nice little Jewish girl like me. (One of the ways that Richard could drive her to fury was to taunt her that she had not a drop of Jewish blood in her veins while his great-uncle had been half Jewish . . .) After the Krupp diamond, which was the star of the show when HTV opened its station—the Burtons' name had indeed helped deliver the lucrative television franchise—came the La Peregrina pearl ($37,000), a pearl, diamond and ruby necklace ($100,000), a sapphire brooch surrounded by diamonds ($65,000), other rubies and diamonds ($60,000), a heart-shaped diamond ($100,000), much more and yet more up to the 62.42 carat Cartier–Burton diamond ($1,050,000).

They bought luxuriously expensive mink coats for each other, paintings, clothes, anything conspicuous, everything expensive. Burton was a curious mixture. In one way he was still a careful self-made boy knocking off the light in the spare room and grumbling over the price of chocolate. In another he was an occasional, but creditable businessman, setting up trusts for the children, trusts for Elizabeth and himself: and yet riding through all this was the easy-come easy-go ("I go my own way"), delighted to blow $100,000, to give away $¼ million, to spend it every way but wisely. His indiscriminate generosity to almost total strangers is well and widely attested in letters I have received while working on this book. The sums could go up to $50,000. It was the getting that mattered.

* * *

1968 began with *Where Eagles Dare*, shot, for the first stint, on location in Austria. It was a straightforward wartime adventure story, "meat and potatoes," Elliott Kastner, the smart young independent producer, described it. Hair-curling stunts, vertigo abounding, standins all round. It was retitled "Where Doubles Dare" by Clint Eastwood. Eastwood, like all the others, had to be okayed by Burton, who got $1 million up front, a hefty slice of what would be hefty profits and living expenses on the Taylor scale, including a limousine standing by twenty-four hours a day and the usual stipulation that he would not have to work on St. David's Day.

Of its kind it is fine. Once again Burton was a good soldier. His convincing briskness and aptitude for command carries the gossamer plot over ravines as deep as those the doubles fight over. He gave it just the weight it deserved and he delivered. It was this capacity to play the straightforward grafting role which was to be of use in the self-murderous years ahead.

In February the Burtons came to London—he to do the studio shooting for *Eagles* and then move on to *Laughter In The Dark*, she to make *Secret Ceremony* with Mia Farrow and Robert Mitchum. As the *Kalizma* was being refitted, they hired another yacht—for $20,000 a month. The reason for abandoning the Dorchester for the Thames was the dogs. British law demanded that all dogs which came ashore be put in quarantine for six months. By keeping them on the boat, Elizabeth kept her incontinent pets near her ($900 every four weeks for new Wilton carpets for the *Kalizma* due to dog dirt) and provided wonderful copy for the pet-crazy British tabloid-press.

In the same month they whisked over to New York for the opening of *Doctor Faustus*. It was slaughtered. "It is of an awfulness that bends the mind," said the *New York Times*. *Time* went for Elizabeth. "When she welcomes Burton to an eternity of damnation, her eyeballs and teeth are dripping pink in what seems a hellish combination of conjunctivitis and trench mouth." "He has exchanged the gift of art for money," they said of Burton. The Faustian label was stuck to his forehead like the scarlet letter. And there it remained. It makes a satisfying scar.

Life in London was fun—old friends, the Welsh, pubs, writers, Burton attempting to get his novel under way, Harlech Television opening and many promises of doing their bit for Welsh TV. Burton moved from *Where Eagles Dare* into a film based on the book of

another novelist he had read widely and admired—Nabokov—
Laughter In The Dark.

He played the part of the Art Dealer and while shooting a scene
at Sotheby's bought a Picasso drawing for £9,000. Elizabeth secured
a Monet for £50,000. Her collection of Impressionists matched her
collection of diamonds.

A fortnight into the film he was fired. The incident which sparked
the row—Burton turning up half an hour late for Sunday filming—
was trivial. Tony Richardson, the director, bawled him out and
Burton—who had brought Liza along for the fun—bawled back.
Both men reached for their lawyers. Burton was replaced by Nicol
Williamson.

This was all very unusual. No satisfactory explanations have ever
been given and the matter was soon washed over by the ever-rolling
tide. Perhaps Burton was affronted in being bawled out when (a)
he had turned up on a Sunday and (b) he had brought his beloved
Liza along to watch the fun. He and Richardson had worked together
most successfully in *Look Back In Anger*. But *Look Back In Anger*
had been a box-office flop and Burton, most unfairly, had carried
the can for that. Richardson and Burton were not particularly com-
patible and perhaps Richardson thought that Burton was too much
the star, perhaps he wanted the suspiciously available Nicol Williamson all along, perhaps Burton slid into one of his Hyde moods
. . . It gave him time to fret and worry over Elizabeth who was ill
again and finding it extremely difficult to get through her film.

> (July 23) I have just spent the two most horrible days of
> my adult life. There was nothing before, as I recall, no
> shame inflicted or received, no injustice done to me or by
> me, no disappointment professional or private that I could
> not think away in a quarter of an hour. But this is the first
> time where I've seen a loved one in screaming agony for
> two days, hallucinated by drugs, sometimes knowing who
> I was and sometimes not, a virago one minute, an angel
> the next and felt completely helpless.
>
> Elizabeth had her uterus removed on Sunday morning.
> The operation began at 9.30 and ended at 1.00. Three
> hours and a half. I tried to read Holroyd's book about
> Lytton Strachey—what a vile, cruel, self-centred man he
> sounds—but during those hours I read about 5 pages and

Edith and Richard (known as Dic Bach) Jenkins, his parents.

Cecilia James (known as Cis), his eldest sister.

Richard Burton as a child. TOP: Richard (left) with Elfed; Elfed's sister Ethel (right) and her son Dilwyn.

With Philip Burton, who gave him his surname.

The school rugby team, 1938–39. Richard is sitting, second from right.

As Professor Higgins, centre, in Pygmalion.

In *The Druid's Rest*, photographed by John Vickers, London, 1944.

In the Royal Air Force, back row, second from left. (INSET: with the RAF in Canada).

With Sybil Williams, before she and Richard married.

With Molly Williams, wife of Emlyn and mother of Brook.

In rehearsal with Emlyn Williams and Andrea Lea for *The Last Days of Dolwyn*.

In *The Boy with The Cart*, 1950.

In *The Lady's Not For Burning*, photographed by Angus McBean, with John Gielgud and Pamela Brown, 1949.

With Olivia de Havilland in his first Hollywood film, *My Cousin Rachel*, for which he gained his first Oscar nomination, 1952.

As Hamlet, the Old Vic, 1953, with Claire Bloom as Ophelia. "He has lashed himself to his own mainmast, steering directly by his own star, the star of absolute self-trust which is within all the best actors and whose courses are unalterable, even by failure"—Kenneth Tynan.

Richard with John Neville alternating as Othello and Iago, the Old Vic, 1955–56. Photographed by Angus McBean. "He was a star. And the Old Vic proved it beyond all question. It was unmistakable"—John Neville.

Richard as Prince Hal, Alan Badel as Poins, *Henry IV, Part I,* Stratford 1951. Photographed by Angus McBean. "Burton is a still brimming pool, running disturbingly deep: at twenty-five he commands repose and can make silence garrulous"—Kenneth Tynan.

As Coriolanus, the Old Vic, 1953–54.

Richard as Ferdinand, Hazel Penwarden as Miranda, *The Tempest*, Stratford, 1951. Photographed by Angus McBean.

Frank Salisbury's portrait of Richard as Henry the Fifth, the Old Vic, 1956. "There now appears a romantic sense of a high kingly mission and the clear cognisance of the capacity to fulfil it ..." —*The Times*.

With Sybil soon after they moved to Switzerland.

With Kate, his first-born, in Switzerland.

With Paul Fillistorf, the chef proprietor of the Café de la Gare.

Richard and
Sybil with
Christopher
Isherwood
and friend.

With friends, John Dearth, William Squire and
Robert Hardy.

Ifor Jenkins, elder brother.

Filming *Alexander The Great* in Spain, 1956.

With Jean Simmons in *The Robe*, 1953.

In *The Desert Rats*, with Robert Newton, 1953.

Four years later in *Bitter Victory*, 1957.

With Claire Bloom in *Look Back in Anger*, 1959.

A Warner Bros. publicity shot for Richard with his co-star in *The Bramble Bush* Angie Dickinson, 1959.

Lerner and Loewe's *Camelot* almost failed to reach Broadway in 1960 following the ill-health of the composer Frederick Loewe and the director Moss Hart. Burton with Julie Andrews and Robert Goulet.

Soon to be known the world over as "Burton and Taylor." Elizabeth wore a blond wig to deceive the paparazzi.

Night shooting on *Cleopatra*, 1962.

"Everything that I wanted to hold or love or have or be is here with me now" —Burton as Antony.

"Without you, Antony, this is not a world I want to live in" —Taylor as Cleopatra.

First marriage to Elizabeth Taylor, 1964.

With his adopted daughter Maria, 1967.

With his new family. Christopher Wilding, Michael Wilding (Elizabeth's sons by Michael Wilding) and Liza Todd (Elizabeth's daughter by Mike Todd), 1965.

*The Taming of
the Shrew*, 1967.

In *Who's Afraid
of Virginia
Woolf?*, 1966.
Elizabeth got a
second Oscar
for the part.
Richard was
nominated only.

With Michael Hordern in *The Spy Who Came in from the Cold*, 1965.

In *Doctor Faustus* at
Oxford, 1966. INSET:
Richard and Elizabeth
with Nevill Coghill.

Burton as Hamlet,
1964. INSET: paint-
ing by Kate, "Dada as
Hamlet".

With Peter O'Toole in *Becket*, 1964.

In *The Comedians* with Peter Ustinov, and Alec Guinness, 1967.

ABOVE LEFT: at a 1966 gala in Rome. RIGHT: the diamonds sparkle at an unrecorded engagement in 1973. BELOW: in aid of the Italian floods.

Daily Mail,
October 2nd,
1970.

London in February, 1968, on yacht with dogs.

Another Oscar nomination. With Genevieve Bujold in *Anne of The Thousand Days*, 1970.

In *Where Eagles Dare* with Ingrid Pitt, Mary Ure and Clint Eastwood, 1968.

With Rex Harrison
in *Staircase*, 1969.

On location filming *Under
Milk Wood*, 1971. He had
played in its first performance on radio.

In *Raid on Rommel*, 1971. With Brook Williams (behind binocu-
lars) and Clinton Greyn.

In *Bluebeard*, 1972, with Virna Lisi.

Divorce His, Divorce Hers, made for television, 1973.

With Alain Delon in *The Assassination of Trotsky*, 1972.

With President Tito and his wife during the filming of *The Battle of Sutjeska*.

As Tito in *The Battle of Sutjeska*, also known as *The Fifth Offensive*, 1972.

Burton as Churchill in *Walk With Destiny* (*The Gathering Storm* in the U.S.).

With Sophia Loren in a television remake of *Brief Encounter*, 1975.

Marriage to Elizabeth, take two, 1975, on river bank in Chobe Game Park, Botswana.

Burton and Taylor celebrating his fiftieth birthday at The Dorchester Hotel, November 11th, 1975.

In *The Wild Geese*, 1978.

Richard and his third wife Susan in the grounds of Le Pays de Galles, Céligny.

On the set of *Breakthrough*, 1979, with Susan.

With Peter Firth in the film of *Equus*, 1977. Previously he had acted in it on Broadway.

In *Absolution*, 1980.

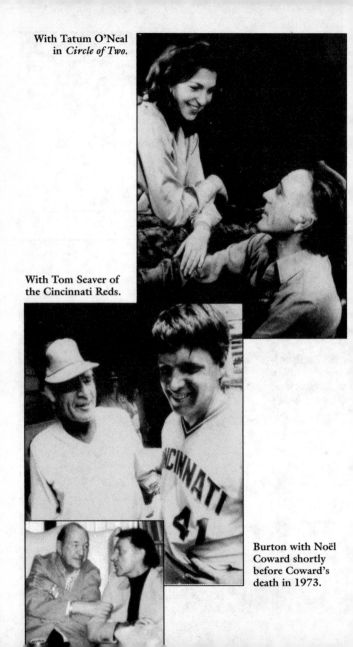

With Tatum O'Neal in *Circle of Two*.

With Tom Seaver of the Cincinnati Reds.

Burton with Noël Coward shortly before Coward's death in 1973.

In *Camelot* again,
1980–81.

In *Wagner*, 1984. RIGHT:
with Sally Hay, who was
working on the film.

In *Ellis Island*, 1984, a mini-series for television, with daughter Kate.

Kate and Richard in *Alice in Wonderland*, the first time they worked together. Kate as Alice; Richard as the White Knight.

In Philadelphia where *Private Lives* was on tour. Richard and Sally had recently married. Elizabeth Taylor had just announced her engagement to Victor Luna.

Marriage to Sally, Las Vegas, 1983.

Taylor and Burton in *Private Lives*, Broadway, 1983.

Richard and Sally at Céligny, 1984.

In *1984* with John Hurt.

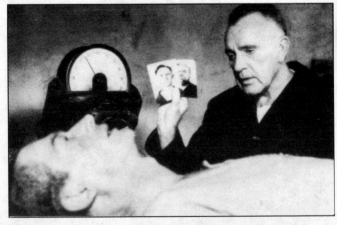

In an episode of *The Fall Guy*, 1983, a television series with Lee Majors.

Burton at a special concert for the United Nations High Commissioner for Refugees in Geneva, 1984.

Richard Burton: "Home is where the books are." The library at Céligny.

Burton reading on the terrace of the house in Céligny.

when I knew she was temporarily safe at least and back in the room I found I had to read them all over again.

But it's the nights that have been so harrowing. I took a room—next door to E.'s—to be near her until the pain had eased somewhat. The walls are like tissue paper and the first night I heard nothing but her groans throughout the night. It is not a normal hysterectomy—there were great complications—and she is suffering far more than normal. In addition they have given her a drug, which eases the pain, but gives her lurid hallucinations. And extraordinary shafts of clarity at the same time. She thought for a long time yesterday that she was on the yacht and, at one point, when flowers were brought in she told them to "put the flowers in Liza's room downstairs." She then sternly told me, looking up from her book (*Public Image*—M. Spark) that I must never shout at Raymond (the steward on the *Kalizma*) again. I said that I wouldn't and she said, "Hush—he'll hear you." "Look," she said at one point, "they're showing *Faustus* in colour on the TV." The screen was blank as a blind eye tho' a greetings telegram had reflected a red into the screen before which it was lying.

Last night she suddenly appeared in my room about midnight supported by a minute Latin nurse and said she was lonesome. She is not supposed to move at all except for the commode. I put her back to bed. Half an hour later I heard her scream "Jim"—she was in the corridor. Back to bed again. I told her she was a naughty girl and she told me to fuck off. I said I would sit in the room with her. She told me to sit in the hall outside the door as she couldn't stand the sight of my face. She turned away from me. I waited 5 mins and left the room. Then there was a shout of "Richard." The nurse and I arrived together. She was sitting on the edge of the bed. Another time she crashed against a chair in the next room. I shot up and out and she was sitting on the lavatory with the door closed.

I've asked them to give her a drug, if possible, that's not illusion-making. Christ, I shall be glad when this week's over. And won't she. She finally fell asleep, or at least remained quiet, at about 4.00 in the a.m. I fell asleep but kept waking with the sort of convulsive wide-awakeness of a man who's afraid of having a heart attack in his sleep.

She is still asleep and it's half past midday. I'm longing to see her.

The press has been pestering us night and day and we're in all the papers this morning. What a vile lot they are— especially the English.

The most alarming lesson I learned about this whole thing was the extraordinary effect that hallucinatory drugs have on the brain. E. looked at me on occasions yesterday with a malevolence that made a basilisk look like a bloodhound.

2.45 and E. is awake and perfectly normal. She is completely aware of everything she did last night! God save the mark!

Her illness, in a curious way, seemed to become the heart of the marriage and, perhaps, for some time sustained it.

The next day, July 24th, Burton began to type the Notebooks. The typing seems to be a signal. In a general sense it signals that the writing is now occupying a serious place in his scheme of things. Page after page stretches on: the Notebooks total about 350,000 words and they cover his reading, his friends, politics, gossip, Elizabeth, speculation, the films, business, anecdotes, acting. If one were to patacake it into shape it could go out as much as a novel as many of the happy new masqueraders under that indulgent umbrella. Elizabeth's illness, which was to continue to have repercussions, was bad enough. Worse came, and in battalions.

(July 24) Janine Filistorf [proprietress of the Café de la Gare] rang today from Geneva with the shocking news that André Besançon, the gardener of Pays de Galles, Céligny, and a very dear and honest man, had committed suicide. Poor bugger. How solitary can you get? We, Kate, Ifor and I will fly in the jet to Geneva on Friday or Sat. to attend the funeral. He hanged himself. I remembered that he had suffered from a nervous breakdown some 12 or 13 years ago after the death of his wife and before we employed him in 1957. He was about to go into a Home this morning at 10 o'clock but it was too late. He killed himself last night. I feel such a bloody fool for not even suspecting it.

He goes back to sleep in the hospital next to Elizabeth, sees Kate up to Hampstead with Ifor and Gwen while Liza and Maria and the boys stay on at the Dorchester with L'Entourage. On the next two days he squares up to Michael and Christopher about their behaviour—loud records at two thirty a.m., cigarette burns in the sheets and curtains. Booze all over the place.

Then he set off to Switzerland to attend the funeral, taking with him Liza, Kate, Ifor, Gwen and Brook Williams. The funeral over, Gwen and the girls were put in a hotel. Brook, Ifor and Richard went to the Café de la Gare across the road from the house for some of the famous fish and some of the drink. Brook, increasingly Richard's pal-on-site (he was in Burton's films as were Ron Berkeley the hairdresser, Bob Wilson the dresser and numerous others in "the family"), is a brilliant mimic, good memory for anecdotes, Welsh. Ifor was the rock of ages, adored still by Richard despite the falling out when he had left Sybil—all mended now, all healed. They decided to stay the night at the house which was just across the railway tracks. Another drink or two taken. The problem was, you were just setting off when the bell went and the level crossing barrier came down and so you were better off going back and having another rather than standing around, might catch a chill. Eventually Ifor, some sheets to the wind, went out to tack his way the two hundred yards in the dark to Le Pays de Galles. He would open up the house.

Richard and Brook drank on. Waited. Ifor was always very conscientious. Rang up. No response. Worried. Set off—hurried across the railway line, the road, ran down the drive to the dark house.

Ifor had caught his foot in a newly installed grille (he didn't know it was there), tripped, fallen awkwardly and broken his neck on the window ledge. He was paralysed from the neck down.

Richard's grief and guilt were uncontainable—his great sport of a father of a brother who had carried him boy and man and outsung, outread, outplayed him all his life, fit, strong, a touchstone, this man he had somehow, in the twisted screw of guilt, "sent to open up the house" like a servant, like an inferior, was now ruined. Ruined for life. Confined to a wheelchair and waiting, as he said, to die. It was unendurable and the world closed in on him.

The Notebooks cease. For two months there are no entries . . .

In the interim they went to America for the Democratic Convention. Burton, as a friend of Bobby Kennedy, did the narration of a documentary film about him. Liza went with them and also Stanley Baker's daughter Sally. Sally was very ill and it was with great reluctance that the Bakers had allowed Richard to take her on the *QE2*. She had to be kept quiet out of all limelight. Burton broke most of the conditions of his trust. He talked to the press about her illness, said there was only one doctor in the world who could cure her, a Russian, but he would get her to him one way or another. The Bakers were distressed and rightly angry. His own alcoholised grief and compulsive fathering of a family had led him to a betrayal and to the assumption of a quite God-like position. Suffer little children . . . 1968 was the year of deaths . . . And his old friends were giving up the struggle to get through to him.

In Paris, Elizabeth was to play opposite Warren Beatty, fresh from *Bonnie And Clyde*, and widely reported as the new Hollywood stud, in *The Only Game In Town*, directed by George Stevens. Burton was to be directed by Stanley Donen in the odd little saga about two homosexual barbers, *Staircase*. The one set in Las Vegas, the other in London's East End and both relocated in studios in Paris to suit the Burtons—a move the studios cursed at the time but which, later, won Zanuck official praise for his altruistic assistance to the French film industry!

Burton said that he played in the film because his old pal Rex had said, "I will if you will." Burton, like Taylor across the road, was getting $1¼ million up front and percentages and lavish living expenses which took them to the Plaza where the five dogs could be incontinent on an entire floor.

He declared that he was "not a homosexual." A needless disclaimer, it might be thought, by the man who, pre-Elizabeth, was the Don Juan of the twentieth century. Yet this has puzzled several writers. Some have pointed to that early intense cohabitation with Philip and doubted the chastity of that bachelor-pupil relationship. While in no doubt that Philip loved Richard, I am equally in not the slightest doubt that it was chaste and paternal. The affection, though, was so strong that it may well have aroused the boy's awareness and branded his emotional development: but "nothing happened."

"I tried it once," he said and the odds are that was in the services when hundreds of thousands of men foreign to the love that dared not speak its name fumbled for comfort and release in the male warrior bondings of war. Like British public schoolboys who for a hundred years have been through a similar bonding—for reasons of class and culture—it tends to fall away, for the majority, once the prison gates are open. Certainly when Burton—quite startlingly attractive—arrived in the post-war homosexual London theatre world of Binkie Beaumont and his lads, he made his heterosexual preferences very plain and his talent made sure he was not discriminated against.

Yet he found it all a strain—like most things after the crippling of Ifor. And there was Elizabeth's illness . . . Warren Beatty on the horizon looking far too handsome . . . Burton threw himself into his writing and their grand social life. For a time he much enjoyed being taken up by the aristocracy and played along as to the manner born. The recording begins again.

Many books were bought and read. Cis and Elfed wrote thanking them for the £500 and saying how excited Tom (a brother) and Hyral (his wife) were when they received theirs. "Can't wait," said Tom, "for the bank to open, they'll hardly get me through the door." "Ifor is to be fitted with a collar which hopefully will enable him to be sat up . . . This should be an enormous help psychologically. He has finally agreed to see Cis." Ifor's shame at his disability was fierce. Burton's unease with Ifor rubs off on the rest of the family: guilt has returned to stalk him yet again. But the present presses out the past. The children are away at school. Filming and socialising and gossip-mongering in Paris begins in earnest on October 1st.

(Oct. 1) Eliz started work yesterday, but without Beatty. Tomorrow he starts. I continued mine with Rex, and oddly enough he was in sparkling form, not worrying about his lines much, and we got along merrily. Hugh French told me that R. Zanuck [son of Darryl Zanuck and a senior film company executive] was more enthused than he'd ever seen him over the rushes from *Staircase*. Well it doesn't mean much but it's better nor a smack in the belly, etc.

But he was in hiding over Ifor's accident; ashamed to meet the family.

> I am much happier in Paris than I am in London. Is it perhaps that I have a dread of seeing my family, i.e. *most* of my family? Is it because I like acquiring new French every day, or that I speak the language, albeit roughly if fluently on occasion? Perhaps I'm ashamed of Britain's weakness. It's awful to see how despised and dismissed she is by the foreign press. Eight in the morning and I must be off to work.

Burton's next dream is to possess a French barge. This he would convert and chug around the European river system with a couple of bicycles on board and all his books, a swimming pool on deck. "It shouldn't be all that expensive." True to form, he begins to search for one. Meanwhile Universal Pictures are threatening to sue him if he does not do *Anne Of The Thousand Days*. He really wants to do *The Man From Nowhere* with Joe Losey but they won't back it. Burton holds out.

The rushes of *Staircase* and *The Only Game In Town* are being scanned daily: Zanuck especially is hoping that the Burton–Taylor moneymaking machine, operating apart but in parallel, will hit a double jackpot. Throughout the filming the reports from the front are ecstatic.

> (Oct. 5) It seems that Eliz has made another success (God my spelling is so uncertain) acc to a telegram from John Springer [publicity man], who is not given to overpraise and who says that he disapproved of E.'s choice of role as a star, but now decided that she was more than a great star, she had proved herself to be a great actress. Weeel Nooooow.

French society begins to claim them. The Rothschilds they know —the Baron is very keen on Elizabeth—but now they have broken through, or are taken up.

> (Oct. 6) We are lunching with somebody called Alex or Alexis who is Baron de Redee. We are going on afterwards

with a party at the running of the Grand Prix d'Arc de Triomphe, the French equivalent of Ascot and Derby day, etc. Though I know very little about horseracing, it might be interesting. Baron Guy & Marie-Helene Rothschild invited us. La Callas will probably be there and possibly Ari Onassis. Aren't we posh?

The pace quickens.

(Oct. 7) We went to lunch at the Baron Redee's house, and had a delicious lunch of fish of some kind, followed by partridge, and a magnificent ice-cream with nuts and cake in it. There were three wines, label-less, and brandy equally anonymous, but all very good. Two devastating wars & crippling taxes, and the moneyed Aristocracy still live like Aristos. They must be cleverer than we think. I noticed that every glass still had wine in it when we left. Is it considered impolite to drain your glass when you rise to leave? If so, I was impolite. There must have been about a hundred people for the lunch. I had a Madame Debreu, American, on my right, and Marie-Helene Rothschild on my left, and a Count de something or other, and a Monsieur de X and astonishingly a lady with a distinct London-Provincial accent. E. sat with La Callas and Baron Guy. The house is huge and very lavish and Marie-Helene said that she considered it the most beautiful in Paris. I said that my favourite house in the world was Ferrières [the Rothschild house]. She said that Guy was a great worrier about legacies to his children, etc, and was going to have it turned into a museum of art, while Marie-Helene would prefer to give it to some branch of the medical profession. Elizabeth said, "Give it to us." Cheek.

Have to go to work, so more later.

Later at the Paddock where only the owners are allowed to go in but we were privileged and went in to the ring. So we were standing there with a great lot of them when suddenly a tall man appeared emaciated and ill and stubble-faced and minusculey-moustached and smiled a lot and was quite incoherent, and had a right hand which was burned to the bone between the index finger and the next. It was Peter O'Toole.

It was the time of the Callas–Onassis Divide.

(Oct. 8) Talking of love-life Maria Callas told us on Sunday that she and Ari had parted. Said he was too destructive and that her singing was affected. I think she's a bit of a bore. She told me how beautiful my eyes were and that they demonstrated a good soul! Said she was a little shy of asking but could she play Lady Macbeth to my Macbeth in the film of it which she had read we were going to do. I suppose she thought Elizabeth was going to play Macduff or Donalbain. Maybe it was merely an off day but she seemed pretty silly to me. She actually described the stage as being undoubtedly my "first love." She is riddled with platitudes. Was on Sunday anyway. Elizabeth who has eyes in the back of her bum and ears on stalks was aware of everything that was going on.

When E., by the way, walked from the paddock to the Loge with Guy and Marie-Helene the thousands of people applauded her all the way. Not bad for an old woman of 36. I am always pleased and surprised by that sort of thing. We have been expecting it to stop for years but it hasn't.

5 past 8 and off to work.

When the point sinks home, Burton is sympathetic and helpful to Callas—little enough you might think though immeasurably more so than the majority of her friends who deserted her. Compared with them, though merely an acquaintance, Burton was stalwart. But even here he cannot talk about a woman without bringing in and building up Elizabeth.

(Oct. 20) Friday began with the English newspapers & the news in headlines that Jackie Kennedy is to marry Ari Onassis. Everybody is intrigued. He is 69, he claims 62, and she is 39. The youngish Queen of the USA and the aging Greek bandit. He is pretty vulgar and one suspects him of orgies and other dubious things whereas the Kennedy woman seems, tho I've never met her, to be a lady. On Friday night I sat beside La Callas who very bravely faced the evening & the press with a bright if rather forced face. I hugged her when I saw her and said in her ear that he was a son of a bitch. This I said not out of moral outrage or because he'd abandoned her but because she learned the news from the newspapers and he'd left her broke. In all those 10 years he, with all his reputed millions, had not given her a cent. Marie-Helene said he would never be invited to her house again but I told her that she was fibbing and that after a time they, the Onassises, would be the toast of Europe. Even we would go to see them, I said, out of pure curiosity. Guy de Rothschild agreed.

I am ridiculously (I hope) jealous of E. nowadays because I suppose she's working with a young & attractive man who obviously adores her. She tells me I'm a fool & that he's like a younger brother. Ah, I say, but there have been cases of incest. They have been known. Oh, yes. But of course I trust her as much as I trust myself, which is considerable, as they say.

We are going out tonight with Maria Callas & Warren Beatty. It appears that the former needs our company & comfort & perhaps the attention we attract, tho' God Knows she can attract enough at the moment in her own right. But I noticed on Friday night that most attention was paid by the press and public to E-beth. She, my girl, looked stunning in a white dress by Dior &, to my surprise as I discovered later, wore for the first time in Paris the great emerald necklace and earrings, etc., which I gave her 3 or 4 yrs ago. My God, she's a beauty. Sometimes even now, after nearly 8 years of marriage, I look at her when she's asleep at the first light of a grey dawn and wonder at her.

The public edginesses, the public testing of their marriage seems non-stop.

(Oct. 9) I read a translation of an article in *Oggi* about a little-known actress who was reported to have said that she could easily have taken me away from Elizabeth, but thought it would be too tedious to try!

Every noteworthy event in their relationship is recorded.

> (Oct. 10) Yesterday was unique. I didn't see or talk to Elizabeth for an entire day. I felt desperate all day long and suddenly about 5 o'clock began to drink Martinis. By the time I got home I was so drunk & tired that I fell asleep, euphemism for passed out, almost before I'd managed to get my clothes off. I think perhaps, though it is good for her, that I don't like Elizabeth working without me. Anyway she must have come in after me, late as I was.
>
> I received telegrams threatening to sue me in "six countries" if I didn't agree to do *Anne Of The Thousand Days*. I am so sick of being sued that I shall probably agree today. But I shall never work with that lot again. The odd thing is that I was never sued when I was poor! At the moment, including the above threat, there are 4 suits against me.

Money.

> (Oct. 11) I have worked out that with average luck we should, at the end of 1969 be worth about $12 million between us. About $3 million of that is in diamonds, emeralds, property, paintings (Van Gogh, Picasso, Monet, Utrillo, John, etc), so our annual income will be in the region of a million. That is God willing, and no wars, and no '29!
>
> We are flying, in the small jet (it's a Hawker-Siddeley De Havilland 125 twin jet) to Nice tonight and going on the *Kalizma* for the wk-end. I'm longing to see it again. We could come back on Monday morning. Sheran and Simon Hornby are flying in the same plane from London and picking us up. They are a charming couple. Off to work and more later possibly.

Sheran Hornby, née Cazalet, was a friend of Elizabeth's from her early childhood in England. Her husband Simon (now Sir Simon) was to become chairman of W. H. Smith.

The Hornbys went down to St. Jean Cap Ferrat, on to the *Kalizma* for the weekend. Burton is as excited as Christmas: the boat is all his Noels.

> (Oct. 12) This morning we are sitting on the poop deck, it is as quiet as prayers with hardly a stir on the waters. We shall go ashore later and probably go to La Ferme Blanche for lunch. Simon and Sheran are with us. They are delightful and so is the boat. The Monet is in the living room or salon, the Picasso and the Van Gogh are in the dining room. The Epstein bust of Churchill is brooding over the salon and there is a Vlaminck(?) on the wall of the stairwell to the kids' cabins. It is ill placed and we will re-place it later when all the other paintings are here. Rex has a touch of 'flu and so we sent him home early and I did close-ups, etc., for the rest of the day tho' we finished early, about 6.45, and I went to pick up E. and the guests at the Boulogne Studios. I saw W. Beatty who gave me a drink and was extremely flattering about Elizabeth. He said how remarkably beautiful she was and how great a film actress. I replied and said that she thought similarly of him. I had a couple of Martinis and went off to the plane. The flight was as smooth as smooth, and took about an hour and a quarter. No one seemed to be nervous but of course we were stiffened by a few drinks. I am having one now as a matter of fact. It is a drink known as a "Salty Dog." That's vodka and canned grapefruit juice with salt around the rim of the glass. We didn't go to bed until 3.30 because we were so excited at the joy of the boat. I can't as 'twere stop touching it and staring at it, as if it were a beautiful baby or a puppy-dog. Something you can't believe is your very own.

> (Oct. 13) Yesterday was a very good day. I'm afraid that I was semi sloshed for most of the day and probably repeated myself but I don't think I was particularly of-

fensive. What a splendidly intelligent couple the Hornbys are. And he particularly is very well read, in some areas as they say, better read than I. There is lots of delicious space left for delicious books. I must too find a corner for reference books and albums, etc., which are very large, and will demand height and depth. The new *Times Atlas of the World* for instance is a couple of feet square or so.

And once more into the breach for Elizabeth.

(Oct. 13) Elizabeth has great worries about becoming a cripple because her feet sometimes have no feeling in them. She asked if I would stop loving her if she had to spend the rest of her life in a wheelchair. I told her that I didn't care if her legs, bum and bosoms fell off and her teeth turned yellow. And she went bald. I love that woman so much sometimes that I cannot believe my luck. She has given me so much.

On the film set the actors wait while the lighting men come and go. The dressing rooms take on the bed-sitter look. Gossip fills in the gaps, like putty to hold the cracks.

(Oct. 16) Stanley Donen told me a funny one about Osgood Perkins [American character actor]. It seems that Perkins was in a long-running melodrama in which he had to kill a character in the last act with a letter opener, stiletto type. One day the props man forgot to put the knife on the table and there was no other instrument around. So instead of throttling his murderee as anybody in his right senses would have done he kicked him smartly up his arse, the fellow fell down and feigned death, and Perkins raked the house with his eyes and said: "Fortunately the toe of my boot was poisoned."

Another letter from Liza which we've been puzzling over. She has a word in the letter which is "irastosable"! I don't know what it means but I shall use it for the rest of my life. A new word has been added to the Anglo-

Welsh vocabulary. What an irastosable day. I found the film absolutely irastosable, etc. "What an irastosable performance."

For pure enchanting malice, this story from Michael Hordern. Count Robert Farquharson of the Holy Roman Empire, 80 years old, pederast and practiser of black arts, reduced in his old age to working at the BBC because he could no longer remember lines, was asked by some mindless young man in the BBC canteen if he'd ever appeared at the Old Vic. This was like asking Gielgud if he'd ever had a shot at Hamlet. Now it so happened that the last time Farquharson appeared there was during Tyrone Guthrie's first season as director. Guthrie is 6ft 6 and at that time weighed about 10 stone soaking wet, as they say. His future and present wife is 6ft 2 and again in those days weighed about 7 stone. The Count's reply: Yes I have worked at the Old Vic. The last time I was there I remember we were directed by a very tall young lady. I remember she wore open-toed sandals, presumably to let the poisonous gases out. And I remember particularly in the middle of the season, to the general astonishment of the company, she grew a moustache, changed into a man, and married her sister.

Letters are written to Kate and Michael and Christopher. News of Ifor being able to move his toes is greeted with enthusiasm. Down to the yacht at weekends.

On the set of *The Only Game In Town* le tout fashionable Paris — its highly bred female cavalry that is, charged in to sniff out Warren Beatty. Elizabeth would return to the hotel and reel off the names of the noblest mares in France whinnying around the man being promoted as the new stud. She also informed an incredulous Richard—still and forever shockable to the roots of his Welsh nonconformity—of open infidelity among the aristocrats, of husbands' lovers and wives' mistresses meeting up, of a wife's lover becoming her ex-husband's lover. "Phew!" writes Burton agog, but more than a touch appalled.

And on the same page (October 23), what might be called, in the spirit of Burton punnery, a footnote.

The waiter just came in with grapefruit juice, stepped in a lump of dog-shit, carried it all over the room and left in a huff & hysterics.

(Oct. 25) The enemy is insidiously attacking again. Beth read in the papers that Ari Onassis had given Jackie half a million pounds worth of rubies surrounded by diamonds. Now Missy already has, as a result of former battles against useless yours-truly, one of the greatest diamonds in the world and probably the most breathtaking private collection of emeralds surrounded by diamonds also in the world. Now the Battle of the Rubies is on. I wonder who'll win. It will be a long attritive war and the idea has already been implanted that I shouldn't let myself be out-done by a bloody Greek. I can be just as vulgar as he can, I say to myself. Well, now to get the money.

Elliott Kastner came from London yesterday and told about flying to the Palace Hotel in Montreux to read Nabokov's new book, *which he hasn't yet finished*, and for which he asks $1 million. All the film boys have been flying into Switzerland in a desperate attempt to be the first to press a million green ones into his hot little Russian palm. How was the book, I said to Kastner? Great, he said. How long is it, I asked? Eight hundred pages. How the devil did you manage to read it in six hours (he had already told me that Nabokov would not let the book manuscript out of Montreux and had given each mogul a time limit)? Well, he said, I read half and Alan (his assistant) read the other half. How then, I said, can you tell it's a great book? You've only read half of an unfinished book. He said he trusted Alan's judgment and presumably Nabokov's too. Funny way to buy a book. Still, I'm glad that a great artist like Nabokov can make them pay through the nose. It happens rarely.

Rachel Roberts was with her husband Rex Harrison in Paris and on the rampage because of her suspicion of an affair. At the premiere of *A Flea In My Ear*, in which Harrison starred, she had gone into a screaming fit against Elizabeth (wrongly) for some suspected slight about whose car was where . . . Some days later she came to have a drink with Richard at about six o'clock.

(Oct. 26) Rachel Harrison proceeded very quickly to get drunk. While she was there Elizabeth called me from the Hotel, she had a day off yesterday and I asked Rache if she'd like to speak to her. Yes, she said, and then, without any preamble, began to bark into the phone. Literally. Like her dog—an adorable Basset Hound called Homer. And that's all she did. Barked and barked. Eliz tells me she was so embarrassed that she didn't know what to do.

Paris in its fabled clichéd sense as the city of sophisticated sin seems to have done the trick yet again.

(Oct. 27) [A friend of theirs] went out with a famous French roué yesterday for lunch. He took her to a Chinese restaurant. As she was forking a mouthful of bamboo shoots into her mouth he said with deadly seriousness, "I would like to penetrate your deepest part." At the party given by Louis Ferraud the night before, where she had met this 57 yr old rapist, he had, without so much as a by your leave, grabbed her by her breast whereupon she had slapped him firmly on the behind. "Beat me more," he said, "I love to be beaten, don't you?" He is apparently very rich and owns newspapers and magazines. I shall find out his name and titles tomorrow from Ron Berkeley. In the car on the way back to the hotel he asked her solemnly to scratch his wrist. Intrigued, she did, at which point he made a great lunge for her sex. She threw him off. I should say that she is getting on for six feet tall and strong as a front-row forward. No easy prospect for an unwilling seduction. He knows somebody, he says to her, who has a room set aside in his house for the sole purpose of orgies. "It is Dunlopillo from wall to wall." Ugh! Strangely enough, though, when E. asked her if she would lunch with the man again, she said, "Oh yes, he's very attractive." Women are very strange.

Burton, out walking one of the dogs, found himself lost.

(Oct. 28) As usual I had gone out without money in my pocket and so I couldn't stop and have a drink, which perhaps is just as well. I was in some very deserted street, very odd that it should be so empty and silent while only, as I discovered later, a stone's throw from the Champs Elysées, when a sort of hard-bitten girl came around the corner. I swallowed my pride at being lost and asked her, "*Ou est l'avenue Montaigne, s'il vous plaît?*" "I don't know," she replied in English. I thanked her and walked on. Suddenly I realised she had turned and was walking beside me. "*Vous aimez Paris?*" she asked. "*Oui, je l'adore,*" I replied, picked up Een So and crossed the road in a sort of urgent half-walk half-trot as if I were the prettiest little virgin in town. I had been made a pass at! First time for years. I wonder if she was a tart.

(Oct. 29) I received a letter from Francis Warner yesterday asking if I could or would become a don at St. Peter's, Oxford, sometime shortly. I am very excited & am going to write to him suggesting that I should go up for the summer of 1970. He will, he says, give us his chambers & I shall offer to swap them for the yacht and our various houses. He needs a sabbatical he says. How funny it will be to be lecturing at Oxford without a degree! Now I've always had this pregnant woman's yearning for the academic life, probably spurious, and a term of smelly tutorials and pimply lectures should effect a sharp cure. I would like to deal with either the medieval poets in English, French, Italian and German and possibly some of the Celtic like Welsh & Irish, or to confine myself to the "Fantasticks," Donne, Traherne, Henry Vaughan, George Herbert. The first poem in English that ever commanded my imagination:

> Sweet day, so cool, so calm, so bright,
> The Bridal of the earth and sky:
> The dew shall weep thy fall tonight:
> For thou must die.

> Sweet Rose whose hue angry and brave,
> Bids the rash gazer wipe his eye:
> Thy root is ever in its grave,
> And thou must die.

> And that's not all. I mean that chap Herbert was indeed
> a box where sweets compacted lay. I am as thrilled by the
> English language as I am by a lovely woman or dreams,
> green as dreams and deep as death. Christ, I'm off and
> running and will lecture them until iambic pentameter
> comes out of their nostrils. Little do they know how priv-
> ileged they are to speak and read and think in the greatest
> language invented by man. I'll learn them.

The zest is unmistakable, the appetite genuine. Not only will the
wild fantasy of an unspoken ambition be realised, this will, perhaps,
confirm, even provoke, that change in the direction of his life which
he wants so naggingly.

There is not a great deal of talk about acting—none at all about
the theory: he could as well be a plumber out on a job and no doubt
he would in some part welcome the analogy.

> I spent much of yesterday in a bath with a lot of body
> make-up on, which meant when I came home Elizabeth
> had to wash my back. I was back to the mines again and
> the women washing their husbands' backs clean of the
> grime of the colliery.

"I feel roughly one thousand years old," he writes, "and have the
old familiar arthritis 'old Arthur' back." He still sleeps badly—
occasionally too much, most often too little.

> (Oct. 31) S. Donen told me just as I was leaving last night
> that the rushes were truly great acting. It was the 'orrible
> black wig scene that he'd just seen. Ah well, we shall
> see.
>
> I had the full actor's nightmare in that heavy second
> sleep one gets. I had awoken at 3.30 and returned to sleep
> after drinking two litres of ice-cold water from the fridge.
> Rex was involved, E. was in the audience sometimes and

sometimes on the stage. Rex was drunk and couldn't remember his lines, and I, little goody two-shoes, was desperately trying to help him out. It was no play that I could
recognise but was full of young irreverent people. Probably that came from the OUDS. Anyway I was glad when
the phone rang & brought me back to this other more
controllable dream.

Must leave for work, it's going on for 9.30 and I mustn't
be late or it upsets my whole day. E.'s still asleep.

The Windsors visit Elizabeth's set and then Richard's. They are
being "taken up" and it gives Richard a chance to have it both
ways. To enjoy a surge of snobbery and undisguised delight that
this twelfth child of a Welsh miner should be hob-nobbing so intimately with the glamorous former Prince of Wales. You can feel
his imaginary postcards going back to Cis and to Pontrhydyfen
saying, "How about *that*!" There was an intellectual snob in him
which he held on to always. The social snob here enjoyed a good
outing and then lost interest. And that was the second advantage.
He could do it—but he could also do without it. If they came, they
were met—for all his understandable bedazzlement at times—as
equals. And it was *they* who came to *him*. And down it went recorded
as use and proof for future works. Then another of the "leaders of
Parisian Society," Princess Elizabeth of Yugoslavia, teams up with
the Burtons.

(Nov. 5) Princess Elizabeth came over to the set. She is
very pretty but quite impertinent. I am not absolutely sure
that she might be a little nasty behind one's back. Tiny
touch of the daggers. Just a feeling. She seemed to enjoy
Rex's inability to remember lines. Can't say likewise for
meself. She was off to dinner with Warren Beatty. She
was quite excited but pretended she wasn't.

Callas is part of the same set and although Richard knows her only
slightly and cannot—in his Notebooks—conceal his reservations,
he does his best.

(Nov. 6) Yesterday I worked on and off all day, Rex going
mad with his lines again. Maria Callas arrived and since

I was in a reading mood she was not very welcome. She seems pathetic to me despite her great reputation as an opera singer-actress. She said how she was meeting some Italian in ten days' time who wanted her to do Medea as a film, but the operatic version, whereas she insists on doing it as in the original, i.e. without singing. I think any second she is going to ask me to play Jason. That's one boring piece they'll never get me to do. I summoned up as much good nature with Callas however as I could & took her on the set a couple of times to watch a couple of snippets that Rex and I were doing. She averred as to how fascinating she found it all, and after a time, much to my relief, went to Elizabeth's studio which she'd already visited once. E. told me later that she too found her rather sad. She was there when E. and Caroline [O'Connor, her nurse] were playing gin-rummy and sat and watched like a child. At one moment E. was beaten easily by a quick gin by Caroline and said "shit." At this Callas shot up and said in great agitation, "Oh no, I've never heard such words. Oh no, no, no, never heard such things." All this time pacing up and down in great ado. E. and Caroline were astonished. Now what was that all about? Next time she comes to see me I'm going to try "*Merde*" on her and see what happens. She is not beautiful but her face has a black-eyed animation which can sometimes be very attractive. She has massive legs and what seems a slender body from the waist up. She has bags under her eyes and wears dark glasses most of the time. Perhaps she cries a lot. She is obviously very lonely after the Onassis marriage. Now she obviously wants to do something that will stagger the artistic world and make him jealous and prove to him that all he's gained is a pretty socialite, while in her he's lost a genius. Quite right too I suppose but without knowing her, and if I had the choice, I'm afraid I'd elect for Jackie Kennedy.

(Nov. 7) The hacking cough that has kept me awake for nights was killed last night by a pill. They had been prescribed for me last summer in England and E. the pill-hoarder had kept them for just such emergency. My sore throat is gone. I haven't coughed once since I awoke. I have a bottle of Perrier straight from the fridge at my right hand, cigarettes at my left, the Ave. Montaigne below and in front of me, it's ten to nine in the morning and apart from the fact that Nixon has won the Yankee election, all's right with the world. Of course a child dies of starvation every minute somewhere in the world, Biafrans are being slaughtered in ambush, napalm is burning babies in Vietnam, and what shall we do about it? "Good Works" as those hideous upper-class Victorians revelled in. A cauldron of soup and a loaf for Mrs. Lewis in the village. She's not too well. Read *Pilgrim's Progress* to dying Mr. Jones, illiterate Mr. Jones, and go home afterwards to a seven-course dinner, swollen with sanctity. A great house, fifty servants, sweeping lawns, follies and vistas and oak drives and no drainage in the village.

Hullo, and what's the matter with me?

Burton's relationship with Stanley Donen, the director, was deteriorating and his usual professionalism was under strain.

Yesterday was a miserable working day. I had to wear again the bald wig, and Donen was so unhelpful that for the first time since the film started I started to become testy. However I controlled myself quickly. I am at that stage, which I reach in every film, where everything seems boring & silly. The same thing happens in the theatre with me too. After a month of a run in a play I become suicidally bored, even with parts of infinite variety like Hamlet. And yet I keep on doing it. I'm a rich man. Why don't I pack it in and do some "Good Works" aforementioned? Grow two blades of grass where one grew before and all that. I couldn't grow grass in a window-box or hammer a nail in a wall without hammering a finger in with it. I'd better just continue to give money to charity.

(Nov. 8) After completing yesterday's entry with milady fast asleep in bed as I thought, I was looking through some scenes in the script when suddenly the bedroom door opened and standing there in a near diaphanous nightgown with one shoulder slipped on to her arm was E. So I went back to bed for ten minutes. I was unquestionably seduced and I teased her about it for the rest of the day when we talked on the telephone. She was very beautiful. It is a fact that after all these years the girl can still blush. I lost that latter capacity a long long time ago.

So after this day is over we have three delicious days off. We plan to hide in the hotel and not go out at all, except perhaps for an occasional meal. I shall read and read and read.

(Nov. 10) Caroline told us some strange little stories yesterday. A woman who came to see the doctor for whom Caroline was working, said that she and her husband had been trying without success to have a baby. The woman was in her late thirties or early forties. When the doctor examined her he found to his astonishment that the woman was a virgin. "How did your husband make love to you?" demanded the doctor. "Why here," she said, pointing to her belly button. Another couple, again very mature, came to see the doctor about their childlessness, and *they* thought one had babies by holding hands! "We've been holding hands for years," they complained, "and nothing's happened." Both these cases were in England and neither couple was illiterate. There are more things . . . I told E. and Caroline a story told me by, I think, a doctor in Hollywood. A man was in the emergency ward one night with a television tube up his bottom, so far up indeed that he couldn't get it down. With very great delicacy the doctors, sweating for hours, managed to get it out without smashing it inside the poor fellow. It would of course have torn his inside to shreds. Having removed it, the man was absolutely OK again. He thanked the doctors and then asked if he could have his TV tube back, *as he was in love with it*!

Both E. and I have had congratulatory telegrams from Richard Zanuck for our "great" "brilliant" "superb, etc." performances in our respective films. Donen and Rex too. It's a long howl to that day in New York, it was actually Shakespeare's birthday, when just about to play

Hamlet at the Lunt-Fontanne, I was served at the stage
door with a writ suing us for $55 million. Settled out of
court, of course, after three ghastly years and innumerable
depositions.

He had been using Liza's word "irastosable" for days. He again
uses it at the beginning of a description of a dinner party which
marks a tidal turning point in his relations with French high society.
Perhaps he suspected that they were merely taking him up: perhaps
some rooted and never eradicated class fury turned the whole thing
sour. He would go again—but much less excitedly. November 13th
cured him of that.

(Nov. 13) I said yesterday that the day might turn out to
be irastosable, and it did. E. said last night that I behaved
like Rachel Roberts. Probably I did, which is just as well
as it means that we'll never be invited again to the Duke
& Duchess of Windsor's soirées. And thank God, he said
fervently. Rarely have I been so stupendously bored. There
were 22 people for dinner and only two names did I know
or remember, and that was from history—the Count &
Countess of Bismarck. And he, the Count, looks as much
like one's mental picture of the iron chancellor as spa-
ghetti. Soft and round and irresolute. He couldn't carve
modern Germany out of cardboard. The iron of his grandfather didn't enter his soul.

It is extraordinary how small the Duke & Duchess are.
Two tiny figures like Toto and Nanette that you keep on
the mantelpiece. Chipped around the edges. Something
you keep in the front room for Sundays only. Marred
Royalty. The awful majesty that doth hedge around a king
is notably lacking in awfulness. Charming and feckless.

E. just reminded me that at one point I said to the
Duchess last night: "You are, without any question, the
most vulgar woman I've ever met." Waaaaash! She also
just told me that we were the only people at the dinner
party who didn't have titles. Little does she know that
we've made her the Princess of Pontrhydyfen. The Duke,
says E., was furious with everybody that he wasn't sitting
next to her, and I was furious that I wasn't sitting next to

the Duchess. I was surrounded by two American ladies, one was a Duchess and the other a Countess. They were hard-faced pretty and youngish. One of them said that she had seen me as Hamlet in New York, and actually asked me how could I possibly remember the lines. I told her that I never did actually get them straight and that some of my improvisations on speeches which I hated and therefore could never recall would have been approved by the lousy actor-writer himself. I told her that once I spoke "To be or not to be" in German to an American audience, but she obviously didn't believe me. I told her there were certain aspects of Hamlet, I mean the man, so revolting that one could only do them when drunk. The frantic self-pity of "How all occasions do inform against me, and spur my dull revenge." You have to be sloshed to get around that. At least *I* have to be. I think I must have shocked her.

Another lady, not a day under seventy, whose face had been lifted so often that it was on top of her head, asked me if it were true that all actors were queer. I said yes, which was the reason I was married to Elizabeth who also, because of her profession, was queer, but that we had an arrangement. Her face, in its excitement, nearly joined her chin. "What," she said, "do you do?" "Well," I said, as straight as a die, "she lives in one suite, and I in another, and we make love by telephone."

At another moment apparently I picked up the Duchess and swung and swung her around like a dancing singing dervish. Elizabeth was terrified that I'd drop her or fall down and kill her. Christ! I will arise and go now and go home to Welsh miners who understand drink and the idiocies that it arouses. Holy mother, they had to have licensing laws to cure us, and we were incurable. I shall die of drink and make-up.

I have been up since about eight. Elizabeth tried to lock me in the spare bedroom, and so I was constrained to try and kick the door down, and nearly succeeded which meant that I spent some time on my hands and knees this morning picking up the battered plaster in the hope that the waiters wouldn't notice that the hotel had nearly lost a door in the middle of the night, and I thought it would be a good idea to blame it on the two pups. E. said that it wasn't a good idea and by tomorrow morning I may think she's right, as ever. Especially as, last night, we only had *one* pup with us. The other, Sebastian, was with his quasi-mother, Caroline. Perhaps it was Caroline who kicked down the door, trying to save me from Elizabeth! You never know, do you?

On November 14th there does not seem much evidence of slowing down.

(Nov. 14) Yesterday was a day as doomed as the Hittites but more delightful, that is to say, nobody died. Many curious things happened. Rachel, who is always pretty good value, showed everybody her pubic hairs, and as a dessert lay down on the floor in a mini-skirt and showed her bum to anyone who cared to have a glance. Outrage, in Rachel's case, has now become normal. If she had a cup of tea with a ginger-snap and made polite conversation about modern poetry, we would all go mad and display our private parts to visiting tourists. I wasn't much help. She said at one point over my dying body to Rex, hooded-eyed and malevolent, "I don't care about his hard-faced blondes." No response. So she said again: "I don't care about hard-faced blondes." "Neither," I said with a laugh as false as a dentist's assurance, "do I."

I'd better be off and to work because I behaved with a fair amount of disgrace yesterday. I drank, so I gather from my friends, three bottles of vodka during the course of the day. And that, naturally, doesn't include the evening when I think I slowed down. But it is not a good idea to drink so much. I shall miss all the marriages of all my various children, and they'll be angry because there'll be nobody around, apart from their mother, to make bad puns.

Little wonder that on November 15th he writes:

I dread today. First I have to act, which I like doing some-times, but not today. Second I have Aaron and his endless questions about legal nothings. Third, I'm likely to have a room full of people again. Fourth, I'd like to be alone with E. for about two hundred years but can't even get two days—we're off to Guy and Marie-Helene Rothschild's house for the weekend. I love the house and love them so maybe it will be alright. We don't go until tomorrow and we'll probably come back on Monday morning.

I think I'll take a kip for an hour. It's ten o'clockish and I don't have to leave until midday. I have all the joie de vivre of a dirge.

Another sadness was that his friend and lawyer—who was afraid of boring him—Aaron Frosch, told Richard that he had the beginnings of multiple sclerosis. Burton's sympathy immediately goes out to him: although he would deteriorate badly, Burton continued to employ him and see him whenever he was in New York. It was only when Susan Hunt and Valerie Douglas later had more say in his business that he employed other lawyers.

Zanuck continues to cable that the rushes are "superb."

(Nov. 16) Aaron said in his cups last night that I was the most intelligent man he'd ever met! And he'd met them all, he went on wildly. Supreme court judges, philosophers, Jack Kennedy, eminent doctors, great actors and Uncle Tom Cobbley and all. I curtsied sweetly but I liked the flattery so much that I've gone to the trouble of putting it down, haven't I? A pebble on the shore of the great sea of knowledge and thank you Sir Isaac Newton. I think I'll try sleeping for an hour to succour my massive brain. No kip so I'll write to the children, *after* a Bloody Mary.

The weekend was spent with the Rothschilds at their magnificent house, Château de Ferrières. Burton himself becomes the grand seigneur.

(Nov. 17) Sunday morning in my favourite house, it is almost midday and the first snow has come in the night and it is snowing again now. Yesterday was a bit wearing with a great deal of talk and oddly enough I was not in a very talky mood but I was forced to. We brought Caroline with us to show her the house and grounds, and E. says that she was very thrilled, as well she might be. It is very massive.

Guy and David were here when we arrived, we met the latter coming out of the trees with a shot rabbit in one hand and a pheasant in the other. The two young boys and a pretty little girl cousin were with them. Phillippe the youngest had shot the rabbit. It was the first bag of his young life. Also here on arrival was Guy's daughter Lily who has to lie down a great deal as she had a clot on the brain about two months ago.

The elevator refused to work at the end of the day so Lily's husband and I carried her, fireman fashion, up to her room. I was puffing a bit as it is two floors up.

Most of the conversation before Marie-Helene arrived was about sexual aberrations. Guy says he knew a man who could only make love if the woman was naked except for *bottines-à-boutons*, that is old fashioned fin-de-siècle button-up boots like one's granny used to wear. Another case, said Lily who works in a psychiatric clinic, was of a man who could have an orgasm only by imagining his mother falling out of a window many floors from the ground and passing the window where he was making love! There but for the grace of God.

Marie-Helene arrived in a great state of excitement having had her make-up done by Alberto di Rossi. It wasn't received very well. She is quite an ugly woman with a large hooked nose and an almost negroid mouth but very beautiful blind eyes, and the vivacity of her manner and her machine-gun delivery in both languages makes her very attractive.

I don't know why I find it surprising when rich people are intelligent, after all they have the advantages from birth of superb educations, and the money to hire the best tutors, etc., but Guy and his son David are as bright as buttons, especially the former. And they both have a very witty turn of phrase. David makes bad puns which I adore. My contribution to the sex talk was David Niven's story of the Hollywood actor who loved to sit naked on a large cake and masturbate. David said he should have told him, "You can't have your cake and have it too."

There were thirteen for dinner so two tables were made up side by side to allay any superstition. At one point I mentioned Onassis' name and a bitter quarrel sprang up between Marie-Helene and Lily. The former adamant that the Onassises would never be invited to her house, and Lily and myself saying that they *would* be invited to ours.

(Nov. 18) Yesterday was a dream day. We slept until noon and discovered to our delight that lunch was a high tea at 4.30. So we ordered breakfast in our rooms. Bacon and eggs and brioche, home-made, toast from home-made bread, little apples, home grown. Then for me, while E. stayed in bed & read a book, a long walk through the woods and the snow. Distantly & occasionally I could hear sounds of the shoot. E. waved to me from the window. The lake was starting to freeze over and the ducks and swans were slowly swimming along the still unfrozen channels, very slowly for some reason, comically.

High tea was a feast. Chicken in the pot with all kinds of vegetables, followed by endless cheeses and desserts. Roasted chestnuts. Raisins. Fresh figs, mandarins, oranges, apples, and obviously and deliciously home-made preserves. There were about twenty-five people sitting at the table. The Minister of the Interior whose name I've forgotten talked to me a lot. He said that his job was more important and onerous than our Home Secretary's. He couldn't explain why satisfactorily. I must find out. My ignorance of French politics is pretty stupendous. Perhaps because, all my life until de Gaulle, they seemed so irresponsibly droll. A new Prime Minister every three weeks and one only for a weekend.

Then upstairs to read and sleep a little and take a bath and so dinner in honour of Marie-Helene and her birthday. This meal was at many tables instead of one large one. I sat between the Countess of Bardolini(?) and Madame Pompidou, wife of de Gaulle's former Prime Minister. She believes, she said, that Georges, her husband, must denounce de Gaulle so that he will stand a chance of returning to power after de Gaulle dies, which she said, perhaps hopefully, cannot be long now. Georges didn't seem very impressive. I took just three words for each and impersonated everyone at our table, vocally that is, which Mme Pompidou found remarkable. So I was told afterwards by Marie-Helene and others. They were very easy voices. The Brazilian Ambassador's daughter with a husky voice and a Portuguese French accent, two people with Italian-French accents, an hysterical gent with a very high-pitched voice. A German-French accent. It was a piece of glottal cake.

Guy de Rothschild, otherwise a sensible man, was beside himself all day because his little Dachshund called Poochy or something like that, was ill. He kept her, wrapped in a blanket in a basket, behind his chair and during dinner must have got up twenty times to check her well-being. The little dog, actually it's a bitch, put on an act of such long suffering as one could hardly believe. But he loves the dog, and there you are—it's something I understand. Marie-Helene told us later that he is so enamoured of the dog that if she dies, she, Marie-Helene, is going to pack her bags & head for the hills, and wait until he's got over his grief. Me too. Practically everyone left for Paris after the party, but we sat up with the German Rothschilds and Marie-Helene and Alexis Redee and Lily until 3.00 in the morning. I spoke Shakespeare and E. and I sang them a Welsh song, "*Ar lan y môr mae rhosys cochion.*" Elizabeth looked so beautiful that strong men were awed, and the children came to sit at her feet. She sang sweetly & unaffectedly and impressed everybody, including me. I'm not blasé yet.

(Nov. 19) We left Ferrières late because of my dilatory Liz but miraculously despite driving slowly because of the snow-slushed and verglassed roads, we arrived on time. A man called Flink from *Look* magazine stayed for about an hour in my dressing room. He asked endless questions about homosexuality which I answered traditionally. Live and let live. It takes all sorts to make a world. Judge not lest ye be judged. Cast not the first stone lest ye be stoned. Some of my best friends are homosexuals, etc., etc.

Two stories about Sunday's party which I omitted, ommited, ommitted—one of them must be right—from yesterday's entry. There were about perhaps sixty or more people in the room waiting to go in to dinner and cocktailing, and Elizabeth and I were sitting in a corner of the room with Lily and other assorted odds and sods when Marie-Helene came over and said to me: "Richard, will you go over and talk to the dark lady in the corner?" I said, "For God's sake, Marie-Helene, I don't know her, etc., and why should I, etc.?" and Marie-H said, "She only wants to listen to your voice, which she thinks is heavenly." And my Elizabeth said in a powerful American accent: "Tell her I'll be over in a minute and give her an impersonation." My broad doesn't muck around. Later, when the children, after dinner, had gone up one by one to the head of the head table and made rather self-conscious little speeches, a man sitting next to E. said, "How boringly middle-class." E. and I decided that if the Rothschilds and Ferrières and eighty guests for dinner in one wing of the house, where trees in the avenues had been planted by reigning monarchs, where there are a hundred servants, was middle-class, then we had just crawled out from underneath a stone. How bored is bored and how middle-class can you be to describe the Rothschilds as middle-class? They are aristos, my friend. It's like Syb once describing the Johnsons (President and Lady Bird) as "suburban." What the hell does she think Ferndale was? Buck House? Anyway, bugger you stranger, Elizabeth and I, famed as we are, rich as we are, courted and insulted as we are, overpaid as we are, centre of a great deal of attention as we are and have been for nearly a quarter of a century, are not bored or blasé. We are not even envious. We are merely lucky.

I have been inordinately lucky all my life but the greatest luck of all has been Elizabeth. She has turned me into a moral man but not a prig, she is a wildly exciting lover-mistress, she is shy and witty, she is nobody's fool, she is a brilliant actress, she is beautiful beyond the dreams of pornography, she can be arrogant and wilful, she is clement and loving, Dulcis Imperatrix, she is Sunday's child, she can tolerate my impossibilities and my drunkenness, she is an ache in the stomach when I am away from her, *and she loves me*! She is a prospectus that can never be entirely catalogued, an almanack for Poor Richard. And I'll love her till I die.

After a few weeks of riding high, a death, which left Elizabeth bereft.

(Nov. 21) Elizabeth's father died yesterday afternoon and I had to break the news to her. She was like a wild animal even though we've been expecting his death for some years. But of course there is no love comparable to a man's love for his daughter or vicky verka. I know to my cost. My passion for my daughters is ludicrous. Whether it's reciprocated as in Elizabeth's case, is another matter. I feel like one who, stabbed in the back, is dying of his wounds. If you know what I mean. I cannot bear suffering in others. I'd much rather have it myself and I'm no masochist, but suffering at second hand is rough enough in its way. Despite all E.'s protestations about her mother over the years, like the good girl she is, she now only wants to protect and cherish her. Me too. Death is a son-of-a-bitch.

He ends that day:

It will be all right if *I* die, but what's going to happen to me if *she* dies? I think I'll turn into a tyre on a bus and roll forever and forever over innocent feet.

The reading goes on—thrillers, *The Double Helix*, the biography of Haldane by Ronald Clark, *The Bible As History*, Osbert Sitwell, more thrillers, Schlesinger on Kennedy read in two-hour slabs and then instantly reread, *Finnegans Wake*—"A Wake For Joyce," who nevertheless is "the perfect writer of the century."

At the beginning of December, he has to go to London to finish the filming of *Staircase*, leaving Elizabeth and her mother in Paris. He returns to find that

> Elizabeth is in such pain that I fancy she's going to end up in a wheelchair. So I'll have my two favourite people in the world, E. and Ifor, tottering about on crutches. *Quelle vie* . . . We dine tonight with the Duke and Duchess of Windsor at a bistro.

His worries about Elizabeth intensify.

> (Dec. 20) I am very worried about E. She is so totally undisciplined about her physical life. The MDs all say she should lie flat on her back for at least a month. The film people have very generously stopped shooting on the film for her to have a rest, and I've yet to see her rest on her back for more than an hour except when asleep. Also she says that the docs say it's alright for her to drink, but it can't be alright for her to drink *and* take the doses of drugs that Caroline is forever pumping into her. As a result of the complete lack of autocare I get impatient when she hobbles around in pain. At this rate her malady will never never get better. And talking to her about it is like talking to the wall. I don't care what the medics say. They've virtually killed her a couple of times, and actually did kill my mother out of sheer neglect. How many really good actors do you get out of a thousand? If you're lucky, about five. The rest are out of work The same proportion applies to doctors but none of them are out of work—they're all busy somewhere prescribing the wrong drugs, mis-diagnosing or butchering some poor unconscious etherised bastard.

And so to Christmas.

> (Dec. 21) We're off to Gstaad today until the 5th of Jan. We have chartered a large plane, I'm not quite sure what it is but it seats about 16 and is a turbo-jet. The reason is that we have so many people coming with us: Sarah, Michael, Chris, Liza, Maria, Caroline, John Something-

or-other who is Simmy's boy friend from Hawaii, and our two bad selves. Otherwise it's going to be one of those quiet, pipe-smoking, slippered, log-fired Xmasses with a well-loved and well-remembered volume of Dickens. It's going to be a screaming mad-house. I shall lock myself in the bedroom for three days and sneak out for walks in the woods when nobody's looking. Maybe I can read *A Christmas Carol* before the log fire in our bedroom. And do all the Xmas puzzles. I forgot to mention that we are also taking four dogs, a cat and a canary. I think I'm going to suggest in future that the family en masse travel without me and I'll go it alone. How lovely it must be to take just the one passport, one bag, a briefcase and a typewriter. And ride in a slow train at night and wake up to cowbells and Swiss chalets. Instead of "Liza, get a move on for Christ's sake and stop patting that stray dog. Maria, sit down, SIT DOWN. Chris, will you for God's sake stop lighting matches all over the bloody airport. Mike, get your feet off the pilot's back. He's trying to drive the plane. Watch out for Fatso. Catch the cat. Clean up Jacob's shit, somebody. Get that bloody cat's claws out of the canary's cage. Will somebody for the sake of sanity stop Oh Fie from cocking his leg against the navigator's ditto. Oh bugger it, where's the parachute? I'm getting out of here." I should have said *five* dogs, I'd forgotten Jacob.

The last entry is on New Year's Eve.

(Dec. 31) The last day of the year and I'm not sorry. It's been an upsiddy-downy year, mostly down than up. The list of calamities I've recounted before. There is however one bit of news to welcome in the New Year which I hope will prove to be propitious. Ifor in the last ten days has been able to stand up three times and has also been swimming three times. Always with assistance of course but at least it's a sign. Give us more signs, Oh Lord! I have a bad chest, nose and throat cold which I cannot shake off. I seem to be having colds much more frequently of late. I've stopped drinking and cut down on smoking to try and clear it up as it makes me, a cold I mean, very irritable and impatient and vile with everybody. I stayed in the bedroom all day yesterday and read or rather reread Schlesinger's massive tome on J.F.K. I must have read without interruption including mealtimes & visits to the lavatory for about 16 hours. The result being that this morning my right eye was bright red. It's the legacy of that fight outside Paddington Station some seven years ago when my eye was so badly kicked by a winkle-pickered boot that I lost the conjunctiva and nearly lost the eye. In middle age those things begin to tell. The base of my spine too gives me hell sometimes, a result of the same fight but perhaps not of the same winkle-picker. There were six of these little monsters against Ifor and myself.

My chief worry for the New Year among the usual worries about children, etc., is E.'s health. It is getting no better and she does maddeningly little to help it. She'll be falling about the place again as soon as she gets back to work for a few days. If she survives this film she is not going to work for a long time. And if she continues to be in trouble with sciatica I'll insist that she *never* works again. It's not fair to her and certainly not to the film companies who employ her. I stayed in bed all day yesterday for instance while she spent the entire day until well after midnight sitting in the main room, gossiping, etc. And of course inevitably sipping away at the drinks. I dread it at night when she has had her shots, etc., of drugs and is only semi-articulate. In addition to all this she is being given cortisone which apparently bloats you up and therefore you have to go on a fairly stringent salt-free diet to combat it. She lasted *two* days on the diet. Oh bugger it. The most frightening thing is that as a result of E.'s total self-indulgence when she moans and groans in agony I simply become bored. And what is more frightening is she has become bored with everything in life. She never reads a book, at least not more than a couple of pages at a time. It took her over a month to read a cheap thriller by Carter Brown that I could have read in an hour. She hasn't asked to read this, to which she has free access and which normally gave her a giggle, for nearly two months. I have always been a heavy drinker but now as a result of this half-life we're leading I am drinking twice as much. The upshot will be that I'll die of drink while she'll go blithely on in her half world. Don't be so depressed, Rich, the world will be new tomorrow.

Zanuck was wrong. *Staircase* was not a success. Though the sight and sound of two thoroughbred goatish heterosexuals being "camp" creased up the studio crews and brought a flush of dollar bills to Zanuck's cheeks, the audience sussed it out for what it was—a trendy piece built on a poor script. The novelty of the idea wore off before it had been executed. It was poorly received and poorly attended. Nor did *The Only Game In Town* fare much better. Burton had *Anne Of The Thousand Days* ahead of him with all the usual loot, perks and glitz.

Elizabeth had a big shock coming her way. She was considered too "mature" to play the part she coveted, Anne Boleyn. She was not one to bullshit any more than Richard. Too mature meant too old. Quite suddenly Richard was out ahead and on his own.

18
Battles Royal

The Notebooks for 1969 begin on January 4th, end on December 12th and are as long as an average novel. Neatly typed, clipped into a Welsh-dragon red folder, roving from Paris to Puerto Vallarta, to London, Gstaad, Geneva, St. Jean Cap Ferrat and the Bell Inn, Aston Clinton, the range of subject more than matches the switch and variety of location. There seems little doubt now that Burton is in training to be a writer—he is writing articles alongside the Notebook—and using the discipline of every day (or most days) to loosen his style, see his mind in print, build up his confidence.

He writes about Elizabeth, their marriage for better and for worse (sometimes unbearable), her illness, her talent, his health, Ifor's incapacity, the children, the dogs, authors—Evelyn Waugh, Octavio Paz, Nathaniel West, Ian Fleming; drink, money, events of the day—the moonshots, Teddy Kennedy's Chappaquiddick, acting, the filming of *Anne Of The Thousand Days*, gossip of grandees and the Welsh past and the circus which passes him by. He writes of places—Puerto Vallarta, London, Paris, Gstaad, of restaurants, of ideas about them, about modern poetry, about sexuality. It is impossible to quote more than a fraction but perhaps the way to do it justice in the context of this biography is to follow him through the year, letting any themes or patterns emerge in the mind of the reader.

The year—in the Notebooks—began and ended in Gstaad which was now the principal land base. The *Kalizma* was the working floating home. In the early part of the year they are back in Paris

329

where *The Only Game In Town* is going over schedule and Elizabeth is finding it very difficult: her operation has left her weak and there is no doubt that she is suffering. (The film will not be any sort of success and it will be her last movie for two years.)

Then off to Puerto Vallarta (the Retreat) for sun and an attempt to build up her health. Caroline the nurse is a constant figure and in true Burton fashion becomes "a daughter." In their Mexican not-so-hideaway until May, Burton reads fanatically, drinks and tries to control it, dreams of retirement and wrestles with the children. This is one of the major stories throughout 1969. There is page after page, particularly about Michael's progress and Burton's worries for Maria.

The children were: Michael, early teens, son of Michael Wilding, not doing well at school; Christopher, two years younger, son of Michael Wilding, doing well, no bother; Liza, daughter of Mike Todd, behind at school but catching up fast and adored by Richard; Maria, adopted, just out of operation, feared by Richard to be rather slow at adjusting and given special attention and much consideration by him; Kate, his own elder daughter, educated in Manhattan, bright, a winner, no problem and the apple of her father's eye; and Jessica, in the Devereux Foundation, deep in his guilt and memory, surfacing as rarely as his remarks about his own health and then heartrendingly so—a mere sentence or two:

> I generally shut Jess out of my mind but sometimes she enters with staggering agony. Well, anyway forget that. Ignore that. Obliviate that. Nowt you can do, *bach gan*, *bach*. Honest to God. All you can do is make her rich, Rich. And she is rich, Rich.

There was also Simmy, a Samoan girl—the adopted daughter of Howard (Elizabeth's brother) and his wife Mara—who lodged with them for some time and whose education was paid for by the Burtons, as was that of a number of children in Puerto Vallarta. He set himself the task of raising $100,000 for a school there. Education mattered mightily to the grammar-school boy.

From Puerto Vallarta they went to London where he was to be Henry VIII in *Anne Of The Thousand Days*. At the time of making it, the view was that it would be another *Becket*. And while he was doing it, news came in that *Where Eagles Dare* was MGM's biggest grossing film of the year. Burton's ability to shift into a totally different career track gave him extra lives—should he want to live them. Elizabeth's career seemed to be rather becalmed although her inactivity could be justified on the grounds of ill-health and her attempt to bring up the difficult and scattered family.

Drink was a serious matter and a battle for both of them. Burton said, "From 1968–1972 I was pretty hopeless. I was fairly sloshed for five years. I hit the bottle. I was up there with Jack Barrymore and Robert Newton. The ghosts of them were looking over my shoulder." It is just another instance of Burton giving an interview. The Notebook for this year shows him far from being "sloshed" all the time. He was, though, having a powerful and thoughtful battle with drink. The problem with using Burton's public interviews—as Brenda Maddox also recognised in her book on Elizabeth Taylor—is that it is unfair. He treated interviews like sport, like throwaway gossip, like the idiocies in drink which bewitched the Welsh early hours after a game of rugby—to be taken, if at all, with a sackful of salt.

We see the marriage on a rack. In many ways it is a miracle. His violence was erupting everywhere. He would turn on his titled hosts and tell them that he "hated all this fucking privilege," call up his aggrieved, oppressed socialist Welsh mining past and blast them as if they had been personally responsible for the privations of his family. He could flip into black moods, viciousness, sarcasm with anyone and most of all with Elizabeth. He flayed her—as he confesses in the Notebooks. She, though ultimately grand and large enough to absorb the shocks of his battering ram of an ego, would fly back at him, often physically "belting him," and he had the greatest trouble in not returning the blows. He did once "and I didn't hear very well for a month," she said. It was indeed one of the matches of the century and as this year goes by the overwhelming conclusion is admiration that they were prepared to try to stick it out and work it out when there was so much—principally their grand Opera House egos—going against it.

Genevieve Bujold, the Canadian actress, ten years younger than Elizabeth, who had been given the title part of Anne Boleyn, was to be a subject of great concern for Elizabeth. In Kitty Kelley's version in her biography of Elizabeth, there is no question but that

Richard had an affair with her. He called her "Gin"—a nickname – a giveaway sign, says Ms. Kelley, for all his women were given nicknames, and Elizabeth "berserked."

There is no doubt that there was suspicion on Elizabeth's side— the Notebooks reveal that. Nor can there be much doubt that, especially in his earlier days, Richard would have flirted with the new girl. However, she had her young husband with and alongside her and, more importantly, Richard denied any affair. And it is in the Notebooks. Two of the actors who were very close to him on the film dismiss the idea out of hand—and they are not part of Taylor's protection agency. They say that Richard—who had a large stake in the film—saw that the girl was overawed, insisted she be treated as a star, treated her as one himself, flattered and "brought her on." This is in character—the *paterfamilias*. His free moments were in the pub with the lads. Alas, as William Squire said. Squire was an Old Vic colleague and brought in under Burton's Old Pals' Treaty. He had hoped to find a sober and serious Burton but instead, as the filming dragged on, found a careless and often half-cut old pal.

It is important, even vital, to be clear about Genevieve Bujold because his boast was that he counted his passion for Elizabeth in terms of his fidelity to her. She was his "Ocean." No one began to match her. No one else need apply. Once *that* was gone, then, as he was to say much later, "the game was up." And although he may have behaved in a way open to misinterpretation, the evidence seems to be that he did *not* have an affair with G. Bujold.

The whole business was very difficult for Elizabeth to digest. She was being told that she could not play a young woman; she could not act this passionate part opposite her husband: she was past it. For someone of her status, rating, proven success, beauty, expectations and character it was a big bad lump to swallow. It was the world's Number One suddenly being dropped from the team. Humiliating. Enraging. Disturbing. No wonder she watched young Gin. It was also, on a straightforward level, distressing: nobody likes to be told that they are too old for the job. Further strain came from the reaction to her serious operation.

Because filming is so "glamorous" it is tempting to dismiss it as "easy." The tension, though, of *having* to deliver, the prospective public jeering, thumbs down to the finished gladiator, if you do not achieve; the deadline and timetable and technical fuss—above all the curiously draining, and even rather insane, effort to "*keep*" the character on the skin of your own personality, like being in a permanent space suit, ever ready to walk out into the alien atmosphere of the set and turn on——that has always had a harrowing and often devastating effect on the strongest and most deeply secure personalities. In the case of Burton and Taylor the effect could be terrible, compounded by the way in which, at their best, they gave the screen everything.

At the end of the year, like ever-migrating birds, they are heading for Hawaii, where Howard, Elizabeth's brother, is Professor of Oceanography, and is to help with the education of the children, especially Michael.

The 1969 Notebooks begin in Gstaad where they are preparing to go back to Paris for Elizabeth's film.

> I stayed in all day and read. I read three books. A history of the *Daily News* journalistically written by somebody called John Chapman "the distinguished theatre critic!!!" *Captain Hornblower* by C. S. Forester, and *Fair Stood The Wind For France* by H. E. Bates. I was fascinated by Bates' notices, quoted on the front & back covers. One would have thought he'd written a towering masterpiece. It is abjectly readable and that's about all.

The next day they receive a letter and a present from the Duke of Windsor and Burton loses his temper completely with the French customs officers. "I told them they were a nation of women and that without the assistance of Anglo-Saxon *men* they would have lost three wars instead of just the war of 1871."

In Paris, at the Plaza Athénée, life goes on.

> (Jan. 7) An odd thing happened last weekend at this hotel which after all is one of the most reputable in Paris. In the lobby beside the lift on the 1st floor John Lee [the assistant of Dick Hanley, Elizabeth's secretary] observed, lying on the divan, a completely naked man with a clothed woman "going down on him." That is to say she was orally masturbating him. John called the Night Manager (it was quite early—about 10.30 at night) who called the police. After a tremendous struggle in which the naked

man threw vases and flowerpots into the well of the hotel he was finally overpowered and carried away in a straitjacket. It turned out that the man was high on drugs, probably LSD, and the lady was of the streets. It is just the kind of thing that one wishes Liza, Maria and Kate to see. What a world!

I read last night in bed some collected articles of Henry Longhurst, the golf correspondent of the *Sunday Times*. I laughed until the tears poured down my face and became quite uncontrollable.

The reading goes on and this is just a section of his comments on one book.

(Jan. 8) Last night I read about a third of a book, which I didn't know he'd written, by Harold Nicolson called *The Age Of Reason*. It is very readable, often very funny but also I suspect too easily written. He repeats himself quite a bit which I know his fastidious sense of economy and style would have rejected if he'd had more time, or given it more time. But nevertheless very enjoyable. What a monstrous set of characters the Age of Reason produced. It might have been called the Age of Monomaniacal Monarchs. Fred the Great of Prussia, Catherine the Great of Muscovy and Peter the Great and the Roi de Solieul. Cor! My spelling! Murder and torture, regicide, suicide, infanticide, banishment and all the vices in the book. Catherine the Great had a lady-in-waiting who was known as the "*eprouveuse*" who as her name implies tried out the Guards Officers in bed first to find out if they would be satisfactory to the Empress of all the Russias. Imagine being found wanting. On second thoughts, imagine being wanted by that raddled old gummy collection of jaded appetites.

Then the first of many many comments on his weight and diet.

(Jan. 9) I've decided to go on a mild diet, one known as the "Drinking Man's Diet," to see if I can lose a few pounds gently. This morning in pyjamas I was 185 pounds which is 13 stone 3 pounds. I'd like to be about 12 stone 7. During the last film I was invited to be fat and I now have quite a pronounced high belly. I can't bear it and it must go.

It sounds rather pleasant in practice.

(Jan. 10) We had a late lunch at La Cascade in the Bois de Boulogne. I stuck to my diet and had a whisky and soda before lunch followed by ½ dozen belons, a steak au poivre, a salad with French dressing and a hefty lump of cheese. I drank Lafite '60, about two glasses, and two or three brandies after the cheese, with sugarless and creamless coffee. Later that night I had a couple more whiskies and soda. Apart from water that's all I took in all day. This morning the scale showed a loss of between four and five pounds. I was very surprised.

Drink and Elizabeth: Drink and his view of the world—which in so many ways is only acceptable through drink—invades the same page.

(Jan. 10) E. was astonishingly drunk even as I got to lunch. I don't recollect her before ever being incoherent from drink. I expect it from the drugs she's forced to take, but not from the booze. Christ, I hope she's alright. It would be frightful to live the rest of our lives in an alcoholic haze, seeing the world through fumes of spirits and cigarette smoke. Never quite sure what you did or said the day before, or what you read, whether wise or foolish, tardy or too soon. God, I'm going to have a whisky and soda right now. There are few pleasures to match tipsiness in this murderous world especially if, like me, you believe in your bones that it, the world as we know it, is not going to last much longer. This is the age of the abyss and any minute now or dark day we could tumble over the edge into primal chaos. Some frigging foreigner will press a button and gone it will all be. Even the Miner's Arms in Pontrhydyfen. Our little lives will be shattered with a cosmic bang. "Those millions of white faces," as Archie

MacLeish says, and then "nothing, nothing, nothing at all." But don't let's be stoned all the time. Let's have days and days of brilliant clarity, etched and limpid, cool and surgical.

I think I had an overdose of History lately. The more I read about man and his maniacal ruthlessness and his murdering envious scatological soul the more I realise that he will never change. Our stupidity is immortal, nothing will change it. The same mistakes, the same prejudices, the same injustice, the same lusts wheel endlessly around the parade-ground of the centuries. Immutable and ineluctable. I wish I could believe in a God of some kind but I simply cannot.

Numerous references to meals and poundage follow. One day he and Elizabeth eat and drink exactly the same: he loses ¾ lb; she puts on 5 lbs—"How can that be? Maybe it has something to do with the drugs she has to take and the vitamins and the anti-bodies." Elizabeth was being slugged daily to take the pain off her back.

Sarah, Burton's mother-in-law, is now with them and, like daughter, never misses a chance to seek help or, charmingly, to enlist the aid of her obliging son-in-law. He takes it all in good part and agrees to trudge along with her to see if a Utrillo is real or fake and again to buy her house if it slides down into a canyon as it threatens to do.

But it is the drink which bites in these January pages.

(Jan. 13) My sins have come home to find me! Who would have thought that a man who has been known in his time to smash windows or fight against odds as a result of drunkenness should be appalled by it in others? At least others close to him. And who's closer than E.? For the last month now, with very few exceptions she has gone to bed not merely sozzled or tipsy but *stoned*. And I mean stoned, unfocussed, unable to walk straight, talking in a slow meaningless baby voice utterly without reason like a demented child. I thought, at first, that it was merely drugs but I understand that the stuff she's having now is merely vitamins so it has to be good old-fashioned booze. I made a desperate attempt this last weekend, when there was no pressure of work on her, to see if I could handle it. Result: the same. The awful thing is that it's turned *me* off drink! So perhaps it has its virtue. There is very little I can do about it. It would be a mistake to have a notorious old pot lecture, with much finger-wagging, a decaying kettle. So I'll continue to pray that it is a psychological reaction from that bloody removal of the Uteris(?) last summer, that it is only temporary, and that gradually she'll come back to normal. I'll have to be very careful that I don't allow myself to join her otherwise we'll have to get a keeper to look after us both. But the boredom, unless I'm drunk too, of being in the presence of someone to whom you have to repeat everything twice is like a physical pain in the stomach. If it was anyone else of course I'd pack my bags, head for the hills and go and live in a Trappist monastery, but this woman is my life. I cannot go to work with her though I will try this afternoon and see how she functions on the set. Last night I was so worried about her and us that I didn't get to sleep until well after dawn. I tried to imagine life without her but couldn't. The intolerable dreariness of her life in that studio is hard to watch. Endless long takes from a multitude of angles, surrounded with possibly the dullest collection of sycophants it has ever been my pain to come across. Apart from little Caroline of course who's a gem. Why in the name of God did I allow her to do this picture? She is indifferent to it to the point of apathy, she never talks about it when she gets home as I did on *Staircase*, she never tells me funny stories about what happened on the set that day. About all I get is: we rehearsed for two hours and shot 13 pages which he will shoot from ten different angles for the next two days.

Elizabeth's condition fills many other pages.

(Jan. 16) A strange thing happened to E. last night. She had been trying on trousers and seemed to be perfectly alright. I was in bed reading a book. She fiddled about for about half an hour. It was about 11 o'clock. Having put her nightdress on she was sitting on the edge of the

bed when out of the corner of my mind I saw that she was
in a very strange position. She had a cigarette in one hand
and a book of matches in the other. There were no matches
in the book. The upper half of her body was at a very
uncomfortable 45 degrees to the perpendicular. I got out
of bed took the cigs and matches away from her. Her arms
were rigid with some sort of temporary paralysis. I finally
tucked her into bed, not without a great deal of effort as
she was a dead weight. She was incapable of speech and
could not tell me what the matter was. Today she only
has a vague recollection of it, if any. In the middle of the
night and her sleep she started to moan and groan sometimes almost to the point of screaming and cried real tears.
Christ, will I be glad when this nightmare is over. Sometimes in the dead vast and middle of the night when I'm
particularly low I feel that I can't stand it any more, but
each new day gives me fresh hope. I must have a long
chat with the doctors and see how long she has to go with
these pills, drugs or not. They obviously don't know the
impact they're having on her and indirectly me!

His world is becoming her world of illnesses. He fears and hates
illness, but follows her there as everywhere else—the lover, the
protector, often angry, sometimes vile, but holding on to her through
one hospitalisation after another. His sympathy—always keen—at
this time appears to enlarge itself even further as he takes on the
upset of one of Elizabeth's make-up men, Frank Larue, who is under
great strain.

(Jan. 17) He has been hovering on the edge of this calamity
for a long time—at least four or five years. Perhaps all
his grown-up life. He is about 50 yrs of age. I've noticed
that if I want to relax him completely I simply ask him
to tell me about his life as a teenaged boy in a hunting
camp in the USA where he describes how hunters would
tell him they'd shot a stag and where to go and find it.
They would then lay bets, when he was gone, on how
long he would take to bring the stag back, or whether he
could bring it back at all, if the animal was particularly
big, and Frank was small for his age. Still is. But they

never beat him, he would tell me proudly. He would describe to me all the tricks he learned and invented to get the prize home. How to drape the monsters around his shoulders, how to take a rest against a certain kind of tree without having to put his burden down, because getting them on to one's shoulders was the hardest task of all if one was alone. Once it took him half a day and part of a night to get one of these giants home. But he made it and when he finally arrived at the hunting lodge all the hunters stood around, toasted him and gave him a dollar each. This was obviously the happiest time of his life. All this confessing came about because one day I was sitting on the beach at Tor Vaianicha and Frank was in a bathing costume. Though small he was a mass of whipcord muscles. I remarked on it and he said it was because of the above. I hope he'll be alright because he is a very decent nice man. Poor lonely old bastard. He has just been in to say goodbye. He looks dreadful.

In this Notebook, at last, there is something of a sustained attempt to talk about himself as an actor, about acting, and, during *Anne Of The Thousand Days*, the film business. He is not always impressed by the perception of journalists.

(Jan. 20) What they don't understand and completely misinterpret is our life-long attitudes to our jobs. I think Mr. Thompson [a reporter] was deeply shocked when I told him that acting on stage or films, apart from one or two high moments of nervous excitement, was sheer drudgery. That if I retired from acting professionally tomorrow that I would never appear in the local amateur dramatic society for the sheer love of it. Could he not understand the indignity and the boredom of having to learn the writings of another man, which nine times out of ten was indifferent, when you are 43 years old, are fairly widely read, drag yourself off to work day after day with a long lingering regretful look behind you at the book you're so interested in. How would he like to face the temperamental goings on of so many of my co-actors, generally the indifferent ones who haven't "made it"? They will never understand that E. and I are not "dedicated" and that my "first love" (God how many times have I read that?) is not the stage. It is a book with lovely words in it. When I retire, which I must do before long, I shall write a screaming diatribe against the whole false world of journalism and showbusiness.

He is writing it all the time. And the references to writing increase.

He is unemployed in Paris and "reads and reads and reads." "I stayed in all day and read a lot of *Time* capsules. E. arrived home from work crocked as a sock, sloshed as a Cossack."

He stops the writing—until March. In late January he goes to London for the premiere of *Where Eagles Dare*—a great *Boy's Own* success: sees Lord Harlech about Harlech Television—in Wales—in which he and Elizabeth have a big investment, makes more plans, sees Ifor and installs Gwen permanently in an hotel—The Bell, Aston Clinton, near Ifor's hospital—and reads and drinks. Then, Elizabeth's film finally done, they take off for Mexico, both exhausted, undermined and bruised. Bowed down, yet with all the privileges of wealth within reach.

He *knows* it is absurd. No wonder that Camus was his favourite writer and the man he was most impressed by.

His honesty in the Notebooks can be endearing, especially with regard to his children with whom he was besotted—particularly Kate and Liza. And yet, even here, he is true to his own mood—a mood no father other than a saint will fail to recognise—and he slams it down in what are now fast becoming not so much Notebooks as Confessions. The marriage is in trouble.

(March 20) Another long silence in this pathetic journal occasioned I suppose by acute unhappiness added to stupendous quantities of guilt, alcohol, laziness, fear for Elizabeth's health and reason, stirred up well with a pinch or two of Celtic pessimism and served as a first-class recipe for suicide. It is by no means over. I am still as tightly drawn as a longbow by John of Gaunt, and as touchy as a fretful porpentine. But it gets better every day.

The last six or eight months have been a nightmare. I created one half and Elizabeth the other. We grated on each other to the point of separation. I had thought of going to live alone in some remote shack in a rainy place and E. had thought of going to stay with Howard in Hawaii. It is of course quite impossible. We are bound together. Hoop-steeled. Whither thou goest, he said hopefully.

Elizabeth has started to read again and I have started to write so there's hopes, isn't there, boys? I dread the children coming down here. My temper is still fine-drawn on the edge of impatience and trying to accommodate that with the warring claims of Liza and Maria and, to a lesser extent, with the demands of Chris & Mike is going to stretch my nerves to the limit. The fact is that children bore me. I discovered after a couple of days of fairly close proximity with Kate in Beverly Hills—and after all I don't see very much of her—that I could do without her too. I long for them to grow up and come to see us only at Christmas time, during which festivities I shall build an igloo in the garden and not come out until the New Year.

Caroline left us a couple of days before we came down here. E. had been in hospital to wean her off the hard narcotics and booze, and to have a thorough, even painstaking check-up on all her bodily functions. She is alright apart from the usual back trouble, which she is going to have for the rest of her life and a rather ominous but not fatal newcomer: her liver is in bad order.

Social life in Puerto Vallarta is neither sophisticated nor stimulating. Sometimes it seems like a remote and very expensive open prison.

(March 24) I became somewhat drunk and was glad to get home. I woke up next morning feeling dreadful and shaky and withal a fiendish toothache which has been nagging me for some time, to find to my dismay that E. had invited several friends for lunch. I downed two vodkas & limeade to sweeten my disposition. The lunch lasted, one way and another, until about six o'clock. [The name of one guest was, something like Honey Beans!] A whole world of vegetables names is spread before us. Darling Turnips, Sweetie Swedes, Cherie Cucumbers, Lovie Leeks, Popsie Potatoes, and so on. She was astounded to find me so young looking, about thirty-five she guessed, and how delightful it was to find us both so beautiful and to be possessed of such "human-ness." I decided to wait until six o'clock before throwing up.

He is writing steadily now. *Look* magazine has commissioned a piece about Wales which he works on consistently. It absorbs him markedly more than anything or anyone else at this time.

(March 26) I wrote it in longhand and then laboriously typed it last night until about midnight, so, since I'd been up since 4.00 o'clock the previous morning and awake for two hours before that, it was a weary man who dragged himself to bed. I'm afraid to look at it this morning in case I don't like it and have to do it all over again. It's about 2500–2600 words. I am falling into a trap as a writer that I should guard against very carefully if my ambitions as a minor scribe persist. The trap of talking myself out. I've always known it to be fatal for any writers but particularly the kind who are as glib and articulate as myself. I will frequently reject a fairly fine turn of phrase when writing because I've heard myself say it a couple of times & therefore seems to me to be a cliché . . .

(March 27) Everybody found favour with my piece about Wales though E. found the end rather lame so I wrote a more powerful ending. She liked it so there it is. Now we'll wait and see if it's too late for *Look* magazine—the deadline was two, no, three weeks ago. If it is I'll sell it to some other mag. *Life* magazine have always said they will publish anything I write. So I could foist it on to them, though they're hardly likely to pay me *Look*'s price which is 2,500 dollars. Also they wanted caption writing to go under photographs of Wales rather than an article, so perhaps they'll reject it for that reason. Anyway we'll see.

I am enjoying this holiday so much that I am beginning to think I really could retire from acting, and write occasional pieces. I will watch myself over the next five weeks and see how my restlessness goes. I love the sun.

I love it when my back is cleared of acne by the beneficent sun. I love swimming and the good scoured feeling after a day of salt and sunburn. Maybe after another year! Perhaps one film, at a reduced fee every three years. And only something really worthwhile.

His reading is indiscriminate but he chews on whatever he finds and turns it into something for himself.

(March 28) Another brilliant morning. I awoke at nine. I went to bed about 9 and read a book of Ian Fleming's called *You Only Live Twice*. A clever schoolboy mind and atrociously vulgar. And every so often he stops his narrative to give little homilies about food, drink, national morals, etc., all of an excruciating banality. Yet ever since the phenomenal success of the films about his hero James Bond and the books—I'm not sure which came first— and of course his death, he is actually being treated seriously by serious critics. I put the light out about midnight and slept for a couple of hours, woke and read a short novel by Nathaniel West, *Miss Lonelyhearts*. What a contrast between that and Fleming. West's book is taut, spare and agonised while the other is diffuse, urbane and empty. West hates himself and postulates a theory that you are always killed by the thing you love, while Fleming loves only himself, his attraction to women, his sexual prowess, "the-hint-of-cruelty-in-the-mouth" sadistic bit, his absurd and comically pompous attitude to food and cocktails "be sure the martini is shaken not stirred." He has the cordon-bleu nerve to attack one of my favourite discoveries: American short-order cooking. I remember with watering mouth the soda fountain on 81st Street, one block west of the park in Manhattan, where in a blur of conjuring the cook would produce corned-beef hash with a fried egg on top and french fries on the side and a salad with a choice of about four or five dressings. All this magically produced and whipped on to the table, piping hot, before you'd finished the comic strips in the *Herald Tribune*, or read Red Smith's wry column. Yet you cannot help liking Fleming. He is so obviously enjoying the creation of his extroverted,

Hemingwayese, sadistic, sexually-maniacal boy-scout that in the end he becomes likeable. I rather like him too for his death line, if the reports are true. He was about 57 and had known for some time that he had a diseased heart. He is reputed to have said: "Well, it's been a hell of a bloody lark." And of course, to that bon viveur, woman-chasing, intelligently-muscled mind it had been.

The sun, the village, the two houses connected by the loving bridge, the ambiance of Puerto Vallarta which, since they "discovered" it, has grown from one thousand to twenty-five thousand people and become a tourist resort with Burton as the unofficial mayor, begins to work.

(March 29) Elizabeth is now looking ravishingly sun-tanned though the lazy little bugger ought to lose a few pounds or so to look at her absolute best. Looking as critically as I can at her yesterday I could detect no sign of aging in her at all, except that she has quite a few grey hairs, mostly at the temples. But the skin is as smooth and youthful and unwrinkled as ever it was. The breasts, despite their largeness and considerable weight, sag very slightly but no more than they did 10 years ago. Her bottom is firm and round. She needs weight off her stomach, not so much out of vanity, but because all the medical men say it will ease her bad back if she has less weight to carry for'ard. She swam quite a lot yesterday and if she keeps that up she should be quite firm by the time we get back to London. Dreadful thought London. Rain and coughs and colds and all those ugly pinched discontented cheerless faces, and that frightful press.

And for him, constant writing and reading. Against very huge odds a good life was threatening to take shape.

(March 30) We roasted in the sun all day and read. E. read *Portnoy's Complaint*, while I read a book translated from the Spanish called *The Labyrinth of Solitude* written by a poet called Octavio Paz. I am finding it very tough going and one of those assertive books which make me long to argue back. Like most books of self-conscious philosophy it is totally lacking in humour. I like merry philosophers. To relieve my mind I would read a fairly entertaining thriller-with-a-message by Simon Raven, between slabs of the Paz book. It is very difficult to understand how any man can seriously discuss Mexico and Mexicans as if they are all one unit. "The Mexican is impassive, he is such a prideful man that he will not reveal himself even to his closest friend, etc." Balls. I know a great many Mexicans and the impassive ones, though the word that is nearer the mark is "sullen," are almost always uneducated and poor. The educated are like their counterparts in Spain, vivacious and wild and romantic. He is equally sweeping about the Yanks.

Like the unofficial Mayor and Mayoress, the Burtons take a day off to "do a tour of the town and do our duty to the various hostelleries." All that happens is that a few minutes after they arrive anywhere the place is packed out, tourists click the cameras, ask for the autographs, and it's back in the Jeep and on to the next bar. Elizabeth reads *The Godfather*—"badly written but un-put-downable": Richard reads "a paperback history of the Mayans by somebody called Von Hagen, famous Spanish short stories with the English text on one page and the Spanish on the other, and am still ploughing through Señor Paz's *Labyrinth*." He was learning Spanish: "the language is giving me hell. I find myself, unless I think carefully, speaking either Italian or French to the servants all the time."

Yet the anger between them could still come virulent and out of the blue.

(April 4) Yesterday was a funny day. It went splendidly for the first half and degenerated into bickering around 3.30 in the p.m. It was largely my fault. I suddenly became testy for no very good reason and remained so for the rest of the day though I tried to get myself better around five but to no avail. E. of course was no help at all and bickered back with almost masculine pride. This was some of the dialogue, roughly speaking:

Me: (Having gone to read upstairs in the bedroom about 8 p.m.) "Is the bathroom still smelling?"

She: "Yes."

Me: "I can't smell anything in there. Perhaps it's you."

She: "Fuck off." (She leaves the bedroom and goes downstairs, while me remains reading on bed.)

She: (Having come back upstairs twenty mins or so later standing at the door with a look of real loathing on her face) "I dislike you and hate you." (It may have been "loathe.")

Me: (Getting into dressing gown) "Goodnight, have a good sleep."

She: "You too."

Me exits and goes to Chris's room where Me lies on bed and reads.

N.B. For the benefit of the actors in this little study of home life among the Burtons, it must be emphasised that though the words used are relatively innocuous, the speaking of them is distinct with venomous malice.

Michael and Chris arrive the next day—"The town is a mad house. Holy Week has brought people in by the thousands . . ."

(April 5) As we arrived back at the house we were hailed by a Negro. It turned out to be James Baldwin and a French boy who spoke no English. He was down here escaping from Hollywood he said. We discussed Black Power, Black Panthers, Black is best, Black is beautiful and Black and White. He said quite openly and not at all sneakily: "Richard, can you let me have 20 dollars?" ("Let me have," mark you, not "lend.")

I was rather surprised, as I would have thought he was fairly affluent and said: "Twenty dollars?"

"I mean 200 dollars," he said. I said certainly and Jim [John Lee] is going to give it to him today. We are seeing him again tomorrow.

(April 9) We think that James Baldwin is a thief! Val [Valerie Douglas] had 220 dollars or so stolen from her purse when J. Baldwin came to lunch on Monday, and, after several reductions ad absurdum have decided that the guilty feller is Baldwin. It may be his French friend but then that's the same thing. More details tomorrow when hopefully my back and my typing will have improved.

(April 10) Well, we decided that J. Baldwin had stolen Val's money for the following, mostly psychological, reasons: the servants have not stolen anything in 7 years, despite my habit of leaving money all over the place in trouser pockets, etc., and E. leaving baubles all over her dressing table and other locations. The children have never stolen anything in their lives . . . [The other guests were old and trusted friends.] Neither E. nor I did.

I have already recorded in this diary that Baldwin had asked me for 20, no 200 dollars. Two days later he asked Jim for a further 50. Then a further 100. Some couple of years ago he had borrowed 10 dollars from Jim (while travelling 1st class on *La France*) and has never payed him back. He was sitting at the table with us over lunch when he saw me give the money to Jim to give to Val (I had been holding it for her) who put it into her handbag. She had later taken it to her room in the lower house and James had made a tour of the houses alone. We shall never be able to prove it and the money doesn't matter, but why does he do it? Does he also steal from black men or does he think that the white man owes him a living? I must find out from others if James has a reputation as a kleptomaniac.

At the same lunch one somewhat sozzled and belligerent guest said something like how could I continue to do a job as degrading and despicable as being an actor. He had prefaced his whole attack on my profession by saying what great potential I had as a writer, and how I was wasting my time acting, etc. His wife later on, so E. tells me, embarked on an attack on E. Her back was worse than E.'s. Liza (E.'s blood) was sullen while Maria (adopted) was delightful. She should have played V. Woolf etc., etc. Envy was out in force that day.

Baldwin on the other hand was kind and generous about

all and is very intelligent. So he can steal some more if he wishes.

The family settles in and Burton feels displaced. But their education continues to obsess him.

> (April 11) On reflection, the school has been bad for them. Their values have become tremendously coarsened, Michael started to smoke there and drink there and found jail-bait companions. Though admittedly he might have found them at any other school. Since coming here I have seen him read nothing but comic strips. Come to think of it though, I haven't seen Chris read anything else either. Maybe they are just not intellectual and that's that. The truth is though, I suspect, that like their Uncle Howard they are slow starters, and won't really begin to move until they're in their late teens or even their early twenties but unfortunately, unless one is a genius, the modern educational system doesn't cope with late starters, and their lives are ruined thereafter.

The sense of a prison is reinforced by the arrival of more media men.

> Yesterday too we had TV cameras outside and incidental photographers who refused to go away. Since we refused to come out, in my case because I could barely walk and also had a three-day growth of beard (for the next film), and in E.'s case because she simply refused, the day, in this case turned into an impasse.
>
> E. is delightful at the moment and has fallen in love with jig-saw puzzles, scores of which had been sent by Val.
>
> Last night as I lay reading in bed and E. was around the corner of the room I asked: What are you doing, Lumpy?
>
> She said like a little girl and quite seriously: Playing with my jewels.

A week later he is trapped once again.

(April 20) I have been going through one of my periodic moods of depression for the last three days. Periods when the very thought of seeing anyone except Elizabeth gives me a real physical pain. And when I'm not drinking which I've not been for the last three days it is at its worst. Actually during the last 12 months or so I have become increasingly anti-social and am only really at comparative ease when fairly drunk. The first two or three weeks here without anyone except E. were happy-as-schoolboys days. It is the damndest paradox. I miss the children terribly when they're not here, especially Liza. My heart does several varieties of dance when I first see them coming off the plane or whatever, and within three days I wish them gone. It is very puzzling. Time was when my chiefest enjoyment after love-making and a good poem was standing at a bar with a convivial few and rambling around poetry and politics and ideas of all kinds—generally second-hand of course—and talking of every subject except the loathed one of acting. And now . . . nothing except to be crouched over a book in our bedroom with the airconditioning turned on to drown the noises of the outside world. The mood is only temporary of course and even this illiterate apologia may go some way towards dissipating the gloom.

Burton is desperately trying to find space for himself—to cut through the ever-growing entanglements of problems—especially the stifling domestic conflicts. Michael figures heavily in the journals at this time. His school problems were no doubt similar to those of thousands of others who finally come through. In this case, Burton's obsession with formal education is as likely to have exacerbated it as helped it. And Michael was Elizabeth's first-born. The undercurrent of jealousy between the stepfather and the growing son can scarcely have been calming. Maria's timidity too sent Burton into a spasm of anxiety. He was a problem solver, an achiever, a doer and that which could not be sorted out quickly and decisively became a burden.

Meanwhile, at times, amid the excess, he can indeed sound like Mike Nichol's description of him, "The loneliest man I have met."

"Most days I read at least three books and one day I read five." He is fashioning himself around writing and writers, cutting himself off in one way, tuning himself up in another. He is also taking on the occupational hazard of the writer which is that the puzzlement and strain of seeking true expression and the weight laid on your resources can bring you often perilously close to depression which shares many of the same characteristics. He reads Elizabeth Longford's biography of Queen Victoria "all night . . . absolutely absorbing . . . I'd forgotten how German they all were . . ." On the same day

> (April 26) Both E. and I went mad last night and started eating Callard and Bowsers Liquorice Fingers. I must have eaten a pound or so and E. somewhat less. The results were evident this morning. I had put on 3½ lbs and E. 2 lbs. Today we are unrepentant but determined to redress the balance. E. longs to be a 129 lbs and I to be a 170. It can be done. But not perhaps by us.

At the end of April worry begins to set in about the film, *Anne Of The Thousand Days*. It is the only time Burton gives any real space to a film in these Notebooks. Partly, perhaps, because of the oddness of it—doing it without Elizabeth, going back to a costume potboiler with historical pretensions; partly because he loves—and indeed makes sure the film employs—lots of old actor pals; most importantly because it comes smack up against his new, modest, underformulated view of himself as some sort of writer. It is an irritant from the very beginning even though, fair to a fault, he scorns himself for complaining "when I get $1M up front and 10% of the gross." Nevertheless:

> (April 30) It's the last day of the month and reminds us of the dreaded date of departure. I am going to loathe London I suspect. And the film. Why am I doing a film that I so patently am bored by? Why do I allow myself to be talked into doing the mediocre when I could have a choice of the choicest properties on the market? I cannot even bring myself to read the script, let alone learn it. I must! I must! Otherwise I shall feel guilty.

While in Puerto Vallarta he gives £50,000 to a relation of Sybil, whose chain of shops has got into trouble. As Burton helped set up the business he takes the problem as a personal insult. Even at that remove it is still family, and therefore into battle. So £50,000 is put in to re-instate his man and Burton's top lawyers are sent in to scare the daylights out of a man who had threatened his kinsman. Apart from that, and the pissing dogs and the barking family,

> (May 2) My guilty conscience about the next film and learning the script has now reached an all-time high. I will read it today if I have to stay up all night. It is absolutely disgraceful and very rare for me, and I would be shocked if I discovered such laziness in another actor. I did once, not so long ago when I played Hamlet last. I was amazed at rehearsals in Toronto that a leading member of the cast did not know a line at the first rehearsals, and while everybody else was bookless at the second rehearsal, he was still muttering around with a book in his hand three weeks later. It meant that he never caught up. The results were obvious in his performance.

It is the reading which consumes him at Puerto Vallarta. And as usual he battles his way through to his own position on the matter in hand.

> (May 3) I've decided that I don't know what poetry is. Last night, in a glut of gloom, I ploughed through the "collected" poetry, "all he wishes to preserve," of W. H. Auden. In ten thousand there is hardly one memorable line. Most of it is type-writing. Some of it is scribble. Much of it is indifferent prose cut up. Almost totally it is formless. When is a poem a poem? I will slash away again at Auden since his aura glitters, and find out.

Burton in his Notebooks always seems to come back to Dylan Thomas, whose personality—especially his pub-personality—appears to have been a bonding attraction together with the poems themselves. Burton was a man who believed that if you had it then it was part of the deal that you showed it.

Dylan was an exception. But listen to Yeats or T. S. Eliot. Or listen, as we had to once, to Archie MacLeish moan without sense or sound his own lovely verse. E. and Ifor and I listened in a tortured agony in a house on a hill in Massachusetts, longing to smash the book out of his hands and read it ourselves. I think that once the mould of form was smashed by a master or series of masters, Pound and Eliot perhaps in poetry and the Impressionists even more perhaps (since I know little about painting) in art, anybody can fool you. And will. And we will never know if they're mucking us about or not.

Wherever Burton landed, he became part of the village. In Switzerland he was giving money to hospitals; on the Thames he was "in" with the Cockney fishermen; in Puerto Vallarta he is a honey pot for all.

(May 4) Charlie, a divine dirty little cheeky shoe-shine boy from the village, came and had a swim in the pool last evening and stayed to have supper with his minute brother. This massive mite is known as Jim. We had tacos with all the trimmings, frijoles and guacamole, lettuce and sundry hot sauces. Jim firmly refused all vegetables. Tacos and chicken only, thank you. Charlie cleaned my boots for his supper. He is very bright and has picked up English quite well. I would love to pay for his education but we tried that before and the parents are useless. They are so ignorant that they can only see to next week and the handful of pathetic pesos it brings in from boot polish. The working class here have none of the self-sacrificing fanaticism of the Welsh or Scots to get their children educated. David Jones, who lived next door to Gwen in Cunard Cottages, worked himself to the bone, denied himself all pleasures except chewing-bacco, went into unpayable debt to put his five or six children in college and then quietly slit his throat.

That last sentence is as toughly compressed a short story as you could wish for. The muscles are rippling. The film rumbles unstoppably into his sights.

(May 4) I have been very unsociable for the last two or three days and recognise it all very well. I am about to start work. Once I'm going all will be fine but from now on until about the fourth of June when the first rushes have been seen and hopefully found adequate, (Will I like the girl? Will I like the director? Will they bore me? Will I be any good?) I shall be, in E.'s words, a basket case.

An example of why the Burtons have to be paranoid. It is a rare reference to his deep worry about the basic safety of his family.

(May 5) Some malicious and dangerous little people put sugar in the petrol tank of the B-Buggy and did something to the brakes the night before last. George was putting it away into the garage when he lost control of the Bug, he was driving it in reverse down the hill from the house, and was forced to run it into the house at the bottom of the hill which, though steep, is quite short, thank God. Our suspicions are directed towards a couple of men from Guadalahara who came up to the house on Sat night and said they represented Volkswagen cars and were having an exhibition or show in the town, and would we, E & I pose by the exhibits for photographs. Jim said no and they were much piqued. It appears that they bought sugar from La Altena next door. If any of us had been driving the car the *other* way down where the descent is really precipitous, something like 1 in 4, there could very easily have been a death. Especially as there are usually quite a lot of children playing around at night in these streets. Well, the luck holds, but malevolence of that kind is frightening and the world is full of it.

This takes him to a remarkable free association.

I remember a small incident at Paddington Station during the war. I was on my way home to Port Talbot and had arrived very early at the station to be sure of a seat. It was the late train leaving about midnight, as I remember. I was travelling 3rd Class of course in those days, coming down, I think, from Oxford. I got me a seat and settled down to read a book by the light of a torch. All seats except one were soon taken. Then a soldier, private, arrived followed by a tiny porter who was carrying his kit-bag, a suitcase and sundry brown paper parcels. The soldier was of medium height and I suppose in his early twenties. He stood by while the porter stacked his bags on the rack. The porter waited for the tip and the soldier said in a horrible towny Cardiff accent: "That's bloody 'ad yew, 'asn't it? You getting no bloody tip from me, boyo. Bugger off." The porter shrugged and walked away. My hatred for the soldier was so overwhelming that I felt like murdering him. I made myself cool down and then very deliberately and without haste stood up and in total silence opened the door of the carriage and one by one threw all his bags and parcels on to the platform. He looked at me with the hatred of a nightmare but he said nothing and went out to pick up his bags. I closed the door behind him and held it so that he couldn't get back in. He must have found a seat elsewhere and I never saw him again. The other occupants of the carriage with typical British taciturnity never referred to the incident at all though we were all together in that compartment for several hours. Odd incident.

At last he gets going on the script.

(May 6) Well, I broke the ice yesterday and plunged into learning the lines of *Anne*. I learned about ten pages which I will have to re-learn today, while learning another ten. By tomorrow yesterday's ten will have fixed themselves in my memory, more or less, while I revise today's ten, and so on. There are quite a few pages of course which contain only a line or two while others, especially in a wordy costume piece of this kind have long uninterrupted monologues. The script is 144 pages long. I do not speak on about 35 of them. That leaves 109. At ten a day that theoretically gives me the whole part in eleven days, though in actual fact it is generally about twice as long because the period of study becomes longer and longer as more and more is committed to memory and the revision extends itself day by day. Also, there are some days when the memory refuses to take in anything at all, and one can only revise.

The script itself is robust and unsubtle but sweeps along at spanking pace. I hope the direction matches it. Henry is mad, I think. If I continue to think so after I've really got the part into my bones, I shall play him that way. He is certainly demonic. Great charm and stupendous outbursts of rage all co-mixed up with a brilliant cynical intelligence. I might be able to make something of it. Especially if the Director & Girl are good and help it all along. Since I gather that the other parts, Wolsey, Cromwell, Howard, Thomas Boleyn, etc., etc., are being played by Hordern, John Colicos and people of their stature I have no worries on that score. Especially Michael Hordern. I think him to be one of the best actors in the world and a rough adversary in a two-handed scene and hard to beat.

He was right to be worried about the script. There is scarcely an original thought or line in it. Nothing is wrong with it but nothing is new or startling either. It is a solid craftsmanlike piece, verbose and lumpen. Burton went to it with a will as he did so many of the projects he was offered—but his intelligence told him from the beginning that it would never be first-rate. Charles Jarrott's conscientious, tableaux direction while suiting the script only served, alas, to emphasise its rather plodding gravitas. Burton's keen interest in Henry VIII and the fun he was to have with the cast kept him going for a while: soon, however, he was seeking, rightly, to "cut down the verbiage."

The writing is wholly in the ascendant.

(May 7) I went to bed early last night, about 9 and read Waugh's *Put Out More Flags* for the umpty-ninth time. I shall have it by heart if I'm not careful. It is astonishing for such a careful writer how often, for a comic effect, he uses the word "distaste." The first time he used it was I think in *Decline And Fall* and the line is something like: " 'This is my daughter,' said the headmaster, with some distaste." I remember being convulsed as a small boy. It is a good trick that he uses a lot. "The Brigadier looked at Basil with revulsion." But these little lapses apart, he is the writer I'd like to write like most. See Tom Thumb wanting to play Goliath, or the Elephant who dreams of being a ballerina. Anyway I'll never write anything except occasional pieces for the magazines unless I spend four or five hours a day on this journal alone, and not 30 minutes.

(May 8) I cannot stop reading Waugh. In the last two or three days I have read *Scoop, Put Out More Flags, A Little Learning, Officers and Gentlemen* & am just finishing *Men At Arms*. The whole thesis is a lament for the death and dissolution of the Squirearchy. They were tougher than he thought. They are still there, as established as ever. A pity for his theme. A greater pity is that he died before finishing his auto-biog. It would have been interesting to read his reactions to what is in essence a socially unchanged world. The same laws of breeding and background and school still apply. Only, it would seem in the arts and particularly in sciences, does it not apply. No school, however eminent, can help you as a painter or writer or physicist unless you have the brains or talent. Most of the brilliant new crop of scientists which we have in GB, and are exporting to the USA, have provincial accents, I'm told. But in essence the old order never changeth.

As they began the move to London, where *Anne Of The Thousand Days* was to be filmed, Burton confesses his terror of aeroplanes— "any man who confesses to me that aeroplanes give him the screaming ab-dabs becomes a friend for life." The bad news in Hollywood included the fact that the "sneak previews" of *Staircase* "were disastrous. Oddly enough, I cared about this film but, what the hell. I'll just grow another callous. I'll end up with a mind like a miner's hands."

In London, after his fittings, he goes, with Brook Williams, now a close friend and frequent visitor, down to the studios to meet the cast on the set.

(May 21) [Tony] Quayle was there and behaved exactly as I expected, eyes twinkling, much smiling, speaking his part with measured and unctuous precision. The girl is very small in every way, in height, in weight and vocally. I could out-project her with a whisper. Her face too is tiny but the eyes and mouth are good. In size and pertness only, she reminds me of the late and lamented Vivien Leigh. It's difficult to tell at a reading but I think she might have difficulty with long sustained speeches, but doubtless we'll be able to fiddle around that with judicious cuts to listening faces, etc., and a spot of dubbing.

Another of Burton's problems surfaced and would not be solved throughout the long arduous summer filming in the heavy costumes—filming preceded and followed by a two-and-a-half-hour drive each way, each day: insomnia.

(May 22) It is 5 in the morn and I've been awake since 4 which is a considerable improvement on the night before. I have a package of Bartlett's pea-soup on the simmer. I took two sleeping pills last night, an unprecedented thing for me to do, and at 4 this a.m. I took another! Junkie Burton has finally arrived. The insurance doctor came to see me about 7 o'clock and told me my pulse rate was twice as high as a year ago! Hullo, I thought to myself. Anyway he suggested at least ten hours sleep to bring it down to normal. Hence the sleeping pills. Actually I managed 8 hrs only and a lot of that was fitful but I feel much better anyway. Yesterday I rehearsed the song I have to sing in the film. It's very pretty but for an amateur, because of funny little stops in it, difficult to learn at such short notice. I record it this morning.

The improvement is temporary, the insomnia worsens as the filming goes on.

One of the advantages, as he sees it, in filming at Shepperton is that it is a reasonable distance from Aston Clinton where Ifor is in hospital and where Gwen is staying, at the famous Bell Inn, at Burton's expense. He goes to see him right away.

(May 23) The improvement in Ifor is considerable. He can wheel himself about in a motorised chair and seemed in very good spirits. We told various and sundry stories some of which made him laugh so much that we had to wipe the tears away from his eyes. Gwen's self-less devotion to him verges on the saint-like. What a marvellous woman. Old-fashioned self-discipline, old-fashioned virtue, old-fashioned devotion to a loved one is not often seen. There's none of that "fuck you, Jack, I'm alright" stuff about her.

On the Thames, at Princess Steps, aboard the *Kalizma*, he thinks of Sybil and then Elizabeth.

(May 25) What an extraordinary world it is. How do you live with one person for 13 years, and another for 8 and find both as alien as strangers. Elizabeth is an eternal one night stand. She is my private and personal bought mistress. And lascivious with it. It is impossible to tell you what is consisted in the act of love. Well, I'll tell you, E. is a receiver, a perpetual returner of the ball! I don't write about sex very often, because it embarrasses me, but, for some reason, who knows why, whatever, is spare, original, stranger. Counter.

The next day.

(May 26) Yesterday's entry, as any man of discernment can tell at a glance, was written while under the strong influence of several vodkas. T.H. (Tim) White once wrote a poem for me and about me called "Vodka Poem to Richard Burton." One night in New York when we were both suitably and idiotically drunk and I had given him the sword "Excalibur" which I used in the play written from his *The Once and Future King*, and after he had insisted on knighting with full accolade many and various and bewildered New York cabbies, we repaired to my apt on 81st Street on the West Park. There we wrote poems to each other. He kept both and some time later to my surprise and delight he had included the one to me in his last book of poems. Mine must be in his papers somewhere. Vodka is the operative word.

VODKA POEM TO RICHARD BURTON

Richard ap Richard
For you are
Your father and your son,
Are you the spendthrift and the spent,
The slayer slain in one?
Believer who does not believe,
Munificent and mean,
Trustless and trusting, insecure,
How will you get you clean?
Do not. But suffer. Understand.
Mascara more the dust of coal
Nor male nor female lashes fanned
Are Gwalia nor the whole.

HAM. I mean HAMEN
Tim

Tim died in his late fifties. If I don't watch myself I'll be lucky to see my late forties. With his huge stature and white hair and beard it was some sight, as they say, to see Tim give the accolade to Harry Schwartz, and Sol Schmuck. Arise Sir Harry! Arise Sir Sol! A few of them actually knelt on the pavement! A barman, used to drunken eccentricity, knelt to be knighted with a glass of vodka in each hand. Quite a lot of actors were knighted also that long-ago wild night. Jason Robards is about the only one I can remember. He didn't bother to knight me he said, because ever since he had first met me he had conferred a mental baronetcy on me. What a crying pity that White is dead. How E. would have adored that madman. And he her. And what a maniacal and lovely mind! I once sat there bewitched while he spoke for a couple of hours on the subject of worms, how each wriggling thing had locked inside him the beginning and the end of man, and that without worms we would all die. When you die, he said, give your body to the worms, they will be grateful. There is absolutely no reason to give it to fire, even the atmosphere might reject the noxious fumes from your burning.

He did his Notebook in the morning before the car came to take him out to Shepperton. Up on his own: tea and a slice of toast—like D. H. Lawrence's mining family before going down the pit.

> (May 28) I am drinking too much again and though I like to drink I have a fear that eventually it might affect my brain. Already, I've noticed, it has affected my memory. Or maybe I am getting old. Anyway I shall now, and hopefully for the rest of the film, slow down, and again hopefully, to a stop.
>
> The film is important despite the fact that both Elizabeth's and my latest films are enormous financial successes. That is to say *Secret Ceremony* and *Where Eagles Dare*. Elizabeth, if you please and with her usual insouciance, impertinence and cheek has managed to win the French Oscar for the former. I am very proud of her because it was an immensely difficult part. I love the old girl very badly nowadays, though I've exactly been indifferent. The last phrase should read "though I've *never* exactly been indifferent." What the hell—it's very early in the morning.
>
> I am very jealous of E. I'm even jealous of her affection for Dick Hanley, a 60-year-old homosexual, and anybody she has lunch with. Girls, dogs—I'm even jealous of the kitten because her adoration of it is so paramount. They'll all die before me though, so I'll win in the end.
>
> And so to Shepperton and work.

The press were there every day.

> (May 29) Barry Norman, another writer, for the *Daily Mail* and bright as a button, asked the unavoidable question. "Why don't you come back to the theatre?" For some reason English people adamantly believe that acting in the theatre is superior (what a funny word) to acting in the films or TV. I've done all three with considerable success, and I'll tell you, Baby Barry, that they are all difficult but with the difference that after, shall we say, 10 weeks of playing Hamlet on the stage one's soul staggers with tedium and one's mind rejects the series of

quotations that Hamlet now is. Has there ever been a more boring speech, after 400 years of constant repetition, than "To be or not to be"? I have never played that particular speech, and I've played the part hundreds and hundreds of times, without knowing that everybody settles down to a nice old nap the minute the first fatal words start. E. was quite savage with Norman, in defence of me, so much so that he perforce had tears in his eyes. So she gave him a kiss! Nobody will understand that I am unlike every actor I've ever met with the exception of Marlon Brando, without his extraordinary talent, but we are both bored!

Marlon's and Elizabeth's personalities, to say nothing of their physical beauty, are so vast that they can and have got away with murder, but Elizabeth—unlike Marlon— has acquired almost by proximity to the camera, by osmosis, a powerful technique. Marlon has yet to learn to speak. Christ knows how often I've watched Marlon ruin his performance by under-articulation. He should have been born two generations before and acted in silent films. The worst thing that ever happened to him was Gadge [Elia] Kazan, the Actors' Studio, and fantastic over-publicity when he was a baby. I love the chap (though the reverse is lamentably not true) and I long to take him in my teeth and shake enthusiasm into him. But deep down in his desperate bowels he knows that like Elizabeth and myself it is all a farce. All three of us, in our disparate ways, know that we are cosmic jokes.

Unusually for Burton, he is prepared to go into some detail about the work-in-progress.

(June 7) I had a hard day yesterday. Gareth [his nephew] had come aboard with us the night before and we spent half the night sitting up & talking and drinking with me insulting E. for most of the time. Then off to work at the crack of dawn to face a long scene with Gin Bujold in which I had to do almost all the talking. She'll be alright I suppose though she doesn't have enough dynamite and spit and venom and arrogance for the part, but of course I always am thinking in the remote rear of my cranium

how marvellous E. would be and how much better. I got
through it well enough and then, Oh blessed relief, I had
to work with Tony Quayle and Michael Hordern. Marvellous pair of pros and no rubbish and cunning as snakes.
I held my own I think. They have every shrug, nod, beck,
sideways glance and shifting of eyes ever invented. I said
to the director that it was somewhat akin to playing between the frying-pan and the fire. All Michael Hordern
had to say was "Yes, your Grace." He must have said
four hesitant "yours" and the three words uttered in his
inimitable way became slightly longer than Hamlet. Un-
cut. They both varied the time of their readings in an
unconscious effort to "throw" each other off, and me.
But I'm too old a hand. I "threw" them a couple of times
too. None said a word to each other about it but all three
old bastards knew bloody well that when that camera is
purring it's every man for himself. Of course if you are
the "star" or the "money" as technicians call it you can
afford to be magnanimous because the "money" is almost
automatically protected but it's as well to know what the
hell you're up to. And to let them know that *you* know
what *they* are up to. There is of course nothing malicious
about it, but it is deep in the subconscious.

Brook was at his funniest yesterday and sometimes
made me laugh so much that I had to wipe away tears.

The two babies arrived from La Suisse and I suddenly
realised that, after work on the film, I had to do the narration for the investiture of the Prince of Wales. And after
that Winston Churchill and 5 Dukes of Marlborough for
the Son et Lumière at Bleinhim(?) Place. Cor! Was I
whacked. Liza is turning into a young lady and I don't
think there's much wrong with Maria's intelligence. Thank
God! It's the first time I've thought that she stands a chance
in the rough world without us.

In the same entry:

I had the frights again yesterday—the second in a weekend
in a row, God Blast It! E. and I were going to make love
in the afternoon and she began to bleed. And I mean

BLEED. Not your pale pink variety but thick clots of blood
that had to be fingered into disappearing down the drain.
I sat with her and stroked her and tried to comfort her as
best I could. It finally stopped but I nightmared a great
deal. In fact, after two weekends of torment on the yacht,
I have mentally re-named the place "Nightmare Stairs"
and not "Princes."

. . . Burton then examined her intimately and carefully. This, as he
writes, was done "with love."

And a little fear. I mean a great deal of fear. She is
better this morning and the excrescences have receded a
considerable amount, but I shall not feel safe until she's
seen a doctor though, *under no circumstances*, is the knife
to be employed. There are other ways.

This passage—and subsequent unsqueamishly detailed descriptions
of Elizabeth's condition—underline the enormous nursing affection
which Burton had for her. The frequency and intensity of her illnesses coupled with the drinking and prescribed drug-taking threatened to make her a perpetual patient. It brings out the best in
Burton. In my opinion, her illnesses prolonged their marriage.
His restlessness and self-doubt are pulling against the grip of that
gypsy domesticity but he will not go while she so openly needs
him.

For him to write it down is curious, but, I suspect, it followed
the same principle as that which he employed when writing about
Rachel Roberts for instance. Nothing human would be alien to him.
And the more strikingly outside his expectation and experience it
was then the more important it had to be for him as a writer to
record it.

Within a few days Elizabeth was up and running again.

(June 11) E. looked very exciting in the shortest mini-
skirt. The slightest inclination from the vertical and her
entire bum was revealed to the admiring gaze.

Kate has now joined them and Burton is over the moon.

(June 11) Scrumptious Kate is with us still and, so far has come to work with me every morning, despite having to get up about 6 o'clock of a morning. All adore her and my leading lady in the film asked if she were for sale. I said that if she were I'd buy her myself.

June 14th, up again at four in the morning, then off to the set.

I love my wife. I love her dearly. Honest. Talk about the beauty, silent, bare . . . Sitting on the Thames with the river imitating a blue-grey ghost. My God, the very houses seem asleep. And all that mighty heart is . . . lying still.

My God again, how easy it must have been in the early days of this language to write poetry. How easy to impersonate the false feelings of a shepherd like Wordsworth's "Michael." Or the impassive massive indifferent passion of my favourite lines, "And I have felt a passion, a sense sublime, of something far more deeply interfused, whose dwelling is the light of setting suns, and the round ocean, and the living air, and the blue sky, and in the mind of man."

Sunday was a day of rest, of reflection.

(June 15) I awoke this morning at about 7 o'clock. I stared at Elizabeth for a long time. I am worried about her and her little bum & the blood. I held her hand and kissed her very gently. Probably no woman sleeps with such childish beauty as my adorable difficult fractious intolerant wife. "When in sorrow," said T. H. (Tim) White, "learn something new." I have changed that injunction to "think something new." I decided to examine my reactions to all the men of talent I have ever met and which company would I prefer. After serious thought, lying on that silent bed, with that killing cigarette between my lips, how I love its round cool comfort, I dropped names all over my brain. Churchill? No! A monologist. Picasso? No! An egomaniac. Emlyn? No. A mind like a cut-throat razor and a tongue to match. Dylan? No! Brilliant but uncomfortable. Willie Maugham? No! he cared only about playing bridge with losers. Gwyn Thomas? No! An impersonation of a chap who would like to be big strong and tough and who is actually fat weak and febrile. Camus? Possibly. But he had the infernal impertinence to die young. John Osborne? No! No leavening of humour. Gielgud? A strong contender for the Burton stakes, but I have a feeling that he finds *me* uncomfortable. Edward Albee? No! A week with him would be a life-time, and he'd feel the same about me. Anyway, why go on? I reduced it to two people. Noël Coward and Mike Nichols. They both have the capacity to change the world when they walk into a room. They are instinctively and without effort and unmaliciously witty. They are both as bland as butter as brilliant as diamonds and never speak with the forked tongue. Noël is an old man and I think he plans to die shortly. Mike plans to out-last Methuselah. What they have, and what I envy, is their absolute assurance. They are totally unafraid. When Noël totters—and he actually does totter—into anyone's presence, their faces light up like lamps. Including mine. Including Elizabeth's. Both E. and I have a remarkable capacity of inculcating the idea of fear into people. I have actually seen people shiver as they cross the room to be introduced to Elizabeth. What the hell is it? Who did it to us? I know that we are both dangerous people but we are fundamentally very nice. I mean we only hurt each other. And we never hurt other persons unless they hurt us first. Somebody once wrote (it was a feller I was at Oxford with called Robinson— can you imagine being called Robinson; I mean it's worse than Jenkins) that when Elizabeth walked into a room for a press conference which he happened to be attending, she gave the impression that nobody else was there. She answered, as it were, from outer space.

The insomnia continues, so does the drinking. The rumours fly about himself and "Gin." From Burton's Notebooks we have the portrait of a man inexorably fixated on himself, his wife, his family and the apparently irresolvable gorgon tangle of associates which prevent him enjoying the Xanadu he has created for himself.

But the acting is driving him potty.

(July 19) Christ Almighty, in whom I firmly believe not, what a week, what a fortnight, what a month. There is no question but that I must stop acting. It is dementing me. The thought of going to work in the intolerably early mornings is like a physical pain. It is all so perfectly boring. Anybody can play Henry VIII—I mean even Robert Shaw who should be consigned for the rest of his life to playing ping-pong against aging former champions— has played it.

He follows the moon landing obsessively, bemoaning the fact that all they can say is "A–OK" but still enthralled by Aldrin and Armstrong. He begins to hate the film. He stops drinking.

And the shock to my system is obviously pretty profound.
   (July 22) I have been like a mad and highly articulate bull in blinding flashes with all kinds of people that I normally have great respect for. I laid into Sheran [Hornby] yesterday at lunch for no good reason. I roughed up Brook and Bob Wilson and Jim Benton [his secretary] with a fine impartiality and to top it all I burned through and around E. today at lunch, in front of the same Sheran, just after she had just come back from one of the most painful operations, the insertion of some dreadful machine up her behind. This is, of course, par for the course when I am drinking heavily, but I'm surprised that I still do it when sober. If it is still the same in a month I shall go back to old father booze and find out how long it will take him to kill me. I might as well enjoy what little might be left me. One of the oddities I've noticed before when I've stopped drinking is that when one starts again the smell of straight liquor is revolting, so much so that one either has to force it down like medicine to get over the initial shock, or mix it deeply with fruit juice or something that will camouflage the taste and smell. I made myself a martini before lunch today and could not drink it. I took one sip and shivered from top to toe. I've only been off it since Friday night and even now it is only withdrawal, i.e. I still allow myself a couple of drinks a day. One

forgets how delicious water is and milk. I shall continue these confessions of an alcoholic at a later date.

(July 23) No drink at all yesterday, to continue the "Confessions," and I am again on a stand-by though I doubt whether I shall be as lucky again today to get the day off. The "moon-men" are already out of the headlines and poor Teddy Kennedy is in them. I feel sorry for him and I suppose understand his panic and indeed it "could happen to anybody" but unless he comes up with something very extraordinary when he appears in court next week, he has had his presidential and possibly even his senatorial chips. The K. family are of course notorious satyrs. I know that when Jack Kennedy was running for President and stayed with Sinatra at Palm Springs, the place was like a whore-house with Pres. Kennedy as chief customer. Christ, the chances those fellers took. But they all got away with it except the last remaining baby.

(July 24) Confessions continued: Last night I fell by the wayside and became drunk. It didn't take much to make me so. Today I shall return to the pavement.

Being (relatively) sober for the last three or four days I have learned a great deal. Drink, for instance, is a great anodyne. I had forgotten how boring people are. I'd forgotten how afraid people are. I'd forgotten how boring I am. And how all of us lead lives of quiet desperation, and bugger you, Thoreau. It is some ungodly hour in the morning.

Uniquely, as far as I can discover, he and Elizabeth sit down to talk about their movies and their movie careers. It is quite impressive how offhand or modest they are about all the fuss they created and all the hits they had. It isn't everyone who is Number One box-office *and* in films for which the critics pause thoughtfully before the Olivetti. Liza set it off.

(July 26) Liza went to see *Becket* the night before last and was I think surprised to see that her father could, despite his dissipation, play a saint. Now she wanted to see all the other films that E. & I had done. We explained that a vast percentage of them were rubbish and not worth anybody's attention but that, however, there were some that would bear re-watching. Which ones, we asked ourselves? Now E. has made around 50 films and I have made around 30. Let us say a rough total of about 80. I guessed that about 10 would bear re-examination. We tried to sort them out. In E.'s case:

National Velvet
A Place In The Sun
Cat On A Hot Tin Roof
Butterfield 8 (for her performance only, I understand)
Suddenly Last Summer
Virginia Woolf
Boom
Secret Ceremony (I think)
Shrew
Faustus (For her eyes and breasts alone)

I'll think of something else in a minute but what is odd is, since actors are considered to be stupid, how E.'s best films have been made *outside* the studio to which she was contracted. And in my case the only films I've made that were any good were the films that *I* chose, again *outside* the influence of contracts. The only two watchable films that I ever made before the end of my 14-year contract with Fox & Warner Bros., were *Look Back in Anger* & *Alexander the Great*. After that, and because of the remarkable impact of E. on my life, I have had virtually free choice. I have, except out of fear, hardly made a mistake. Since Elizabeth I have practically caught her up. I have done, now let's have a look:

Becket
Woolf
Spy
Shrew
Boom (Support)
Iguana
Faustus
Staircase

Not, if you have a careful look, a bad record, for two

people, who happen to be in love, and compete with each other, and who have the same temperament.

So, in some way it proves that we have our own taste. And if they allow us free rein, we will manage not to let anybody down. I think we should revert to being splendid amateurs, and if E. wants to shoot the love-life of a turtle, with herself as the vet, we shall do exactly that. I'll be the turtle.

We are, for a minute or two, at the absolute zenith of our ragged professions. So they, before they start tearing us apart again, should gracefully withdraw. The last sentence does not make any kind of sense, so let us stop. NOW. It is still a beautiful morning.

I think he undersells himself. There are scenes in *Dolwyn* and *A Subject Of Scandal And Concern*, there's *Where Eagles Dare* and *The Desert Rats* (of their kind) and bits in *Now Barabbas Was A Robber* and *The Prince of Players*. *Anne Of The Thousand Days* I would exclude save for four or five scenes.

The attempts to put real energy into the part of Henry VIII have drained away. William Squire who appeared in the film with him blames the drink. But he had drunk before and made fine films. It all came back to the words. When there was no grand writing involved—in an action film—then Burton gave himself the order to get on with the job and did it well. But when the part called for eloquence, for poetry, for oratory, then he measured the words against those of his favourite writers. If they failed to measure up, he could not sustain any real interest. It was a kind of intellectual arrogance and impatience. It was also honest. He was an actor who could not pretend. His gift was inspirational. He had to believe. In this plodding, bluff, unsurprising king of six wives he could have no faith and soon the Notebooks switch their focus.

He gives money to a polio-crippled boy who is walking on his crutches for charity. A. P. Herbert comes on to the *Kalizma* for lunch and Burton listens alertly but it is Elizabeth, once more, who is demanding his real attention.

(July 30) I knew there was something wrong yesterday. I could feel it in my primitive Welsh bones. E. had gone into the surgery for her 3rd and last injection. The first word I had was from a doctor, who, twixt lines as 'twere, made it blatantly clear that my baby child had nearly kicked it. I can forgive a "panel" doctor in S. Wales making a mistake, seeing a miner every minute on the minute, because the pressures are so enormous.

But not their expensive equivalent.

I am still dazed by the potential enormities of their ill syringes. That is why I am writing this long before the dawn will crack. It is 3.30 of the a.m. Well, she has defeated their best efforts to kill her many times. I wish she would realise, like me, that good doctors are as rare as good actors.

Anyway, she's alright, though I am still night-mared. What could life possibly be without her? Where would I go? What would I do? Everybody else pales by comparison. It's no use picking up a mini-skirted chick of 18—she wouldn't last a week, if that. I would die, I suppose, a greatly accelerated death. Anyway, she's alright. Bastards.

(Aug. 1) Aaron arrived at the studios yesterday. He seems to me to be very groggy and prematurely old tho' he assures me that the disease [multiple sclerosis] has not only been arrested but has "regressed." It doesn't seem so to me. I asked him how much money we have. Could we really afford to retire. He told me that in "quick" money I have roughly 4 to 4½ to five million dollars, and E. has slightly less. This is quick money and not to be confused with the various houses, the *Kalizma*, the paintings, the jewellery, etc., which would amount to about 3 or 4 million more. *If*, I said, we stopped acting, what sort of income would we get without touching the principal. He said: At least ½ million dollars a year. Let us give away a 100 thousand of that in keeping R. Hanley and Benton and Wilson in the style in which they are accustomed and all the godsons, god-daughters, nephews, nieces and Howard and Sarah and Will and schools. Let us give another 100 thousand running the *Kalizma*. Let's allow another 50 thousand for odds and ends and we, E. & I, will have to make do on 250 thousand a year. All the children are now rich, some more than others, and so we don't have to worry about them. Financially, I mean. I think, with some blank paper and a typewriter and some amiable but not furious vodka and Jack Daniels we could manage alright. As it was pointed out to me, it is a greater gross income, because of no taxes than the French Roths-childs. And, of course, if we don't touch the capital, as Aaron points it, by the time I am about 50 the capital will have at least doubled. Short of a war we shall be worth about 20,000,000 dollars. Twenty million. Joking of course, aren't you. Money is very important, not *all* important, but it helps a lot. That's why I have written about it so much today because it means that if E. & I have the strength of mind to give up being famous we can at least live in more than lavish comfort. I might even be able to buy her the odd jewel or two. We'll spread our time between Gstaad and the *Kalizma* & Puerto Vallarta. We'll nip over to Paris occasionally and give a party for the Rothschilds. We'll take the Trans-Siberian Express across Russia from Moscow to Vladivostock. We'll go to the hill stations in Kashmir. We'll muck around among the Greek Islands. We'll visit Israel and bury dead Egyptians. We'll re-visit Dahomey again and look at the washing on the line at the Palace—we can slide down the coast there in the *Kalizma*. And Spain and the West Indies and Ecuador and Paraguay and Patagonia and go up the Amazon. We'll take a month and do a Michelin Guide of France. There are many worlds elsewhere, Coriolanus. I can write pretty books with photos by E.

Two days later.

(Aug. 3) Today, however, I have lost all sorrow for myself & am really thinking of stopping this acting lark alto-gether.

The next day.

(Aug. 4) So off to work and another round of repetition. "I must have a son to rule England when I am dead. Find a way, Cromwell. Find a way. The Pope. The Cardinal. Orvieto, My Lord Bishops. Divorce Katherine. Divorce Anne. Marry Jane Seymour." I use every trick I know to make it credible but it's a losing battle. It's all medicore rubbish.

Cheered up by

(Aug. 5) Quip from Tony Quayle: "Michael Redgrave is in love with himself but he's not sure if it's reciprocated. That's his problem." I laughed for a long time.

Word comes in that *Eagles* has grossed over $21 million in the States "and is still going strong." Burton's calculations whirl into action. He can certainly retire now. His own dissatisfaction with acting is reinforced by Elizabeth.

(Aug. 20) That's why I know E. to be right when she says that I should pack it in for a bit—acting—and start to think.

He sees Emlyn Williams with great delight.

In first-class order and subtly wicked as ever. Age has not withered nor custom staled . . . It's a hard task not to be overwhelmed by Emlyn. The slightest suggestion of mock-modesty, of false values, of sentimentality and with a couple of words he will stab you right under the heart.

As is not unusual on such films, out-of-school tales about the leading man and his co-star abound on the set. On August 28th the Gin Bujold case hits the Notebooks.

Despite my protestations E. is still apprehensive about Gin Bujold. It is a dangerous situation but the danger lies to Miss Bujold and not to us. I imagine she is going to find it very difficult to go back to Montreal to the suburban house after the false glamour of this particular production. Well hew to the line and let the chips fall where they may.

Three days later.

(Aug. 30) Well, it's over. All I have is a couple of shots left to do and then I'll clean myself and go home and dry. I have rarely been so desperate. I remember waiting for the letter from Oxford and the terror of not being accepted. I remember the torment of choosing between Kate and Elizabeth. I chose the later and perhaps I shall never forgive myself for it. Though I love them both very badly. E. will not believe me but I have never done anything to betray her trust.

Does he, you may legitimately ask, protest too much? I still think he was innocent. And the next day on the rampage.

(Aug. 31) Yesterday was yet another terrible day. I behaved in a way to make a banshee look kind good and sweet. Insulting Elizabeth, drunk, periodically excusing myself rather shabbily and then starting the rough treatment all over again. Sometimes I am so much my father's son that I give myself occasional creeps. He had the same gift for damaging with the tongue, he had the same temporary violence, he had the same fidelity to Mam that I have to Elizabeth, he had the same smattering of scholarship, he had the same didactitism (bet I spelled that wrong), we wave the same admonitory finger at innocence when we know bloody well when we are guilt-ridden, when we have to attack when we know we're in the defensive position.

The running row with Elizabeth erupted in the hotel at Aston Clinton when Elizabeth suddenly ordered what Richard thought (rightly) were a totally unnecessary stack of towels, sheets, etc., and flooded out Gwen's room with these supernumerary gifts. He exploded. She retaliated.

Well, I went mad which ended up with Elizabeth smashing
me around the head with her ringed hands. If any man
had done that I would have killed him, or any woman
either, but I had sufficient sense to stop myself or I most
surely would have put her in hospital for a long time or
even into the synagogue cemetery for an even longer time.
I still boil with fury when I think about it. I took myself
off on a long walk to some farms that are around the
corner and thought of every possibility and its consequences. I decided that for a time anyway we are stuck
with each other. I thought that what E. needed was a long
rest in a quiet place and that so did I and we might get
together again. We are fighting & have been fighting for
a year now over everything and anything. I have always
been a heavy drinker but during the last 15 months I've
nearly killed myself with the stuff, and so has Elizabeth.
She has just come out to this minute back room where I
type and we're at it again. Neither of us will give in and
if one of us doesn't something is going to snap. And *I'm*
not going to give in. I'm too small a man and not feminine
enough. I prided myself on not having the shakes this
morning but the minute E. came out and sat down they
started up again. Now what the fuck is the meaning of
that? Anyway this naturally is one of the black celtic
melancholy days. I see nothing ahead of me but a long
grey waste. This afternoon I may see a little colour in the
desert and tomorrow perhaps even an oasis. But at the
moment I am in despair. If we cannot understand each
other or what is worst not stand each other we'll go our
separate ways pretty soon and go back to work . . . She'll
film again and I'll write.

Writing is now seen as a salvation, even the only hope of sanity.
But in Gstaad there is relief.

(Sept. 28) We have been here for about two weeks—I
will look up the exact date later—and already it has done
me a world of good. Shortly after we'd arrived Lillabetta
and Brook arrived with Maria. And we, i.e. B. & L, have
played badminton every day in the morning and occa-

sionally in the afternoons. We have taken long fast five-mile walks and for about a week I was so stiff that I could barely turn over in bed and my hands shook so badly that drinks had to be held up to my lips by E. Now however I am as steady as a rock and although still somewhat stiff in the arms and the back of the thighs and the lower calves I am infinitely more limber than I have been for a long time. I have reduced my boozing to practically zero—by my standards. A vodka martini before lunch, and wine with dinner. And I frequently don't touch the wine. I have taken up the Drinking Man's Diet again about three days ago.

But the booze cannot be left alone for long.

(Sept. 29) I fell off my disciplined wagon last night with a thunderous crash and sat up with Brook until 5:30 in the a.m. drinking in the meantime a whole bottle of Scotch alone. I am feeling it today but have abandoned the diet and stopped all alcohol.

The real pleasure—perhaps the greatest pleasure of the year—was the receipt, at this time, from Elizabeth, of that complete uniform edition of the Everyman Library, "one thousand, numbered, gleaming, uniform books." The publishers had taken over five years to collect them. Burton himself had begun to collect them at the age of twelve and then scattered them all over his many homes and passing residences. The books were in packing cases and now at Gstaad he unloaded them and put them on the shelves. "I shall browse in that place for the rest of my life. They will take up one wall of the room. It is a fantastic reference library with the index in my head."

This leads into a story.

(Sept. 30) I told E. that while up at Oxford and in the RAF I would, whenever I could, go to London for the weekends and steal books from the giant Foyle's in Charing Cross Road. I told her how I used to do it. During the war, when I did my best stealing, there was an acute shortage of paper and Foyle's couldn't wrap the books up as they do nowadays. I would buy one book and pay for it. The assistant would give a receipt which I would ostentatiously leave hanging out of the pages of the legitimate purchase. Now whether one bought one book or ten you still had only the one slip of paper to show for it. I would then pick up one or two Everymans, taking a long time —as much as an hour sometimes before I sauntered quietly out of the shop. I must have stolen scores of Everymans in this way. One day I was up to my usual tricks in Foyle's while a friend of mine called N. was doing likewise in the corner. I had been bold this day and had about five books in addition to the one I'd bought, when N. came and stood casually beside me. Out of the corner of his mouth he said softly: "Put all the books back, Taffy. Put 'em *all* back." Very slowly and acting the part of a man who could not make up his mind I, one by one, put them all back. Later on when we were safely away from the shop N. told me that he'd seen one of the male assistants go into the little glass walled office that Foyle's used to have then, put on a raincoat and follow me around. I never stole a book again, and indeed, within a year, having almost immediately become a "star" I didn't need to any more.

In Gstaad he plays badminton with Brook Williams whom he frets over—saying that Brook should be a writer, delighting in his "unmalicious wit." They go to the art gallery where several of Elizabeth's paintings are hung and to see Dr. Rossier in the paraplegics ward of the local hospital. They bought $50,000 worth of equipment, partly so that Ifor could use it when he came over to stay as they were determined he should.

Again they went to the hospital to discuss Ifor's bed and then:

(Oct. 2) Somewhere between the hospital and dinner brooding set in. Between long silences deadly insults were hurled about. At one point E., knowing I was in a state of nastiness, said to me at the lousy Italian restaurant we went to: Come on Richard, hold my hand. Me: I do not wish to touch your hands. They are large and ugly and

red and masculine. Or words to that effect. After that my
mind was like a malignant cancer—I was incurable. I
either remained stupidly silent or, if I did speak, managed
an insult a second. What the hell's the matter with me. I
love milady more than my life and I adore Brook. Why
do I hurt them so much and spoil the day?

I am very contrite this morning but one of these days
it's going to be too late, cock, too late. E. has just said
that I really must get her the 69 carat ring to make her
ugly big hands look smaller and less ugly! Nobody turns
insults to her advantage more swiftly or more cleverly than
Lady Elizabeth. That insult last night is going to cost me.
Betcha!

On November 1st he catches up on some of the previous days.

(Nov. 1) Then to England and Ifor and he looked to me
that he was dying fast. He is, of course, but I should
expect it and not be as stricken as I was. It threw me for
a long time, lasting until this minute. I am not used to
death and Ifor has always been a kind of God to me. He
never treated me harshly, despite his short-temper, all his
life. He only hit me once and then I deserved it.

And then came the RING.

(Nov. 1) But now on to other things: *bought the ring for
Elizabeth*. Its acquisition was a tremendous excitement. I
had set a "lid" on it of one million dollars, if thou pleasest,
and Cartier outbid me by $50,000. When Jim Benton [his
secretary] called me and told me (we were at the Bell Inn
visiting Ifor and Gwen) I turned into a raving maniac and
insisted that he get Aaron on the phone as soon as possible.
Elizabeth was as sweet as only she could be and protested
that it didn't matter, that she didn't mind if she didn't
have it, that there was much more in life than baubles,
that she would manage with what she had. The inference
was that she would make do. But not me! The relief
in Jim's voice was unmistakable and, an hour later

when I finally got him on the phone, so was Aaron's. I screamed at Aaron that bugger Cartiers, I was going to get that diamond if it cost me my life or two million dollars whichever was the greater. For 24 hours the agony persisted and in the end I won. *I got the bloody thing.* For $1,100,000. It will take two weeks or more to get here. In the meantime it is on view in Chicago and has been in New York and 10,000 people a day go to see it. It has also been a star on the Ed Sullivan show and both Jim Benton and Aaron Frosch have entirely changed their minds about the wisdom of my buying it. It turns out that one of my rivals was Ari Onassis but he chickened at $700,000. But apart from the fact that I am a natural winner, I wanted that diamond because it is incomparably lovely. And it should be on the loveliest woman in the world. I would have had a fit if it went to Jackie Kennedy or Sophia Loren or Mrs. Huntingdon Misfit of Dallas, Texas.

The excitement and the hubris is unmistakable. It is another conquest: this time on the open market of *gross* extravagance. Brook Williams fills in the details. That phone call was made from a public box in the passage outside the public bar at The Bell. Inside, men sipped pints of mild and bitter and no doubt cocked an ear. The operator became more than a little fussed about the reverse charges. Locals were patiently waiting to phone through their bets to the local bookie. Elizabeth, according to Brook, was *indeed* sweet, as Richard reported, but tears were shed. *The* ring was the 69.4 carat job.

It was brought over with security guards and a man with a machine gun gave it his protection. The *New York Times* deplored the crowds outside Cartier's where it was displayed and lambasted the Burtons for vulgarity. Princess Margaret too thought it vulgar: Elizabeth asked if she would like to try in on: yes please. "It doesn't look so vulgar now, does it?" said E.T. Not much later, John Gielgud went to stay and, helping with the washing-up, found it lying on the draining board next to a saucer. It is also surprising—and something of an insight—to learn that Elizabeth Taylor washed up!

The sparkle from the diamond seems to have dimmed rather quickly.

(Nov. 18) This morning in the early hours the pot decided to have a go at the kettle and won handle down. E., the pot, gave this particular kettle, me, a savage mauling. I was coldly accused of virtually every sin under the sun. Drunken-ness (true) mendacity (true) being boring (true) infidelity (untrue) killing myself fairly quickly (true) pride envy avarice (all true) being ugly (true) having once been handsome (untrue) and any other vice imaginable except homosexuality and ungenerousness. Otherwise this personal kettle was not black at all but shimmered in aluminium. I mean I practically got away scot-free.

Ifor's condition continued to be a preoccupation throughout the Notebooks.

(Dec. 8) Ifor goes up and down, but catastrophically he had a stroke in his sleep last September, which was hidden from us. He has great difficulty in speaking and has retreated more and more into himself. Apart from an occasional spirited flash of old, he has changed into another person. He is mortally afraid, he tells me, *not* of death itself but of leaving this world and all its varying excitements. The physical pain of death he discounts. "I will die in my sleep for sure anyway and won't know anything about it. My stroke in my sleep at Stoke Mandeville didn't wake me up and I didn't know anything had happened until the orderlies came in in the morning and I found I couldn't speak." What a blow on a blow. He'd have lived until he was 90 were it not for that trip in the dark at Céligny. Gwen too is a semi-cripple with arthritis.

The news of *Anne Of The Thousand Days* is good.

(Dec. 12) Today received a telegram from Edd Henry of Universal Pics saying that *Anne Of The Thousand Days* has been shown to the press in N.Y. & L.A. and the reaction is "nothing short of sensational." And "superior to *Man For All Seasons* and *Lion In Winter*." We shall see, Mr. Henry, we shall see. It would be rather nice if it was a blockbuster as I have a hefty percentage of the

gross. And rings and farthingales and things and hospital
wings could be bought. It would be a good thing if Gin
Bujold won an Oscar which, since she's unknown & *if*
the film is as successful as Universal believes it's going
to be and if she keeps her trap shut about how horrible a
place Hollywood is, she is quite likely to do.

She did not win the Oscar but claimed Hollywood's Golden Globe.
In her acceptance speech she said, "I owe my performance to Richard Burton. He was generous, kind, helpful and witty. And generosity was the one great quality."

You can take that as rubbing it in or stirring it up. The evidence
from his actor friends on the spot points to the latter.

At the end of 1969, the Burtons were harassed and planning to
take a year off. Elizabeth was genuinely seriously ill: her recovery
was sporadic and slow. The children—Michael, chiefly; Maria had
suddenly "come through," almost miraculously, to Richard's unabated joy—needed sorting out. There was an ominous emptiness
about Elizabeth's future and Burton was now fighting the drink, his
terribly unreliable and violent mental state, his fear of the marriage,
and the typewriter.

There was no doubt that now they genuinely wanted to quit. They
were on top. It was a good time to go. They had the money. He
had the alternative occupation of writing. They loved not working.
She had scooped the diamond pool. To quit at the very top. They
would attempt it. It was to be their year of living dangerously, their
year of discovering what inner resources they really had.

19
The Sabbatical

So 1970 was to be the year of the sabbatical. Time out, time off. Risk time, time to re-route the caravan, time to rest and do all the things undone as their meteors had burned through the Sixties. Most of it was spent at Puerto Vallarta, with the model Bridge of Sighs connecting the two houses which made up Casa Kimberley. Elizabeth was thirty-eight in February; Richard forty-four; *Cleopatra* was nine years behind them and they had been married for six years.

At the beginning of the year they were joined, for three months, by John David Morley, now a novelist, then a young ex-pupil of Nevill Coghill, fresh from Oxford and delighted to be tutor to the children. He has written and spoken about his "Brief Encounter with the Burtons" and his insights are valuable.

He stresses how powerful Burton was as a presence. His first sight of him prompts him to think of Heathcliff. The first conversation he records has Burton reciting twelve stanzas from a Scottish poet, Dunbar, with the sonorous refrain "Timor Mortis Conturbat Me"—"Fear of death anguishes me." He speaks of Burton's superbly handsome looks, his undeniable aura and presence, his staying power as a parent—he wrote the letters to the children, Elizabeth added the postscripts. He uncovers, kindly and I think accurately, the mask of gruff dismissive intellectuality and shows us a man genuinely devoted to books and words, truly impressed by learning, a keening intellectual underneath all the brainy bluff.

Elizabeth told Morley that she was afraid that she would bore

Burton. She is the playful one, the children's playmate, the delighter in trifles. Burton, taking thought to weave them all together, anxious over Maria, now finding the meat of the marriage, according to this perceptive tutor, in the family.

Yet Burton was still deeply bound to Taylor. In the balance of fame and the notoriety of success, Taylor outgunned him. At her peak, she outgunned almost everyone in the world in weight of tabloid interest, crowd curiosity, face space. He competed now and then but there is no indication that he took it very seriously. On the contrary, the indications—especially in the Notebooks where he was speaking true—were that he relished her fame and adored the glamour and, most of all, understood the spunk and power of instinctual genius which went into it. She would indeed bore him with her retellings of the innumerable operations: just as he bored her with the retelling of that stock of stories which he used like the handbook of a thousand and one Welsh and theatrical nights. But overwhelmingly, she could fascinate him still. It was when this went that the marriage hit a rock.

In 1970 she could still seem the joy of his life. He was interested in her, as a zoologist might be if he discovered a valley full of new species hitherto unknown to the world. And she blossomed under his scrutiny—enriched by the insights he brought to bear on her. He valued her with an intelligence which had never before given her a second thought. Many of the women who have spoken lovingly about Burton have highlighted this aspect, the feeling of being enormously valued; women responded mightily to the concentration of attention he gave them.

So did men. Whenever he was engaged he was fully engaged and the power of his character (Morley is yet another witness to this) could be dramatic and memorable. He could connect: with a single person, a company, a family, an audience, the black space beyond the lights or the lens. But not, perhaps, with the blank space within.

Yet those close to him are forever recording him to be isolated and detached. He can be economical with the truth about himself. Having mentioned his arthritis once or twice—the effect of which can clearly be seen on the screen beginning about now, the hunched shoulders, the stiff neck movements, the unfluent arms—he drops it. Perhaps he is ashamed, perhaps he is embarrassed, thinks it sissy—but out it goes. No mention at all of the epilepsy. Plenty about the booze but then the booze was a character in his life—a foxy old friend, a confidant, an opponent, a chance to slide out of himself, and, eventually, an instrument in his toying with the depths of himself which approached and then became an obsessive essay in self-destruction. For some time, his absorption with Elizabeth staved that off.

He was forever considering alternative lives. What would have happened if he had stayed on in the Valleys? Or gone back to Oxford? Or taken up Olivier's offer of the National Theatre? Considering them, though, playfully, in rather a melancholy way. His central intuition into the brevity and strangeness of life was too potent to lead to minor career regrets. "Timor Mortis Conturbat Me."

Morley talks about Burton carrying the typewriter about with him. He would go to an eyrie atop Casa Kimberley, above their modest bedroom, and pound away in the mornings. The typewriter would be carried about with him like a pen. Morley says that there were a lot of crumpled sheets and that once, when he opened one up, he discovered it to be blank. The implication is, just a touch, that Burton wanted to be seen as a literary, even as a writing, man but had nothing to say: and so wrote nothing.

In fact, during that year, Burton was attempting his first full-length novel. He was also, after March, deep into his Notebooks. Typically he kept them from Morley even though he respected Morley as a literary man. No one could be wholly trusted except family—and even then . . .

About 20,000 words of the novel were written. But there is no trace of it. Burton once told a reporter that he had lost the manuscript while in LA that year—1970—when he had been nominated for an Academy Award for *Anne Of The Thousand Days*.

The laconically admitted loss undoubtedly conceals a good deal. This sabbatical year had been engineered partly for a rest, partly to see if they could live contentedly and comfortably off their investments, doing no work at all, and partly to see if he could set himself up as a writer. He was already in a position to contribute to several newspapers and magazines: the *Observer*, *McCalls*, *Vogue*, the *Daily Mail*, among others, would always be in the market for pieces on Wales or acting, while the world and its mother wanted anything on life with Elizabeth. He did not underestimate or dismiss the value of that, but to set up shop he needed something more substantial.

It's of interest that he turned to fiction. Most actors when they write—after that first fine poetical fling which marks almost all scribblers—go for the stage. Many of the best dramatists have been actors. In choosing the novel, Burton was again, in a small way, showing himself apart. The novel was then the Bible of the working-class scholarship boy: poetry the Prayer Book. The writing—as he had once suggested—was to come from his roots rather than his later branches.

Perhaps he thought the loss of the novel was an omen. Perhaps he thought he was no good. He was always hard on his own performance, although, and in parallel, always certain of the existence of his talent.

In Puerto Vallarta, then, with a tutor for the children, a life at the typewriter, on the sun roof, not much in the town—too harassed—occasionally tempted out to sea to fish, inland to ride or off to some grandiose estate. There was always Elizabeth, and he was a man who did not despise his own company. The reading went on, the drinking, the Notebooks.

> (Mar. 24) It's a long time since I wrote in this thing. I fell by the wayside at the Sinatra house. It must be confessed that he is a very unhappy man—apart from his fundamental moroseness he was at the time plagued by writs, etc., by the State of N. Jersey which is his home state, about complicity with local gangsters. I believe Sinatra to be right that he was in no way implicated and we have read since that he finally appeared in N.J. without the necessity of extradition or whatever they call it between state and state, and has been clean-slated. So that's alright. His house is a kind of super motel in shape and idea. A series of very elaborate suites with every possible modern gadget included, vaguely surround a small swimming pool. There is what is known as the rumpus room which contains a pool table and a magnificent toy train set given to Frank by the manufacturers and which he has arranged to have transferred to some children's home or something. He is a very nice man in short doses but I imagine a bore to live with, especially now with the energy gone and where he is obviously watching his health. His library was quite extensive but "Prince" Mike Romanoff told me that Frank had asked him to choose the books. That may have been of course Mike's intellectual conceit, but I did see

lots of copies of *Encounter* around and I'm bloody sure
Francis doesn't read that. Elizabeth made sheep's eyes at
him the whole time, and sometimes he at her. I've never
seen her behave like that before and apart from making
me jealous—an emotion which I despise—I was furious
that he didn't respond! We out-stayed our welcome and
over-stayed it by three or four days, though I was longing
to get away. Eventually we did and came back down here
to Vallarta. We flew up to Palm Springs and back to LA
in Sinatra's jet plane which is called a Gulf Stream jet or
something like that. It's a lovely plane and E. of course
immediately wanted to buy a similar one. It costs no more
than $3¼ million dollars. That's all. What with that and
a $1 million dollar hospital we'd be flat. And the world
has changed—I mean our world. Nobody, but *nobody*,
will pay us a million dollars a picture again for a long
time. I've had two financial disasters, *Staircase* and *Boom*,
and Elizabeth *Boom* and *Secret Ceremony*. *Anne* is going
steadily along and will more than make its money back.
So is E.'s picture *The Only Game* but *Anne* only cost $3½
million whereas *The Only Game* cost $10 million so that
one will never get its money back under twenty years. I'm
afraid we are temporarily (I hope that it *is* only temporary)
out in the cold and fallen stars. We haven't of course
fallen very far—we could doubtless still pick up $750,000
a picture which aint chicken-feed. What is remarkable is
that we've stayed up there so long.

   This is going to be a long entry presumably to be continued tomorrow. As a promise to Elizabeth I went into
Hollywood Presbyterian Hospital to have a complete
check-up. And what a check-up! It took 24 hours which
meant I had to stay the night in the hospital. By the time
they had made me get into bed, taken what seemed like
several pints of blood out of my left arm—no—right arm,
and said I must take some funny little pills every five
minutes for until there were no more left, and Rex Kenemer, the Dr., assuring me just by feel that I unquestionably had an enlarged liver as a result of 30 years of
excessive drinking. So with Elizabeth in the next room to
comfort me I had a very uneasy night. I was not a little

afraid of the tests though I comforted myself with the thought that apart from two toothaches and an appendix removed when I was 8 yrs old and an occasional heavy cold or a light 'fluenza I had never been ill in my life. The tests were excruciatingly boring. They took off-and-on hours and hours and between times agonies of waiting in little cubicles like locker boxes in a golf club while they found out if the X-rays had "taken." They told me after some hours that they were afraid the gall-bladder test hadn't turned out too well. Did this mean I asked that my gall-bladder was a mess or simply that the snap hadn't come out too well. "It could be either," said the little round-faced chap with sparse blond hair (about 35 yrs old). Anyway it turned out alright so I didn't have to stay in for another night. Next day Kenemer came to see me and told me that I simply had to stop drinking for at least 3 months. Why, I asked? Because apparently, at my present rate of booze I would have sclerosis of the liver within about five years which would get progressively worse. Whether I drank or not. I mean after five more years. Very well, I said, I shall stop drinking totally. I have done so before for an occasional week and sometimes longer. This will be the longest time of the lot. This is my 10th day without booze of any kind & I must confess I feel immensely healthier. We are off to the Garza Blanca for lunch.

Some news! The next three or four months record much but the progress of the non-drinking is watched unceasingly. His will-power is strong. The gains are obvious and noted. But drinking has not only been a compulsion—it's been a pal and a passport to other worlds. Without it he was truly alone.

Up it crops two days later. The ache of the new convert can be seen in the rather comical inclination to preach:

(Mar. 26) Hard liquor in whatever form before eating is a taste-bud killer, though a burgundy, rich and deep, with beef and port with a powerful cheese is delectable. So is a good very dry light white wine with fish. Standards, but ones I had not appreciated before.

It will never be out of mind for long. The next day he receives a long "and I suspect slightly drunk" very affectionate letter from Laurence Olivier and another from Anthony Quayle mentioning his success in *Sleuth*. Burton begins an intensive course of Spanish lessons and once more nods at the bottle.

> (Mar. 27) Today or tomorrow will make it a fortnight without drinking—the longest since I played *Camelot* and I haven't missed it at all but had a severe time at a party given by a family called the Gunsbergs, a surprise luncheon birthday party for dear Phil Ober. Everybody was stoned when we arrived, everybody was repetitious. I was vastly tempted to down a huge dollop of vodka and join the general boredom but desisted and smiled and smiled and hoped for the best.

On the following day it erupts into the text several times.

> (Mar. 28) It's a sod of a world today. I am extremely unhappy and as melancholy as a Sankey and Moody hymn. My instinctive aversion and distrust of the human race is brought to a head periodically, drunk or sober. And this is one of those days. The sun is bright. The people around me in the house are all engaging but today, at least, I don't want to see any of them. I am writing this on the top private-patio of the house wearing a Mexican hat, Mexican fashion over my nose because at the moment I could easily play Bardolph without any make-up . . . The trouble with total sobriety is that if you are a born misanthrope and if your base is an essential cynicism, and my birth and base are both, you do not see the world through a glass darkly (in my case a glass of alcohol) but suddenly face to face. I find that, alcoholless, I have become for me relatively silent. I do not as before tell incessant stories, most of the audience having heard them before, especially poor Elizabeth who has had to suffer them endlessly for 8 or 9 years. There was an out-burst at lunch today. Norma [Heyman] said how marvellous I was looking since I gave up booze . . . it's only been a fortnight for God's sake . . . And I said "there's someone

who could never give up drink" pointing at E. Whereupon she said (E.) hated my guts and furthermore disliked me savagely. "Ah," said the little stirrer-up Norma, "but you do love him, don't you?" "No," said E., "and I wish to Christ he'd get out of my life. It's been growing on me for a long time." "Piss off out of my sight," she added. So like the Arab I picked up my tent and stole silently away up here—my tent being the typewriter, my sombrero and Madrigal's Magic Key to Spanish. She has said all those things before and I to her, but never before, as I recall, when *sober and* in front of people. If, of course, she *was* sober. Raymond makes extremely powerful drinks. She has had the above out-burst so often recently—going back about a year, I would say, that it undoubtedly smacks of the truth. The eyes blaze with genuine hatred and contempt and her lovely face becomes ugly with loathing. I have to face the fact that E. may be going to take off one of these days and perhaps sooner than I expect. I have known it deep down for some time but have never allowed it to surface. Well, perhaps when we have all come out of this slough of despond we can still make it work. Tomorrow is always a surprise. Our quarrel sounded like the quarrels one hears from the next room in a cheap hotel by two middle-aged people, 20 yrs married and bored witless by each other. A good shouting match is sometimes good for the soul, cathartic, emetic, but I can't be bothered to shout back when I'm sober. Pity.

(Mar. 29) As for E. & I there is a kind of armistice. Both sides are fully armed, the bombs are ready to go off but so far nobody has pressed the button. The first six months of the sabbatical have been completely wasted. Except when we were alone we have bickered and quarreled incessantly, and we have hardly ever been alone.

That last confession is the saddest of all. Elizabeth had always had an entourage—you were never alone as a star. But Richard had known a life before all that, a life without a court, a life with space and privacy. Even allowing for the vast difference between his marriage to Sybil and his marriage to Elizabeth, it is still sad and foolish that he could not engineer what he knew they needed. But that, perhaps, is a measure of the paralysis which was fast setting in to the marriage.

On April 2nd:

> Another worry is that I have temporarily lost all sexual urge which is very frustrating for E. Presumably because of the terrific change in my body as a result of total abstinence for (now approaching) three weeks, after thirty years of steady and sometimes unsteady drinking is taking its time to re-assess itself. When it does come back it will be a vast explosion. If it does come back which it better had.
>
> I read last night Aaron's precis, which runs to several thousand words, of our respective financial positions. It seems that we have approx 5¼ million dollars each but that our overheads are approx 600,000 dollars a year. Insurance alone for jewellery and paintings is 200,000 dollars a year. The *Kalizma* is 100,000. Vallarta is 20,000. Salaries and fees—lawyers, etc., and agents' Xmas bonuses, *et al*, is 370,000. The latter sum includes some of the former. It is in any case a lot of money. And extremely worrying, not for me but for E. She could blow her whole assets except, thank God, her trust fund in 6 months.
>
> I must find out from Aaron how we can cut down from 600,000 to about 400,000 dollars a year. That should stop us going into capital. We'll hammer it out.

And so, on April 3rd, to Beverly Hills for the Oscars.

> (Apr. 3) We arrived smoothly from Vallarta in Sinatra's jet in 2½ hours. I have lost roughly 18 lbs in two weeks on the low carbohydrate diet and have yet to have a drink in three weeks.

While waiting for the Oscars, he dips into sport—buying dozens of table tennis balls, some "travelling cues" and Minnesota Fats's book on the game, watches golf, and broods a little about the award.

(Apr. 6) There is apparently an outside chance I might win but I give it no mind or else I shall become morose if I'm a loser. I have now gone over 3 weeks without a drink and never give it a thought, though win or lose tomorrow night it's going to be another test of my willpower, because certainly everybody else will be intoxicated. It's one of those nights.

In fact as that entry shows drink is never very far away from his thoughts.

(Apr. 7) Today is Hollywood's big day—the day of the Oscars. It's curious that the whole world makes fun of it, but that all actors want to win one and in the obits of actors it is invariably mentioned as the summit of their achievements. Even in *The Times* or *The Guardian*. For instance one of the reasons is that if the Oscar for leading actors is won tonight by John Wayne it will be out of pure sentimentality because, though I haven't seen his performance, I'm told that it is little more than his usual walk through. His performance is not comparable with Voight's or Hoffman's. I haven't seen O'Toole's and I am no judge of myself. The supporting actress will probably be won by one Goldie Hawn because she is a famous TV personality. The leading actress will probably be Liza Minnelli because her mother died last year—Judy Garland, a great and sentimental favorite here. And so on. That's what makes it absurd and still it's coveted, even by me! My only chance is that I am a Kennedy–Adlai Stevenson associate and a "Dove," while Wayne is a Republican, "My country right or wrong" Birchite Hawk, and the "artistic" Hollywood fraternity is usually very liberal. Also, John Springer says that a great many people thought we wuz robbed when I didn't win for *Who's Afraid*. We shall see. I shall be bloody furious if I don't have a chance to show off my new dinner jacket which has a brocaded waistcoat and lots of fol-de-rols, especially as I am now 169 lbs as of this morning and was around 186–8 when I was measured for it a month or less ago.

The rest of the day is going to be chaos and I look forward to Vallarta with longing. One more day.

(Apr. 8) John Wayne won the Oscar as predicted. We went to the party afterwards and sat with George Cukor the Pecks and the Chandlers (owners of the *LA Times*) but were surrounded by scores of photographers, who, to my delight, took very little notice of anybody else including the winners. Barbra Streisand who fancies herself a big star was completely eclipsed. And a whole queue of people, literally hundreds, passed the table to stare at E. and tell me that I was robbed and after all these protestations we began to wonder who in the world voted for Wayne. We got out with great difficulty because of the hordes of photogs, visiting Gig Young, who won best supporting actor, en route. Hawn won best supporting actress, also as predicted. We couldn't find Duke Wayne so came home, then the family came home, Brook and Liz [his wife] and later and very tearful—because "everybody had left her" came Norma. Later still came Wayne himself also very drunk but, in his foul-mouthed way very affable. I survived another night without booze but I did take at the dinner party a couple of Elizabeth's "pink pills" which are supposed to be pain-killers and muscle-relaxers. They certainly eased the boredom. I shall try them again instead of Valium when I'm surrounded by drunks.

Anyway, I lost again, and am now the most nominated leading actor in the history of the Academy Awards who has never won. So I have carved my tiny niche in the wall of Oscar's *Wisden*.

Burton then flung a cocktail party for the "losers" including

Jane Fonda who talked of nothing but the Black Panthers and got $3000 each out of E. and me . . . it went on until about 9.30.

(Apr. 10) By this time we all thankfully returned to the bungalow with everybody drunk except me of course (still no drink) and E. really sloshed. I asked her not to talk to her mother but she insisted and then there ensued a slanging match with accusation and counter-accusation which all of us could hear through the walls. Later, after another call they appeared to become reconciled. What a pair. I went to bed and Elizabeth went to the bathroom. Then I heard her calling me and she was bleeding . . . I called Kenemer who told me to wrap some ice in a towel and for her to hold it against the bleeding. But she still wanted to see poor Kenemer, so I rousted the poor sod out of bed—it was now the middle of the night—and he came over within ten minutes. By this time naturally, it always happens, the bleeding had stopped. However he mucked about and put a bandage around her arse, stayed for half an hour.

The tone has changed decisively. The tender care shown previously in the nursing and in the prose are absent.

A fortnight later they were guests of General Garcia Barragan,

who, I'm told in whispers, is the real power in Mexico. He will decide . . . who will be the next President . . . Echeverria apparently. It's all very Graham Greenish. They, the family, have given Elizabeth everything she's pointed at and said—"It's yours." A horse that she saw from their plane . . . was given to her on the spot—a Palomino . . . Tonight they gave her a splendid Mexican saddle. What is behind it all?

Bored after a day, he went in for long slugs of reading and weighing himself.

(Apr. 27) I have lost so much flab that I am now only 165–167 lbs. A loss in six or eight weeks of over 20 lbs. (This has been done by cutting out booze entirely—my 7th week without alcohol in any form—and otherwise eating well on the low carbohydrate diet, supplemented by the Swiss sweetener—"Hermesetas"—and sugarless sweets if the urge is too strong for sweet things.) As a result of this dramatic drop—the lightest I've been since my early twenties when I played rugby night and day—

all my trousers are many inches too big around the waist and behind. They measured my waist at 34 inches but even they were too big and I settled for 4 pairs of 33s. I could get into a 32, I think, but the 33 will allow for minor breaches of discipline. I had been 38.

As he gets fitter, Elizabeth is still the victim.

(May 5) Slept well and woke at a civilised hour—about 8.30–9.00, having gone to sleep around 1.00–1.30. Showered, shaved and exercised with a "sauna belt" around my waist. 100 toe-touches, 100 sideways bends, breath expulsion and trying to drive the stomach wall against the backbone while totally exhaled. Boring but gives one the idea of being virtuous. I am somewhere between 160 and 165 pounds roughly—both weighing machines differ. Anyway I feel about 160ish.

E. suffering tortures from "chigger" bites—the unseen creature that digs into your flesh and lays eggs, but suffering worse from open wounds, one of them quite deep, from riding at El Tuacon without riding boots.

After a few days on the beach, their own, about 10 acres, they return to Los Angeles with Brook Williams and his wife, who have been their house-guests.

(May 9) We leave for LA tomorrow and Lucille Ball's show, rehearsing Mon, Tues, Wed and shooting before a *live* audience on Thurs. Then E. goes into hosp for the (we hope) final operation on her piles. Shall be very glad when that's all over for poor E. They say it is among the most sustainedly painful businesses. Nobody wants to go to LA but I must confess to a little excitement about the show because, I suppose, I haven't worked for so long. I'm told that L. Ball is very wearing to work with. We shall see.

(May 14) Those who had told us that Lucille Ball was "very wearing" were not exaggerating. She is not "wearing" to us because I suppose we refuse to be worn. She lives entirely on that weekly show which she has been

doing and successfully doing for 19 years. Nineteen
solid years of double-takes and pratfalls and desperate
up-staging and nervously watching the "ratings" as she
does so.

Burton's mounting fury with Lucille Ball and his perception of her
methods of work represent, crudely and commercially, the head-on
clash of two totally different methods of working. Burton waited
for his gift to materialise: if it did not, he was helpless. Lucille Ball
worked on her talent like an engineer, forever shaping and restruc-
turing, driving the machine of her shows through to performance
whatever. It was the first American situation comedy Burton had
been involved in and he was completely unprepared for the relentless
professionalism. As a result—characteristically—he stood back and
slammed it. Perhaps his growing anger was fuelled by guilt. Why,
after all, was he doing it? For exposure? (Did he fear he might need
it?) For money? (Surely not. He was very wealthy by now.) For
fun? That is most likely. In which case it back-fired badly and what
had promised to be a romp turned out to be Burton on the rampage
with a very fierce view of Miss Ball and all her works.

I loathe her today but now I also pity her. After tonight
I shall make a point of never seeing her again. We work,
or have worked until today which is the last day, thank
God, from 10 a.m. to somewhere around 5 p.m., and
[she] can thank her lucky stars that I am not drinking.
There is a chance that I might have killed her. I said very
loudly after yawning prodigiously and being asked by the
director, a nice man called Jerry Paris, whether I was tired
or bored or what, that I was not particularly any of those
things but was puzzled as to why anybody who didn't have
to for financial reasons, *et al*, would submit themselves
to this mindless routine week after week for 19 years.
Miss Ball and her husband who were sitting beside me
said nothing at all. It is possible to imagine a series for a
couple of years perhaps being reasonably tolerable as a
way of life and a way of money—enormous money it'd
have to be—with a congenial director and a happy few
relaxed repertory of actors. But for a lifetime! Ah no. It
is fascinating to watch her reaction to Elizabeth. She calls

her for the most part Mrs. Burton or Miss Taylor and occasionally Elizabeth but corrects it to the more formal immediately. She calls me in the third person His Highness or Mr. Burton and sometimes Mia. This is a joke that E. made on the first day when she, E., said that I had become so thin—I am now about 160 lbs—that sleeping with me was like sleeping with Mia Farrow who is first cousin to a match-stick.

She ignores Brook and her brilliant straight man who's on, poor soul, week after week with her, a man called Gale Gordon, and Cliff Norton who plays a small part and the director. Between shots yesterday she summoned us, Norton, Brook and myself to her dressing-room with a tap on each forehead—we were all sitting down chatting with Hugh French—and proceeded to tell us how to play the scene which we had just walked through. With faces as straight as freeways we then all proceeded to shout every line at each other in ludicrously loud voices. "That's better, Richard, now I can hear that word, you're making me laugh." And laugh she did, every time we did it and we did it about three times. Brook's face was a study in disbelief. The other actor was obviously used to it and took it all as if this were normal for an actor to tell other actors how to do a scene without the director being there. I warned the director to warn [her] that if she tried any of that stuff on Elizabeth she would see, in person, what a Thousand Megaton Hydrogen Bomb does when the warhead is attached and exploded. It will all be over tonight and again Lucy will be lucky that I am temporarily such a little saint. Tomorrow to Fresh Fields.

Burton's comments on the show—which went very well—were all about Elizabeth.

(May 16) E., as ever, took everything in her stride. Everything she did—E. that is—worked like a charm, and the audience quite clearly adored her. Her stage presence (this is the third time I've felt it happen) is quite electrifying. She held the audience like a vise in *Faustus* at Oxford, at the Poetry Reading in New York and now in the Lucy

Show. Now that we can afford it though I will be as tense as a tigress with her young, she should try the living legitimate stage as they call it. Since she has decided to do it anyway there is no point in my getting in the way of a juggernaut . . . As a reaction from the nerve-rack of the Lucy Show combined with E.'s fears of the surgical knife on Monday and my fears of her fears and my natural irascibility & impatience when not drinking led to two bitter exchanges yesterday. E.'s telling me to "fuck off and get out of my sight" and me replying in kind.

The British government gave him an honour—making him a Commander of the British Empire.

My disappointment at being offered a CBE (which nevertheless I accepted, tho' E. wanted me to turn it down thinking only a knighthood good enough) and not the bigger prize. The trouble with a CBE is that it is so easily confused with the pathetic MBE and OBE in the public mind though it is a much more important honour. Like the OM and the CH it means nothing because though it is a title—I suppose one is entitled to be called "Commander"—it doesn't have the nice rolling sound of Sir Richard and Lady. I am nevertheless immensely pleased. Pleased that it wasn't a "Beatles" award [the "inferior" MBE]. Pleased that it was obtained without any attempt on our part to get it. Pleased that it means we are no longer notorious but officially posh. Pleased that it will please the family. Pleased by the fact that a knighthood is not after all out of reach of a divorcé and a non-tax-paying citizen. Noël Coward was the first man in my profession to get a CBE (and now a knighthood) while hoarding money away in Swiss banks and he may have made a break-through. We might, in effect, have our cake and eat it at the same time . . .

These outbursts of longing for respectability strike back to his roots. They saddle a recognisable British contradiction between the democrat—"a man's a man for all that"—and the historical romancer—to belong to the pageantry of the place.

I wish to Christ that E. didn't have to have that operation. I am convinced that it could be cured by other means. By a proper diet and a savage cut down on other drugs and exercise I bet it could be cured without the knife. But it would take a lot of discipline and a fair amount of time —perhaps as long as a year. But I feel sure it could be done.

Again and again in the Notebooks, Burton loved to tell a story. In Malibu in May, after recording with pleasure the fact that "Kate can be with us for a month this year so *that's* OK," he launches into the retelling of a story told him by a friend and doctor. In this case the story has more than one level of interest.

(May 17) An account of a few days with Nick Hilton a few months before he died was particularly hair-raising. It seems that Hilton, towards the end of his relatively short life (he was about 40 when he died), became dominated by and dominated a sort of [guru] who had quit his medical training and turned analyst when still an intern. [The Dr.] knew the analyst noddingly but had never met Nick Hilton. One day the [guru] had to leave town for a week or so & would he, Dr., act as locum while he was gone. Dr. agreed. Within a few hours of the psychiatrist's phone call there was another from the Hilton mansion in Holmby Hills. The voice on the other end of the line asked him to come to the house immediately. Dr. asked who was calling and the voice identified itself as a male nurse who was in attendance on Hilton. This surprised Dr. who had been given no indication by the guru that Nick was sick enough to warrant a male nurse. Off went Dr. to the house and was met by a woman who told him, again without a warning of any kind to go immediately to the bedroom. Dr. did so unaccompanied, knocked on the door, a voice told him to come in and in he went to find Nick Hilton sitting up in bed with a loaded gun pointing at him. There was no question, acc to Dr, that Hilton was a lunatic— one glance was enough—and that the slightest mistake on Dr.'s part would have meant that he would be killed. There were three male nurses, not just one. There was nothing

Dr. could do except shiver in his shoes, stand there and
suffer a torrent of vile abuse from the raving idiot in the
bed. He got out as quickly as he could and sought information from the [woman] who said that Hilton had been
like this for a long time, that there were loaded guns of
all kinds all over the place and that the vanished head-
shrinker was a terrible and evil influence over Hilton and
stayed with him only to get his money. Dr. went away
convinced that Nick should be locked up as soon as possible. Thereafter he was called every hour or so by the
male nurses until Dr. himself began to think he was going
to go mad. Eventually he called for assistance from a very
famous and also very great LA psychiatrist. Reluctantly
and only as a favour to Dr. the great man went along with
him to the house and, like Dr., took one look at the patient
and knew that he was far gone almost to the point of no
return but that there was a chance that he could be helped
. . . he was prepared to go into court the next morning
and testify that the patient not only should but must be
removed immediately to Mennengers—the top place in
the States apparently—by private plane. That he should
be either strong-armed into this and if necessary knocked
out to get him there as soon as possible.

It turned out that the missing guru *had* been in town all the time—
but in hiding from Hilton. Nick Hilton died six months later from
unspecified causes. He, of course, was Elizabeth's very first husband. Burton's fascination is understandable.

And once more Elizabeth went into hospital. She had thus far
had twenty-seven operations.

(May 18) Held Elizabeth's hand while she was given two
or three pre-operative shots, one of which hurt her a bit
but she only winced and made no noise. She's very brave
compared with me as I am scared always of the needle in
any form. She gradually, while I held her hand, sloped
off into a semi-coma but awoke immediately when they
came to take her away. That was ten minutes ago and
presumably they are now hard at it. They said it would
take no longer than a half hour and that she would be a

further hour in the "recovery room." During that time I shall go out for breakfast and buy a few drug-store sundries. Rex [Kenemer] has just been in to tell me that things are underway and that he is going to be very firm about the amount of hard narcotics supplied to her tomorrow and will cheat a great deal as to what she is getting since she is so susceptible to drugs . . . The half hour is up and over but no sign from Dr. Swerdlow or Rex. So keep on typing Rich Bach with crossed fingers. It's a lovely day, he said with trembling chin and he has just noticed that a thriller story by John D. Macdonald which he brought in for his wife to read when she is recuperating is called *One Monday We Killed Them All*. It is Monday today. Happiness is a successful operation.

Dr. Swerdlow has just come in to say that everything is perfect. I'm off to have breakfast. Hip. Hip. Hooray.

(May 20) Have just talked to Elizabeth who has just had her first bowel movement since the operation. She says it is unbelievably painful and unfortunately occurred before anticipated by the doctors so she, as it were, did it all by herself without the assistance of lubricants and soothing laxatives, etc. Result: screaming agony. I don't think I can face Aaron today, i.e. this morning. And much as I love E. and sympathise with the pains which no one else can understand who hasn't suffered it, the thought of going into the hospital for yet another endless visit with continual interruptions from all kinds of people—e.g. no one, no single one person brings in E.'s food but always 2 or 3, and they are never the same people twice. It follows that they are taking turns to have a glimpse of my girl. Crazy people abound and sometimes get into the room. A lady who said she represented the Ministry of Love was only just caught in time. Once when the nurse was out for a second a hippie Negro entered the room with only the most perfunctory knock on the door and said he just wanted to "have a look at E." I coldly told him to get out. On another occasion when I was fast asleep on the couch in the room two hippie gents walked in casually with a bird's nest, beautifully made and aromatic and chose a place on the wall to hang it and then left. It turned out that the nest was from a dress-maker well known to E. called Elizabeth Courtenay, but it could just as well have been a couple of off-shoots from the branch of lunatics who killed Sharon Tate and Jay Sebring. I then remembered that Rex Kenemer had told me that rapes in these huge sprawling hospitals were by no means uncommon. He thought it was funny. I was appalled.

(May 21) E. called me early this morning at about 7.30 —I had been up since 6.30 and had showered, shaved, had a cup of coffee, dressed, ate a piece of cold and delicious filet mignon med-rare out of the ice-box and smoked my first cigarette of the day. She was very tearful and complained bitterly about Rex's treatment of her in the hospital. What, I asked, was the matter? She said that the pain was awful and that she had been getting 2½ ccs of Demarol but that now they refused to give her any more and that they were giving her, orally, Emp & Chodine #3 and a yellow pill called Pergadon—at least, that's what it sounds like. I talked to both doctors and both had pretty feeble arguments against her irrefutable one that if she were going to be in pain and if she didn't need a nurse to give her shots and was to receive only oral pain-killers why shouldn't she be at home where it was much more pleasant, less "up-tight," as she put it, than a hospital the very thought of which after all these years of operations strikes terror into her heart. Their argument is that during the last phase of the withdrawal they would like to be near her in case anything goes odd. Her argument is that they could get to her in half an hour from the hospital and that when she was in the hospital they were never there anyway. So I shall try and get her out later today and, short of a catastrophe, certainly before lunch tomorrow. I did, however, after polite slanging matches with Rex, find out that she had not been receiving 2½ ccs of Demarol but only a minute fraction of that amount for the last 36 hours. So the withdrawal had started without even my knowledge. I don't fancy that much. I don't fancy E. & myself being treated like children. I will tell E. the truth about it all one day but not now as the one thing she finds intolerable is to be lied to like that. She will forgive Rex for telling her that he refused her Demarol today and keeping his word. She will not forgive him very readily when she finds out that for the last 36 hours she has not been getting, as she thought, Demarol at all but an ordinary tranquilliser. God save the mark, the phone is ringing again. I seem to have been on it for days.

He occupies himself by doing the first draft of a rugby article for Cliff Morgan: "The place I physically think of is the awfulness of Tonmawr tho' I have never actually played there." His past was forever in his present and the distance between the two was never lost. It could jack up his pride; it could make him feel isolated; it could and would tempt him to turn to examine the depths of himself.

Meanwhile there was the waiting and Elizabeth's condition. His devotion to her continues to be admirable. She is sneaked out of hospital in a wheelchair.

(May 23) There were no photographers, thank God, as one of the reasons for E.'s relative lack of offers from film companies is because nobody is prepared to risk the gamble of what they think to be her precarious health. If I didn't know her and relied only on papers and rumour for my information neither would I. So the less publicity of that kind the better. The way things are going in the business temporarily I shall be forced to write films for ourselves, produced by ourselves. Money is unobtainable and the market keeps on falling . . . E. seems pretty comfortable for most of the time but has the expected and usual spasms. I wondered, not for the first time yesterday, why any man would specialise in that particular part of the anatomy. So much more romantic to specialise in brain surgery . . .

(May 25) I am extremely glad it is not last Monday. Crossing everything within sight and praying under one's breath, there seems to be a chance that E.'s operation is a total success. There may not even be any "tidying up" to do. The next and hopefully the last anxiety will be next weekend. After that, home and dried.

The preoccupation with Elizabeth's health leads to interest in diet which Burton addresses briskly.

> (May 26) So all food is poisoned [he had been reading books on nature foods] and acc to Kenemer who was here for the birthday dinner of Liz, all sun was bad for everybody and made you old before your time—"Under this tan, is a little Jewish man" he reports one of his patients saying on being complimented on how well he looked after a few days at Palm Springs. So food, out. Booze, out. Sun, out, drugs out and God is dead. Otherwise OK.

As Elizabeth improves, his attention moves across to Ifor.

> (May 29) Elizabeth is *much* better, almost in fact back to normal and I am so delighted that I spend my time counting my blessings. Humming under my breath I fill lighters, wash my socks and underpants, empty ashtrays, read books at tremendous speed—I couldn't concentrate even on a detective story properly while she was ill.
>
> I talked to Gwen yesterday. Ifor is back in hospital in Geneva. One kidney is malfunctioning. I wish him to die now. I can't bear to see him so helpless and childlike—not in his mind, that's alright—but in his querulousness, his hatred of being helped. And he is in continual pain since a kind of moribund life came back into his body. Why did that slip in the dark have to happen. So slight a slip, so gigantic a fall. A nightmare night that will haunt me forever. Thank whatever Gods may be for money. At least we don't lack that. He will die in first class which is the only way he has ever wanted to travel—a Pullman to the grave.
>
> (June 2) Still no booze . . . it is now 11 weeks since I last had a drink and ordinarily feel no desire for it.

The energy was taken up by Elizabeth.

> (June 4) Elizabeth started bleeding yesterday from her behind, great gouts of blood which were frightening to

behold. I cleaned it up periodically—on one occasion the bathroom floor was awash with it—and thanked the Lord that I was a non-drinking man and felt no nausea at all. I am convinced that were I a drinker as I used to be I would have thrown up convulsively. The blood was richly dark red and had the consistency and appearance of half-set jelly. The poor little thing had about 8 of these emissions before we finally got her to hospital. The doctor gave her a sedative which only succeeded in making her very jumpy and nervous. Today is going to be a battle to stop them giving her "hard" narcotics otherwise it's going to mean another period of "withdrawal" which is more than human flesh and blood can stand.

Endless telephone calls were made to Kenemer and Swerdlow who both obviously thought that it was a minor thing and that she was trying to swing for some hard shots again. Finally we got Sisler, who has done a great deal of proctology and who is the doctor of and known to Dick Hanley, to come over. After more phone calls it was decided to remove her to the Desert Hospital. Swerdlow drove from LA in what must have been a hair-raising 90 minutes and waited to examine another dollop of blood. It was not long in coming and he decided to knock her out and have a look at least and see if she was haemorrhaging and she was knocked out and they wheeled her in to the theatre and found out that one of the stitches was ripped out, re-stitched it and she was all out in 30 mins. I aged another ten years. She was pathetically frightened and kept on saying like a child as she was being wheeled down the corridor, "I love you, Richard." "I love you too, Baby."

They are in Palm Springs, the temperature 115–120 in the shade.

(June 5) I wanted to open the windows of Elizabeth's hospital room yesterday, French windows which led on to a terrace on which there were comfy looking chairs. They were unopenable. The nurse obtained a "maintenance man," a large slow man. He opened the window with wrenches and pliers, etc. Later I asked the administrator why all the windows in the hospital were locked. Because two years ago, she said, a patient on the third floor, an old dying man of 87, had thrown himself and his chair to which he was strapped out of the window of his room to his death below. But we are on the ground floor, I said. Yes, I know she said. The eyes cross . . .

(June 7) E. still in hospital with her blood-count very low and weakening and depressing for her, but if the count has remained the same or gone up this morning she will come out today. She is to rest a lot and not strain herself or overtire herself, etc., until the blood has been restored. This should take about 6–8 weeks. It means she won't be able to come to Mexico with me probably when I make the film [*Raid on Rommel*]. It will be very strange without her but perhaps it's not altogether a bad idea as I shall be working terrible hours and will hardly see her at all, going to bed early and up at the crack of in intense heat and so on. She might as well take it easy with somebody congenial in LA or Malibu. Female of course. Also, unlike E., once I start a film I want to get it over as soon as possible and will work any hours and seven days a week if necessary to do so. E., having grown up inside the MGM machine, gives them nothing free and considers adding to their costs fair game. I couldn't care less about that but with all the energy of a profoundly lazy man wish to get it over as soon as possible so that I can laze again or go to fresh fields. There is no film or play that I've ever been in that hasn't bored me after about six weeks so I like to get them over fast.

(June 8) I have now been a teetotaller for 3 months, so have kept my promise. Will probably keep it up too.

For a drinker of Burton's capacity and for a man who enjoyed much of his life much better with a glass in his hand, this was no light achievement. He was to retain the ability to "knock off" at will for the rest of his life. He was, on the other hand, to get much weaker, physically, and the long drag of pain—which he repressed and refused to acknowledge ninety-nine per cent of the time— together with the tremendous shock to his system of the massive surgery he would have to go through later, finally left him very vulnerable to the few drinks he would once have put back before any lunchtime. Drink was also a drug in the sense that opium was a drug for De Quincey—an enlarger, a soother, a realiser of dreams, a prompter of stories, a way to fend off "Timor Mortis." And it was also a drug in the sense of Jekyll and Hyde. Burton could be spectacularly nasty and vicious in drink—especially to Elizabeth and, often as not, to those whose privileges seemed unearned and somehow offensive to the Welsh background which he held on to like a good Cardinal holding on to his first hairshirt. As an actor he was at his finest when his "knack," his gift, met a part he could suit or was challenged by a mind he admired. He also had the characteristic—not uncommon in nonactors—of enjoying playing many roles in his own life. Indeed the extremes of his yearly existence led him into hugely varied contacts—now with the Duke of Windsor, then coaching Maria, then talking rugby, now on a film set, now buying a ludicrously expensive diamond, wining in Monte Carlo, talking to writers, back in Port Talbot with ex-miners, and so on: drink enabled him to do all that without leaving the bar. And it was his Valhalla: a few drinks, a few men, talk of sport or stories of wild heroes . . . in giving it up he was carving a large slice out of his existence. But he did it. "3 months, so have kept my promise."

Elizabeth's recovery is slow and difficult; his concern unabated.

(June 9) Elizabeth is alright this morning but yesterday was one of the worst days I remember. She was in terrible pain and cried a great deal in the afternoon. Eventually I summoned the Dr. who gave her a shot and she became dopy but easier. I felt as helpless as a leaf in a whirlwind, a cork in a tempest . . . I expect another couple of bad days from E. before we turn the corner but nothing short of a catastrophe can be as bad as yesterday. The nervous tension created in me when she's in pain is quite extraordinary. I am incapable of dispassion and keep on thinking how nice it would be if I had the burden of pain instead, except that I'd be far worse than she.

Otherwise he writes on as the small house fills up with children and their house guests—Brook and Liz Williams who stayed four months

– and Elizabeth's every bowel movement is a cliffhanger. He retreats to the patio with his typewriter.

One of the entertaining things about Richard is his open interest in the progress of himself and other acting animals up the Gilbert and Sullivan ladder of British gongs.

> (June 13) The *LA Times* today announce that Larry [Olivier] has been made a life peer, that Sybil Thorndike has been made a CH, Freddie Ashton the same as I am, a CBE, and David Frost an OBE. Nothing still for Emlyn and he could have done with one. Larry told me years ago that he was determined to be the first "actor-peer." It was a reply to my asking him what worlds did he have left to conquer in our profession.
>
> Shall send a cable to Olivier today. It is a remarkable achievement considering that he has never been a "clubbable" man in the Wolfit, Richardson or Guinness sense. He has remarkable stamina and it's about time they separated him from the herd.

Earlier in 1969—March and April—the Burtons had done two extremely cheerful interviews with David Frost. Richard did most of the talking but this was not camera-hogging: it was to Richard that most of the questions were addressed. He spoke of his Welshness and his father with great affection; his references to Philip were loving and grateful; he was funny, looked astoundingly handsome and reamed off paragraphs from the Old Testament which he had learnt by heart when he was ten. Elizabeth was wearing two diamond rings: the ping-pong diamond—which cost just $14 and which he had given her after promising her a diamond should she take ten points off him at table tennis. "I got him sloshed," she said, "and I not only got the ten points, I beat him. So he had to go down and buy me the perfect diamond." .042 carats. The other was "the most expensive diamond in the world, 69.42 carats." "Not chopped chicken liver," she said as the camera moved into close-up. They looked in fine fettle.

Elizabeth's mother Sarah then landed on them and Richard had to keep the peace. Meanwhile he was winding himself up for an odd enterprise. Thousands of feet of "war" footage had been shot for *Tobruk* and never used. The plan was to make a film—*Raid on*

Rommel—around it, shot as fast as an old silent. "The writing is to be dialogue sufficiently credible to get us from one explosion to another. There is to be no overt attempt to give it any 'artistic' merit whatsoever." Burton saw it rather like an agreeable game of rugby. "The schedule has been reduced again to 3 weeks and 2 days. If the film does a mediocre gross only I shall pick up at least a million dollars. I could make as much as a million pounds. For 20 days' work. Morally indefensible." Brook Williams and the gang were all written in. "Made sure that Brook was treated with due respect both artistically and financially."

In Malibu he is trying to set up *Don Quixote*.

> (June 22) Dustin Hoffman I understand is either very fearful or very conceited as he says he cannot make up his mind whether to take Sancho Panza or not as he's afraid that as Quixote I will steal the film from him. What a funny reaction from such a good actor. He obviously wants to play a one-man show where no other actor stands a chance. Reasoning that way, he would turn down Othello and/or Iago. I must be supremely self-confident as no such considerations cross my mind, or ever have.

And house-hunting for the family. They went to see one house.

> (June 24) The owner was so much a red-neck Republican that I was tempted to become a hippie rebel on the spot. "I want to give you three words, hey, stand here, Valerie, so that I don't have to talk over my back, it's a toast that was taught me by a Swedish-American many years ago, I give you three words. Steal, Lie and Drink. Don't steal from your friends, lie only with a woman you love and drink to present company. The Burtons and Valerie I give you a toast." That's what the man said. He was about 60ish, though difficult to tell with a reptilian face set on an abnormally thick neck which was wider than the top of his head but the same thickness as his jowl. He said later to Valerie that his father said: "When you see a beautiful woman tell her she can put her socks in your coffee any time." The mind boggles. Elizabeth is thinking of sending over her socks. I read most of my next epic.

I shall finish it today sometime. It is very laboured but I bet can be very watchable. I shudder to think what the posh critics will say. Well, actually I don't shudder. I shall rather enjoy them . . . I must strip my part in *Rommel* down to the bone. I talk too much in it and destroy what little mystery the part might be invested with.

Brook read the script yesterday and said he wanted to play Reilly, a nothing part, a man who drives the half-track and is in all the action and said, "The part of the CO disappears after one speech in the early pages. Says he won't be involved in killing anyone and walks out of the film." On the contrary I discovered that the CO seduces the Italian girl, etc., and has the only "love-interest" in the piece. Reminds me of Jimmy Granger being sent the script of *Odd Man Out* by Carol Reed and flipping through the pages where he had dialogue, deciding that the part wasn't long enough. He didn't notice the stage directions, so turned it down and James Mason played it instead and made a career out of it. It's probably the best thing that Mason has ever done and certainly the best film he's ever been in while poor Granger has never been in a good classic film of any kind. You could after all have a "James Mason Festival" but you couldn't have a "Stewart Granger" one. Except as a joke. Granger tells the story ruefully against himself.

And "still the non-drinking Burton." Life beyond the money-making movie is more in line with the original intention of the sabbatical.

(June 25) They want me to go up to Oxford for Michaelmas term Oct 11th to December 5th or Hilary in Jan until March. What am I going to lecture about? I must write today to Francis Warner and get some direction and hints. What, for instance, does he lecture about. It's a great platform to get rid of a lot of spleen. I can do lethal work on some public figures and clast a few icons.

And the Notebooks are bursting with sketched notions which a university life would have enjoyed knocking into shape.

(June 25) The world is in a terrible state of chassis as Joxer has it and I want to watch its chaos from a little distance and make a leisurely and I hope long preparation for death. I love the world and its insanity. There is no difference basically in humanity now than there was 5000 years ago. The same cruelty, the same vices and virtues as ever. The same stupidity and intelligence and in the same proportion. Who can possibly take seriously a student who says "down with Nixon and Mao for ever" or vice versa. Both are clowns. Neither commands our gravity only our laughter. The "Thoughts of Mao Tse Tung" are a laugh a thought. Nothing can happen overnight. The betterment of mankind will be a triumph of the inevitability of gradualness as the Baron Passfield [Sidney Webb] said in another context. That is if there's to be a triumph at all. So far the gradualness has been so minutely graded that it is invisible to the naked eye. There must be a holocaust one day soon. All the practical man's hope can be is that he is not at its centre, that he is peripheral and do his duty to survive and if possible see that his family survives with him. Here is one man who firmly believes the world to be a delightful place, nicely balanced by its horrors. Without sorrow there can be no joy. True happiness is as transient and as ephemeral as true misery, thank God. *Plus ça change plus c'est la même chose*. The French, American and Russian revolutions changed nothing. Privilege and money still dominate mankind.

These rather lofty thoughts smack a little of the saloon-bar philosopher. Viewed through the wrong end of a telescope all men are worms, no change matters, all is vanity. Burton's scepticism and his foreboding about death were real enough, however.

His spirits go up as Elizabeth recovers and drop at the prospect of *Rommel* which seems to be "chaotic." He is now out on the hunt for new film material.

(June 27) My favorite hour of the day. 6 in the a.m. but grey again, the sky. I read after a month's procrastination the script called *Hammersmith Is Out* which P. Ustinov had sent. It is very wild and formless but just the kind of thing that I would like to do at the moment. Particularly as it has a splendid part for E. too, and a film for both of us is what we've been looking for for a long time. Ustinov is to direct so that should be alright. He should also play one of the smaller parts. The whole thing begins and ends in a lunatic asylum and my role is a deadly and totally insane killer called Hammersmith. The idea is not new. Who are mad? Those inside the bin or those outside? In this case both. We might be able to shoot it this fall. I have a fear that I may have left it all too late. We shall know within the next few days, I suppose. It should be wildly funny and fun to do, especially with somebody as congenial as Ustinov and as brilliant, and might be a big commercial success to boot and spur.

The Rommel film is imminent.

(June 28) Two more days before I go to Mexico. Tales I hear of the place—San Felipe—are not too encouraging. Mean temp 113. Only two restaurants. Population 800. Shark-infested waters. Hurricane season. Only 33 beds in the whole town for visitors, most people living in caravan trailers and tents. No telephone. Only expert pilots can land there. Otherwise OK.

Two days later, in San Felipe, Mexico, on location, the first thing he does is to write to Elizabeth, beginning "Dearest Scrupleshrumpilstilskin" giving her all the gossip about the film, the food, the weather, "still no booze," the cast and, about a thousand words later, ending, "Very very very odd curious strange bizarre unattractive without you. Millions of kisses and hugs. *The bed is huge!*"

They had scarcely been apart for more than a day since the marriage. Having seemed threadbare, the marriage now seems to be finding nourishment again.

And the business of making the film gets under way.

(July 1) I have been learning the German I have to speak in the film from a German actor. He invented the reason for yawning. He is so boring that it is almost hypnotic. All I ask him to do is speak the lines for me and I will

write it down phonetically in my own way and then learn
the whole thing off like a machine-rattle. BUT he expa-
tiates on every line. "I do not zee Cherman think would
say to a check-point man dese thinks mit deses words."
So doing a page of script consisting of perhaps 3 lines of
German for me, takes a full hour. I faint with ennui. "I
disapprove of all military thinks and should not be doing
ziss film but one must work I suppose and you are much
admired in my country."

He talks to Elizabeth and she announces that she is on her way.

(July 3) She said she missed me as badly as I missed her
and that she mooned about at night and felt almost tearful
over a pair of my socks that she saw hanging about. I've
told everybody that she went to bed with my socks. It's
a new fetish, I say, that might sweep the world and replace
Marijuana.

I feel extraordinarily fit since I talked to her and feel
as young as 25 or something. Stopping drinking is the
best thing I've ever done for my physical well-being.
Twice since I arrived I was immensely tempted to have a
drink—once when I was alone. This is the kind of place
and the kind of situation where one is naturally driven
to booze. Waiting for the film to start, waiting for the
tanks and guns, etc., to get here, the uncertainty of the
Mexican immigration, "we start tomorrow with you, but
on the other hand we may not, we'll let you know in the
morning . . ."

One of Burton's great pleasures over the next month was to study
the very tough, very Army, director Henry Hathaway.

(July 4) I am going out on the set to see the film begin
and wish luck to my fellow prisoners. This film shows
every sign of being the most eccentric I've been in for
a long time. Perhaps since *The Night Of The Iguana*.
Hathaway said yesterday to a perfect stranger who was
sitting in the bar: "Get your Goddam hair cut and get
rid of those Goddam side-boards. How many Goddam

times do I have to tell you?'' The innocent was an astonished tourist.

(July 5) It seems that Hathaway gave the German actor Carl Otto Something a dreadful time yesterday and did 57 takes on one scene, most of which takes were cut by Hathaway on the first line with suitable endearments like ''You are the Goddamnest stupidest actor I've ever met.'' Lucky I wasn't there. Such behaviour against a defenceless small-part player makes me angry to the point of blindness.

He continues to rail about politics and the lies (by omission) that even the best seem forced to tell. The expectation of Elizabeth's arrival and the grind of a film in the desert with much rushing about and action in temperatures over 110°F preoccupy him but there is a surprising amount of political comment.

Hathaway again.

(July 7) This Hathaway is fairly mindless as a director. He doesn't give the actors any respite between shots. Brook and the others sat on the back of a truck for several hours yesterday with a break only for lunch. Brook says that for most of the time they weren't even seen. I simply don't understand that kind of mentality though I mentioned yesterday that a man who so patently couldn't care less whether he was liked or not couldn't be all bad.

And then she flew in.

(July 8) A horrible day. The heat in the desert was insufferable and I spent half the day laying in the sand with my mouth agape pretending to be unconscious while the sand, stirred up by the wind which was blowing in exactly the wrong direction, blew up my nose and into my mouth. However I was excited at seeing E. so I was stoically good-natured. The plane carrying E. and the kids and Norma [Heyman] buzzed a couple of times and I panted with impatience to finish and get home. Like all things too eagerly awaited the meeting was a fiasco. I arrived and tore into the ''suite'' and there was nobody there!

Kate came in and said "Hi" and went out again. Somebody had turned the air-conditioning off and the living
room was like an oven. E. came prancing in and we hugged
and kissed though I was filthy and covered with grease
and sand and wasn't very huggable. Immediately everybody started making cracks about San Felipe and what a
terrible place it was, and one would have thought they
had attacked Pontrhydyfen—I was so defensive. Never
has a man been so chauvinistic about a shit-house. I feebly
pointed out the beauty of its beach, and lamely said the
sea was wonderful. Kate said it was too warm and it was
like taking a hot bath. I lamely and bravely said that there
were horses for hire. I said it was much more cosmopolitan
than Bucerias which is like saying that Hell is better than
purgatory. We went in a sullen silence to dinner at Reu-
ben's and it was as stickily uncomfortable as I'd ever
known it or perhaps it was just the same as usual but I
imagined it to be the worst night of the year and that the
weather gods were conspiring against me. E. made me as
jealous as vengeance earlier on by saying that she'd called
Marlon on the phone and that they had talked for an hour
and that he was very solicitous about me. He really is a
smugly pompous little bastard and is cavalier about everybody except Black Panthers and Indians. "He's been keeping tabs on you," said E. That infuriated me even more.
That sober self-indulgent obese fart being solicitous about
me. Sinatra is the same. Gods in their own mirrors. Dis-
torted mirrors.

Things are a bit better this morning and E. is coming
to work with me though the heat will drive her insane. I
keep on forgetting that people can't take the sun as well
as I do. A few people have fainted on the set and I had
mistakenly forgotten that E. is still lacking blood from
that haemorrhage.

But the magic starts to work in the morning.

(July 9) Yesterday was a lovely day. I left for work for
the day at 7.00 and E. came with me, despite the heat—
and it was very hot. I thought she would only stay for an

hour or even less and then return to the air-conditioning as she has hardly ever been out since the emergency in Palm Springs and even then only half an hour or so. But she stayed until after lunch—something like 2.30. Everyone was delighted that she was there and everybody said afterwards that it was the best day they've had on the film yet. Hathaway was mellow by his usual standards and at one point when he started screaming at one of the actors I told him he was mistaken and that he had told the actor to move earlier. He said, "Goddamn it, I did not." "Goddamn it, you did," I said. "I apologise," he said to the actor. Everybody was astounded and one chap said to Ron that it was the first time in thirty years of working with Hathaway that he'd ever known him apologise to anybody. So I was a little hero, the leader of my little band, the little Robert Emmet . . .

(July 11) It seems that we've been here for 10 weeks and not ten days. The heat to which we are all thoroughly acclimatised is tremendous. And humid with it. Were it not for air-conditioning it would be a case of continual sweat morning, noon and night. As a matter of fact, it is hotter and more uncomfortable—or seems to be—in the mornings when there is not a breath of a breeze to cool the burning brow. The work consisted of throwing a German across a truck while four or five of my men render him unconscious. Next stint was jumping off the back of the lorry. Today there will be knifing in the back and lots of firing, etc. Might even get to say a few jokes . . .

And letters to Chris, talks with Kate, watching Liza grow, chats with Brook and Ron and the pals, resisting getting another dog when they already have five dogs and four cats. Politics are still closely monitored—especially the rise of Reagan and the fall of Wilson. But Elizabeth is never far from the centre.

(July 13) Elizabeth took the sun very well yesterday and felt faint only a couple of times when she bent over to pick things up, but otherwise she seems to be in roaring good health. She has remarkable recuperative powers and has confounded the doctors who said she'd be a semi-invalid for three or four months. By the fall she should be fitter than she's been for many years. When she loses a little flab she'll also look fitter than she has for years. Her sexual appetite is as eager as ever and so is mine though I don't think either of us attaches the urgent importance to it that we used to. I had a fear that the complete cessation of drink would decrease my sex desire, and so it did for a time probably because I concentrated so much on stopping the alcohol that everything else became diffuse—I had difficulty in concentrating on reading for instance—and I found that my mind raced and flitted from thing to object to idea at a bewildering speed. Now that the poison is nearly out of my system—I'm told it takes six months to dry out totally—I can think clearly again. I don't see the world whole, but I see it steadily. I have lost the hungover nightmarish fear of imminent disaster and early death and all its concomitants and am better balanced. I am not a nervous wreck for days before I fly as I used to be, and am indeed so calm about it that I have to remind myself of the helpless hazards of flying so that I don't stretch my luck too far. I think that in about two or three months I'll be able to settle down to a sustained piece of writing and in this new sober world I don't have the desperate urgency that I used to have that I would never do anything with any permanence, even semi-permanence. Now slowly, I believe I can.

After such a calmly optimistic assessment of his life and prospects, after as clear a recognition of the perils of alcohol—at the rate he sucked it in—it is almost impossible to believe that he would ever touch a drop again. Life is going well again. The film is fun, unpretentious, and on schedule. Elizabeth and kids and pals are all about him. And his wicked pen is in good order.

(July 15) I read yesterday in the *LA Times* that Frankie Sinatra has "come out for Reagan." That's like Laurel coming out for Hardy. I shouldn't think either of them has had a thought of their own in their lives except about themselves. Frank was asked by Haber of the *Times*, "Knowing your justly deserved magnanimity and interest in charitable organisations and support of ethnic minorities and the under-privileged, etc., how do you feel about Governor Reagan's slashing of the funds for the aged and the blind by $10 million?" "Has he done that?" said Frankie. "I must talk to him about that." Big, as they say, fucking deal. If we hear shortly that Reagan has only cut the aid-fund to 9,900,000 dollars we shall know that Francis Albert Sinatra's fine hand has been behind it again. All either of 'em can do is count—using their fingers of course. Hathaway suggests that it's pique on Frankie's part. "He was given the brush-off by Jack Kennedy." "Don't call us, Frankie, we'll call you," he is reputed to have said to Frankie who had been plaguing him with phone-calls after he was President. Even Frankie, however, despite his monomania, should be able to see that Reagan is patched cardboard and dangerously stupid. Now let's hope that Jesse Unrah beats him in November and leave Frank with egg on his face again. Silly sod.

He never felt the same about Sinatra after he suspected Elizabeth flirted with him.

Elizabeth has been away. "Tomorrow comes Snapshot back home and life will be richer again and a bit more mad. Without her I could easily become a recluse." Hathaway unbends.

(July 18) Hathaway told me yesterday that many many years ago he had an idea for a film—"Christ as the unknown soldier." He needed a writer to write it. He saw William Faulkner who thought it was a "hell of an idea." Faulkner went away & months later he called Hank and said I will write it as a book first, because I don't know how to write scripts and then we'll do it as a film. "Great," said Hank. 15 yrs later the book came out dedicated to Hathaway called *Fable*. Hank asked me if I'd read it and I said yes. He had read it, he said, but couldn't get through it because "it didn't have one, one single one of my Goddamn ideas in it."

The household continues to rattle and moan like a Russian dacha in an autumn of discontent. Liza came up to run in the adolescent steeplechase. A beautiful girl, she attracted the boys and Elizabeth was as protective as a mother superior to a novice. Such normal ceremonies, that of the maturing of children with all the normal problems, crop up somehow unexpectedly in the exotic life of the Burtons. Their life together was so strange, so chaotic, so public that these times of private ordinariness can seem like an intrusion. But the Burtons would have it all and as Liza approached the sexual hurdles, parental prickliness surfaced here as it does in every other family.

Burton is reading William Manchester's biography of Krupp and being very wary of the reports of "great rushes." *Staircase*, he says, cured his belief in such reports. The film—perhaps because it is so physical, so mindless and so short—continues to be hard work and good fun.

> (July 22) Everybody is convinced that [one of our cast] is an amiable nut. Yesterday it seems he had to get hurriedly into a car and drive or be driven off at great speed in pursuit of me and my men. He hurried to the car alright but then did a kind of Charlie Chaplin high kick and gave a wild cry as he leapt into the car. Hathaway went "spare" and bounced up and down in uncontrollable anguish. Everybody was so astounded that it wasn't until later that everybody laughed and were still laughing at ten o'clock at night.
>
> Carl Otto dresses up every Saturday night in tight black "charro" trousers, an ornamental black shirt of many silver decorations and a black sombrero low on the forehead. It is an unbelievable sight as he is a very white man with a huge belly and a face like two melons one on top of the other, joining around the eyes. He becomes very wild when dancing in the bar and after "dancing" with elephantine grossness and awkwardness one night he leaned ponderously over a table and said to the boys— Brook, Ron and others—"I wish people would learn to use their bodies with beauty," indicating the other dancers with scorn.
>
> When he came into the restaurant last Saturday night

> where E. and I were dining alone sitting by the window
> she said in genuine wonder: "What is that?" "That," I
> said, "is our tame German." I added urgently, "Do not
> look in his direction or we will have him for the night."
> "Hullo," she said immediately, "what a splendid costume
> you have on." "Sank Zew," he said, "I am always wear-
> ing dis on every Saturday night in honour of mein host
> country." "How thoughtful," said milady. From there
> on neither she nor I understood a word he said.

Reading about Krupp prompts him to speculate on why there was
not a successful assassination attempt against Hitler. He worries
about the blotches that keep coming out on his back, the severe
"acne"—his word—which began, he thinks, at Oxford. The state
of his skin concerns him now and then—but the concern does not
appear to be out of vanity. He is puzzled.

> Why is it that none of my brothers and sisters have ever
> had this amazing disease? I am frantically clean and always
> have been. I've discovered that it is exactly 140 days or
> five four-week months since I stopped drinking so it cannot
> be the booze. Anyway, it's little enough to live with.

His back gives him trouble but

> (July 26) apart from that I am pretty limber largely from
> climbing in and out of tanks and lorries and running across
> the sand and diving into various holes when explosions
> are supposed to be going off. Hathaway said to me yes-
> terday what a revelation I was to work with. He had heard,
> he said, that I was a consummate professional but that I
> was super-pro and super-on-time, etc. I said how much I
> admired his thoroughness too and that we should try some-
> thing really ambitious together one of these days. There
> was nothing he'd like more, he said. So there. How to
> make friends.

What is quite clear is that he finds it difficult to keep sober when
he spends so much time rowing with a boozy Elizabeth. Ill again.
The piles seem to have cleared up but a trip to the dentist results

in nightmare pain, drugs and abuse. "Jesus, it's hard work when other people have had a few drinks and you haven't, even when that people is someone you deeply love."

Trouble, too, back at the ranch in Wales where Richard's only younger brother, Graham, who had already upset him very much by going to the press in the past (about which Richard has fiercely cutting things to say), does it again.

> (July 28) Brother Graham has been entertaining the press again re my early life. The press concerned is that rag of all rags—*The People* newspaper. They are about to do a several part article on my life and loves. This will be shame-making for a day and then will disappear into a just oblivion very rapidly, but it's a bore nevertheless. Why does little Graham do these things—even after the outrageous mess-up with the *News of the World* some years ago. He has entertained the writer of the article in his house and taken them round to the other members of the family, etc., and generally aided and abetted them in every way. He will never learn. I don't know whether I should write him a scathing letter or forget the whole thing. There is a letter from *The People* man to Aaron which indicates that he is well down to barrel-scraping standards. Ah well.

And so on to Beverly Hills where Richard enjoys the luxury of baseball on the colour television—he became an addict of the game and a very eager learner—and Elizabeth fights her way through gaping crowds to continue her treatment at the dentist's and Richard deplores American crossword puzzles. "They are all—even the *New York Times*—uncomplicated synonyms except on Sundays when they are general knowledge tests for the solving of which you must be armed with reference books. There are no plays on words, no puns, no anagrams . . ." The search begins for a co-star for *Hammersmith Is Out* and Robert Redford is considered.

> (July 31) Saw *Butch Cassidy and the Sundance Kid* last night. A charming film, very derivative of *Bonnie and Clyde*. The man Redford that I'd heard so much about is disappointingly ordinary and Newman is much more impressive. It is just as well that he has turned down *Ham-*

mersmith as he has a quality of dull-ness and I can see quite easily why he has taken so long to become a star. I think he would have ruined our film simply because he seems so sluggish and certainly doesn't suggest for a second the kind of demonic idiotness that Billy Breedlove must have. [Beau Bridges got the part.]

On August 2nd, he notes, while on the train to New York:

(Aug. 2) Nice to be alone with E. too. We worked out that it is the first time we've been with [out] attendant guests or servants or both since this time last year. And we have more time on the *QE2*.

And then adds at the end:

Forgot momentous news. I had a Jack Daniels and soda and two glasses of Napa Valley red wine last night with dinner. Felt immensely daring and all it did was make me feel very sleepy and not elated or anything like that. E. had the giggles most of the time. Can't think why as I was in great control. Can't help if the train sways.

Elizabeth accused him of being boring when he was not drinking. So, although it would be a while before he was in the ring with the drinking champions again, he was off the wagon. A fall.

It was not only the taking of a drink, it was the decision to abandon a life which clearly suited him. A life in which he was physically fit and had recovered his looks and his stamina. A life which was largely free of the hurricanes of melancholy and the terrible depressions. A life which could cope with Elizabeth's apparently endless illnesses and reactions to illnesses and imminent illnesses and the whole tribe and talk and ceaseless preoccupation with illness. He wrote in the undrinking life and was balanced: he lost none of his wickedness or his anger but seemed to gain interest in larger areas of the world and his mind. Later he would give up for nine months: he could always give up when *he* wanted to. But the plain and simple fact seems to be that he concluded life was better or more tolerable, or both, with booze. So, gradually, booze again it was. Considering the strain—and the provocations—of Elizabeth, his protracted abstinence might be thought to deserve the alcoholic's purple heart. A couple of days later—a bottle of Burgundy with some liver and bacon.

Down to the Mediterranean and on to the boat at Portofino. He reads Machiavelli and applies it to American presidents. Drinks again, not too much until September 1st: "Missed yesterday as I was more or less stupefied with drink all day long." On September 8th from Le Verniaz, Evian:

> We arrived here on Sunday having felt that we needed to be alone together—if the paradox is pardoned—for a couple or three days before the hurly-burly of London and work again. A horrendous night on the yacht much compounded by a mighty sullen drunken-ness on my part prompted us after hours of accusation and counter-accusation to a reconciliation and finally to a resolution that we were both happier when we are utterly alone. This done and agreed we ordered the jet and got out of Ajaccio and off the boat and into Geneva and on to a helicopter and are here at our favourite little hotel with our favourite little chef who flatters Elizabeth so. When we arrived and walked through the "tea garden" we were applauded!

Alone! They created their own fish bowl wherever they went.

And so the record of the sabbatical year comes to an end. More resolutions which seem impossible to maintain: applause from the crowds—the world still their stage, a film together in the offing, Elizabeth seemingly well at last. And Richard back on target. But the sabbatical as an essay in redirecting their life had failed. *Raid On Rommel* was a hit. Burton was still a good soldier.

20
Five in a Row

Between autumn 1970 and the end of 1971, Burton made five films—*Villain*, *Under Milk Wood*, *Hammersmith Is Out*, *The Battle Of Sutjeska* (in which he played Marshal Tito) and *The Assassination Of Trotsky*. In the second half of that period he wrote heavily, especially while on the Tito project. Not only the Notebooks—there was a four-thousand-word story first published in the *Daily Mail* and a ripple of articles for American magazines. We see him in the Notebooks not only "practising"—whether describing a day with Tito or an evening with the Duke and Duchess of Windsor—but musing over what he could write: autobiography? A novel? A mixture of the two? The family still preoccupied him: the cheques continue to go off to Wales on the dot on the date; the children continue to pile in all around the clock; friends stay for weeks and even months on end. He and Elizabeth keep saying how much they enjoy being alone but they very rarely manage it. That lack of privacy, of domestic intimacy, must have been starving.

There was also the question of money. They had enough. Oh, they would invent minor panics and worry about "eating into the capital" but the drive to grab the lot to feed all the mouths and secure all the futures and build themselves a fortress against an enemy world was gone. They had done all those things. Unless there was a world war—they were financially safe. In fact a war might just as easily have increased as decreased their fortune. At one stage in the Sixties they were coining more money per year than any individuals on the planet apart from the Aga Khan and one or two emperors of oil. The money drive, like the sex drive, had been a serious matter for Burton: he was able to fake neither. Now the real money drive was gone. He had to fake it and he was not much good at that.

Elizabeth's severe illnesses had taken a toll not only on her health and possibly on their marriage but on her career. She was to make *X, Y and Zee* or *Zee & Co* in the autumn of 1970, one of her worst films. Edna O'Brien, who wrote the film, describes her as "surprisingly nervous," at that time, "very watchful over Richard as if every woman was a threat." This was a constant in both their lives. In the gamey world of movie marriages, the Burtons were the tops and everybody wanted a shot. To get Liz away from Dick! To get Dick away from Liz! Bull's eye! Edna O'Brien, a beauty as well as a fine writer, was rightly sensitive to Elizabeth's fears.

Burton was a shrewd man. As we can read in the Notebooks, he was soundly aware of his career. He registered the change in fortunes in the film industry even though he ignored movie magazines and, perhaps fatally for his craft, only rarely saw films. But he knew that there was a sea change and he was perfectly capable of facing up to it and getting on in the new dispensation. Elizabeth's instincts were better than his in many areas—movies most of all. Yet she seems to have gone adrift badly about this time. Her judgment was out, her acting was not on song. Both of them seemed lacking the energy and crackle of nervous conviction they had once brought to the screen. It was as if their inner lives, her ceaseless illnesses and his wearying bouts of melancholy, fits of alcohol, fears of disabling ailments, drained some essential strength from them. They had little left for the screen.

Burton made some bold and, on paper, well-calculated choices. Each one of those five films could be defended and even welcomed in prospect. None of them quite worked. Two were terrible to behold. Cumulatively they drummed up the notion that his career was on the skids. But the Burton–Taylor story was still hot, after all, and "on the skids" was a nice new chapter for the tabloid editors.

In *Villain*, Burton again took a chance with a new director— Mike Tuchner—a chance he had taken successfully with Mike Nichols and Zeffirelli. He played a Cockney gang-leader and batted quite well on a dullish wicket. The interest for him was not the money—which by his standards from the Sixties was small—but the part. He liked thrillers and had always wanted to take part in one. As in *Rommel* he was criticised, especially by American reviewers, for betraying his "great talent" by taking part in what they thought was a commercial romp. In fact, his nasty villain was a credible figure and grows more valid with age and East End memoirs. They were much more concerned about the image of his career than he was. He was always careless about it; and always arrogant. He went his own way. The critics missed a point—Richard was a genuine democrat, as loved by Arthur Ibbetson, the cameraman, as by the teaboys and the leading ladies. He was a decent fellow, surprisingly un-grand: even at the end on the set of *1984*, his geniality and approachability were still much in evidence. This profound lack of snobbery (although he was capable of all manner of superficial snobberies—intellectual and social) meant that he did not categorise certain genres as Inartistic or Unworthy. He took great pleasure in reading John D. MacDonald's thrillers and grabbed a chance to be in a movie which had some of those elements. Just as, fascinated by twentieth-century history and enjoying the Boy's Own games played, at that time, in war films, he took up the offer of doing *Rommel*. And again it has to be stressed that in prospect, *Villain* was a bold step. It worked well enough in the UK and Europe; flopped in America where the Cockney accents had to be re-dubbed.

He was drinking in *Villain* and now and then it shows. Whether he was on two bottles of vodka a day or three is difficult to nail down but he was hitting the bottle hard. Bernard Weintraub for the *New York Times* was on the set doing a profile. He was an interesting man and as such gained Burton's confidence and respect. Burton was in a fierce downer. Perhaps it was the drink, perhaps the strain of being nurse to Elizabeth—remember how much he feared and hated illness in himself and others—perhaps the stress, still there and never lost, of knowing he had abandoned Jessica and to some extent Kate or that terrible black dog which bit him from time to time and would not let go. "Fame is pernicious," he told Weintraub, "and so is money." Weintraub wrote: "Despite the bravura voice and style, he appears, at this point, oddly vulnerable, even frail. Somehow the shadows of the past have deepened. The drinker, the lover, the celebrity have flattened into a surprisingly weary figure."

On his forty-fifth birthday, he went to Buckingham Palace with Elizabeth and Cis—typical Burton touch—to receive his CBE. That part of his life which still wanted to impress the English at their own game had hoped for a knighthood—but a CBE was very respectable: halfway there.

Elizabeth was still filming *Zee & Co*—which was running way over schedule—and Richard announced he would spend some time in Wales. Andrew Sinclair, novelist and contemporary historian, had bought the rights to Dylan Thomas's *Under Milk Wood*—the radio play in which Burton had acted at its first performance. It was an audacious, even an eccentric choice of subject but Sinclair is one of a special breed of polymaths and he had the idea that he could pull it off. The film was to open the Venice Film Festival in 1971 and but for the entirely political decision to award no prizes, it would certainly have been given a major award. Of course there were those who said the attempt was doomed from the start *whatever* anyone did to it: that radio into film just did not go.

Sinclair had persuaded Peter O'Toole to play Captain Cat. Burton came in to be the First Voice and Elizabeth came in as Rosie Probert, but only after persuasion by O'Toole for which he claimed "a sort of VC"—as he had fallen out with E.T. since his time on *Becket* when he was anti-the-marriage. Small fees were accepted; huge percentages given. At one meeting, Sinclair announced that he would give away "all 200 per cent" and left the room. The total budget was £300,000.

Sinclair's first encounter with Burton was in Squire's Mount, Hampstead—which Burton still owned—and Burton "started the game immediately," said Sinclair. "I hear you have a very big house, Andrew." Sinclair was then leasing a Nash Terrace house on the edge of Regent's Park: very grand, very fashionable. Sinclair explained that the lease meant that he was getting a cheap deal and would have to be out soon. But Burton played on. Sinclair had complimented him on the paintings—a Van Gogh, a Matisse, a Monet—"These aren't our best pictures," Richard said, grandly, "our best pictures are on the yacht." "Oh, then these are your travelling pictures." Burton liked that, brightened up: the phrase struck home.

He was delighted to discover that Andrew had been at Cambridge (First Class Honours), knew his literature, was "an intellectual." There is always something touching about Burton's lifelong reverence for learned men. It is, for instance, so clumsy. It betrays the poverty of his general acquaintanceship at this stage in his life— that he should so greedily seize on scholarly credentials. A reminder and a measure of how isolated his success and wealth had made him.

He then unburdened himself about his hero Dylan Thomas—recounting again how Dylan had asked him for £200—or he would have to go to America (the trip that killed him) and Burton's guilt "even though I didn't *have* the money—I was working at the Old Vic then—but I keep thinking—I could have *found* it." There are too many true stories in Burton's life about the essential power of money for anybody to be critical about his interest in it: yet the British theatre establishment of the Fifties and even the Sixties thought there was something distinctly "tradesman's entrance" about it.

Then he threw one at Sinclair. "Would you agree, Andrew, that I am the greatest actor in the world?" The eyes were merry but the voice was powerful. "It was the impossible question," Sinclair said. "The Zen test. If I'd said yes—*he* had the film: 'no' and he'd be offended." "What did you say?" "I said something that sounded like 'Bleah!' and Burton laughed his head off."

On the film Burton was "totally professional." "You're lucky I'm sober, Andrew." "Define sober." "Never more than one bottle of vodka a day." One or two of the actors thought that he looked a little drunk now and then. Aaron Frosch, his lawyer, had advised him heavily against doing the film but by that time Burton had announced that he was going back to Wales, land of poetry and song, "And he was hoist with his own PR," says Sinclair, who was one of those who could see the man plain, weaknesses and all, but still be stunned by the force and distinction. As for Elizabeth —"he totally supported her. He was there with her for every shot, helping her with the accent, everything. He was marvellous with her."

Burton also became very fond of Ryan Davies—who played Second Voice to his First Voice. Towards the end of the film, Sinclair, Ryan and Burton were drinking and talking happily: there were two silver goblets on the mantelpiece, given to Richard by "the people of Wales." He handed one each to Ryan and Andrew. Enter Elizabeth in "a long Donald-Duck-yellow dripping mink coat, the tails trailing on the ground and underneath—the first pair of hot pants I'd seen. They may even have had tassels on them. She opened the coat and swirled around. 'Well, Richard, what do you think?' 'Very nice, Elizabeth,' said Burton, patiently, clearly wanting to be back in the talk." She twirled again and then noticed that the two men had the silver goblets. "The storm broke! We handed over the goblets to Elizabeth and fled." The evidence that she bored him and could retain his attention chiefly by her illnesses and temper begins to build up.

Yet for all that, Burton once said to Sinclair, "You and I may be intellectuals, Andrew—" he *was* full of vodka—"yet Elizabeth is more intelligent than both of us." Still the fascination although whether it was with Elizabeth as he found her or Elizabeth as he invented her . . .

Seen today, *Under Milk Wood* is, in parts, remarkably effective.

Back to Mexico to do *Hammersmith Is Out*, written and directed by Peter Ustinov. Burton plays a demonic mental patient who escapes to wreak havoc: Taylor a ripely sexy waitress who accompanies him. The film had a good idea in the middle of it, but for whatever reason, Ustinov told it in such a mixture of styles that the result did not jell. As in *Villain*, it was a part which made Burton unsympathetic to his audience. It was badly botched and flopped.

The interest of the film is to try to work out why Burton and Taylor were *so* bad in it. She is all over the place, slipping in and out of character like a loose kneecap: painful. He stares and stares in a possessed-*looking* way—but that inner intensity, that concentration, was not there—not evident on the screen at any rate. They don't spark off each other; there is no magic at all. It confirms Elizabeth's falling away—worse even than *Zee & Co*. Was it the illnesses which had taken so much out of her? Or the drugs which were first a by-product and then perhaps a cause of, even an excuse for, the illnesses? Or had things now turned bad between them— which they would not admit. They look like two heavyweight champions who had fought each other to exhaustion but cannot quit. She is out of it. Burton is further away from a character than ever in his life. He looks lost, ravaged and isolated. It cannot only have been the drink.

All three films had qualities to recommend them in prospect. The next offer—to play the young Marshal Tito who was said to resemble the Burton of *Where Eagles Dare*—was accepted against *all* advice: the script was 250 pages of Serbo-Croat. But yet again one can see Burton's reasoning. Tito *was* a great man: it would be an adventure. He took it on.

The disaster unfolds in the Notebooks.

The final film in that set of five yet again had much to recommend it. The director was Joseph Losey. The screenplay was by a fine novelist and screenwriter, Nicholas Mosley. The co-star was Alain Delon. And the subject—Trotsky's assassination—was powerful. But Losey was not only off-form but, apparently, so tired/drunk he was hardly a presence at all. The script became, increasingly, long monologues which relied totally and cruelly on Burton's ability to "carry" whole scenes in restricted spaces with words culled from written speeches and letters. The pace was turgid. Another commercial flop.

The commercial flops were bad enough. The movie business was in a state of utter disarray better described as hysteria. Nobody knew what would sell. The studio system was sunk. Television ruled. The audiences were still falling. Stars shone and then, blink twice, they guttered out. Five financial flops in a row was not a record to encourage the nervous backer. Was he any longer "bankable"? It seemed not.

Burton's rebelliousness—his deeply Celtic "sod you" attitude—now worked against him. He was a man to make friends but his manner was not one to influence his so-called masters. Most of them he thought of as sharks or charlatans. He had a wicked tongue and gossip always got back. A lot of bruised husbands and envious lovers, a lot of dumb producers and bone-headed executives took some satisfaction in what appeared the fall and fall of Richard Burton and queued up to be the next to say "No." It was of no relevance or importance to them that there was *something* to be said for *all* five of the shots: working with Ustinov, paying a tribute, even a debt—and Burton paid all his debts—to Dylan Thomas, enjoying the challenge of doing a thriller, involving himself with two of the more important men of the century, Trotsky and Tito. That mattered not. Five financial flops. The new accounting age ruled in Hollywood now and the boys added up.

More importantly—and this was going to become even more evident after this year—there was undoubtedly a quality of deadness in the man's performance. It was as if he were waiting for, hoping for, the "knack," the inspiration—but waiting in vain. Of course, other factors were involved, scripts, directors, production and, except in a couple of instances, he had a bad run there. But behind all that and despite occasional flashes, there is undoubtedly a growing deadness. It is as if his spirits had moved elsewhere. As if he knew in a profound way that a phase in his life was coming to an end and all his energy went into puzzling over that, trying to work out where to go next, brooding over the signs. *Burton* is less and less present in those movies.

Yet the Notebooks show a man still entertained by the external world, still plunging into it. The absurd and frantic pace of work went on, seeming, in this context, more a fight against whatever force was pulling him down than an embracing of opportunities.

In the middle of all this Michael (18) married and Elizabeth became a grandmother and soon became involved in a struggle over her grandchild, resolved only when the distressed Beth, her daughter-in-law, took herself and the baby back to America.

The Notebooks are silent on *Villain*, on *Milk Wood* and on *Hammersmith*. They open in June 1971, in Gstaad, where Burton is preparing to play Tito.

> (June 27) Feel inordinately lazy and somewhat disappointed as the Tito treatment is not very good. A series of loud bangs like any other old war film. I will attempt to get them to make it more Tito than guns and local partisan heroics, which, though probably true, have been seen in every Hollywood film ever made. If they do not I shall have to withdraw. I will still struggle away with learning Serbo-Croat. I find it fascinating.

Domestic life, which now means sickness, is the draining and dominating factor.

> (June 28) Am getting another extra day off from Heathfield for Liza. Don't like to do it but she is so persistent that I give in just for a quiet life. Like W. C. Fields I really have no patience with young people. I find them all inordinately boring.

And the arthritis has returned.

> (July 1) My left hand and wrist are now completely useless so this piece will have no capitals. I was so uncomfortable

last night that in bed the slightest movement made me to groan as if demented.

The pain grows, pills are taken to deaden it.

(July 11) The doctor came to see Elizabeth and gave her some new pills to take which have worked very well. Meanwhile I asked him to have another look at my arm which is still very painful when I forget and do something sudden with it. He prescribed some tablets, actually capsules, called I think Endocin which have cleared the thing up no end. I still wince now and again but the wrist and hand are incomparably more comfortable. It seems inconceivable now that I cannot, I mean couldn't, get my thumb to meet any other finger on that same hand. Now I can pick up light things. Since I am obviously going to be plagued with the differing forms of gout, all its cousins like bursitis, arthritis, etc., I must make a point of finding out what is the diet I should stick to to make the attacks less frequent and more amiable.

About this time he was writing an article for *Vogue*. After an over-elaborate opening, it got down to business: Elizabeth and himself at a local circus in Puerto Vallarta. The high point is the dagger throwing at a live target:

Now came the big moment. This was it. This was the culmination of the evening. The lights went out and then while they allowed us a breathless pause a light, one enormous light, came on. It illuminated a pretty girl crucified against a backward leaning board. She looked uncertain and fated and doomed to her few remaining breaths because facing her was a young man of ferocious aspect who announced he was going to surround her with hurled daggers. I examined the daggers afterwards and found they were roughly about ten inches long and as sharp as La Rochefoucauld and as desperate. I shudder even now at what I allowed my wife to go through. I shudder even more when I think of what they made me go through.

Let me tell you about it which I've been trying to do

for the last thousand words or so but I keep distracting myself on the way. So there they were, the blinding light, the nervous girl, the nervous man and those terrible daggers. With studied and sadistic fury he slammed them around her gentle body and sometime or other in the past he must have erred a little because she flinched at every thud. And I mean those daggers really went into that board. It took a strong man to get them out. And then the man on the mike said: *Tenemos sta noche las muy famosas actores del mondo* or something like that and I waited for them to announce Elliot Gould and Jane Fonda but it turned out—tricked again as we were by modesty—to be us. I longed for it to be George C. Scott because he would have turned it down or caught the daggers in his mouth and swallowed them. But it was us. What can you do? My wife undulated exquisitely into the arena without any apparent qualm and addressed herself to the task of having scimitars thrown at her by a mad Mexican man she'd never met. I stood on the edge of the abyss and waited for a landslide. After all, it was a small itinerant circus and who was to know that that dark Mexican would not be overwhelmed by dreaded twitches by the prospect of throwing lethal instruments at a world-famous attitude. The possibility of reducing 38, 23, 35 to zero, zero, zero must have daunted his mind. He made no mistake. He missed the 38s by a breathtaking whisper, he diced with eternity by a millimetre as he investigated the 23 and surrounded her 35 with a closeness that could only have done justice to a man of iron nerve or a sex maniac who promised himself surcease in the middle of nights at the remembrance of things past.

I had not left my seat because, misunderstanding the Spanish tongue, I assumed he was simply going to ask her to take a bow, until, to my increasing puzzlement, he led her ballet-fashion up to the board and placed her in position and I knew at once and shockingly that he was about to throw assegais at my wife. By the time I arrived in the ring the first javelin—they were getting bigger all the time—had thudded and thunked into the board a safe two inches from her left ear and then another howitzer an appalling inch from her right ear. Eyes wide open, the other girl had kept her eyes closed, and smiling, Elizabeth whispered, "Don't move, Richard, you might make him nervous or something." I obeyed. Lot's wife could have taken lessons. It took Alejandro Fuentes (the dagger-man) no more than a minute perhaps to throw those daggers during which time the hair on my chest turned grey.

Then there was the ovation from the crowd, as at a bullfight and I shook hands with Fuentes, kissed Elizabeth, tousled heads and started to lead the heroine back to the box and the champagne, when to my horror there was a roar from the audience and I was dragged silently screaming up to the deadly board. Unlike Elizabeth who had faced Fuentes with superb dignity in the attitude of a brave man facing a firing squad, they turned me sideways, stuck a balloon in my mouth and one in each hand. My left side faced the thrower, my right hand was placed high over my head in such a way that when or if he burst the balloon clamped between my teeth the dagger would go into the wood and not my upper arm. The other in my left hand was put back behind my knees. I looked like a soldier of powerful homosexual tendencies who was being shot for effeminacy in face of the enemy and was defiantly saluting his own demise. I looked, in short, like an idiot. As the daggers went true to their targets—three for the balloons and one each side of my head for good measure—I gave several more lessons to Mrs. Lot.

We drove home and sat on the balcony with the Obers and looked over the town and listened to the mad cacophony of Saturday night and Phil Ober kindly held the vodka to my mouth as by this time I had turned from Mrs. Lot into St. Vitus. There was lots of talk and some silences. Out of one of them Elizabeth said, "We must have been out of our minds."

He is not reading as much as he wants to—a Kingsley Amis novel, *The Green Man*, is an exception. His weight preoccupies him as it did for the rest of his life. There are very few references to his looks—only curses now and then against his erupting skin. But his weight seemed to be a matter of great importance—as if he marked his will-power and well-being by the measurement on the scales. This is typical of several entries:

> (July 12) My weight is down to approx 175 lbs. Will continue to 168 and then indulge myself a bit. Still the Drinking Man's Diet but without the drinking. Gout still nudging but nothing to complain about. Am trying to do without pills today. So far so good.

Another running preoccupation is the fate of the children: Maria, Liza, Michael, Christopher, Kate, they are forever coming in and out like the extended family in a Chekhov comedy.

After a furious eight months on the booze, he is off it again. The Notebooks start up. The even tone is quickly found. Drink is a force to watch. On July 26th, when Beth's baby was born—making Elizabeth the "World's Most Glamorous Grandmother" at forty:

> Great excitement and I broke my drinking fast for the first time since June 15. Had a glass of nasty champagne and two or was it three stiffish martinis. Knocked me sideways and I slept for 3 or more hours this afternoon . . . I don't like drinking but I do miss the conviviality of bar hopping, etc.

The enduring problem of Michael and the long slow death throes of Ifor continue. Burton feels both keenly and angrily, and is, perhaps, too harsh on Michael, still very young, whose childhood has been, to say the least, no easy passage.

> (July 28) I think E. and certainly I would abandon Mike to his own idiocy for a while—were it not for the baby and Beth. We are auto-blackmailed by our own concern for Beth and the child. Sometimes I fear that Michael is in danger of earning E.'s hatred. I know certain aspects of her so well—like for instance when she is enjoying somebody's company and when she is not. On his part, I think he thinks of his mother simply as a beautiful woman who because of her looks alone is a highly paid film star. He has no idea that she is a major talent and therefore resents her wealth.

With Burton, the crossword fanatic, problems had to be solved. Other people's especially. Lack of a solution brought on a terrible impatience. His style was to get out of the way and leave space for what was really important.

> Ifor is very near the end. Death is written all over his face. He did not know me when I saw him yesterday. He can barely speak. He is already dead. I wish he were. The sight of Ifor, after the emotional disturbance of baby and Beth and Michael, finally reduced E. to tears and she sobbed all the way back to the Dorchester and sometime afterwards. Liza was an angel to Elizabeth and watched her as [if] the positions were reversed as 'twere and Liza was the mother and E. the child. I love that child. She can be a bit of a bastard at times but she is fundamentally an angel and great in a crisis.

He is setting up a film, *Absolution*, which he will not do until some years later. He meets

> (July 29) Christopher Miles—brother of Sarah Miles the actress—the director of the film. A tiny fellow with bright sharp humorous eyes. He looks as if he knows what he wants and will insist that he gets it . . .

Family life takes an upward swing.

> The delightful Kate was with us from noon on and was her usual charming self. Giggles a great deal and professes to be appalled by my occasional irreverencies. She is a joy . . .

And off to Claude Gill's

> to buy books for the yacht . . . A couple of Dickens and a few thrillers and horror stories for Liza and Hornblower for Chris and a few volumes of poetry in French, Welsh and English for myself . . . also bought books for the chauffeur's sons who are showing interest in schoolwork.

Pass on the knowledge wherever fertile ground is sighted.

And so to Yugoslavia where they met President Tito. Burton is aware of his great war record and his independence within the Communist bloc and is prepared to admire him.

> (Aug. 1) The Pres is surprisingly small and delicate. Little short arms and legs and a small head with little features. He wears slightly tinted glasses and I can't really tell the colour of his eyes. He has quite a pot-belly but the rest of him is slim—no bottom and thin chest and legs. He walks slowly and with short steps. When he sits down behind a table he seems most formidable. I'm slightly put out by the nervousness with which the servants serve us all. They live in remarkable luxury unmatched by anything else I've seen and can well believe Princess Margt. who says the whole business makes Buck House look pretty middle-class. After lunch the Pres and I talked a great deal about the war and Sutjeska in particular. I asked him if he liked Stalin. He took a long time to answer and finally said he "liked him or rather admired him as a politician but disliked him as a man."

But soon the old symptom returns.

> (Aug. 2) Were it not, actually, for E.'s delight in the power and the glory of it all I would do my best to cut and run—so great is the strain of boredom—especially the interminable translated conversation. Both Tito [real name Broz] and Madame Broz tell long stories which they don't allow the interpreters to interrupt, result being that by the time the latter have finished one couldn't care less what the story is about. Madame has a very penetrating voice which, after a time, becomes extremely tiresome. And protocol demands that I'm always with her and the Pres with E. And they have a professional interpreter whereas I have a Minister's wife whose English leaves a lot to be desired.

It doesn't help that he is off the booze.

(Aug. 2) It is as well that I'm not drinking or I might be asking some very awkward questions. There were occasional bright moments. Tito in English: "I was very glad when my grandmother died." E: "Why?" Tito: "Because it meant she stopped beating me." E: "That's an awful thing to say." Tito: "She was small but strong and always angry."

He met Churchill who was in the vicinity on Onassis's yacht. Winston C. accepted a very small whisky. Tito had his usual large one. "Why so small a portion," asked Tito, "you taught me to drink large ones." "That was when we both had power," said Winston C. "Now I have none and you still have yours."

Power does corrupt. I doubt whether Tito sees the ordinary Joe Soap from whom he came except when the latter waves a flag and carries a banner.

And later:

Am still worried by the atmosphere of dread which surrounds Tito. Cannot understand it. Neither can the rest of us.

He has been off the booze for two months and congratulates himself regularly. It also leads him to write more and reminisce.

The Notebooks are now emerging more clearly as a draft for an autobiography. What is fascinating is to see his later reflections and insights into what he considers key events in his life. This provides the opportunity not only to see these events from a different perspective, but to gauge how he has changed since he lived through them. Passages of this autobiographical nature, used not at the time to which they relate, but now, are essential to emphasise the way in which, throughout this particular period, Burton was reassessing his whole life. With a view to writing about it—certainly. But also with a view to measuring it against his expectations, finding a meaning in it, deciding what to do with it.

He decides to take the *Kalizma* into Porto Santo Stefano to clear up some of the many difficulties arising from the Tito filming, which was appallingly badly organised. Often Burton took up the task of sorting it out. Autobiography takes over: back to the time of Cleopatra.

(Aug. 13) The other reason for going in is to visit the café where we had our first and near-fatal drink one near-dawn morning on our way to the next bay for a clandestine weekend. I had driven E. from Rome in the small hours in a rented car—a small two-seater Fiat as I remember— in order to escape the paparazzi. The town was a grave at that hour and in the bar-café were only a couple of people and a boy and a dog and a waiter. All the world press were searching for us. We thought we had got clean away. One of the anonymous gentlemen in the bar was a newspaper man on a humdrum assignment from his newspaper to cover the arrival of Dutch Royalty. And lo & behold there in front of his eyes were the "hottest" and most scandalous couple in the world. We left the place after a coffee and cognac apiece or perhaps we had two and drove in smug blissfulness to the hotel who had set aside for us a half-finished and small villa which was half a mile from the hotel, looked stupendously over the sea and was completely isolated. We gambolled like children, scrambling down the rocks to the sea and enjoying ourselves as if it was the last holiday. We found out soon enough that every bush—and there were hundreds of them—contained a paparazzo. We were well and thoroughly trapped. The weekend turned immediately from an idyll into a nightmare. We drank to the point of stupefaction and idiocy. We couldn't go outside. We were not married. We were impregnated with guilt. We tried to read. We failed. We couldn't go out. We made a desperate kind of love. We played gin rummy. E. kept on winning and oddly enough out of this silly game came the crisis. For some reason—who knows or remembers the conversation that led up to it?—E. said that she was prepared to kill herself for me. Easy to say, I said, but no woman would kill herself for me, etc., with oodlings of self-pity. Who knows what other kind of rubbish was said. Who remembers from so long ago with everything shrouded in a miasma of alcohol what was said. Out of it all came E., standing over me with a bottle or box of sleeping pills in her hand saying that she could do it. Go ahead, I said, or words along those lines, whereupon she took a handful and swallowed them with gusto and no dramatics. I didn't believe they were sleeping pills at first. For all I knew they could be Vitamin C or anything else. She then, I think, took herself off to bed in an adjoining room. From then on I hardly remember any detail. Vague memories of trying to get her awake, or realising that she wasn't joking. Loading E. into a car and a hair-raising drive to Rome and a hospital and hiding at home because officially E. had a tummy complaint or some other excuse which the press told immediately to the Marines. Not being able to go to the hospital because of the snappers and not answering the telephone to Roddy McDowall and Mankiewicz and almost everybody.

So now we have just come back from the very same café where E. had a *café latte* and a cognac as she did that time ago, and I noticed that it was Friday the 13th. I mean today and decided that I didn't want any repetition of that awful Easter. By God, what if she'd died. Worse, what if she'd lived with an impaired brain? I'm perfectly sure that I am incapable of suicide so presumably I would still be alive. What would I be doing? Maybe I would have drowned myself in booze by this time. Anyway, it's all over though never forgotten. It certainly has cured any thoughts of suicide from this family. In that year also Sybil also had a go at knocking herself off. I was furious with her but not furious oddly enough with E. I suppose I must have been thinking of Kate being motherless and didn't think similarly of Liza, Maria *et al* being likewise because they were still little seen, known or loved by me at that time.

It is the double perspective which gives it such poignancy.

Back to his study of Tito. It was a rare position—to play a living hero—and Burton studied his man.

(Same day, Friday, August 13) Tito told me that he never ever raised his voice above ordinary conversational level during his whole life, except when distances were involved—shouting across a valley for instance—and that he had always found it infinitely more effective and on occasions much deadlier than a Hitlerian or Mussolinian storm.

And as the boat drifts across the Mediterranean to Capri, the forays into the past continue and they show their own version of home movies.

(Aug. 15) E. saw *Cleopatra* last night with all the kids. I popped in at one point for about 10 seconds and went away and slept for another couple of hours. No reflection on the film! As a matter of fact E. said this morning that the film is not at all bad—marvellous spectacle and all that. My lack of interest in my own career, past, present or future, is almost total. All my life I think I have been secretly ashamed of being an actor and the older I get the more ashamed I get. And I think it resolves itself into a firm belief that the person who's doing the acting is somebody else. That accounts presumably for my fury if anybody shows me anything about my acting in the magazines and journals. I don't mind the gossip stuff like "seen walking on the Via Veneto last night" or "The Burtons on their luxury yacht," etc. And I am equally angry whether I am praised or damned tho' mostly I'm praised. The press have been sounding the same note for many years—ever since I went to Hollywood in the early Fifties, in fact—that I am or was potentially the greatest actor in the world and the successor to Gielgud, Olivier, etc., but that I had dissipated my genius, etc., and "sold out" to films and booze and women. An interesting reputation to have and by no means dull but by all means untrue.

Wherever they go they are besieged by holiday crowds and an attempt to buy a pair of sandals becomes a violent scrum. This onerous limitation on a life is not heavily underlined, but the occasional references highlight the paradox of their known-to-all celebrity and their isolation.

Despite the difficulties with the script and the *manana* methods of the Yugoslavs, he next attempts to grapple with Tito's character by questioning him directly.

> (Aug. 18) I also want to show in as low-key a fashion as possible Tito's life-long refusal to shoot captured enemies, even Cetnik traitors. He told me of one terribly bitter story. He had a few hundred German prisoners and was at a point where he was forced to retreat. To carry the prisoners with him would have been a tremendous strain on his ever-slender resources. So he informed the senior German officer that he was releasing them to find their own way back to their commands. They were astonished but delighted, naturally. The usual treatment in that kind of warfare was to shoot all prisoners. He also hid his own injured men who were not able to move in what he thought was a safe place. He found out later that the released Germans returned as soon as he had disappeared and slaughtered the helpless partisans. Even so, he never wreaked vengeance.

This impresses Burton, but it also alerts him. The observation continues—the study of a living "part."

> Among many little oddities I found from Tito that he shaved every day of the war except one day, the one day when he was wounded in the left upper arm by bomb splinters. And that he dressed as impeccably as was possible throughout the whole madness. Another bit: He had sent a message to Stalin telling him of his release of the German prisoners. He received a brutally nasty telegram from Stalin in reply to which he sent a cold reply saying that unless Stalin could send him, Tito, material assistance, or at least the morale-lifting presence of a military mission, he should mind his own business. When later Tito went to Moscow to see Stalin there was a small party at which, among many others, was the dreaded Beria, chief of the Secret Police. Many toasts were drunk and all inevitably to Stalin. Tito had not had a drink of any alcoholic kind during four years and the eternal vodka was hitting him very hard. When his turn to toast came he

toasted the inevitable Stalin, whereupon Stalin said with
deadliness, "Why do you toast me now after sending me
that insulting telegram?" Tito mumbled some placatory
answer but the atmosphere was charged with menace.
Later, feeling sick from the vodka, Tito went out into the
grounds to throw up. A shadow appeared among the trees.
It was Beria, who said: "Don't worry, it is only your
friendly policeman!"

The filming itself begins as it will go on—a nightmare.

(Aug. 22) To my astonishment the actor with whom I have
most to do in the film doesn't speak a word of English
and was prepared to speak all his dialogue in Serbo-Croat.
I refused to do this saying it would give the dubber into
English an impossible task and ruin the film for distribution
in the Western world. As it is, I don't see it having a
chance even with them speaking all the dialogue in broken
English with me speaking in perfect Oxford. We can, I
think, write this film off before we start.

And the temper slips badly.

(Aug. 24) And I was at bursting point. I had been very
cruel to Liza this morning—viciously so. She had said
that I ought to keep the film dog with me at all times while
I was doing the work. I said the bloody dog was so in-
fatuated by his master that he would whine and scratch
all night and in any case I said the bloody master was
reluctant even to have me tickle his ears. Liza said, "But
he's your dog." And out of that cess-pool of cold cruelty
which some people call a brain came, "Don't be bloody
stupid. He's no more my dog than you are my daughter."
Liza was as brave as hell and said with a strained little
laugh, "That was very nice." E. was quite rightly livid
and I wanted to cry or slit my jugular.

"Eventually I made it up with both of them," he writes, "but 'taint
good enough."

Burton adored Liza and it must have cost him dearly to write this down. We sense the uncontrollable demon which could, it seems, literally "possess" him (and epilepsy was long thought to be evidence of possession), but is all of a piece with his talent which also surged into him from a hidden, unknowable source and possessed him. The interest though also lies in this utter determination to have the truth about himself on the page—warts, wounds and all. As a man of easy conversational and public deceits, it was vital, it seems, to tell the whole truth and nothing but the truth in this way at this time. He swore on the Bible of these Notebooks. It is important at this juncture most of all to read them, not only for what they say in themselves, but for what they say about his underlying intention. Here, fighting the drink, struggling with the never-ending illness of the woman he loved, afraid of his destructive boredom with his career, his encroaching loneliness and his own growing ill-health, he was finding a root to life, forcing himself to give evidence and sit in judgment on what he was. He was in short, looking to change himself profoundly and the Notebooks were his couch and his laboratory.

Elizabeth continues to be on the injury list.

> (Aug. 30) E. had cut her shin on the right side of her right leg just above the ankle to the bone by slamming down my other red typewriter and hitting her leg by accident. A very nasty cut indeed and which took a couple of hours or more to stop bleeding. Poor little dab. She probably is the all-time World Champion for being minor-accident-prone. However having established her injury she hasn't mentioned it at all since.

It begins at times to seem like an occupation. Her mother, too, is ill and Elizabeth is ready to fly off to the USA at a moment's notice . . .

> (Sept. 5) E. is in the worst state of lassitude I ever remember of her. She has always been naturally somewhat indolent—not the kind of girl one finds rushing off to play golf and tennis, God forbid—but now, I mean for the last couple of days, she can barely move one foot in front of the other. It's largely of course the reaction from the tension of the past week but it's bloody worrying. She isn't

boozing any more than usual so it isn't that. She just seems to find everything just too much trouble.

There had been talk of her having a small part in the film but in the end she declined: she would have played a nurse. The battle is still to find time alone together and to discover an equilibrium in drink: him off the booze and her on it tends to work badly and there are curt reports of bad quarrels. The odd thing is that Burton is fully aware of the disruption caused by the entourage but seemingly powerless to change it.

(Sept. 9) Heyman told me that everyone is agreed that The Burtons are as easy as pie to handle but that The Burtons' Entourage is a pain in the ass and every producer, when they are mentioned, hopes fervently that they will all die in the night of galloping heart attacks. Too bad, I said, though I agree about some. The great exception is of course Ron and though I like the others I don't think that any of them are necessary to me. I like Bob Wilson to be around and be the barman and man of distinction and Jim is useful with mail but lacks the charm so essential when handling so many different kinds of people. He's no Dick Hanley. All the others actively bore me if they are around for any length of time.

The film dragged on with Burton talking to actors who had no knowledge of the language, on locations arrived at by kamikaze helicopter flights, Elizabeth uncertain, no booze. He buried himself in the Notebooks and over the next month or two they grow enormously.

(Sept. 13) Yesterday received a long and incoherent letter from Larry Olivier re the National Theatre. He must have been very drunk the last times we talked to him as nobody could have turned down the job with more firmness. But he has obviously been persisting so I wrote a long letter, longish anyway, explaining that he mustn't worry about his not being able to get me the job and that I wouldn't take it if offered. Not at least unless there were drastic changes. That is to say, I couldn't see myself being overruled by a board of governors over some project I had in mind. As Larry was over the Hochhuth Churchill play [*Soldiers*]. Granted the play was a travesty and badly written or translated or both but I would have resigned. He also said in the letter that they hadn't been allowed the money to put on *Guys and Dolls*. Well, what sort of National Theatre is that? Those Old Etonians, etc., would drive me mad in five months . . . (Evening) Sitting on the poop deck with my infinitely beloved wife who has acquired an even greater weight of love. I keep on mentally looking around to make sure she's there. For why this new and massive re-affirmation of adoration and worship and a promise to myself that I shall never be nasty to her ever again? I will tell you for why. For because for about 3 mins this afternoon I thought that I was about to be killed instantaneously and at once, without time to re-tell her how much I love her, to apologise for breaking my contract to look after her forever, for letting her down with a bang (hysterical pun intended), and for having no time to tell her the million things yet to be told and for not realising and demonstrating my full potential as husband, provider, lover and all.

I did not work today which is rapidly becoming the norm for this piece and all I did was to sit around in Tito's hut and drink tea and Nescafé and try to read the script *Gingerbread Lady* [by Neil Simon] which they want E. to do and which she wants to do and was interviewed by a man with one of those curious beards that are only about half an inch wide and run meticulously along the edge of the jaw-bone and I wrote half a page of a letter to Kate and munched on cheese and morsels of the celebrated local ham, of which I am getting a trifle sick, and finally and of course inevitably word came that work was over for the day and that it was "a wrap" and so we set off back to the 'copter and Kupari. I settled in on the port side right behind the pilot while Vesna, the interpreter, sat beside me with Brook on her other side. Ron sat in the rear row with Gianni. And off we went. There was a low cloud ceiling which we went into immediately we'd gained some height and, as so many times before, we threaded our way through the vicious peaks to right and left. Suddenly and without warning we were completely blacked-out, tho' I believe the technical description is "whited out." There was nothing to be seen outside the cabin of the chopper except nothing. A white nothing. On top of this it began to rain torrentially and the windscreen wipers whipped back and forth like insane crickets sharpening their legs. The co-pilot frantically tried to turn himself into a human demister. We flew like this for perhaps half a minute though it seemed like an hour when there it was! We were going at an angle of about 45 degrees into a peak. The pilot, God bless his marvellous reflexes, flung the copter to the right and there appallingly was another rock face. The co-pilot slapped the pilot on the arm and we pulled away again to the left. I don't know how close we actually were but it seemed to be the length of the rotor-arm and six feet. Whatever the distance, it must have been very close otherwise we wouldn't have seen the two peaks at all. Still we ploughed on with everyone except Gianni and I—and the pilots of course—with their eyes closed tight. Ron I saw curl himself into a ball and cover his head and ears, with his knees on the floor waiting in what they say is the classical position for a plane crash. I stared to the side with hand ready poised to warn the pilot if anything appeared on our side. The pilot was straining his eyes forward. The co-pilot was rubbing his side window with hand also poised to warn the pilot. Gianni just stared over Ron's semi-kneeling position like a man who saw nothing except eternity. Apart from my saying Holy Shit in a strangled whisper nobody uttered a sound. No sound, at least, that could be heard. So we continued to fly blind for another aeon (possibly a minute, possibly two, who knows?), dreading the head-on how-de-do from which there would be [no] way of turning. Then, the machine began to lose height pretty quickly. I could feel it tho' I daren't take my eyes away from the window to check the altimeter. I thought the pilot had gone mad. Later I found out why and how right he was. We dropped and dropped until there suddenly and miraculously was the much ma-ligned road curling around the mountains. Rarely have I seen such a beautiful road, a masterpiece of the road-maker's art, an example to the Romans of ancient time, I could not think how I had ever said that the road was a fucking nightmare and an elongated version of a shit-house, a ruined shit-house. I would have gladly apologised to every kilometre of its lovely length. The pilot had lost height, he said, to be able to see, to try and go above the clouds was certain suicide because in order to gain height quickly he would have had to circle and he knew, as indeed we all knew, that there were a hundred peaks of a different height, width and also there was no knowing how high the cloud was. He was however fairly sure that the cloud base would not cover the bed of the valley. What is night-marish on recollection is how many close shaves we must have had during those 2 or 3 minutes. Glimpses of eternity that we had never seen.

What is also frighteningly revelationary too is the num-ber of levels on which the mind functions at moments of imminent catastrophe. "Believe me, sir [Burton quotes Dr. Johnson not wholly correctly], when a man knows he is to be hanged tomorrow morning it concentrates the mind wonderfully." There was one blazing mental image that seemed to last right through the enormity. It was E. lying in bed on the yacht with a book open at the page where she'd stopped reading with the title front cover and pub-lisher's blurb on the other face up on the bed near her right hand which was out of the covers. She was wearing one of my favourite nightgowns, a blue thing and shorty which she may have been wearing this morning when I said goodbye to her. (I've just asked her and she was.) She had one leg bent and the other straight. On another level I was telling her over and over again that I loved her, I loved her. At one fractioned point I kept trying to remember a line of Alun Lewis's, "If I should go away, beloved, do not say . . ." and I couldn't remember the rest which I've known for 25 years or so. Immediately the crisis was over I remembered it immediately.

> If I should go away,
> Beloved,

Do not say,
He has forgotten me.
Forever you abide
A singing rib within my dreaming side.

The mind is a remarkable instrument. If I wrote down
everything I could remember from those interminable seconds it would be a million words. It is in fact what James
Joyce's *Ulysses* is all about except he took a whole day
for Bloom while he could have taken 3 minutes because
the "mind concentrates so wonderfully." A shorter catastrophe of this kind happened to me before when I was
perhaps 19–20 yrs old but I hadn't learned to love then
and to love obsessively. Going to stop now until tomorrow
morning. I must read *Ulysses* again.

After a conversation, Burton is reminded of a famous actress he
knew in Hollywood and her discovery of the joys of masturbation.

(Sept. 15) "Why the hell didn't someone teach me all
about it when I was in that fucking convent?" she demanded. "Think of all the emotional involvements I could
have saved myself instead of having to get myself laid by
guys I didn't even like just because I was horny. For
Christ's sake I spent my youth looking for big cocks when
I could have screwed myself with a brush handle." And
so on.

All this revolutionary talk took place in an apartment
hotel, rather shabby, where most of the New York actors
used to stay, on Sunset Boulevard. I think it's still going
and is called the Sunset Towers. In the middle Fifties it
was the thing to do if you were a New York stage actor,
and to show your contempt for the contract stars, to stay
there in that stucco monstrosity making it quite clear that
you were your own man and not owned by some studio
and the minute the fucking lousy film you were in was
over you were going back to the great New York THE-
ATRE where you re-found your soul as an artist and where
the Real Work was done. I, because I was a real stage
actor and had played your standard classics, was accepted

there despite the fact that I had a million-dollar contract with Fox.

Marlon and Monty Clift were habituees too for a time because they were always going to go back on stage (and actually did for a second—Marlon did a couple of months in summer stock playing *Arms And The Man* and Monty went back off-Broadway to do *The Seagull*) but gradually Marlon shifted further and further away until he eventually had a permanent house of his own. For Marlon, it must have been a harrowing time because he was their natural leader. They all worshipped him and comforted their own failure with "Marlon is the greatest Goddamn actor in the world and the greatest Goddamn film star too but he's one of us and next season for Chrissake he'll be playing Richard the 3rd and Hamlet and fuck 'em all here in this shitty phony town." But he never did and slowly he also began to fail as a film star and the great disillusionment set in. Then it became fashionable to denigrate Marlon. "He's sold out." "Let's face it, Marlon isn't any good unless Gadge [Kazan] is there to tell him what to do." Etc. Arguments with which I'm only too familiar because I was the British version of Marlon. In my case it was even worse because I was, from the beginning, held up against Paul Scofield. We were the natural heirs to Gielgud and Olivier, Paul being Gielgud and me being Larry. "But Burton let the side down, etc." What they don't seem to realise is that Paul tried like mad to be a film star. I remember his testing for film after film and being turned down largely because nobody knew how to photograph that magnificent face. It was the era of pretty boys: Rock Hudson, Jimmy Dean, Paul Newman and even Marlon and myself. But, largely out of a kind of obligation to my background and because I felt that I owed it to Phil Burton to become a great classical actor I continually destroyed my film career by going back again and again to the theatre. And I did it against all the odds. It was still, up to my middle thirties, "Scofield and Burton."

But then everything changed. I went to live in Geneva, made me a million dollars quickly, did any bloody thing to get out of the contract with Fox, even to the extent of doing two truly appalling films called *Bramble Bush* and *Ice Palace* and at last I was free to do anything I wanted and, more importantly, not to do anything I didn't want to do. I spent a whole summer in Céligny blackening in the sun—it was a particularly splendid summer all over Europe—turning down film after film. I remember turning down an offer of 350,000 dollars to play Christ in a film called *The King of Kings* that summer. It was very tempting. Five months in my beloved Spain and though the script was unspeakable it was to be directed by Nick Ray who had after all made one good film, *Rebel Without A Cause*, and might pull it off again. But I turned it down and just as well. Both Stratford and the Old Vic offered me whole seasons to myself. Play anything you like. Turned them down. I was offered plays by the score. The only thing I did for a whole year was the film of *Look Back In Anger* which was a flop and a TV special of another short Osborne play called *A Subject of Scandal And Concern* for the BBC. I stayed at the Savoy during rehearsals. It was for BBC TV and it seems ludicrous now to think that we had to hold a press conference with Tony Richardson, Osborne and myself while we defended the BBC against the fact that they were paying me 1000 pounds— one thousand pounds indeed to God—for an hour's play and three weeks' rehearsal. The most ever payed before was 500. The thing was a huge success and I must try and get a copy for the boat. It seems odd too nowadays to think that the BBC solemnly warned all its viewers that the play was being put on deliberately late at night to give them, the viewers, a chance to put their young ones to bed as the play was about a man "who didn't believe in God." Wow!

The fact is that I was in a very enviable position. Though I was knocked about by the press—British press particularly—for being a bloated millionaire and a traitor to my country for deserting a sinking British Empire on which the sun was at last setting, I was more courted than almost any actor in the world. I knew bloody well that I was not considered box-office after *Bramble Bush, Ice Palace* and *Anger* but I also knew that any film sub-

mitted to Marlon and turned down was automatically sub-
mitted to me and of course any play of significance came
to me first and then went down another line of stage
actors. I had an adorable girl baby, I was very fond of
my wife, I was a millionaire, I had a sweet little estate
in Céligny. I had a superb convertible Cadillac (still
among the favourite cars I ever had), a large library, an
insatiable thirst for knowledge and the means to satisfy it
and every opportunity to play anything I wanted and I was
terribly unhappy.

The autobiographical line hardens up. As in many autobiographies
there is self-justification as well as self-revelation. The breeziness
is characteristic: the no-nonsense, non-whingeing man who is
pleased to report that he is riding a wave of luck. The lack of boasting
or vanity is also noteworthy as is the realism about his film rating.
What is most effective, however, are those last four words. And
yet again it is presented as something which came out of nowhere.
In the middle of all these riches—which he appreciated, for which
he was grateful and which he relished, "I was terribly unhappy."
It could of course be no more than a common condition said to
affect those who get everything they want. It could be a way of
motivating himself: unhappiness would provoke restlessness which
would seek activity and bring yet more rewards. No explanation is
offered. But it fits in with another pattern: that of a man massively
endowed with heroic strengths and terrible weaknesses who was
somehow fundamentally at the mercy of forces which rose up in
him as volcanically as those never-explained boils rose up on his
skin. And he sensed himself to be at the mercy of these forces, now
dark, now dazzling . . .

He reads Dickens, Solzhenitsyn, Anthony Powell—"not a writer
for every mood"—and puzzles away at the character of Tito who
has grown very fond of Elizabeth (who, in turn, presented him with
a dog).

(Sept. 24) I have been a little put out by something Ron
Berkeley told me and which I have yet to verify. I have
predicated my still unwritten article or whatever it might
turn out to be about Tito on the belief that he never ordered
anyone, including captured Germans who had behaved

with atrocity to his defenceless people and Cetniks who betrayed and murdered the partisans, to be shot. Now Ron tells me that he was in a bar in Dubrovnik the other night and in the course of conversation with a group of Yugoslavs he said that I was particularly fascinated by Tito because of this. Whereupon two men immediately stood up from the table and left the café-bar without a word. Ron asked why this, as Yugoslavs are generally polite. The propr. who is a Cockney Slav, believe it or not, said that the fathers of the two men had been shot in the Yugoslavian "purge" of 1948. I must now try and find out if these two killings (altogether, Ron says 41 people from Dubrovnik were shot at that time) were personal settling of scores or whether the orders came from the top. If so I shall be a disappointed man. I mean if the orders came from Belgrade. I must also find out if people are willing to talk. So far, after countless conversations with all kinds of people, I have never heard one bad word about Tito and very few pejorative remarks about Communism, though quite a lot about bureaucracy and its attendant evils—particularly nepotism and the fact that a member of the party, though inferior in merit to a cardless Slav, will always get the vote. I asked Branko, a veteran Slav actor who speaks good English, why nobody, but simply nobody, spoke ill of Tito. Was it caution or fear perhaps. Branko said that it was neither, that Tito was still a father figure. To the older generation—people of my age and his (57? 62?)—he and Sava had been the legendary saviours and to the younger generation—those of 30 and under—there had never been any other President. Tito and President had become synonymous. Rather, I suppose, the way in which Caesar came to mean King. Kaiser and Czar are probably etymologically derived from Julius and his namesakes. The young ones know that he saved them from Bosch beast and the Red Bear and those who might have opposed him in the crisis of 1948—if Ron's story in the pub is to be credited—were presumably knocked off or incarcerated. I must ask more of Branko and find out if I can detect in him any signs of caution or fear when next he chats at my instigation. I think I'll be able to tell. I

must ask about Djilas and whether it would be possible
for me to meet him or even whether it would be advisable
of me to ask somebody like Popovic who is a member of
the party.

Elizabeth's cut leg causes her great pain and the Notebooks record
the pills, the insomnia. Burton builds up his paperback library on
the *Kalizma*—buys and "devours" *Ulysses*, thereby fulfilling a
promise in his journal a fortnight before. These are times of innocent
enjoyment with Burton—as always when he was with a couple of
pals.

(Sept. 30) I ask for tea. A middle-aged lady of fearsome
aspect, though she smiles for me, goes off to get it. In
ten minutes she is back *without* milk. I ask for milk as
well. My Serbo-Croat is rippling off the tongue. She comes
back in ten minutes with the milk by which time the tea
is cold or gone. This happens three times a day and has
just happened again. This morning I cunningly put the
small jug of milk on the window-sill—outside—so that
when she next forgot I would be equal to the situation.
But with even greater cunning she had removed the milk.
Touché. I am now hiding the milk outside on the balcony.
At least she won't be able to get at it at night. Not unless
she is the direct descendant of a cat-burglar. Or crawls
over my bed in the dark having picked the lock of my
room.

But next day:

(Oct. 1) My friend the maid defeated me yet again.
Milk all ready on the balcony and all prepared she archly
brings the milk with the tea. So now I have two jugs of
milk . . .

(Oct. 5) Last night after dinner Gianni Bozzachi reduced
me to tears of laughter when he told me some of the items
put on our weekly bill at the house. Now, the number of
people staying at the house is five—Gianni, Claudie, Ray-

mond, E. and myself, tho' E. and I have spent very little
time there as we usually stay at Cavtat in the *Kalizma* –
and of those five only Elizabeth drinks *but* she drinks *only*
booze brought from the boat, Smirnoff and Jack Daniels,
both of which products are unobtainable in Yugoslavia.
So, in effect, nobody at the house of our party drinks at
all. The bill however for one week had us down for 5,000
dinars, new dinars, and the following week it had jumped
to 8,000. I asked how much a bottle of Scotch was in
dinars. Johnnie Walker Red Label is 100 dinars. It therefore follows that *if* we were all drinking and *if* we drank
only the most expensive drink available which is Johnnie
Walker and other whiskies we would have drunk 50 bottles
the first week and 80 the second. Again assuming we all
drank the same amount it would mean that the first week
we drank 1 and ⅗ths of a bottle per person per day, and
in the second week 2 and ⅖ths of a bottle per day. Only
five raving alcoholics of the classic pattern could keep up
such a pace. I have in my time and at my best put away
I'm sure the occasional 3 bottles of vodka a day but not
for two or three days in a row and certainly not for a week
or a fortnight. Otherwise it would be Dead Dad. No, that
kind of consumption demands the presence of Bobby Newton, Bernie Lee, Trevor Howard, Errol Flynn and Jason
Robards to name but a few of my friends only two of
whom oddly enough are dead. If we had taken the local,
and apparently very drinkable, wine which costs 10 dinars a bottle we would in two weeks have put away 130
bottles. Correction: 1,300 bottles. As for the food, it is
a riot of over-charging. It is reminiscent of the time when
Dick Hanley found that the monthly bill in the house
in Rome on the Via Appia Pignatelli for bread alone was
500 dollars . . .

(Oct. 6) Have just heard from Brook that we are off
to Sarajevo again tomorrow, back to that house and a
continuance of the battle of the milk with the charmer
who "did" for me. I will not cheat by buying a carton
of milk in the local dairy but will fight the good fight
straight down the line.

He takes the private jet to London to see Liza who is in hospital having been slightly concussed in a fall from her horse, and goes up to Hampstead to find Ifor in surprisingly good form.

He leaves the Tito filming later in October to begin on *Trotsky* in Rome: the Tito will be finished later. He is, rightly, wary of the massive speeches he is forced to undertake: long enough in the script, even longer on the set when Losey—who admires Richard greatly—throws in an extra few paragraphs of direct quotation from Trotsky. Because Burton can manage the speeches, he is overburdened with them. They become a short-cut for an unsure director.

Michael and his marriage still nag away in his private life—just as the world and its mother continue to nag away in his public life.

> (Oct. 21) There's been a man called Jeffrey Archer, MP, plaguing the life out of me through Raymond [Vignale] for weeks. I've always refused to talk to him and have told Raymond to tell him to tell Raymond what he wants to talk to me about. This he has refused to do as it was very important stuff and had to do with Pr. Margaret, HRH. Then would he write it as Mr. Burton will not speak on the telephone . . .

The letter arrives: all about appearing in a play for Sir Lew Grade.

> At the receipt of our agreement to perform this so far unread [television] play, Sir Lew Grade would make over a cheque for 100,000 pounds to the St. John's Ambulance lot. We would be paid nothing.

Then came the sequel, a typically extravagant Burton squib.

> (Oct. 25) I talked to Princess Margaret last night at about 7.25—she had said 7.15 but not too bad for Royalty, and amazingly for the Italian Telephone Service which gave us a very good line. She asked me whether the Lew Grade thing was acceptable and I told her that in principle the idea was fine though we thought the plays were not very good and we had two far better ones by John Osborne (I hope we have) and that we would do them in March next year and that the 100,000 pounds would come anyway

only simply from a different source. What did I mean? she asked. Well, I said, we had already contracted to do the two Osborne plays for Harlech TV and therefore Harlech had a prior call on our services and the plays were being, had already been financed by USA TV and that the 100 thousand would come from us and not Lew Grade. Do you mean from Harlech, she asked? No, I said, from Elizabeth Taylor and Richard Burton. Good Heavens, M. said, how very generous of you. I am absolutely staggered and other fatuities. Then we went on to talk banalities about Tito and we must simply spend some time together when we were all back in England and swap family albums and stories about Tito and Yugoslavia. She told me she had lost her voice and I thought that it was rather a good idea as she sounded so gentle and long-suffering. That's how I feel, she said. She sent her love to Elizabeth and I sent E.'s and mine back and to Tony as well I said. I shall give it to him when he comes back from America she said. Well, goodbye, I still can't get over your extraordinary generosity. Not at all. Goodbye. It was nice talking to you. Nice talking to you too. Goodbye then. Goodbye, your Highness.

He enjoyed that, but worries crowd in about the quality of the film in which he has risked himself. He can't jump ship and yet he sees potential disaster all around him in the *Trotsky* filming.

(Oct. 23) Yesterday work was very strange again—I thought I'd left all that kind of thing in Yugoslavia—for the second time this week I played a scene with two people who couldn't speak a word of English and who were found to be incapable of learning, even like parrots, the few lines they had to say. It was an all-day agony of frayed nerves for everybody, including Joe, tho' we all kept our tempers and were very patient. But why did Joe cast them in the first place.

(Oct. 28) Joe is definitely not himself. He doesn't seem to know the script as well as he usually does. Time and time again I, or the continuity girl, have to remind him of things that are very obvious. For instance: In one of the scenes I am pacing up and down and around the garden dictating. Every so often I pause as I hear myself talking to the now dead Sheldon Hart, killed in my defence. I am remembering my last conversation with him. Joe asked me why I was pausing. I told him why. Oh really let me look at the script. Yes, you're quite right. Yes. Very odd.

Burton is being generous. Losey was drinking hard and his private worries interfered with the film-making.

Burton turns to his domestic life—with unexpected relief.

(Oct. 28) What an enchanting evening yesterday's was. It was as if we'd turned the calendar back five years and Michael was himself again. He was loving with the baby, fun to talk to *and to listen to*. Elizabeth was as happy as only a grandmother can be. Beth was in good form. Even I was pleasant and though I longed to I daren't touch the baby as my cold (much better but still there) might have been given to her. She is the kind of baby that everyone should have. It kicks little legs and makes minute fists and blows spit-bubbles and smiles a lot but hardly ever cries. Everybody hates a crying baby—in fact distraught mothers, generally from the working classes, have been known to kill them—and everybody loves a charmer as Layla unquestionably is . . .

(Oct. 30) Just had a long talk with Liza about masturbation—prompted by a Dear Abby column she is just reading. I told her that it was a perfectly normal part of growing up—especially I said in boys. Why especially in boys? Because I said I knew about boys, having been one believe it or not, but never having been a girl I wasn't too sure. I told her some of the frightful and stupid things I was told and heard as a kid. That you'd go blind and bald before you're 21, etc. All rubbish. Also told her that excessive masturbation might lead to an onanism which might spoil one for more normal sex tho I wasn't too sure about that either.

Elizabeth is off alcohol for a full week (save the odd martini and beer); Cassius the cat is trodden on and has to be nursed through the night.

(Nov. 3) E. is a funny girl. When a human being is injured—as when the man fell off the balcony in the small hours in Mismaloya and broke his back and fractured his skull E. gave points and a beating to Flo Nightingale while everybody else, including me, looked the other way. Her agonised frustration at the spectacle of dumb animals in pain is sad to see. But the whole family have it. Once we were telling a story to Liza about some dreadful accident that had occurred to some people who had a dog with them. I've forgotten who the people and the dog were and what the accident was. Listening with rapt attention until we'd finished Liza said: Oh the poor dog.

The reading passion continues unabated.

(Nov. 5) My chief joy at the moment in reading is Baudelaire. It is a magnificent thing to discover poetry in middle age. Most men take in their quota of verse before the age of 25 and live on it for the rest of their lives— those, that is, who have a feeling for it at all. I mean, of course, to discover new poetry, new at least to them and not simply regurgitate the old and well-known. Baudelaire I had, of course, read in English, in which language he is unrecognisable. Why was I not properly educated to French in my early years, tho' perhaps I should prefer it this way round.

And the dieting.

(Nov. 7) Both of us dieted yesterday. I am 76 kilos. Have not started with my usual 2 kilo drop. The virtual cessation of drink has made a terrific difference to E. She is more active, more spirited and at the same time more relaxed. And she looks even more beautiful than before. Her face has thinned very subtly and her ever present baby double chin is much less. Even with E. there is bound to be a certain amount of bloat from booze. If she loses 5 or 6 lbs with this diet she will look 25 again. And there is no doubt that less grey in the hair takes a few years off too.

And the chat became less doom-laden.

(Nov. 8) I read David Niven's autobiography yesterday in one sitting. It is very funny tho' not very well written and is, like all actors' biographies, very anecdotal and full of "and then Mike Todd called me and said 'Get your ass over here,' " etc. He describes one scene on Bogart's yacht which is not what happened at all as I was there. He describes Sinatra singing all through the night on a motor yacht with a lot of other yachts around "awe-struck" he says. Frankie did sing all through the night it's true and a lot of people sat around in boats and got drunk it's true but Bogie and I went out lobster-potting and Frankie got really pissed off with Bogie. David Niv., who describes himself as bewitched all through the night, was trying to set fire to the *Santana* at one point, because nobody could stop Francis from going on and on and on. I was drinking "boiler-makers" with Bogie, rye whisky with canned beer chasers so the night is pretty vague but I seem to remember a girl having a fight with her husband or boy friend in a rowing dinghy and being thrown in the water by her irate mate. I don't know why but I would guess that she wanted to stay and listen to Frankie and he wanted to go. And Bogie and Frankie nearly came to blows next day about the singing the night before and I drove Betty [Bacall] home because she was so angry with Bo-gie's cracks about Frankie's singing. At that time Frankie was out of work and was peculiarly vulnerable and Bogie was unnecessarily cruel. But any way it is not at all like Niv's description. He's very sweet about E. and indeed about practically everybody.

. . . Another year.

(Nov. 10) I am 46 yrs old today. I am sometimes surprised that I got so far. I always had the feeling that I would die at the age of 33. This belief was induced in me by an Irish (Welsh—Irish) idiot many years ago in a drinking club in London on a wet Sunday afternoon, late afternoon, when we were having a break from a poetry reading. Dylan was there and Constant Lambert, Louis MacNeice and Esme Percy—by God all of them are dead—and we were drinking well with no particular thought for the fact that we were broadcasting "live" in an hour's time some intricate verse—at least Esme and I were. No, we weren't, we were doing Thomas Love Peacock's *Nightmare Abbey*. The club was and is a most unattractive, badly run, filthy hole in a wall. I have never found out if I was a member, tho' I must surely be one now as I "loaned" them £500 last winter via John Dearth. Its only use was as a place to drink when the pubs were closed. Anyway this particular afternoon we had the usual "break till 6.30, run-through until 7.30, the red light comes on at 8" injunction and Esme and I repaired to the club. It was my idea of total bliss. A Sunday in London at the BBC on the Third Programme—surely the best radio channel in the world —playing Shelley in Peacock's marvellous piece, surrounded by a melodrama of brilliant English actors—Esme himself, Count Robert Farquharson of the Holy Roman Empire who was reputed to be a Satanist, Ernest Thesiger, Andrew Cruikshank, Robert Speaight, Michael Hordern and sometimes Dylan and James Crock of Gold Stephens and always the BBC stock company one of whom was, if such a thing is possible on radio, a truly great actor— James McKechnie. So there you are in my drab paradise of magnificent language for the speaking of which you were actually paid money, on a Sunday in Studio 8 of the BBC Portland Place, the Sunday papers strewn hither and thither and much chat between the boys who matched story after story and, because the competition is so intense, no one person was able to hold the floor for too long even if Dylan was there, for Dylan—the most compelling talker I've ever met—was oddly constricted by these precise cold

English actors with their impeccable accents. Lunch was at somebody's club—I would sometimes go with Esme to the Savile—but more often it was in the BBC canteen, a hellish place appositely placed in the sub-basement of the huge building. It was a serve-yourself café and a pretty sight it was to see the august Count Farquharson, cloaked like a bandit, and all the other great presences queuing up for the appalling BBC fare. The drinking men however lunched out of a bottle at the George or—not quite so popular as it was that bit further away—the Stag or the Roebuck or some such name. But it was the work itself that was the wonder. The audience was of minor consideration as it was so small. Apart from the fact that the channel for the Third Programme was unfindable in most of Great Britain, this brain-child of the BBC would play plays in the original Greek and was indeed deliberately steered away from the mass audience. If they accidentally hit on a smash success it was almost always re-played on the Home Service or Light Programmes. The best work I have ever been associated with was with that Programme. I did endless poetry readings there and every kind of adaptations from great works, particularly the lesser known stuff. Your *Hamlets & Henry Fifths* were common fare and one did those on the vulgar air-waves but *'Tis Pity She's a Whore* and Love Peacock and Bessie D'amboys [sic] and Chaucer and Jones's *In Parenthesis* and *Anathemata* and Joyce's *Finnegans Wake* and *Ulysses*, etc., were all done on "our" programme.

Anyway this Cardiff Welshman—a feature of the sleazy drinking houses in those days and vividly remembered tho' I can't remember his name—a writer who never published and an actor who never acted elected to tell us from our hands when we were going to die. My father was up for a week from Wales and I'd taken him to the BBC to have a look at it and was going to send him back to Hampstead after the afternoon drinking session was told he was going to die when he was 81, Dylan when he was 39, Lambert when he was 55 and me when I was 33. I was very impressed—so much so that I have remembered

it to this very day. It was made more frightening as Dylan
did die when I was 29 at the age of 39 and Dic my father
died when I was about the same age at 81. My brothers
say that my father was 83 but there has always been some
confusion re the old man's age and in any case he was,
the prophet, only a couple of years out. Lambert died but
I don't know at what age and I can't remember whether
he foretold Esme's death date, but Esme also died. My
behaviour to anyone who didn't know during my 33rd
year to heaven was high comedy. I turned down a film in
Durango with Burt Lancaster and Audrey Hepburn and
directed by Huston because of the unavoidable flying.
Were it not for the fact that I was ashamed to tell anyone
I would not have worked that year at all & celebrated my
34th birthday with a stupendous booze-up. I was already
very rich & kept on saying to myself as the offers came
up, "Why should I risk my life for a mere 150 thousand
dollars when I have a million in the bank, why don't I
settle here in Céligny and never leave the grounds of the
house even until the year is up? I can learn Hebrew or
something. The thing is not to give the gods of retribution
the slightest chance." The anomaly is that I am not even
mildly superstitious ordinarily and am certainly not a fa-
talist. I must find out, as a matter of mild interest at what
age Lambert died. I wonder too if in death Lambert is still
considered to be the genius he was thought to be when he
was alive.

Again there is the conviction that life—especially the vital and
defining aspects of life—is a force over which he has no control
whatsoever, a force whose plaything he is. Superstitious thoughts
of a sudden or early death are not uncommon, but Burton surely
took the case to a bewildering, even a ridiculous extreme. Clearly,
though, he felt warned and alarmed by it. At times such snatches
of self-revelation show a character more understandable in terms of
a credo of witchcraft and spiritual possession, of the roving psychic
forces recognised by older tribal societies rather than a product of
a Western rational society. Burton seems to have been both—very
distinctively—leading "as it were" a biographical life—in which

external events could be reduced or at least made to work and an internal, autobiographical life which had moods and imperatives of an entirely different order.

Both he and Elizabeth got very drunk. "The rot set in when I made a large martini each about 1 o'clock." Elizabeth developed a cyst on her nose and Paris was chosen for the operation. There's dinner with Peter Sellers and an Indian mystic friend of his at which, again, both Richard and Elizabeth get spectacularly drunk: flowers and apologies are sent around the next morning. Meanwhile the offers keep coming in (letters delivered by the hand of Bob Wilson, his dresser and friend).

(Nov. 20) Bob just brought me a telegram from Tony Richardson asking me to play with Vanessa Redgrave in *Antony and Cleopatra* "early next year." I said no. Politely. That man must have the thickest skin in and out of Christendom. This is his 2nd offer to me this year—the other being to do the film of *I, Claudius*. After our bitter debacle about Nabokov's *Laughter In The Dark* one would think that he would be scared witless to approach me to play Scrabble. But not our Tony.

And now for Paris . . .

(Nov. 23) Frings [a producer] came in about 6 and we discussed the script which I'd read in the afternoon. It's rubbish but it's something I've never done which is a "horror film" and which the kids have been anxious for one or the other of us to do for many years. I play Blue-beard, a German or mittel-European Count or Marchese or something complete with Ruritanian or perhaps Transylvanian would be better castle. Booted and spurred and tails-clothed and impotent and kill eight wives—all of great beauty—the moment they expect me to go to bed with them. There is a great deal of horror though everywhere. Can't make up my mind whether I should do it or not. Any road, if they wish to do it in January as they say they do, I must decline. Its other attraction is that they shoot in Hungary, to which country I've never been, and I could do with a little lightness after Tit & Trot. Am supposed to have lunch at Fouquet's with the director—

one called Dmytryk who—I've only just discovered this morning—I've been confusing for years with a man called Siodmak. Both have their similarities in that they started off well and then tapered off into the usual mediocrity.

The battle to achieve an acceptable domestic life appears to be ceaseless.

Back at Gstaad . . .

(Nov. 27) I've lighted the fire in the main room and am on my second cup of tea and E. is still sleeping and I cleaned up the inevitable dog shit. The dogs are house-trained in a way. If there is an acre of a room completely bare except for a rug one foot square they will crap on that rug, taking turns. Their habits in this house are pretty regular. Two of them use the rug in the visitor's lavatory while two use the rug in Raymond's room. At least one knows where to find it and when they are all healthy and their ordure is dry the job presents no great disgust but when one or more or all have the trots then it's an odious job indeed. At the moment they are all dry.

(Nov. 29) The devil over my shoulder, E., is trying to press me to have a martini before lunch because she wants one and doesn't like drinking alone. I'm dickering with the idea but think I will have one this evening if at all. As I've explained to E. ad nauseam, I find one drink simply not enough. I guess two or three stiff ones are what I'd find satisfactory but that means slowly reverting to being a drunkard again and I simply will not tolerate a return to that. E.'s problem is that unlike me, she does not smoke at all except when she drinks, therefore giving her a per-manently large appetite. There are months when her hun-ger is bad and she has to be coaxed into eating reasonably when naturally food watching is easy but now, and for the last month or so, her appetite is voracious. She has this morning, e.g. been in agony poor old thing and cannot read or do anything to assuage it. We've tried lots of tea with lemon, bouillon, chunks of cold chicken from yes-terday's dinner but to no avail. Now she has gone upstairs to make us Steak au poivre for lunch and I am going to make her a martini with vodka. I am not going to have one myself.

The next day, November 30th, contains an unusually sustained reference to the book that Burton is seeking to write.

Searching desperately, well, not desperately but continually, for a book to write that would not be autobiographical, at least not overtly, I have come upon an excuse. I have been much impressed by a Yugoslav "novel" called *The Bridge of the Drina* which I think I must have mentioned before in this haphazard daily exercise. For it is not a novel at all but a series of semi-legendary stories purporting to take place in and around the bridge. By this means the author gives one a saga of the many invasions and changes of family and fortune, in small, of the entire South Slavs of Yugoslavia. I thought of our pearl, the famous or infamous Peregrina, and its extraordinary history. Found by a slave in the 16th century or perhaps even the late 15th, it was part of an argosy that took it to the Court of Spain. The slave who found it was given his freedom. Who was the slave? Are there any traceable descendants? Were the sons of slaves free too? Where were my ancestors at the time? Where were Elizabeth's? The tracing of the pearl's history will be complicated. I shall have to imagine my and E.'s ancestors, unless E.'s mother's story that she is descended from Mary, Queen of Scots could be substantiated! That would be a great coup for the book. The thing would of course take years to write and would demand a great deal of specialised reading and almost certainly the employment of searchers, I believe they call them. It has been done before. There was a rather good film on the subject I remember—the object being a tail-coat. But the Pearl involved famous dynasties and is authentic history in itself. I could elaborate on my cynical-comical views of mankind and a small page or two of its history. The whole and vast personal question is Do I have the intellectual stamina to sustain such a big undertaking and is my writing good enough? I shall need to be fairly near a great library which means Oxford or London. Not all the time but from time to time to frequent time at least. I think the first person to consult would be Nevill Coghill who would introduce me to the methods of scholarship, what sort of people to employ and consult. Now I will sleep on it for 6 months until we get to England again.

It is a massively, almost laughably, ambitious project, but impressive and touching for that. Yet it could have been one of the maverick books of twentieth-century English literature, which form a persistent subversive alternative to the main-stream and the officially accepted avant-garde. That would have been consistent with Burton's line. The interest lies in the fact that Burton is now taking a view that the writing he does need not be autobiographical. That step outside the exploitability of himself and his own life—so well rehearsed in so many cups—is yet another measure of the way in which he is screwing himself up to the sticking point to find some expression of life which will satisfy and fulfil him in a way in which nothing else does, at least not for very long.

Meanwhile the Maharajah–Maharanee lifestyle pursues them even into their own home.

A salesman from Van Cleef visited the Burtons with about three million dollars' worth of gems.

(Dec. 1) E. had changed a gold belt she had bought from them—or I had rather—when she was doing *Zee & Co* and he had come up with the new belt-cum-necklace in exchange. With us of course, and probably with everybody, he brought as I said an extra two or three millions in temptations. I was not to be drawn however except for a pair of matching earrings for the already bought necklace which E. had been "loaned" for some time and naturally (sarcastically) became attached to. That, by the way, is a good ploy of such salesmen. They let you have a splendid but not overwhelmingly expensive piece on loan, or for a specific occasion, an opening night or the Rothschild party for instance, and hope that the wearer or the spectator,

me, decides to buy it what the hell. The necklace and
earrings are a perfect example since I bought the earrings.
They cost about 6 thousand dollars.

The Rothschilds were giving a ball—described, of course, as the
Ball of the Century—and the Burtons were invited. Hence the jewellery for Elizabeth. The Burtons were guests of the Rothschilds at
Ferrières. He loves the snobbery and goes like a reporter, alert for
material. Writing it up becomes an exercise in itself. And he was
off drink.

(Dec. 3) So the Ball was had. It was had until 7 a.m.
when the music at last stopped and the do-or-die-ers
crawled into their cars and lumbered off with the early
morning traffic to Paris. We had come up from the party
about 4.30 a.m. but, after packing away the ''big'' jewellery and putting it in the house coffre, we sat and chatted
desultorily away until the orchestra stopped at 7. I managed, tho' I was sorely tempted during dinner, not to have
the mildest form of alcohol so despite only about 4 hrs
sleep I feel as bright as a button. We have just had tea,
as indeed we did at 5 this morn also. It is 1.15.

We picked up Grace at 32, Avenue Foch, which doesn't
seem to be the Embassy and I forgot to ask Son Altesse
if it was or not. A very amiable Rainier brought Grace to
the gate carrying her two small bags—a considerable difference from Son Altesse E.T.B., even despite the fact
that Grace was not staying the night. We were delayed
by E.'s being 12 mins late and hitting heavy traffic in the
Champs Elysées and it therefore took us nearly 2 hrs to
get to Ferrières whereas Gianni & Claudie who actually
left *after* us were there almost an hr *before* us. There is a
highly sensitive 15 or 20 minutes or so in these city journeys and had we not had to pick up Grace in the ''wrong''
direction as 'twere, we wld have had a quick run. There
was one massive pile-up somewhere in the outskirts where
we took about ½ an hr to do ½ a mile. However, Grace
and E. chatted away at the back of the car while I sat in
front beside the driver. Grace was nice and relaxed and,
after the initial awkwardness which I always feel with

people like Grace who are in a somewhat false position and know it, everybody talked freely. Grace went into a blow by blow description of the Shah of Iran's famous or infamous party. Grace defended its extravagance with extraordinary obtuseness though neither of us attacked it. It was meant, she said, as a tribute to the people of Persia and as self-advertisement for the Shah's magnificent governing which was bringing literacy to the illiterate and hygiene to the unwashed and culture to the brutish. She described the Shah as a marvellous man and once called him a great man which is going a titch too far. She said how monstrous it was of the Western press to be so vulgarly cynical of the whole show, all of them she said she knew for a fact writing their stuff before the thing had got really going. E. was sweet and said that yes I mean Tito and the Hungarians and other Communist countries were there and didn't seem to be particularly put out by the obvious "capitalism" of the whole thing. Absolutely, said Grace and said it was a marvellous thing to see people of such enormous disparity in religions, politics and races finally warming to each other after the birth-pangs of meeting and how a little Chinaman who was stiff and unsmiling and reserved and talked only through an interpreter was by the last day chatting a mile a minute radiant with smiles in impeccable English to all and sundry. So there. It all goes to show that we are brothers under the skin. And why for heaven's sake doesn't the Western press attack its own spending of zillions a year on advertisement, corrupting the minds of the young and the stupid with their idiotics? And so on. One didn't suggest that it might perhaps have been more helpful to his appallingly poor people if he had promoted a sort of World's Fair, an Expo 72 or something and have the other people pay for the advertising. The "do" of the Shah's was supremely silly under any circumstances and if it was to celebrate the extraordinary advances made for the benefit of his people then it was inane to the point of simple-mindedness.

Enough of the car journey. As we approached the last few miles to Ferrières there were policemen, mostly motor-biked every few hundred yds and learned later that

Guy had arranged for a policeman or van every ½ mile from Paris. All the way from Paris! Now President Pompidou used to be employed by Guy de Rothschild before and after he became Prime Minister and the new Prime Minister was also to be here last night but was unable to come and rang M.-H. this afternoon while we were there to apologise not only to M.-H. for not being able to come and telling the reason why but also asked the names of his two side by side companions in order to apologise to them too. *Toujours la politesse*. So it is no wonder that Guy can commandeer the entire Parisian police force if he so wishes. As we turned into the drive the entire house faced us and for the first time since we've been coming here was lighted up. It looked magnificent and were it the clop-clop of horses and the smell of saddle leather and blankets round the knees and not the low hum of a heated Cadillac we could have been back a hundred years. The main entrance however was only for the herd—we entered by the side door as we usually do and went straight up to our rooms, having some difficulty in finding out where was which and who was where. Sorted out finally, we found ourselves in the Chambre Rose while Grace used the Chambre Balcon to change in and do her hair. We are changing from our *chambre* to the Balcon tonight while at dinner. The Rose, while very nice and suitably rosy with all the decoration à la Wedgwood, panelling and all, has an outside bathroom which though exclusively for our use meant having to put on a dressing gown, if you happen to be in shorts in case of running into M. Oliver who lived next door and shared our little hallway. Also, to our surprise, we could hear everything in the two adjacent rooms quite clearly, it therefore following that everybody could hear us. So it will be nice to gossip at normal *voce*.

I sat around and waited for all the girls to be ready— my girls including the Duchess of Windsor and the Princess of Monaco and of course my very own "girl." Grace was ready and waiting about 10 minutes before time and came to our room for a drink. E. would have been ready but Alexandre, the hairdresser, took forever to arrive and longer to do M.-H.'s hair-do. We had been told that we were to descend strictly at 9.10 and sit down to dinner at 9.30. We descended at 10.30 and sat down at 11 p.m. The great hall had been made into a dining room for the occasion and was impossible before we began. It took me 15 minutes to get to my table from the door—I timed it —and after having trod on endless trains and knocked aside several expensive coiffures, virtually climbing over half a dozen people, I found myself at table No. 11 with Madame de Montesquieu on my left and the former Mme Louis Malle on my right, both of whom, thank God, I knew. Now for an hour or more of absolute agony. The waiters simply had no way of being able to get round the tables so most tables including ours elected one person to receive all the services and pass them on from hand to hand. The food was divine, or perhaps I was so hungry that it seemed better than it was, and I made an arrangement with Mme Malle, who is a very beautiful but giant of a woman, for her to pass me all her re-fills of water while I passed her all my wines. She must have a powerful head for she must have had well over a dozen glasses of various wines—champagne, a white wine, the inevitable Lafite and a second white wine which I guessed from its vicuousness [sic] was Château D'Yquem and it was. My attention was however riveted from the first by a man sitting opposite me. He looked like a cadaver when still and a failure of plastic surgery when he moved which was seldom. He was eye-brow-less and eye-lash-less and atrociously wigged or dyed with snow-white hair at the front of his head and to the crown and nondescript brownish, rather like mine, hair at the back. His face was hideously pasted with make-up and had odd lumps on it, a face made of funny putty by an inept child. I had just asked in Mme Malle's ear who was that extraordinary thing over there when he leaned forward and said, ''Where's my Elizabeth?'' Ah, I said, well now, she is ah, over the other end of this room ah sitting and ah eating indeed at the ah corresponding table to this but ah at the ah other end if you ah what I mean. I wish she was here, said he, the inference being that far better her than me. So, as a matter of fact, do I, I said with a speed which would have done the Rev. Sydney Smith no harm to admire . . . After the strangely delivered question from Andy Warhol, for that is who the horror film gentleman was, we all settled down to the battle of the food. I discussed on my left with Madame de Montesquieu, who is indeed descended from the great Charles Louis Secondat, Baron de Brede et Montesquieu who wrote *L'Esprit des Lois*, poetry which all started by her saying that she had been at somebody's house and they had played records of me speaking ''The Ancient Mariner'' and how this woman who had given the party and played the record said that she had heard me speak poetry at the Rothschilds' ''and even Guy listened'' and that she (the hostess) had gone out and found all the records she could find of me speaking verse. I asked Montesquieu twice who the woman was and twice she told me but I shld have written it down as I have forgotten it already, but wld like to know who this lady is. Just out of curiosity. It wasn't Lily Rothschild who I know has some of my poetry things. So we talked about French poetry which I told her I was only just beginning to read and enjoy. Mme Malle and her sideman were much more amusing and I think that E. would like Malle. She, the latter is nicely unhappy, almost desperate I wld guess and she and I and the man on her right discussed painting. I said my usual and quite true things about Art, that I didn't understand it at all and derived pleasure only from the occasional picture but that, quite clearly, I was artistically ''tone-deaf.'' I said that we had what was by common consent a very fine Van Gogh but that though I was impressed by it I didn't know why it was remarkable and that to me the most impressive thing about it was its estimated value in cash which was enormous. Apart from the written and spoken word—preferably the former—the only other art-form that genuinely could disturb me was music, some cheap, some deep. Malle and the man protested that music at its greatest was so much like painting at its greatest that I must try again with painting. I said I would.

Meanwhile at the other table E. and Grace were having a marvellous time. The lucky bastards had Guy, the Duchess of Windsor, Maurice Hertzog, Jean-Paul Binet and a few others. The star turn according to E. and Grace was the Duchess who is perhaps getting slightly ga-ga. She had an enormous feather in her hair which got into everything, the soup, the gravy, the ice-cream, and at every vivacious turn of her head it smacked Guy sharply in the eyes or the mouth and at one time threatened to get stuck in Guy's false moustache which was glued on. She made one bon mot which had Grace in tears. After having got her incredible feather into everything possible she then called in her very penetrating voice, having a desire to write down her tel. no. for E. and me which has changed since they sold their house, "*Est-ce que quel-qu'un qui a une plume*?" She was most insistent that E. and I shld see the Duke before we left for Gstaad, giving E. the feeling that he is probably on his last legs. We are going to dine with them on Monday night. Binet flirted blatantly with E. but in the best French manner and they had the same hysteria with the serving of the food—Grace being the hander-over.

After the dinner, Guy asked E. if she wld help him remove his moustache which was now becoming a bore. They went into a gents lav, or rather a lav for either sex while a servant stood on guard outside. Bettina elected to choose this time to try and get into the same loo, not knowing that E. and Guy were inside. E. had removed the moustache and was cleaning around Guy's mouth when Bettina finally burst past the servant and found them in this odd situation. It looked for all the world as if E. and Guy had been having a necking session and E. was now removing the evidence. Bettina was delighted by the whole thing.

By this time the rest of the guests, as it were the "B" list, were arriving. They were announced in a stentor voice by a gentleman with a large voice and a large intricately carved staff—I've forgotten what they call those things —with which he pounded the floor and boomed Madame et M'sieur Harry Dogface to which fascinating information nobody except the people who had just whispered their names to him paid the slightest attention. I squeezed past them followed by Mme Malle and her friend and Elsa Martinelli and somebody else (uninvited) to take them to the lav of our room. E. was already in the room repairing her maquillage with Bettina. I sat thankfully & smoked before we went back into the whirlpool below. We both sat for a time with Grace in the normally intimate corner of the first room. Scores, perhaps hundreds of people flocked past on some pretext or other to view E. and Grace. I wandered about after a time talking to this one and that including Jacqueline de Ribes, Pierre Salinger and wife, Sam Spiegel and M.-H.'s lovely big brother that we call "Broken-nose" and occasionally I caught glimpses of E. being avidly though covertly gazed at wherever she went. And I congratulated Salinger on the success of his book and how much I'd enjoyed it and that I had read it in one sitting and had he yet sold it for a film and he had—to CBS—and we then talked of the splendid night in LA when Bobby Kennedy and I insulted each other's races, bloody Irish v. bloody Welsh and the usual Kennedy–Burton quotation match, and Rudi Nureyev and his wickedness and how horrified and struck dumb we all were by Bobby's assassination and how much we all loved him.

After a time wandering about, Grace asked me to see her upstairs and help her remove her borrowed choker and get her to her car. I suppose it was about 1.30. This I did, nearly strangling Grace to death while trying to get the necklace off. For a minute she was in bad trouble as the necklace got twisted up as a result of my inept handling of the clasp as the bloody thing was too tight in the first place and, in fact, I had told her before we went down to the ball that she ought to remove it, telling her she didn't need it. However, we finally twisted it around so that she herself could see it in the mirror and finally we released her. Even when off it took considerable strength to unclasp it. So down the stairs we went together. At the bottom, alone, was Sam Spiegel. Where are you going you two? "For God's sake," said G., "don't, Sam, say a word to Elizabeth. She's at the Ball, she's dancing, she's happy, let us go. Richard will let Elizabeth know. It's going to be a shock but . . . these things happen. Etc." For a full

half minute Sam, because of Grace's normal seriousness
and because of her very good piece of acting and my
deliberately stricken-with-guilt face, was taken in. We
made off. Found Grace's car not before a lot of waiting
in the piercing cold and she was gone. She was quite the
nicest she's ever been & David Rothschild expressed astonishment that she could be so gay. She had always, he
said, been a bit of a dead weight. On the contrary, we
said, but she does need a little drawing out. Actually it is
the nicest she has been in all the years since we've known
her as a Princess. At one moment during the choking
choker episode I saw mental front-pages in *France Soir*'s
and *News of the World*'s lurid headlines. Famed Actor
Strangles Princess in Bedroom at Rothschild Mansion During Grand Ball.

For the rest of the evening we wandered about and ran
into Audrey Hepburn and her ludicrously named Italian
psychiatrist husband Doctor Dotti who is not very nice I
think. We had snaps taken of us by Cecil Beaton who is
also not very nice in a different way. Then in another room
we had snaps with Audrey Hepburn and M. Dotti and
Doctor Troques and his wife and after an encounter, very
strange, with M.-H.'s sister-in-law Gabby Van Svillen,
who insisted that she was the Tsarina of All the Russias.
Did she, I asked politely, feel this because she had in fact
some Romanov blood—Mike Romanoff blood, I added.
No, she said, everybody is someone else and I am the
Tsarinevitch. What about you? she said. I want to be a
Fellow of All Souls, I said. A what? she said and lost
interest. I was saved by a man called Valery who is the
son of the poet. He was charming and again we discussed
poetry. He told me of the time when everybody assured
his father that he was a dead certainty to win the Nobel
Prize for Lit that year and with what excitement, sitting
in the garden, the maid came out in a hurry to say there
was a long-distance call from Stockholm for him; he went
bounding into the house to hear the great news only to
find it was a wrong number. He never did get the Nobel
Prize . . .

At one moment Marie-Helene came up to me at the bar

where I was talking to Salinger's wife about Tours and
the surrounding country which I love and said, "Where's
Richard? There's a woman who's dying to meet him."
"It is I, Hamlet, the Dane," I said whereupon she
screamed a little and went off at a tremendous pace forgetting to take me with her, and I never did meet the
woman who was dying to meet me and Marie-Helene has
already forgotten who it was and indeed the entire incident.

. . . And the comedy of Parisian High Life goes on.

(Dec. 7) We went to the Duke and Duchess's house last
night for dinner with half a dozen of the most consummate
bores in Paris. I don't know their names but I shall never
need to remember them for I have an idea they are people
who only go to the Windsors and one of them—probably
the old Duke—must die very soon, though it is she who
is now nearly completely ga-ga. It was a sad and painful
evening and needs a long time to write about and I haven't
got the time. They both referred continually to the fact
that he was once the King. "And Emperor," I said at one
point. "And Emperor," she repeated after me. "And Emperor, we always forget that. And Emperor." He is physically falling apart, his left eye completely closed and a
tremendous limp and walks with a stick. Her memory has
gone completely and then comes back vividly in flashes.
She derided Grace Kelly all night as being a boring snob.
I defended but she wld have none of it. I finally gave up
as I knew that half the time she didn't know what she was
saying. There was one woman there, a French woman
who protested violently that she was not Swiss—what's
so wrong with being Swiss?—and who is married to a
Hungarian Count who obviously didn't realise that the
Duchess was gone away from us and attempted pathetic
rational argument. I gave the word. Her husband said that
Tito was the natural son of a Hungarian Count who had
exercised the Droit de Seignor or whatever that's called
over Tito's mother's family. I said I wld tease him with
it when next we saw him. I doubt it. Both the allegation
and that I wld tease him.

The final entry is on December 21st. The two main preoccupations are a 3,000-word article he has written for the *Daily Mail* and Elizabeth's health.

> I am worried about my sweet E. She doesn't seem to be at all well and her back is kicking up again like fury. It's a dreadful thing to think when we love this house so much but I am beginning to have the horrifying suspicion that the altitude is too much for her. She sparkled in Dubrovnik, she was radiant in Rome, she was a young girl in Paris but here she seems listless and slightly bored all the time, not just with me, but with everybody and everything. I think that already she is wishing that we were here just the two of us. We must use this time as a testing period for if it *is* the altitude then we must simply go lower down.

Superficially, all normal: Elizabeth ill, Richard writing, film offers coming in, films coming out, a huge acquaintanceship—Tito, Rothschilds, Bob Wilson, the Duke of Windsor, Niven—heavy reading and, even better, long stretches of time when the drink problem has been cracked. But these five films, cumulatively, were to depress Burton's reputation badly. More than that, they were to unseat his confidence in his ability to pick quality winners. Elizabeth's illnesses and demands were becoming wearing and although he keeps reassuring himself—in those Notebooks which she occasionally dipped into—that she continued to be the absorbing focus of his life, that was soon to be disproved. He had been wearing a mask, even for Elizabeth. In *Bluebeard* he was to rip it off. Part of his life died.

21
Bluebeard

If you can judge a man by the range of his friendships and acquaintanceships, there is also something to be said for understanding him through the letters sent to him. Burton wrote many letters and received many in return. He was not scrupulous in keeping all of them. But those he did keep, to take a selection simply from the year or two around this period, reveal an impressive range. There are serious letters, which were seriously answered, from the Invalid Tricycle Association, Port Talbot and District Group, of which Burton was President; and the letters from Laurence Olivier in which he asked Burton whether he was interested in taking over the National Theatre after him. Olivier suggests they do it in tandem first, and then sadly and at length reports that the Chairman is unwilling to go along with this plan. There are long and detailed letters from Cis (partly in Welsh) and others in the family, cheek by jowl with correspondence from J. K. Galbraith, Christopher Isherwood and Sir Stephen Spender. The latter, poet, essayist and human rights' campaigner, writes most enthusiastically about Burton's company, as indeed so many of them do: "I haven't laughed so much in years," writes Peter Ustinov after a dinner party. The Aberavon Rugby Football Club (Ground and Dressing Rooms: Talbot Athletic Ground) keep him up to date with local news of the game and thank him for his donations—one of many grateful letters from beneficiaries large and small. Burton had the charity of an amiable medieval abbot. John Ormond, the poet, writes to him, and Frank

Sinatra; A. L. Rowse the historian—in the most flattering terms—and just before his death T. H. White, a long letter describing his drink, his melancholia. Pals from school and the Air Force; Richard Nixon; "Tim" Hardy—a great number, usually signing himself "Tsar" and more often than not thanking Richard for a favour, lending him the private jet to go to Greece, for instance, for the honeymoon of his second marriage; Nevill Coghill and Francis Warner from Oxford; Gielgud of course and Warren Mitchell; Emlyn Williams; Richard Findlater, asking him to write more for *The Observer*—on it goes. And the children.

Burton blames himself for not writing often enough to the children. But Kate speaks of numerous letters—"he loved me so much he didn't know how to handle it"—and the tone of such letters can be seen from a couple he didn't post. One to Maria:

Miramonte Majestic Grand Hotel,
Cortina, D'Apezzo,
Italy.   28 March, 1973

Dearest Maria,
How thrilled we were to get your letter. Everybody in the film, with very few exceptions, is very ill except for your very tough old Dad. Even Mama is a bit rough though she confines herself to saying things like "I feel as if somebody has beaten my bones with an axe" or "Did you kick me a lot last night, Richard?" or "Are you quite sure that Maria didn't sleep with me last night because the last time she slept with me I found myself on the floor four times?"
   I reply, very sternly, that I have never bashed her with a hatchet and that my daughter would never dream of kicking her out of bed. "How dare you," I say, "infer that two of the most loving people in the world, your husband and your daughter, would dream of hacking you about with an axe or kicking you about as if you were a lump of coal that had to be extricated from the coal-face so that we could have milk for breakfast. How dare you, Good God almighty, even dream of such a compound of errors?"
   You know how much Mama loves Art Nouveau. Well,

all she talks about now is a silver and lavender vase. It is, she says, the most tactile but ironically the most untouchable object of art that she has ever seen. If ever, she says, you would like to buy me a present I wouldn't be averse to be given that! And, like yoxu, oops, sorry, when your Mama wants something she pulls out every feminine wile ever invented.

Now, we miss you very much and love you even more and we talk about and boast about you to the point of silliness. I have deliberately used some long words, and some short ones. Will you look up every word that you don't understand, find out what they mean, and use them when you write to us. Mama says she loves you better than raclette and I love you better than Huckleberry Finn. The next time I see you I am going to pick you up and hurl you about and smother you with kisses. Mama asks if she is invited to the same party.

All our love.

And one to Kate a couple of years later:

Ariel,
Gstaad,
Switzerland.   23rd Sept., 1975

Dearest Ivy League,
Thank you for your letter duly stamped, received and in a minute answered.

Glad that you find Brown "cute." I can't say that I found Oxford "cute." I was scared out of my wits and, as a result of copious reading about the City of Dreaming Spires, rook-racked river-rounded, and Shelley, Bowra and the ghosts of a million scholars wearing the walls away it was anything but cute. Awe-inspiring would be a more bon mot in my case . . .

Israel was a mad-house, the only respite being a long dissertation with Nancy and Henry Kissinger. Nice of him to call me "very intelligent"—you missed out the "very" in your missive. It is no accident that the Middle East's problems were solved so quickly after our chat. Strong men, hardened and calloused by the wear and tear of interminable negotiations, were heard whispering in hallowed tones: "Kissinger, Sadat, Rabin and Perez have spent three years commuting between Alexandria, Cairo, Tel-Aviv (but don't tell anybody else) and helicopter pads and can it be possible that after three hours with Burton the whole thing was signed and sealed in three days." What can I have said to resolve the murderous balance of power? My lips are sealed and are not to be opened until thirty years after my death, by which time you are likely to be Katherine Kissinger Burton and the secret of my subtlety—that's an odd word—will be a lesson in diplomacy and doubtless incorporated in the Torah and the Talmud, elbowing its way past Moses and all the other prophets. I am sometimes astounded at my own modesty but I feel that you can make up for it.

Tonight—it is 7 a.m.—we fly to Johannesburg to help black people play tennis or something. I'm not quite sure what it's all about but am assured that it is "a good thing." Everybody is terrified that superbly sober as I am I may yet start sounding off on "Apartheid." Elizabeth has crossed everything including her incomparable eyes that this street-corner evangelist, which is to say your shrinking violet of a father, in the frantic hope that I will not have one of my murderous out-bursts against injustice and be locked up forever by what is a fascist police state whose God is Hitler. Stand by . . .

A word of advice from an old old man. Whatever you decide to major in and whether you goose-step or dance, try and get a little science in on the side. It is one thing that is terribly hard to teach yourself, physics, biology—another interesting word, anthropology. If you do "International Affairs" the preceding sciences will give you a solid base. I will always regret that I didn't take higher mathematics instead of Eng Lit and Med Italian. Those things come to us without instruction, but the sciences need a helping hand. It is no longer possible to be an ossimath but is possible to have a stab at it. Darwin and the inexplicable mystery of numbers is a continuing fascination. I love you to the point of agony so be a bad girl.

If international affairs is going to be your major let me know and I will send you the pick of English, French and Italian magazines. (Even though you don't know the latter very much you'll be able to read it with reasonable fluency in three weeks or so . . .)

So now to pack and drive down to Céligny with Brook while Elizabeth follows later. We are Mini-Moking it. Brook sends his undying love.

And of course there are the business letters, hundreds, thousands of them, clipped neatly in beige files, an autobiography by numbers.

1972 was to be a fateful year. It is worth taking a brisk look around the Burton estate before plunging into it. Although he had drifted away from the theatre he still spoke about it and had plans which were often very near fulfilment. He was being accused, in London, of betraying his talent but this seemed to worry him very little. He had built up a big career as a box-office star and thrown in several excellent and two superlative performances for good measure. Over the past year or two he had taken risks with material (Trotsky, Tito), worked with unusual directors (Ustinov, Andrew Sinclair) and was forging ahead on projects that interested him. There was always a good reason for his choices and he was always gambling: friends could say he happened to be on a losing streak. Just one of those things? Closely observing critics could see the retreat, the withdrawal of his powers as an actor. Something was draining him.

He had heavy loads to bear. The Welsh family never got any smaller and he took his responsibility seriously. Graham continued to be a source of desperate embarrassment. Nephews and nieces, in-laws and neighbours joined the band and as Elizabeth's dresses were sent over to Hilda at Pontrhydyfen to be picked out by the ladies of the village, Richard's cheques winged their way to similarly ever-open Welsh banks. It was all a pleasure he said. What did tire him and turn on corrosive guilt was Ifor, getting worse now, the paralysed giant, father, friend, brother, for whose paralysed state he was somehow directly responsible.

The children too—Liza, Kate, Michael, Christopher, Maria and the rarely referred to Jessica—were a concern. So was Elizabeth. Her illnesses, her reliance on prescribed drugs, her obsessive demands for his presence. And yet, he still declared he loved her and the heavy odds, at this stage, were that he had been faithful to her. This meant denying a philandering nature or compulsion which he had cultivated since the age of eighteen. Quite unacceptable in these times but with its vivid place in history and no doubt in biology—Burton was a lover of many women, and he had rejected all that in the marriage with Elizabeth. Monogamy was the penalty he exacted from himself for the crime of leaving Kate and Jessica and Sybil. And he had been as good as his word for about ten years now. At this stage in his life he could have been thwarting his nature.

There was the drink—but he appeared to have some control over that. It was crude. Stop-go. But it seemed to be working and the medical check-ups were not unduly worried about that. There was more worry about the arthritis, the gout, the painful and crippling seizures in his neck and back. Pills, or so he thought, would see to that.

He had surrounded himself with an entourage—and been further surrounded by Elizabeth's entourage—to an extent which he did not really appreciate. He was too interested in reading the next book. But the pulse of gossip, information, peer-group fun, small opportunities, good talk—all that was beyond the thorn stockade of the self-perpetuating entourage. Never alone.

He was never a whinger. The problems he grappled with were always real—love, family, sex, poetry, drink, money, security; a career was something he cared little about. He was increasingly drawn to the fascination of self-destruction and increasingly obsessed by the unthinkable notion of death. Almost without exception, whoever met him, whatever gender, class, race or level of intelligence, found in him a man they could love, admire or respect. He was still his own man, still a one-off. But the sands in this particular hourglass were beginning to run out.

The 1972 Notebooks begin in Arizona, where he has gone with Elizabeth to look after her mother, Sarah. Sarah is ill again and the family gathers around to set her on her feet and put her into society. Burton had expected a true democratic American town. He admired the openness and republicanism of the USA. He was very quickly disillusioned.

> (Jan. 28) Last night I had an unique experience—for me that is. I went to have dinner with the Ws in the swankest country club in the area, or the richest, or both. However,

the uniqueness was that I discovered towards the end of the dinner that the club was restricted to Gentiles only. NO JEWS ALLOWED. Mary Frances told me so. She said that they, the club, had told them, the Jews, that there are just too many of you and before long you'll be running the place so why don't you form a club of your own. I was flabbergasted. I shld have immediately announced this to the rest of the family and we wld have undoubtedly swept out en masse. However I thought of Sarah and that the only reason why we were dining with the Ws was to get her out as easily and unrancorously as possible, but I simply couldn't sit there and say nothing. She promptly gave me an opportunity to salvage my conscience as she said with twinkling glee, "And do you know, Richard, they ran into financial difficulties and had to appeal to us Gentiles for help. What about that!" I swooped. "How strange to hear that," I said. "Our lot doesn't usually get into that kind of difficulty." She took the blow with an air of not knowing quite whether I was making a little British joke or not. I now laid it on. "Elizabeth, as you obviously don't know, is a convert to Judaism and our daughter Liza is of course a Jewess and my grandfather was a Jew." She was helpless. She said "Yes" but it had several additional vowels in it, impossible to write down but it was something like "Yeaaeahowes."

To re-iterate here the platitudinous idiocies of their conversation would be tedious. E. and I and Howard and Mara had gone there knowing what to expect but so exactly did they react to any given suggestion that they were little different from Pavlovian dogs. One rang the bell of this idea and they tolled the precisely expected answer. To the very anticipated word. We all agreed afterwards that they were so brain-washed that nothing, no argument, no appeal to intelligence, cld possibly change them. For instance, and only one example will I give, W. said that the thing that had made this country great was that it was a melting pot for all the peoples of the world. Yawn. Yawn. But they had just said that Jews were not allowed in their club! There was therefore absolutely no point in asking about the blacks.

We reduced ourselves to hysteria in the course of the post mortem in our suite but under it all we were sick at heart.

They move on to Beverly Hills, taking with them Elizabeth's brother Howard and his wife Mara. The celebrities continue to drop by and he judges even the best of them astringently.

(Jan. 29) At one time Paul Newman came in. Paul is what I call a real actor. A nice man, extraordinarily youthful looking with a complexion so peaches and cream that at first I thought he had make-up on. Every move he makes is like one practising—with no need to look any more— in front of a mirror. I don't mean that unkindly. He doesn't even know he's doing it. He is a keep-fit fanatic and my God the results are remarkable. He must be at least my age and yet with a little care around the eyes and a dye-job on the hair he could still pass for 24 or so. I would hate to look like him. I did once before acne re-mapped my face and I hated it. I abhor mere prettiness.

Burton is gearing up for Hungary where he is to play the title part in *Bluebeard*. The director was Edward Dmytryk whose films included *The Caine Mutiny* and *The Young Lions*. Burton had previously described his work as "tapering off into mediocrity." The eight "victims" of *Bluebeard* included Raquel Welch, Virna Lisi, Nathalie Delon and Joey Hetherton. It was to be made in and around Budapest and although Burton's financial deal was not a record breaker, it was not bad either: were the film to succeed he would reap a fortune. He complains that ". . . it is impossible to find any literature on modern Hungary . . . I can't believe there is so little stuff about a famous modern state. Lack of interest must be the answer." He stocks up on paperbacks and stalks the intention to cut down on smoking (he is on about 100 a day). Both of them are pleased to read that they are still very comfortably placed in what he calls "the Top Ten Box-Office things." More anticipation of Hungary: more paperbacks.

(Feb. 6) Tomorrow to Hungary. I am looking forward to it with excitement. The very name Budapest smacks of romance and tragedy and wild Magyar music. It cannot, simply cannot be dull, regardless of friends' warnings that it is the most depressing capital in Europe. I shall start out, at least, refusing to be talked into disliking it before I find out for myself. And again the Communist experiment is eternally fascinating. There must be some alternative to the idiocy and rat-race murderousness of "democracy" and I'm pretty sure that Communism is not it but it is different so one more look at one more Communist country.

I went to the Lion bookshop yesterday and bought yet another pile of books for the ten-week stay in Buda and Pest. Cadogan's diaries, A. L. Rowse's two vols, *The Early Churchills* and *The Later Churchills*, Solzhenitsyn's *Full Circle, Chosen Words* by Ivor Brown. Two dual-language Penguins on Mallarmé and French poetry of the 19th Century. A book by Auberon Waugh—son of Evelyn. Isaac Deutscher, *Red China, Russia and the USA*—I think it's called. A Hungarian grammar. And a handful of thrillers. So we should have more than enough to get through ten weeks.

Before he goes he writes at some length about the great Hungarian film producer and entrepreneur—Alexander Korda.

(Feb. 7) As for Hungarians, the only ones I have consciously known have been successful exiles—George Tabori and he who gave me his word and a contract for £100 per week while I was still slogging away in the theatre—the incomparable Alex Korda. When I think of Hungarians I emblematise them in the person of that great scoundrel of ineffable charm, huge generosity and large lies, of living grandiosely beyond his means, of telling me of poverty in Paris where he lived at one time—he solemnly assured me—on one gigantic cake sent him by his mother, for 6 weeks. When, out of the blue, I was invited to have lunch with him at 146 Piccadilly, which turned out not to be lunch at all but coffee and cigars, and he said with his growling Hoongarrian English "Would you like to work with me?" I stammered a sort of "Yes, but of course I have to . . ." "It will hardly inconvenience your stage career. In fact I insist that the theatre must come first. I am going to give you £100 a week for five years. I have never seen you act but I have heard from a friend or two that you are going to be an actor of importance. My friend and colleague Laurence Olivier told me that you are a natural aristocrat & now that I have seen you I know that he is right. I am therefore investing £5000 on a belief that Olivier and I are right. So learn all you can in the theatre. Try not to get in long runs, do as many plays as you can. Go to Stratford. Buy a car, get your wife a mink. Enjoy yourself." I was in a daze of delight. I was about 24— no, 23 yrs old—and the most I'd ever earned was £12 a week. "Sign this," he said, indicating one sheet of paper with only one side worded. I began to read it. "Good," he said, "never sign any paper you haven't read and understood." It said roughly that I was to be available to Sir Alexander Korda for a maximum of 12 weeks a year at *my* convenience, for a maximum of 5 years during which time—if I did a film for anyone else—I was to get my usual 5000 plus half of whatever price the other film company were prepared to pay. The other half was to go to Korda's company "London Films." I danced down Piccadilly to the nearest pub and phone. I called home and told Syb. I called Stanley Baker. I told the publican—a complete stranger. I called Ifor through Dai John Philips. When the pub closed at 3, I suppose it was, I took a taxi, undreamt of extravagance, to a club near the BBC where I was sure that there would be a few congenial well-wishing friends. To cap it all the late and beloved Dylan was there and the even later and equally beloved Louis MacNeice both of them well on the way to stupefaction. Vague figures loomed out of the haze of smoke and alcohol and I had pretty well run through my first week's salary by the time I arrived home in the little hours.

This was an astonishing step forward. Many young actors, some of them good like Dirk Bogarde, Donald Houston, Andrew Crawford, Jimmy Granger—I think—and Jean Simmons were under horrible contracts to the Rank Organisation but I was under contract to Sir Alexander

Korda and his other contract actors were Olivier, Vivien Leigh, Ralph Richardson and a host of other giant names. A very much posher and distinguished lot than the Rank "stable." In the end I never did do a film for Alex. He loaned me out to Emlyn Williams and Tolly de Grunwald [for *The Last Days of Dolwyn*] and then to Fox for a film called *My Cousin Rachel* with Olivia de Havilland as my leading lady. I was still agent-less (unless one considers Korda as my agent) and Fox offered me 50,000 dollars. I had told Syb and the family that I was going to stick out for 7000 pounds. When the Fox representative, whose name was oddly enough Freddie Fox, offered me roughly twice what I was so ruthlessly determined to hold out for I agreed at once. I must confess to lying about it all to my friends and saying that I had fought them every inch of the way to get that enormous sum. To ice the cake Korda said that he was not going to take his cut but that I should go out and buy a Rolls-Bentley immediately. I bought a Mark 8 Jaguar instead.

There was more to come. The man who insisted I played in the film was George Cukor, an infinitely wicked and lovable man as well as being, at his best, one of the very fine directors. He had seen me and was seeing me in a play of Lillian Hellman's, *Montserrat*. I didn't think much of the book or the script but I thought a lot of Cukor and my leading lady was, he assured me, to be either Garbo (who told me mendaciously but charmingly some months later, having seen the film, that she wld have done it had she known I was so good) or Vivien. So I left with Syb and her brother Dai Mogs—just down from Cambridge with a deliberately indifferent degree—who was supposed to be my secretary tho' I ended up answering not only my own post but his too—on the *Queen Mary* First Class and all found.

By the time we got to NY 5½ days later Cukor had been either fired or had withdrawn (I never did find out which) and my leading lady was Olivia de Havilland who had just won two Oscars in three years and was, in the language of Hollywood, "hot, hot, hot." She was married to a very eccentric man, very forgettable. I was also told by Zanuck's hatchet man—one of the baldest men I've ever seen—Lew Schreiber—that Miss de Havilland would not permit me to have co-starring billing with her. I didn't mind about the billing a bit and to this day I have never cared about it but I did get the impression, later confirmed, that they were hoping I wld do a Rex Harrison and arrogantly walk out as they wanted somebody else, or Miss de Havilland wanted somebody else—I seem to remember it was Greg Peck—to play my part. I said somewhat testily to Schreiber that I had worked with the greatest living actors and actresses and they hadn't fussed about billing. So I stayed but with a little murder in my heart for Miss de H. The film, for some forgotten reason, was delayed for 7 weeks and we lived in a small—large to us—duplex apartment on Charleville Boulevard. It was during those seven weeks that I started the hunt for Jean [Simmons]. It didn't take long. What has this to do with Hungary? Well, eventually it will lead back to the lovable larcenous Sir Alex Korda. (To be continued.)

He continued it the next day. The autobiography was afoot.

(Feb. 8) But back to Korda. As a result of the enormous success of the *Rachel* film and the one following it—a terrible thing called *The Robe*—Fox offered me a million dollars for 7 years for 7 films. It was only later that I found out that in addition to paying me a million they had—forced to because I was still under contract to Korda—paid him a ½ million on the side. A few years later, after I'd found this out, I went to have dinner with Alex in Millionaire's Row, to which he had moved after living for years at Claridges, taking his new wife with him. His brother had found a Canaletto and when I admired it Alex said, "Enjoy it, my boy, you paid for it."

Once again, Burton's hindsight view is beguiling, for what he now considers important. It was all a breeze, he says. A golden age. He was fortune's child. Written in that way in this later period it has the tone of most references to a golden age—the past is seen as a time of innocence, ease and glory. This usually signals dissatisfaction with the present and a longing to overturn it and somehow find a way through the needle's eye of time to a future as glowing as that seductive past.

They established themselves in the presidential suite at the Intercontinental in Budapest and domestic life stakes out its claims. There is a time for comedy and laughter. Bluebeard beckons.

> (Feb. 9) Both E. and I did our going to bed exercises last night together. It is difficult to keep a straight face when she is doing her numbers as she goes at it with a solemn ferocity which is hilarious. It is especially droll when we do running on the spot as she has to hold her breasts— one hand on each—for firm as they are, really like a 30 yr old's more than a nearly 40 year old's, they are pretty big and the resultant wiggle-waggle would be pretty odd as well as bad for her. It's a very fetching sight and were it open to the public would fetch a lot of people. Like 10 million.
>
> Rather than do a double-crostic or *The Times* crossword yesterday I started out on the Hungarian language. It is the kind of potted grammar which I adore, somewhat like "Hugo's" grammars, which have little vocabs and exercises at the end of each lesson with the answers in the back half, third, of the volume. And all my answers were right. Since it is neither a Slav or Romance language the acquisition of the vocab alone is a formidable task. It has, the vocab, no association with anything I know.

Elizabeth sleeps an immense amount and is said to have gone out of the hotel only once in four weeks. Burton takes the part seriously.

> (Feb. 11) I had forgotten what an enormous part and opportunity it is and gives. Also I've got to learn to act this kind of Maria in the Red Barn melodrama. It has to be done with immense tongue in cheek. I try to remember how the master—whassisname—Vincent Price plays it. Plays that kind of thing, I mean. Even voiced, measured in speech, purposeful in movement with the occasional violence in voice and movement. Must be funny serious. Shall know the minute I begin how to do it I hope. I go

in today for the first scene rehearsal. But don't shoot until
tomorrow.

The trouble was that Richard had only fleetingly seen "the master
—whassisname—Vincent Price." He saw so few movies that when
he went to Hollywood he moved in a swarm of totally strange faces
and called everyone "luv" to take the sting out of his complete lack
of knowledge. Michael Hordern has pointed out that Richard "was
no good at wearing a wig": by which, of course, he meant that all
the clever and convincing details which go into "character" roles
—over and above the talent—were simply not in his range. So it
would prove here. "Whassisname" could have done it well: Richard
could not escape that bold heroic look, aspect, feel, which crashed
through his make-up and then through the lens. Still, he is
conscientious—Dmytryk, like so many other directors, cameramen,
lighting men, props men, picks out that willing characteristic and
praises it. He tries to build up the part of the mad, rich Count who
takes one beautiful woman after another and then kills her because
she falls short of his ideal. He is no good at it: no Burton in it?

Norman Parkinson arrives to photograph Elizabeth. After dis-
trusting him, Burton comes to admire his skill—and it prompts
thoughts of *anno domini*.

(Feb. 14) Saw last night many lovely snaps of E. taken
by Norman Parkinson who turns out to be a very amusing
and nice man and, indeed, of the scores of photographs,
only about 5 or 6 made E.s face look a little full. He must
be used again. Those old aristos—Beaton & Parkinson,
really know what they're doing. I suddenly realised the
difference in quality between a Parkinson or a Beaton and
the others. Not a brush of touch-up is necessary. Partly
by his lighting and mostly from E.'s having lost 8 lbs or
so I would say, the fullness of the chin—the under-chin
is never obtrusive.

He didn't make me look very fetching but I gather that
he's not very good with gents. Anyway I've never been
—at least not for 20 yrs or so—and am never likely to
be the pin-up type. Too many excrescences and twisted
bones. My hair is at last getting very thin though it still
covers my whole scalp but when wet, soaking wet, one

can see its barren-ness. Since it's such a bore to have Ron pencil in lines all over the place I think I might one of these days try one of those transplants. It won't be like those idiots who are really bald and on whom it is still obvious and I only need a few strands around about the crown of the head. I don't think however that I will get me a face lift like that abject [. . . . . . .] who not only admits to it but it makes him look like one half of a naked ass-hole.

Meanwhile he is still holding hard to his health. *And* "I am still as purely non-alcoholic as the scion of two AAs." He has a hard job claiming any sustained sleep but the film rolls on: he plays the organ, a falcon flies around, a kitten will be killed—Elizabeth gets into a state in case the kitten really *is* killed. The writer Wolf Mankowitz turns up to work some more on the still unfinished *Tito* and Burton relishes his company.

(Feb. 20) He was at his most engagingly Cockney and obviously adored Elizabeth who reciprocated and said, "Now that's the kind of man I could love if you weren't around, I adore him." Bloody daft thing to say, I said, hurting. But good taste all the same, I thought. There is always an oddity about people's preferences in types. I've always lusted for medium-height dark-haired Jewesses, or those who could be first racial cousins. Elizabeth has always fancied Jews, period. She seems to have a rapport with them which she doesn't have with the ordinary Anglo-Saxon. She and Wolf could obviously have talked all night. And about all kinds of things. They touched lightly on Wedgwood for instance last night and later, when I wasn't there, on what sort of securities there shld be made against malignant gate-crashers at next weekend's parties, etc. And it has nothing to do—in E.'s case—with male beauty, for Wolf is a mess, about my height with a great pendulous belly that is big enough to turn after the rest of his body has turned, double chinned, grubby looking without being unclean. But his mind is astringent. There is no shit about him & he is a Renaissance man. He opens shops to sell Wedgwood, having first made himself an expert on the subject, writing a lavishly illustrated book to prove his own provenance as an expert and then—as he just has—sold the shops owned by his sister and himself for half a million nicker, tax-free capital fackin' gain. "And who to, d'yer think? Fackin' Wedgwood that's who." He has now either started or resurrected a small private printing press in Cork or Dublin—anyway in Eire somewhere—and his first publication is a book of his own poems. Now he wants me to write for them. "Anything," he says, "rondeaux, frigging triolets, belles lettres, the story of your life, graffiti, anything you like, old mate." He is superlatively intelligent with a considerable smattering of the poet about him.

But all this is as a preamble to Elizabeth's Fortieth Birthday Party.

There were cynical views of the party: there always were about everything the Burtons did. It was said that Elizabeth's career was in such a perilous downward spiral that she needed to show that she could pull the publicity. If this was the case, she succeeded—the newspapers were loaded with photographs of the family (Jenkins) and the Famous (Princess Grace, Ringo Starr, Michael Caine, David Niven, Susannah York, Stephen Spender) taking their pre-paid tickets to Budapest. Journalists went there too and the Hungarian prose wound back around the gossip columns of the world. It was said that Elizabeth feared the pull and the strain of eight leading *Bluebeard* ladies on her husband and in the light of subsequent events this may also be true. Up until then, however, Burton had remained sober and, from the evidence, loyal. Nevertheless, when the party list grew too long, Elizabeth decided to "disinvite the *Bluebeard* broads." Raquel Welch came anyway. It is more likely that Elizabeth just wanted to have a party. She loved all parties, all anniversaries, name-days, birthdays, Christmas Days, anything that brought the world back to the MGM nursery. And besides, there were the presents.

Two hundred invitations left the capital of Hungary.

We would love you to come to Budapest as our guest for the weekend of 26 and 27 February to help me celebrate my being 40 Birthday STOP The hotel is very Hilton but there are some fun places to go STOP Dress slacks for

Saturday night in some dark cellar and something gay and pretty for Sunday night STOP Dark glasses for languorous in between STOP Lot of love Elizabeth and Richard STOP P.S. Could you RSVP as soon as possible to Intercontinental Hotel Budapest so I know how many rooms to book.

After the telegrams went off, Richard wanted a follow-up to insist "NO GIFTS." "But I invited Bulgari," (the jeweller) said Elizabeth.

Richard gave her a $50,000 heart-shaped diamond, assuring her of everlasting love. It was Indian, seventeenth century, designed by the man who built the Taj Mahal—"I would have liked to have bought the Taj Mahal for Elizabeth, but it would have cost too much to transport it." Never one to miss a shot at the grandiose in public.

Dmytryk described it as the best party he had ever been to. The Welsh seemed to have taken it over, the family, led by the actor Victor Spinetti, retreating to the top floor early in the morning for the "real party": singing.

The only rub came from Alan Williams, novelist son of Emlyn, brother of Richard's great friend and companion, Brook. Alan Williams had written about the Hungarian revolution and began to question Elizabeth on her attitude to that event: further he criticised her for her lack of interest in contemporary Hungary. He then appears to have challenged a sober Burton who avoided unpleasantness; but he persisted and Bob Wilson and Gaston the chauffeur chucked him out. Nevertheless, his point had been made and it was reported back to the London press, including his description of the new forty-year-old as "a beautiful doughnut covered in diamonds and paste." Emlyn Williams spent the next day walking moodily by the Danube with his son: letters were written; Richard let it pass. It was at the same party that Francis Warner offered him an honorary fellowship to teach at St. Peter's, Oxford. Here too that Dmytryk observed a beautiful young woman who had talked with Burton, apparently casually, for about ten minutes, tear across the room and say, "He loves me." "There is no doubt he had this quite phenomenal effect," says Dmytryk, an experienced man. "He would talk to a girl for a few minutes and she would be convinced he had fallen in love with her or would very soon." Whatever the case, they fell for him. "I am," Burton admitted, once, laughing and undercutting his own rare immodesty, "considered to be sexually attractive." For Burton, to love many women was not a disease—as many psychiatrists insist: it was a delight—as many women agreed. The following day, at a brunch, Burton promised to give the equivalent of the price of the party to a good cause. True to his word, on July 8th, 1972, he gave $45,000 to Peter Ustinov, roving ambassador for UNICEF.

The party took up a couple of pages in his Notebooks.

(Feb. 26) A day of enormous excitement for all. Some 80 odd or so people arrived at various times of the day for the big week-end. Chief pleasures were of course the families—mine and Elizabeth's or should I say rather ours and ours. The next were Grace who again qualified for five stars and Nevill Coghill and Spender and Mrs. Ladas and Simon and Sheran. What exquisite manners they all have in their very different ways. I taught all the girls to curtsey and all the lads how to do a proper hand-shake with Royalty and each by each and one by one they all performed admirably. We had a cocktail party in our suite—hastily re-arranged for the purpose—which went with a swing—at least until the last reluctant group left at about mid-night with Howard Mara and the kids staying until the end, as it was the only chance we had of talking properly to them. I had several clec-clecs with my lot in one of their rooms. I took wee Maria along—not so wee, she is a very tall girl—and introduced her to her 1000s of heretofore unknown and un-met aunts and uncles and, completely forgetting, we went babbling on in Welsh until we suddenly all realised that Maria was completely be-wildered. She had been told by me of course many times that certain percentages of Welshmen spoke a tongue en-tirely alien to English but I don't think, until she heard us all at it last night, that she realised quite how alien it actually was. I think that vaguely she thought it was the equivalent of an Irish brogue or a Highland Scottish. The family adored her of course because she looked so like Kate. In fact Will Cross-eyes and a couple of the others thought she was Kate. There is superficially a fleeting resemblance. Round face, cherubic cheeks, same colour-ing. The family were in tremendous form—Tom at 71 being the dynamo. The flight was as smooth as silk and

was a particular thrill for Verdun who had, *to my astonishment*, never been in an aeroplane in his life and a jet
at that. That alone has been sufficient excitement for him.
They, with their still retained sense of wonder, were
bowled over by everything. The very bathrooms, the fact
that there was a bar in each room, the view of the legendary
Danube, the meetings with Elizabeth and of course Grace
were high points. Both E. and Grace behaved superbly.
E. is down to 128–9 lbs and is going to look her usual
wonder tonight and tomorrow. Little Mickey Caine had
flown from LA with one of his exquisite "birds," a Marlon
Brando Asiatic as usual, and How. and Mar. and my lovely
[Margaret] Leighton and the equally lovely Chris and Al-
leyn had come almost exactly halfway around the world
and are going to be a trifle jet-lagged today and tomorrow
I wld guess but the parties will keep them going. Victor
Spinetti and a friend were, are here, and Ringo and wife
and Susannah York and Mick and Liz & Brook and
Grace's lady-in-waiting, a certain Mme Aurelli, Professor
Warner and Doris Brynner and Bettina and Marie Lou
Tolo (one of the girls in the film), Yves le Tourneur and
wife, Vanhattan of Van Cleef—Cartiers, NY, I mean—
Hebe Dorsey, Vicky Berkeley complete with Ron, Billy
Williams and wife (Williams is the great cameraman who
shot *Zee & Co*) and our very own Chris and Liza who
gave me thunderous goodnight kisses several to each side
of the face and Kurt Frings, John Springer and too many
to recount them all. Frings went into business as usual
and after extracting a promise from me that I wld not
throw him into the Danube said that the Lerner-Loewe-
Donen consortium were still desperate for me to play *Little
Prince*. They are all so abject in this mishandling of me
that I said I wld think about it. He also thinks that E. shld
postpone *Nightwatch* in favour of another film called *Twig*
for which she is "on my mother's life bound to win an
Oscar" and that I really shld do the *Little Prince* for now
they were beating a path to my door on their knees. He
also said that representing E. and I was the greatest experience of his life and that we didn't realise what magic
our names were and that after *Zee & Co* E. is hotter or

as hot as she's ever been. And that the respect and even awe at the mention of our names in a meeting is quite extraordinary, that he has been in the business forty years and that plural noun "Burtons" is almost synonymous with Royalty. Another incidental exchange in the brouhaha of the party was that Francis Warner said that he wld like to see me alone for ½ an hour or so today and I said I wld call him as soon as I arrived back from the studio. I didn't ask what specifically about but he was obviously bursting to tell me and said something very quickly and in tone of espionage. "Fellowship at Oxford." I am intrigued. It cld be a step towards a D. Litt., which is the only honour I really covet. So I look forward to the after-shooting chat.

The world press is here in droves. From everywhere. Literally, it seems. Japanese, India, as well as every other place you can think of in the Western hemisphere. I think I will have to talk to them today—perhaps en masse. Dread of dreads and hell's damnation.

The brothers (and their women too for that matter) are agog about the Welsh rugby team of the last three yrs and have brought 16mms copies of "highlights" of the All Blacks and various other games. Shall try and watch it all this afternoon while everyone else is kipping.

(Feb. 29) The party was a huge success. That means four parties—the cocktail party when we arrived, the cellar party, the brunch party next day and the post party at night. All, apart from a nasty incident with Alan Wms at the cellar party, went without a hitch. There was a press conference which went alright. I had to do it alone. Just as well I suppose, as E. gets fractious at the slightest hint of criticism. I saw a couple of hrs of Welsh and Lions rugby on 16mms and by God they're really good . . .

I have shaved and in half an hr I shall set off to the studios. The wkend was an undoubted success. I am sure that were it not for the fantastic exuberance of my family that it wld not have been half so good. They seemed to relax everybody and nobody has ever seen Grace let her hair down—literally and figuratively—as much as she did.

Her lady-in-waiting too a Mme Aurelli was a ball of fire.
Grace confesses that she never knew she had it in her.
She danced wild Hungarian dances and at one time as I
was sitting in a booth with Frankie Howerd, Susannah
York and husband and Ladas and Spender the rest of the
party swept past us doing the conga. I was goggle-eyed.
Led by the family, the whole thing passed before our eyes
with Grace in the middle of it all. Unbelievable.

And so to work.

(Mar. 1) It was nightmarish yesterday going into work
and finding, as I walked on the set, that the scene was yet
another party, dinner jackets and ladies in evening dresses.
For a second I thought I was doomed to parties for the
rest of my life. I finished a little early and went straight
home, only to find that E. had gone out to lunch an hour
before (at 4 o'clock) and did not come back until about
6. I talked to Aaron and at last we have decided to return
to England and pay our taxes. I also—they have come
back to me with a bang—finally and irrevocably turned
down *Petit Prince*.

We have asked Simon and Sheran to look for a place
near theirs and not too far from Oxford, with plenty of
ground to keep a horse or two and a large dog or two, so
that I can nip into Oxford when I feel like it.

I have to send telegrams, etc., this morning setting the
wheels turning for the return to England. We shall do our
damnedest not to winter there tho' we shall pay the taxes.

This was one of the several indications that Burton's restlessness
was now over. He had spent eight or ten years storing up the finances
against any eventuality—now, he decided, he could live the life he
wanted. Be near Oxford and its libraries: teach now and then. Be
near Stratford and London. Attempt *King Lear*. Work with the new
theatre directors. Meet the old pals every Sunday down at the village
pub. Do the occasional movie. Talk. It was a dream which at last
seemed possible of fulfilment. He had waited long enough for it.
On March 15th it was their eighth wedding anniversary. ''By some
standards it is nothing. By others it's a monumental achievement.

During that time too we have the rare distinction—in our business — of having been faithful to each other.'' But the next entry is the last in the Notebooks for eight years, and the blackest.

Ifor died.

Richard had longed for this, dreaded it, willed it away and lived with it ever since the night that Ifor had stumbled over to the house from the Café de la Gare and slipped on the grille, breaking his neck. Richard had allowed him to go alone: perhaps in a way— unconsciously—he had expected Ifor to go, rather in the manner of a major-domo. Whatever it was, in the enormous, insatiable over-protectiveness he felt towards his family and friends, he had been in some manner responsible. More than that. He loved Ifor. Ifor had replaced Dic: given him the envied bicycle; been the hard man of the mines, of the local rugby team, loved poetry, loved only Gwen. Richard and Elizabeth went straight back to London and Wales and when they returned he was a different man. Dmytryk reports on him growing older and more desperate by the week. He had been sober: now he took to vengeful drinking. The day began at 8 a.m. with a very large vodka and orange juice, after which Bob the dresser and Gaston the chauffeur carried him—upright between them—from the Rolls to his dressing room. The devil which he had fought so hard against—losing often enough in drink but still in the ring; winning in fidelity; steady in building up the security for all his dependants; selfless in going for what bolstered Elizabeth—that devil was now out and on the loose. He was in pain. Ifor was dead and the game was up.

When a young actress romped too intensely with Burton on the set and he responded, Elizabeth—scenting his mood instantly— delivered what she referred to as a ''knuckle sandwich'' at the actress right there on the set. She was not quick enough the next time, as Hollis Alpert related. Burton was to do a night shot walking Nathalie Delon down a street. So he did. Around the corner. The crew waited for him to reappear. Dmytryk sent the second assistant. No Burton. No Nathalie. Gaston the chauffeur had been waiting with the Rolls and off they went. No shooting the next day either. Elizabeth took revenge by flying to Rome to have a 'quiet dinner' with Onassis who arrived without Jackie. The quiet dinner turned into a brawl between twenty-seven paparazzi, the restaurant staff and the Rome police. Elizabeth and Ari left at dawn in separate cars to separate hotels. Back in her bedroom Elizabeth picked up the phone, rang the Intercontinental in Budapest and screamed, "Get that woman out of my bed!" "How did she know?" Burton asked Dmytryk the next day. "Don't you realise that you are surrounded by her agents?" the wise old bird replied, amazed at the Welshman's naivety.

The change in Burton was cataclysmic. Burton and Taylor went to the British Embassy for a grand and official dinner. Burton insulted two ambassadors and their wives, swore at his hosts, condemned all privilege and walked out. Elizabeth gamely stayed on and talked about her operations and her children. He was out of control. Even when Kate and Liza made a pact and went to plead with him to give up the booze he could do no more than promise, weep, break his promise and reach for the bottle. Ifor's death had unhinged him. Just as he was poised to come home, to live the life he truly wanted to live—in the English countryside with old pals, the Bodleian Library nearby in Oxford, the London theatre, a movie. All abandoned! His deep and furious affair with self-destruction was under way. Ifor's death had killed too big a part of him. He was adrift.

22
"The Game's Up"

The life of Richard Burton between 1973 and 1975 is that of a man with his foot jammed on the accelerator going as fast as it is possible to go. Occasionally he switches to the brake, slams down on that and uses the dazed crashed pause to regroup. He went like a hornet out of hell and ended up being carried into hospital and given two weeks to live. The devil was driving him. He was breaking up with Elizabeth. But just as their coming together had progressed in a series of melodramas, ultimatums, spaces of illusory calm and emotional earthquakes, so their separation shuddered with similar seismic forces.

It began quietly enough. Soon after Budapest they borrowed Simon and Sheran Hornby's Oxfordshire home at Pusey and for a few weeks Richard achieved one of the great ambitions of his life. He taught literature at Oxford to undergraduates. All accounts agree that he was a quirky but inspiring teacher. Had Philip Burton had the educational bug only, and not harboured the theatrical dream, perhaps a don is what Richard would have become just like other bright scholarship boys and . . . Ifor would not have died. But the cosy English long-term future was off. His restlessness was only controllable in the anaesthetic of alcohol.

He went to Yugoslavia to finish the film on Tito and was drunk much of the time. Then he decided he had to do something for Harlech Television. His name had helped to get them the franchise—i.e. the right to broadcast in Wales and collect the mo-

nopoly advertising revenue for doing so—and he had promised that
some day he would do something. However, it was well enough
known in the trade that not all franchise promises would be kept
and very few believed or were even unduly bothered that the Burtons
might in the fulness of time find it just too tricky to do the dramas
they had said they would do. But he felt obliged. His sense of
obligation was as vast as his reservoir of guilt. Fed by the same
springs.

Just as they came together on a film—*Cleopatra*—which staked
out their private and their public roles plainly and juicily, so the
first truly public signs of the collapse of the famous marriage which
meant life and death to the couple themselves showed in the far too
aptly titled *Divorce His, Divorce Hers*—two seventy-five-minute
films about the break-up of a marriage, first from his point of view
and then hers.

John Osborne wrote the original scripts. Osborne was one of the
few contemporary playwrights known to Burton who admired him
greatly. The plan to move to England had now evaporated and
Osborne was asked to "set" the action worldwide—on the *Kalizma*,
in Rome, Acapulco, anywhere to save on tax. Osborne however
wrote the script as he saw it and it is a measure of Burton's lack of
stability and sense of what was good for him at that time that he
rejected it. John Hopkins, an extremely good playwright whose
reputation had been made in television, rewrote it. His version fitted
in with the tax imperatives.

Elizabeth was making *Nightwatch*, another of her sadly deteriorating movies, and it was overrunning. Waris Hussein, the young
director of *Divorce*, who thought that he would have a few weeks
with her, was told most bluntly that he would be lucky to get a few
days as she (British Citizen) had to leave the island or be caught
for £2 million taxes. Ifor's death saw them back into old and worn
patterns which would no longer hold.

Hussein gave a detailed interview to Paul Ferris in which he
described the terrible rows that Burton and Taylor were having—
she taunting him about his supposed excellence as a stage actor, he
retorting in kind on her film performances—all done over long,
liquid lunches while the costly unit waited. Hussein was acute and
generous. His first sentence encapsulates a great deal. "I think a
lot of what happened was due to their own personal unhappiness,"
he said. Certainly his version, and the catty account of Carrie Nye

(a supporting actress) point out a new unprofessionalism in Burton. He came and left as he felt like it. He ignored the director. He behaved uniquely badly. Hussein is now sympathetic. He says as if addressing Burton, "I'm sorry I didn't get to know you better. I'm sorry for what happened. Because I admire Burton." He describes an excellent week's shooting in Rome with Burton alone and almost sober. Elizabeth arrives in police-escorted, paparazzi-boggling, headlight-flashing splendour at a night shoot and says, "Just ignore me, Waris." Burton takes to the bottle and a simple walk down the street takes for ever. The death of Ifor appears to have released the demon against Elizabeth. Yet still he tried. And friends like Spinetti turning up could report that everything was just fine. No problems. The two *Divorce* films were poor and they were heavily panned. "A matched pair of thrilling disasters" (*Time*). "Holds all the joy of standing by at an autopsy" (*Variety*). Pointless to say that there were some good moments—as Hussein himself observed, the quiet moments; or that there was real tenderness now and then and anguish: it did not matter, it did not fit in: the Burton–Taylor act was on the skid—official.

Burton said, "Once I started being attracted to other women, I knew—the game's up." It was the brief truth. What he saw as the sacrifice and betrayal which had gone into the marriage with Elizabeth rested on his commitment to fidelity. Now that was broken. It might be forgiven—by Ifor's death—but it had been broken. Burton had made a pact with himself—that Elizabeth would be the completion of his life. He had held nothing back. Now the contract was broken. The mixture of shame and relief, the feelings of liberty and guilt, of failure and hope were ignited. But it would have to be a slow burn. Elizabeth would not give up easily: in fact, she never gave up until his death. And he, too, was still locked in the kind of embrace which drags drowning couples to the bottom of the river bed.

The atmosphere around them was always melodramatic: bodyguards, private jets, threats of kidnapping, gangsters after the jewels, sudden illness (E.), abrupt drunkenness (R.). Their lives were still global-gypsy but without that wonderfully nourishing sense of defiance which had given them such outlaw energy in the Sixties. Now it was traipsing around, patently unnecessarily, no longer pirates on the main taking booty from the great galleons of studios and governments to hand it over to their own deserving, but snatch and grab merchants, jaded. The dogs messing up all the carpets were no longer quite as much fun. Burton's lack of interest in films compared with his reading and his writing began to be insulting: and Elizabeth was on a terrible downer.

But they had unbelievable stamina. Elizabeth had lived through traumas and stresses which on most medical and psychological counts ought to have crippled her: and, temporarily, they had done. But she always came back. Richard too took on challenges and strains which, coupled with his own physical weaknesses and the drink and the hundred fags a day, ought to have floored him. He too went on: The marriage held together in the vise of their own making.

At the beginning of 1973, Burton was in Italy doing *Massacre In Rome* with Marcello Mastroianni, a film based on the true story of German reprisals following action by the Italian Resistance. Burton played the German officer who had to deliver the executions. He played the part well—as most critics said, nearly two years later, when the film was released—but there was so little to play *with*. Again and again he is given what must have *read* like an interesting character but asked to play it in a series of speeches—the directors believing that his voice and his looks in their intensity will be enough to carry the part through. He is given no one to play off: he is given little or no incident or business to help him: he is there to *be*. In *Hammersmith* and *Trotsky*, it was the same thing and it would continue to be. The extraordinary thing was that he succeeded, manacled in monologue, in giving any convincing performances at all.

Elizabeth went on to make *Ash Wednesday* in which once again she played a super-rich woman. Burton, who was turning down easy offers, trying to set up *Don Quixote* and other projects, drinking, reading and working on pieces for magazines, declared himself disgusted with her choice of role. Another aspect of this new post-Ifor character was that the principles which he had held tenaciously as a young man began to surface again. He hated the jetsetters, he said, they took all sorts of dubious substances, they did not know the proper value of life, they were disgusting parasites, they were . . .

Hold on! This is the Richard Burton whose company owns several private jet planes; who loves to go to the Rothschilds at Ferrières and eat in bistros with the Duke and Duchess of Windsor; whose yacht is the best-known boat in the Mediterranean and whose wife can walk around like a Christmas tree, dangling baubles which were real diamonds, emeralds, rubies . . . Yet there is no doubting his sincerity. The dichotomy is not unique. The greatest Jew-scorners are often Jews; an English aristocrat can be bitchy and lethal about the aristocracy in a way which would astound an outsider; set a thief to catch a thief. Burton had delighted in the game of outbidding Onassis and Cartier, of lording it with the Rothschilds, of capping the Sinatra jet—but there is little evidence that it had been more than an adventure, even a lark. His own tastes and preferences were unaltered throughout the twelve-year cloudburst of—was it $70 million, $80 million? A good book, a good bar, a few pals, a wife he loved—prospect of a decent job. Not a little but not nouveau riche either. He was re-aligning himself, not only in his marriage but in every aspect of his life. The new eruption wanted to smother all that had moved in the decadence of his Pompeian period and bring back the cathartic cleanliness of his old fire. To be worthy of Ifor.

The ropes began to snap, the masts to splinter, the storm of their own making hit them full on. Zeffirelli, a skilled marriage-watcher, commented that Burton was now openly restless and aggressive at Elizabeth's ceaseless possessiveness. She demonstrated her affection in punches to the arm and shrill commands across a room—all excused in the name of obsessive love. But after a while, after the spell had been broken and she was no longer the fairy creature with whom you had made the Faustian pact, it could pall and dwindle into mere hen-pecking. Not very agreeable statements began to creep out of the two camps. In June 1973, Richard said, "When Elizabeth loves you, she is not happy until she owns your soul . . . And me? I must have my own way. Our natures do not inspire domestic tranquillity." Elizabeth flew to California ostensibly to see her sick mother but her meetings with old pals Peter Lawford (who was wrongly and bewilderingly dragged in as "the other man" for a week or two by the headline hatchet men now gathering around like poor relations at the dying bedside of their grand and opulent kinswoman), Laurence Harvey, ill but stalwart, Rex Kenemer and Roddy McDowall were well reported. To none of them did she conceal her distress.

Instead of joining her in California as had been planned, Richard went to stay at Aaron Frosch's guest house at Long Island, near

New York. He phoned Elizabeth and, apparently, ordered her to join him immediately. He met her at the airport but by the time they got to Long Island the quarrel between them was so bitter that she took the car back into New York where she checked into the Regency Hotel.

On July 4th—Independence Day—she issued a statement which shared the front pages with Nixon and Watergate! It had been hand-written. It was no less than the declaration of someone who knew that the world saw her as the people's dream queen: she lived up to her responsibilities. It is quite extraordinary.

> I am convinced it would be a good and constructive idea if Richard and I separated for a while. Maybe we loved each other too much. I never believed such a thing was possible. But we have been in each other's pockets constantly, never being apart but for matters of life and death, and I believe it has caused a temporary breakdown of communication. I believe with all my heart that the separation will ultimately bring us back to where we should be—and that's together. I think in a few days' time I shall return to California because my mother is there, and I have old and true friends there too. Friends are there to help each other, aren't they? Isn't that what it's all supposed to be about? If anybody reads anything lascivious into that last statement, all I can say is it must be in the eye of the reader, not in mine or my friends' or my husband's. Wish us well during this difficult time. Pray for us.

A confidential letter addressed to millions: the sort of thing any distressed woman might say to a confidante—but Taylor knew her public and delivered it to them. All the world was her confidante and she was in some way its representative in celebrity and glamour. She had shared her marriage with the public, now it received the "official" separation. In between, she fought for privacy. But she always paid her public dues and her touch was as sure as that of a great mob-orator.

The press flowed across to Long Island the next morning where Burton, vodka at the ready, chatted away quite openly, amused at the latest revelation from this mystifying woman he had married. But he seemed very happy to play the game. To Nigel Dempster, the *Daily Mail* (London) diarist, leading the pack, and to others he said, "It was bound to happen. You can't keep clapping a couple of sticks together without expecting them to blow up." . . . "I have only twenty-four hours a day. I read and write and film. Elizabeth is constantly seeking problems of one kind or another . . . she expects that I drop everything to devote myself to these problems. I cannot." That rang very true and is evidence that even here where Burton saw himself as the relaxed interviewee, he was on the case. The game was up. Never before had he publicly said anything as simple and as damaging. But "there is no question of our love and devotion to each other," he said, reaching out for the ever-available heroic mould, "I don't even consider that Elizabeth and I are separated."

Friends rallied round. Elizabeth in California was said to be seeing one Henry Wynberg, a businessman with interests in used cars. Richard made his raids into Manhattan. He also began his first serious, under doctor's orders, attempt to dry out.

Drink was given up for a week or two and he took off for Rome to stay in Sophia Loren's guest house. The explanation was that he needed to be away from the ceaseless badgering of the paparazzi: it was plausible. The lawyer announced that the drinking was over, the Burtons were reconciled; Elizabeth flew to Rome where she was to shoot *The Driver's Seat* while Richard and Sophia, under the great Italian director, Vittorio de Sica, would film *The Voyage*.

The reconciliation lasted nine days. For the first time Burton spoke of divorce. "I don't approve of divorce as a blank thing. But if two people are absolutely sick of each other or the sight of one another bores them, then they should get divorced or separated as soon as possible. That is certain." She moved out of the guest house, into the Grand Hotel.

Elizabeth was devastated and under tremendous strain. She had to begin filming the next day and did not turn up on the set until 5 p.m. She begged forgiveness of the crew and was wildly applauded. She told the producer that she thought that she would never have another day like that on which Mike Todd died. "I was wrong. Today is the second sad day of my life. I am desolate." Whatever else, her grief was serious and led her into an otherwise inexplicable spin of behaviour—most notably allowing herself to be taken up by Henry Wynberg.

When news of this reached Burton his laconic response was that he was certain that, just as one of "Mr. Wiseborg's" (he never *did* get the hang of the name) used cars, "at the psychological moment it would drop off." Elizabeth spoke several times about "using him"—ruthless in her own crying need to staunch the blood: and when she had used him up she dumped him. Losing Burton seems to have cut her off from her moorings and she veered around widely.

But her distress was real and very hard for her friends to live with. Two versions of her emotionalism at this time have her lying on his bed alongside Laurence Harvey when he was dying of terminal cancer, mumbling something about "going together." After his death she gave him a memorial service in a Californian Episcopal church which puzzled all of Harvey's other friends who knew that he was a Lithuanian Jew. She nailed Andy Warhol and told him about her life, whereupon the pop artist uttered the cry of many housewives in Middle America: "Gee. She has everything. Magic, money, beauty, intelligence. Why can't she be happy?"

She could not be happy without Burton who was on a spree of his own. Vittorio de Sica reported that Burton was "killing himself." His only love, the love of his life, declared Vittorio, was "Elizabetta." Friends became like war correspondents, sending off despatches compulsively. Anyone within twenty miles of Taylor or Burton could rely on a good spread with just such an enlightening observation.

Then a few weeks before Christmas 1973, Elizabeth rang him up and is reported to have said that she did not want to live and die alone. Could she come home? She was in hospital in LA, Burton in Sicily filming. He immediately flew over the Pole. "Hello, Lumpy," he said. "Hello, Pockmarks," she replied. He chucked Wynberg out, spent a night with her in hospital and wheeled her out, on to the plane and back first to Italy and then to Puerto Vallarta for Christmas, 1973. Another declaration hit the cuttings. "I believe in Santa Claus," said Elizabeth. And, clearly heartfelt, this would be the happiest Christmas of her entire life. It is sometimes difficult but important to accept that beneath the baby language there is a real, mature and unique woman making serious comments on her life.

On NBC TV, John Chancellor announced to his fellow citizens

in the USA, ''Elizabeth Taylor and Richard Burton are reconciled permanently . . . as opposed to temporarily.''

Meanwhile Elizabeth was convinced that Richard had had an affair with Sophia Loren. Her instinct was unbudgeable despite the denials of both Richard and Sophia. His case was not altogether helped by an article on Sophia he was writing (for the *Ladies Home Journal*) which contained phrases such as ''as beautiful as erotic dreams.'' Oddly, Philip Burton (a strict non-gossip) refers to it in his unpublished manuscript. He is writing of the time when he and Richard got together again (after a very long time: another reaching back to the roots), when Burton was on one of his lightning trips to New York in autumn 1973.

Richard was in the Regency Hotel. I called him there; I said I wouldn't pester him with calls—I knew how much he disliked using the phone—but looked forward to hearing that he was coming down to see me. He did call me a few days later but to tell me of his latest dilemma resulting from an involvement with Sophia Loren; he might be leaving for Rome in a few days' time. Aaron called me the following day and suggested that Richard was exaggerating his dilemma. That was on a Saturday. On the Monday Richard called; he was not going to Rome; instead, he was coming to see me the following day. But he didn't come; he couldn't; the doctor said he shouldn't travel because he had intestinal 'flu. On the Friday I went to New York, and the doctor reassured me about Richard. He certainly looked well but had some difficulty in walking. Still, he decided to come back to Asbury Park with me and stay until the Sunday evening.

There followed a wonderful weekend in which we made up for a backlog of years of needed conversation. I think it helped him; I was told later that he was ''a different man'' after the weekend. Although it was painful for him to walk, he insisted on coming out with me a few times for a brief walk. An amusing episode happened on one of our excursions. We were sitting on a bench at the unfrequented end of the boardwalk. A small group of young teenage boys came by. One of them recognised

Richard and, very tentatively, came over to speak to him. When he was told that he was indeed speaking to Richard Burton he became starry-eyed and stammered. Richard dealt with him delightfully and ended by giving him a twenty-dollar bill. When the boy had gone with his friends, all of them repeatedly looking back, Richard said with a smile, "His mother will never believe it, and as for the twenty-dollars. . . !"

On the Saturday we called Elizabeth who was in Rome. It was not an easy conversation and got nowhere. I felt the situation was hopeless. My sympathy was with her when Richard left me on the Sunday evening because in the car which came to fetch him was a pleasant and pretty young actress. I felt protective towards her too because she was so vulnerable. But, in spite of all, it had been a very worthwhile weekend. I was not surprised to hear on the following Wednesday that Richard had flown to Montana for solitude, but he was soon back in New York on his way to Italy. I went to see him, but failed to see him alone. I felt his condition had deteriorated, both physically and psychologically, and I was depressed by this. I longed to have a private hour with him, but it was not to be. (Incidentally, he gave me a new typewriter, which is being used now to type this.) The next time I heard from Aaron was that Richard was again in Quogue, and with him was another young woman, not the one I had met in Asbury Park.

During our weekend together Richard and I had had a preliminary discussion on a subject that was to occupy us for years, and only his untimely death was to prevent it from coming to fruition. It was to do a play about Shakespeare's *Richard III* as he appeared not only in the play of that name but also in the plays of *Henry VI*, Parts 2 and 3, where he is the Duke of Gloucester. His best and most revealing soliloquy is in *Henry VI*, Part 3. I was by no means the first to think of this. Colley Cibber had had the same idea in the year 1700 . . .

Nevertheless there was some time at Puerto Vallarta before Richard went to Novilla in California in 1974 to play in *The Klansman*—a story about the Ku-Klux-Klan before the Civil Rights movement. Lee Marvin co-starred. Terence Young was the director.

Burton arrived drunk and stayed drunk throughout the film. Marvin drank him a close second. Elizabeth arrived accompanied by a nurse. Elizabeth too was drinking but not too drunk to object violently when the headlines and photographs told her that Richard had bought a $480 ring for an eighteen-year-old waitress "who reminded him of Kate"—and there was another ring for a shop assistant and at least a couple of women bit players in the film . . . She left. He was on three bottles of vodka a day.

Meanwhile, as Hollis Alpert relates, a charming publicist announced to the world's press that "if you want to interview a drunk or see a drunk fall in the camellia bushes, come ahead." They did. And like an old bull, Burton was looked over. Kerwin of the *Chicago Tribune Magazine* wrote:

> His thin wrists branch out of a baggy shirt. His loose brown trousers are an old man's trousers. The once robust and forceful face has a powdery pallor. The irises are bright blue but the whites are deeply red, with only flecks of white. On his face is a dazed grin as if he's been shocked awake under those heavy lights in the midst of surgery.

Good writing. Pitiless. And then they all crowded in to crow out their stabbing picador questions. He gave them words they used only against him. "There's something to death. Something to death and something to truth and we're after them all our beautiful lives on earth. Liquor helps." Or "One drinks because life is big and it blinds you. It's grabbing at you from all directions all the time and you have to tone it down. Poetry and drink are the greatest things on earth. Besides women." They gobbled it up and pulped it out. He told them wild stories about all his family eating nothing but poached (pun intended) salmon, he spoke poetry by rote and the customers of the publicist rattled this copy around the world. One curious note is that although the director, Terence Young, was sympathetic to Burton and aware of the degree of the problem— there is a harrowing account of Burton trying to get a line right and failing again and again and all but bursting into tears—he kept him on to the end before calling a doctor. He was given no quarter by anyone. Nor is there any record that he ever asked for it. Finally he was told that he had two or three weeks to live. With typical fearlessness and gallantry he told the doctors, "I'm amused you think I can be killed off that easily."

He was taken to St. John's Hospital in Santa Monica, where he stayed in the hospital for six weeks while they fought to repair his system. Physically and emotionally he would never be the same again. While he was still convalescing Elizabeth decided on divorce. It would go through swiftly.

While he was in the middle of this fierce treatment, he called his lawyer to make sure that his immediate family, his sisters and brothers, nephews, nieces, friends, were all provided for *and* to ensure that Elizabeth would have enough cash besides the jewels and the paintings and the property! In the grounds of the hospital he met Susan Strasberg, whom at first he failed to recognise. She described him as worn, frail, an old man. He left the hospital in May. Elizabeth got the divorce in a Swiss courtroom on June 26th, 1974. I have tried everything, she said: the differences were irremediable. They had been married just over ten years. There was no doubt that she was deeply upset and was still in love with him.

Lee Marvin made the wisest and truest comment on Burton at the time of *The Klansman*. "The man's suffering," he said. "Who knows what it is?" The signs were clear enough. The physical deterioration so lovingly described by visiting hacks. The limp which some thought was part of the character he was playing but was in fact caused by acute sciatica. The bunching of the shoulders and pain in the left arm. Marvin was right: Burton was suffering.

"Who knows what it is?" The external evidence of alcoholism was treated with no sympathy even such a short time ago. Witness the publicist inviting the world's hacks to come and be in at the death. Drunkenness was something to be ashamed of, something others giggled at, something to boast of, a fool's complaint, something to endure. It was not regarded as a step towards alcoholism and alcoholism itself was seen as a serious illness only in limited medical circles. Widespread awareness was some years off. As always, Burton was ahead of his time. It was pre-Betty Ford, pre-the big health cult/craze/education. Alcoholics got neither sympathy nor understanding from the general public.

Even after he was treated, even after he had come within a few days of dying, Burton could still not deeply accept the truth of the matter. Would not. His culture and his nature were wedded to drink. Drink was the way to turn conversation into street poetry, it was the meeting place of disarmed minds and bodies, it was proof of machismo in a world where it mattered to be a man, to be proud, keep your word, not back off, have guts: and it was fun. The lows, the hangovers, the sickness—these were the bills you paid but you paid them willingly, finding even there a space for humour.

It was the recklessness of Burton's drinking which impressed his friend Lee Marvin and that came from something deep. The death of Ifor was vividly present and in the hospital the recurrent dream he had was of Ifor. Burton described how he could only sleep for stretches of about forty-five minutes and of how he would wake up to see Ifor "perfectly fit and well, in the room with me." During these weeks of treatment, Burton lost three stone.

And there was of course the split with Elizabeth. As she said in her July 4th document, they had lived in each other's pockets constantly and when they wrenched apart, the arteries snapped. Whatever he thought of her, however many times he told her—as he did—to "get out," however much he wanted her to go, he knew that in her going was a life of ten years, promises made to himself and others, promises broken to himself and others, suffering laid on her and on himself.

Beyond even that was yet another layer and this one impenetrable. He would talk of the Celtic problem of needing to drink; he would talk of the shame of wearing make-up and being an actor and the need to drink to get over that; he speculated that acting was essentially an appeal to the homosexual in a man's nature and therefore you drank for fear of that. But in the end it was inexplicable except in terms of secret self-destruction.

"Each man kills the thing he loves." There are those who say that the human organism contains an affinity for that which will destroy it. The idea of self-destruction as a poetic romantic force—as distinct from the classical, logical hemlock of Socrates—has been active in Western literature for at least the last two hundred years and it relates to the truth about some human beings. To destroy what has been so wonderfully and mysteriously wrought can become an exquisite intellectual pleasure in pain. The pleasure can come through the method chosen and in this case drink was always a pleasure to Burton. Non-drinkers can never quite appreciate the sheer unmistakable smack and relish in drinking, the drink itself.

"Each man kills the thing he loves"—and if the thing you love, as in most cases is true, is yourself? And it is also and at the same time the thing you hate? Two reasons there. Burton was a fantastical creature. A miner's body; a hero's monumental head; a fine intellect, perhaps an outstanding one; a demonic acknowledged talent; a huge capacity for competing and winning in so many of the arenas in which men prove themselves; an inordinate love of women inordinately returned; a capacity to make friends of all manner of men; an unusual, even freakish, loyalty to all who had known him or were in any way connected with those who had known him in his Welsh past; a terrible carelessness, the voice of a sorcerer. These characteristics could so easily be at war with each other. Instead of sailing in single convoy they could scatter across his brain, and he could have the nightmare of non-being restrained only by the solid matter of drink: like love; like poetry; the real thing.

He was certainly driving towards a death to compete with that of his hero, Dylan Thomas. In the hick town of Novilla, Lee Marvin saw it and knew how to deal with it. You stood aside, if you were that type of man, and let him settle it with himself. And he almost did. Compared with the intensity of this struggle, the business of whether he should have stayed in London as a theatre actor or gone into films was the merest bagatelle.

As he drew some strength together to come out of the hospital, wraith of Burton, frail man not yet fifty, a life seared in passions and giant achievements, the telephone lines and gossip columns of the world still buzzed over the divorce proceedings. Once again, as they had been so often since that first frantic dawn on *Cleopatra*, Burton–Taylor were on the front page. Why had they split up?

The old wiseacres of course pointed out that they had known all along: that it had never stood a chance anyway—she too film, he too theatre, she too glam, he too bright, she too flash, he too reckless, she a monster, he a monster—ego v. ego = no-go. But that scarcely explained almost thirteen years together.

Her friends plumped for the booze theory. He was too drunk too often and Elizabeth simply could not cope with that at the end. Nobody could. In drink he became a different man, he became George and she had long ago stopped being Martha. Add to that the return of the Don Juan in Burton and yes, indeed, the game was up.

That was certainly plausible and no doubt contained much truth. It does not wholly explain why *forever* afterwards she was on the scent or the scene whenever there seemed the slightest possibility of his availability. But in any court she had a case and he could be said to have driven her into that court against her deepest and constant wish: to be married.

His defenders would say that the burden had become intolerable. Her illnesses were an illness. He was male nurse first, last and always. If not her illnesses then her other problems—the need for prescribed drugs—or the children or the dogs or the unholy untidiness or the compulsive lateness or the shrill voice squawking "Richard! Richard!" across the set or across a room whenever he addressed anyone of the female gender, or her need—greed for presents and perks: too much to bear. After a while, suffocating. And always having to explain and then defend the long words . . . There were reasons enough on both sides.

The cut which had severed the bonds between them had been the death of Ifor. Burton's grief and guilt were immeasurable. Death was imminent and final and all the structures he had built up—the gypsy, but domestic life, the organisation of work, the move towards writing—all appeared the merest vanity. He took his revenge on death by wrecking everything around him—again a dark visceral response—and his vengeance came hardest on himself. Perhaps in some way he left Elizabeth because that was the greatest hurt he could at that time inflict upon himself and according to his own mysterious and singular religion, that alone would serve.

Even so he gave up with the greatest reluctance and he saw it as a defeat. Perhaps this was his first real defeat. The Old Vic had been stormed, as had Stratford; he had become Number One at the box-office and made fine films; writing was under way and he had taught at the University of his Jude the Obscure dreams; the most beautiful woman in the world had fallen and he had plucked diamonds like pebbles from a stream; European society invited his company and poets spoke to him as to an equal. But he had tired of holding to Elizabeth: tired perhaps of holding her up.

Certainly when she went away to Wynberg she gave the impression that what she needed was simply to be propped up. Anyone would do. Anything could help. Without Richard she felt that she was without her character. For Richard had paid her the profound compliment of taking her seriously and treating her not as a "broad" (which was how she described herself) nor as "just a movie star" (another self-appellation) but as a woman of intelligence and sensitivity, full of surprising and unique mysteries to be pored over like the most beguiling Celtic rune. In his eyes she had been Somebody. And she had seen them all—the directors, the writers, statesmen, other actors, friends, all listening to Richard, respecting his intelligence, even conceding to him: and she had seen his quality and he had laid it at her feet. Although he was to do poor work he was also to do very fine work in the future, indeed some of his best was to come and the mind, the humour still moved and impressed those who had ears to hear. Elizabeth's career never recovered. Far from being Taylor who had carried the two of them through those Laurel and Hardy years, the separation proved—to doubters—that it had all the time been Burton who had fed her, nourished her, supported her and discovered her. Nobody had taken the trouble before. Nobody had thought her worth it. Nobody had had his intelligent passion for her.

She had given him a great adventure. As a lover of women he had found his "Ocean," the first nickname he gave her, and he charted it as thoroughly as a Captain Cook. Her sheer delight in externals—clothes, jewellery, possessions—and her sudden passions of sympathy for people, cats, causes—all this entranced him. She became a project. And there was the glamour, the steel in her power battles with the studios. She flourished in Burton's awareness of the complicated kind of courage and nerve it takes for a star to *be* a star and fight the battles that need to be fought and keep the public watching and wanting. He could trace almost to its seed the complex of will, nerve and the surfing on chance which made and kept an Elizabeth Taylor for so long such a star. To be known is the greatest comfort and flattery of all. To be understood and recognised for what you hope you are. Burton gave her that and its absence drove her wild.

But he had fought the good fight. Like a lone warrior sent out on some fabulous mission, he had conquered castles, captured towns, taken the golden princess, showered her in even greater splendours. But now it was time to move on. A few weeks out of hospital when for some days he had been very near death, fragile, pale but undaunted, Burton shrugged off the illnesses, cast aside all the warnings, and literally sailed out of the New World and back to the Old, declaring to the ever-present reporters: "I intend to rove the globe searching for ravishing creatures." Nobody like him.

The game, once more, was afoot.

PART
THREE

PART
THREE

23
The Remake

After a few months in 1974 Burton simply ignored the drinking warning delivered by those six weeks in hospital. He would never have the drinking capacity he once had—but that was not to stop him. He was now a serious prey to arthritic attacks—which he dismissed. He was up and away and the devil take the hindmost.

At first he was careful. He had been asked to play Churchill for a joint BBC–NBC ninety-minute production sponsored by Hallmark Greetings Cards. The producers had visited him in Puerto Vallarta where he was recuperating, drinking a little white wine, but somehow, as they described it, lost. He read portions of the script aloud and then fell asleep over it. They tiptoed away. He was unquestionably a sick man but Jack le Vien (the producer) was determined to have him in the picture. Everyone remembered his wonderful impersonation of Churchill's voice in *The Valiant Years* and besides, who else had the stature? He would recover.

As he was doing that, a call came to do *Brief Encounter*: Robert Shaw had been penned in for the part but he was still grappling with *Jaws*, which was over-running. Sophia Loren suggested Burton and for £200,000 plus expenses, and for Sophia Loren, Burton walked into that disastrous remake. He must have been extremely fond of Sophia. Trevor Howard and Celia Johnson had made the parts their own in David Lean's masterly version and everybody involved in the remake was on a hiding to nothing. Alan Bridges, the director, has commented that Burton showed scarcely any interest at all in the project. No wonder. Burton the actor was always a heat-seeking missile: if the part were there, or the words, or occasionally another actor or director he liked (or, gloriously, all three) then he would and could deliver. If the thing was a sham he nosed it out in an instant, shut up shop and went through the motions very professionally. Which is what he did here. Looking far too slick, smiling far too much at Sophia, conveying all the emotion of a pocket calculator.

Brook Williams was in Winchester with Burton for the filming and remembers with some amusement the attitude of the crew. "It was—watch out! Here he comes! They'd worked with him before, a lot of them, and it was 'Hello, Rich!' 'Hello, luv!' 'Time for a quick one, Rich?' 'No thanks, luv.' He was strictly on the wagon all through the film. He went cycling in the mornings to try to build himself up—the hospital treatment had left him like a twig." Burton was never to regain that sense of muscular bulk, that lumberjack vitality, the physical presence which gave him the odd double edge—a brilliant head on a powerful frame. "There was once he went into a pub and ordered a double vodka. 'This is it'—you could feel the lads say. 'Here we go, Here we go, Here we go!' But he took one sip and pushed it away. Back to the soda water. The gasp of disbelief was as loud as a clap of thunder."

It was noted that when Sophia declared in the film that she could not leave her husband to live with him—Burton—she had "real tears" in her eyes.

Perhaps it was also the £200,000. Burton, in his usual generous and careless manner, was being very easy about the settlement. Elizabeth was being tough. The jewellery (which at current rates could be worth anything up to $15 million) had been bought as a *joint* investment but *all* of it stayed with Elizabeth. Cruel observers at the time were heard to say that she almost cleaned him out. If she did, there is no evidence that he did anything much to defend himself. And his aloof attitude to money, coupled with his princely confidence that one way or another he would always be able to look after those who needed his support was, of course, yet another of his attractions for Elizabeth.

After *Brief Encounter*, he turned his attention to Churchill, to drink, to Princess Elizabeth of Yugoslavia and to Jeanne Bell. Jeanne Bell, a beauty, was the first black model to be a *Playboy* centrefold. She had been around the set of *The Klansman* and Burton had said,

"You look nice, why don't you join in?" A small part had been arranged. They kept in touch. Princess Elizabeth of Yugoslavia was related to the British Royal Family and a long-time acquaintance of Burton and Taylor. At this period she was separated from her merchant banker husband Neil Balfour and a divorce was pending. She took Burton along to meet Lady Churchill who was delighted that he was playing the part, her husband had been such an admirer, remember the *Hamlet* at the Old Vic? Immediately afterwards Richard and the Princess were seen around town together. When their engagement was announced, Elizabeth's back gave way and she was put in traction declaring, violently, that it was nothing to do with Princess Elizabeth who was a "good friend."

The rumour was that Burton did not turn up for the first day's shooting of *Walk With Destiny*. Whether that happened on day one is unclear. It certainly happened later. He was drunk. The director, Robert Wise, found it very difficult to reach out to him. Parts of the early sequences in the film, when Churchill was supposed to be lighthearted, had to be cut because of Burton's sombre, even stygian, characterisation. When reporters came to the set, he went through the old routine: Churchill at *Hamlet*; met him at his home at Hyde Park Gate; honoured, great man, great Englishman. The PR purred.

The *New York Times* asked Burton to write a piece for them. Burton's response was a portrait in vitriol worthy of John Osborne. His colleagues on the movie were bemused but if we take the alteration in his character seriously—from the detonating death of Ifor to the trauma of his own near-death and the divorce—then this is yet more evidence of his return to an older self to rebuild anew. Before the privacy of his typewriter, he thought hard about Churchill and the conclusions he came to were those of the young Welsh actor full of anger at the oppression in the Valleys, the pragmatist and man of generous sympathy horrified by the slaughter of war, the democrat unimpressed by and apprehensive of the power of those men who seek and find power. "I realise afresh that I hate Churchill and all his kind," he wrote, "I hate them violently." He goes on to castigate Churchill out of his own mouth. When in 1939 Churchill said of the Germans "they must bleed and burn, they must be crushed into a mass of smouldering ruins" was it a simple exercise in hyperbole . . . or was it what he actually meant? Similarly Churchill on the Japanese. Churchill, after hearing of the atrocities committed against prisoners of war, said, "We shall wipe them out, men, women and children. There shall not be a Japanese left on the face of the earth.'' Burton commented: ''Such single-minded cravings for revenge leave me with a horrified but reluctant awe for such single-minded and merciless ferocity—but then so am I awed by Attila the Hun, Genghis Khan, Tamberlaine the Great, Lenin, Hitler and Stalin.'' So it went on, imputing personal timidity to Churchill, criticising his prose style, admitting that ''he was one of the few people—two others were Picasso and Camus—who have frightened me almost to silence when we came face to face''; he nevertheless attempted a demolition job.

The uproar went through the Richter scale. Burton was condemned in Parliament, his own service career was raked up and ridiculed, ''friends'' from that time were quickly sought out to decry him; real friends—Sheran Hornby, Tim Hardy—sent him telegrams of protest and anger. Hallmark Cards got the jitters and dissociated themselves from the comments. NBC distanced itself. The audience was un-usually big for such a programme. The reviews on the whole were good. Le Vien did not ask Burton to play in the sequel a few years later.

Yet again, what Burton said and did in today's context seems not such an extreme point of view. Not one for which a present-day writer would be threatened with a lynching. Burton certainly fore-shadowed a more general mood which would gather and question some of the actions of the Allies including Churchill. The problem was that he said it too boldly, too early and too publicly and he was ''only an actor.'' Any remaining thoughts of settling down among dreaming spires to meld into the pastures of Gilbert and Sullivan England must have disappeared for ever.

On becoming engaged to Princess Elizabeth he took her on a trip around Morocco, stopping off at all the souks and casbahs he came across, always safe though always unguided since, according to a letter he wrote to Philip:

> I was called unceasingly by solemn djellabahed old wiz-ened men, possibly no older than I am, Saint Becket or Major Smith. The latter puzzled me for a time until I discovered from John Huston whom we found casually in the middle of the Atlas Mountains, that *Where Eagles Dare* had been a huge success in Morocco and had been playing for months, while *Becket* seems to be a perennial.

Burton went down to the Riviera to make *Jackpot*, which was never completed; judging from the story this can be seen as a blessing. However, celluloid passed through the camera for a while until all broke up over unpaid bills. Jeanne Bell had a part in the film. Princess Elizabeth, back in London, saw a photograph of Ms. Bell and Mr. Burton arm in arm on the promenade. He went back to London to explain. All was forgiven that time but it was not the only time and there was the occasion when both women were in the same club and Burton, outside in his Rolls, several over the eight, seemed undecided for whom he was waiting . . . A final reconciliation meeting with Princess Elizabeth at the Dorchester was delayed by her for two hours while she prepared herself. Those two hours he spent in the bar. "I didn't realise that it takes more than a woman to make a man sober," she said. The engagement was off. Elizabeth Taylor was almost immediately on the phone and kept phoning from then on in.

She was in Leningrad doing a Russian–American co-production, *The Blue Bird*. Wynberg had been brought along. Elizabeth went down with amoebic dysentery among other things—most of the cast were ill—and lost eighteen pounds during the six months the filming eventually took. Richard, unemployed in Switzerland, was attempting a convalescence. His drinking was down to a severe minimum. He dieted, exercised, read, made plans to do a play by Sartre. Jeanne Bell was living with him and he set up her son in an expensive Swiss school. Elizabeth's phone calls persisted and became more frequent.

In August 1975, she flew into Geneva with the hapless Wynberg. She met Burton. The next morning Wynberg flew back to LA. Jeanne Bell quit the chalet and the Burtons were together again. She was determined that they re-marry. He was not in favour. The remake was on.

Was it her determination overcoming his inertia? Was it to show the world she could get her man whenever she wanted to? Explanations such as these don't fit the case.

Elizabeth Taylor was desperately and obsessively in love with Richard Burton and, from her public utterances, even after his death, remains so.

They went to South Africa—as Richard explained in the letter to Kate—to help a good cause. First there was a twenty-four-hour scare that Elizabeth had cancer. Soon Elizabeth's ceaseless campaign

– including notes made public, "I love you, Richard, and I leave it up to you. Please answer"—won her the prize. She teased and cajoled him into proposing and he did. On his knees, apparently, mockingly: she accepted, promptly, delightedly. He had been sober for some months. Now he hit the bottle.

Elizabeth sailed on in what seems a miasma of fantasy. They would be married, she declared, "in the bush, amongst our own kind." They were married in Botswana by an African District Commissioner from the Tswana tribe. Once again she bravely declared to the world that it would be "for lovely always." They toasted each other in champagne while "their kind"—two hippos and a faraway rhinoceros—looked on. "It was like a huge dream," said Burton. "I remember thinking: what am I doing here? Odd place to be married, in the bush by an African gentleman. It was very curious. An extraordinary adventure, doomed from the start of course." He went down with malaria. A young pharmacist, Chen Sam, was helicoptered in, went back to London with them and ended up in Elizabeth's entourage. In London for his fiftieth birthday he sipped mineral water and was described by friends as looking "worn," "world weary." That could have been the after-effects of malaria.

One thing that *was* commonplace about the wedding was that Richard gave Elizabeth a costly diamond. Elizabeth declared to the world that much as she loved the diamond she was going to trade it in to provide hospitals in Botswana. Kitty Kelley tracked this through and alleges that it did not happen, but that as of 1979 she had contributed only $25,000 to a hospital project there.

She was never less than the true fairy tale. Now she had recaptured her prince and installed him in the ice palace in Gstaad on top of the Swiss mountain, safe from harm, accessible only to her.

The cracks though had already begun to show in London. Elizabeth had come back from South Africa and yet again gone into hospital. After a while, Richard refused to keep spending the nights there with her—she was in for back and neck pains—and she excoriated him for this. Those near to them at the time sympathised with Burton: she was suffocating in her demands on his time, his presence, her problems. He wheeled her out of the hospital and over to Gstaad for a White Christmas in 1975. All the sentimental things were done and children came and friends, Brook Williams, and gifts were sent over to Wales. The old firm seemed to be back in business.

But it was as ill-judged a remake as *Brief Encounter*. The original was too strong in the memory to tolerate the pallid second go. As he had said, "The game was up." Now, Burton thought, he had given it every possible chance. His health improved. He would not be dragged once more into the clinic on the inveigling Magic Mountain. He went out skiing. In a ski lift, with Brook Williams, "I turned around and there was this beautiful creature about nine feet tall," he said. "She could stop a stampede. I kept wondering when she was going to turn up again. Brook knew her a little and my luck was in. She started coming to the house—two, three and then four times a week."

The blonde was a model, Susan (known as Suzy) Hunt, in the process of a divorce from her husband, the racing driver, James Hunt. Suzy looked new, uncomplicated, English, middle class, stylish, healthy, and very attractive. "Instinctively, Elizabeth recognised that Susan was something special," said Burton.

When he went to New York to begin rehearsals for *Equus*, he called Suzy Hunt to join him. She took the risk and flew across the Atlantic. Elizabeth went to the local disco and seized on a thirty-seven-year-old Maltese advertising executive called Peter Darmanin. "Don't leave me, please, whatever you do," she repeated, as they danced together. Both pitiable and tyrannical, her plea drafted him into her service for a few weeks, he boasted to Kitty Kelley. "What was I expected to do?" she had asked a reporter who had criticised her for moving on to Eddie Fisher so soon after the death of Mike Todd. "Sleep alone?"

Burton summoned her to New York and Darmanin was dumped. In New York Burton faced her and asked for a divorce. He wanted it quickly as it was his intention to marry Suzy Hunt. "Why the hell did you have me come all this way to tell me that?" But, knowing as well as he that it was all over, she went across the States to California to her friends, briefly and disconcertingly back with Wynberg, and then with the Iranian Ambassador Ardeshir Zahedi and finally with John (later Senator) Warner, whom she would marry. And all the time the phone calls went through to Burton. She would delay the divorce until publicity about her maintenance forced her to accede.

Burton now considered himself free of her. He was a deeply serious man about those he loved and any criticism of Elizabeth would be most mild and most rare. He had been fascinated by her, obsessed by her, in love with her, and although his feelings had changed they would no more entirely fade away than his feelings for Cis, for Ifor, for old friends. He was loyal to all those who had joined him on the trail. But now he was after new conquests.

24
Regrouping

"You have the guts of a blind burglar." That could serve as Elizabeth's parting shot, her comment on his decision to go back to the stage and take over the long and exacting role of Dysart in Peter Shaffer's *Equus*.

The play is about a young man who has blinded six horses because they saw him making love to a young woman. Dysart is the psychologist who unravels the causes of this terrible act. It is an immensely exacting role. For someone who had not done a serious stint on the stage since 1964 (*Faustus* intervened but only for a week and it could not be said to be in the same league) it went beyond audacity and touched on the foolhardy.

Stage acting has much in common with athletics, ballet or musical performance. Regular practice is essential. The loss of a month or two can be dangerous: of a year or so, near-fatal. One of the reasons for the clamour of his acting friends to bring Burton back to the stage is that they were very well aware of that. Stay away too long and rust turns to a decay of parts. The voice goes, the sense of an audience, playing live with others, the command of a text, of a stage, the sheer stamina of eight performances a week, each one of which is expected to hit Top C. The muscles turn to flab and it shows. Especially so in a part which demands so much of the actor and the audience as Dysart. It *did* take tremendous guts.

The stakes were upped in two other ways. He was third into the part, following acclaimed performances by Anthony Hopkins and

Anthony Perkins. And he was being auditioned. Marlon Brando and Jack Nicholson had been thought of for the film—which was to be directed by Sidney Lumet. In the end they went for Burton but tales of his alcoholic days and nights had circulated around the industry and the producers wanted, as t'were, a dry run. The last time he had been on Broadway he had broken the record for the number of performances of *Hamlet* and had he wanted to double that number the crowds would have continued to come in. Now he was on trial.

Susan came. "She saved my life," he said then and for some years afterwards. She did not hide the booze—the bottles of vodka and gin stood around—but she steadied him in his resolve. He was an alcoholic who would not yet accept the fear and insult of that word. "Drunk" he could live with because drunks in his book came out fighting the next night. But he would not be an "alcoholic." And so from time to time he would take a glass, or several. And almost invariably "go." The severity of his condition had left his system with a much lower tolerance than before. Years later, observers noted that a single glass of brandy could turn an utterly sober man into a zonked, aggressive wreck. That was still far away. But he needed to hold back and the nearness and freshness of the twenty-seven-year-old daughter of a brigadier-barrister proved just the ticket.

Brook Williams was also in New York to help him with the role. Burton was meticulous about going to rehearsals but he always liked to work alone as well. He had been brought up as an outlaw to organised theatricals, a loner, someone who strode in "out of nowhere" as Gielgud had so tellingly said, and commanded the stage. His power was alchemised in solitude or with one single aide. He had to gather up his forces in his own way. Seek out that unaccountable instinct. Hitherto that aide had been Philip. But Philip was in Key West, unable to travel to New York. Brook, a friend since Richard had "adopted" him in boyhood, an actor, the scion of a theatrical family and a man who deeply understood Burton, was at hand.

They arranged the furniture in the suite of the Lombardy to match the layout of the stage and while Brook read and played all the other parts, Richard sweated and drove himself through his lines. Susan was there to bring him confidence and refreshment: milk.

There is a view that John Dexter, the play's director, was very annoyed with Burton in rehearsals and indeed the man's lack of recent experience and his reticence about releasing the power of the part *until he had to* could well have given Dexter nightmares. However Brook Williams, who was there, denies that Dexter—as reported—dressed Burton down in front of the cast and called him "a drunk." (He touched no alcohol throughout rehearsals and until way into the run.) He also says that the idea that Dexter "forced" Burton to appear in the matinée on the Saturday before his Sunday première is erroneous. The matinée was Burton's idea. He desperately needed to test himself before a live audience.

"It was the first time in my life I'd been on stage without a drink," he said. This is 1976. "I've never been so bloody scared." The terrors of all actors—drying up, getting stage fright, suddenly forgetting whole passages—were immensely accentuated for someone who had not done this seriously for twelve years. And this was Broadway! There would be no second chance. There was no safety net. The world thought it knew about the erratic, boozy, Flying Dutchman Burton, Film Star and International Celebrity, jewel buyer extraordinaire with pretensions to be a writer, grandee of glamour: now let's see what he does with nothing between himself and his critics but a few yards of dark auditorium.

Elizabeth came over towards the end of the rehearsal period and after two days of violent quarrels, she left, but not before she had visited his dressing room and scrawled on the mirror in lipstick, "You are fantastic, love." He never wiped it off. But it was to Susan he turned. And on Brook he relied to go through the entire play night after night.

Burton is of the stuff of heroes. Again and again he does those feats which heroic youth can only dream on. Out of severe illness, out of nowhere as a recent stage actor, nerve shot, sober, headline-hunted by the cannibals around the fresh corpse of his marriage, he came on stage and, according to Walter Kerr of the *New York Times*, did "the best work of his life." Clive Barnes in the same paper added that it was "undeniably a star performance. [Burton] is the most promising middle-aged English speaking actor of his time." Burton liked that. There were dissenting voices: the *New York Post*, for instance, thought him "implausible" and there were those who preferred their Hopkins or their Perkins to their Jenkins. But the major critics waved him on. The twelve-week run was packed out and a two-week extension merely nibbled at the box-office queues. There were standing ovations every night. And whenever Susan and himself went to a restaurant, they were applauded. "Suzy saved my life," he said and, "I thought, if I don't take the plunge now, I'll never go back." The crowds outside the theatre escorted him to his car. The Welsh hero, boyo, genius, had done it again. A special Tony Award was struck saying "Welcome back to Broadway."

Now he made plans for more stage work and it had to be Shakespeare. *King Lear* was his aim. It was thought that *Lear* alone could not hold and so the idea was to alternate it with *Romeo and Juliet* in which Burton would play the relatively undemanding part of Friar Laurence, using the *Equus* company—now near the end of its New York run—as a "rep." Dexter would direct. Alexander Cohen would produce. It would be staged in the Metropolitan Theatre in the Lincoln Center. The scheme seems to have fallen down on Burton's insistence that he could only play six times a week, i.e. once a day with one day off. It was thought that without him in the two matinées, the scheme would not work. Further difficulties and confusions proliferated. The plan fell through.

In August he married Susan in Virginia. She was on time. He was sober.

Before moving on to the *Equus* film, he squeezed in *The Heretic* or *Exorcist II*, designed to capitalise on the runaway success of *The Exorcist*. John Boorman, the fine British director (*Deliverance*), seemed a guarantee of class. $750,000 which, with overage, turned into $1 million, was a further inducement. Burton was—yet again —a priest. Soon on in the long shoot, he confessed to being puzzled and bewildered by a film of which Boorman was to say "I made the wrong film." Robbie Lantz, Burton's agent, had seen it as precisely the right sort of money-spinner between stage *Equus* and film *Equus*. There were those who thought that though it might not be quite the *worst*, it was certainly the stupidest film ever made. Yet again, with a great deal going for a movie he had willingly walked into, Burton walked out with egg all over him.

Perhaps the $1 million was more than tempting. In the second divorce settlement, Elizabeth seems to have cleaned him out. She took all the remaining jewellery, the house in Puerto Vallarta, Richard's rights in the *Kalizma* and all the remaining art works. She was always much tougher than he was—than anybody was—over contracts. As ever, he appeared maddeningly grand and unconcerned about it all which, considering his origins, his sense of the value of money and the energy he had used up to get it, reveals the reach of the man: whenever necessary he could find another cylinder. He would not cheapen himself.

In June of that year, 1976, his old boyhood acting friend, Stanley Baker (*Sir* Stanley), died. Burton was grief-struck. In a peculiar mood—anger, mourning, rage against the loss, he wrote a "Lament For A Dead Welshman" which was published in *The Observer*. Stylistically it was the least impressive piece he had written—but it is also the most moving. It offended Lady Baker deeply with its insistence on Stanley's lack of culture, his roving devilment, the image of the street-fighting philistine. What is significant about it is how very much it mattered to Burton to write it. He was not commissioned. He offered the piece. In one sense it spoke a little for Ifor, and he himself was in it of course. But the portrait was so far from the truth about the brothers—and about Baker—all of whom came from those Valleys in poetry and song and victory, that a puzzle remains. Perhaps Baker's death opened, yet again, the constantly fresh wounds which Burton carried, the wounds of a man who has stepped out of his class and finds it unacknowledged by those with whom he now passes his life. Burton's occasional vicious flares of anger against hosts and hostesses coming from the British—eternally privileged—upper-crust, and his eruption about Churchill, are all part of the same pattern. In the world of middle-class England there was more space and sympathy for any Colonial, or any foreigner, than for a working-class Britisher. The class from which he came, he and Baker, was an under-class, oppressed for centuries, and still ignored. When its message surfaced it was included—and so ridiculed—only in the music hall. Popular songs became its stock in trade. When its messengers brought news of what it was *really* like down there—they were jeered at, patronised, or, most usually, accused of being boring. The door of understanding was shut in his face. Burton's cry in that article is the cry of a man saying—Look! Do you realise the odds against Stanley Baker? The will and intelligence and the cunning and nerve it took him to get even with the privileged. Look at him fully! Acknowledge him!

And then he went beyond it. He came from terrible poverty, terrible disadvantage. Admire the journey.

One of Burton's problems as an actor was that when he was on form he was so astoundingly "professional," i.e. good, that he was easily taken advantage of. Sidney Lumet shot Burton/Dysart's eight great monologues in the film of *Equus* in a single day! Despite that — no time to breathe, to sense the character developing through the narrative, to find the truest pitch of a changed tone—*Equus*, shackled to the word though it is, produced a more than creditable performance. He was nominated for an Academy Award, his seventh. And again failed to get it. There is no doubt, though, that the cylinders are firing, the power is back in the eyes, the face. The interpretation is open to criticism as over-dramatic, even as over-heroic, but it is the performance of a star and at times his intensity rivets you. He was back on the case.

To cap off what had been for him a year of vital reconstruction of his health, his confidence and his career, he went back to what he called his "first love," BBC Radio, where for £4,000 he narrated twenty-six episodes in a series called *Chronicle of an English Crown.* "This is home," he said. The voice was a little thinner but still fully able to switch you into its mood, grip your mind with its intelligence, mesmerise you like the running of a stream.

Now he was back in his stride. He had held on to Céligny and Susan began to add to it, decorate it, settle down. Both of them were extremely keen to have children but they had not yet been lucky. There was time. She polished up the dining room, added a little here, a little there and, most dramatically of all, had some cunningly carpentered bookshelves built into an entire wall of the long upper barn which now became Richard's den and study. To go there now is to be in a place in which you know he was often perfectly content. A log fire, an easy chair or two, the desk, the typewriter, and the books. In the settlement with Elizabeth all he had insisted on were the books. Thousands, but none particularly valuable. The library stands today and it is the library of a reader: books thumbed, reference books, the rich higgledy-piggledy of someone whose curiosity was sharp, whose tastes were catholic, who loved words, words, words.

While Elizabeth languished unhappily as the wife of husband John Warner, whom her charisma and campaigning zest had turned against high odds into a Senator, out of the film business and fast becoming a national lampoon for her fatness—she went up from 130 to 175 pounds—Richard appeared to be thriving.

It was while he was with Susan that he finally took a firm grip of his financial affairs which had slithered all over the place. No longer the careless prince.

July 27th, 1978

Dear Aaron,

First of all, let me say at once how enormously impressed and thrilled (inadequate word) I was at your very obvious physical improvement, both speech and movements. I must get hold of that vitamin B13 or is it 15? that you've been taking.

Now as to business: For the first time in my life I examined with minute care all the statements, accounts, debits, credits, etc. When, with the use of a calculator, I had finally worked out the over-all financial situation, I became extremely alarmed. Not so much for what I shall refer to as the Elizabethan period, but since. Since, in fact, I stopped drinking almost entirely about 2½ years ago.

What I would like and I know it's an onerous task, is a complete breakdown even unto minutiae of how Mrs. Warner and I spent something in the region of 30 million dollars. I would like it in detail. There is for instance no reference anywhere to the Tenerife property and what happened to that investment. On a vastly smaller scale there is no reference to the 50 acres and a shack in Ireland. I would like all those details, please.

I realise that I lived the life of Riley and that there were enormous inroads, deductions, fees, etc., e.g. assuming you received 10% of Elizabeth's income as well, you or your organisation acquired approximately three million dollars, the various agents, another 3. So there goes 6 million dollars at one gigantic swoop.

Let me repeat again that more out of curiosity than what was fury—I gave myself a day to calm down—I want to know how the rest was spent. My fury, may I say was directed mostly at myself in not having someone responsible enough to steal, hide, rob me of my own monies and put it safely in a trust—a trust, incidentally, which was formed for precisely that reason—to protect me against my over-generosity. That is however in the cauchemarish past.

He then goes on into minute detail about the previous year and follows that with a heavy burst of angry questions.

Why is there no indication of my "deferred" monies?

Where is the information that indicates Lantz's and your percentages of 10% each?

Why is the earning statement only to the end of 1977, yet expenses for major items goes to the end of June 1978?

Above all, *again*, why is my personal trust fund now reduced to less than a half a million?

Why is some real estate shown at "acquisition" figures and others shown at current market value? Again, what of Tenerife and Ireland holdings?

It is lamentable that in the past I have not taken an active, positive position in relation to my business affairs. However, I am now keenly interested *in each and every detail* and will anticipate receiving at once, any and all statements that relate to my "worldly goods." In actual fact, Aaron, after much moaning and groaning, I enjoyed the mathematics involved.

As Valerie [Douglas] told you, I would like Susan to own an insurance policy in her name on my life, that will amount to $500,000.00. If it is possible, and it should be, after all these bloody tests to which I have been subjected, I would prefer not undergoing yet another physical examination. I am, incidentally, in perfect order.

I am considering a new will. Would you also please advise the actual position on Squire's Mount and Bushel Investments Ltd., i.e. Gwen's share, her will, etc. This has never been clear to me.

Would you also please send copies to Valerie on the requested statements and any and all "personal and confidential" matters pertaining to Susan's and my affairs. Additionally, please send her copies of all contracts in which I have either deferments or continuing percentages.

I am sorry that our plans changed and that our airport meeting was aborted, as I had planned to hand you this letter and discuss certain aspects. But we should be coming through New York in the Fall and we both hope you will continue your magnificent physical improvement.

Much love,
Richard

The next film, for $500,000 up front, was *The Medusa Touch*—an Elliott Kastner package directed by Jack Gold. Gold had a remarkable track record in British television and had made some good feature films. This movie was an oddity—a man has "a gift for disaster," he can *will* explosions and debacles—an oddity but in the event well made and well enough received. Burton was off the booze, no tantrums at all. If he gave very little in the way of general bonhomie, if he seemed very quiet off the set, the reason, unadmitted, was that he was fighting two hard battles.

He considered that he was winning the battle of the drink. A little wine some of the time, the occasional lapse into spirits. But on the whole a well-disciplined diet alternating with periods of total abstinence especially when he was working.

The second battle was with his health. The pain in the shoulders, in the arm, the arthritis and sciatica and gout, these had threatened again in *Equus* and he took heavy pills to deaden the pain and, so they promised, bring not only relief but cure. It is arguable that the pills did as much, if not more, long-term damage than good. He didn't whinge but nor did he dissipate his strength in his usual generous social talk.

All the more remarkable, then, that he accepted the role of Colonel Faulkner in *The Wild Geese* and went for it with such physical recklessness. But he was always a good soldier. This was 1978.

It is worth dwelling on *The Wild Geese*. Burton greatly enjoyed doing the film. He turned in a spanking performance with the likes of Richard Harris and Roger Moore. The film grossed a considerable profit, proving yet again that Burton could do it. There are two good and reliable witnesses to what happened there—Euan Lloyd, the producer, and Brook Williams, who took a small part in the film. And, most importantly, it spotlights and identifies Burton's real and increasingly worrying enemy.

Andrew McLaglen was the director. Reginald Rose, who had written *Twelve Angry Men*, was the screenwriter. He wanted Burton. It was shot in the Northern Transvaal, at Tshipise, in temperatures well over 100 degrees, sometimes up to 120. Lloyd made deals which ensured that, for those days, a remarkable number of black Africans were on the unit. Burton played Colonel Faulkner, based on "Mad" Mike Hoare, a mercenary who led a bunch of former soldiers on a raid to release an imprisoned African leader. It was action, action and action. First rate of its kind—in the thriller mould which Burton unsnobbishly liked.

I spoke at length to Euan Lloyd, who had known Burton since just after the war. "At that time he was the most handsome, dashing, strapping fellow you could imagine." He remembers him at Twickenham for a big game, at the end of the Forties, "shinning up the goalposts with Stanley Baker and Donald Houston helping him and hanging leeks on the crossbar—the crowd roared . . . he always led the singing, bottles of beer in his coat pocket . . . and he was always Jack the lad . . ."

The problem that Lloyd encountered was not the booze—"he said he wouldn't drink and he didn't." It was his back trouble. "It was so bad, so severe, that we couldn't get any insurance on him. It was a $10 million movie and if his back went, we would be finished. And it was full of very strenuous activity—jumping on planes, fights, action all the way. But we all wanted him and so we took the risk. He was very gallant. I would say courageous. Sometimes he was in absolute agony but all he would say was that it was 'a touch hot today.' If that. Only once did we hold up the film. That was when he could not move at all. A specialist was helicoptered in and he gave him some big shots, very heavy injections. Burton was back on the set next day. The only luxury he wanted was a baby grand piano for Susan—she was a good pianist and played for two or three hours a day, I believe. Burton had about five hundred books shipped out and he read in the evenings. And he was very clued up about the part and the politics of it all. The homework was done."

Richard Harris, also known to like a drink or two, was on the film and the deal with him was that fifty per cent of his fee was deferred, to be withheld if he drank. Brook Williams remembers the "Night That Richard Harris Fell Off The Wagon." The place was a shack which the unit had turned into a pub christened the Red Ox. Roger Moore, Harris and the lads got down to it. Burton was there with his non-alcoholic Tab. The Welsh singing began. Lloyd saw the glasses rise and empty, the voices rise and rise and he panicked, called out "Time, gentlemen, please. Time, please," bringing the party to an end. The next day Harris turned up holding his head. "Sorry, Governor. It won't happen again." And it didn't. Burton asked Lloyd to go and see him and read him the riot act. He considered that Lloyd had insulted them all, especially him, by treating them as children. He was white with fury. An hour later, it was all over. Back on the set.

The film has one or two self-indulgent jokes. When Burton, as Colonel Faulkner, takes his first drink, and is challenged as to his drinking, he replies that he never drinks when working but adds, "There's a special clause in my contract which says that my liver has to be buried separately, with full honours." Later in the same conversation, he says, "I work for anybody if they pay me. It's an irredeemable flaw in my character." The most interesting aspect of that scene, however—he is sitting on a large sofa in the house of the international tycoon industrialist who is hiring him—is to watch him drinking. He has to hold the whisky tumbler with both hands and even so dip his head a little to take the drink. He could scarcely lift his arm even to shoulder height. Later it was discovered that there was a nerve trapped and pinched in his spine which, coupled with the arthritis and the other spinal pain which had dogged him since his rugby playing-fighting days, caused him the most terrible "discomfort"—that was the word he would use. He took strong pills to deaden it and those, in turn, had side effects which would make him extremely irritable, morose, depressed.

This, then, was the real enemy. There would still be the occasional night when he would tumble off the wagon. Humphrey Burton, the television producer, remembers going to a dinner at Leonard Bernstein's: Richard had a couple of drinks in a small company beforehand and was "gone." Susan was escorted by Humphrey Burton on that night. Richard was an obstinate man. He watched his drinking but he would never give in, as he saw it, to the surrender of total abstinence.

It was this apparently incurable, irreversible, physical decline which took his energy. The "distance" one or two people describe, the quiet life he led, the increasing seclusion—all of it makes sense when you realise that this active, powerful, all-the-world's-my-stage man was battling with a literally crippling illness. In his frustration and anger he lashed out—as happens—to those nearest: Susan had to take a lot on the chin.

She responded by taking over more of his life. Euan Lloyd noticed how she was forever fussing over him. She could not stop flicking her hands through his hair, ceaselessly bringing him undrunk cups of tea, untasted bowls of fortifying soup. John Springer, his friend and long-time publicist, found access increasingly difficult and eventually sent a letter via Bob Wilson to say that he was ceasing to charge Richard for services because he found it impossible to do any. Ron Berkeley, the hairdresser and make-up man, whose passage Richard had wangled on so many films, went next and Susan appointed herself in that role. Brook Williams, who had been around Richard since his, Burton's, teens, felt unwelcome.

"She wanted rid of all the old mates," Brook said, "which left him terribly isolated. That was bad enough. But then she and Valerie Douglas took over the whole shooting match and the results, I think, were disastrous. They read the scripts, they decided on the contracts. And as far as I'm concerned they didn't know Richard. For instance, Andrew McLaglen, who'd done *Wild Geese*, wanted to get much the same bunch together and do *Sea Wolves* over in Goa. Lovely. Richard would have adored it. Good fun. Good money. But no. He would have had such a good time. Missed it. We sent him lots of postcards."

One film he did do was *Absolution* written by Anthony Shaffer, brother to Peter (*Equus*) Shaffer. He had been trying to get that going since 1970 which made it pre-Susan. The front money was $125,000—much less than his usual fee at the time—but the part of the priest (again) who heard a confession of a murder in the context of an English public school intrigued him. His performance is well up to scratch and the film did him no harm. Billy Connolly, the Scottish writer-comedian, was also in the film and, like a great number of the new generation of British writers, actors, directors, took fondly and admiringly to Burton. What Burton did not realise was that there was, in England, a constituency for him still: all he had to do was to come and claim the crown.

For the next three movies—*Tristan and Isolt*, shot in Ireland, in which he played the King of Cornwall; *Breakthrough* with Rod Steiger and Robert Mitchum; and *Circle Of Two* with Tatum O'Neal, directed by Jules Dassin—he was paid $750,000 a time. All the films were dreadful.

In those three films and in those two years he dived from a substantial peak into the doldrums. In *Equus* the play and *Equus* the film he had showed his boldness and his class; in *The Wild Geese* he had proved his box-office appeal and in *Absolution* he had kept in touch with some of the newer, brighter talents of the day. But the next three movies were dire. The finances were sorted out excellently but at the expense of his reputation.

It is difficult to see why he allowed it to happen unless it was again through his wasteful fault of over-generosity. Perhaps he thought that Susan was not getting what she had a right to expect. There were no children—why, whose lack, if either, it was, is not clear. But she gave the impression that she was treating him at times as something of a child and, to please her, he connived at this, some of the time. It was not an easy role for him to play and Kate, his daughter, was one of many who noted how much it irritated, even maddened him, and how he battled to subdue that. Yet Susan made him very happy, gave him a home, a library, time to read, looked wonderful whenever they went out, was straight and loving. What more could anyone want?

Like all extraordinary people, what Burton wanted was often at odds with apparent common sense. The itch of restlessness or the fertile unease which makes great talent began to work in him again. He knew he was becalmed. An ageing man, treated increasingly like an invalid, cut off from old friends, on a treadmill of money-spinning flops, his reputation oozing away by the hour. He knew, too, that he had not his old strength. And he worked out his strategy.

What he came up with would require the strength of a fit man half his age; it would expose him in the cruellest light in the most savage amphitheatre; it would galvanise him or finish him off. He decided to do a strenuous tour in the States, coast to coast, the most wearing travel, new cities, new premières, new opportunities for the critics. It would be a relaunch of *Camelot* in which he would have to act, sing, sword-fight and sustain an immense production night in night out for twelve months. Kill or cure.

And so he came out of Le Pays de Galles and, once more, headed West. The strategy—as always with Burton when he felt in danger—was to go on to the attack.

25
Camelot Revisited

For some of the time he again kept a journal. The show opened in Toronto—Burton was on $60,000 a week—and in June 1980 it came into New York. Susan was becoming a nurse and personal assistant as much as a wife.

> (June 29) Did little but ate, breathed, dreamed and rode the nightmare of Camelot. We might be winning the race—I'm not sure—but, if the Toronto audience reaction is anything to go by, then we have a massive hit whatever the critics might say here in the Empire State. We open the previews in two days.

The illness is there, now a permanent feature.

> Am going to see "the daddy of all the neck and shoulder specialists in the Western world" . . . am having enormous difficulty in sleeping . . . proper sleep—oh sleep it is a gentle thing beloved from Pole to Pole, To Mary Queen the praise be given she sent the gentle sleep from heaven that slid into my soul. Shall try again to sleep. It's now 5.30.

Camelot opened with more *réclame* than the first time round.

(Aug. 12) The show is a super smash hit. Particularly, apparently, for me which is gratifying but surprising as only now, six weeks after the opening, am I beginning to get the piece safely under my belt. We broke records week after week. I find it an unfathomable fiscal mystery that we have standing room only the first week and break that record the second week and again the third and fourth and fifth.

Frank Rich in the *New York Times* wrote, "Burton doesn't merely command the stage, he seems to own it by divine right." Yet again, after a five-year lay-off, partly crippled, stemming his drinking by the powerful drug Antabuse, Burton went out and delivered.

He had judged himself well. The demands on his talent, his nerve and his guts far from draining him reinvigorated him—at least for the first few months. His writing is one sign.

(Aug. 12) I am writing to please myself tho' there's a feeling in some place in my head—the pineal gland for instance which is seemingly an appendix to the brain and just as useless as the abdominal one—that this might be publishable. I haven't been writing for nothing. I am still having, from time to time, extreme discomfort from my neck—a pinched nerve and not bursitis—but now from both sides! Have I pinched another pinched nerve?

Burton and Susan began to see quite a lot of Henry and Nancy Kissinger. Burton was clearly delighted to be on equal, chatty terms with the statesman. He recalls that Kissinger took a dim view of Carter's possible re-election and had a low opinion of him because of his lack of grasp of foreign affairs. A great many high reputations were assassinated over the Tab.

(Aug. 14) We supped at the "21." The Doctor had about 6 guards within shouting distance. I remembered the contrast. In Jerusalem I was told there were 750 guards. 250 Yanks, 250 Israelis, 250 Arabs—for *one* man. The conversation went on for hours (we closed the "21") although it was more a monologue by Kissinger. I was, and sometimes Susan, the feed or stooge. "The presidency is now open for any unemployed megalomaniac'' was one of his bon mots.

Camelot continues to have great impact, often bizarre in its repercussions.

> (Aug. 16) Last night some strange man in the audience offered a thousand dollars if we would do the last Act again as the audience had not understood me profoundly enough when I bellowed "Long live the King." Towards the very end of the play, when I had the boy Tom of Warwick (Thor) underneath my arm this same strange one came up on to the stage and tried to wrest a sword from one of the "knights" saying, "I must have his eyes . . . I must have his eyes" and "I have a message from God" and finally, "I've failed. I've failed." He was, apparently, taken away by the police. I kept on going willy-nilly. This almost child-like piece of Lerner and Loewe's has most extra-ordinary effects on people sometimes. Weirdly eerie. Some people, intelligent ones too, come backstage and are seemingly struck dumb, apparently speechless or incoherent with emotion. Others wait until they have stopped crying before they come to see me. Others though are untouched, or appear to be so and are as bland as bananas. One thing I've learned though or understood rather from personal experience: the emotional impact of a supple voice speaking lovely sounding banalities can shatter even the most cynical and blasé of audiences. They tell me that Lloyd George was a genius at it and I suppose too Senator Ed Kennedy's speech the other day was something of the same thing.

The audience's reaction is so dramatic that he puzzles over it.

> (Aug. 17) The audience reaction to the play: When we were in Toronto and we received *without fail* standing ovations at every performance I warned the cast not to take it for granted, that it would only happen occasionally, if at all, in NY. But I was wrong. The same thing happens here with unfaltering regularity. I used to get the occa-

sional house to stand up for me in previous plays but now they always do. Will they in Chicago and the rest of the places? It's a phenomenon that I am puzzled by. Is it nostalgia? The roars I get when I take my second solo calls are almost exultantly savage. Is it a ferocious hunger for the past, a massive "hiraeth," a sort of murderous longing for "home" and security and simple peace. I don't know. It cannot be simply the performance. Some nights unavoidably, tho' I try like the devil to climb to the audience's expectations every time I play, I am not so good—but the final reaction is exactly the same. Is it that the audience know so much about me—or think they do —from my highly publicised and infamous past? Is it because my performance is now truly dynamic but no, it can't be that because only in the last couple of weeks have I taken absolute control of myself on the stage. Is it a combination of all? I shall never know. But let me say at once that to this little shrinking Welsh violet it is highly gratifying.

The journals continue to explore his own particular ache of enquiry.

(Aug. 19) "Only our concept of time makes it possible for us to speak of the Day of Judgment by that name: in reality it is a summary court in perpetual session." That is from a letter of Kafka's. It haunts me. The supreme judge at that severe searching of the soul is oneself. It is I who act, I who do the deed or have the thought and it's I only who can judge the action or the thought. I am prosecutor and defender, Satan and Saint. I am totally responsible for all my sins and goodnesses. And I am alone. That great storehouse of knowledge and memory, ignorance and idiocy, brilliance and banality, good and evil is in my own brain and only my own brain can call itself to the bar for the agony of self-examination. An endless, life-long viva voce. I wish I had more time to think.

And the chatter is back in full flow.

(Aug. 19) Bernstein is indeed a fascinating creature, genius and dolt, a man and a woman. A boy and a girl. There is no personal hell quite like the hell Lenny lives through. All the time, all the time night and day there is the battle between his super ego and his utter self loathing—a Mahatma Miserable. I think that master means to die shortly unless the will to live reasserts itself. And all those faceless sycophants around him. Repulsive. It's his birthday next Sunday and neither Susan nor I can face the people who are certain to be there. Fortunately we cannot go anyway. Not with a previous date and packing and Chicago the next day. I've written and thought myself into a state of depression. Ah! How I'd love the panacea of a drink now. A double ice cold vodka martini, the glass fogged with condensation, straight up and then straight down and the warm flood of pain-killer hitting the stomach and then the brain and an hour of sweetly melancholy euphoria. I shall have a Tab instead. Disgusting.

Susan, with him of course, continues to give him exactly what he seems to need and after noting that, gratefully, the Notebooks move along as busily as ever they did.

(Aug. 22) Yesterday was our Wedding Anniversary—the 4th. Susan gave me a life-saving present. A portable book-case, immensely durably strong which, at a rough calculation will hold a hundred or so really heavy thick tomes and I suppose twice that number of paperbacks. She had conspired with the stage hands, props man and carpenter to make it. Was it not Francis Bacon who said that books make the best furniture. He's right. I can't stop musing at it. It is painted *my* colour. Red. Very fetching and a delight. My beloved John Neville just phoned. He is coming to play tonight. A remarkable man—brilliant actor, administrator, director and, with the possible exception of John Gielgud and Larry Olivier, knows more about the practical side of the theatre than anyone I know. I spoke in a whisper as Susan still asleep—she packed all our clothes and bric-à-brac, or most of it, yesterday and is very tired. She should finish it all today. I am useless to help her as my right arm—which is now affecting my left arm as well—is dead for lifting the lightest weight beyond diaphragm height. After the show I can only eat food that is possible to lift to my mouth with one arm. Ridiculous.

After the opening night, the most sensational event in New York was when the curtain had to come down half way through a performance as Burton staggered around the stage, incapable. "Give him another drink," called out a witty member of the audience. The understudy replaced him but hundreds walked out and asked for their money back.

It was not drunkenness or only very slightly. The drugs he was taking made all drinking impossible. But he *had* taken a couple of glasses of wine with Richard Harris that day—the amount was not questioned—and by the evening he was on the way out. He woke up at 3 a.m. the next morning asking Susan what had happened. He called Mike Merrick the producer the next day. "He said it would never happen again and it didn't."

Being Burton, he went into battle. He appeared on the Dick Cavett show on no less than four successive nights. Cavett's introduction included, "On the rare occasions when he misses a performance it is headlines around the world."

You can see why Cavett loved Burton. He makes most talk-show guests look like sponsored sleepwalkers. He was funny, racy, touching, playful, honest, rugged-faced—the gossip about his having had a face-lift must have seemed rather foolish. His face was as worn as that of a man who'd spent a few years hacking granite. He was open about the one-night failure and, as ever, bold before his time and beyond the call of the chat show when it came to the crunch. Alcoholism? At last he was unequivocal.

"Alcoholism is a dreadful disease. My sympathy for American alcoholics is profound. They come up to me as being a representative of this dreadful disease and they tell me their stories. I can't say that I've beaten it." Typical of Burton—yet another of the reasons why across the world and across the board save for a few English snobs and Hollywood squealers he was thought to be the "real McCoy." "Irving Berlin, a dear friend of mine, wrote to me a few years back when I was in trouble with drink. He said, 'Don't forget, you're always fighting. The other fellow is booze. You're evading, always evading, but one of these days, unless you're careful, he's going to nail you.' When you get through the day you say: I've beaten the boxer. So, for the rest of your life you're stuck with that shadowy figure. There's every conceivable cause to take a drink. I get a bad notice. I think I'll take a drink. A good notice. I'll take a drink."

The night after he had blacked out, he stepped on stage to a three-and-a-half-minute ovation. "I gave possibly the best performance I've ever given. The entire evening flew on wings. It was one of the most extraordinary experiences I've ever had in the theatre."

The show moved on to Chicago. The theatre was so big (capacity 4,200) and so distant that Burton had no idea of what the audience was feeling: this unnerved him. But the standing ovations went on and on. They went along to a party at the Kissingers.

(Aug. 28) The Kissinger tea, cocktails and dinner was v. interesting though somewhat nerve-racking esp for Susan, who didn't know who everybody was not having caught their names. I filled her in as quickly and as often as they were out of earshot. "Joe Alsop famous, sometimes brilliant and always instinct with probity, political writer." "William F. Buckley (Bill), TV talk show star, political writer too, brilliant too, not too sure of him." Harry Evans we had to be told about as he was new to both of us. Editor of London *Sunday Times* with a provincial accent. 42 yrs old or 44, I'm not sure. Irish-Welsh, he said of himself. Did a very good Welsh accent. "Happy" Rockefeller very *un* "happy." Not surprising after the death of Nelson Rockefeller. And the manner of his death. I spent a long time comforting her. Susan too. The Kissingers and Susan and thy humble servant all sober. Ed of the *Times*—careful. Joe Alsop impeccably spoken at all times. He spoke with a veddy veddy English upper-class accent. "Where on earth did you, a Yankee, get such an English accent?" I asked. "I was very badly educated," he replied. Buckley, whose face looks a triumph of plastic surgery after a bad car accident—he must have had monumental acne in his youth or had indeed, quite seriously, a bad burn or smashed-up face or something of that nature, very red in the face and tried desperately to make it a brilliant evening. Much talk of the Middle East. Only

Jordan (the kingdom not the politico) could solve the situation with the PLO, etc. We like the Kissingers more and more and Susan now feels at home with them. I always have done. I reasoned that after our first meeting in Jerusalem they wouldn't ask me back unless they liked me for my little timid self alone.

All of them seemed to have read one or other of my occasional published writings and seemed to my relief far more interested in that part of me than the acting part. I couldn't have been better pleased. The Ed of the London *Sunday Times* suggested that I write about the American hinterland. I was going there for the first time—why didn't I make it a book? Any good and he would publish extracts in the *Sunday Times*. He'd paid 32,000 or was it 38,000 pounds? to William Manchester for six or eight extracts from his latest. Why not me? Why not indeed, I thought? I said I would ponder over it and perhaps send him a few thousand words to see if or how he liked it. I still don't know if I will but it is an intriguing temptation. But what can I do about getting out and around. I cannot sit in a public park or any public place, restaurant or bar or church without being recognised within minutes. Like Hamlet but not for the same splendid reasons I am the observed of all observers. Being famous or infamous depending on whether you're Dean Acheson or Harry Goldberg the cab-driver has that disadvantage, and there are others but, I quickly must add, the ads greatly outnumber the disads. One curiosity about being as peculiarly well known as I am, is that almost everywhere I go, it's the other people who change—not me. In the restaurant for instance, once it is known that I'm there and, gradually, Susan too, it's the other diners who begin to be self-conscious and start unconsciously to act. Women especially become arch or arrogant, simpering or ultra sophisticated, etc., at once, and everybody covertly, they think, stare at Susan— searching her hair, her jewellery, her clothes, her finger-nails, face, figure, legs and feet. A great many restaurants in these limited States have mirrors and it is sometimes amusing to sit at a mirrored bar with Susan beside me, while waiting for a table, me with my inevitable Tab or

Diet Pepsi and Susan with her invariable and diabolically insulting "Chivas Regal and Coca-Cola over two lumps of ice, please" and watch the subtle changes of attitude and posture and pose and poise of the others. I taught Susan, who, unlike me, is shy almost to the point of being in pain, to watch them and I think it has greatly eased her shyness but she is still indignant that whenever she goes to the loo she is always followed by a gaggle of women who are hoping to see her at close quarters and her underclothes as Bill Buckley would zeugmatically say.

Later, in what is one of his relaxed pieces, he writes about telling the truth, when sober, but "In vino, which I never am nowadays, I lose all control and will lie in my teeth about anybody or anything and viciously too. I am not a nice man at those times. I hope they never recur."

He loves Chicago. "Unless I am careful it will erode my affection for London and New York as being my first and second favourite cities. (Rome, LA and Paris are villages *avec beaucoup de banlieus*)." The preoccupation is to get Susan's sister and her baby out of a disastrous marriage in South Africa and over to join them in the States. Burton pursues this with his usual tenacity until it is accomplished and is utterly delighted with the child. "I have played with her for hours. And I'm trying to remember what my other babies were like at that age—Kate, Jessica, Maria. I cannot remember of course." On the way back from a performance he is annoyed with himself because he can't quote T. S. Eliot's "Rhapsody On A Windy Night" word perfectly. He tugs away at it in his Notebook, gets most of it but "not the whole thing. That means a walk to a bookshop tomorrow."

It's in Chicago that he ventures into one of his rare extended passages on actors and acting. Rex Harrison's opening of *My Fair Lady* in New Orleans is the cue for it all.

(Sept. 23) I think Rex is, of his genre, the greatest actor in the world—the highest of high comedians. No less a person than that delicious Noël Coward once said, "Rex is the greatest light-comedian in the world"—pause— "after me." I would say they were at least even, with

Rex having the edge. I shall be thinking of him all evening long. Both Susan and I have sent him telegrams separately and one to the entire company together. Rex's brand of acting and his off stage personality are inextricably bound together. Most obviously, for instance, Rex's normal private-life voice is the same as the voice on stage—only projected a little more. I think mine is. So is George Scott's, so is Gielgud's, so was Coward's, so is Jason Robards's, so is Fonda's, so is Richardson's, but Olivier's is totally different, and Scofield's, and Guinness's. Alec and Paul tend to "boom" on stage though cathedrically quiet off and Larry Olivier's develops a machine-gun metallic rattle with an occasional shout thrown in "to keep," as he said to me once "the bastards awake." I'm not quite sure whether Larry meant his fellow-actors or the audiences or both. But one has to be careful with Larry—he is a great dead-pan leg-puller and one is never quite sure whether he is probing very subtly for weak spots or majestically sending one up. Superb good value though all of them. O'Toole's voice, too eccentrically accented in private, is the same on the stage. I wonder what it means. Does it mean that Olivier, Guinness and Scofield are basically and essentially character actors while the rest of us mentioned above are simply extensions of ourselves? Well, the more I act and the more I think about it (which is not very often) the less I know I know of the heart of its mystery. Why one believes absolutely in one actor and knows he's blazingly honest and not in another equally dazzling player is beyond my competence to explain. I can only accept it and hope for the best.

Talking of O'Toole I only knew by chance that he had taken such a terrible hammering—a front-page hammering —from the British critics for his performance in *Macbeth*. I knew only because Onllwyn Brace came to supervise my narration in the documentary film about Welsh rugby football. "Your pal O'Toole," he said, "has been murdered by the English critics." "For what?" asked I. "For *Macbeth*," he said. I phoned Peter that night as soon as the hours were right and managed to catch him before he'd left the Old Vic. I said "a couple of boys from the BBC were over today to record my voice and they told me you've had a bit of stick from the critics." "Yes." "How are the houses?" I asked. "Packed." "Then remember, my boy," I said (he is 4 years younger), "you are the most original actor to come out of Britain since the war and fuck the critics."

"Thank you." "Think of every four letter obscenity, six, eight, ten and twelve letter expletives and ram it right up their envious arses in which," I said, paraphrasing Robert Atkins, "I'm sure there is ample room." "Thank you." "Good night, Peter. Don't give in and I love you." "I won't and it's mutual." "Good night again." "Good night, Richard, and thank you."

That was the extent of our conversation but my fury at the critics took me through the night—another sleepless one—and I thought of all the things I should have said to Peter and didn't and thought I should write him a letter and didn't and prayed to God I hadn't sounded like a false sympathiser secretly rejoicing in his critical debacle. But no, I comforted myself, he knows I too have been through the fire and understand. And by God I have too. It's a phenomenon that is again inexplicable that a few of us— O'Toole, Sinatra, Brando, Elizabeth Taylor, Jane Fonda, Barbra Streisand, *et al*—carry something sanguivorous and the parasite is called "press-envy"—especially in our own countries. Why is it? Because we take risks and run against the conventional. It cannot be because we are, albeit patchily, successful and earn millions because one never hears of viciousness anent Robert Redford or Dustin Hoffman, Paul Newman or De Niro or Jon Voight but one does about Al Pacino—my dear, he has—an American Film Star yet—dared to play Richard III! And what's more—horror of horrors—he's going to have a go at *Othello*. Shakespeare's *Othello*, no less. I can hear the critics and the gossip-mongers and the Sardi-set already stirring up the vitriol. Mr. Pacino is certainly not lacking in courage—he has my deepest admiration. Live acting and film or TV acting are so different in their demands on the nervous system but more anon.

There was no more.

He is beginning to suffer badly but the references are bald: "Both my shoulders seized up again." It is worth remembering that this is while continuing a stage performance at full pitch for upwards of three hours, with fast costume changes, stage fights, singing, huge stretches of dialogue, and an audience of over 4,000 demanding to be drawn into the very soul of the man you are acting. "Can't stop sweating. From discomfort in the shoulders, I suppose."

The reading goes on. He reads Peter de Vries because he had been told that he was like Evelyn Waugh and does a brisk comparative analysis ending "except superficially, poles apart." They move on to Dallas where, at the beginning of October, the journals end.

The show made for Mexico.

Richard had taken Susan to Wales where she had been welcomed and admired. He had also taken her to Key West to meet Philip who recalls the event in the unpublished memoirs.

> In such an intimate place as Key West it would be impossible to prevent the news of their arrival from spreading quickly. Would Richard have to be a prisoner in the house? Susan would be free to roam around, but not Richard. All worked out well. Only twice did the three of us venture out together, to St. Paul's Church on Sunday morning— I introduced them only to the Rector—and once to a restaurant . . .
>
> I had planned some special meals only to find that they wanted very plain food and very little of that, but it was good to find that Richard was in one of his "dry" spells; he would not touch even a glass of wine. Susan loyally followed him in his choices of food and drink.
>
> I immediately approved of Susan, and my instinctive liking for her increased during their stay. But then, I have heartily approved of all four wives once I got to know them. Susan was destined to have the hardest time with him, because she virtually had to become his nurse during a long illness, and he was a very difficult patient.
>
> Richard spent much of the time reading, a habit of long standing. He was eager to read my Burgoyne autobiography, and he genuinely enjoyed it. Then he wanted to

hear the recording of my lecture-recital on *Hamlet*; he smiled as he listened to it because it brought back many memories.

On their third night Susan stayed up after Richard went to bed. She wanted a long talk with me and I was grateful for it. My diary comment on her after that talk was, "She's a fine person."

What did Richard and I talk about? We relived the past, we talked about Kate whose twentieth birthday would be two days after they left, and, of course, we talked Shakespeare. He became excited about my ideas for the new version of *Richard III*, but chiefly he wanted me to talk about *King Lear*. He had an increasing desire to play the title role and that thrilled me.

A few pages on, Philip reprints part of a letter Richard sent him—it was enclosed with "Rowse's New Annotated Shakespeare. He's as usual, very waspish and sometimes witty," Philip quotes from Richard's letter. His affection for his schoolteacher father continues with undiminished enthusiasm.

Word of your enormous success with the latest lecture reached me from all kinds of sources. I smiled modestly and said I'd taught you all you knew! I tell people you don't do anything as common as lecture; that we must coin a new word for what you do to that audience. I tell them that you explode with more passion in one "lecture" than I do in ten performances of *Hamlet*. What shall we call them? Lectureagonistesappassionata? Impressive on a billboard don't you think? My eldest brother Tom died, as I think you know, a few weeks ago—no, several weeks ago—nearly making his 79th; not bad with two lungs full of coal. Susan and I went to the funeral. Susan was overwhelmed by the singing; the whole valley was out in force. It was a curious irony that his only child, Mair, who has been married for twenty years, suddenly found herself pregnant *for the first time* at the age of 41 yet. What's more, the baby has arrived, a girl, and mother and child are in splendid order. The Lord giveth . . .

Cis was at the funeral and angelic as ever. Naturally

she sent especial love to you. "Oh, I wish I 'ad all that's in 'is 'ead." Imagine if you'd caught that bright loving creature when she was young.

If we get a chance we'll nip in and see you. If not, we'll try and get *Camelot* to Miami.

When is the next lectureagonistesappassionata? Tell those idiots to get the taping right for once, will you? Am in splendid health (apart from a temporary cold) and Susan too. Cannot, however, give up smoking, whereas booze is a distant (and regretfully delightful) memory. Will try again with the nicotine and tar. Dangerous though, as the last time I gave it up—for five days—I *totally* lost my memory. Apparently it's not at all unusual.

Happy birthday. Much love, and from Susan too. Usual apologies for long silence.

P.S. Kate is at the Yale School of Drama if you want to drop her a line.

There is some evidence that Richard insisted that *Camelot* went to Miami in order that Philip could see it. Philip was not allowed to travel far, but the Key West–Miami journey was within his tolerance. His report on the event bubbles through the pages. There was time for a graze over the past, a summation, regrets.

I had not told Richard about our coming because I knew he would have wanted to postpone the visit, but when we got to the theatre I decided it would be unfair not to let him know that I was there. I went to the stage door alone—my friends could see him after the performance —but there was such strict control on admittance to see him that someone in authority had to be fetched before I was allowed in.

When we got to the dressing room the first thing that struck me was that Susan was doing Richard's make-up; his right arm was virtually useless; on stage he wielded his sword with his left arm. When he had recovered from the surprise of seeing me and I had explained the circumstances, he asked me where we were sitting. I told me we had good seats halfway back. He called the House Manager and asked him to change our seats to ones nearer the stage. The house was completely sold out, so how the Manager could change our seats I didn't know, but he did it; we had centre seats in about the sixth row.

The script had been skilfully adapted to allow for Richard's added twenty years; it began with a prologue in which King Arthur was middle-aged, and then the tale became a reminiscence. I did not have to maintain my usual critical appreciation of the show and Richard's performance— they weren't on their way to Broadway—so I was free just to relax and enjoy it, and I did.

At the end of the performance Richard received a standing and vociferous ovation, and then he made a speech about me which was so deeply moving that I wasn't the only one in the audience with tear-filled eyes. He said that he had been more nervous at that performance than at any since the opening night because his father was in the audience. Then he went on to sing my praises, and said that he owed everything to me.

I had assumed we would be going to a suite in a hotel, the usual accommodation for a star on tour, but to my surprise we were taken to a beautiful house in a very select part of Miami, Golden Beach. It had been rented for a month. Staying with them were Vivienne, Susan's sister, and Vanessa, Vivienne's little girl.

After our enjoyable tea-party Richard beckoned me and led the way upstairs. He took me to a lovely front bedroom overlooking a private beach, and he said, "This is your room." I told him I couldn't stay and began to explain why. He broke in with "Why do you think I took this house?" I was deeply touched and agreed that I would come up for a week in early November and be there for his 55th birthday on November 10th . . .

By my insistent choice, my second visit was made by bus; Richard had wanted to send a car to Key West for me.

After a two-performance day Richard usually stayed in bed until noon, but not this time; he was up at nine. Apart from the excellent meals which she provided for us, Susan left us alone and we talked almost all day, not about *King Lear* and *Richard III* and future plans, but about intimate personal matters. My diary says, "I learnt astonishing things, and much to admire." The man revealed to me in such talks was very different from the one known to his theatre friends; them he entertained with tales from his past which became embellished with the years. He needed to talk to me about his hidden self. The boy I had grown to know, admire and love was still there. He didn't try to mitigate or justify the hurt he had caused others, but faced it with deep regret. He remembered gratefully the times of deep happiness. He shared his dreams with me; to the end of his life he was a frustrated scholar and writer. One thing I had long esteemed him for was his instinctive generosity. His divorced wives were lavishly provided for. His several brothers and sisters and their children were always treated generously. He had established trusts for his children. The urge to make money to give him the power to help so many had resulted in his doing much film work he despised, and this, in turn, had resulted in his drinking to drown the sense of artistic guilt . . .

The next day, Monday, November 10th, was Richard's 55th birthday.

The never-to-be-forgotten wonder of the day was the after-theatre party which Susan had arranged. The whole company had been invited; there were at least a hundred people present. Susan had engaged the premises and services of a really distinguished Miami restaurant. We had the exclusive use of four rooms: a dining room, a dance-floor, a bar, and a buffet which had a most tempting display of delicacies so that guests could continue eating, after the served dinner, through the early hours of the morning. Our family group didn't get home until 2 a.m. and we seemed to be the first to leave.

Richard and I sat at a table for four; the other two places were for Susan and Valerie, but they had so much to see to that they sat down for only an occasional mouthful. Prior to the actual dinner I had enjoyed talking to some members of the company in the bar; some of them seized the opportunity to ask me how they could improve their performance. This had happened with other companies. Richard had always painted such an advance-picture of me as the Wonder Man of the Theatre that meeting me must have been a sad disillusionment for many.

When we had come to the end-of-the-meal coffee and liqueur, an imposing gentleman, who may have been the proprietor of the restaurant, came to our table and invited Richard to go with him to the cellar to see their famous wine collection. Richard was away a long time. Two of the chairs at our table had been taken by Franz Allers and his wife. Franz had been the conductor of the original production of *Camelot* and had returned twenty years later to supervise the local orchestras. The three of us enjoyed our conversation so much that they said they were coming to Key West to visit me the following Friday; later they were forced to postpone their visit to January; it still hasn't taken place.

Throughout our conversation I had been concerned about Richard, and events proved that I was right to be. Susan came to tell me that we were going home. She didn't have to tell me the reason; Richard was drunk. He had always taken pains to avoid my seeing him in that state, and apparently he had been commendably sober for months. During the ride home I couldn't make contact with him, and gave up trying. He talked nonstop in an effort, I suppose, to appear normal.

When I saw him the following morning he seemed astonishingly normal, and we had a good talk, with no reference to the wine-cellar. Then he said he wanted to get an orange-juice, and I didn't see him again. He had lain down on his bed and fallen fast asleep. I was leaving that afternoon, again travelling by bus, and Susan and I decided we shouldn't wake him because he had a performance that evening.

And back to Key West he went, by bus, a rightly proud and happy man.

One feature of Philip's memoir is the devotion of Susan and, equally, the constriction of her life in what became—for long periods—a matter of total service. She has maintained a well-defended silence about her time with Burton. Those who know them are slow to lay on her any blame for the eventual divorce. One version is that he allowed her to manage and nurse him but soon resented being managed and nursed and turned on her for it. It may well have been that her more conventional nature simply tired of the exceptional demands of the man.

As the tour went on, Burton's physical pain increased until it was all but intolerable. Close observers noted that the intensity of the pain and the will and force he had to employ not only to combat it but to give eight full performances a week to packed house after packed house would have killed anyone else. For whatever reason —his stubbornness, the fury of a man of great former physical strength and grace who cannot abide this thing of weakness his body has become, hates and fights the illness like a mortal foe—he went on. Perhaps, for such a man as he was, the very nerve and anguish of it took him into regions of illumination which fascinated him. He was always and truly spellbound by the unthinkable notion of death. ''Timor Mortis Conturbat Me.'' ''The fear of death anguishes me.'' But also tells me the fragile and precious value of life. In that period he went down from 175 pounds to 140.

For far too long he fought it. In San Francisco it was discovered that he had an impinged nerve in the cervical area. The pain was now so bad that his right arm was useless and he could not lift his left arm up to his shoulder. The pills he took made him nauseous. But still he went on. In LA the advance booking broke all records. Despite constant sweating and nausea he went on. Between scenes he made for the men's room and vomited. Then he returned to the stage. Rapturous ovations. A good press. Finally he collapsed and only then did he allow himself to be taken into St. John's Hospital in Santa Monica. It has been suggested since that the operation was not wholly necessary, although at the time it was genuinely thought to be. Its after-effects could be most damaging. They were in this case. His neck muscles were permanently weakened and from then on he would be in unremitting pain.

He went to Céligny to convalesce but was soon in more distress. A major operation for ulcers was carried out in October.

By the end of the year he was separated from Susan. She was to take the second home he had bought at Puerto Vallarta, and $1,000,000. He did not demur. She had had enough and he was the first to sympathise. What he needed now was a long and deep rest. A break from the peculiarly nerve-tearing tensions of his very strange profession. None of the burden of leading a large company or carrying a big project. Peace he needed and tranquility and both he could afford to have—despite the money flung out to former wives and strangers, brothers and sisters, nephews, nieces—all twenty-nine of the family. He had earned a rest. Cis, from so far back, saw him about this time and said, most simply, what many wanted to say: "Why don't you give yourself a rest, Rich, I asked him. You've done your bit."

His reputation could afford it. Indeed could benefit from the maturing quality of absence. *Camelot* had proved yet again his ultra star status, his pulling power. The four bad films would drop off the branch, the memory of *Virginia Woolf, Becket, The Spy Who Came In From The Cold, Look Back In Anger, Night Of The Iguana, Equus* and *The Wild Geese* all in their different ways would rise with the yeast of time. He could wait, sit it out, come back when he was refreshed to be welcomed as one of the Great Survivors.

But whatever it was that drove Burton, whatever genie or devil that worked away would have none of it. Like some legendary Celtic king who, bereft of army and even of arms, will neither surrender nor retreat but attack and attack again, he was not to be restricted nor even seem to be defeated. His arms had no strength. His back gave him constant agonising pain. His body cried to heaven for rest. But he feared death would scythe him down even sooner were he to give in.

At the beginning of 1982 he took on the biggest and most punishing film role he had ever accepted. Once more, despite all advice to the contrary, he went into battle.

26
The New Campaign

"If he wanted to reach across the table for the marmalade," said Brook Williams, "then he had to lift one hand with the other and most likely bend forward his entire body as well. The muscles across the neck and the upper arms were gone. He couldn't raise his arms up in the air. But he never complained; never heard him say a word about it, nobody did." This was during the filming of the life of Richard Wagner, the composer whose operatic life was some match for his operatic art. It was to be a long television "art-film" mini-series. Burton played Wagner.

Now that Susan was gone, Brook Williams, his most enduring and his closest friend, moved in to be Richard's entourage. He was his stand-in during the Wagner filming—besides playing several minor character roles—and his wit, shared literary passion, showbiz nous and mimicry were just what Burton needed. Besides, and perhaps most importantly, Brook was from the old days . . . Emlyn, his father, had given Richard his first film and big theatrical break, Richard had gone to Brook's school plays. Brook knew the Welsh and all the London actors, continued to be friendly with Elizabeth, had himself survived a difficult marriage, knew about professionalism à la Coward—learning the lines and not bumping into the furniture. Burton was lucky and canny in securing such a friend at that time. *Wagner* would nearly finish him off: but also it would restore him.

It would be the most tremendous haul. Seven months' filming—

all over Europe—forever striking camp: "It was a luxury to be able to unpack," Brook said, and Burton at the centre of almost every scene as Richard Wagner the composer not only of the new style of opera but the new vision of Germany. There would be a ten-hour version and the more generally viewed six-hour version.

The hospital insisted on sending a physiotherapist along and Brook thinks this was a mistake. "He was a great guy"—Brook mimics him—" 'The last time I was in Europe I was seven thousand feet up bombing the shit outa the place.' But the last thing Richard needed after a ten- or twelve-hour day was to be pummelled and thumped for an hour. An *hour*! He needed to put his feet up. But anyway—being Richard—he stuck to the contract."

Wagner was directed by Tony Palmer, whose reputation rested on award-winning arts documentary profiles—of Benjamin Britten, William Walton, Stravinsky. He was and remains fascinated by Burton and over that intense period came to know him quite closely.

"Even now—although there were criticisms—I can't think of *anybody* who could have brought it off better than he did. Apart from anything else they were so alike—the women, the drink, the grandiloquence, the sense of destiny: and the name! *And*, both had very large heads. We did a photo of Burton as Wagner—modelled on a famous photo—and they are uncannily alike. He used to say 'I am Wagner.' "

Palmer is now aware of the quite extraordinary physical strain being put on Burton. But he never complained. Even young and fit men flaked as this pounding caravan slugged around Europe. "Forty per cent of the time he's marvellous, forty per cent he's very good, twenty per cent he's terrible. But most of that is my fault. I didn't have the experience to cut around it and when *he* suggested a younger man should play the young Wagner, I, mistakenly, resisted. The amazing thing about him was his talent. He shot for 152 days and on *every* day—no matter what had happened the night before—he was word perfect. Sometimes for the most incredibly long speeches. And he would often get them in take one. Storaro" (the brilliant Italian cameraman) "and myself would work out very very long single takes so that we could get the rhythm and sense of a long long speech and he would just do it! But often, when I'd say 'wonderful,' he'd say 'didn't you notice that I said "across" instead of "towards"—let's do it again.' And if I *hadn't* noticed, he'd be quite cutting."

Palmer says that "Burton was more riddled with insecurities than any actor I've worked with." As evidence for this he cites, "He would literally be shaking with nerves before a big take." I don't think this was insecurity. David Lean once remarked that "no actor worth a damn *isn't* nervous before a big take. Only the mediocre are unworried." Besides which, Burton's whole art was to do with calling up forces he did not understand, nor did he pretend to or want to understand them. As this is all but impossible to imagine, it is all but impossible to explain but that does seem to be the truth of it. He had very little technique—his arms, for instance, as Gielgud pointed out early on, were "too short" and "flopped about" and so he rarely used them. He abhorred technique: he did not *want* to be the same night after night or film after film. He knew that his talent was a gift, of some sort. This is one of the many reasons why all sorts and conditions of men and women liked and trusted him. They too believed and believe in "the gift": that, totally unaccountably, some human beings are "given" a talent. In the experience of many of us this is indeed the case—a talent for sport, for figures, for gardening, for affection, for business, for writing, for acting: a "gift." When that gift is as powerful as Burton's and when the man who received it comes from a terribly underprivileged class—then the combination seems miraculous. Burton had the sense and the superstition to know the strengths and limitations of this gift. He had to summon it up or nothing at all happened. In several films—*Hammersmith Is Out, The Klansman, Bluebeard, Circle Of Two* and, alas, others—nothing at *all* happens. He is a presence without a motor. At most he is so bored—as in *Circle Of Two* for instance—that his *boredom* is the single most powerful factor around and everything else fades on the celluloid. He shook before the long takes in *Wagner* because he knew he needed to conjure up a great spirit and he knew also that the deep shocks to his system of those massive operations—never mind the years of drinking, the apocryphal crystals of alcohol discovered on his spine, the five packs a day—might have destroyed the source of the talent, the gift. I think that his nervousness was something quite other than insecurity, although it displayed some of the same characteristics.

Palmer asked him once or twice the old old question—had he wasted his talent? "He never thought he had wasted his life at all. He thought he'd been unlucky once or twice, that was all. He was miffed about not having done *King Lear* in New York some years before—and he still had plans to do it, if he could build up strength in his arms to carry Cordelia—and, really, he rather resented the fact that Sir Peter Hall had never asked him to do anything at the National Theatre." Partly because by contrast Olivier had been so generous in his offers, I suppose.

He drank now and then during *Wagner*—not often but with dire results. It was here that Palmer learnt of Burton's occasional tendency to epilepsy. "He said it had come on first when he was a young actor, about 20. He had been found shaking uncontrollably in the wings, given a couple of brandies and sent on." His fourth wife Sally's sad responsibility was to carry around in her handbag a special stick—with a small sponge on the end of it—which was to release the tongue after an attack. "It helped a few times," she said. He went—briefly—to hospital twice during *Wagner* when he felt it coming on. Drink, then, had once and early been the fatal cure. Alcohol had been the best medicine to hand. And acceptable.

The imperious portrait is of an indomitable fighter, a warrior who would not be licked: and yet, despite the odds, that grace—"he could not have been more courteous—to everyone"—and the fatal carelessness both remained.

There was a terrible party.

Sir Laurence Olivier, Sir John Gielgud and Sir Ralph Richardson were all acting together, in *Wagner*, for the first time since Olivier's film of *Richard III*, thirty years before. Burton was delighted: they were too. All of them were long-time friends. Their scenes were early in the shooting, in Vienna. Each decided to give a party for the other three. At Richardson's party exotic food was served but the service was awful. Gielgud flew in food and presents but alas the food was a touch tasteless. Olivier seemed set to win (yet again?) when he had special menus printed and laid on a magnificent feast. Unhappily the directions got muddled and everybody was late, some very late. Burton seemed set to clean up. It was a game—the art of "upstaging" which he, like the others, loved. It was often mistaken as his chief view of a performance—who upstaged whom—whereas, in fact, it was the chief *fun* of a performance, pro-to-pro.

His party was at the famous Palais Schwarzenberg. The three knights were there, the director, Palmer, Storaro the cameraman, Shirley Russell the designer, Lady Richardson and Burton who, as customary, had before him one glass of wine (which would be untouched all evening) and a glass of water which would be constantly replenished.

Burton arrived in storming form and held court for two hours. New stories, funny old stories, the three knights enchanted and giving as good as they got. He was winning and no one grudged it. As the evening grew to a crescendo of splendid mimicry and anecdote and competitive out-quoting and fun, Burton suddenly began to grow tired. His body began to flag. The ten-hour day; the pummelling of the physiotherapist; the strain. In the middle of one rococo story about the Jenkinses of Wales, his hand shot out and grabbed and drank the wine. About five minutes later a transformation had taken place. It was, so it is utterly reliably reported, quite extraordinary: Jekyll to Hyde.

He became as vicious as he had been generous, as savage as he had been affectionate. One by one he picked them off. Olivier was "a grotesque exaggeration of an actor. All technique. No true emotion." Gielgud was subjected to biting references about his sexuality. Richardson's famed timing was nothing more than forgetfulness: he could not remember his lines and had to look around for the idiot-boards. The odd thing was, says Tony Palmer, that whenever one was being attacked, the other two did not rise to his defence, perhaps even seemed to agree just a little. The atmosphere was Mephistophelian. Richardson was very laid-back: "Poor Richard," he murmured. Gielgud looked disdainfully and sadly down his nose: Burton was perhaps his greatest pupil and, he knew, his greatest admirer. Olivier said nothing at all but watched, and noted, and you felt it would all come out some time later in a performance. On the way to his car, Olivier said, "I know now why you chose Richard to play Wagner." On the way to *his* car, Burton said, "O God, O God, I went too far, didn't I?" None of them referred to it again by word or nod.

"It was quite scary," says Palmer, "the power of the man."

Palmer praised the thoroughness of Burton's research: "He had a library of Wagner books with him and he was a stickler for accuracy; he must have been a menace on those earlier historical feature films." He was also impressed by his professionalism. "He would have a night out, say, with Franco Nero and Nero would want to continue the larking around on the set the next day. Burton wouldn't have any of that at all." Work was to be got on with; put in a proper shift; be the good soldier. And finally, Palmer, who has met some very civilised people, was "amazed by the range of his knowledge. He was always the best read person around."

In week four of the shoot, he and Susan announced that they were to be divorced. Many of their friends were shocked and dismayed. She had given him immense support. Her mother blamed the drink. Burton blamed himself. A dispassionate outside view might have pity on a man who had endured the surgery and hospitalisation which Burton had gone through but he never referred to it. He said that their quarrels had become violent, that Suzy had all the reasons in the world to leave. She had wanted children; he, too, at first and then he had grown unwilling. Since leaving Sybil, since the birth of Jessica, the only "child" had been Maria who had served Elizabeth and himself as "theirs."

Elizabeth had divorced US Senator Warner a couple of months earlier. Her life with the cattle-loving Senator had been a touch limited. She described it as largely lying on a bed, watching television and eating. Her obesity became a national joke ground into a routine by another national joke, Joan Rivers. Warner got on with his career. Elizabeth, whose work and charisma had hoisted him up a ladder his inborn talent seemed destined never to mount, swelled into boredom. There were those who were convinced that she was mourning Richard. That after the dozen years of his attention, his intense understanding of her, his appreciation of her and the excitement of the danger of the man, the alternatives were rather thin stuff. Burton had given her an idea of herself which was grand—and, it seemed, true. Without him she felt no more than "a broad." Or, put simply, she was still in love with him. Certainly when Susan left him, the phone began to ring—at least three times a week—and she asked if she could come out on to the location in Venice. Burton asked Palmer, and Palmer demurred, and Burton said no. But the phone kept ringing.

And Mohammed went to the mountain. Inspired, some thought, by Burton's success in *Camelot*, Elizabeth had slimmed down, lost forty pounds, called up a play, *The Little Foxes* and, unpredictably, been a hit, critically and at the box office. Now it came to London, where it would open a few days after her fiftieth birthday party. As usual, Elizabeth allowed no occasion to escape quietly.

Coincidentally, Richard had long before arranged to be in London that weekend. He was to play in a one-off charity performance of

Under Milk Wood. He rang her. She asked him to be her escort. He hired a private jet. "Where's my present?" she asked. They danced, "as t'were" (a favourite phrase of Burton's) the night away and then, still on track though way off the wagon, he entertained the world and its wife to the sort of melodrama and interviews that put him in the five-star category of the journalist's guide to top class copy. Maria was there—a swan, a model, just married; Liza was there. He had, he said when he returned to the film—on time and sober enough to act—had a "blinder." The engine of war was still in tune.

Taylor's friends and entourage feared his coming—wanting to protect their girl from the man whom they knew could snatch her away with a nod: and they resented his going because he went alone. Richard said that the weekend, though "terrific," had reaffirmed that it was and always would be "all up" between them—however much she continued to fascinate him.

As if to confirm this, he had begun a circumspect stalking of Sally Hay, who was to become his fourth wife. Sally had worked at the BBC and then gone freelance, successfully, as a PA. In London she had a flat, some liaisons had come and gone, she was an attractive thirty-four-year-old career woman who had worked with Palmer before and was "thrilled to be on *Wagner*. To get away from London again. And it was a good career move." From November she was at base camp in Vienna. Richard joined the film in January; Brook, who became and remains her good friend, two weeks later.

"He was very thin," Sally recalls. "But very sun-tanned. I thought he looked great. We all thought he was taking on a massive challenge. Somehow he wanted to prove himself again. And at the very beginning he was still hoping to get together with Susan. 'I must go and telephone my wife,' he would say. He was very proud of her. He worked hard. Most of all he enjoyed the actors who came out—the three Sirs of course—but Dicky Pasco, Ronald Pickup— he wouldn't drink for two or three weeks and then a little binge. He was terrific at holding us all together. But he would read a lot. The physio was at him every night. Bob Wilson came out later on when he began to get really tired."

The pilgrimage began—Vienna, Munich, Venice, Siena, back to Venice, Germany, Hungary, Austria again, Dublin, the night of the three Sirs, the weekend with Elizabeth, or E.T. as Sally playfully calls her. "After the Suzy thing had gone there were other ladies around. I'd been attracted to him—he was gorgeous. But I thought—forget it. There was one point in Venice when he was having dinner with a girl and I got tremendously jealous and I thought 'Watch out. You're in trouble.' Then there was one night—about three months in—I went down to one of Ludwig's castles—Vittorio [Storaro] was running a little behind. I went to explain to him what was happening on the set. I was staying in the same hotel. He asked me to join him for dinner. It took off from there. I remember thinking—I'm not going to blow it. I'm not going to be frightened. Or carried away. I'd just see what happened. It seemed to work. What I mean is a few days later I moved in with him.''

Brook Williams's version is more complimentary to Sally, as indeed was Richard's—and includes a stalking, waiting, hoping period on Richard's part which Sally herself does not mention. She was very cautious.

''I thought—it will only run for the film. I didn't want to get hurt. It'll be great (it was)—I'll have a wonderful time (I did) and then it'll be over (no). About six weeks in he discussed marriage. I knew that Richard was into marriage and I was worried. He was serious. Let's give it a year, he said. Then talk about it again. I still didn't believe it.''

By the end of the film ''he was not very well. His back was hurting badly. Tempers were short. We were all exhausted. He worried about the film. 'I think it will become a cinematic curiosity,' he said. After the filming we went off to LA to have his back checked. I realised I was in his life then. They really wanted to do another operation on his lower spine but Richard was against it. Just as he was against all pain killers after the ulcer operation. But ultimately he had to take them.''

Richard became devoted to Sally. ''She can do everything,'' he boasted to Brook Williams, ''she can cook, type, do shorthand—there's nothing she can't do. She looks after me so well. Thank God I've found her, Brookie.''

Several of Richard's friends pointed out the similarity to Sybil—in temperament—cheerful, clever, as well as attractive and a home-maker. There was one other factor. Sally's father was an alcoholic—a fact which the British press dug up quite quickly—she knew the terror and the difficulty of all that.

After being in hospital in LA, they took the sun at a beach on the way to Malibu. ''A funny little shack, a supermarket along the street, cooking for ourselves, reading a lot, drinking a little, now and then. He got very interested in diets and the house seemed overwhelmed with diet books. Whenever he went on one he stuck to it rigorously."

The question was—what next? Burton was still restless, still determined to throw off the shadows and the failures of the past few years and go out and show them. Perhaps *Wagner* had done it but there was no way of knowing until it was released. He wanted to be on the trail again, like a cowboy wanting to be back in the saddle after a fall. But where was the horse?

Elizabeth Taylor had very pointedly swum back into view. Mike Todd Junior was to produce a film, *Herself Surprised*, and Richard was to be in it. That would take him through autumn '82: in spring he would do *A Long Day's Journey Into Night*. He was beginning to re-establish the pattern which suited him. Both fell through and gradually he was inveigled into doing *Private Lives* for the "Elizabeth Theatre Group" which she had set up with Zev Buffman. Three plays were on the agenda: the Noël Coward, *The Corn Is Green* and the third "to be announced."

It happened by fits and starts, but suddenly, one Sunday, in the middle of the *New York Times*, there appeared a massive heart pierced by an arrow announcing, "Together again!" Tickets were on pre-sale.

"It all seemed accidental but now I'm inclined to think it was very clever on Elizabeth's part, unconsciously perhaps," says Sally. "The original idea had just been to tape it. And then it was decided to stage it first. Then it was suggested that it be the lead play in Elizabeth's instant new theatre company. The taping was put back and back. It never was finally taped. Had the deal been: 'Do you want seven months on tour with *Private Lives*,' Richard would have fled. But it only came to that when he was too far in."

At the beginning of 1983, Burton went to Haiti for his divorce from Susan. Before that he began a diary which he kept up for about six weeks. It is much thinner than the Notebooks—more a jotter than anything else. His urge to attempt to be a writer appears, at this stage, to have abated. Yet the entries are not without interest especially as they re-introduced Elizabeth to the scene. Sally, incidentally, had been "terrified of meeting her. But she was very very nice. After I did meet her I felt very secure and I continued to feel that."

The Notebooks begin again in Switzerland and, typically, the opening entries home in on Sally and his Welsh family.

> (Feb. 14, 15, 16, 19) Sally v. depressed all day. Worried about Haiti, divorce, NY, and attendant publicity she thinks. Poor thing. I went back to work . . . S. still depressed and fed up with being a slavey no doubt. Being with me is not as glamorous as people think . . . Sleepless until 5 or so. Got up at 12.30 or thereabouts. Verdun back in intensive care with yet one more heart attack. Will he repel the swine this time again? Pray that he does. He has been v. overweight since he gave up fags. He is the lynch pin of the family since Tom died. His loss wld be terrible . . . Watched Ireland v. France. Heard Wales v. Scots. Not much in it, either side cld have won.

The old ways and days were back. It could have been Sybil in Hampstead thirty years before.

10 Feb 83

Dear Sally,

Or dearest Sally or most beloved Sally or undo-without-able Sally or lovely Sally especially with a minimum of clothes on, or clever Sally or sexy Sally, dress up for me this evening or rather dress down and let's see what happens for I love you and adore you to the point of weakness sometimes—sometimes abjectly—sometimes with a species of pain. So after dinner you and me and then back to that beastly Coward. I warrant I'll sleep too!

This is the first time I've touched a typewriter for two years or more and my first exercise in it or on it is directed to you. My use of the machine—like me—has detiorated in speed but not much in accuracy. Who knows that I may not start writing again. For money I mean. Or even for my own enjoyment or yours.

So it shall be an early dinner and an early night for you and possibly not too late a night for me.

God, how I shall miss this place after we have been thrown into the mealstrom again. That seemingly inevitable cauldren of public attention. Never mind we shall undercome. This machine a ecrire slips a line now and again. Not my fault. Honest.

See you later.

Love and hugs and cwtches and other things.

My arms, so far, are not hurting. Good. No?

As the time for the rehearsals draws near, he gets down to learning his role—as Elyot, the part written for and played by Coward himself.

(Feb. 25) No appetite again—beginning of nerve tension I suppose. Milton Katselas (director) phoned to say r'he'sals put two days forward so perhaps a longer stay in what we hope will be sun in Haiti. It is due for the first of the rainy seasons in Port au Prince. I wonder if E.T. is behaving herself in her film so hence the delay in beginning work.

Sally worked like a miner all day long packing—quite a task as we're going to be away so long. All I did was pack the book-bag with reference books and foreign grammars and had at it with Noël again. Going thru' a blank and boring spot with it. Roll on work when it shld all fall into place. Talked to Verdun. Seemed in good form.

And so to Haiti and divorce from Susan.

(Feb. 28) I was divorced yet again today here in the Palais de Justice. Took ½ hr or so. Interpreter was sent for who took (a woman) 10 mins or so to get there before which time the Judge and I decided we cld do without her as my French was fluent enough. He spoke no English.

Delighted all over.

Strongly tempted to buy a place here. Relatively cheap to buy and very cheap to live here. Shall go to see some houses. People gay and delightful and no servant problem. Sally pleased too and it's so helpful to know the language. Easier to get to than Mex (P.V.) and only 3 hrs to NY.

Lines are read over with Sally and he builds himself up.

(Mar. 4) Slept like a rose. Awoke at 6 a.m. Brilliant day. Lay in sun, had b'fast. Supine for a couple of hours going thru' *Private Lives* in my head after breakfst. Very hot. Frequent dips in the pool. Have developed new stroke in swimming since I can't still do the crawl. The underwater butterfly. One breath each five strokes. Next Olympic championship.

In New York he made all the connections immediately.

(Mar. 13) Sunny day. Talked to Kate—coming over Monday night. Working off-B'way. Irish play. Maria came over with baby. Went with them to see E.T. who's using Rock Hudson's flat in the Beresford. Little or no library. Horrid flat. E.'s face OK but figure splop! Also drinking. Also has not yet read the play! That's my girl!

The struggle is there with Elizabeth's lateness and her fight over lines.

(Mar. 14) E.T. bad. Couldn't even read the lines properly. Doubtless she'll come up to scratch eventually. E.T. as exciting as a flounder temporarily. Sally went health-store-hunting. This is going to be a long long 7 months. E.T. beginning to bore which I wld not have thought possible all those years ago. How terrible a thing time is . . .

(Mar. 15) E.T. only 15 mins late but then spent 15 mins more doing her eyebrows. She stinks of garlic—who has garlic for b'fast? She is also on something or other b'cause there are lines here and there which *she can't say at all*. Very worrying. It's appalling, but I'd not mind if she found she couldn't do it and we had to get someone else. She is also terribly low in energy. Tells me twice an hour how lonely she is. I pity that poor Buffman . . .

(Mar. 16) Still lovely weather. E.T. 1 hr late today. Two Veganin stuck in her throat and in trying to shift them (with Fernet Branca) she vomited. Then her car wouldn't start so mine was sent for her. On the white wine today. Bought me a quite unnecessary Cartier scarf "Le Must" . . .

(Mar. 20) Ran thru 2nd act with E.T. Abysmal. She was quite crocked by this time and couldn't even *read* the lines let alone remember them . . .

(Mar. 22) Fury recollected in relative tranquillity. E.T. impossibly sloshed all day long. So much so she cldn't even *read* the lines. Same at dinner with the Simon Hornbys.

Only occasionally do other considerations intrude into what is becoming a battle to get under way a production which seems irredeemably waterlogged. Though even here E.T. is still present.

(Mar. 23) Worked from 12 noon 'til 7 p.m. without ceasing. E.T. had an eternal costume fitting (2½ hrs) so worked without her. Less sloshed but didn't know a single word of second act which Brook and I went over with her endlessly on Sunday last. Have been forced to promise to go to a memorial service (as "one of the stars") for Tennessee Williams. Did two films of his—both goodish, I believe. I didn't even like the chap. As a matter of fact hardly ever saw him sober tho' we were together for months. A self-pitying pain in the neck. Also he made a pass at my Chris when Chris was 8.

Then the light began to dawn. Elizabeth delivers.

(Mar. 27) E.T. tremendously better in 1st act—still rocky in 2nd and reads 3rd. For the first time in this piece I enjoyed r'h'sals. Hope it continues.

And it goes on.

(Apr. 2) Two runs-through today and the difference in perfs was sensational in comparison with a mere 1½ days ago. The play and players began to invent. J. Callum [playing Victor] now spot on. Odd man out is me at the moment. I suspect I'm too dangerous to play Noël. My

bloody voice is too rich or something. Well, I'll see what
I can do.

And that is the last entry in the Notebooks.

Elizabeth's troubles are understandable. If she had engineered this
reunion it was in order to be with Richard—"together again"—
only to find Sally firmly in residence. Her figure was too bloated
and she was about to show it off not on the magical screen with its
sympathetic lights and experienced flattering cameramen, but on
stage where exposure would be inevitable. And she had her own
methods of preparing for a role. She paced herself and nothing had
to interfere with that. It had always been the case. She divined her
way to the part and learning the lines was not high on her list of
priorities, although she would, and on time, be word perfect. Richard's equally odd mixture of old fanatical army discipline and his
own secret inner quest to turn on the light of the part from the
darkness of his own unconscious personality provided an uneasy
match. He was not drinking, still recovering from the savage surgery
and the seven months of *Wagner*. And she, as came out later after
her spectacular Betty Ford cure, was not only drinking but seeking
extra relief and/or energy from the drugs she could get as medication.

Her later admission of the drug dependency throws a sad but also
an illuminating retrospective light over the years of her marriage to
Richard. Over drink he was his own harshest critic and never con-
tradicted or tempered the authorised version which said that Elizabeth had finally left him because of the drink. This is what she
told Sophia Loren. This is what she told Ava Gardner—bursting
into tears and saying that she could not stand it, watching him commit
suicide day after day. This is what she told all her friends and Richard
took it on the chin. On the other hand, her numerous—compulsive,
endless—visits to hospital may have a second possible explanation:
that some of them were to get at the drugs she craved. Since her
adolescence she had been addicted to all manner of medication and
prescribed drugs. The drug dependence had increased over the years.
Mixed with the amount of alcohol she took it must have given her
body and brain a terrible pounding, and yet Richard rarely mentioned
it—and then only to blame the doctors. Either he did not see its
danger—which is possible in those pre-hyper-health-conscious days,
or he knew but wanted to protect both of them from the full realisation of the consequences. Or he knew and was prepared to take

on the burden. There is always a sense in which Burton is looking for a pilgrim's burden: setting up families he will have to support, helping a network of old pals, being the Godfather to all who needed him.

Brook Williams was with Richard and Sally throughout the long tour. "The notices were very bad—partly because the opening night was a circus. The curtain went up thirty-five minutes late and the first interval was longer than the first act! Then four performances were cancelled because of Elizabeth's laryngitis. And so it went on. But make no mistake about it—it made a *fortune*. And audiences *loved* it. Loved it." Burton had made $1 million out of *Wagner*: he made over $900,000 in *Private Lives*. Even by the standards of the Eighties, this was not bad going. The Miners' Midas had not lost his touch. And yet, by this stage, there is something which does not interest him about the Klondyke fees. That time was past. He wanted to replant his life in an intelligent domesticity with Sally and regroup his resources. *Private Lives*, which like Topsy "just growed," was helping him do neither and his great problem was to rein in his resentment and call on yet another of his talents—staying power. "He didn't drink at all during the entire run," says Brook and this is confirmed. "It would have been impossible."

"Her tardiness drove him crazy night after night. He would be there over an hour before—make-up—chat—have a cup of tea. 'Where is she, Brook? Is she here yet?' He would get tremendously agitated. She'd arrive, making-up in the car, with a couple of minutes to spare—but then half the audience was out on the streets waiting for her. So *they* had to be herded in. The curtain never went up on time—fifteen minutes late was the minimum and this just drove him crazy. 'This has proved it,' he would say. 'I can never get together with that woman again.' "

But that very statement indicates that he was aware of the pressure. "And I think she was a little jealous," said Brook. "Not just of Sally. But of Richard and me as well. We were having a good time. We had friends. 'Rich' was sober and funny. Elizabeth had all that boring entourage, all the bitching and in-fighting, and the body-guards and the drugs and drink and when she looked across to *our* hotel—we must have seemed rather enviable. Then she brought in the parrot: Alvin."

Alvin came to the theatre every night but stayed in her dressing room. Eventually, Elizabeth began to bring him on for the last scene—Alvin would be on her shoulder—another round of applause of course. And Alvin would take a bow—standing ovations, flowers thrown at the stage. The parrot got very upset. One night— "Where's Alvin?" Brook asked. Elizabeth was very sad: "He can't be with us." "Oh, why not?" "The applause disturbs him." "So where is he, Elizabeth?" Silence. "Oh no! He isn't with a parrot psychologist!" Elizabeth nodded. "But it's so unnecessary," said Brook. "The real reason is that Alvin is very upset because Senator Byrd was in the audience last night and didn't come round afterwards to congratulate him."

"Elizabeth enjoyed that," said Brook.

One of Brook's jobs was to field unwanted or untimely phone calls. Apart from Burton's hatred of the phone, he liked to be in bed before midnight. Elizabeth's calls—always from a nearby hotel—were whenever. "She would ring about three in the morning," says Brook. "Once, for example—phone rings. 'Can I speak to Richard?' 'I'm awfully sorry, Elizabeth, he's asleep.' 'Oh.' Pause. Sob. 'Brookie . . .' 'Yes, Elizabeth?' 'I've gone blind.' 'Oh dear. How very upsetting. This is very serious news.' " Then, says Brook, there was an almighty crash at the other end accompanied by "Shit!" "Hell!" and other Elizabethan expletives. "Are you all right, Elizabeth? What happened?" "Alvin knocked my Jack Daniels over." "I see." "What am I going to do, Brookie—I'm blind again." "Well: you could call your doctor. Or you could contact Sammy Davis's doctor. (She starts to giggle.) Or you could finish the Jack Daniels, have a sleep and see—if you'll pardon the word —what happens in the morning."

An eyelash had got stuck, causing a temporary blindness.

When she was on form, though, Brook avers, "she never lost a line and she could be very very funny."

It was during the run of *Private Lives* that Sally and Richard were married. "Elizabeth was off sick," says Sally. "Richard had five free days. 'Let's get married,' he said. I didn't think he meant it. I couldn't believe life could be so good to me. As a result, I'm wearing the most boring dress. I thought—I might as well get something that's useful! No one-off designer number." Brook and Valerie Douglas were the witnesses; in Las Vegas. Richard was sober—had a couple of glasses after the wedding; stayed sober.

Elizabeth sent them flowers and congratulations. Immediately afterwards she became engaged to a charming Mexican lawyer, Victor Luna.

What upset Sally most on the tour was the physical wear and tear on Richard. "As you know, there are fights and so on and I'd be standing in the wings getting very frightened. Elizabeth at that time was a very heavy lady. And she's not the most co-ordinated person. You should be able to stage a fight so that you do it exactly the same every night and no one gets hurt. It didn't happen like that. It was different every night. She would just grab at him or throw her whole weight on him. I could see the spasms of pain as he braced himself—just where he had had that terrible operation. It worried him but he would say, 'What can I do? That's Elizabeth.' Even simple things didn't work. She had to break a record on his head—it was the usual 'sugar'—but she couldn't do it properly. He would come off bleeding every night. I had to mop him up and re-do his make-up. It was very upsetting but all he'd say was, 'That's our girl. She'll surprise us all.' "

The basic story is similar to the first *Camelot*. Despite the troubles with the director and with Elizabeth and with the pain "and, frankly," Sally says, "neither of them was rightly cast. They are not my idea of Elyot and Amanda," the performance soldiered and staggered on with Richard holding it together. New York, Philadelphia, Washington, Chicago, Los Angeles—a gruelling tour for fit juveniles—a seven-month roller-coaster to hell, it could be assumed, for a man so recently so ill and already overstrained. There was no opening night in Chicago because Elizabeth was ill. In Washington, where Elizabeth had once voiced a desire—not pursued with any of her famed tenacity—to be a great political hostess, in the Washington of Warner, her Senator, where she could be seen to have failed so publicly, become the repository for the cheap jibes of Joan Rivers, Elizabeth played a scorcher. "She was very very good," says Sally. "Every night. Very funny. And she was punctual. She looked great." That, as Richard would say, is our girl.

But the tour petered out in Los Angeles and no one was very sorry.

It had been a disastrous error and at a critical time. He had gone back on the boards—always a courageous thing to do and in his condition quite crazily brave—but he had received none of the refreshment or satisfaction such ventures had given him previously.

One specific loss typifies all of it. While they were in Boston, John Huston rang to ask him to be in *Under The Volcano*. Richard was to have played the Consul, from Malcolm Lowry's marvellous novel. The Consul's drunkenness, his vanishing elegance of mind, the relationship with his wife, with others, the whole part seemed made for Burton and he knew it. But he was stuck in *Private Lives*, heaving Elizabeth across the stage to raspberries from the critics, undiscriminating applause from the audience, and scorn from those, like Lauren Bacall, who thought that they were "merely selling themselves." He had made at least one exceptionally good film with Huston: this could be another—and he needed it, just the right sort of success at the right time. Could Huston wait? "I might die," Huston said. "I've got to do it now. I don't have time to wait."

At the end of 1983 they went to Haiti for sun and rest. It seemed an odd choice of location to Sally but Richard regarded it as no more than a place on the map where he could get some sun and restore his energies for the next campaigns. He had endured two massive engagements—the epic *Wagner* for seven months and the comic epic of *Private Lives*, another seven months—both would have stretched a young, fit man to the limit. Burton had come through, and, some thought, in no little style, partly due to the depth of his character, but also to his strength in his new marriage. And writing again. A new life. He was back on course.

27
1984

In Haiti, Sally and Richard furnished the house, read a lot, swam a lot—he totted up the lengths and increased them steadily—drank hardly at all and wondered what to do next. It was a good moment to make a radical assessment.

He had no reason to be disappointed about his campaigns of the last two years. *Wagner* had shown he could still command the screen, *Private Lives* the stage; both had been endured and here he was with a new wife getting in top shape. The wider world was still interested. At the end of 1983 he had given a speech of honour at the Variety Club Party for Frank Sinatra—an encomium written by himself. It had drawn a posse of acclaim, led by Sinatra's letter, ". . . You moved me as no other man ever has. And I will be grateful to you every day of my life," and a letter from Richard Nixon, "Your tribute was moving without being maudlin and sincere without being sappy and eloquent without being stilted." So, as he would say, that was all right!

For a while he thought, yet again, that he might retire altogether. His coffers had been depleted by the double departure of Elizabeth and then the exit of Susan and he was always as good a giver and spender as he was an earner, but even so, Sally and he calculated, it could be managed. But he wanted to work.

There was talk of *The Tempest* with Anthony Quayle—Burton to play Prospero, the play to open in Bristol; negotiations finally broke down. "He wanted to work with Anthony Quayle again," says

577

Sally (it was Quayle who had given him his first great classical "break" as Young Hal at Stratford), "but going back into Shakespeare would be *so* demanding that he wanted to take all the risks and do it in London." But letters were exchanged, views proposed at length. As always he was "terrified" of going back on the stage; as always he was summoning up the guts to do it. The idea of King Lear—"Shakespeare's great Welsh king," he called him—still haunted him: had he the strength in his arms?—he ploughed up and down the pool. Had he it in him to be an old man?

They were in Haiti for four or five months and over that time Burton unravelled his life for Sally. On his childhood. "He spoke of the difficult relationship with Elfed," says Sally. "I always thought that this was because Richard must have been an extremely difficult teenager. I think that Cis and Elfed, both of them, must have been incredible to have taken him in as their child when times were so bad." Stories of Hilda doing the shopping for all the family, of Ifor banning the purchase of chocolate and scanning the weekly accounts, of Hilda buying chocolate anyway and putting it down as "jam" until the terrible day of reckoning when Ifor's throaty strong Welsh voice demanded, "So where's all this jam, Hilda?" Simple, warm stories belonging to many close families in adversity. "Cis was a Madonna figure. An unearthly creature. As a child he absolutely adored her." And the Madonna was transferred to others for whose essential quality he would disregard all blemishes, excuse all faults.

Sally and he talked about Elizabeth. "I always knew that E.T. would be part of our lives. He would read something or hear something and say, 'You'll never guess what she's doing now, the old girl. She'll surprise us all, that one.' " Sally, as I interviewed her over a couple of years, visibly came to a settlement in her mind about the "other wives." "He needed different women at different times."

About Susan. "He was immensely proud of her beauty. I think Susan was an important part of Richard's life. And after the divorce—she just disappeared. I admire that. There's a tendency to dismiss her. He loved her classiness. When he was having such a success in New York with *Equus* and then walked into a restaurant with Susan on his arm—Wow! They applauded. She worked very hard at the image."

Sybil. "He used to say they were so young. It was great fun—he had some wonderful times with Sybil—they became like brother and sister."

"There were no 'failures.' Different phases needed different people and different times. It was just Richard moving on. None of the wives would have worked in another time."

While they were buying the local hand-painted furniture, soaking up sun, trying to bring real strength back to the spine and shoulders and the thin arms, he talked around the evening meal about many of the figures from his past, mapping out his days for his newest wife. "He would talk about John Neville and 'Tim' [Robert] Hardy, Stanley Baker, Paul Scofield—about the times they had. They were his real friends. It was at the time he *had* real friends. In Elizabeth's day there was the Entourage and a rather grand lot—Brook was the only one who seemed to get through the barrier to him successfully."

I remembered Tim Hardy's story about being "summoned" to a party at the Dorchester for Richard and Elizabeth and, as the evening went on, the better friends drew in closer and closer to the great couple. Like being at the court of a minor German prince, says Hardy: bugger "minor," says Burton. "In Susan's day it was the Gunther Sachs type—seen now and then—not really friends. When I met him," Sally went on, "it seemed strange that he didn't seem to have real pals. And he was such a pally chap in one way. But it does seem to happen to the big stars."

She was "surprised at the number of things he knew and had absorbed." This is from someone whose work had introduced her to a large number of well-read, well-informed people. "He had a vast knowledge—and sometimes it would just pour out of him." About his ambition. "He would go back on the stage but he simply wasn't interested in spending his whole life on the stage doing the same thing every night. He very occasionally spoke of being an academic—but that was a fantasy, I think. His great contentment—and he would have been most proud of himself—would have been to be a writer. He was wondering whether he could put together an autobiography and the Notebooks were referred to as being useful for that."

In spring, brown, fit, calm, they came back to Céligny. "He was in very good shape," says Sally. And from photographs at the time he certainly looked good. The assault of time was still evident but the ravaged haunted look which had seen possibilities in self-destruction had gone. They stayed there until May: and Burton laid out his next campaign.

In August he would do *Wild Geese II* with Euan Lloyd: that would be fun, it would most likely do well at the box-office, it would remind that commercial world that he could still do it when he had a mind to. In October he would move on to *The Quiet American*, to be directed by the young Englishman Charles Sturridge. He was delighted about this: the quality of the book, the relevance of the subject, Sturridge's credentials—he had done *Brideshead Revisited* for Granada Television—all appealed to Burton's sense of style, literariness and sense of adventure with a new talent.

He was asked to appear in an American mini-series, *Ellis Island*. He did not want to do it. Kate, his daughter, had been offered a very large part—an important break for her. "Without actually anything being said, I suppose I was the bait for Dad," she says, over-modestly. But there was something in that and, quickly, Burton sniffed it out. He accepted a small part which would take a couple of weeks and justified it by talking about "looking into this new world of television series." And there was a play, *Painting Churches*, which he wanted to do at the end of the year on Broadway.

He had put together a formidable package but the best was to drop into his lap. *1984*, the film adaptation of George Orwell's novel, directed by Michael Radford. Six weeks' work in June–July which he could fit in. He was utterly delighted. He telephoned Philip.

In May I received two long calls on the same day from Richard who was at home in Céligny. The ostensible reason for the first call was that he wanted me to send him a copy of my book, *The Sole Voice*, for A. L. Rowse. I was to send it to London where he was going very soon, and where he expected to meet Rowse. Richard was obviously in an unusually good mood. He said he felt better than he had for years, and it was all due to Sally. He longed for me to meet her, and he was definitely going to bring her to Key West in late January or early February of 1985. What's more, they would stay for several weeks so that we could study *King Lear* together and my new version of *Richard III*. He was excited about his part in George Orwell's *Nineteen Eighty-Four*, because he would bring some humanity to the apparently inhuman O'Brien. Then he talked about *Ellis Island*, a television series based on the novel; he had agreed to take part in it because Kate would be in it, and he would have some scenes with her. After that came a film to be made largely in Germany, and at the end of the year he would go to India to make Graham Greene's *The Quiet American* . . . and then Key West. It was years since I had heard such a happy Richard.

The second call was, prompted by something he had forgotten in the first call. It was to ask me to write to Cis; she was feeling her age and would welcome a letter from me. He would be seeing her soon at her home which was near London. Mention of Cis unleashed many memories. Richard was not a man who wore his heart on his sleeve, but in that conversation he revived deep memories that we shared and treasured. It was a revelation of his true values, and as such warmly remembered by me.

He was not the first choice for *1984*. Paul Scofield had the part but broke a leg. A considerable amount of shooting had already been done before Richard arrived on the picture and Mike Radford showed it to him. John Hurt figured largely. Richard already knew and admired him. When he saw the shot film he said to Sally, "I've got to pull out all the stops this time."

"Radford *directed* him," says Sally. "He enjoyed that." Indeed in many ways, Richard was just what the new wave of young British film-makers were looking for. A grand star who yet had instant connections with the sort of style and radicalism which permeated the ideas of many of them. The intelligent British movie was on its way up and Richard was a natural for the big but not leading parts which required men who looked experienced, intelligent, world-wise. O'Brien in *1984* was right for him. He dropped the "Burton voice," played it quietly, even casually. This torturer and pillar of the state is simply doing his job and with plenty of time to spare; able even to sympathise a little, certainly to understand, quite interested in the victim but in the beginning and in the end utterly immune to any trace of feeling which might take him away from his task: to break the opposition. It is a very fine performance and was reviewed as such.

Richard was buoyant. He exchanged stories and gossip with Hurt, loved his style, liked the man. He was back on track.

"Richard was just perfect to work with," says Hurt. "He helped you. He knew what you were doing. He made no fuss. If he had to do it again, he'd do it again. I thought he was bloody marvellous." Hurt, not unknown as a drinker, had one or two nights out with Burton and all seemed in order: no sudden pallor, no descent into hell, no Jekyll to Hyde.

In July he did *Ellis Island* and both Kate and Sally remember it for the attention he gave to his daughter. "He was so *proud* of her," says Sally. "When she was doing a scene, he would just hang around, out of the way, and look at her so intently. It made me want to cry." "I think he just wanted to take my hand and lead me into his world," said Kate. "If I asked him anything he was always very practical. He would tell me how to help the other actor when you stayed behind for *their* close-ups. The crews all thought he was great—he was 'the man.' I was very proud of *him*, too."

It was at this time, Kate told me, that she got to know him best. "He told me about his childhood, about his shame at some of the parts he'd been in, his shame over the drinking. I learned a lot about his insecurity. We got very close."

It could be said that it takes a man of considerable fundamental security to confess insecurities to a daughter. There is no doubt that at times he *was* insecure although my interpretation is that this was more to do with the way he prepared for acting than a fear of any deep inadequacy. This time with Kate, these conversations in *Ellis Island*, now seem like a valedictory, a last testament to his daughter, telling her how he had failed, yes, but in so doing telling her how he had tried, making himself a reality to her, not a god-the-father figure who would be of no use to her own maturity.

Back to Céligny to prepare for *Wild Geese II* and *The Quiet American*. He made another buoyant call to Philip.

> He called me again after he had finished both *Nineteen Eighty-Four* and *Ellis Island*. He was very happy about the former but wanted to emphasise that the only reason he was in the television series was to be with Kate. Both to him and, when I had seen it, to me, *Ellis Island* was

a shameful exploitation of a great subject. He had had a fine time with Kate, both on and off the set. I had long felt that he had had a sense of guilt about his neglect of Kate, so that meeting and working together must have been a very rewarding experience for both of them. Again he went on about how well he felt and how happy he was with Sally. This was in mid-July.

There were a happy few days. John Hurt was in Switzerland working on another film and they had a couple of nights out. Sally was at the Café de la Gare the night Richard drank and got drunk. That· was Friday, August 3rd. He had come to an accommodation. In a recent television portrait he had spoken of himself as an alcoholic, but typically he had decided to deal with it in his own way. Mostly he was sober—totally abstinent for weeks, months on end. Then he would have a binge and accept the consequences. He still smoked heavily. He was not a man to give up any of his guaranteed pleasures. Nor would he ever be anyone who did anything but "go his own way."

On August 4th he admitted to a headache and Sally gave him a couple of aspirins. She now thinks she ought to have been alerted by his complaint. "But there was never any way of telling. He scarcely ever complained and even if it was serious you couldn't tell." She drove John Hurt back to his hotel in Geneva—he had stayed the night at the chalet. It was hot and sunny.

Brook had gone on ahead to work on *Wild Geese II*. Elizabeth, almost supernaturally slimmed down after her drastic Betty Ford cure, was up in Gstaad "having another go," says Sally. "Making phone calls. Making suggestions that they should work together." Burton told John Hurt, "I'm still fascinated by her." Sally knew this and was quite secure about it all. "They were very content," says Brook Williams. "It was back to basics. Him and Sally and now and then myself to do a spot of organising."

That evening he went to bed early—about ten—as he often did, to read or make a few notes on the pad he kept on his bedside table. He was asleep when she turned in. When she awoke early on Sunday morning he was breathing very heavily and she could not wake him up. She realised something was very wrong.

She got the doctor there in twenty minutes. He did not think it was especially serious and had the ambulance take him to the little local hospital in Nyon. When they discovered how serious it was, they sped him to Geneva. He had had a cerebral haemorrhage.

At the Geneva hospital, Sally was told that they were operating, it would take a long time, the best course for her was to return home and make any phone calls or arrangements. He would be in hospital for a long time. She sensed—this was later confirmed—that had the operation been successful he would have ended up confined to a wheelchair, unable to speak . . . that was a nightmare too. Almost as soon as she reached Céligny, the phone rang. Could she go back?

When she arrived at the hospital she was informed that he was dead. She went to see him. Alone. "I remember quite clearly thinking—Well done! You've thrown off that old body. You're on your next adventure. Well done!"

When we talked she said, "I had a strong feeling that it was a tragedy for us but not for Richard. That helped me through the next weeks. My feeling was that Richard had many lives in him, but not that of an old man."

He was fifty-eight.

The next few days and weeks were turbulent.

"I never thought," said Emlyn Williams, the Welsh lilt flowing, "when I gave that boy his first part in a film that when he died he would be front page and *headlines*."

At the Festival Theatre, Stratford, Ontario, John Neville heard the news, stepped forward at the end of the performance, announced it to the audience, praised Richard, "a truly great actor and friend," and wept. "He was so young," said Olivier when told, "so young." In Hollywood Valerie Douglas began to telephone around the world. One of her calls went to Key West where Philip Burton broke down. "I was devastated." Sybil also phoned Philip and in New York Kate received the commiserations of scores who had known and loved him. No one knew how to break the news to Cis in London but her two daughters went together and told the woman who had been his mother and his sister that she had lost the boy whom she had always loved because she "couldn't help herself." The news spread over Wales and must have been registered in every pub and home in the land. Television. Radio. The press crowded in . . . And then came the funeral.

Brook flew back from *Wild Geese II* which now had a "multi

million dollar problem" and Valerie Douglas came in from California to help Sally. There was confusion everywhere. The press were all but laying siege. Speculation was wild. Would the body go back to Wales? Would Elizabeth Taylor show up? And the other wives? And the family?

He had long before decided to be buried in Switzerland. That was plain in the will. Fear of the press and the crowds and worries over his brother Graham Jenkins's association with the press which had given Richard so much trouble over the years, led to the suggestion that Graham be dissuaded from making the journey. Brook made the phone call to Graham as tactfully as possible but offence was taken. Somehow it was transmitted that none of the family was welcome, and to Sally's added grief, Cis came along convinced she "wasn't wanted." Sally was finding it extremely difficult to cope with putting people up, arranging services, meals, flowers . . . When Graham turned up with a BBC reporter she flew off the handle.

The funeral was up the hill in the village of Céligny. The church there is very like a Welsh chapel. Small. A curved wooden ceiling. A Welsh friend came over to play the organ: just to be sure he went to the chapel the night before and tuned it to his satisfaction. Brook and Kate read in the church. A packed, moving service, the Welsh singing as if they were at home. Brook spoke "And death shall have no dominion." Sally put a poem in an envelope and dropped it on the coffin. Photographers and newsmen and television jostled all around them.

Questions of precedence became positively courtly. Sally thought she could not take Elizabeth's presence at the funeral—"the press would have gone mad"—and rang Elizabeth to tell her so. "I regret that now." But Elizabeth accepted and came on her own, at first making the understandable mistake of going to the new cemetery and being unable to find his grave. Distressed enough, she retreated and returned later in semi-darkness to be led to the small ancient sliver of a burial ground down beside the fast mountain river. Susan came to the memorial service in Los Angeles, Sally was alone at the New York service, Elizabeth came to Wales where the singing in the chapel at Pontrhydyfen brought out the tears in everyone. "Richard would have loved the singing!" Several of them said that. Susan and Elizabeth came for the memorial service in London and Sally was thrown to see Elizabeth—cosseted by Graham—seated in the middle of the Welsh family, next to Cis.

Sally had set out on what must have appeared an amazing adventure with a man who seemed to be getting stronger and fitter by the month. Now it was all abruptly cut off. It was to take her two or three years to absorb it and truly accept it.

When the guests had gone from that funeral at Céligny and Sally had her first few hours of quiet and her first intimation of the encroaching loneliness, she began to tidy up. On Richard's bedside table, she came across his scribble pad. He used a red pen to write on it, often waking in the middle of the night to jot down a thought. These lines had been jotted down on that last night.

> The multitudinous seas incarnadine,
> Making the green one red.
>
> Tomorrow and tomorrow and tomorrow . . .
>
> Our revels now are ended . . .
>
> Cap a pi . . .

The last line is unfinished.

The blood vessels burst and flooded into the brain and there were no more words.

28
"Rich"

Those who knew him best called him "Rich." From childhood. Those who scarcely knew him at all saw his riches too. A man who stormed and captured so many citadels which in his boyhood and youth must have seemed as fantastical and unobtainable as Ali Baba's cave. A man of many lives. A man who had his own centre, something untouchable about him, perhaps something he did not know about himself, did not want to know – perhaps, as Emlyn Williams's old teacher said, the devil in him, certainly a terrible power.

Not least the power to leave his mark on so many. Scores of people wrote to offer their memories of him. Those I did talk to addressed themselves with the utmost concentration to their recollections. It was important to them, a serious matter, to do him justice. He was a great figure in so many lives.

His social range was extraordinary, a tribute to his charm, his modesty and his Welsh sense of equality. He knew, to quote another Celt, that "a man's a man for a' that" – and acted on it. Whether with miners or the Duke of Windsor, with the Baron de Rothschild or Bob Wilson, his black dresser, with Dylan Thomas or Princess Margaret, Gielgud or a novice, Kissinger or a bar-stool politician, Burton was himself, had his own touch, went his own way. He was, and effortlessly, "one of the lads," and marked out for the "elite" – a "natural aristocrat," in Tim Hardy's opinion, just a Welsh working man, in his own. Wanting the respect of Ifor.

His range and generosity were represented in his will with bequests to his several families: the family he came from in Wales; the family he inherited through Elizabeth; his own family; and the various families – friends, Bob Wilson, Ron Berkeley, pals around the campfire whom he had written into so many films over the years; Philip Burton of course; and specific gifts spread abroad. The will took three years to sort out – there were companies in so many different countries from the good old days of Burton – Taylor Global Enterprises Unlimited and the lawyers licked their paws very happily. Going through that was part of Sally's trauma and, finally, part of her recovery; struggling through that gave her both a chance to continue and even deepen her knowledge of Richard – which had been cut so cruelly short – and, the job done, provided the end of a chapter.

She has sold the house at Céligny and moved to London, published a novel and set out on a career as a writer and television journalist. Kate's career as an actress blossoms and she has just had her first child. Liza is a sculptress, Maria, having been a model, now married, also a mother. Michael an actor in New York, Christopher a film editor in Hollywood. Elizabeth is still charting her own public and inscrutable course. Susan off the radar but, when spotted, as stunning to look at as ever. Sybil cheerful, content, silent as a myth on the subject of Richard. Philip living a life of study and friendships in Key West. Cis cared for by her daughters, still a bell in every tooth, on the green fringes of London. Jessica as she has been for more than twenty years, silent.

Perhaps much of Richard's unbearable melancholy can be traced back to Jessica. Not only the guilt, the possibility that the manner of his leaving Sybil somehow exacerbated the affliction, the "ordinary" guilt of leaving a helpless child, but the preying, insistent thought of her terrible non-thought isolation. Her condition was the nightmare he dreaded. "Timor Mortis Conturbat Me"— the fear of death anguishes me—there *are* those whose awareness of death is so much fiercer than that of the rest – Burton was of that company. He was hugely aware—in some haunted way which hints at that telepathic knowledge of so-called "primitive" people—of the fragility of existence, the darkness ready to swallow him up, the extreme, absurd brevity of the sparrow's flight through the lighted hall, from night to night. In some way his acting was a divination of that darker self. All he had was a knack, he said—that was his modesty: it has been called "the knack of the devil." His force as an actor—to which there are far too many witnesses to doubt—the power of melancholy which he had to fight as a man both came from the same source. And somehow, as part of it, was his beautiful, schizophrenic, autistic daughter, Jessica, whose one word that we know of was a cry—"Rich!" His shadow, his fear, his horror.

His own illnesses, borne so lightly, would have worn anyone down. The creeping, crippling onslaught of arthritis, the dislocating fear of epilepsy, the assault of massive surgery—he was rich in his misfortunes too.

But it is the good fortune which made him. He was fortune's child. But fortune favoured him only because he had the guts and the talent. What would have crushed, what did and does subdue millions of people, Burton overcame. It was an incredible leap, a journey to figure in a fairy tale, an epic life.

It was built on talent, his own, given talent. The looks of course were striking—the statuesque head, wide-apart green-blue eyes, pocked skin, grandeur and suffering. The voice was thrilling—many consider it his very greatest gift. Harley Usill, who produced his records of poetry readings, said, "I have never worked with a voice like Richard's—it was the intelligence as well as the sense of rhythm—but the voice was not the essential and crucial gift. He had what everyone recognises and no one can interpret. Something which is found in the back streets and in the great houses, on playing fields and in drawing rooms: he had 'presence.' " His singularity was unmistakable. He was like no one else and the power of that singularity was what he drew on. And, since this happens so arbitrarily and is something we all recognise when we see it, there is both a democratic and an aristocratic dimension to it. For his talent to act, to still an audience and to fill the screen, this was drawn not from technique, nor from imitation, but from himself. And yet it was his life, always, that mattered—and into that he put his genius.

Of the many tributes which followed his death, that which would have pleased him most came on BBC Radio in a special edition of the arts programme *Kaleidoscope*. The producer assembled a notable cast to talk about a man who had, according to Douglas Cleverdon, the great drama producer, been peerless in the medium. It began with Burton speaking the opening line from *Under Milk Wood*. The portrait opened with a recording of Richard very straightforwardly describing his background and then the contributors, like a Greek chorus of distinguished mourners, filled it out. Professor Nevill Coghill said, "There was an element of Welsh Glendowerish magic or mystery to remind us of the unknowable things in life." John Gielgud: "He arrived at the first rehearsal and just walked into a part. I had never to tell him anything except to stop yawning when it was lunchtime . . . he had the most wonderful instinct, immediately." Of his first West End starring role—*The Boy With A Cart*—Harold Hobson, the critic: "He brought his own cathedral on with him." Paul Daneman, who was also in the play, talked of the very first reading. "He read it magically. I mean quite magically. We all sat there transfixed by this wonderful voice and extraordinary feeling for poetry." Anthony Quayle, who took him to Stratford: "There was absolutely no doubt at all. He was going to be a thumping great star. He had this inner concentration on himself and on his destiny, on his journey through life, on his adventure. He wasn't that concerned in contributing to great art or anything. No. He was concerned with the odyssey of Richard Burton and that is what made him such a fascinating man."

He fought all his life to be a man. A man he could be proud of. A man who looked after his family and friends. A man who could look out for himself. A man who would hunt for pleasure and prizes. A man who would not kow-tow but always go his own way. The ideal of that stern hard poetic coalfield hero never left him even when he was surrounded by the squalid spoils of success and the riches of Arabia. Even when he tempted self-destruction he did it in a way which would be comprehensible to those from whom he had come – through drink. The excess the Celts like to claim as uniquely theirs, releasing poetry and song, fortifying for battle, reminding you of the brevity of life, numbing you against its grief.

The outward splendour of his meteor streak through life shows the bold, fearless warrior from the hills; the Notebooks reveal the steadier, funnier, more tormented, more sane man. Coming from where he did, aiming at the moon, there would always be tensions, furies, guilt, remorse, loss: the wonder is that there was so much humour, so much friendship and loyalty and solid achievement. His library at Céligny is where he was as happy as anywhere: an open fire, a comfortable chair, a good reading light, and hundreds, thousands of books to read and re-read and perhaps to add to as he looked out of his own darkness to the light that mattered most to him—words.

In the end he retreats back to the spellbound past of the tiny everlasting country of Wales whose language he spoke so richly. There is something untouchable about Burton—calculating he called himself and he hated to be touched—maybe he was indeed "a genius" as Nevill Coghill said—maybe the devil was indeed there because he could erupt into a violence which transformed him and equally into a performance which transformed others. Needs must when the devil drives. But always the sad dark centre. That very isolation, though, that detachment, that deeply withdrawn character is allied to openness, the interviewer's gift, the journalist's pay packet, the most quoted actor of the century and very often the quotes were good. But the talk took you no nearer to him. In the end you have to track him through the life, from "Rich," the boy brought up by Cis, to the man who made conquest after conquest — fame, women, money, words, celebrity—and yet would put all those riches aside for a drink with a pal, a new book, the dream of writing. Terrible and physically painful melancholy switching to roaring humour. Heathcliff to young Prince Hal, a man of so many parts and all of them himself. Nobody like him.

His grave is in a modest, small cemetery above a clear fast stream. The plain stone carries only RICHARD BURTON 1925–1984. When I was last there it was dusk on a winter's day. Only the sound of the water, a little wind in the trees. Lime, ash and pine. He had made a good decision: a Welsh hero fallen in battle on a foreign field. Much mourned. Rich now in the memory.

Acknowledgments

A great many people contributed to this book and I am grateful to them. For each sequence in Burton's life, I went for the key witness. There was considerable generosity and a determination to "do right" by him, warts—yes, but splendour as well.

One feature of writing the book was the widespread general interest. For instance, while I was in Australia at a literary conference a woman who had travelled to Switzerland to see Burton's grave gave me some photographs she had taken and a piece she had written after the experience. Walking on Hampstead Heath—where Ifor and Richard used to work up an appetite for a pub lunch—I was hallooed through autumn woods by a very Welsh woman who announced—at a distance of about twenty metres—that Burton, aged about fourteen, had once walked out with her cousin until her Uncle Jack "threw him out. Nobody knows her name," she sang through the bare trees, "and nobody's going to know." And these examples can be multiplied. From Wales have come letters, encouragement, insights from contemporaries, a tribute in themselves to the affection and esteem in which Burton's country holds him. Several people wrote to tell me of gifts—sometimes substantial—which Burton had made them. While in London and New York in theatrical bars and on any territory sympathetic to acting, Burton stories have come out to play as fresh as ever. Passing recollections—from his old friend Simon (now Sir Simon) Hornby, who holds to the Faustian notion of Burton: from Nick Garland the cartoonist who described, vividly, seeing Burton at the Old Vic in *Henry V* and thinking—"if I were Olivier or Gielgud I'd have been terrified": from the actress and director Maria Aitken, who talked about his magnificent eccentricities while appearing in the Oxford University production of *Doctor Faustus*; from Gore Vidal—so it went on. Burton had a huge constituency and the odds are that he had very little idea of its size or the warmth of its regard.

The family is one key element to Burton and I was most fortunate to be able to talk to the sister, Cecilia (Cis), who brought him up from the age of two until he left for Philip Burton's house at seventeen. Cis's daughters, Marian and Rhianon, his nieces brought up as his sisters, could not have been more helpful and their description of their father Elfed was an important contribution. I am also grateful to Gareth Owen, Hilda's son.

Philip Burton's generosity in giving me the right to use his unpublished memoirs calls out the deepest gratitude. The passages from his book carry the authority and affection of a man who, even now in his eighties, can inspire intense admiration from anyone interested in scholarship, the theatre, ideas. Richard was a most extraordinary boy: it was his great good luck to be spotted and nourished by an extraordinary man. The man to whom Philip in some sense passed him on, playwright and actor Emlyn Williams, was most co-operative, as was the third of his great mentors, Sir John Gielgud, who made notes before our interview and read from them at a hundred miles an hour with perfect diction.

Burton made several good friends among actors in London and they have been most willing to discuss the man and his career. Robert "Tim" Hardy—met at Oxford, "The Tsar," always a special pal; Michael Hordern ("The waste! The fleshpots!"); John Neville, whom I talked to in Stratford, Ontario, and was moved both by the strength of his feelings and by the fact of his vitality and energy—a man almost exactly the same age as Burton; Warren Mitchell, who once stood in for Burton in real life; Bryan Forbes, who tapped the post-war brew of West End theatre politics; William Squire, whose recollections included—as others did—tales of Burton's sudden, Arabian generosity.

From Burton's beloved radio days I had the great good luck to talk to Douglas Cleverdon and listen, with him, to the tapes of *In*

Parenthesis and *Under Milk Wood*. Frank Hauser, who produced his radio version of *Henry V*, was also someone who has followed his stage and screen career. He, too, was invaluable.

Conversations with actors spread across the range of Burton's experience—Lord Olivier, Sir Alec Guinness, John Hurt. Sir Peter Hall was one of several directors who spoke of the dynamic impact Burton created as a young stage actor.

There were those sought out for particular occasions—John le Carré (David Cornwell) for the filming of his novel *The Spy Who Came In From The Cold*; Andrew Sinclair, who directed the film of *Under Milk Wood*; Tony Palmer, who directed *Wagner*; Euan Lloyd, who knew Burton over a long period and produced *The Wild Geese*; Jeremy Treglown, who saw the Auden–Burton poetry reading at Oxford; Lauren Bacall, who helped pave the way for Burton's first entry to Hollywood; Donald Trelford and Richard Findlater at the *Observer*, for which Burton had written; Frank Delaney, who spent some time with him in Dublin; Cliff Morgan, who knew the rugby man; Arthur Ibbetson, the cameraman, who saw him clearer than most. Harley Usill, who recorded the poetry readings.

Burton as a family man, the father to several children, was described by his daughter Kate, the actress, who also spoke a little of her mother, Sybil's, very busy and cheerfully fulfilled life—after Richard.

Burton as a lifelong friend was the concern, for a while the central preoccupation, of Brook Williams, the actor whose help was unstinted. It is easy to see why "Rich" found him to be such fine company and the quality of Brook's friendship speaks very highly for the man who greatly valued male friendships.

There is a growing Burton industry and books by Philip Burton, of course, Paul Ferris, Penny Junor, Fergus Cashin and John Cottrell, and Hollis Alpert and an essay by Bryan Forbes are all interesting and enjoyable in their various ways. The lead title in the Elizabeth Taylor industry is by Kitty Kelley, but books by Brenda Maddox, Ruth Waterby and Dick Shepherd are equally absorbing. *The Cleopatra Papers* by Jack Brodsky and Nathan Weiss is excellent on that period, as are Richard L. Sterne's *John Gielgud Directs Richard Burton* and William Redfield's *Letters From An Actor. The Broadway Hamlet*. Susan Strasberg's *Bittersweet*, Claire Bloom's *Limelight And After, Lauren Bacall by Myself*, Zeffirelli's autobiography, Joseph Mankiewicz's autobiography, Mel Gussow's biography of Darryl F. Zanuck. There are many television interviews—with David Frost, Dick Cavett, James Fenton. David Frost was typically generous with his recollections. The screen and stage of Burton's time have spawned a monstrous quantity of print. He left a mountain of cuttings. I owe a debt of gratitude to Annette Balfour-Lynn for her research—most especially for her work on the appendices (and to St. John Howell who researched the radio and recordings section). And particular thanks—for her work on the text—to my good friend Julia Matheson.

The words which have not until now been in print are Burton's Notebooks. These 350,000 words were a marvellous discovery which, together with his letters and the many files of contracts, gave me a unique opportunity to study the man in detail. Seeing all the films again, listening to the records, reading his published work, talking to those who knew him—none of this was as revealing as the Notebooks—even his battles with spelling—(Sophia Loren could beat him at Scrabble—in English!)—which drew me into the fortress of the man. This book is in some part the autobiography he often spoke of writing.

One thing the Notebooks and other writings gave me was a line on Sybil, Susan and Elizabeth. His first three wives are all largely described in his terms. In the case of Elizabeth, of course, her interviews and her autobiographical writings have also been most helpful.

My deepest debt is to Sally, who woke up to a tragedy so cruelly soon after she had set out on a new life. I have greatly admired the patience with which she has coped with the unravelling of the will, the disposition of gifts and the volatility of the press. She has held steadily to her idea of how Richard Burton should be respected and represented. She was extraordinarily generous with her gift of the Notebooks and other material. She has made no attempt whatsoever to censor the book.

Finally, to Cate my wife, much love and thanks for all the patience and encouragement.

MELVYN BRAGG
1985–1988

APPENDICES

A compilation of Richard Burton's work
in theatre, on film, in television,
in radio and on record.

Theatre

Early walk-on parts while under contract to H. M. Tennent have not been included.

November 1943
Royal Court Theatre, Liverpool
January 1944
St. Martin's Theatre, London
Druid's Rest
First professional stage appearance as Glan, the elder son of publicans in a comedy set in the back parlour of a small public house in Wales, early this century. Gladys Henson and Roddy Hughes appeared as his parents. Written and directed by Emlyn Williams.

Summer 1944
Christ Church Cloisters, Oxford
Measure for Measure
Originally hired as understudy to Angelo in this Oxford University Dramatic Society production. He took over the role when the actor cast as Angelo fell ill. Directed by Nevill Coghill.

February 1948
Lyric Theatre, Hammersmith
Castle Anna

A drama set in Ireland at the turn of the century, in the drawing room of a country house. Burton played Mr. Hicks, a young officer stationed nearby. With Hazel Terry, Richard Leech and Arthur Sinclair. Written by Elizabeth Bowen and John Perry; directed by Daphne Rye.

May 1949
Globe Theatre, London
The Lady's Not For Burning
Burton as the orphaned clerk in Christopher Fry's period comedy, set in the house belonging to the Mayor of a small market town. With John Gielgud and Claire Bloom. Directed by John Gielgud and Esme Percy.

January 1950
Lyric Theatre, Hammersmith
The Boy With A Cart
Christopher Fry's play begins in a Cornish village, and moves to Steyning in Sussex, with Burton playing the role of Cuthman. With Mary Jerrold, Hazel Terry and Diana Graves. Part of a double bill which included *Shall We Join The Ladies* by J. M. Barrie. Both plays directed by John Gielgud.

March 1950
Dolphin Theatre, Brighton
A Phoenix Too Frequent
Christopher Fry wrote this one-act play and also directed. Burton played Tegeus the Roman soldier, comforting the grieving widow in the mausoleum. With Diana Graves.

November 1950
Royale Theatre, New York
The Lady's Not For Burning
His first stage appearance in New York. A repeat of his role as the orphaned clerk. Also with John Gielgud, who directed.

Summer 1951
Shakespeare Memorial Theatre, Stratford-upon-Avon (Season)
Henry IV (Part 1)

Directed by Anthony Quayle and John Kidd
Henry IV (Part 2)
Directed by Michael Redgrave
Henry V
Directed by Anthony Quayle
As Prince Hal, Henry IV and Henry V in the Shakespeare Memorial
Theatre's season for the Festival of Britain.
The Tempest
Directed by Michael Benthall
As Ferdinand son to the King of Naples with Alan Badel as Ariel.

December 1951
The Plymouth Theatre, New York
Legend of Lovers
As the Musician in Jean Anouilh's adaptation of *Eurydice*. With
Dorothy McGuire and Hugh Griffith, directed by Peter Ashmore.

April 1952
Lyric Theatre, Hammersmith
Montserrat
Lillian Hellman's free adaptation from Emanuel Robles's play is set
in the Governor's Palace in Valencia in Venezuela during its fight
for independence in 1812. Burton played the title role with Noel
Willman as Colonel Izquierdo. Willman also directed with Nigel
Green.

September 1953
Assembly Hall, Edinburgh
Hamlet
In the title role in the Old Vic production. With Claire Bloom as
Ophelia, directed by Michael Benthall.

1953–1954
The Old Vic Company (Season)
Hamlet
Directed by Michael Benthall
Title role.
King John
Directed by George Devine

As Philip the Bastard, with Michael Hordern as King John.
Twelfth Night
Directed by Denis Carey
As Sir Toby Belch, with John Neville as Orsino, and Claire Bloom
as Viola.
Coriolanus
Directed by Michael Benthall
As Caius Martius (Coriolanus) with William Squire as Menenius
Agrippa.
The Tempest
Directed by Robert Helpmann
As Caliban, with Michael Hordern as Prospero and Claire Bloom
as Miranda.

1955–1956
The Old Vic Company (Season)
Henry V
Directed by Michael Benthall
In the title role, with John Neville as the Chorus.
Othello
Directed by Michael Benthall
The roles of Othello and Iago were alternated between Burton and
John Neville.

November 1957
Morosco Theatre, New York
Time Remembered
Patricia Moyes adapted *Time Remembered* from Jean Anouilh's
Léocadia, a romantic comedy about a Duchess, a Prince, a ballerina
and a milliner. Burton was Prince Albert, with Susan Strasberg as
the Milliner and Helen Hayes as the Duchess of Pont-au-Bronc.
Directed by Albert Marre.

December 1960
Majestic Theatre, New York
Camelot
As Arthur in the Lerner and Loewe musical, directed by Moss Hart.
Based on T. H. White's version of the legend of King Arthur, *The
Once and Future King*, it won Burton the New York Drama Critics

Award in 1961 for the best performance in a musical. With Julie Andrews as Guinevere.

April 1964
Lunt-Fontanne Theatre, New York
Hamlet
In the title role in John Gielgud's production. With Hume Cronyn as Polonius and Linda Marsh as Ophelia.

February 1966
Oxford Playhouse
Doctor Faustus
Marlowe's dramatisation of the medieval legend of the man who sold his soul to the devil, had Burton in the title role and Elizabeth as Helen of Troy. An Oxford University Dramatic Society production, directed by Nevill Coghill. This production was filmed in Rome later that year, with Burton co-directing.

March 1976
Plymouth Theatre, New York
Equus
Burton took over the role of the psychoanalyst Martin Dysart from Anthony Perkins, a role he later re-created on film. Peter Shaffer's play was directed by John Dexter.

1980–1981
American tour, including New York
Camelot
Revival of the Lerner-Loewe musical. Burton as Arthur once again.

May 1983
Lunt-Fontanne Theatre, New York
Private Lives
Noël Coward's sophisticated comedy about a divorced couple who fall in love with each other, whilst on honeymoon with other partners. Burton and Taylor appeared as Elyot Chase and Amanda Prynne. Directed by Milton Katselas.

Films

The dates are generally first release, following the style of Leslie Halliwell's *Filmgoer's Companion*.

The Last Days of Dolwyn   1948
Film debut as Gareth, foster son of the widow Merri, played by Edith Evans. A melodrama about the flooding of a Victorian Welsh village. As well as taking a leading role Emlyn Williams also wrote and directed; produced by Anatole de Grunwald.

Now Barabbas Was A Robber   1949
As Paddy, an Irish saboteur in a prison drama centred around an execution. With Richard Greene, Sir Cedric Hardwicke as the Prison Governor, Kathleen Harrison and Beatrice Campbell. Screenplay by Anatole de Grunwald who also produced from the play by William Douglas Home; directed by Gordon Parry.

Waterfront   1950
His role as Ben Satterthwaite, an out of work ship's engineer, highlighted the problems of unemployment in Merseyside in this adaptation of John Brophy's novel. With Avis Scott, Robert Newton, Kathleen Harrison and Susan Shaw. Screenplay by John Brophy and Paul Soskin who also produced; directed by Michael Anderson.

The Woman With No Name   1950
A romantic role as the Norwegian airman, Nick Chamerd, who
bigamously marries Yvonne Winter, played by Phyllis Calvert,
whilst she is suffering from amnesia. Adapted from the novel *Happy
Now I Go* by Theresa Charles, produced by John Stafford and directed by Ladislas Vajda.

Green Grow The Rushes   1951
The leading members of the cast accepted lower fees and deferred
a percentage until the box-office profits in this first film made by
ACT Films Ltd., the film industry's union. With Roger Livesey and
Honor Blackman. Adapted by Howard Clewes from his novel of
the same title, with Derek Twist who also directed; produced by
John Gossage.

My Cousin Rachel   1952
First US film. As Philip Ashley, the young heir who falls passionately in love with his foster-father's widow, played by Olivia de
Havilland. Adapted by Nunnally Johnson, who also produced, from
Daphne du Maurier's psychological mystery set in Cornwall. Directed by Henry Koster. Academy Award nomination for best supporting actor.

The Robe   1953
First full-length Cinemascope film. Based around the Crucifixion of
Christ. As Marcellus Gallio, the Roman officer whose role as ov-
erseer to this event led to his conversion to Christianity. With Jean
Simmons, Victor Mature, Michael Rennie and Ernest Thesiger.
From the novel by Lloyd C. Douglas, screen adaptation by Gina
Kaus, produced by Frank Ross and directed by Henry Koster. Acad-
emy award nomination for best actor.

The Desert Rats   1953
As Captain MacRoberts, the English officer commanding a group
of Australian soldiers defending Tobruk against Rommel, played by
James Mason. With Robert Newton and Robert Douglas. Written
by Richard Murphy, produced by Robert L. Jacks and directed by
Robert Wise.

Prince of Players   1954
This film follows the fortunes of the Booth family, a traditional
theatrical hierarchy, whose squabbles amongst themselves lead to
the assassination of President Lincoln. As Edwin Booth, the surviving brother of assassin John Wilkes Booth, played by John Derek.
With Raymond Massey, Charles Bickford and Elizabeth Sellars.
Based on the book by Eleanor Ruggles, adapted by Moss Hart,
produced and directed by Philip Dunne.

The Rains of Ranchipur   1955
Set in India during the monsoons and earthquakes, adapted from
Louis Bromfield's novel, *The Rains Came*. Burton played an in-
scrutable young Indian Doctor Safti, with Lana Turner, Fred
MacMurray and Michael Rennie. Screenplay by Marle Miller, pro-
duced by Frank Ross and directed by Jean Negulesco.

Alexander the Great   1956
In the title role as the legendary scholar and warrior who conquers
the world of his day undefeated in battle. With Danielle Darrieux,
Claire Bloom, Peter Cushing and Fredric March. Written, produced
and directed by Robert Rossen.

Sea Wife   1957
A poignant story about survival on a desert island by a group of
four people adrift in a dinghy after their ship has been torpedoed.
With Joan Collins as the nun whose nickname is Sea Wife, and
Burton as the RAF officer whose nickname is Biscuit. Screenplay
by George K. Burke, produced by André Hakim and directed by
Bob McNaught.

Bitter Victory   1958
As Captain Leith with Curt Jurgens as Major Brand, leading a British
Army patrol in the desert behind enemy lines in an effort to capture
some German documents, and Ruth Roman. Screenplay by Rene
Hardy, Nicholas Ray and Gavin Lambert. Produced by Paul Graetz
and directed by Nicholas Ray.

Look Back In Anger   1959
As Jimmy Porter, adapted from John Osborne's play of the same

name. With Mary Ure, Gary Raymond and Claire Bloom. Screenplay by Nigel Kneale, produced by Gordon L. T. Scott and Harry Saltzman and directed by Tony Richardson.

The Bramble Bush   1960
Set in a small town in Massachusetts, this film deals with mercy killing, blackmail and adultery, culminating in Dr. Guy Montford, played by Burton, standing trial. With Barbara Rush and Angie Dickinson. From the novel by Charles Mergendahl, screenplay by Milton Sperling and Philip Yordan, produced by Milton Sperling and directed by Daniel Petrie.

Ice Palace   1960
This adaptation of Edna Ferber's novel follows the fortunes of Zeb Kennedy, played by Burton, and the development of Alaska from 1918 until it achieved statehood in 1958. With Martha Hyer, Carolyn Jones and Robert Ryan. Screenplay by Harry Kleiner, produced by Henry Blanke and directed by Vincent Sherman.

The Longest Day   1962
Film of D-Day, June 6th, 1944. Burton played the role of an RAF pilot. The large cast included Robert Mitchum, John Wayne, Red Buttons, Henry Fonda as Brigadier General Roosevelt, Trevor Reid as General Montgomery and Henry Grace as General Eisenhower. Screenplay by Cornelius Ryan, based on his book. Produced by Darryl F. Zanuck. Directed by Ken Annakin, Andrew Marton, Bernhard Wicki and Darryl F. Zanuck.

Cleopatra   1963
Adapted from Plutarch, Suetonius Appian and C. M. Franzero's *The Life and Times of Cleopatra* by Ranald MacDougall, Sidney Buchman and Joseph L. Mankiewicz. With Elizabeth Taylor in the title role, Burton as Mark Antony, Rex Harrison as Julius Caesar. Produced by Walter Wanger and directed by Joseph L. Mankiewicz.

The VIPs   1963
Burton and Taylor together again as Paul and Frances Andros, the couple to whom the delay of a plane on a fog-bound afternoon, along with other notables in the VIP lounge, meant rather more than

just being late for their intended destination. With Louis Jourdan, Elsa Martinelli, Margaret Rutherford, Maggie Smith and Rod Taylor. Screenplay by Terence Rattigan, produced by Anatole de Grunwald and directed by Anthony Asquith.

Becket 1964
In the title role, with Peter O'Toole as King Henry II, Sir John Gielgud as King Louis VII of France, Sir Donald Wolfit as the Bishop of London and Martita Hunt as the mother of King Henry II. Screenplay by Edward Anhalt, adapted from Jean Anouilh's play, produced by Hal Wallis and directed by Peter Glenville. Academy award nomination for best actor.

The Night Of The Iguana 1964
Burton as the Reverend Laurence Shannon, a de-frocked priest, trying to find his way back to God. With Ava Gardner and Deborah Kerr. Screenplay by Anthony Veiller and John Huston from the play by Tennessee Williams. Produced by Ray Stark and directed by John Huston.

Hamlet 1964
The title role. A filmed recording of two public performances of the New York theatrical production (by John Gielgud). Produced by William Sargent Jr., and Alfred W. Crown, directed by Bill Colleran.

What's New Pussycat? 1965
Cameo role as himself in comedy with Peter O'Toole. Directed by Clive Donner.

The Sandpiper 1965
Another Burton and Taylor collaboration. Filmed mostly against the background of the Big Sur in California. With Eva Marie Saint and Charles Bronson. Original story by Martin Ransohoff, screenplay by Dalton Trumbo and Martin Wilson. Produced by Martin Ransohoff and directed by Vincente Minnelli.

The Spy Who Came In From The Cold 1965
Based on the novel by John le Carré. Burton played the spy, Alec

Leamas, with Claire Bloom and Michael Hordern. Screenplay by
Paul Dehn and Guy Trosper. Produced and directed by Martin Ritt.
Academy award nomination for best actor.

Who's Afraid Of Virginia Woolf?   1966
Burton and Taylor again collaborated in adaptation of play by Ed-
ward Albee. With George Segal and Sandy Dennis. Screenplay by
Ernest Lehman, who also produced; directed by Mike Nichols.
Academy Award nomination for best actor.

The Taming Of The Shrew   1967
Director Franco Zeffirelli shared the production credit with Burton
as Petruchio and Taylor as Kate. Screenplay adapted from Shakespeare's play by Paul Dehn, Suso Cecchi D'Amico and Franco
Zeffirelli.

The Comedians   1967
Set in Haiti, against the background of voodoo, corruption and the
Tontons Macoute, Burton is Brown, a middle-aged lapsed Catholic
stuck with a decaying hotel and a love affair with a Latin-American
Ambassador's wife, played by Taylor. With Peter Ustinov, Alec
Guinness and Lillian Gish. Filmed in Dahomey. From the novel by
Graham Greene, who also wrote the screenplay. Produced and di-
rected by Peter Glenville.

Doctor Faustus   1968
Burton financed, co-produced and co-directed the version of Marlowe's *The Tragical History of Doctor Faustus*. Filmed in Rome,
with Taylor as Helen of Troy, co-director Nevill Coghill playing a
professor and many of the supporting roles played by students from
Oxford University. See Theatre section.

Boom   1968
This adaptation of Tennessee Williams's play *The Milk Train
Doesn't Stop Here Any More* had the Burtons acting together again,
with Taylor as the beautiful dying millionairess and Burton as the
Angel of Death, Noël Coward as the Witch of Capri. This allegorical
tale is set on an island in the Mediterranean. Produced by John
Heyman and Norman Priggen, directed by Joseph Losey.

Candy 1968
This psychedelic sexual fantasy was based on Terry Southern's novel of the same name. Burton was the wild Welsh poet McPhisto, with Marlon Brando, James Coburn, Ringo Starr, Walter Matthau, Charles Aznavour and John Huston, and Ewa Aulin as Candy. Screenplay by Buck Henry, produced by Robert Haggiag, directed by Christian Marquand.

Where Eagles Dare 1969
Burton and Clint Eastwood are part of an Intelligence Commando unit on a mission to rescue an American general from an impregnable castle in Bavaria. This thriller was adapted by Alistair Maclean from his book. Produced by Elliott Kastner and directed by Brian G. Hutton.

Staircase 1969
Rex Harrison and Burton portrayed a pair of homosexual barbers. With Cathleen Nesbitt. Screenplay by Charles Dyer, based on his play of the same name. Produced and directed by Stanley Donen.

Anne Of The Thousand Days 1970
Based on Maxwell Anderson's play chronicling King Henry VIII's relationship with the unfortunate Anne Boleyn. Burton as King Henry with Genevieve Bujold as Anne Boleyn, Irene Papas as Queen Katherine and Anthony Quayle as Wolsey. Screenplay by John Hale and Bridget Boland, adaptation by Richard Sokolove. Produced by Hal B. Wallis and directed by Charles Jarrott. Academy award nomination for best actor.

Raid on Rommel 1971
Director Henry Hathaway's film is set during the events leading up to the battle of El Alamein. With Burton as Captain Foster, Wolfgang Preiss as Rommel. Written by Richard Bluel and produced by Harry Tatelman.

Villain 1971
Burton as a violent psychopath. With Nigel Davenport. Screenplay by Dick Clement and Ian La Frenais, adapted by Al Lettier from the novel *The Burden of Proof*. Produced by Alan Ladd Jr., and Jay Kanter, and directed by Mike Tuchner.

The Assassination of Trotsky   1972
An historical reconstruction by director Joseph Losey of the events
leading up to the death of Trotsky, played by Burton. With Alain
Delon and Romy Schneider. Screenplay by Nicholas Mosley and
co-produced by Norman Priggen and Joseph Losey.

Hammersmith Is Out   1972
Burton's Hammersmith is a dangerous escapee from a mental institution, involving Elizabeth Taylor as Jimmie Jean Jackson and
Beau Bridges as Billy Breedlove, a male nurse, in his life of destruction. Screenplay by Stanford Whitmore, produced by Alex Lucas and directed by Peter Ustinov.

Bluebeard   1972
In the title role as Baron Kurt von Sepper, the legendary Bluebeard,
with seven wives frozen in a refrigerated vault tucked away in his
castle. With Raquel Welch, Nathalie Delon, Virni Lisi and Joey
Heatherton. Filmed on location in Budapest and Rome. Screenplay
by Ennio di Concini, Edward Dmytryk and Maria Pia Fusco, produced by Alexander Salkind and directed by Edward Dmytryk.

The Battle of Sutjeska
A reconstruction of the mountain battle where the embattled Tito
and his 20,000 partisans break through the German encirclement.
Burton persuaded the producers to refashion and rewrite his role as
Marshal Tito to fall in with a first-hand account of the battle by F.
W. D. Deakin in his book *The Embattled Mountain*. With Irene
Papas. Video title, *The Fifth Offensive*. Screenplay by Branimir
Scepanovic, Sergei Bondarchuk and Wolf Mankowitz. Produced by
Nikola Popovic and directed by Stipe Delic.

Under Milk Wood   1973
Burton is the Narrator in Andrew Sinclair's adaptation of Dylan
Thomas's radio prose-poem. With Elizabeth Taylor as Rosie Probert
and Peter O'Toole as the blind Captain Cat. Produced by Jules Buck
and Hugh French, Andrew Sinclair directed.

Rappresaglia (Massacre in Rome)   1974
Burton as Colonel Kappler has the unpleasant task of selecting 320

names as victims of a reprisal for 32 German SS troops killed by partisans in Rome towards the end of the war. With Leo McKern and Marcello Mastroianni. Screenplay by Robert Katz, based on his book *Death in Rome*. Produced by Carlo Ponti and directed by George Pan Cosmatos.

The Klansman   1974
A drama centred around racial conflict in the Southern state of Alabama. Burton is Breck Stancill a liberal landowner in conflict with the activities of the Ku Klux Klan. Lee Marvin is Big Track Bascomb, the sheriff, trying to maintain law and order. Based on the Pulitzer Prize-winning novel by William Bradford Huie, screenplay by Millard Kaufman and Samuel Fuller. Produced by William Alexander and directed by Terence Young.

The Voyage   1974
This turn-of-the-century love story set in Sicily was director Vittorio De Sica's last film. Burton is Cesare Braggi, deeply in love with his younger brother's wife, played by Sophia Loren. Filmed in Sicily, Palermo, Naples, Milan, Venice and Rome. Based on a short story by Luigi Pirandello, screenplay by Diego Fabri, Massimo Franciosa and Luisa Montagnana, and produced by Carlo Ponti.

Jackpot   1975
Filming was suspended when only half of the film was made. This thriller, from the story of the same name by Charles Long, cast Burton as Reid Lawrence, an actor, paralysed by a falling lift. James Coburn is Reagan, an insurance investigator. Screenplay by Millard Kaufman and Peter Draper, produced by William Alexander and directed by Terence Young.

Exorcist II: The Heretic   1977
In this sequel to *The Exorcist*, Burton plays the role of pagan priest Father Philip Lamont appointed by the Vatican to exorcise the mind of a young child by "synchronised hypnosis" with linked electrode headbands. With Linda Blair and Max Von Sydow. Screenplay by William Goodhart, produced by Richard Lederer and John Boorman who also directed.

Equus   1977
In this film adaptation by Peter Shaffer of his stage play of the same name, Burton plays the role of the psychoanalyst Martin Dysart attempting to uncover the deep-seated neuroses of the teenager Alan, played by Peter Firth, who savagely blinds horses. Produced by Lester Persky and Elliott Kastner and directed by Sidney Lumet. Academy award nomination for best actor.

The Medusa Touch   1978
Jack Gold co-produced with Ann V. Coates and also directed this film, with Burton as the demonic writer with a gift of telekinetic catastrophe. With Lino Ventura and Lee Remick. Screenplay by John Briley.

The Wild Geese   1978
Filmed in Tschipise in the Northern Transvaal in South Africa, this adventure film follows a band of mercenaries on a mission to rescue a black African president from a rival dictator's jail. Burton is Colonel Allen Faulkner, hired by Fleet Street press baron Sir Edward Matheson, played by Stewart Granger, and Roger Moore, Richard Harris and Hardy Kruger are enrolled on the mission. Screenplay by Reginald Rose, produced by Euan Lloyd, and directed by Andrew V. McLaglen.

Breakthrough   1979
Burton is Sergeant Steiner in this sequel to *Cross of Iron*, set in Europe near the end of the Second World War. Steiner is trying to procure an honourable ceasefire and surrender. With Curt Jurgens and Robert Mitchum. Screenplay by Tony Williamson and Lucas Heller. Produced by Wolfgang Hartwig and directed by Andrew V. McLaglen.

Absolution   1979
Anthony Shaffer's screenplay has Burton cast as Father Goddard, a repressed teacher priest at a Catholic boys' school, drawn into a lethal game by two of his pupils. With Dominic Guard and Billy Connolly. Produced by Danny O'Donovan and Elliott Kastner and directed by Anthony Page.

Tristan and Isolt   1980
Burton played the role of the ageing King Mark of Cornwall in this
film of Wagner's opera. With Kate Mulgrew and Cyril Cusack.
Filmed in Ireland. Screenplay by Claire Labine, produced by Tom
Hayes and Claire Labine and directed by Tom Donovan.

Circle Of Two   1982
A generation-gap love story between a sixty-year-old failed artist
and a sixteen-year-old. Burton is the fading painter Ashley St. Clair
and Tatum O'Neal is Sarah Norton, the wilful schoolgirl running
the gauntlet of parental disapproval as she pursues the artist. Screenplay by Thomas Hadley, producer Henk Van Der Volk, directed by
Jules Dassin.

Wagner   1983
Tony Palmer's nine-hour biographical film on the life of the composer cast Burton in the title role, Vanessa Redgrave as his second
wife Cosima, and Gemma Craven as her predecessor Minna. Shot
on location in Switzerland, Bavaria, Venice, Siena and Hungary, it
had a large cast with many distinguished names including John
Gielgud, Ralph Richardson and Lawrence Olivier. William Walton
played Friedrich August II of Saxony. Screenplay by Charles Wood,
produced by Alan Wright and directed by Tony Palmer.
   An edited six-hour version of this film has since been shown on
television in Britain.

1984   1984
George Orwell's futuristic vision for 1984 under the Inner Party's
Big Brother was adapted for this screen version by Michael Radford
who also directed. Burton is O'Brien, the ambiguous Inner Party
member, and John Hurt is Winston Smith, his brainwashed victim;
produced by Simon Perry.

Television

A selective list

Wuthering Heights   1958
As Heathcliff, playing opposite Yvonne Furneaux as Cathy, directed by Daniel Petrie.

The Fifth Column   1960
John Frankenheimer directed this adaptation of Ernest Hemingway's novel with Burton, Maximilian Schell and Sally Ann Howes.

The Tempest   1960
As Prospero, with Lee Remick and Roddy McDowall. Directed by George Schafer for Hallmark Hall of Fame.

A Subject of Scandal and Concern   1960
As socialist lecturer George Holyoake on trial for saying he did not believe in God. John Osborne's play was set in 1842 with John Freeman as the narrator, and George Devine as the Judge. Tony Richardson directed.

Divorce His, Divorce Hers   1973
A television melodrama in two parts documenting the differing views between a husband and wife of the cause of their marital breakdown.

Burton and Taylor as Martin and June Reynolds looking back over their marriage, first from his point of view, and then from hers. Screenplay by John Hopkins, produced by Terence Baker and Gareth Wigan and directed by Waris Hussein.

Walk with Destiny   1974
As Winston Churchill in this NBC-BBC co-production with Virginia McKenna as Clemmie, his wife. Written by Colin Morris, co-produced by Jack le Vien for NBC and Andrew Osborn for the BBC, directed by Herbert Wise.

Brief Encounter   1976
As the country doctor whose love affair with a married woman, played by Sophia Loren, is doomed never to be consummated. John Bowen wrote this adaptation of Noël Coward's play. Alan Bridges directed.

The Fall Guy   1982
As himself helping Lee Majors during a cross-country train journey.

Alice in Wonderland   1983
As the White King with daughter Kate in title role. Adaptation of Eva LeGallienne's stage production.

Ellis Island   1984
Mini-series following the fortunes of immigrants into the United States at the beginning of this century. Burton is the wealthy US Senator Phipps Ogden, with Kate Burton as Ogden's daughter. It was Burton's last role and was shown on television after his death. Also starring were Claire Bloom, Peter Riegart and Faye Dunaway. The period filming of New York was undertaken mostly in Billingsgate in London and Shepperton studios. Screenplay by Fred Mustard Stewart and Christopher Newman, based on Stewart's novel. Produced by Nick Gillott and directed by Jerry London.

Radio and Recordings

A selective list, excluding interviews and chat shows.

Between 1949–52 Richard Burton broadcast in a considerable number of schools educational programmes: *Junior English*; *Senior English*; *Book of Verse*; *Prose and Verse for Schools*; and *Religious Interlude for Schools*. He also appeared in *In Parenthesis* (11–1948, producer: Douglas Cleverdon), experience of an infantryman in the First World War; *Last Days of Dolwyn* (20–7–49); *Nightmare Abbey* (7–11–49); *Hippolytus* (3–50); *Sea Flood* (5–50); *Birth of a Giant* (15–7–51); *Night Birds* (29–9–51); *Taffy Was a Welshman* (23–10–51); *Good for the Boy* (11–53); *Younger Generation* (12–53).

In 1954 he was in Douglas Cleverdon's production of *Under Milk Wood*, followed by *The Old Vic Comes North* (6–54). His own work, *A Christmas Story*, was broadcast on 25–12–65.

His first radio play was probably *The Corn is Green* (27–1–45), but many of the early records seem to be somewhat fragmented.

The following recordings are held in the BBC Archives:

In Parenthesis, experiences of an infantryman in World War I. Producer: Douglas Cleverdon. 1948.   MX/14950–9

The Lady's Not For Burning, play by Christopher Fry. Producer: R. Raikes. 150.   X/15424–7

New Judgement: Thomas Love Peacock. Producer: D. Cleverdon.
1949.   MX/15717–8

Men of Steel, the Birth of a Giant. Producer: E. Evans. 1951.
                                                          MX/19982–4

Under Milk Wood, play for voices by Dylan Thomas. Producer: D.
Cleverdon. 1954.   X/20227–8

The Dark Tower. 1956.   LP/24575–6

Henry of Agincourt, a sequence from *Henry V* (Shakespeare).
1956.   LP/23889–90

Night Must Fall, play by Emlyn Williams. Producer: A. Whitaker
—Stars in Their Choice series. 1953.   MX/21723–6

Thanksgiving Service for Life of Richard Burton held in St. Martin-
in-the-Fields, London 30–8–84. With Stuart Burrows (tenor),
Sioned Williams (harp) and the Rhos Cwm Tawe Male Voice Choir.
Lesson read by Rev. Charles Hedley. Other readings by Paul Scofield, Kate Burton, Sian Owen, Emlyn Williams, John Gielgud.
                                                          T46555

Vivat Rex (narr.): A Dramatic Chronicle of the English crown
through 200 years of its history as seen by the Elizabethan playwrights. Adapted in 26 parts by Martin Jenkins. 1976–7.
                                                          T42431–T42456.

The following records featuring Richard Burton were issued commercially.

ARGO   *The World of Dylan Thomas*: "Poem
PA/A 166   in October," "The hunchback in the
                            park," "Fernhill," *Under Milk
                            Wood*—excerpts (as First Voice).

ARGO RG 43 SW 503	"In my craft or sullen art," "The force that through the green fuse," "A Winter's tale," "The hand that signed the paper," "Ballad of the long-legged bait," "Fernhill," "Hunchback in the park," "Deaths and entrances," "Before I knocked," "I see the boys of summer," "Lament," "Lie still, sleep becalmed," "Do not go gentle into that good night," "Poem in October," "And death shall have no dominion." All Dylan Thomas.
ARGO RG 21–2 SW 501–2	*Under Milk Wood* (4 sides) as First Voice
RG 41	"Rime of the Ancient Mariner," "Kubla Khan," "Frost at Midnight." Coleridge. With John Neville and Robert Hardy
RG 438 PLP 1039	*The English Poets* "Rime of the Ancient Mariner" (as The Mariner), "Frost at Midnight." Coleridge.
ARGO RG 29 PLP 1060	"A Hunchback in the Park," "Poem in October," "Fernhill." From *Homage to Dylan Thomas* (recorded at the Globe Theatre 24–1–54)
ARGO ZDSW 714s	*A Personal Anthology* "The leadon echo and the gold echo"—Hopkins; "The boy with a cart" (extract)—Fry; "The good-morrow"—Donne; "Song: Go and catch a falling star" —Donne; "To Christ"—Donne; "At

the round earth's imagined corners"
—Donne; "Death be not proud"—
Donne; "The passionate shepherd to
his love"—Donne; "The nymph's
reply to the shepherd"—Ralegh;
"The passionate man's pilgramage"
—Ralegh; "Non sum qualis eram
bonae sub regno Cynarae"—Dow-
son; "Yasmin, a ghazal"—Flecker;
"Welsh incident"—Graves; "Exe-
quy on his wife" (extract)—King;
"Lament for the makers" (extract)—
Dunbar; "The Rev. Eli Jenkins—
'Morning Hymn' " (from *Under Milk
Wood*)—Dylan Thomas; "Elegy"
(for his father)—Dylan Thomas;
"Desiderata"—Anon; "Adlestrop"
—Edward Thomas; "Autumn"—
Clare; "Priest and peasant"—R. S.
Thomas; "The lonely farmer"—
R. S. Thomas; "in memoriam Wal-
ter Ramsden"—Betjeman; Hunter
trials" —Betjeman; "The hound of
heaven"—Thompson; *Richard II*
(Act 4 sc 1)—Shakespeare; *The Tem-
pest* (Act 4 sc 1)—Shakespeare.

CAEDMON
SRS M. 239/1

"The Rape of Lucrece"—Shakespeare.

SRS M.226/A–C
SRS 226/A–C

Coriolanus (as Coriolanus, 1962)—
Shakespeare.

CAEDMON
TC.1140

The Poetry of Thomas Hardy "In Te-
nebris I," "The Souls of the Slain,"
"Shut out that Moon," "Reminiscences of a Dancing Man," "Let me
enjoy," "Channel firing," "Beyond
the last lamp," "Wessex Heights,"

"At Casterbridge Fair"—The Ballad Singer: Former Beauties: After the Club Dance: The Market Girl: The Inquiry: After the Fair. "I found her out there," "The Voice," "After a journey," "Weathers," "The Phantom Horsewoman," "She charged me," "In the Servants' Quarters," "In the Study," "Timing her," "Great Things," "Old Furniture," "The Sunshade," "At Castle Boterel."

CBS (Embassy) S CBS 31845s	compilation 8/80 *Broadway Magic Vol 2—The Great Performers*, "What do the simple folk do?" (From *Camelot*) with Julie Andrews (vocal) and Orchestra/Frank Allers (Original Broadway cast)
CAEDMON TC 1141s	*Love Poems of John Donne*. "The Good Morrow," "The Rising Sun," "The Canonization," "The Triple Fool," "Go and catch a falling star" (song), "Sweetest love, I do not go" (song), "The Legacie," "A Feaver," "The Flea," "The Anniversary," "The Curse," "A Nocturnall," "The Apparition," "A Valediction —Forbidding Mourning," "The Extasie, The Funerall, The Extasie," "Jealosie" (Elegy I), "The Comparison" (Elegy VIII), "Natures lay ideot" (Elegy VII), "The Relique."
CBS SBPG 63189s BPG 63189	*Doctor Faustus*—excerpts as Faustus. Marlowe.

CBS S CBS 6477s	Dead London (from Jeff Wayne's musical *War of the Worlds*) Orchestra/Jeff Wayne
CBS S CBS 6496s	"The Red Weed," with instrumentalists and orchestra/Jeff Wayne
CBS S 82671–2s CD 96000/a–Bs CBS 85337s	*War of the Worlds*—as the Journalist with vocalists, instrumentalists, chorus and orchestra/Jeff Wayne
CBS 32356s	*War of the Worlds*—highlights.
COLUMBIA DOL.302 (8 sides)	*Hamlet* (1964 Broadway Production) (as Hamlet)
CBS BRG 72259 72259s	*Hamlet* (highlights) (1964 Broadway production) (as Hamlet)
COLUMBIA KOL 5620 or CBS APG 60004 or BRG 70009 COLUMBIA S 32602s (CD)	*Camelot*—Lerner and Loewe musical (1960). "What do the simple folk do?" with Julie Andrews (vocal), "I wonder what the king is doing tonight," "Camelot," "How to handle a woman," all with orchestra conducted by Franz Allers (Original New York cast)
COLUMBIA ML 4440/1 + AML 4440–1	Conversation Piece—Noël Coward. (as the Marquis of Sheere)
DECCA DL 9508–9	*The Lady's Not For Burning*—Christopher Fry (as Richard)
DRG DARC 2100/B	*Twenty-Five Years of Recorded Sound from MGM Records—Vol 1* (Record 2) "A Married Man" (from the musical *Baker Street*) with Orchestra/Richard Hayman (recorded November 5th 1964)

EMBER NR 5012 POWDERWORKS POW 401s	*Zulu*—film soundtrack, Isandhlwana, 1879. "The VC roll," "Men of Harlech," with John Barry conducting an orchestra
EXPLOSION SE 8008s	*Revisited* Isandhlwana 1879 with John Barry and His Orchestra
HMV ALP 2270	*Doctor Faustus*—Marlowe (as Doctor Faustus)
LIVING SHAKESPEARE DEOB 5 AM	*Henry V* (abridged) (as King Henry) Shakespeare
STATESIDE SL 10045	*The Longest Day* (condensed version) with cast and orchestra
UNITED ARTISTS UAS 30136s	*Equus*—film soundtrack. Monologues and dialogue with Peter Firth and orchestra conducted by Angela Morley
VICTOR LOC.1091 or RCA VICTOR RD 7679	*Becket*—Highlights from the soundtrack (as Thomas Becket)
RCA VICTOR VDM 117 or RB 6711	*The Taming of the Shrew*—Zeffirelli (director) film (as Petruchio)
WARNER 2B 1657	*Who's Afraid Of Virginia Woolf?*—Screenplay: Ernest Lehman based on Edward Albee's play. (As George.)
WARNER 3XXX 2737C	*Fifty Years of Film* (1923–1973), *Who's Afraid Of Virginia Woolf?*—dialogue from film as George (Soundtrack recording)

WARNER BROTHERS B1635	*The Days of Wilfred Owen* Preface to Poems; "The send off," "Arms and the boy," "Sonnet," "Strange Meeting," "Le Christianisme," "Soldier's dream," "The last laugh," "At a calvary near the Ancre," "The sentry," "Anthem for doomed youth," "Apologia pro poemate meo," "The show," "Conscious," "Greater love," "Asleep," "Futility," "The next war," "Dulce et decorum." With incidental music.
WARNER BROS W 1656	*Who's Afraid Of Virginia Woolf?* Soundtrack selection with Elizabeth Taylor (speaking) and orchestra conducted by Alex North

INDEX

630   Index